INTRODUCTION TO
ORGANIZATIONAL BEHAVIOR THIRD EDITION

The Scott, Foresman Series in Management and Organizations

Lyman W. Porter and
Joseph W. McGuire, Editors

INTRODUCTION TO
ORGANIZATIONAL BEHAVIOR

THIRD EDITION

Richard M. Steers
University of Oregon

SCOTT, FORESMAN AND COMPANY
Glenview, Illinois   Boston   London

Credits for Photographs

Page 3, © 1986 Zigy Kaluzny.
Page 91, © 1987 Ed Young.
Page 321, © Michael Schneps.
Page 491, © Greg Pease.
Page 623, © Gary Landsman/Folio Inc.

Library of Congress Cataloging-in-Publication Data

Steers, Richard M.
    Introduction to organizational behavior / Richard M. Steers.—
3rd ed.
      p.   cm.—(The Scott, Foresman series in management and
organizations)
   Bibliography: p.
   Includes indexes.
   ISBN 0–673–16724–0
   1. Organizational behavior.   2. Industrial management.
3. Psychology, Industrial. I. Title. II. Series.
HD58.7.S74   1988
658.3′001′9—dc19   87–28775

*Dedicated with sincere appreciation
to Dorothy Wynkoop*

PREFACE

Several years ago, Richard K. Irish wrote a book called *If Things Don't Improve Soon I May Ask You to Fire Me* (Anchor Books, 1976). Dedicated to all those who labor in the vineyards, whether they "press the grapes or work in top management," the book was a humorous—if accurate—exposé on life in contemporary organizations. The major conclusion was that organizations are, more often than not, mismanaged, leading to an employee work climate that is not only inefficient but also stressful and dissatisfying. Although Irish may have overstated the problem slightly, significant improvements *could* be made in contemporary organizations, if only managers knew what to do.

The problems that plague modern organizations include low morale, poor motivation, high job stress, high turnover and absenteeism, poor product quality, distrust and conflict between groups and levels within the organizational hierarchy, and poor decision making. These problems—and how managers can attempt to solve them—represent the major focus of this book. Students are introduced to the topic of organizational behavior by examining in detail the nature of people at work, exploring individual differences, group dynamics, work environment, and individual and collective behaviors. This serves to develop students' appreciation for work-related problems and managerial solutions.

The text is organized into five parts. Part One introduces the study of organization behavior by examining the nature of work itself, problems of the work place, and a model for analyzing behavior in organizations. Several macro considerations are presented in a discussion of the related concepts of organization design and effectiveness. Various contingencies in organization design are incorporated into the discussion. Throughout, practical examples of how theory relates to the work place are included. This section of the book creates the foundation for understanding how organizations function so that individual and group behavior can be studied in an organizational context.

Individual behavior in the work place—perception, employee abilities and traits, job attitudes, and motivation processes—is examined in Part Two. Group behavior, the subject of Part Three, includes the topics of communication, decision making, power and politics, conflict and intergroup behavior, and leadership, and highlights the way each of these relates to group effectiveness. Several applied topics are introduced in Part Four as the focus shifts to people at work. Stress, work design, career development, and organizational change are examined here. Part Five concludes with predictions about the future of the work place and changes that may occur. A special Appendix is included that provides an overview of scientific method in organizational behavior research.

Theory, research, and application have been carefully and deliberately integrated in this text. Although the organization and contents of this edition are similar to those of the first and second, you will find that the third edition includes several new features. For example, such macro considerations as organization design are given more extensive coverage. In addition, more international examples have been included for cultural contrast. And throughout the text, numerous practical examples from the work place have been incorporated to increase the relevance of the material. Finally, the substantive cases and exercises at the end of the chapters have been enhanced, applying concepts from the book to real world situations.

Many individuals have contributed to this text throughout its three editions. Initially, I must recognize a special debt to my colleagues and doctoral students at the University of Oregon, who have provided the challenging intellectual environment necessary to stimulate new ideas and ways of thinking about organizational behavior. Many of the ideas expressed in this book are the result of prolonged discussions with them.

In addition, I should like to express my sincere appreciation to several valued colleagues who provided helpful comments and suggestions to various editions. They include Robert H. Miles, Harvard University; Richard T. Mowday, University of Oregon; Douglas T. Hall, Boston University; Benjamin Schneider, University of Maryland; Ricky Griffin, Texas A & M University; William H. Mobley, Texas A & M University; Ralph Katerberg, University of Cincinnati; Philip G. Benson, Auburn University; Rodger W. Griffeth, Kent State University; William E. Rosenbach, U.S. Air Force Academy; Chris A. Betts, California State University, Fresno; David Churchman, California State University, Dominguez Hills; Ronald W. Clement, Arizona State University; William B. Snavely, Miami University; Eric J. Walton, New York University; Jack M. Feldman, University of Florida; Thomas J. Naughton, Wayne State University; M. Jamal, Concordia University; Angelo S. DeNisi, University of South Carolina; Harriet Kandelman, University of Portland; and David A. Bednar, University of Arkansas.

I would also like to express my thanks to Lyman W. Porter, University of California, Irvine, for his assistance and patience as academic editor at Scott, Foresman and Company. Moreover, I am indebted to Jim Sitlington of Scott, Foresman for his expert help and guidance throughout the production process.

A special note of appreciation is also due my wife, Sheila, for her patience and support during the rather lengthy periods of cloistering while the revisions took shape. Finally, I should like to acknowledge a debt of gratitude to Dorothy Wynkoop, to whom this book is dedicated, for her enthusiastic support of the project and her continuing dedication to management education. Without people such as these, a project of this magnitude could never have become a reality.

Richard M. Steers

CONTENTS

PART FOUR
PEOPLE AT WORK   490

CHAPTER SEVENTEEN
Work and Stress   492

CHAPTER EIGHTEEN
Work Design   529

CHAPTER NINETEEN

Careers and Organizational Attachment   563

CHAPTER TWENTY

Organizational Change and Development   599

PART FIVE

PREDICTIONS FOR THE FUTURE   622

CHAPTER TWENTY-ONE

Managing People at Work: The Future   624

INTRODUCTION TO
ORGANIZATIONAL
BEHAVIOR THIRD EDITION

PART ONE

INTRODUCTION TO ORGANIZATIONS: THE WORK SETTING

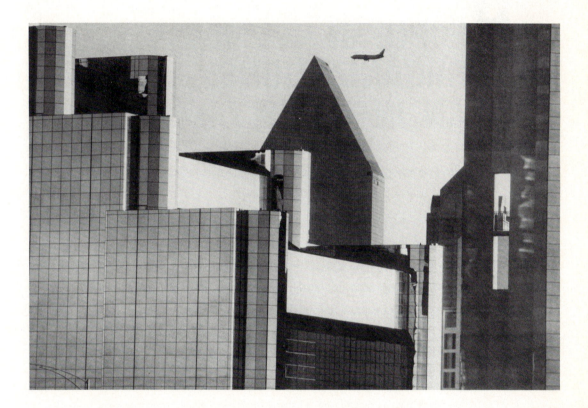

CHAPTER ONE

PEOPLE IN ORGANIZATIONS: AN INTRODUCTION

When we ask managers to discuss human problems in the work place, we usually hear such questions as the following:

- Why don't my employees work harder?
- Why are absenteeism and turnover so high?
- Why do we have so many communication problems?
- What kinds of characteristics should I look for in hiring people?
- How can I improve job satisfaction among my employees?
- How can I reduce—or at least cope with—job-related stress?
- How do I evaluate and reward employee performance?
- How can I become a more effective leader?

Questions such as these reveal a general frustration among many managers who seek to deal effectively with individuals and groups on the job. These questions also indicate an inadequate understanding among managers of the nature of people at work.

Being a manager is no simple task. In fact, the manager's job is often cited as an example of a high-stress position because of the many conflicting demands and pressures placed on managers in our society. Every day, managers are involved with people, production, finances, marketing, and accounting. The particular concern of this book is *people problems:*

employees, the work environment, and the interaction between the two. By learning more about people at work—how employees see, perform, and react to their jobs—we can perhaps make the job of manager a bit easier. Our goal is to increase understanding and minimize future frustrations by reviewing what has been learned from the behavioral and social sciences about organizational behavior and people at work. Throughout this book, we will concern ourselves with four central topics: people, the work people perform, the environment or organization where the work is performed, and the role of management in coordinating people, work, and work environment. Our intention is to facilitate a better understanding of how these four variables interact and how they relate to employee need satisfaction and organizational effectiveness. Before discussing these relationships, however, it will be useful to consider what we mean by the term *work,* as well as its role in modern society. Based on this understanding, we can begin assembling the building blocks that are necessary for understanding and appreciating organizational behavior.

THE NATURE OF WORK

Meaning of Work

What is work and how do people feel about the work they do? This question could be answered in several ways. Perhaps one of the best ways to understand how people feel about their jobs is simply to ask them. This has been done in an interesting book, *Working,* by Studs Terkel (1972). Terkel interviewed scores of people in a wide variety of jobs. How do these people feel about their jobs? Listen.[1]

[1]*Working: People Talk About What They Do All Day and How They Feel About What They Do,* by Studs Terkel. Copyright © 1972, 1974 by Studs Terkel. Reprinted by permission of Pantheon Books, a Division of Random House, Inc., and by permission of Gower Publishing Company Ltd.

I'm a dying breed. . . . A laborer. Strictly muscle work . . . pick it up, put it down, pick it up, put it down. . . . You can't take pride any more. You remember when a guy could point to a house he built, how many logs he stacked. He built it and he was proud of it (p. 1).

Steelworker

I changed my opinion of receptionists because now I'm one. It wasn't the dumb broad at the front desk who took telephone messages. She had to be something else because I thought I was something else. I was fine until there was a press party. We were having a fairly intelligent conversation. Then they asked me what I did. When I told them, they turned around to find other people with name tags. I wasn't worth bothering with. I wasn't being rejected because of what I said or the way I talked, but simply because of my function (p. 57).

Receptionist

I think switchboard operators are the most underpaid, 'cause we are the hub of everything. When you call somebody, you want immediate service. Of course, I chose the job. If you choose the job, it's your responsibility. Just because I feel I'm not paid enough doesn't mean I'm not gonna give 'em good work (p. 63).

Switchboard operator

People ask me what I do, I say, "I drive a garbage truck for the city." . . . I have nothing to be ashamed of. I put in my eight hours. We make a pretty good salary. I feel I earn my money. . . . My wife is happy; this is the big thing. She doesn't look down at me. I think that's more important than the white-collar guy looking down at me (p. 149).

Sanitation truck driver

I'm human. I make mistakes like everybody else. If you want a robot, build machines. If you want human beings, that's what I am (p. 186).

Policeman

The almighty dollar is not the only thing in my estimation. There's more to it—how I'm treated. What I have to say about what I do, how I do it. It's more important than the almighty dollar (pp. 259–60).

President, Lordstown Local, UAW

I usually say I'm an accountant. Most people think it's somebody who sits there with a green eyeshade and his sleeves rolled up with a garter, poring over books, adding things—with glasses. I suppose a certified public accountant has status. It doesn't mean much to me. Do I like the job or don't I? That's important (p. 351).

Accountant

These other people, they work, work, work, work and nothing comes of it. They're the ones that catch hell. The ones that come in every day on time, do the job, and try to keep up with everybody else. A timekeeper . . . she's a fanatic about time. She would argue with you if you were late or something. She's been working for the government twenty-five years and she hasn't gotten a promotion, 'cause she's not a fighter. . . .

The boss whose typing I messed up lost his secretary. She got promoted. They told this old timekeeper she's to be his secretary-assistant. Oh, she's in her glory. No more money or anything and she's doing two jobs all day long. She's rushin' and runnin' all the time, all day. She's a nervous wreck. And when she asked him to write her up for an award, he refused. That's her reward for being so faithful, obedient (p. 461).

Process clerk

Examples such as these—and there are many, many more—explain how some employees view their jobs and the work they perform. Obviously, some jobs are more meaningful than others and some individuals are more easily satisfied with their jobs than others. In any case, people clearly have strong feelings about what they do on the job and about the people they work with. In our study of behavior in organizations we shall examine what people do, what causes them to do it, and how they feel about what they do. As a prelude to this analysis, however, we should first consider the basic unit of analysis in this study: work itself. What is work and what functions does it serve in today's society?

Work has a variety of meanings in contemporary society. Oftentimes we think of work as paid employment, the exchange of services for money. While this definition may suffice in a technical sense, it does not adequately describe why work is necessary. Perhaps a more meaningful definition of *work* is to view it as "an activity that produces something of value for other people" (Dept. of Health, Education & Welfare, 1973, p. 3).

This definition broadens the scope of work and emphasizes the social context in which the wage-effort bargain transpires. It clearly recognizes that work has purpose—it is productive. Of course, this is not to say that work is necessarily interesting or rewarding or satisfying. On the contrary, we know that many jobs are dull, repetitive, and stressful. Even so, the activities performed do have utility for society at large. One of the challenges of management is to discover ways of transforming necessary yet distasteful jobs into more meaningful situations that are more satisfying and rewarding for individuals and that still contribute to organizational productivity and effectiveness.

Functions of Work

We know why work activities are important from an organization's viewpoint. Without work there is no product or service to provide. But why is work important to individuals? What functions does it serve?

First, work serves a rather obvious *economic* function. In exchange for labor, individuals receive necessary income with which to support themselves and their families. But people work for many reasons beyond simple economic necessity.

Work also serves several *social* functions. The workplace provides opportunities for meeting new people and developing friendships. Many people spend more time at work with their co-workers than they spend at home with their own families.

Work also provides a source of *social status* in the community. It is a clue to how an individual is regarded based on standards of importance prescribed by the community. For instance, in the United States a corporate president is generally accorded greater status than a janitor in the same corporation. In China, on the other hand, great status is ascribed to peasants and people from the working class, whereas managers are not so significantly differentiated from those they manage. It is important to note here that the status associated with the work we perform often transcends the boundaries of our organization. A corporate president or a university president may have a great deal of status in the community at large because of his or her position in the organization. Hence, the work we do can simultaneously represent a source of social differentiation as well as a source of social integration.

Work can be an important source of *identity, self-esteem,* and, for some, a means for *self-actualization.* It provides a sense of purpose for individuals and clarifies their value or contribution to society. As Freud (1930, p. 34) noted long ago, "work has a greater effect than any other technique of living in binding the individual more closely to reality; in his work he is at least securely attached to a part of reality, the human community." Work contributes to self-esteem in at least two ways. First, it provides individuals with an opportunity to demonstrate competence or mastery over both themselves and their environment. Individuals discover that they can actually *do* something. Second, work reassures individuals that they are carrying out activities that produce something of value to others, that they have something significant to offer. Without this, the individual feels he or she has little to contribute and is, hence, of little value to society.

We clearly see, then, that work serves several useful purposes from an individual's standpoint. It provides a degree of economic self-sufficiency, social interchange, social status, self-esteem, and identity. Without this, individuals often experience sensations of powerlessness, meaninglessness, and normlessness—a condition called *alienation.* In work, individuals have the possibility of finding some meaning in their day-to-day activities, providing, of course, that their work is sufficiently challenging. When work is not sufficiently challenging and when employees are not involved in their jobs, organizations run the risk of jeopardizing productivity and organizational effectiveness by creating situations where employees simply see no reason to contribute or to maximize their efforts on the job. This situation has given rise among managers to a general concern with declining productivity and work values. In fact, concern with this crisis has caused many managers to take a renewed interest in learning how the behavioral sciences can help them solve many of the problems of people at work.

EXHIBIT 1.1   U.S. TRADE DEFICIT, 1967–1984

Source: President's Commission on Industrial Competitiveness, *Global Competition: The New Reality* (Washington, D.C., January 1985), Vol. I, p. 13. Based on statistics from the U.S. Department of Commerce.

The Problem of Productivity and Work Values

During the past several years, it has become apparent that both the United States and Canada are not as competitive in world markets as they once were. As inflation increases, unemployment rises, and other industrialized nations surpass our previously unchallenged rates of productivity and output, there is concern that today's managers and workers are simply not doing enough to compete successfully in the economy of the 1980s.

The problem of lower relative productivity and reduced industrial competitiveness can be seen in several ways. First, consider the sharp decline in the U.S. trade deficit with foreign nations (see Exhibit 1.1). In industry after industry, the United States and Canada are losing market share, and future prospects do not appear promising. Perhaps a major reason for this decline in markets is the relatively low rate of improvement in worker productivity compared to such countries as Japan, Korea, France, and Germany (see Exhibit 1.2). Simply put, we are losing ground to foreign competitors in the production of goods and services. Reduced productivity, combined with the

EXHIBIT 1.2   PERCENTAGE INCREASE IN PRODUCTIVITY RATE, 1960–1983

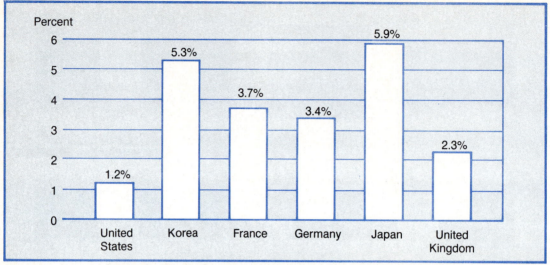

Source: President's Commission on Industrial Competitiveness, *Global Competition: The New Reality* (Washington, D.C., January 1985), Vol. I, p. 11. Based on unpublished statistics from the U.S. Department of Labor, Bureau of Labor Statistics, December 1984.

relatively high wage rates of North America, provide the ingredients for a bleak future. In short, it is clear that there is a "crisis" of productivity facing us today as we attempt to compete and survive in increasingly challenging environments.

A search for the root causes of this problem yields a variety of possible answers. As Yankelovich (1979, p. 61) notes:

> Our productivity is slowing for many reasons: the cost of energy, the crippling effects of government regulations, the distortions of inflation, environmental costs, a slackening of investment, a shift to services, and so on. But careful studies show that, collectively, all these factors can account for only a fraction of the present slippage.
>
> If you look at changing American attitudes toward work, you catch a glimpse of what is a major factor contributing to the decline. People who work at all levels of enterprise . . . are no longer motivated to work as hard and as effectively as in the past.

As proof, Yankelovich cites the following statistics. In the 1960s approximately 50 percent of employed Americans considered their work a source of personal fulfillment; now the total is fewer than 25 percent. Moreover, in the 1960s, 58 percent believed that "hard work always pays off"; now only 43 percent hold this belief. Today only 13 percent of working Americans find their work truly meaningful and more important to them than their leisure-time activities.

Based on this survey of employees, Yankelovich estimated that the work force can be divided into five categories. He further estimated the number and type of employees in each category as follows:

- *Go-getters (15% of the work force).* Young, ambitious, predominantly in sales, motivated by money and getting ahead.
- *Work before pleasure (19%).* Older, dedicated, hard-working, want to make a contribution.
- *Habitual workers (22%).* Older, poorer, mostly blue-collar or clerical, want job security, structure, and guidance.
- *Middle-management (17%).* Young, highly educated, managers and professionals, hungry for responsibility and challenge, seek interesting and vital work.
- *Turned off (27%).* Poorly educated, low income, largely blue-collar, least motivated, living for today.

Although one may argue with the classification or the estimated percentages in each category, this analysis highlights the fact that today's work force is highly diversified, characterized by different educations, skills, age groups, responsibilities, and job challenges. Perhaps most important are the different levels of motivation and drive.

This issue is further emphasized when we consider the current debate over the relative motivation levels of younger and older workers. We frequently hear comments about younger employees' lack of dedication and unwillingness to work hard. The image is that younger workers are lazy, lack direction and purpose, and are untrustworthy. Available evidence fails to support this image. Rather, while younger employees (or prospective employees) still appear to value hard work, there has been an apparent shift in their *expectations* of their jobs.

Several studies have shown that younger employees have higher job expectations than they did in the past. A survey by the American Institutes for Research (1971), for instance, surveyed over 400,000 high school students in 1960 and a comparable sample again in 1970. It was found that, while the 1960 sample valued job security and opportunity for promotion, the 1970 group placed a higher value on "freedom to make my own decisions" and "work that seems important to me." Either job security or promotional opportunities have become less important, or more recent students have come to assume such things as given and demand more from a job. In either case, younger employees have apparently come to expect more meaningful input and responsibility from the jobs they select instead of "waiting in line" to move up the hierarchy.

In another survey, Taylor and Thompson (1976) found similar results. In their study of a large sample of workers, they found no generation gap between younger and older employees. Differences were noted, however, between the two age groups. Younger workers were found to value self-expression through work to a greater extent than did older workers. Younger workers attached particular significance to opportunities to learn and chances to make responsible decisions. Workers of all ages, especially more educated workers, showed a strong sense of pride and valued both intrinsic (job-based) and extrinsic (economic) rewards.

Based on their findings, Taylor and Thompson (1976, p. 534) conclude:

> The study suggests that managers, union leaders, and public policymakers will face new challenges in the years to come. Young workers will be demanding both more job satisfaction and higher income. At the same time, more educated persons entering the labor force are less likely to trust existing institutions to meet their needs. Young managers may have as much difficulty as their older superiors in relating to young workers.

In summary, it appears that younger workers do not value hard work less than they did in the past. They want to contribute to organizations in meaningful ways but get frustrated by what they perceive as bureaucratic obstacles to effective job performance. The challenge for management is first to design a work environment in which employees are motivated to perform well in their jobs and then to provide the necessary leadership in this environment.

Social Problems of Work

In addition to the general problem of the value placed on work, a series of social problems associated with work have been identified. These problems result largely from an individual's reactions either to the work itself or to the work environment (Argyle, 1972).

One such problem is the inability of many employees today to identify with their work or with their employer. They work in jobs that have little meaning and under conditions over which they have little control. Hence, it is not surprising to find workers who are *alienated* and have *low job satisfaction.* In addition, contemporary managers are finding that employees—at all levels—exhibit a *lack of motivation.* Turnover and absenteeism are high, and even among those workers whose attendance records are good, many show little enthusiasm for their assigned tasks. If we were to ask workers what they wanted from their jobs, we would get answers similar to those shown in Exhibit 1.3. The challenge for organizations is to determine whether they can provide these outcomes for employees to such an extent that the employees will remain in their jobs and perform at high levels.

Difficulty of communication is another social problem experienced by many at work. As organizations grow in size and complexity, patterns of communication (the lifeblood of organizations) become more structured and formal. Delays and distortions of information increase, leading to misunderstandings and to decision making based on information of poor quality.

EXHIBIT 1.3   WHAT WORKERS WANT FROM THEIR JOBS

Question: If you had to choose, which two or three of these are most important to you on the job?

Answers:

A good salary	63%
Job security	53
Appreciation for a job well done	40
A chance to use your mind and abilities	39
Medical and other benefits	36
Being able to retire early with a good pension	20
A clean, quiet, comfortable place to work	19

Survey of 967 employed adults, conducted May 30–June 2, 1985. Overall results should be accurate to within 4 percentage points either way. Data: Louis Harris & Associates Inc. for *Business Week*.

Source: Reprinted from July 8, 1985 issue of *Business Week* by special permission, ©1985 by McGraw-Hill, Inc.

Failure to communicate may contribute to another problem that exists in some work environments: *conflict within and between groups.* Some conflict is unavoidable in contemporary work environments. Individuals and interest groups work toward different goals despite the fact that their differing objectives may create problems for others. Such conflict can be a constant source of stress in an organization as each group looks out for its own interests. This intergroup conflict is perhaps best exemplified by recent tensions concerning discrimination against females and members of minority groups. The slow progress being made in placing women and minorities in certain types of jobs (management and professional positions, for instance) is causing many to be concerned. Consider, for example, the percentage of women in management positions at AT&T (see Exhibit 1.4). Clearly, few female executives can be found in the upper echelons of the organization. Similar findings emerge for other companies (see Exhibit 1.5). However, as more women assume top positions in corporations, we can expect their male counterparts who are vying for the same elite positions to become concerned.

Finally, employees face *problems of technological change.* Organizations today must adapt to environmental pressures and market opportunities. Changes occur with alarming frequency, creating anxiety among members of the organization who wonder how the changes will affect them. One example of this can be seen in the dramatic rise in the use of industrial robots in the United States. As shown in Exhibit 1.6, the number of robots on the shop floor will rise significantly in the early 1990s. Will such a change put people out of

EXHIBIT 1.4   PERCENTAGE OF WOMEN IN MANAGEMENT LEVELS AT AT&T

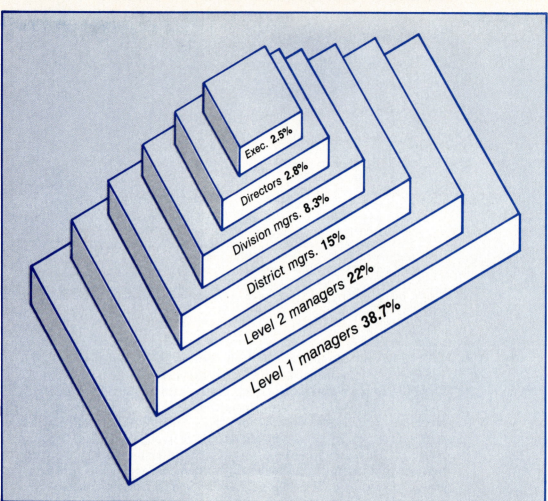

Exec. **2.5%**

Directors **2.8%**

Division mgrs. **8.3%**

District mgrs. **15%**

Level 2 managers **22%**

Level 1 managers **38.7%**

Source: From Carol Hymowitz and Timothy D. Schellhardt, "The Glass Ceiling," *Wall Street Journal,* March 24, 1986, p. 4d. Reprinted by permission of *Wall Street Journal,* © Dow Jones & Company, Inc. 1986. All Rights Reserved.

work? Will it reduce their job security or influence their job status? Will it make their jobs less enjoyable or more stressful? Managers must deal with change and its accompanying anxieties if their organizations are to remain in balance with (or ahead of) environmental, technological, and societal pressures and demands.

There are other social problems at work that could be mentioned here, but citing them all is not the aim of this discussion. The point is that managers have a responsibility to recognize the existence of such social problems and to recognize the extent to which these problems inhibit productivity and the

EXHIBIT 1.5   PERCENTAGE OF MANAGEMENT JOBS HELD BY WOMEN (1985)

	Management Jobs Held by Women	Women in Company
Industrial companies		
DuPont	7%	22%
Exxon*	8	27
General Motors*	8	19
Goodyear Tire & Rubber	6	14
UAL Inc.	25	39
Technology		
AT&T*	32%	48%
General Electric	6	26
IBM	16	28
Xerox	23	38
Consumer products		
Johnson & Johnson*	18%	47%
PepsiCo	28	46
Philip Morris (excluding General Foods)	14	31
Procter & Gamble	17	28
R.J. Reynolds	20	40
Retailing and trade		
Federated Stores	61%	72%
Kroger	16	47
Marriott	32	51
McDonald's	46	57
Sears Roebuck*	36	55
Media		
ABC (excluding Capital Cities)	36%	43%
Time Inc.	46	54
Times-Mirror	27	37
Financial services		
American Express	37%	57%
BankAmerica	64	72
Chemical Bank	34	57
Prudential Life Insurance*	32	53
Wells Fargo Bank	58	71
Average for companies with more than 100 employees	24%	44%

*1984 figures

Source: From Karen Blumenthal, "Room at the Top," *Wall Street Journal,* March 24, 1986, p. 7d. Reprinted by permission of *Wall Street Journal,* © Dow Jones & Company, Inc. 1986. All Rights Reserved.

quality of working life. Many of the topics discussed throughout this book focus both on these work-related problems and on what managers can do to alleviate such problems. Throughout our study of organizational behavior we shall develop a conceptual appreciation of the nature of work problems as well as analyze the theoretical basis for their solutions.

EXHIBIT 1.6   ESTIMATED NUMBER OF INDUSTRIAL ROBOTS IN THE UNITED STATES

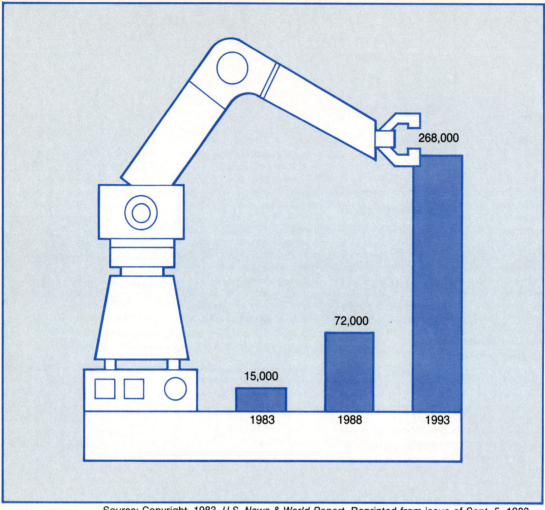

Source: Copyright, 1983, *U.S. News & World Report.* Reprinted from issue of Sept. 5, 1983.

A MODEL FOR UNDERSTANDING ORGANIZATIONAL BEHAVIOR

A major responsibility—indeed, many feel *the* major responsibility—of managers today is to make organizations operate effectively. Bringing about effective performance, however, is no easy task. As Nadler and Tushman (1980, p. 35) note:

Understanding one individual's behavior is challenging in and of itself; understanding a group that's made up of different individuals and comprehending the many relationships among those individuals is even more complex. Imagine, then, the mind-boggling complexity of a large organization made up of thousands of individuals and hundreds of groups with myriad relationships among these individuals and groups.

Despite this difficulty, however, organizations must be managed. Nadler and Tushman continue:

Ultimately the organization's work gets done through people, individually or collectively, on their own or in collaboration with technology. Therefore, the management of organizational behavior is central to the management task—a task that involves the capacity to *understand* the behavior patterns of individuals, groups, and organizations, to *predict* what behavioral responses will be elicited by various managerial actions, and finally to use this understanding and these predictions to achieve *control.*

The work of society is accomplished largely through organizations and the role of management is to see to it that organizations perform this work. Without it, the wheels of society would soon grind to a halt.

Understanding the nature of people at work is fundamental to the effective management of an organization. Nadler, Hackman, and Lawler (1979) have developed a conceptual framework for understanding organizational behavior (see Exhibit 1.7). Their model identifies the following five basic units of analysis:

- *Individuals.* Clearly, the basic building blocks of organizations are the individual employees. As we note in Part Two of this book, individuals vary considerably in their skills, motivation, learning abilities, and so forth. These differences can have a marked effect on both behavior and performance in organizations.
- *Groups.* A second aspect that is central to organizational behavior is groups and group processes. Here we are concerned with communication, decision making, power, and leadership. These topics are discussed in the text in Part Three.
- *Tasks and technology.* Based on a knowledge of individuals and groups, we can focus on how individuals and groups react to the technology of the workplace. That is, how do people respond to the work itself? In Part Four we consider such topics as job attitudes, conflict, stress, performance appraisal systems, work design, and turnover and absenteeism. Throughout, emphasis is placed on the interactive dynamics between people and jobs.
- *Organization design.* Putting together all three of these factors —individuals, groups, and tasks—is the subject of organization design. That is, how do we structure an organization so it effectively coordinates and controls employee behavior to facilitate performance? Because of the central importance of organization design to understanding individ-

Source: Adapted from David A. Nadler, J. Richard Hackman, and Edward E. Lawler III, *Managing Organizational Behavior.* Copyright © 1979 by David A. Nadler, J. Richard Hackman, and Edward E. Lawler III. Reprinted by permission of Scott, Foresman/Little, Brown College Division.

ual and group behavior in organizations, we begin our exploration of organizational behavior with this topic.

- *Environment.* Finally, it must be recognized that organizations do not exist in a vacuum; they must interact with their external environment. This subject is also examined as a prelude to a more detailed examination, throughout the remainder of the book, of people at work.

We will begin our study of organizational behavior by considering what are called "macro" variables—the external environment and organization design. This sets the stage for later discussions about various "micro" variables—individual and group level analyses. Given our model and approach to the study of organizational behavior, a useful first step, however, is to examine the role managers play in organizational dynamics.

THE ROLE OF MANAGEMENT

Many years ago, Mary Parker Follett defined *management* as the "art of getting things done through people." Managers coordinate and oversee the work of others to accomplish ends not attainable by individuals alone. Today our definition has broadened. Management is generally defined as the process of planning, organizing, directing, and controlling the activities of employees in combination with other organizational resources to accomplish common objectives. In a broad sense, then, the task of management is to facilitate the organization's effectiveness. Management exists in virtually all organizations seeking to achieve goals, whether in the public or private sector and whether in a socialist or a capitalist economy.

Managerial Responsibilities

An important question often raised about managers is: What responsibilities do managers typically have in organizations? According to our definition, managers are involved in planning, organizing, directing, and controlling. A recent survey of 600 managers in a large electronics manufacturing organization provided detailed insight into managerial responsibilities (Gomez-Mejia, McCann, and Page, 1985). Responding to questions about their activities, managers described responsibilities that suggested nine major types of activities, as summarized in Exhibit 1.8. The basic activities of planning, controlling, supervising, and coordinating are four of the types of activities reported. Managers also monitor business indicators; help develop and produce primary products and services, customer relationships, and external contacts; and provide technical expertise and advice to other members of the organization.

Variations in Managerial Work

Clearly, all managers do not perform the same types of work. Every manager may have responsibilities in all the categories listed in Exhibit 1.8, but the amount of time spent on each activity and the importance of that activity will vary. The two most important influences on managerial activities are the manager's level in the organizational hierarchy and the type of department for which the manager is responsible.

Management Level
We can distinguish between three general levels of management: executive, middle, and first-line (see Exhibit 1.9). Executive managers are at the top of the hierarchy and are responsible for the entire organization. Middle managers, who are at the middle of the hierarchy, are responsible for major departments and may supervise other lower-level managers. First-line manag-

EXHIBIT 1.8   MANAGERIAL RESPONSIBILITIES

LONG-RANGE PLANNING

Engaging in planning, strategy development, and decision making for major divisions and functions. This includes determining the annual performance objectives of major divisions and functions, developing major plan revisions, revising the structure of one or more divisions, giving guidance in planning, determining international business potential, and consulting on corporate-wide problems.

CONTROLLING

Having responsibility for controlling the allocation of human, financial, and material resources through activities such as assignment of supervisory responsibility, expense controls, performance goals, and budgets. Also included are employee relations responsibilities, establishing parameters to guide the planning of functional units, developing operational policies and procedures under which managers are expected to perform, and allocating and scheduling resources to assure that they will be available when needed.

MONITORING BUSINESS INDICATORS

Being concerned with monitoring key business indicators, such as total new income, five-year return on equity, total assets that have been acquired, net income as a percent of sales, optimum return on investments of the organization, debt-equity ratio, and market conditions and indicators.

SUPERVISING

Planning, organizing, and controlling the work of subordinates, including face-to-face contact with subordinates on an almost daily basis. The concerns covered by this factor revolve around getting work done efficiently through the effective utilization of employees. Activities include analyzing subordinates' strengths/weaknesses and training needs, reviewing their work methods for possible increases in productivity, providing them complete instructions when giving assignments, and scheduling their work so it flows evenly and steadily.

COORDINATING

Coordinating the efforts of others over whom managers exercise no direct control. These activities include working in close association with individuals from other units, sharing information required by other units, coordinating interdependent activities of different groups, handling conflicts or disagreements when necessary, and consulting many different people before making major decisions.

CUSTOMER RELATIONS/MARKETING

Being involved in providing, promoting, and selling products or services to external customers; negotiating with customers; identifying and developing new

continued

EXHIBIT 1.8   *continued*

markets for products or services; monitoring sales volume and market conditions affecting the users of products or services; anticipating new or changed demands for products or services.

EXTERNAL CONTACT

Interacting with individuals external to the organization other than customers. These activities involve first-level contact and negotiation with employees of suppliers, representatives of community organizations, and representatives of federal or state governments.

CONSULTING

Applying technical expertise to special problems, issues, questions, or policies, having an understanding of advanced principles, theories, and concepts in more than one required field, and being asked to apply highly advanced techniques and methods to issues and questions.

PRODUCTS/SERVICES

Being involved in planning, scheduling, and monitoring the design, development, production, and delivery of products and services; tracking their progress, quality, and profitability.

Source: Luis Gomez-Mejia, Joseph E. McCann, and Ronald C. Page, "The Structure of Managerial Behaviors and Rewards," *Industrial Relations* 24 (1985), 147–54. Used with permission.

ers supervise rank-and-file employees and carry out day-to-day activities within departments. Exhibit 1.10 shows differences in managerial activities by hierarchical level. Top managers rate high on such activities as long-range planning, monitoring business indicators, coordinating, and consulting. Lower-level managers, by contrast, rate high on supervising, because their responsibility is to accomplish tasks through rank-and-file employees. Middle managers rate near the middle for all activities. These findings suggest that the skills required of managers change as they move up the hierarchy and acquire greater responsibility.

Departmental Function

Managerial responsibilities also differ with respect to the type of department. Exhibit 1.11 illustrates differences for manufacturing, quality assurance, marketing, accounting, and personnel departments. Manufacturing department managers rate high on products and services, controlling, and supervising. Marketing managers, in comparison, rate low on planning, coordinating, and consulting, but rate high on customer relations and external contact. Managers in both accounting and personnel departments rate high on long-range planning and low on products. As the exhibit shows, managers in

EXHIBIT 1.9   LEVELS IN THE MANAGEMENT HIERARCHY

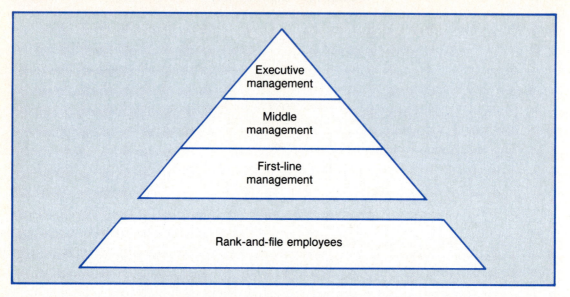

accounting are also concerned with controlling and with monitoring performance indicators, while personnel managers provide consulting expertise, coordination, and external contacts. Exhibit 1.11 illustrates that the emphasis on and intensity of managerial activities varies by department.

In many firms managers are rotated through departments as they move up in the hierarchy. In this way they obtain a well-rounded perspective of the responsibilities of the various departments. In their day-to-day tasks they

EXHIBIT 1.10   IMPORTANCE OF MANAGEMENT ACTIVITIES BY LEVEL

	Management Level		
Managerial Activities	**First-Line**	**Middle**	**Executive**
Long-range planning	25	45	84
Controlling	38	50	61
Monitoring business indicators	30	49	74
Supervising	65	50	33
Coordinating	31	52	70
Customer relations/marketing	27	49	69
External contact	38	45	57
Consulting	30	52	70
Products and services	33	50	58

Source: Luis Gomez-Mejia, Joseph E. McCann, and Ronald C. Page, "The Structure of Managerial Behaviors and Rewards," *Industrial Relations* 24 (1985), 147–54. Used with permission.

EXHIBIT 1.11   IMPORTANCE OF MANAGEMENT ACTIVITIES BY DEPARTMENT

Management Activities	Department				
	Quality Assurance	Manufacturing	Marketing	Accounting	Personnel
Long-range planning	21	39	21	68	72
Controlling	66	70	53	80	48
Monitoring business indicators	21	30	62	73	32
Supervising	51	65	50	40	44
Coordinating	42	38	22	51	71
Customer relations/ marketing	25	31	93	39	22
External contact	34	31	61	42	67
Consulting	32	41	26	61	80
Products and services	66	70	52	19	20

Source: Luis Gomez-Mejia, Joseph E. McCann, and Ronald C. Page, "The Structure of Managerial Behaviors and Rewards," *Industrial Relations* 24 (1985), 147–54. Used with permission.

must emphasize the right activities for their department and their managerial level. Knowing what types of activities to emphasize is the core of the manager's job.

SUMMARY

It should be clear from reading this chapter that the major focus of this book is the role of managers in facilitating organizational effectiveness by working through people. The nature and meaning of work was discussed, as well as the functions work serves in our contemporary society. The crisis of productivity and work values was also examined. It was noted that North America is becoming increasingly less competitive with respect to Japan and other Asian countries.

Next, we considered several of the more serious social problems commonly found in the work place. It was noted that such problems must be recognized and addressed by managers interested in removing barriers to effective organizations.

A model for understanding human behavior in organizations was introduced. The model, based on open systems theory, incorporates individuals, groups, tasks, organization design, and the external environment as they jointly influence organizational dynamics and managerial effectiveness. This model represents an overview of what is to come in the remainder of this book.

Finally, the central role of management in developing effective organizations was discussed. Variations in managerial work were examined.

KEY WORDS

alienation   self-actualization
informal organization   self-esteem
management   social status
productivity   work
role differentiation   work values

FOR DISCUSSION

1. Define what is meant by *work*.
2. What functions does work serve in modern society?
3. Describe the extent and nature of the crisis of productivity and work values. What can be done about this crisis?
4. Are younger workers less committed than older workers? Explain.
5. Discuss several major social problems associated with work in contemporary organizations.
6. Discuss the role of management in the larger societal context.
7. Identify what you think are the critical issues facing contemporary management. Explain.

EXERCISE

CLASS GOALS AND STUDENT INVOLVEMENT

1.1

Purpose
To consider class objectives, student concerns, and the students' role in making the class a success.

Instructions
Groups of six to eight students should meet for a period of twenty minutes, discussing their answers to the following three questions. Answers should be listed on a sheet of paper.

1. What are your goals and expectations for this class? (This question should be answered with reference to the course syllabus, the table of contents of the text(s), the instructor's introductory comments, and your own goals and expectations. In short, gear your answer to what you hope to gain from taking the class.)
2. What anxieties or concerns do you have about the class?
3. What exactly are you willing to do to achieve your goals and make the class a success? (It might be useful here to set forth specific goals for your participation in the class.)

After 20 minutes, the class as a whole should discuss and compare their answers. Through discussion, the class should attempt to clarify what the class will and will not accomplish; how to reduce student anxieties and concerns; and what students are willing to contribute to facilitate the accomplishment of class goals.

CHAPTER TWO

ORGANIZATION DESIGN AND EFFECTIVENESS

This book examines people at work, both as individuals and as group members. Before it is possible to understand a person's behavior, however, it is important to understand the environment in which he or she works. This working environment, the *organization,* is the vehicle through which people coordinate their efforts for task accomplishment.

What exactly is an organization and how do organizations differ? How is organizational effectiveness measured? What are some classical and contemporary approaches to organization structure and design? The primary emphasis of this chapter is organization design and effectiveness, and these are some of the topics that are discussed. Chapter Three will continue the examination of organizations by focusing on how various technological and environmental contingencies affect organization design and success.

IMPORTANCE OF TOPIC FOR MANAGERS

Why is it so important that managers thoroughly understand the dynamics of organizations? To begin, people work in organizations. It is difficult to understand employee behavior on the job without understanding the social environment in which such behavior occurs. In fact, the structure of an organization places considerable constraints on behavior. Nor is it possible for a manager to fully comprehend such issues as job design, stress, turnover, and absenteeism without knowing something about how the organization influences them.

We often hear talk about what "organizations" do to people. Such comments imply that most organizations are alike. Of course, this is not true. Work organizations vary, and their differences can have a profound impact on employees. It is important to have a clear picture of the diversity that exists across organizations. It is also essential that managers have at least a rudimentary understanding of the related concepts of organizational effectiveness and efficiency, particularly if the primary function of management is to facilitate an effective level of operations. Such knowledge can help managers to assess their own performance and the performance of others.

Finally, because many organizations are currently experimenting with new forms of organization design, such as the matrix design, these new designs may be studied and the information applied to managing other organizations. Such knowledge can be useful to managers striving to maximize organizational effectiveness.

THE NATURE OF ORGANIZATIONS

Definition of Organization

In the literature on organizations, a wide variety of definitions can be found for *organization*. One of the earliest definitions was advanced by Barnard (1938, p. 73), who viewed an organization as "a system of consciously coordinated activities of two or more persons." According to this definition, organizations are considered to have stated purposes, communications systems and other coordinating processes, and a network of individuals who willingly cooperate on tasks necessary for organizational goal attainment. Similarly, Etzioni (1964, p. 4) describes organizations as "planned units, deliberately structured for the purpose of attaining specific goals." Finally, Porter, Lawler, and Hackman (1975) argue that organizations are typically characterized by five basic factors: (1) social composition; (2) goal orientation;

(3) differentiated functions; (4) intended rational coordination; and (5) continuity through time.

Several common themes run through these different definitions of organizations. First, organizations are seen as groups of people working together for common goals. They are goal-seeking systems in which individuals coordinate their efforts (through differentiated functions, rational coordination, etc.) to create a viable system capable of accomplishing common objectives. Each member of an organization may not value all objectives similarly. Instead, individuals might pursue less-valued goals (e.g., goals valued by the organization) in exchange for securing the efforts of others for goals that are more highly valued by the individuals. Through coalition and cooperation, individual members of an organization try to satisfy their own diverse needs and goals commensurate with available resources.

Diversity in Organizations

Organizations come in many sizes and shapes. Consider, for example, a particular local chapter (organization) of Mothers Against Drunk Driving (MADD), shown in Exhibit 2.1. As we can see, the structure (lines of authority, communication channels, decision-making mechanisms, etc.) is quite simple. Now compare this structure to that of the Sumitomo Group, one of Japan's largest conglomerates (Exhibit 2.2). The Sumitomo Group is involved in a wide range of often unrelated industries and businesses. The organization's structure is complex, and the potential organizational problems are tremendous. Still, both the local chapter of MADD and Sumitomo have found ways to be effective and efficient in the pursuit of their objectives.

Requirements of Organizations

In order to maintain a certain amount of stability and predictability within the surrounding external environment, organizations must meet a series of *organizational requirements* for survival. The extent to which organizations can successfully satisfy these requirements will largely determine their ability to persist in the pursuit of their goals and objectives. If an organization cannot fulfill these requirements, severe threats to its stability can occur that jeopardize its chances for survival. These threats may take the form of loss of resources, loss of legitimacy from the supporting environment, or organizational stagnation. Such losses have obvious implications for the people who work for the organization.

Organizational requirements include the following (Etzioni, 1975; Gross, 1965):

- *Resource acquisition.* Organizations must be able to compete successfully for scarce and necessary resources to serve as inputs for organizational work activities.

EXHIBIT 2.1   ORGANIZATION CHART OF A LOCAL CHAPTER OF MOTHERS AGAINST DRUNK DRIVING (MADD)

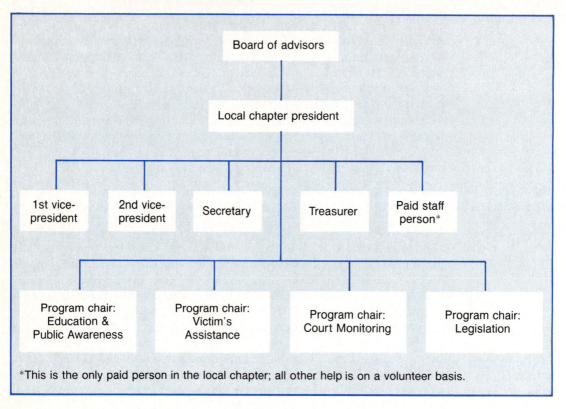

*This is the only paid person in the local chapter; all other help is on a volunteer basis.

- *Efficiency.* Organizations must strive to secure the most advantageous ratio of inputs to outputs in the transformation process.
- *Production or output.* Organizations must produce and deliver their goods and services in a steady and predictable fashion.
- *Rational coordination.* The activities of the organization must be integrated and coordinated in a logical, predictable fashion consistent with the ultimate goals of the organization.
- *Organizational renewal and adaptation.* Most organizations must invest some resources in activities that will enhance the net worth of the organization in the future (e.g., R&D investments). Without renewal efforts, organizational survival is often threatened by short-term shifts in market demands, resources, etc.
- *Conformity.* Because of the close interrelationship between an organization and its external environment, organizations (and their members) must often follow the prevailing dictates and norms of the environment. Wide deviation from social norms, laws, regulations, and shifts in moral standards can result in a variety of sanctions being levied against the

EXHIBIT 2.2   COMPANIES OF THE SUMITOMO GROUP (JAPAN)

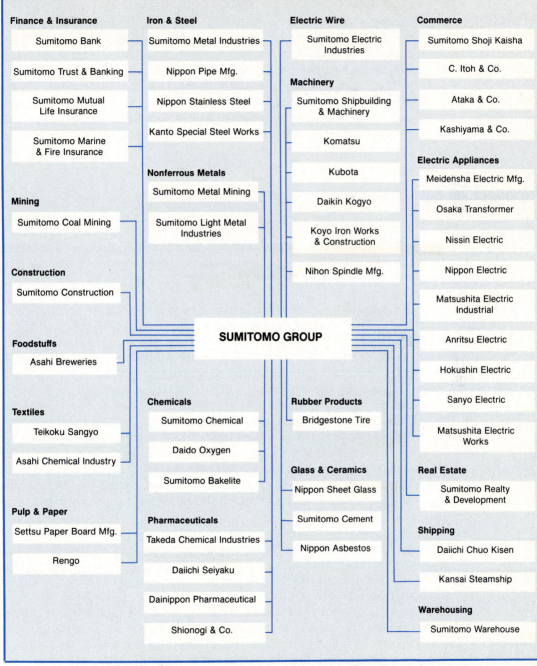

Finance & Insurance
- Sumitomo Bank
- Sumitomo Trust & Banking
- Sumitomo Mutual Life Insurance
- Sumitomo Marine & Fire Insurance

Mining
- Sumitomo Coal Mining

Construction
- Sumitomo Construction

Foodstuffs
- Asahi Breweries

Textiles
- Teikoku Sangyo
- Asahi Chemical Industry

Pulp & Paper
- Settsu Paper Board Mfg.
- Rengo

Iron & Steel
- Sumitomo Metal Industries
- Nippon Pipe Mfg.
- Nippon Stainless Steel
- Kanto Special Steel Works

Nonferrous Metals
- Sumitomo Metal Mining
- Sumitomo Light Metal Industries

Chemicals
- Sumitomo Chemical
- Daido Oxygen
- Sumitomo Bakelite

Pharmaceuticals
- Takeda Chemical Industries
- Daiichi Seiyaku
- Dainippon Pharmaceutical
- Shionogi & Co.

Electric Wire
- Sumitomo Electric Industries

Machinery
- Sumitomo Shipbuilding & Machinery
- Komatsu
- Kubota
- Daikin Kogyo
- Koyo Iron Works & Construction
- Nihon Spindle Mfg.

SUMITOMO GROUP

Rubber Products
- Bridgestone Tire

Glass & Ceramics
- Nippon Sheet Glass
- Sumitomo Cement
- Nippon Asbestos

Commerce
- Sumitomo Shoji Kaisha
- C. Itoh & Co.
- Ataka & Co.
- Kashiyama & Co.

Electric Appliances
- Meidensha Electric Mfg.
- Osaka Transformer
- Nissin Electric
- Nippon Electric
- Matsushita Electric Industrial
- Anritsu Electric
- Hokushin Electric
- Sanyo Electric
- Matsushita Electric Works

Real Estate
- Sumitomo Realty & Development

Shipping
- Daiichi Chuo Kisen
- Kansai Steamship

Warehousing
- Sumitomo Warehouse

Source: K. Bieda, *The Structure and Operation of the Japanese Economy* (Sydney: John Wiley & Sons, 1970), p. 237. Reprinted by permission of Jacaranda Wiley Ltd.

organization that can reduce its sources of legitimacy and threaten its survival.

- *Constituency satisfaction.* Finally, organizations are composed of a variety of constituencies, including employees, investors, and consumers. For system effectiveness, organizations must satisfy—or at least partially satisfy—these various constituencies to gain their necessary support and cooperation. In view of the often conflicting demands made by these various constituents (e.g., employees want more money, investors want more profits, and consumers want lower prices), a major function of managers is to somehow achieve a workable balance so that all parties are at least marginally satisfied and willing to continue participating in the venture.

Organizational Subsystems

In order to accomplish their goals, organizations must obviously divide and distribute the various tasks and engage in some form of specialization. When we view organizations as open systems, these various areas of specialization can be categorized into five such *subsystems* (Katz and Kahn, 1978):

- The *productive* subsystem, where concern is focused on the major functions or work of the system (e.g., a manufacturing department).
- The *supportive* subsystem, which acquires necessary raw materials for the productive subsystem or distributes the system's finished products (e.g., a purchasing or marketing department).
- The *maintenance* subsystem, which maintains and protects the organization's structural integrity and character (e.g., training programs, compensation plans, company newspapers).
- The *adaptive* subsystem, which focuses on the adaptation and long-range survival of the organization in a changing environment (e.g., an R&D department, long-range planning functions).
- The *managerial* subsystem, which coordinates, controls, and directs the other four subsystems so that maximum effort can be directed toward goal attainment.

All five subsystems, when taken together, represent the concept we call an organization. As shall be seen throughout this book, the study of people at work is colored by all of these subsystems since people in various roles and capacities operate all five subsystems.

It is important to note that the characteristics of each of these subsystems can vary considerably across organizations. In fact, a major problem that continues to complicate the study of organizational behavior is the heterogeneity of organizations. That is, organizations differ not only in their size and shape (tall vs. flat), but also in the technologies they employ, the external environments in which they function, the work climates they create, and the types of goals and objectives they pursue. It is this property of uniqueness

—that is, every organization is an original—that complicates attempts to draw meaningful generalizations concerning what managers can do to improve their operations. Such a fact cautions against the search for hard and fast *principles* of management and instead suggests a contingency approach to the study of organizations and the people who work within them.

ORGANIZATIONAL EFFECTIVENESS

The term *organizational effectiveness* has been used and misused in a variety of ways in the literature on organizations. Some people equate the term with profit or productivity, others view it with regard to job satisfaction, and still others see it in light of societal good. However, such simplistic definitions tend to be far too narrow to be useful; they are situation specific and value laden. Instead, as noted earlier, organizations are quite diverse in their nature and mission. As such, a more comprehensive approach to defining organizational effectiveness is to follow Talcott Parsons and Amitai Etzioni and define it in terms of an organization's ability to acquire and efficiently use available resources to achieve specific goals.

The definition of organizational effectiveness requires elaboration. To begin, we are focusing on operative goals, not official goals. Our concern is with what the organization is really trying to do, not with public relations statements concerning what it says it is doing. For many years, a major company used to say "progress is our most important product"; obviously this was not the case. Second, inherent in this definition is the realization that effectiveness is best judged by an organization's ability to compete in a turbulent environment and successfully acquire and utilize its resources. This emphasizes the fact that managers must deal effectively with their external environments to secure needed resources. Finally, this approach clearly recognizes that the concept of efficiency is a necessary yet insufficient ingredient of effectiveness.

To be effective, an organization must obtain and efficiently use resources to achieve operative goals. However, as stated previously, members of an organization may not completely agree on the importance of a particular goal. The value that the board of directors places on a goal is likely to differ from the opinions of employees or society as a whole. In short, it seems logical to conclude that organizational effectiveness is best assessed by those whose goals are involved. That is, it is necessary to take a "multiple constituency" approach and recognize that various groups have a stake in the organization's success. As Friedlander and Pickle (1967, p. 293) argue:

> Clearly, effectiveness criteria must take into account the profitability of the organization, the degree to which it satisfies its members, and the degree to which it is of value to the larger society of which it is a part. These three perspectives include systems maintenance and growth, subsystem fulfillment and environment fulfillment.

In other words, in assessing effectiveness, clear recognition must be given to simultaneously satisfying diverse—and often opposing—interest groups. This balancing act represents a real challenge to managers.

Effectiveness and Efficiency

Many managers equate the terms effectiveness and efficiency. However, treating these two related but distinct concepts as interchangeable only serves to confuse the assessment process. While *effectiveness* is the extent to which operative goals can be attained, *efficiency* is the cost/benefit ratio incurred in the pursuit of those goals. Efficiency considers the issue of how many inputs of raw materials, money, and people are necessary to attain a given level of output or a particular goal. If two companies making the same product finish the fiscal year with equal production levels, but the first attained the level with fewer resources invested than the second, then the first company would be described as more efficient. It achieved the same level of output with fewer inputs. An example of this can be seen in Exhibit 2.3, which shows the number of employees required to make automobiles in various companies in the United States, Europe, and Japan. (Note the extensive use by the Japanese of robots to replace humans on more mundane jobs.)

It is easy to see how decreased efficiency could be detrimental to organizational effectiveness. The more costly it becomes to achieve a goal, the less likely the organization is able to survive. For instance, consider the results of recent job enrichment experiments by Volvo and Saab-Scania, automobile manufacturers, where efforts were made to improve the quality of working life. However, as noted by several prominent investigators, while job enrichment may have desirable social consequences, the costs associated with such efforts may be so high that they increase the price of the product beyond what customers are willing to pay, resulting in decreased sales. This is obviously self-defeating for both the auto firm and its employees.

Relative labor costs, productivity per man-hour, costs of raw materials, and technological advances are just a few of the many factors used to determine the efficiency of a given organization. In the last decade, for example, many business enterprises have moved their factories from one state to another because of lower taxes or labor costs, or because they would be closer to their sources of raw materials and thus reduce transportation costs. Such moves may be seen as attempts at improving efficiency, if not effectiveness.

The concept of efficiency, then, may be viewed as being closely related to effectiveness. Whether or not efficiency is a determinant of effectiveness apparently depends upon several additional factors, such as the availability or scarcity of resources. In general, efficiency is defined here as the extent to which resources are rationally utilized in the pursuit of organizational goals. In this sense, factors such as employee turnover and absenteeism (that is, the wasting of human resources) may represent more a statement of organizational inefficiency than ineffectiveness, as has been suggested by others.

EXHIBIT 2.3   EMPLOYEE EFFICIENCY RATIOS FOR VARIOUS AUTOMOBILE COMPANIES

Company	Number of Cars Produced	Number of Employees	Efficiency Ratio
British Leyland	500,000	130,000	4:1
General Motors	4,000,000	517,000	8:1
Volkswagen	1,600,000	150,000	11:1
Renault	1,700,000	100,000	17:1
Toyota	2,000,000	45,000	44:1

Source: Based on information in *Fortune,* May 4, 1981, p. 284.

Influences on Organizational Effectiveness

If managerial success is defined in terms of organizational performance, it is necessary to ask what managers can do to facilitate effective performance. Based on recent work in the area (Goodman and Pennings, 1977; Steers, 1975, 1977), it appears that organizational effectiveness is influenced by four major categories of variables over which managers have some degree of control: (1) organizational characteristics, such as structure and technology; (2) environmental characteristics, such as economic and market conditions; (3) employee characteristics, such as job performance and job attachment; and (4) managerial policies and practices (see Exhibit 2.4). Examples of organizations that failed to coordinate these four major influences are discussed in Close-Up 2.1.

Organizational and environmental characteristics are discussed in this chapter and the next; employee characteristics and managerial actions are the subject of the remainder of the book. Based on this brief study of organizational effectiveness, we are now in a position to consider how people affect organizational performance. For example, what influences employee behavior and job attitudes? How do variations in the work environment affect such behavior and attitudes? What is the role of the work group in such outcomes? Finally, what can managers do to facilitate employee performance and job satisfaction?

Two general conclusions result from this discussion of organizational effectiveness. First, the concept of organizational effectiveness is best understood in terms of a continuous process rather than an end state. Marshalling an organization's resources for goal-directed activities is a never-ending task for most contemporary managers. Because of the changing nature of the goals pursued in most organizations, managers must continually be sensitive to environmental changes, restructure available resources where necessary, modify technologies, and train and retrain employees so maximum use is made of available talent and resources. In this way, the organization is in its most advantageous position for pursuing goals.

Second, it is incumbent upon managers to recognize the unique qualities that define their organization (e.g., its goals, structure, technology, people,

EXHIBIT 2.4   MAJOR INFLUENCES ON ORGANIZATIONAL EFFECTIVENESS

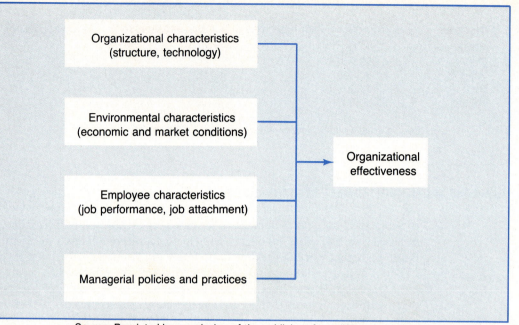

Organizational characteristics
(structure, technology)

Environmental characteristics
(economic and market conditions)

Organizational
effectiveness

Employee characteristics
(job performance, job attachment)

Managerial policies and practices

Source: Reprinted by permission of the publisher, from "When Is an Organization Effective? A Process Approach to Understanding Effectiveness," by R.M. Steers, *Organizational Dynamics*, Autumn, 1976, ©1976 American Management Association, New York. All rights reserved.

etc.) and to respond in a manner sensitive to this uniqueness. Arbitrary use of rules or principles for achieving success is not advisable because such principles may be of little use when applied to diverse organizations. Instead, responsibility must fall to management to develop employees who can successfully recognize and understand a particular situation and respond accordingly. When viewed in this manner, organizational effectiveness is the extent to which managers and employees can pool their knowledge and efforts to overcome obstacles that inhibit the attainment of the organization's goals.

ORGANIZATION DESIGN: THE BUREAUCRATIC MODEL

About the same time that industrial engineers such as Frederick Taylor and Henri Fayol were formulating the basic principles of scientific management (see Chapter 18), Max Weber was developing a model of organization, later to be known as *bureaucracy*. Weber, a German sociologist of the late 1800s, examined the work organizations of his day and found that organizations were

What differentiates an effective organization from an ineffective one? In many cases, a major factor is the extent to which an organization's managers can successfully balance and integrate organizational, environmental, and employee characteristics with managerial policies and practices. One of the best ways to understand this interaction is to examine instances of organizational *in*effectiveness. Consider the following two examples.

Farm Tractors. Here we have an example of a company that correctly identified a problem and set relevant goals, but then employed a less than optimal strategy for attaining those goals. Specifically, during the depression of the 1930s, Ford Motor Company decided to use its production facilities (underutilized because of sagging auto sales) to produce farm tractors. Within a short period of time, Ford designed and built a versatile yet inexpensive tractor. Unfortunately, however, Ford attempted to market its new product through the company's existing automobile distribution channels, primarily located in the cities and not attuned to the needs of farms. Hence, the product never reached the intended market and sales were minimal until Ford realized the mistake and developed a separate distribution system that was suited to market realities.

Slide Rules. If the above example represents an attempt to apply the wrong strategy to the right goal, this next example may be described as an attempt to apply the right strategy to the wrong goal. Specifically, for many years, this organization had a strong reputation for producing and selling high quality slide rules for a variety of applications. However, with the advent and widespread dissemination of inexpensive electronic calculators, sophisticated calculations could now be made more quickly and accurately than ever before. As a result, demand for slide rules decreased almost immediately and product sales dropped by 75% in just two years. Now, it is almost impossible to find a slide rule in any store. They have gone the way of the buggy whip. The company had either failed to predict environmental changes accurately or was unable to adapt to such changes in order to achieve its profit goal.

Examples such as these highlight the importance for managers to accurately diagnose environmental changes and to structure their organization and its people in such a way that a satisfactory response can be made to environmental demands.

Source: R. M. Steers, *Organizational Effectiveness: A Behavioral View* (Glenview, Illinois: Scott, Foresman and Company, 1977).

run primarily on the basis of custom and politics, not merit or efficiency. People secured administrative jobs principally through contacts, not expertise. Moreover, lines of authority and accountability were often scattered. In response to this, Weber (1947) sought to create what he felt was an ideal organization—one governed by rationality rather than politics.

Characteristics of a Bureaucracy

According to Weber, the ideal bureaucracy was characterized by the following:

1. *Specialization and division of labor.* Tasks required to accomplish the organization's goals were broken down into highly specialized jobs so that everyone would become an expert in his or her area.
2. *Rules and procedures.* Weber believed it was important that each task be performed according to a consistent system of abstract rules; thus, the beginning of "standard operating procedures." Such rules and procedures were to lead to a standardized high quality of output, since everyone would know precisely what was expected.
3. *Authority.* All positions in an organization were arranged in hierarchical form with domains of authority clearly established.
4. *Impersonality of office.* Position holders were required to assume an impersonal attitude in dealing with others. Authority was vested in the office, not in the individual; the individual simply acted impersonally as a trustee of the office.
5. *Employment and promotion by merit.* Instead of the previous practice of political appointments to office, Weber argued that office holders at all levels should be selected based on merit and qualifications. Here we have an impetus for civil service examinations in Western Europe (although curiously such examinations were used in China since the time of Confucius).

Problems with Bureaucracy

These ideal characteristics of bureaucracy were meant to result in organizations that were both more productive and more equitable to employees. Stability, efficiency, and control of the organization were all theoretically enhanced. Unfortunately, however, the gulf between theory and actual practice can be great, and the bureaucratic model has been criticized on several grounds.

For example, many people feel that the bureaucratic approach creates *excessive red tape.* When an organization is faced with a new problem, however small, it typically responds with new rules or procedures. The ever-increasing multitude of rules serves to constrain creative behavior. Instead of finding solutions to problems, people often spend their time following rules. This may contribute to another criticism—that bureaucracies have *reduced flexibility* of operations. The nature of a highly structured organization makes adaptation and innovation difficult. Instead, the organization continues on its preordained path.

In some situations, bureaucracies create conditions in which there is a *dominance of authority.* That is, having more and more authority—and exercising that authority—becomes almost an end in itself. Likewise, people

EXHIBIT 2.5   DIMENSIONS OF ORGANIZATION STRUCTURE

Dimension	Definition
Decentralization:	Extent to which power and authority are extended down through the organizational hierarchy.
Tall vs. Flat:	Number of levels in the hierarchy (controlling for organization size).
Division of Labor:	Extent to which jobs are specialized and broken down into small units of work.
Departmentation:	Primary mechanism for grouping units in the organization, either according to function, product, or some other criterion (e.g., matrix).

with less authority tend to blindly follow the dictates of those with more authority, regardless of whether such dictates are wise, prudent, or ethical.

Finally, the hierarchical progression of careers proposed by bureaucratic theory is supposed to create the condition where people rise in rank as a result of merit. In actual fact, however, people often rise by seniority. Hence, a psychology of *position protection* is created in which employees exert energy to maintain and protect their positions (and the prerequisites that go with such positions) instead of exerting energy on organizational goals or effectiveness.

Although other shortcomings could be mentioned here, the point is that bureaucracy in practice is often at odds with bureaucracy in theory. Although bureaucracy was designed to reduce inefficiencies and incompetence in organizations, modern bureaucracies often contribute to such ills. Because of this, recent efforts in organization design have attempted to develop new approaches that minimize these negative influences on organizational life.

ORGANIZATION STRUCTURE: CONTEMPORARY APPROACHES

Simply put, *organization structure* refers to the way in which an organization puts together its human resources for goal-directed activities. The way the various human parts of an organization fit together into relatively fixed relationships defines patterns of social interaction, coordination, and task-oriented behavior. The role of structure in the success and functioning of an enterprise has long been a topic of concern among both organizational analysts and managers (Blau, 1955; Dubin, 1959; Worthy, 1950).

The concept of structure can in turn be broken down into various *dimensions* of structure. At least four such dimensions have relevance for the study of organizational behavior: (1) decentralization vs. centralization, (2) tall vs. flat, (3) division of labor, and (4) departmentation (see Exhibit 2.5).

Decentralization

Decentralization refers to the extent to which various types of power and authority are extended down through the organizational hierarchy. The more decentralized an organization, the greater the extent to which the rank-and-file employees can participate in and accept responsibility for decisions concerning their jobs and the future activities of the organization.

Historically, an increase in organization size typically brought with it an increase in centralization of authority and power in the upper echelons of management. As organizations grew, the distance between the relevant sources of information for decision making (often located near the bottom of the hierarchy) and the decision makers themselves became greater, resulting in poor communications, unfortunate decisions, and reduced effectiveness. Although it is not possible to pinpoint precisely when this trend toward increased centralization plateaued, Chandler (1962) has suggested that it may have been during the 1920s when Alfred P. Sloan, Jr., then president of General Motors, introduced the concept of the *central office.* The central office was to concentrate the more important organization-wide *policy* decisions in the hands of major corporate executives, while decentralizing responsibility for *operating* decisions to the lowest level possible in the various operating divisions. In theory, most decisions would be made closer to their information sources, leading to increased flexibility of operation and increased divisional autonomy, while maintaining corporate control over major policy matters.

Increased decentralization in organizations often leads to improvements in several facets of organizational effectiveness, including managerial efficiency, open communications and feedback, job satisfaction, and employee retention. In some cases, decentralization has led to improved performance and greater innovation and creativity in organizations, although the findings here are not entirely consistent (see Close-Up 2.2). These findings suggest that decentralized organizations allow for greater autonomy and responsibility among employees at lower levels in the hierarchy, thereby utilizing more effectively an organization's human resources. This explanation is consistent with recent findings among individual employees indicating that increased autonomy and responsibility often lead to increased job involvement, satisfaction, and performance.

It should be pointed out, however, that a close relationship between decentralization and improved effectiveness is not always found. For example, one study discovered that decentralized control led to improved performance in research laboratories, but caused poorer performance in production departments (Lawrence and Lorsch, 1967). Such findings may be attributed to differences in individual or situational factors that can affect the decentralization-effectiveness relationship. It has been shown, for example, that different personality traits and other individual differences can affect the amount of participation that employees seek in decision making (Steers, 1977b). Some employees may simply want to avoid the added responsibilities that are brought on by decentralization of authority and influence, while other employees eagerly accept such responsibilities.

CLOSE-UP 2.2   DECENTRALIZATION AT 3M

A good example of decentralization in organizations can be seen at the 3M Corporation of Minneapolis. For a company with 87,000 employees and annual sales of $6 billion, 3M spends a lot of time "thinking small."

As Gordon England, vice-president, says, "We are keenly aware of the disadvantages of large size. . . . We make a conscious effort to keep our units as small as possible because we think it helps keep them flexible and vital." For example, 3M's average manufacturing facility employs just 270 people, while management groups with as few as five members often guide the fortunes of many of the company's household, industrial, and scientific products.

Does decentralization pay off? For 3M, apparently so. The company has seen its sales and earnings grow fourfold over the past decade, while its work force has increased forty percent.

Increasingly in the U.S., sagging corporate performance is blamed on inflexible company structures and entrenched operating methods. In many cases, the economies of scale made possible by bigness are nullified by organizational rigidities and bottlenecks. Because of this, the decentralized, flexible company (even a big company) has a greater capacity to adapt to changes in the external environment.

Managing consultant Robert Heller says, "U.S. companies are often nominally decentralized, but in fact operate under a top-heavy headquarters staff." And Olivetti's Carlo De Benedetti adds that there is "a dramatic decline in the entrepreneurial skills of American managers and an enormous growth of bureaucracy in American companies."

Hence, a case is made that one remedy for North America's lagging productivity (see Chapter One) may be increased decentralization, in which authority and action are pushed downward to involve more people at the bottom of the hierarchy where the actual work is done.

Sources: *The Wall Street Journal,* February 5, 1982, p. 1 and p. 25; *Fortune,* October 20, 1980, pp. 147–48.

Moreover, it is possible that differing job technologies, work environments, or goals may call for varying degrees of decentralization in order to be successful. While clearly recognizing the benefits of decentralization in work organizations, Duncan (1972) noted several potential weaknesses that should also be recognized. These include the following:

1. Innovation and growth may tend to be restricted to existing projects or functional areas since fewer means exist to coordinate and integrate the various decentralized units.
2. In some cases, it may be difficult to allocate pooled resources such as computing facilities or laboratories.
3. Decentralization makes it more difficult for certain shared functions (e.g., personnel, purchasing) to be executed.
4. Decentralization can lead to jurisdictional disputes and/or conflicts over

priorities since each unit essentially becomes an independent entrepreneurial area.

5. Decentralization may create conditions in which a deterioration of in-depth competence and expertise transpires. It may become more difficult to attract technical specialists.

6. In general, decentralization in the extreme may lead to ultimate ineffectiveness of operations due to a lack of high-level coordination and integration.

Managers of effective organizations must seek the optimal amount of decentralization or centralization. Hence, the decentralization concept should not be seen as good or bad in itself; rather, based on the goals of the organization, efforts should be made to decentralize power and authority to an extent that allows organizations to make full use of the knowledge and expertise of lower-level participants, while simultaneously maintaining the necessary degree of centralization to insure coordination and control.

Tall Versus Flat Organizations

A second aspect of organization structure focuses on the vertical structural arrangements of the organization—that is, the extent to which an organization is *tall* or *flat*. As shown in Exhibit 2.6, a "tall" organization typically has more levels of management than a "flat" one. Both the tall and flat organizations shown in the exhibit have the same number of employees; they are simply arranged differently.

What difference does such variation in organizational structure make? To begin, tall organizations allow for closer *control* over subordinates. Since a manager has fewer subordinates, he or she has more time to focus on the activities of these few people. Managers in flat organizations, on the other hand, must oversee the activities of more people, thereby placing greater responsibility for task accomplishment on subordinates. In a very definitive manner, flat organizations facilitate increased decentralization of power and authority.

Second, tall organizations allow for greater *personal contact* between manager and subordinate, again because the manager has fewer people to oversee. The risk, however, is that the manager comes to know two or three subordinates very well, but fails to become acquainted with those further down the hierarchy. In contrast, a flat organization forces a manager to get to know more people, albeit on a somewhat more superficial level.

Finally, tall organizations often serve to inhibit *interpersonal communication*. This occurs because the increased number of levels through which a message must be transmitted allows for more distortion of the message (see Chapter Thirteen). In contrast, managers in flat organizations come into direct contact with a greater number of subordinates, thereby allowing for increased direct communication and accuracy of message transmission.

In summary, it would be inappropriate to conclude that one type of

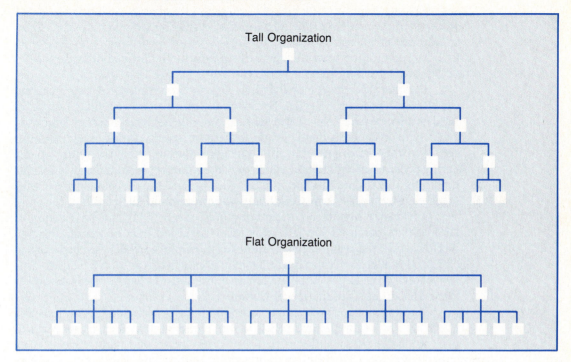

Tall Organization

Flat Organization

organization (tall or flat) is superior to the other. The appropriate number of levels in an organization depends upon many factors, including the purpose of the organization, the people, the technology involved, and the resources available. For instance, one can make an argument that an R&D organization (which requires an open exchange of ideas and has rather long time horizons for planning) requires a flatter organization structure than a military organization (which requires quick and unquestioning response in times of crisis). One form is not "better" than the other. Instead, each utilizes the form that is more suitable for its purpose and environment.

Division of Labor

The concept of *division of labor* (or functional specialization) traces its origins to the scientific management movement around the turn of the century. Taylor (1911) and his associates argued that a major determinant of organizational success was the ability of an organization to divide its work functions into highly specialized activities. As support for specialization, these writers (looking at effectiveness from the standpoint of industrial engineering) cited Adam Smith's example of the manufacture of straight pins in England. Smith noted that in the late eighteenth century (before the advent of the Industrial

Revolution) one worker by himself could make 20 straight pins per day. However, when the tasks required to make such pins were divided into ten separate operations and each worker carried out only one such operation, ten workers could make 48,000 pins per day, or 4,800 pins per worker. Thus, specialization brought about a 240-fold increase in productivity. Examples like this represented a major source of support for Taylor and other advocates of increased specialization.

Perhaps the concept of division of labor is best seen in many current experiments with job redesign. For instance, as shown in Exhibit 2.7, a major innovation of the new Volvo and Saab automobile plants is that they largely do away with the traditionally high degree of specialization seen in most contemporary auto assembly lines. Instead, they represent a return to the "craftsperson" approach in which each employee is trained in multiple functions and supposedly has a better idea about how the whole product fits together. Employees form work teams to jointly build subunits.

The major hypothesis underlying the concept of increased division of labor is that increased specialization (also called job fractionization) leads to increased effectiveness because it allows each employee to develop expertise in one particular area to maximize his or her contribution to production. This hypothesis formed the basis for Henry Ford's introduction of the assembly line and the mass production of cars.

Unfortunately, few rigorous attempts have been made to examine this hypothesis in organizational settings. The evidence that does exist seems to indicate that increased specialization is often associated with reduced labor costs and increased innovation and creativity—both inputs into organizational effectiveness. However, specialization has also been shown to be related to increased friction and conflict within organizations. Apparently, increased specialization causes frustration among some employees because it limits their behavior and their attempts to satisfy their personal development goals. The employees may express their dissatisfaction through various forms of industrial conflict.

In other words, although division of labor is frequently beneficial in terms of employee performance, it may simultaneously be detrimental to employees' job attitudes, mental health, and propensity to remain with the organization. Thus, the benefit of increased productivity derived from a high degree of specialization may be more than offset by such negative consequences as strikes, sabotage, turnover and absenteeism, and so forth. Again, management must decide how best to balance costs and benefits in its attempts to discover the optimal organizational design.

Departmentation

The final aspect of organization structure to be discussed here is departmentation. In brief, *departmentation* focuses on how the various primary tasks of an organization are grouped. Although many approaches to departmentation have been taken by various organizations, three rather general types can be identified: departmentation by function, product, and matrix.

EXHIBIT 2.7   TWO DIFFERENT APPROACHES TO DIVISION OF LABOR AT SAAB-SCANIA

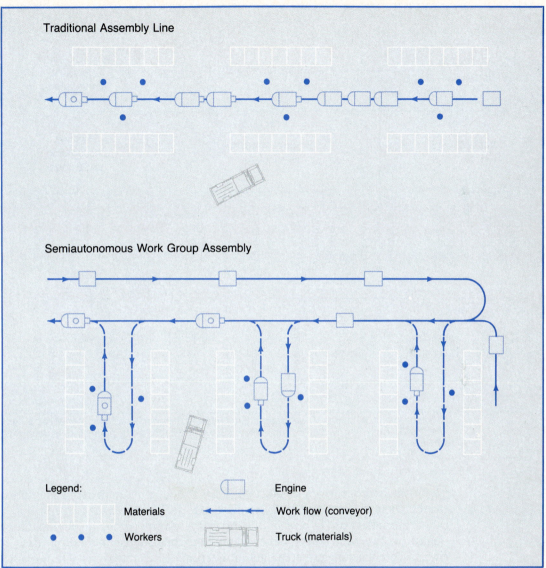

Traditional Assembly Line

Semiautonomous Work Group Assembly

Legend:

Engine

Materials   Work flow (conveyor)

Workers   Truck (materials)

Source: J. P. Norstedt and S. Aguren, *The Saab-Scania Report* (Stockholm: The Swedish Employers' Confederation, 1973), pp. 35 and 37. Reprinted by permission.

Functional Departmentation. We often hear managers refer to the various "functions" of an organization. By function we mean a particular specialized activity that is central to an organization's continued survival. Such functions for a typical business organization include marketing, finance, manufacturing, research and development, etc. *Functional* departmentation, then, organizes

EXHIBIT 2.8   FUNCTIONAL DEPARTMENTATION AT THE DICTAPHONE CORPORATION

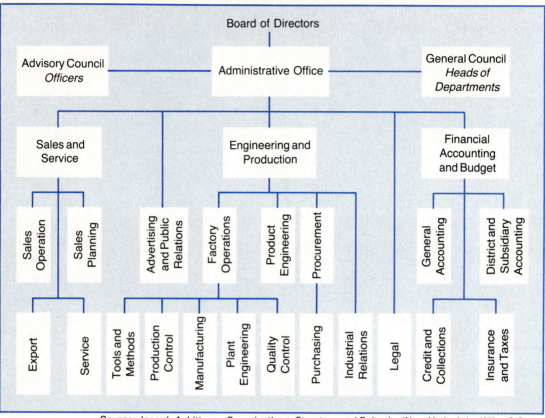

Source: Joseph A. Litterer, *Organizations: Structure and Behavior* (New York: John Wiley & Sons, Inc., 1963). Copyright © 1963 by John Wiley & Sons, Inc. Reprinted by permission of John Wiley & Sons, Inc.

the work force according to specialized activities. Functional departmentation at the Dictaphone Corporation is illustrated in Exhibit 2.8.

Specialization is one of the primary advantages of departmentation based on function. Many believe that functional departmentation leads to increased efficiency and economic utilization of the employees. On the other hand, functional specialization may also lead to situations of goal suboptimization as each department focuses on its own specialty or function at the expense of others. This problem can be clearly seen in a classic study of Dearborn and Simon (1958), described in Chapter Four.

Product Departmentation. A second approach to departmentation, often favored by larger organizations, is *product* departmentation. Under this approach, work units are organized based on products rather than functions, as shown in Exhibit 2.9. Within each product group, all of the various functional areas are represented.

EXHIBIT 2.9   PRODUCT DEPARTMENTATION AT TEXAS INSTRUMENTS

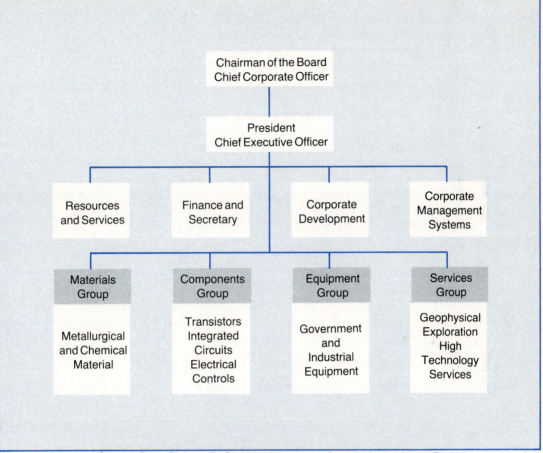

Source: From Richard P. Olsen and Jordan J. Baruch, *Innovation at Texas Instruments, Inc.,* 9-672-036. Copyright © 1971 by the President and Fellows of Harvard College. Reproduced by permission of the Harvard Business School.

With product departmentation, each product grouping (consumer products or industrial products, for example) becomes essentially a "company" of its own, or more accurately, a cost center of its own. General Motors, for example, has different divisions to manufacture cars and trucks, locomotives, refrigerators, automobile accessories, and so on. In this way, each division manager focuses all of his or her attention on one business (see Close-Up 2.3). This allows control of the division to be more easily accomplished and conflict between functional areas to be reduced somewhat.

Matrix Organization. A third approach to departmentation is the *matrix organization.* In essence, a matrix design represents nothing more than a product departmentation superimposed on a functional departmentation. The managers for the functional areas represented (e.g., marketing) have

CLOSE-UP 2.3 THE PRODUCT MANAGER AT GENERAL MILLS

When General Mills completed its new headquarters building in Minneapolis in 1980, it was discovered that all of the telephones could not be installed at once. The order came down from senior management: "Hook up the product managers' first. The business can't run without them."

Even though a product approach to organization design has been in use since 1927 at Procter and Gamble, the approach remains popular today with many companies. A product management approach essentially creates an environment in which each product manager runs his or her own show. Often ranging in age from late twenties through the thirties, these managers are provided with an opportunity to demonstrate their expertise early in their careers by shepherding one product or group of products in the marketplace. The company benefits by knowing that one individual is exclusively responsible for the particular product or product group.

The product manager is responsible for developing a marketing plan and a budget, which is reviewed by upper-level marketing managers. Once approved, the product manager is responsible for carrying out the plan. For instance, one twenty-eight-year-old manager was given a $10 million budget to introduce a new cereal.

For those who succeed, there are rewards. In fact, of the three new top executives appointed at General Mills in 1981, each had risen through the product management ranks.

How does the company benefit? Says one General Mills executive, "Profit responsibility is fundamental. If a product manager has it, it pushes him into manufacturing efficiencies, productivity gains, ingredient substitutions, and anticipating commodity fluctuations." In short, an entrepreneurial system is established, using company products as the basic units of organization design and providing a training ground for aspiring young managers.

Source: Ann M. Morrison, "The General Mills Brand of Managers," *Fortune,* January 12, 1981, pp. 99–107.

direct-line authority over the specialists in their own departments. This provides for good control and accountability by function.

In addition, each functional specialist is assigned to a project group or profit center, such as industrial plastics, as part of a focused team. As such, a particular sales representative, for example, would be responsible both to the general sales manager and to the project director for industrial plastics. In other words, almost everyone has *two* bosses instead of one.

An example of this approach in practice can be seen in the case of Dow Corning. In order to facilitate better communication, planning, and control, Dow Corning implemented a matrix organization design in the late 1960s. (See Exhibit 2.10.) It set up a "business board" for each of its ten businesses, consisting of a business manager (who was primarily responsible for the profitability of the business) and representatives from marketing, manufactur-

EXHIBIT 2.10   MATRIX ORGANIZATION DESIGN AT DOW CORNING

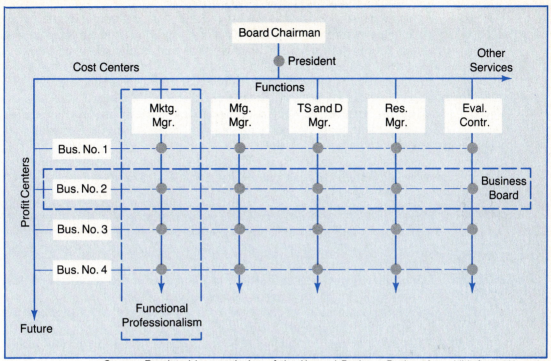

ing, finance, research, and technical services and development (a trouble-shooter who ensures that the customer is satisfied with the technical workings of the product).

At Dow, each functional representative reports *directly* to his or her functional department, but contributes to the design, implementation, and success of the particular business to which he or she is assigned. Thus, each person essentially has two bosses. As a result, care must be taken to ensure that both the functional and business board managers are given sufficient authority and accountability to attain their respective objectives. Coordination and trust are essential ingredients if such a system is to work.

After long experience with the matrix design, the company concluded that the system had both advantages and drawbacks. On the positive side, the matrix design led to: higher profit generation, even in industries squeezed by competition; increased competitive ability based on technical innovation and product quality; sound, prompt decision making facilitated by open communications; resource allocations proportionate to expected results; more stimulating tasks and on-the-job training; visible and measurable results; more time for top management to focus on long-range planning instead of day-to-day operations; and accountability that is more closely related to responsibility and authority.

But the matrix design was not without its costs, including: the necessity to cope with resistance to change; strong top management support for extended periods; the need for an intelligent and highly motivated middle management anxious to see the whole organization progress; a determination to minimize internal politics; and the need for board members, top management, and middle management to exercise abundant patience.

Overall, however, the matrix design at Dow Corning has proven to be an effective tool that facilitates both individual managerial self-development and increased corporate profitability.

Proponents of matrix organizations argue that such designs have the following advantages (Cleland and King, 1968; Davis and Lawrence, 1977):

1. Each product or project is given special attention in that a product manager is appointed specifically to look after that product.
2. Employee utilization is flexible in that a reservoir of specialists is kept in the various functional organizations.
3. Specialized knowledge is available to all product or project areas and this knowledge can be transferred from one project to another.
4. Project people have a functional home to return to when they are no longer required on a given project.
5. Response to market fluctuations or customer needs is typically faster because decision making is centralized within a project group and because each group has the needed functional expertise to act quickly.
6. A system of checks and balances is established between concerns for product and concerns for function in which both areas of responsibility can receive necessary consideration.

In summary, matrix organizations hold considerable promise for organizations in dynamic environments in which rapid managerial response is a central consideration. Integrating various functional areas and focusing attention on specific product areas allow for both expertise and flexibility in management. Thus, it is no surprise that major organizations like General Electric, TRW Systems, Dow Corning, Shell Oil, and others have come to rely on such designs.

SUMMARY

In this chapter, we began our discussion of formal organizations by examining the concept of organizations. Included in this discussion was a recognition that organizations need to meet certain requirements in order to survive. Moreover, it was noted that organizations can perhaps be best understood in terms of subsystems; that is, different parts of the organization perform different functions.

Next, we turned our attention to the topic of organizational effectiveness, noting how effectiveness differs from the related concept of efficiency. Several major influences on effectiveness were discussed.

The bureaucratic model was introduced, and several potential problems with this "ideal" form of organization were considered. Following this, the concept of organization structure was explored in detail. In particular, we considered four basic dimensions of structure: (1) decentralization-centralization, (2) tall vs. flat organizations, (3) division of labor, and (4) departmentation based on function, product, or matrix.

To conclude, this chapter provides a foundation for understanding general organization design principles upon which to base the discussion in the next chapter of contingencies in organization design.

KEY WORDS

bureaucracy
central office
decentralization
departmentation
division of labor
efficiency
functional departmentation
matrix organization

organization
organization structure
organizational effectiveness
product departmentation
rational coordination
subsystems
tall versus flat organizations

FOR DISCUSSION

1. Discuss the various approaches to defining organizations.
2. Describe some of the requirements of organizations. Which ones do you feel are most important for organizational survival?
3. Identify the five subsystems of organizations.
4. What is meant by organizational effectiveness?
5. Compare and contrast organizational *effectiveness* and *efficiency.*
6. Identify the major influences on organizational effectiveness.
7. What are the defining characteristics of ideal bureaucracy? Identify several problems with the bureaucratic model.
8. What is meant by organization structure? Identify the various dimensions of structure.
9. What are the advantages and disadvantages of tall and flat organizations?
10. Compare and contrast functional, product, and matrix departmentation.

CANADIAN MARCONI COMPANY

On the fifth of April 1968, the employees of the Avionics Division of Canadian Marconi Company in Montreal, Canada, were advised that the division would undergo a significant organization change. Mr. K. C. M. Glegg, General Manager of the Division, posted a notice which described some of the changes Avionics anticipated as it reorganized to a matrix:

Managing Change
The general approach to our organization is intended to reflect the following three features:

1. *Most of our work is made up of large separable tasks having a unique character with regard to customers, equipment, schedules, contractual conditions, test requirements, and so on. This is our program activity and requires program management.* The program manager breaks the main task into subtasks to which other people are assigned, and so on, until a complete program team is evolved.
2. *A relatively small fraction of our work, somewhere between 10 and 20 percent, cannot usefully be viewed as having a unique program character. This is usually initiation and follow-on activity and needs special provision.* Examples are redesign of small areas of a product; updating of a manual; production of spares for an inactive program; and early study and experimental phases of new products.

3. *Most of our work requires similar facilities: selling, design, contracts, manufacturing, purchasing, quality control, scheduling and planning, pricing, and so on. These are functional activities and require functional management.* The total capacity required in any one facility far exceeds that required for any one program or follow-on activity. This "facility management" or "functional management" is clearly complementary to "program management."

Details of Organization. Using the foregoing discussion and nomenclature, the various groups can be regarded as falling into the following two categories:

1. *Functional (facility) groups*
   Mechanical design
   Procurement
   Manufacturing support
   Assembly and components
   Marketing
   Quality control
2. *Functional and program groups*
   Products and programs group I
   Products and programs group II
   Product support and programs

These groups will contain all program activity and, in addition, a certain amount of functional activity.

Exhibits 1 and 2 show the organization of the division and a typical program.

Predeterminates of Change
Keith Glegg had worked his way up

Case 2.1 from S. M. Davis and P. R. Lawrence, *Matrix*, pp. 58–68, © 1977, Addison-Wesley Publishing Company, Inc., Reading, Massachusetts. Reprinted with permission.

EXHIBIT 1   CANADIAN MARCONI COMPANY—AVIONICS DIVISION

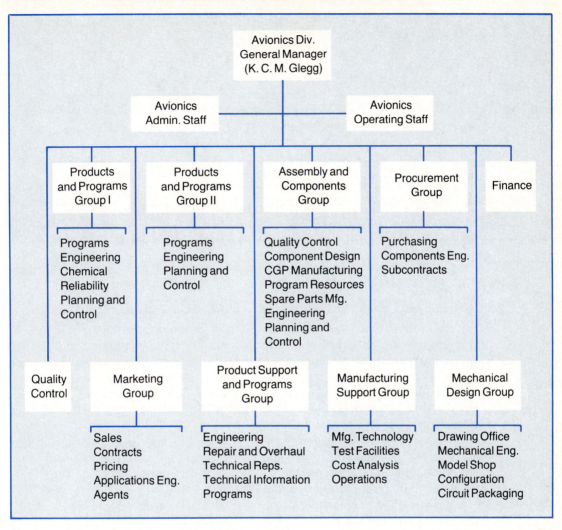

through the technical arm of Canadian Marconi to become chief engineer and then General Manager of the Avionics Division (see Ex. 1). He was an important inventor and innovator in basic frequency-modulated continuous wave (FM-CW) Doppler radar technology. This FM-CW technology gave Avionics a world leadership position in Doppler radar equipment design and production. All Avionics' equipment designs were at the state of the art of the technology in their field at the time of their design, a result of the importance Glegg attached to the role of innovative research and development engineering for the department's future.

Doppler radars were used in airborne navigation systems to determine aircraft velocity and distance by bouncing microwave signals off the terrain and calculating the desired parameters from the

EXHIBIT 2   AVIONICS DIVISION—TYPICAL PROGRAM ORGANIZATION

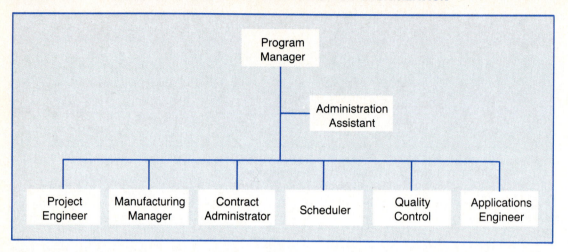

"Doppler effect" of returning signals. A typical Doppler system was composed of several "black boxes" of electronic and electromechanical equipment. The Doppler systems in the Avionics product line sold for prices that ranged between $20,000 and $80,000 per system.

As the division grew and Avionics' success with Doppler systems brought large increases in sales, Glegg's preoccupations became considerably more managerial than technical. He began to reassess some of his own thinking about organizations. The organization appeared too weak, both structurally and managerially, to cope with the increasing complexity of his division's activities.

Glegg was finding it impossible to cope with the number of major decisions that had to be made. Six major programs and several minor ones were in different stages of design and/or production (see Fig. 2). All had different customers, sometimes in different countries. Every program's product, although they were all Doppler radar systems, was significantly different from every other one, particularly in its technology. Nevertheless the programs had to share manufacturing facilities, major items of capital equipment, and specialized functions. Glegg felt he had to find some way to force the whole decision process down to some level below his own. He described some of his thinking.

> Even in all the difficulties that we found ourselves in at the time, many of us saw that if we could succeed in managing the place effectively, we could get out of difficulty and into more products and the necessity for still more decisions. I started looking for a way of making the system nonlinear; a way of decoupling the number of decisions that I would have to make from the number of involvements of the division. Eventually one has to decouple the one nervous system from this linear attachment to all the involvements. And the way you do it is to put another nervous system between you and it.

Glegg identified the uniqueness of the task as one of the key factors determining the particular approach taken to matrix design. He felt that in Avionics'

business the task could be isolated cleanly and simply. More important, however, was his feeling that the isolation of task was something that could be understood by all the people in the division. After extensive discussion with his subordinates, it was decided that a matrix should be the general form towards which Avionics must move.

Corporate Management Unfreezing . . .

Convincing himself and his managers was one task for Glegg. Convincing corporate management was quite another.

> First of all, I had to get agreement from the corporate management that they would allow me to implement such a scheme. There was a tremendous amount of opposition. There were people opposing it for the usual reasons, such as one man reporting to two people. That's not just against organization—it's against God. It's agin' the Bible.[1] No man should serve two masters. You shouldn't do that. There were people on the accounting side of the house saying, "It's going to cost too much." Obviously, it's a much more expensive way of managing than a straight functional way of managing.
>
> You could break down the objections they were presenting into two classes. One of them was semiphilosophical notions of management and people, that you could overcome simply by talking enough. The practical objections such as, "But it's going to cost more," were more difficult. I guess the way I ended up putting that one out of the way was to say, "Look, what you're telling me is that I'm going to end up with a system that is overmanaged. Now if you ask me, I can tell you what the cost is of this overmanagement. But now I have to ask you a question. What is the cost of undermanaging? I can give you a bounded cost for the overmanagement. That is, I can count up the pieces and multiply them by their salaries, and I can tell you what the cost of overmanagement is. I can give you absolute upper bound.

Now you tell me, what are the costs of undermanagement? Are they $100,000 a year? Are they $1 million a year? What are they?"

> Well, at the time we had so many problems of undermanagement on our hands, it was easy for me to illustrate that the number was almost catastrophic. So I got a kind of grudging understanding that I could go ahead, but it had better work or both it and I would go.

. . . And Unfreezing Everyone Else

Glegg then went about selling matrix to the rest of the organization. A series of meetings for middle managers answered some of the immediate questions, and an extensive notice posted throughout the department was designed to inform the rest of the department members of the intended changes. However, Glegg was aware that neither notices nor speeches could supply the real answer. The people would have to see the system function to have faith in it. He described how he believed the process of acceptance took place for many.

> It took the better part of two years to work through enough of the cases to remove the question whether it could work. People are still left with the question as to whether it works for them. If a change has caused them to lose something or other, then it still isn't working for them. But at least over two years, if the thing works in some objective way for most of the people, then it does work.

Establishing the Program
Manager's Boundaries

Glegg and his immediate subordinates then faced detailed decisions about the structure. In many matrix organizations the program manager reports directly to the organization's head: the department general manager or divisional vice-president. Should the program manag-

ers report to Glegg or should there be a level between him and the program managers? While it was evident that Glegg could have coped with the number of program managers initially envisioned, it was also evident that as their number grew he would be unable to manage both them and the functions. Glegg commented:

> The program manager is the first level at which integration occurs. It is the first level at which the company's business is conducted whole. When he is not available, either because he's sick or traveling or something, it is not practical to go down in the organization to replace him. You have to go up.

Although it was the functional managers that one had to go to when program managers were unavailable, Glegg went to considerable effort to make it clear to the functional managers that the program managers were nevertheless their seniors. They were senior in the sense that they were responsible for "the business whole," and no functional manager enjoyed that privilege. This was also reflected in their salaries.

> We had to decide on the extent to which a program manager would control his facilities and his resources. That is, what would a program manager be? We decided on an arrangement which took us far over on the side where the program manager controls everything. There are some problems with this kind of an arrangement. For example, how do people who are attached to this guy, on an essentially temporary basis, get their progress review done? That's a hard, practical question. The way it was resolved was that the employee's progress review would be done jointly by the program manager and by his functional shop. It seemed important that when a person was reporting to two people, that the two people were indeed contributing to the assessment of

performance, and that the person with two bosses felt it.

Selecting Program Managers

Engineers dominated the Avionics Division. Glegg and six of the eleven group managers held formal engineering degrees. In addition to the very large numbers of engineers within the formal engineering groups, many of the marketing and applications personnel were engineers and a substantial number of the senior personnel in the production and manufacturing areas held engineering degrees. Any consideration of the characteristics needed to be a program manager under the proposed matrix had to face this issue of professional background squarely.

> We wanted to start with an engineer and turn him into a program manager, because the root of the most serious problems is technical. But the object was not to get an engineer and turn him into a program manager so he could solve the problem. The real object of starting with an engineer was to make certain that there was someone who could assess how to commit resources to the solution; someone who could give order to the problems a program manager was bound to encounter.
>
> There are difficulties inherent in the notion that you're going to retread an engineer. One of the things you have to do is help him suppress a tendency to want to become his own project engineer. You have to help him resign himself to the fact that he's no longer an engineer; but that he's going to have to use what he knows about engineering to run the risk of the generalist.

From Program Management to Product Management

In the late 1960s the division expanded rapidly with the economy, and the aerospace industry enjoyed the tail end of a long economic boom. Mid-1970 sales reached a peak of $36 million and employees numbered in excess of 2000.

However, the year 1970 also ushered in an end to North America's economic boom and the aerospace industry was about the hardest hit of all. Avionics' dependence on programs with fixed termination dates left the division in a very vulnerable position. In some cases, follow-up contracts didn't come. In others, cancellations left design and production areas with little or no work. Avionics needed a different type of business to ensure its survival. It needed products that would endure and applications that went beyond only one narrowly defined program. It also needed an organization that would support such a strategy. Avionics' response was to change the program management form of matrix to a product management form; from an overlay to a more permanent balance. Glegg explained the difference.

> The product manager's object in life is almost exactly the opposite of the program manager's. The object of the product manager is to take an opportunity that he has and extend it as far into the future as he possibly can. To start with an idea, a product, someone else's product, and make of it whatever he can; as big, as long-lived, and, of course, as profitable and productive as he can make it.
>
> The object of the program manager is to take a task which is well defined with respect to its schedule, cost, and function, and to execute it. A program is really a special case of a product. A program represents a kind of singularity in the product where the intensity of management it needs simply requires that you attach one nervous system to it exclusively.
>
> So far as I can tell from the literature, there's a lot of experience with the program management idea, with the fixed

time, fixed money, fixed outcome situation. There is much less experience with the product manager, of the type we have tried putting into existence. What we're finding, however, is that it's an extremely powerful way of getting motivation into the system, because what the product manager has become is a kind of mini-general manager.

Modifying the Control System

To have product managers make the most of their own decisions, Glegg insisted that the accounting system reflect the organization design. With appropriate cost information and profit and loss data available to them, program and product managers could contain decisions at their level. They only had need to approach the group manager level on financial matters when major capital demands were being placed on the division.

Program or product reporting was broken out by total sales and further subdivided to provide as much managerial visibility as possible. Within each category, program and product managers could also determine individual charges by the cost centers which represented the different functional activities. A parallel system recorded functional costs. Every direct charging employee had to be accounted for by a "legitimate" charge number so that only overhead people in the functions could remain unassigned to a particular program. As a consequence, slack personnel in the functions were quickly identified by their charges to program or product numbers.

Communication and Openness

In the early phases of implementation, few people fully understood the matrix concepts. Others understood them hardly at all. Believing that effective and open communication was central to successful implementation, Glegg went about creating an atmosphere to support his beliefs.

One way of ensuring that the matrix would work was to ensure that functional shops always had the best possible grasp of what the business side of the house was likely to want. It seemed vital that all the resource pieces have the longest possible view of what the demands on them would be if they were to offer the most help.

To do this, I decided that we would have meetings every Friday and talk about all the problems in the division. The people who attend these meetings are group managers in charge of resource functions and group managers in charge of task groups.

At this point, the meetings are as open, frank, relaxed, and productive as one could hope to find in any industrial organization. We trust one another and, maybe what's even more important, they trust one another.

Glegg felt that these meetings lay at the core of successful matrix management. It was a mechanism whereby every part of the organization could question every other part and come to understand better each other's contribution. After approximately two years, one meeting a month was expanded to include program and product managers in addition to the group managers. With the variety of experiences that was building up among the product and program managers, they could learn extensively from each other's problems, successes, and failures. Two years later, this meeting was expanded to the second-level functional managers and a function-by-function critique of each of the areas had commenced. Glegg described the contributions gained from adding the product and program managers to this communication process.

This allows people to hear from one another and understand that they all have problems; to build a kind of confidence in themselves because they hear about other people's experiences and solutions in similar circumstances.

I'm getting the impression that the communication propagation down through the product manager is more effective than through the functional shop because they are more closely knit to each other.

Holding this clearly delicate "net" together is the most challenging part of my work. The most powerful tool one has, and it is really simple after you get living this way, is openness. I don't have any secrets at all. Anything they want to know, I'll tell them. Furthermore, it's easier for me to know things now, with a lot more activity going on, than it was even two years ago. I don't have to go after information. People come in and tell me things they think I should know. In fact, they'll come in and tell me things in the presence of whoever else is in the room, since we've no more secrets in the division.

Maintaining the Product/Program Versus Function Balance

As a final comment, Glegg talked about the problems of achieving the "right" balance between the two sides of the organization.

That was a very hard part of living with group managers early in the program. What I had to say to these people who report directly to me was that the people at the next level were, in a sense, organizationally in more control than they were. It was hard to do initially. For a functional manager to derive satisfaction from such a system is very complicated. It's difficult for him to find a way to achieve success because the organization is structured so that its main success indicator is attached to the task and not to the functions.

So he has to derive his pleasure in vicarious ways, and get his satisfaction sideways. They have learned to do that

largely by identifying with me. At first, it was very, very difficult and frustrating for them. This would often lead to impasses since the functional manager would see his so-called prerogatives challenged. The program manager will come into the procurement shop, for instance, and say, "I don't like the way you're buying my stuff," and be answered by, "Look, I'm buying it better than you could." Then the program manager will say, "Well, I'll show you. Just give me two people out of your shop and I'll attach them to the program and buy it myself."

Well, we have gone from that unhappy state of affairs to the situation today where we foresee two months ahead that a program is going to develop a heavy procurement requirement. We'll agree that the functional manager will go to the product manager or program manager and say, "Look, you're going to develop a need for a very heavy procurement operation. We can do it in a number of different ways. We can get one or two people on your job, or I can keep them and try to do it for you here—over in the shop. How do you want it done?" We're that extreme. The functional managers long ago ceased worrying about their prerogatives. They see that the real satisfaction will come from allowing people to perform in the most effective way.

Something reciprocal has also happened. The necessity for product managers to go bashing functional managers has largely disappeared. The system has become supportive. I know that we'll all live longer for it.

It's now a real beauty to observe. You can see people anticipating, talking to others about a need that they can see others are going to have, and asking how they can help. The functional shops are now receiving the most unbelievable bouquets from product managers. It's been a long time coming. But the average functional manager today knows now that he performs an important function. And he now knows how to perform it in order to be most useful.

Note

1. "No man can serve two masters: for either he will hate the one, and love the other, or else he will hold to the one, and despise the other." Matthew 6:24.

CASE DISCUSSION QUESTIONS

1. Why did Glegg decide to implement a matrix organization?
2. What happened when Glegg first introduced his idea for a program management matrix design?
3. What form did the second matrix organization take?
4. How was resistance to the new plan overcome?
5. Do you think it was appropriate for the Avionics Division to convert to a matrix system?

CHAPTER THREE

CONTINGENCIES IN ORGANIZATION DESIGN

In the previous chapter, we examined the effect of culture on organization design. As might be expected, however, organization design is shaped by a variety of variables, and two such variables are the subject of this chapter. The first variable discussed is *technology* and its role in organization design. What is technology, and how do technologies vary in organizations? What is known about the influence of technology on organization structure and design? What is the relationship between organizational technology and effectiveness?

The second influence on organization design to be discussed in this chapter is the organization's *external environment*. Organizations interact with the outside world—the external environment—in a complex, dynamic relationship that affects organizational goals and the lives of employees. Thus, it is important for managers to understand the role of the external environment in organization design.

IMPORTANCE OF TOPIC FOR MANAGERS

Why study the variables that influence organization design? First, consider the role of a manager: to initiate actions to improve productivity and the quality of working life. To accomplish this, however, a manager must have a thorough understanding of two important factors that may affect any actions taken.

In our world of increasing innovations and sophistication, technology plays an important role. Management must plan for the influence of technology in long-range forecasts, new product introductions, and research and development. Technological change is continuous, and if an organization is to survive, it must keep pace.

Moreover, organizations simultaneously face various pressures from the external environment. These pressures come from the government, the marketplace, competitors, and the economy. For example, job security and salary levels are influenced by competitors and the economy. Strict regulations for disposal of industrial waste have been imposed and enforced by the government. And the increase in the marketplace price of gasoline had a tremendous effect on organizations and people. As was evident in the U.S. auto industry, to ignore such factors almost ensures organizational failure.

It is essential that managers anticipate change and adapt to the external environment. In doing so, actions can be taken to buffer the organization from adverse environmental effects, and sometimes an organization may even be in a position to turn an external environmental pressure into an opportunity.

TECHNOLOGY AND ORGANIZATION DESIGN

Consider the example of Paul Laincz, age thirty-two, who works for AT&T (*Fortune,* June 28, 1982, p. 59). Like most telephone installers and repairpersons, known now as "systems technicians," Laincz used to go to work wearing jeans, with a tool belt around his waist. Now he makes his calls wearing a suit and tie, carrying his tools in a briefcase. Instead of a van, he drives a company sedan. Instead of receiving his job assignments from a supervisor and having each job closely timed, Laincz works with only five corporate clients. He decides himself what needs doing, and when. Paul Laincz's experience is similar to that of thousands of employees across North America. Laincz has not experienced a job change; he has experienced a *technological* change in the same job.

Technological changes are evident in most every aspect of work. For example, it is estimated that the number of industrial robots in use in the

United States will grow from a few thousand today to approximately 100,000 by 1990. Moreover, the number of desk-top computers or terminals will increase during the same period from four million to over 30 million (*Fortune,* June 28, 1982, p. 58). The advent of computer-based technology leads to fundamental changes both in the way work is done and in the kinds of jobs available. As such, it is important to examine how technological changes affect organizational behavior and effectiveness as managers attempt to adapt to a changing work environment.

Definition of Technology

The word *technology* refers to anything that involves either the mechanical or intellectual processes by which an organization transforms inputs (raw materials) into outputs (finished products) in the pursuit of organizational goals. In discussing the role of technology in organizations, we are in essence focusing our attention on "who does what with whom, when, where, and how often" (Chapple and Sayles, 1961, p. 34). An example of technology at work can be seen in such processes as the way a computer transforms data into a usable report, or the way an assembly line transforms steel, rubber, and glass into an automobile. In both cases, we see examples of transformation processes in organizations in which mechanical and intellectual energies are exercised in the efficient utilization of scarce and valued resources.

Types of Technology

Because of its important influence on structure and behavior in organizations, technology should not be viewed in oversimplified terms. In fact, it is more appropriate to discuss the *technologies* in a single organization, rather than the technology. Managers and researchers are obligated to understand the variations and intricacies of all of the technological processes employed in a particular organization under study. In order to allow managers to study more precisely how different "types" of technology influence organizational structure, performance, and effectiveness, several researchers have identified categories into which various technologies can be assigned.

One of the earliest and most widely used typologies was developed by Woodward (1958). Focusing specifically on industrial firms, Woodward suggested three categories of technology based on the level of technical complexity of the production process. These three categories are:

- *Small batch or unit production.* The product is custom-made to individual customer specifications (for example, airplanes, locomotives, and printing jobs). Operations performed on each unit are typically nonrepetitive in nature.
- *Mass production.* The product is manufactured in assembly-line fashion (for example, automobiles). Operations performed are repetitious, routine, and predictable.

- *Continuous process production.* The product is transformed from raw material to a finished good using a series of machine or process transformations (for example, chemicals and oil refining).

Woodward argued that the technical complexity of an organization increases as it moves from unit, through mass, to continuous process production. Although such a trend may occur in many cases, it is easy to envision exceptions. For example, one could argue that the development and production of a DC-10 or a Boeing 767 (small batch technology) is far more complex technologically than either mass production or continuous process production. Thus, it may be necessary to differentiate standard or routinized from nonstandard forms of small batch production technologies when discussing technical complexity. Although the printing process may employ fairly routine production techniques, designing and manufacturing an airplane certainly does not.

A somewhat different approach to the classification of technological diversity has been proposed by Thompson (1967). This typology is based on the manner in which individuals or units are organized for task accomplishment:

- *Long-linked technology.* This technology is characterized by interdependence of a number of different operations or departments. It is roughly equivalent to Woodward's (1958) "mass production" technology, where various pieces are "added" to the product as it moves through the manufacturing process.
- *Mediating technology.* This technology is characterized by a linking of otherwise independent units or elements of a system, where the various units are made compatible through the use of standard operating procedures. Examples include a bank where customers are classified into depositors and borrowers, then dealt with based on standardized procedures.
- *Intensive technology.* This technology is characterized by uniqueness of task sequence. Here, the choice of techniques and the way they are used to alter an object are varied and are largely influenced by feedback from the object itself (that is, how it responds to what happens to it). An example of an organization using intensive technologies is a hospital, where a variety of techniques, services, and skills are applied in varying combinations, depending upon the particular illness of the patient and his or her response to treatment.

Compared to Woodward's, Thompson's method of classification includes a wider variety of organizations. Woodward addressed herself specifically to the industrial-manufacturing domain; Thompson sought to include almost every type of work organization. Perhaps broader still is the typology proposed by Hickson et al. (1969). In their analysis of British organizations differing considerably in size, shape, and purpose, the following categories of technology were suggested:

- *Operations technology.* This focuses on the techniques used in the work flow activities of an organization (for example, handcrafting vs. mass production).
- *Materials technology.* This focuses on the types of materials used in the work flow.
- *Knowledge technology.* This focuses on the amount, quality, level of sophistication, and dispersion of information relevant to decision making and production in an organization.

In contrast to Woodward and Thompson, the Hickson et al. (1969) categories are not mutually exclusive. That is, organizations may exhibit some form of all three technologies at the same time in the same place. For example, one organization may employ a highly advanced manufacturing process (operations technology) on a relatively simple raw material (materials technology); moreover, such a process may require skilled, well-educated, versatile employees with a high degree of interdepartmental communications (knowledge technology).

Other methods for classifying technology could be discussed here. However, the important point is that there are different types of technology influencing organizational structure and behavior. Managers of modern organizations are faced, not with a single technology, but with a range of technologies, and it is essential that they understand the variations and intricacies of each type.

TECHNOLOGY, STRUCTURE, AND EFFECTIVENESS

The complexity of the organization's technological dimension makes it difficult to pinpoint just how it relates to organizational performance and effectiveness. Two of the more important studies on this topic—the Woodward Studies and the Aston Studies—yielded some interesting hypotheses that will be presented here. A brief discussion of some additional related studies will follow.

Woodward Studies

The earliest detailed examination of the relationship between technology, structure, and organizational success was carried out by Joan Woodward and her colleagues (Woodward, 1958, 1965). Woodward, a British sociologist, began her research in the early 1950s by addressing the question of whether "the principles of organization laid down by an expanding body of management theory correlate with business success when put into practice" (Woodward, 1958). She and her associates surveyed about one hundred British manufacturing firms, varying in size from one hundred to over one thousand

EXHIBIT 3.1 RELATIONSHIPS BETWEEN TECHNOLOGICAL VARIABLES AND ORGANIZATIONAL STRUCTURE

Structural Variables*	Unit or Small Batch	Mass	Continuous Process
Supervisory span of control	23	48	15
Executive span of control	4	7	10
Number of levels of authority	3	4	6
Ratio of administrators to workers	9:1	4:1	1:1
Ratio of staff/specialists to workers	8:1	5:1	2:1
Relative labor costs	high	medium	low
Degree of formalization	low	high	low

*Data reported are median scores.

Source: Developed from Woodward, *Industrial Organization: Theory and Practice* (London: Oxford University Press, 1965).

employees, and collected information on a variety of structural variables. She examined span of control, organization size, levels of authority, degree of formalization, and the relative success or effectiveness of the various enterprises.

Initially, Woodward focused her attention on the relation of organization size to structure; however, no consistent pattern emerged. This absence of relationship may have been accounted for by the relatively restricted range in the sizes of the firms surveyed, however. Moreover, no association was found between size or other structural variables and organizational success. These findings led Woodward (1958) to question the validity of the early "principles" of management: indeed, they did not appear to have universal applicability in all types of organizations.

In an effort to account for the variations in managerial practices and the absence of a clear structure-effectiveness association, the researchers decided to classify the organizations in their survey *by technology*. As discussed previously, technology was classified into small batch or unit, mass production, and continuous process categories. Following this classification, a reanalysis of the data yielded these important findings (see Exhibit 3.1):

1. There was no significant relationship between technological complexity and organizational size.
2. The span of control of first-level supervision increased from unit to mass production technology, but then decreased markedly from mass production to continuous process technology.
3. The span of control of the chief executive increased with increasing technological complexity (from unit to mass to continuous process).
4. The number of levels of authority in an organization increased somewhat with increases in technological complexity.
5. The ratio of administrators to workers increased with increases in technological complexity.

6. The ratio of supporting staff and specialists to workers increased with increases in technological complexity.
7. Relative labor costs decreased with increases in technological complexity.
8. Formalization (clear definitions of duties, rules, amount of paperwork) was greatest under mass production technology, tapering off considerably under unit and continuous process technologies.

Next, Woodward asked what impact these findings had for the study of organizational effectiveness. Firms were classified according to relative degree of success, and structure and technology were again compared. The surprising conclusion resulting from this analysis was that "the organizational characteristics of the successful firms in each production (that is, technology) category tended to cluster around the medians for that category as a whole, while the figures of the firms classified below average in success were found at the extremes of the range" (1965, p. 69). In other words, there appeared to be an optimal level for several structural characteristics (such as span of control) for successful firms in each of the three technological categories. Less successful firms in each category exhibited structural ratios that were either too large or too small. It is important to stress here that the optimal level for success was different for each technological category.

From these findings, Woodward (1965, pp. 69–71) concluded that "the fact that organizational characteristics, technology, and success were linked together in this way suggested that not only was the system of production (that is, technology) an important variable in the determination of organizational structure, but also that one particular form of organization was most appropriate to each system of production." In short, Woodward was arguing in favor of a contingency approach to management whereby different technologies require different structures and interpersonal styles. This *technological determinism* concept essentially proposes that under mass production technology, a highly structured, formalized, bureaucratic managerial style may be more appropriate for organizational success. However, at the two opposite ends of the technological continuum, small batch or unit and continuous process, more successful firms employed less structured, less formalized managerial styles with fewer rules, fewer controls, and a greater degree of interpersonal interaction (see Exhibit 3.2). As we shall see below, however, not all investigators have agreed with this position.

Aston Studies

A second major study that focused on the relationship of technology and organizational structure was carried out by several British social scientists led by Pugh and Hickson. Collectively, this research team has become known as the "Aston Group" because much of their early research was carried out at the University of Aston. Although a good deal of this research focused on

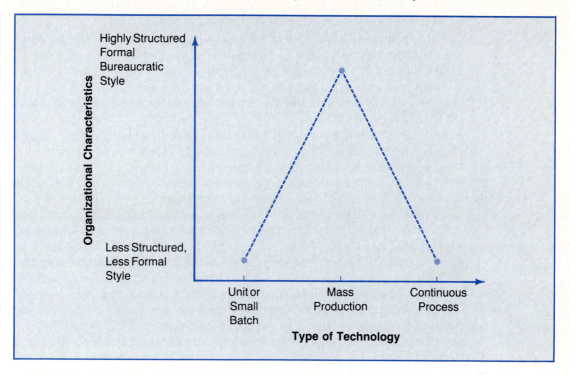

relationships between structural variables, our primary focus here is on the findings pertaining to the structure-technology relationship and organizational performance (Hickson et al., 1969; Pugh, 1973, 1981).

Hickson et al. (1969) view technology in terms of a general factor called *work-flow integration.* Included in this concept are such variables as the degree of task interdependence, the rigidity of work-flow sequences, the automation of equipment, and the specificity of evaluation of operations. The greater the automation, task specificity, and so forth, the greater the extent of work-flow integration. Using this concept, Hickson and his associates surveyed forty-six firms and calculated a numerical index of work-flow integration for each organization. Hickson et al., like Woodward, carried out their analysis on an organization-wide basis; that is, it was assumed that each organization employed only one general type of manufacturing or service technology.

Their index of work-flow integration was then compared to a variety of structural variables with several interesting results. To begin, no general relationship was found between technological complexity and structural characteristics (specialization and standardization). This finding was in direct contradiction to the earlier findings by Woodward. "In general, our studies have confirmed that the relationship of technology to the main structural dimensions in manufacturing organizations is always very small and plays a secondary role relative to other contextual features such as size and interdependence with other organizations. . . ." (Pugh, 1973, p. 32).

On a more detailed level of analysis, however, technology was found to be related to various aspects of structure in a number of highly specific job ratios, referred to as *configurations* by Pugh and Hickson. Specifically, Pugh, Hickson, and their associates found the same curvilinear relationship between span of control of first-line supervisors and technological complexity that had been found by Woodward. Moreover, the ratio of quality inspectors and maintenance personnel to workers was also greatest in mass production and tapered off for both unit and continuous process technologies.

When the Aston Group findings concerning technology are considered as a whole, though, there appear to be two related conclusions. First, the evidence indicates that "only those [structural characteristics] directly centered on the production work flow itself show any connection with technology. Away from the shop floor, technology appears to have little influence on organization structure" (Pugh, 1973, p. 33). In short, technology appears to affect organization structure only in those departments actually using the technology—for example, production. Other departments such as accounting or marketing appear to be largely unaffected, according to these data. Second, and almost a corollary of the first point, the evidence appears to support the position that "the smaller the organization the more its structure will be pervaded by such technological effects; the larger the organization the more these effects will be confined to variables such as job counts of employees on activities linked to the work flow itself, and will not be detectable in variations of the more remote administrative and hierarchical structure" (Hickson et al., 1969, pp. 394–95). In other words, variations in technology have a more pronounced effect on organization structure for small organizations than for large ones.

Thus, Pugh, Hickson, and their associates interpret their findings within a contingency framework, whereby technology can affect the structural design of an organization, but only as moderated by additional intervening variables such as organization size or department function. In small organizations, technology largely dictates structure; in large organizations, technology dictates structure *only* in production-related units. Such findings raise questions concerning the validity of the technological determinism point of view advanced by Woodward and others that suggests that technology determines structure. The Aston Group would argue that determinism is contingent upon several mediating variables, such as size of organization and departmental function, that may serve to intervene in the technology-structure relationship. Moreover, it is possible that technological determinism may be operative only for specific aspects of structure such as formalization and span of control, and not for others, such as complexity of department and levels of authority. In any event, although some disagreement exists concerning the exact role of technology, both studies clearly point to the relevance of this variable in any consideration of the determinants of organizational effectiveness.

Additional Studies of Technology and Organizational Effectiveness

Several other studies have examined the impact of technology on organizational processes and performance, and when compared to the Woodward and Aston studies, several important conclusions emerge. To begin, no consistent or simple relationship was found between organization structure and organization success. That is, variations in the degree of complexity, formalization, levels of authority, size, and so forth did not appear to be related to organizational success (Miles, 1980). In other words, there is no universally desirable structure that can facilitate effectiveness in any environment. Management must understand the uniqueness of its own organization's situation and structure its resources accordingly.

The evidence is equally clear in demonstrating the absence of any simple relationship between technological complexity and overall effectiveness, although there does appear to be some relationship between technology and worker attitudes (Fullan, 1970). In a study of employees working in a variety of technological settings, Fullan found that workers in continuous process technologies were more satisfied and identified with the company to a greater extent than did employees in mass production organizations.

Also, the majority of the available evidence tends to support the contention that technological complexity or variation affects the resulting structure of an organization to a substantial degree. For example, Harvey (1968) found that the more stable an organization's technology was, the greater was its degree of "structuring"; that is, higher specialization, centralization, task specification, and so on. Thus, an automotive firm with a highly stable technology exhibits far more structuring behavior than an aerospace R&D firm, where the technological state is much more volatile. Similar findings concerning the impact of technological stability on structure have emerged in a wide variety of organizations (Miles, 1980).

These findings, which on the surface provide support for the technological determinism hypothesis, appear to be in conflict with the findings of the Aston Group. For instance, although Hickson et al. (1969) found support for technological determinism only in small organizations, Harvey (1968) found such support, both before and after organization size was controlled for, in his study of industrial firms of varying sizes. The majority of the evidence appears to support Harvey's conclusions. Thus, it would appear, based on these findings, that technology does indeed often play a central role in the determination of organizational structure.

Finally, we come to the issue of how technology and structure *jointly* relate to effectiveness. Although it has been demonstrated that neither technology nor structure by itself shows any appreciable relationship to effectiveness, several investigations have suggested the existence of an interactive relationship between these two variables as they affect ultimate organizational success. This contention has been called the *consonance hypothesis* (Mohr, 1971). Specifically, it is argued that organizational effectiveness is largely a result of the extent to which an organization can successfully match its technology with an appropriate structure. Thus, an organization that employs very routine, repetitive technology, for example, may perform best when it relies on a highly formalized structure. Evidence in support of the consonance hypothesis can be found in several studies (for example, Burns and Stalker, 1961; Lawrence and Lorsch, 1967; Perrow, 1967; Zwerman, 1970).

Those that take issue with the validity of the hypothesis, however, argue that such factors as "social class traditions" may affect structure far more than technology (Mohr, 1971; Pennings, 1975). Although the data from these latter studies clearly do not reject the hypothesis in its entirety, they do suggest the existence of a series of individual and social factors (which have been ignored in earlier studies on technology) that might influence effectiveness. Therefore, it may be necessary to expand the consonance hypothesis to include a recognition of the role of human behavior. Thus, effectiveness may be seen as a function of an organization's ability to successfully integrate technology, structure, *and* personal characteristics and social factors into a congruent, goal-oriented entity. For instance, not only would the use of assembly-line technology call for a structured approach to organizing human resources, it would also suggest the need for individuals who were willing, and had the capacity, to work in such an environment. It appears that the inclusion of this human variable in any consideration of the technology-structure relationship would considerably increase our understanding of organizational dynamics and success.

DIMENSIONS OF THE EXTERNAL ENVIRONMENT

Organizations obviously do not exist in a vacuum—they must interact with the outside world. The outside world, referred to as the *external environment,* is made up of customers, suppliers, competitors, government, and certain specific aspects of technology, and each has an influence on an organization's goal-directed activities. The external environment plays a critical role in organizational dynamics (see Exhibit 3.3).

Why does the external environment so significantly influence the shape and nature of organizations? First, recognize that all inputs used by the organization ultimately come from the environment; for example, the supply of raw materials. Moreover, outputs must find a market in the environment. Finally, many aspects of the transformation process are limited or regulated by environmental factors such as legal or governmental regulations. Because each of these factors can affect the lives of people at work, it is important for managers to know something about differences in environments. In an effort to simplify the multitude of environmental characteristics, Thompson (1967) and Duncan (1972) have identified three major dimensions by which environ-

EXHIBIT 3.3   GENERAL ENVIRONMENTAL CHARACTERISTICS FOR ORGANIZATIONS

Cultural. Including the historical background, ideologies, values, and norms of the society. Views on authority relationships, leadership patterns, interpersonal relationships, rationalism, science, and technology define the nature of social institutions.

Technological. The level of scientific and technological advancement in society. Including the physical base (plant, equipment, facilities) and the knowledge base of technology. Degree to which the scientific and technological community is able to develop new knowledge and apply it.

Educational. The general literacy level of the population. The degree of sophistication and specialization in the educational system. The proportion of the people with a high level of professional and/or specialized training.

Political. The general political climate of society. The degree of concentration of political power. The nature of political organization (degrees of decentralization, diversity of functions, etc.). The political party system.

Legal. Constitutional consideration, nature of legal system, jurisdictions of various governmental units. Specific laws concerning formation, taxation, and control of organizations.

Natural Resource. The nature, quantity, and availability of natural resources, including climate and other conditions.

Demographic. The nature of human resources available to the society; their number, distribution, age, and sex. Concentration or urbanization of population is a characteristic of industrialized societies.

Sociological. Class structure and mobility. Definition of social roles. Nature of the social organization and development of social institutions.

Economic. General economic framework, including the type of economic organization—private vs. public ownership; the centralization or decentralization of economic planning; the banking system; and fiscal policies. The level of the investment in physical resources and consumption characteristics.

Source: F. E. Kast and J. E. Rosenzweig, *Organization and Management,* 2nd ed. (New York: McGraw-Hill, 1974), p. 136. Reprinted by permission.

ments can be measured: simple-complex; static-dynamic; and environmental uncertainty.

Simple-Complex Dimension

The simple-complex dimension of the external environment concerns the intricacy and qualitative nature of the environment. A simple or placid environment is one in which the external factors with which an organization must deal are few in number and are relatively homogeneous. For example, consider a company that exclusively manufactures spark plugs for the major automotive companies. Its product line is restricted, its technology is fairly stable, and its market is relatively constant. Moreover, its customers are few in number. In short, it exists in a fairly simple environment.

Contrast this example with a company that builds commercial aircraft, such as Boeing. The manufacture of various components of the aircraft is subcontracted to dozens of other firms, increasing significantly the coordination problems among major production units. Moreover, the jet engines themselves must be purchased from still other companies. The technological aspects of manufacture are tremendously complex and varied, and the final product must meet not only the specifications of domestic and foreign airline companies who purchase the aircraft, but a series of U.S. government regulations as well. Certainly, this environment is a more complex one than that of the company manufacturing spark plugs.

Just as the manufacture and sale of a spark plug differs from that of a Boeing 747 aircraft in terms of complexity and cost (approximately 1 dollar versus 50 million dollars), so, too, are there differences in the manner in which an organization must manage itself in response to such divergent environments. The degree of environmental complexity can have a significant impact both on organizational behavior and on organizational effectiveness, as we shall see presently.

Static-Dynamic Dimension

In addition to environmental complexity, one must also consider the relative degree of stability in organization-environment relations. For example, compare the stability of our automotive parts company, which will make spark plugs year after year, to an aerospace firm, which may receive a contract to build a satellite one year and modular houses the next. One environment is fairly stable; the other is quite dynamic. Environments that are in a constant state of flux often require different organizational structures and approaches to management than do more static, predictable environments.

To complicate the picture further, it should be recognized that the static-dynamic dimension is, in reality, a multifaceted phenomenon. Certain portions of the environment may remain static, while others change radically over time. Automobile companies provide a good example of this. While the production technology of automotive manufacturing has remained relatively stable with few new technological breakthroughs, the *marketing* component of the environment changed dramatically as people shifted from large cars to small cars to no cars and back again. In part, this volatile marketing environment is a function of environmental complexity. Oil prices, general economic conditions, and governmental regulations are all considerations. Even so, such environmental turbulence has little effect on the stability of the *technological* environment.

Environmental Uncertainty

An understanding of the simple-complex and static-dynamic dimensions of the external environment is needed in order to comprehend their influence on the degree of environmental certainty or uncertainty in which organizational decisions are made. Environmental uncertainty is a result of three conditions: (1) a lack of information concerning the environmental factors associated with

EXHIBIT 3.4   **CHARACTERISTICS OF VARIOUS ENVIRONMENTAL STATES**

	Simple	Complex
	Cell 1: **Low Perceived Uncertainty**	**Cell 2:** **Moderately Low** **Perceived Uncertainty**
Static	1. Small number of factors and components in the environment 2. Factors and components are somewhat similar to one another 3. Factors and components remain basically the same and are not changing	1. Large number of factors and components in the environment 2. Factors and components are not similar to one another 3. Factors and components remain basically the same
	Cell 3: **Moderately High** **Perceived Uncertainty**	**Cell 4:** **High Perceived Uncertainty**
Dynamic	1. Small number of factors and components in the environment 2. Factors and components are somewhat similar to one another 3. Factors and components of the environment are in continual process of change	1. Large number of factors and components in the environment 2. Factors and components are not similar to one another 3. Factors and components of environment are in a continual process of change

Source: Reprinted from "The Characteristics of Organizational Environments and Perceived Environmental Uncertainty" by R. B. Duncan, published in *Administrative Science Quarterly 17* (September 1972): 320, by permission of *Administrative Science Quarterly.*

a particular organizational decision-making situation; (2) an inability to accurately assign probabilities with regard to how environmental factors will affect the success or failure of a decision unit in performing its functions; and (3) a lack of information regarding the costs associated with an incorrect decision or action (Duncan, 1972).

In an effort to integrate the stability and complexity dimensions with the issue of uncertainty in organizational decision making, Duncan (1972) proposed a model that describes the environmental states resulting from the interrelationships (see Exhibit 3.4). The model builds upon the earlier theoretical formulations of Thompson (1967), Emery and Trist (1965), and Terreberry (1968), suggesting that the "static-simple" environments contain the least amount of uncertainty for organizational planners and decision makers, and the "dynamic-complex" environments contain the greatest amount of uncertainty.

An empirical investigation provided general support for the model (Duncan, 1972, 1973). Not only was the dynamic-complex environment found to be associated with the largest amount of perceived environmental uncertainty, it was also discovered that the static-dynamic dimension was a more important contributor to perceived uncertainty than was the simple-complex dimension. Commenting on his findings, Duncan (1972, p. 325) concluded:

> Decision units with dynamic environments always experience significantly more uncertainty in decision making, regardless of whether their environment is simple or complex. The difference in perceived uncertainty between decision units with simple and complex environments is not significant, unless the decision unit's environment is also dynamic.

ENVIRONMENT, STRUCTURE, AND ORGANIZATIONAL EFFECTIVENESS

Is environmental variation a determinant of organization effectiveness? A number of studies have examined in detail the joint effect of organization-environment relations on the success of an enterprise. In order to determine more precisely the role played by environmental factors in ongoing organizations, four of these studies will be examined here. Pay particular attention to the concepts of stability, complexity, and uncertainty in each of these investigations.

Burns and Stalker Study

One of the earliest studies of organization-environment relations was carried out by Burns and Stalker (1961). They surveyed twenty British industrial firms, most with interests in electronics, in an effort to identify relationships between certain environmental characteristics and resulting managerial practices. The researchers focused on the rate of change in both the relevant technology and the market; in other words, on environmental stability as it related to managerial behavior.

Based on their analysis, they concluded that there existed two relatively distinct approaches to management—*mechanistic* and *organic*—that were largely a function of the relative degree of stability in the external environment. As indicated in Exhibit 3.5, these two styles are quite different. Mechanistic systems are characterized by centralization of control and authority, a high degree of task specialization, and primarily vertical (and particularly downward) lines of communication. Organic systems, on the other hand, generally exhibit a higher degree of task interdependence, greater decentralization of control and authority, and more horizontal (that is, between departments) communication. Moreover, mechanistic systems are seen as relatively fixed and inflexible entities, while organic systems are viewed as being more flexible and adaptable.

Burns and Stalker argued that each system of management had its proper place in organizational effectiveness. In highly stable and predictable environ-

Mechanistic	Organic
1. Tasks are highly fractionated and specialized; little regard paid to clarifying relationship between tasks and organizational objectives.	1. Tasks are more interdependent; emphasis on relevance of tasks and organizational objectives.
2. Tasks tend to remain rigidly defined unless altered formally by top management.	2. Tasks are continually adjusted and redefined through interaction of organizational members.
3. Specific role definition (rights, obligations, and technical methods prescribed for each member).	3. Generalized role definition (members accept general responsibility for task accomplishment beyond individual role definition).
4. Hierarchical structure of control, authority, and communication. Sanctions derive from employment contract between employee and organization.	4. Network structure of control, authority, and communication. Sanctions derive more from community of interest than from contractual relationship.
5. Information relevant to situation and operations of the organization formally assumed to rest with chief executive.	5. Leader not assumed to be omniscient; knowledge centers identified where located throughout organization.
6. Communication is primarily vertical between superior and subordinate.	6. Communication is both vertical and horizontal, depending upon where needed information resides.
7. Communications primarily take form of instructions and decisions issued by superiors, of information and requests for decisions supplied by inferiors.	7. Communications primarily take form of information and advice.
8. Insistence on loyalty to organization and obedience to superiors.	8. Commitment to organization's tasks and goals more highly valued than loyalty or obedience.
9. Importance and prestige attached to identification with organization and its members.	9. Importance and prestige attached to affiliations and expertise in external environment.

Source: Adapted from T. Burns and G. M. Stalker, *The Management of Innovations* (London: Tavistock Publications, Ltd., 1961), pp. 119–22.

ments where market and technological conditions remain largely unchanged over time (for example, the automotive industry), the mechanistic system may be more appropriate. Because the environment is highly predictable under such conditions, it is possible to routinize tasks and centralize directions in order to maximize efficiency and effectiveness in operation. (Note that Burns and Stalker do not suggest that such a system of management is personally satisfying to employees—only that it is efficient.) Where the environment is in a constant state of flux, however, and where an organization has to change direction constantly to adapt to its environment (such as in the aerospace industry), organic systems appear to be more appropriate because of their added flexibility and adaptability. Thus, Burns and Stalker really argue for what might be termed an *environmental determinism* point of view, where the organization design is determined as a function of external factors. The role of management thus becomes one of properly understanding environmental conditions and adapting organizational structure and practices to meet and exploit those conditions.

Chandler Study

Taking an historical and evolutionary approach to the study of organizational effectiveness, Chandler (1962) traced the growth and development of nearly one hundred major U.S. business concerns. Based on these case studies, he concluded that each major change in the design or structure of these organizations resulted from environmental shifts that necessitated such changes. More specifically, changes in the external environment were seen as creating demands on an organization to modify its strategies for dealing with the environment. These strategic changes in turn necessitated modifications in organizational structure so that it would be consistent with the revised strategy. As Chandler (1962, pp. 18–19) describes it:

> Strategic growth resulted from an awareness of the opportunities and needs created—by changing population, income, and technology—to employ existing or expanding resources more profitably. A new strategy required a new or at least refashioned structure if the . . . enterprise was to be operated efficiently. The failure to develop a new internal structure, like the failure to respond to new external opportunities and needs, was a consequence of overconcentration on operational activities by the executives responsible for the destiny of their enterprises, or from their inability, because of past training and education and present position, to develop an entrepreneurial outlook.

Chandler sums up his point by adding that growth or change "without structural adjustment can lead only to economic inefficiency" (1962, p. 19). By way of example, he cites Henry Ford's venture into farm tractors in the late 1930s. This is discussed in Close-Up 2.1 on p. 35. In an effort to expand his base of operations and find substitutes for the declining automobile market of the time, Ford and his engineering staff designed and built an inexpensive tractor that had the potential of competing effectively against the existing tractors then on the market. However, Ford attempted to sell his tractors through his car dealerships, which were inexperienced in farm needs and which were principally located in cities. The new tractor failed commercially until a new structure (particularly a new marketing structure) was designed that was consistent with Ford's marketing goals and strategy. Chandler concludes: "The incredibly bad management of his enormous industrial empire, which was so clearly reflected by the lack of any systematic organizational structure, not only prevented the Ford Motor Company from carrying out a strategy of diversification, but also helped cause the rapid drop in Ford's profits and share of the market" (Chandler, 1962, p. 462).

The point here is not to single out one company for criticism. On the

CLOSE-UP 3.1   PIEDMONT AVIATION: A CASE OF STRATEGIC ADAPTATION

A good example of strategic change can be seen in the airline industry before and after deregulation. Prior to deregulation in 1978, airlines had protected route structures. New airlines could only enter into competition on a particular route with the approval of the Civil Aeronautics Board, and such approval was seldom given. After deregulation, however, it became much easier for new competitors to enter the market, and existing airlines had to compete harder or lose ground.

A case in point is Piedmont Aviation, a commuter airline serving primarily the southeast United States. When deregulation was being debated in Congress, Tom Davis, president of Piedmont, says, "We opposed it. We thought bigger airlines would pick off our best routes." Even so, the company did more than complain. "We saw it was going to happen, so we decided to get ready."

In response to a government policy he didn't like, Davis quickly developed a strategy of change—a succession in the basic corporate goals—that has created the largest growth ever experienced by Piedmont. Since 1978, Piedmont revenues have grown by over eighty percent, reaching $484 million in 1981. Earnings per share have tripled, and Piedmont stock was one of the best performers on the New York Stock Exchange for 1981.

The strategy for change basically rests on Piedmont's identifying new short-haul routes overlooked or not adequately served by the major air carriers (for example, from Raleigh-Durham to Tampa or to Dallas). Deregulation allows Piedmont to initiate such new service easily and to change service when market conditions warrant. In short, because of a major shift in government policy, Piedmont had to reexamine its conservative and traditional goals, leading to more challenging goals for the future. Says Davis of Piedmont's response to deregulation, "We're not trying to split up the existing pie; we're cooking a whole new one."

Source: Adapted from "Fly Me, I'm Little," *Forbes* (April 27, 1981), pp. 112–13. Adapted by permission of *Forbes* magazine. © Forbes Inc., 1981.

contrary, many examples can be cited in which organizations showed an inability to adapt structure to corporate strategies and goals. Instead, recognize that a key factor in effectiveness and efficiency is the ability of managers to properly understand their environment, make strategic decisions based upon their understanding, and then organize their human resources around these strategic decisions. A good example of this principle in practice can be seen in the case of Piedmont Aviation, as shown in Close-Up 3.1.

Lawrence and Lorsch Study

Following the lead of these earlier studies, Lawrence and Lorsch (1967) and Lawrence (1981) carried out among a small sample of American firms an extensive investigation of environmental influences on organization design and effectiveness. They began by posing four specific research questions (1967, p. 16):

1. How are the environmental demands facing various organizations different, and how do environmental demands relate to the internal functioning of effective organizations?
2. Is it true that organizations in certain or stable environments make more exclusive use of the formal hierarchy to attain integration, and, if so, why? Because less integration is required, or because in a certain environment these decisions can be made more effectively at higher organization levels or by fewer people?
3. Is the same degree of differentiation in orientation and in departmental structure found in organizations in different industrial environments?
4. If greater differentiation among functional departments is required in different industries, does this influence the problems of integrating the organization's parts? Does it influence the organization's means of achieving integration?

To find suitable answers to these questions, Lawrence and Lorsch studied organization-environment relations in three widely divergent industries: plastics, packaged foods, and standardized containers. The external environment for firms in the plastics industry was typically characterized by a high degree of uncertainty and unpredictability. The rate of technological innovation and shifts in market demands in this industry were quite high, requiring organizations to change products, procedures, and sometimes structures fairly rapidly. The container industry, on the other hand, was typically characterized by a highly stable and predictable environment. Competition in this industry centered around the quality of the product or service, instead of on product innovation, as was the case in the plastics industry. In between the plastics and container industries, in terms of environmental stability, came the packaged foods companies. These latter organizations were characterized by a moderate amount of predictability and stability in environmental relations.

The central issues concerning Lawrence and Lorsch were how organizations adapted structurally to diverse external environments and which adaptation processes were generally more successful. Structural variations within organizations were defined in terms of the amount of *differentiation* and *integration* existing within each organization. Differentiation, as defined by Lawrence and Lorsch (1967, p. 11), refers to "the difference in cognitive and emotional orientation among managers in different functional departments." It refers not only to the degree of specialization of labor or departmentalization, but also to what might be termed the "psychological" departmentalization; that is, the extent to which managers in different departments are characterized by different attitudinal and behavioral orientations. The greater the psychological distance between managers in different departments, the greater the differentiation.

On the other hand, integration refers to "the quality of the state of collaboration that exists among departments that are required to achieve

Industry	Organization	Average Differentiation*	Average Integration
Plastics	High Performer	10.7	5.6
	Low Performer	9.0	5.1
Foods	High Performer	8.0	5.3
	Low Performer	6.5	5.0
Containers	High Performer	5.7	5.7
	Low Performer	5.7	4.8

*Higher differentiation scores mean greater differences between functional
units; higher integration scores mean higher degrees of integration.

Source: From P. R. Lawrence and J. W. Lorsch, *Organization and Environment.* Boston: Division
of Research, Harvard Business School, 1967, p. 103. Republished as a Harvard Business
School Classic: Boston: Harvard Business School Press, 1986. Reprinted by permission.

unity of effort by the demands of the environment" (p. 11). In short,
integration refers to the nature and quality of interdepartmental relations, as
well as the processes by which such relations are achieved. Integration can be
brought about by several means, including the creation of rules and standard
operating procedures that govern behavior, plans and objectives, and mutual
adjustment and agreement.

Several important findings emerged from the investigation. To begin, as
indicated in Exhibit 3.6, organizations operating in more complex environments such as plastics tended to exhibit a greater degree of differentiation
between functional departments than did firms operating in less turbulent
environments such as containers. The more effective plastics firm had a score
of 10.7 on the differentiation measure, compared to 5.7 for both container
firms. The packaged foods firms, which operated in a moderately dynamic
environment, exhibited a moderate degree of differentiation. In other words,
the greater the instability in the external environment, the more psychological
distance was needed between departments in order to be effective.

Second, it was noted that, with one exception, more successful firms
within each industry had higher scores on both differentiation and integration.
Thus, it would appear that one component of organizational effectiveness, as
defined and measured here, is the capacity of an organization to achieve an
optimal balance of differentiation and integration consistent with environmental demands. One hallmark of less effective organizations is an inability to
grant various departments sufficient latitude and autonomy to increase their
contribution to organizational goals through functional specialization, as well
as an inability to integrate and coordinate these diverse departments for the
common good.

Finally, it was concluded that different environments call for different
structural approaches to integration. In the dynamic plastics industry, the
more effective organization employed a formal integrating department, whose

purpose was to ensure that the various functional areas worked toward common goals. In the moderately dynamic food packaging industry, the more effective organization used individual integrators; that is, individuals whose primary responsibility was to ensure mutuality of purpose. In the more stable containers industry, integration was facilitated in the effective organization by direct managerial contact through the chain of command. Thus, when we consider the *effective* organizations in the study, each is characterized by an ability to achieve integration commensurate with its respective environment. The more complex the environment the more elaborate the integrative mechanisms.

In summary, Lawrence and Lorsch (1967) emphasize the need for an organization to understand its environment and to structure itself accordingly. Although these findings are more comprehensive than those of Burns and Stalker, Chandler, and others, the basic conclusions are the same. Environment does play an important role in the relationship between structuring activities and organizational success.

Pfeffer and Salancik Study

Taking a significantly different perspective, Pfeffer and Salancik (1978) examined organizational-environmental relations by focusing on the extent to which the organization is dependent upon the external environment for its resources and the consequences resulting from this dependence. Their *resource dependence model* suggests that organizational actions, and indeed organizational effectiveness, depend on the extent to which organizations can successfully manage environmental relations.

The model begins by defining organizational effectiveness as the extent to which an organization can satisfy the demands of those in the environment whose support is necessary to ensure continued existence. An organization is said to be dependent on another group to the extent that an important input or output of the organization is controlled by others outside the organization. And the fewer outside groups control the input or output, the more dependent the organization is on the outside. For example, a mining company that can corner the titanium market would exert considerable influence over aircraft manufacturers who require titanium for new airplane designs. The manufacturers would be dependent on the mining company for an essential resource.

The resource dependence model, then, focuses on situations in which organizations are dependent in varying degrees on outside forces for their essential resources and on how such organizations deal with their dependency. An essential part of the model deals with the extent to which organizations accurately assess their true degree of dependence on the environment. Misreading the environment can result in major corporate failure, as described in Close-Up 3.2. Pfeffer and Salancik (1978) note four possible reasons that organizations fail to properly assess the extent of their dependence on outsiders or fail to adapt to such dependencies:

CLOSE-UP 3.2 JARI: ANATOMY OF A FAILURE

A good example of how Pfeffer and Salancik's resource dependence model works can be seen in the well-known attempt by American billionaire Daniel Ludwig to set up a self-contained industrial empire in the jungles of Brazil. Ludwig's idea was to develop a major enterprise known as Jari in an area rich in resources. His project included plans to cultivate a supertree for high-grade paper, to mine a mother lode of bauxite, and to erect a fully modern pulp mill and a smelting plant. However, in 1982, after fifteen years' effort and a $1.1 billion investment, the operation failed.

Why? Several problems emerged. First, managers at Jari failed to adequately test the soil for their "supertree," only to discover later that soil conditions were inappropriate for the trees they planted. In addition, the peasants who were recruited at high wages to leave their homes and move far into the Amazon jungle got homesick and returned in droves to their villages. And managers came and went like a revolving door; Ludwig had over twenty directors who often complained that he tried to run Jari "by remote control" from New York.

However, the fatal blow came from the Brazilian government and from Ludwig's inability to deal successfully with it. Known for his independence, Ludwig set his own course at Jari and refused to discuss what he was doing with government authorities. Soon Jari became a hated symbol of U.S. imperialism. When, in 1980, Ludwig finally had to ask for government financial assistance, it was not forthcoming. His threats to pull out unless he received government cooperation were seen as heavy-handed and a further example of U.S. imperialism. Finally the Brazilian government announced that the title to the land at Jari was in doubt. With this, it became impossible to secure nongovernmental financial aid and the project collapsed. While a Brazilian consortium has taken over the project in an attempt to make it work, it has yet to succeed.

If there is a lesson from the Jari experience, it lies in the importance for managers to recognize their dependence on the external environment and to successfully deal with this problem. Ignoring environmental demands can only hasten confrontation and possible ruin for the organization. On the other hand, as noted by Pfeffer and Salancik, the companies that accurately interpret environmental conditions and take steps to deal with them are far more likely to succeed.

Source: Based on information in "Anatomy of a Failure," *Newsweek* (January 25, 1982), p. 45.

- *Misreading interdependence.* An organization may simply be unaware of all of the external groups on which it depends, or the relative power of each group. The auto industry in the 1960s showed a lack of concern with safety and pollution control and faced subsequent problems of regulation. The automakers were simply not aware of the power of these outside forces.
- *Misreading demands.* A second problem emerges when an outside force

is recognized as being important but the organization misreads what demands the outsiders are making. For example, partly as a result of the antiwar rallies in the late 1960s and early 1970s in major U.S. universities, and partly due to student concern that university education was lacking in relevancy, major declines were experienced in university budgets, student enrollments, and alumni contributions. Universities responded by tightening managerial control and reevaluating program costs. However, producing student revolutionaries more efficiently or delivering irrelevant education for less money was not the issue. The environment was asking for changes in output, while universities were perceiving a need for improvements in efficiency.

- *Commitment to the past.* Often, organizations feel threatened by change and rely on past practices to get them through today's crises. In a changing market, Henry Ford's commitment to the old Model T, produced in one style and one color only, almost ruined the company.
- *Conflicting demands.* Organizations sometimes face situations where responding to one outside pressure aggravates another outside pressure. Consider, for example, the plight of the corporation that decides to discriminate against white males to compensate for past discrimination against females and minorities. Either way, someone becomes alienated.

How does an organization respond when confronted by external demands from a source it is dependent upon? Pfeffer and Salancik (1978) note several response mechanisms. To begin, a most obvious response is simple *compliance* with the demands made by outsiders. However, compliance leads to a loss of credibility for the organization. This can be seen in the case of OPEC, where oil companies (and governments) took a passive role in the formation, growth, and development of OPEC and complied until OPEC became so powerful that organizations risked disaster if they refused the demands.

A second strategy for responding to environmental demands is to attempt to *avoid* the efforts by outsiders to influence the organization. For example, the organization may be secretive about what it is doing so that those making the demands do not know what others are receiving, or even how well they themselves are doing. For example, the American Petroleum Institute, an organization supported by the oil industry, reports information on oil supplies and forecasts. This industry-sponsored organization is the U.S. government's source for most of its information used to control the very same oil industry. And the organization may also avoid being influenced by pitting one pressure group against another (for example, unions vs. equal employment organizations) so the organization itself may be left alone.

The third approach to responding to environmental demands is to *manage or avoid actual dependency itself.* For example, an organization may attempt to develop alternative resources of supply or markets. The development of synthetic rubber (for tires, etc.) was hastened during World War II by the enemy control of most of the world's natural rubber supply. Alternatively, organizations can seek laws or regulations that restrict the power of outside influences, such as antitrust laws. Finally, organizations can engage in cooperative efforts or coalitions with other organizations to reduce external dependence. Many farmers band together in farm cooperatives, for example, to share risks and buffer themselves against the effects of outside pressures.

If an organization is to be effective, it is essential that it discover ways to gain greater control over its own destiny. Whether this is done by winning more independence from others or by establishing long-term coalitions, it is necessary that dependence on hostile or threatening forces for resources be reduced. As noted by Pfeffer and Salancik (1978, p. 1), the central thesis of this model is that:

> . . . to understand the behavior of an organization you must understand the context of that behavior—that is, the ecology of the organization. This point of view is important for those who seek to understand operations as well as for those who seek to manage and control them. Organizations are inescapably bound up with the conditions of their environment. Indeed, it has been said that all organizations engage in activities which have as their logical conclusion adjustment to the environment.

MANAGING ENVIRONMENTAL CONTINGENCIES

In any discussion of the impact of organization-environment relations on organization effectiveness, several critical variables appear to be consistently interrelated. They are: (1) the degree of predictability; (2) the accuracy of perception of environmental states; and (3) the notion of rationality in organizational actions. Based on the available evidence, these variables —predictability, perception, and rationality—are important factors in managing environmental relations. Because an optimal response to environmental conditions contributes to organizational effectiveness, it is essential that managers fully understand each of these variables.

Predictability and Control of the Environment

First, consider the issue of predictability and control. In discussing the degree of complexity and stability in the environment, we are in effect raising questions about the degree of uncertainty in organization-environment relations. The greater the uncertainty, the less the predictability and control. The capacity of an organization to successfully adapt to its environment is largely facilitated by its ability to know what the external environment is going to be like in the future. The more certain managers are about future environmental states, the more opportunity they have to respond accordingly. For example, managers in the plastics firms discussed by Lawrence and Lorsch (1967) were not unduly hampered by the instability of their market so long as their organization was structured to accommodate market changes with relative

EXHIBIT 3.7   ENVIRONMENTAL INFLUENCES ON ORGANIZATIONAL EFFECTIVENESS

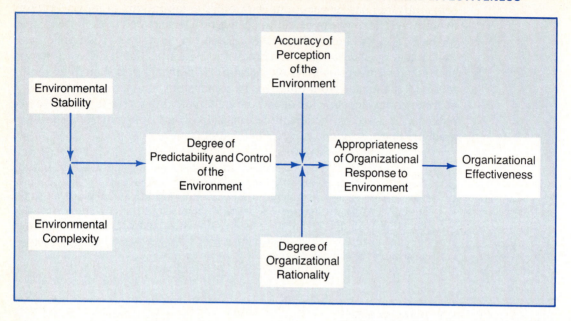

ease; that is, they had the appropriate amount of differentiation and integration.

Thus, environmental instability is not necessarily detrimental to effectiveness. Its impact on organizational adaptation is more a function of the extent to which the instability and the direction of changes can be predicted in advance. Research indicates that if the environment is highly unpredictable, a more organic structure may be more effective. A mechanistic structure may be more appropriate for predictable environments. In conclusion, then, it would appear that the greater the predictability concerning environmental states, the greater the potential for appropriate organizational response (see Exhibit 3.7).

Perception of the Environment

At least two "filters" may affect the ultimate response of an organization to the existing environment. First, there is the problem of the accuracy with which management perceives the environment. As pointed out by Weick (1966) and others, managers respond to what they perceive, and such perceptions may or may not correspond to objective reality. Weick calls this the *enacted* (or created) *environment.* If management accurately perceives the degrees of complexity, stability, and uncertainty existing in the external environment, the probability of appropriate organizational response and adaptation is enhanced. If, on the other hand, an organization "enacts" an unrealistic environment, either through managerial myopia, lack of expertise, insufficient time, or whatever, the negative effects on organizational success could be substantial.

Second, there is the question concerning which cues are picked up by organizational decision makers. As individuals and in groups, managers often exhibit certain response biases about what they see or how they see it. This phenomenon has been alternatively referred to as the "organization man" syndrome, the "corporate mentality," "groupthink," and so on. Executive managers work together, socialize together, and often think along similar lines. Thus, it is not surprising that their perceptions of the environment may be filtered by similar work experiences and professional associations. When these perceptions are in error, or when only part of the relevant cues are received from the environment, decisions concerning appropriate responses are made on the basis of distorted or incomplete information. Inaccurate perception can severely constrain organizational response to the environment.

Degree of Organizational Rationality

A third problem that can affect managerial reaction to environmental events deals with the extent to which managers behave rationally in making environmentally relevant decisions. Although organizations may strive for rational behavior, it has long been recognized that, because of insufficient information or because of a decision maker's inability to adequately process all the relevant information, managers likely engage in some form of *bounded rationality* (Simon, 1957). That is, they attempt to optimize instead of maximize on the quality of their decisions. The concept of rationality is important for the following reason: no matter how predictable the environment and no matter how accurate the perceptions concerning environmental states, organizations and managers still have to determine a course of action to respond to changes in the environment. The more rational the choice processes are for selecting viable alternatives, the greater the probability that the chosen response will be appropriate to meet environmental demands.

A case in point is the Women's Christian Temperance Union. During the era of prohibition, the WCTU was an active and powerful foe of the legalization of any type of alcoholic beverage. However, as environmental demands changed and popular support shifted in favor of the legalization of liquor, the WCTU remained firm in its opposition. Even though the environment in which this organization operated had changed, and even though it clearly recognized the change, it made a decision to continue its support for prohibition. As a result, the organization lost most of its popular support and virtually all of its power. One might argue that, under the circumstances, a more "rational" decision for the WCTU would have been to compromise on the issue while it could still bargain from a position of strength. Instead, the organization chose to remain firm in spite of environmental changes with the obvious consequences to the organization's effectiveness.

In conclusion, based on the available evidence, predictability, perception, and rationality are all important factors in environmental relations. Moreover, there is a pattern to this relationship, where the actual degree of predictability of the environment is "filtered" by organizational decision makers through their accuracy of perception and through their rationality. The resulting selection of a particular course of action can be seen as leading to organizational effectiveness to the extent that it is appropriate for a given environment. If the environment is in fact highly unpredictable and management perceives it to be stable, one would not expect a high degree of organizational success over the long term. Similarly, if the environment is unpredictable, but management chooses to ignore the fact for whatever reason, again one would not expect a high degree of success. Thus, only when accurate perception and high rationality of decision making are both present would we predict that an organization's response to environmental conditions would be optimal in contributing to effectiveness.

SUMMARY

In this chapter we continued our discussion of organization design, giving particular attention to the role of the technological and environmental variables. It was noted that variations in technology and in the external environment can have a marked impact on the structure and design of an effective organization.

There are at least three approaches to developing classifications for technology. The point here is not that one typology is superior to another; rather, it is important to note that the role of typologies in understanding organization design is to help management better understand their own particular organization. Two prominent studies of the role of technology in structure and effectiveness were reviewed: the classic Woodward study and the studies by the Aston Group. While the particular conclusions reached by each of these studies were somewhat different, both studies nevertheless pointed to the role of technology as a central variable in facilitating organizational effectiveness.

Next, attention shifted to the role of the external environment in determining organization design and effectiveness. We began with a discussion of Duncan's model of environmental states. This model consists of three major variables: the simple-complex dimension, the static-dynamic dimension, and environmental uncertainty. Using these three dimensions, we can fairly readily categorize a particular organization and thereby understand its relationship with the external environment.

We then went on to examine several classic studies of the relationship between the external environment, organization structure, and subsequent effectiveness, studying the models by Burns and Stalker, Chandler, Lawrence and Lorsch, and Pfeffer and Salancik. The resource dependence model represents a fairly recent attempt to understand organization-environment relations in terms of a balance of power between the two entities.

At the conclusion of the chapter the various models were integrated to illustrate how they jointly help in understanding organizational effectiveness. Organizational effectiveness is largely a function of the extent to which an organization appropriately responds to the external environment. The appropriateness of the response is influenced by at least three variables: the accuracy of perception of the environment; the degree of predictability of the environment; and the extent of organizational rationality. The manner in which an organization responds to changes in the external environment greatly influences the capacity of that organization to become effective.

This chapter concludes the discussion of organization design and effectiveness. Based on the information provided in Chapters Two and Three, we are now in a position to examine the role of the individual in organizations. It is to this topic that we now turn.

KEY WORDS

bounded rationality
consonance hypothesis
differentiation
enacted environment
environmental complexity
environmental determinism
environmental stability
environmental uncertainty
external environment

integration
mechanistic
organic
resource dependence model
strategy
technological determinism
technology
work-flow integration

FOR DISCUSSION

1. Compare and contrast the three approaches to classifying technology. Which approach do you prefer? Why?
2. What was the major finding of the classic Woodward study? Is this conclusion still valid today?
3. What is technological determinism? How valid is the concept?
4. How do the findings of the Aston Group differ from those of Woodward?
5. Describe the consonance hypothesis as it relates to organization design.
6. What is meant by the external environment of an organization? What are the dimensions of such an environment?
7. Describe Duncan's model of environmental states.
8. What are the major conclusions of the Burns and Stalker study?
9. Discuss Chandler's basic hypothesis concerning the relationship between strategy and structure.
10. Define and discuss the relationship between integration and differentiation according to Lawrence and Lorsch's model.
11. Describe the resource dependence model of organization-environment relations. How does this model differ from the one proposed by Lawrence and Lorsch?
12. Discuss the practical significance of the enacted environment concept.
13. Define bounded rationality. Discuss the role of this concept in organizational decision making.

UPSTARTS IN THE SKY: THE CASE OF AIRLINE DEREGULATION

On September 8, 1980, New York Air announced plans to begin daily service between New York and Washington, D.C. In doing so, it intentionally challenged Eastern Airlines' lucrative Air Shuttle head-on. The philosophy behind the new carrier was a simple one: hire young, nonunion employees and offer low-cost, frequent service using a standardized fleet of 115-passenger DC-9s.

By the time New York Air began flying on December 20, it had already embarked upon a highly visible media campaign that openly taunted Eastern, decrying that carrier's "cattle car" approach to air travel. To lure passengers, New York Air offered off-peak fares of $29, compared to the $59 fare on Eastern flights. The airline was soon competing with the Washington and Boston shuttles, matching Eastern flight for flight on both routes. In just six months, the new carrier managed to capture thirty percent of the traffic in these markets. Next, the feisty upstart added Washington–Boston, Washington–Newark, New York–Cleveland, and New York–Louisville runs, and its competitors began waging a battle to protect their threatened markets.

New York Air is just one of a growing collection of "upstart carriers" formed since deregulation. Midway Airlines, People Express, and Muse Air are now airborne, and several other new airlines are preparing for entry. Ironically, few observers anticipated this flood of new entrants. In fact, during the debate over airline deregulation, many experts predicted that the major carriers would eventually swallow up their smaller competitors in a nonregulated environment, leaving the nation just a handful of mega-airlines. That prediction proved woefully inaccurate. Instead, deregulation has spawned a swarm of highly efficient, low-cost airlines anxious to challenge the major carriers.

At present, these new airlines carry only three percent of all passenger traffic. But their rate of growth far exceeds that of established major and national airlines. More important, it's the upstarts—not the older carriers—that are calling the shots in today's competitive industry. So pervasive is their influence, in fact, that these new entrants may ultimately revolutionize the air transportation system in the United States.

Before the Airline Deregulation Act of 1978, a protectionist Civil Aeronautics Board effectively prohibited new carriers from serving interstate routes. But CAB jurisdiction never extended to *intra*state routes. As a result, between the late 1940s and the mid-1960s, no fewer than sixteen new airlines began service within California. One of the most successful was California Central, which operated a highly profitable network of intrastate flights. In 1953, California Central's maintenance employees went out on strike, sending the carrier into bankruptcy the following year. Determined to capitalize on California Central's demise, a then-tiny California upstart called Pacific Southwest began expanding to fill the role left by its former rival. Ultimately, Pacific Southwest was the only carrier of the original sixteen to survive in California. In fact, until the mid-1960s, PSA was consid-

ered a textbook example of how a no-frills airline offering frequent flights could compete profitably against the major carriers.

Then came Southwest Airlines, modeled after Pacific Southwest's success in California. Southwest entered the Texas intrastate market in 1971 by inaugurating service between Dallas and Houston. The carrier's strategy was simple: provide frequent service on heavily traveled routes, offer minimal in-flight services at substantially reduced fares, maintain high labor productivity, and use one standardized type of equipment. To carry out this strategy, Southwest opted for high-density seating on its Boeing 737s, cash-register-style ticketing, no in-flight meals, and fares up to sixty percent below competitors'.

In time, Southwest became so successful it outdid even PSA. Today, the airline flies twenty-five Boeing 737-200s to fourteen cities. Passenger volume has risen from 108,000 per year in 1971 to more than six million passengers in 1980. In 1980 Southwest earned an astounding 25.6 percent profit margin —easily the best in the industry.

For the majority of the new upstarts, Southwest's "keep it simple" philosophy has taken on all the trappings of a holy writ. With few exceptions, most new entrants are flying standardized fleets of used DC-9s, 737s, or BAC-111s. Although such aircraft often burn more fuel than later models, their relatively cheap price—roughly $3 to $5 million —greatly reduces the initial capital outlay. People Express, for example, is purchasing a fleet of seventeen 737s from Lufthansa for $62 million, the same price the carriers would have to pay for four new 737s. Also like Southwest, the upstarts are shunning interline services. Most will not write tickets for flights on other airlines. Few will interline luggage

at connecting airports (that is, forward luggage to another airline). By focusing on point-to-point markets, the upstarts are confident they can meet passenger needs while avoiding the costly interline agreements that are a traditional service of their mainline competitors.

The upstarts have consistently shown a willingness to introduce innovations into the air transportation system. For example, at People Express, passengers never grumble about standing in line at the ticket counters. There are no ticket counters. Although reservations are required, the carrier sells tickets in flight, as Eastern does on its Air-Shuttle.

To trim costs, People Express refuses to accept cargo or mail, and discourages passengers from checking baggage. The airline charges a three-dollar fee for each piece of checked luggage. To encourage passengers to carry their luggage on board, each 737 is equipped with oversized luggage compartments, and seat bottoms have been raised higher off the floor to provide additional storage room.

Muse Air has adopted a no-smoking policy aboard all of its flights. "From the public's standpoint," says Ed Lang, Muse's senior vice-president for marketing, "this has probably been the most positive thing we've done. We feel it's attracting more new customers for us than what we've lost." Muse Air offers a free bottle of wine or champagne to any passenger who is assigned a middle seat. To lure passengers from Eastern's shuttles, New York Air offers free cocktails during business hours—an amenity never afforded veterans of the Air Shuttle.

Finally, by avoiding jet-clogged O'Hare, Midway Airlines exploits the advantages of Chicago's underutilized South Side airport, frequently reminding air travelers of its proximity to downtown and its lack of congestion.

Of all the innovations, however, pricing policies of the new entrants are the most significant. "What's important is not just how low the fares are, but the design of the fares," says Roy Pulsifer, associate director of the CAB's Bureau of Domestic Aviation. "The unique feature of what the new carriers are doing is offering a peak/off-peak fare structure. What this does is allow the smoothing of traffic flows so that flights right around the clock and on weekends are all filled at about the same level. If you can keep the planes full, you've licked the worst problem in air transportation, which is traffic imbalance." According to Pulsifer, proper pricing can theoretically increase load factors to as high as ninety-five percent. It also results in equity aloft, as every passenger aboard a given flight pays exactly the same fare.

A major reason the new entrants can offer fare reductions of as much as seventy-five percent is lower labor costs per unit of output. Once again, Southwest provides the classic model. Despite the fact that nearly all of the carrier's employees are unionized, Southwest has one of the most productive work forces in the industry. Pilots, for example, fly an average of seventy-five hours per month, twenty-five percent more than most union pilots. Between July 1979 and June 1980, Southwest's 737 labor costs were sixty-five percent below those of major carriers. "Southwest pays good money," says Pulsifer, "but their people work their tails off."

Not surprisingly, nearly all of the new entrants are hiring nonunion personnel. When seniority is factored out, the salaries paid by the upstarts are on a par with those of established carriers. Yet the cost advantage of hiring a fresh work force is substantial. Pilots often start at salaries of $30,000, far less than the $70,000–$100,000 paid to senior pilots at established carriers. Many of the new entrants are also determined to cross-utilize their airport personnel. New York Air, for example, trains employees to become reservationists and ticket-counter agents as well as flight attendants, rotating individuals among all three jobs depending upon demand.

To encourage greater productivity, People Express has devised a program that *requires* each employee to purchase stock in the company. "You have to see these people in operation to believe it," says a spokesperson for the carrier. "When all employees are stockholders, it's one-hundred percent hustle every day." No wonder the new entrants boast labor cost advantages of thirty percent or more over the established carriers.

Not only have the new entrants succeeded in luring passengers away from their airline competitors, they've also snared many travelers who would otherwise have journeyed by car. Consider what happened when People Express began offering low-cost service between Newark and Norfolk. Traffic on the route increased eighty-two percent during May 1981 compared to the same period in 1980. "At the fare level of the new entrants," says Pulsifer, "air becomes very attractive against substitutes, namely the automobile. It's possible that there will be a whole new transportation market, one that never existed before."

New entrants meet resistance from carriers already serving an airport. When Midway Airlines tried to sublease gate and ticket-counter space from the carriers serving LaGuardia, all refused. Only after intervention by the New York/New Jersey Port Authority, the airport's operator, was Midway able to secure the space it needed at LaGuardia.

For the major carriers, the emergence of a vigorous group of highly competi-

tive upstarts couldn't have come at a worse time. Saddled with large, fuel-inefficient jets, steep labor costs, and expensive frills, the major U.S. carriers lost more than $400 million in 1980. Last year, airline ticket prices soared more than twice the rate of inflation, sending their traffic plummeting seven percent. Besides driving away business, such steep fares have also aggravated the threat from the upstarts.

Established airlines are keenly aware of the threat posed by the upstarts. Some, such as Pan Am, maintain they are unable to compete with new entrants on point-to-point service and have given up trying. Others offer little more than knee-jerk responses, matching new entrants' fares in specific markets.

Ultimately, the majors will find that such stopgap measures don't address the problem. "It's pure Darwinism," says Pulsifer. "If you're challenged by another species to occupy the niche you're in, you have two choices: either you give up and retreat and go out of existence, or you can adapt yourself to whatever is required by the environment." According to Pulsifer, such adaptation means that the trunks and regionals will have to find a way to hold the line on costs. "From now on," he says, "the cost level of the industry will be determined by the cost level of the new entrants."

Angered by the intrusion of new entrants into their markets, some established carriers have suggested that the CAB is deliberately showing favoritism toward the upstarts to "prove" that deregulation works. This summer, four carriers accused the CAB of "blatant discrimination" after the board granted People Express the right to lower its limits on baggage liability and ease de-

nied boarding compensation rules. The CAB denies the charge, and at least one trunk official agrees with the board. "To the CAB's credit," says Neil Effman, TWA senior vice-president for airline planning, "I think . . . it has been a fair referee in the game and given no one an unfair advantage."

One thing is clear: many more upstarts will appear in the years to come. In light of such a prediction, it may very well be that the upstarts of today will face their biggest challenge from the upstarts of tomorrow. Already there is evidence of this trend. Founded by the former president of Southwest, Muse Air is now competing head to head with Southwest on the lucrative Dallas-Houston route. Air Chicago, the brainchild of two former Midway Airlines execs, is now poised to set up its own hub-and-spoke system, also from Midway Airport. Not all of the new carriers will survive. "When you have lots of entrants," says Jordan, "you also have lots of failures. This is to be expected."

CASE DISCUSSION QUESTIONS

1. What makes an upstart like New York Air successful? How long do you believe this success can last?
2. Describe the upstarts in the context of: (1) environmental determinism; and (2) the resource dependence model.
3. Will the upstarts survive? If so, how? Do you feel their strongest competition will come from larger airlines or from new upstarts?

Source: Based upon D. Martindale, "Look Who's Calling the Plays Now," *OAG Frequent Flyer*, November 1981, pp. 47–51, 72.

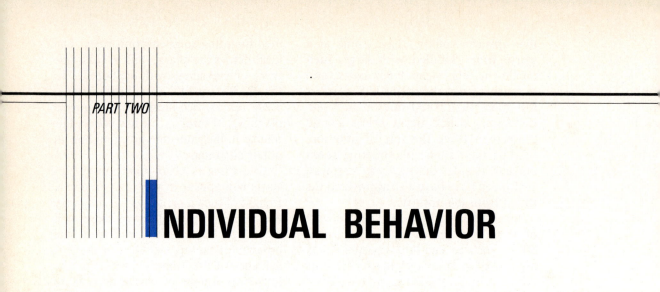

PART TWO

INDIVIDUAL BEHAVIOR

CHAPTER FOUR

PERCEPTUAL PROCESSES

Many years ago, Kurt Lewin (1937) suggested that a useful way to study human behavior was to consider behavior *(B)* as a function of the interaction between a person *(P)* and his or her environment *(E)*. In short, Lewin proposed that $B = f(P, E)$. It is clear from this simple formula that an understanding of the person is central to understanding organizational behavior. Thus, several chapters are devoted here to the study of the person, or more specifically, to the study of individual differences. This chapter will focus on perception in the work environment. In the following chapters we will consider employee ability and traits, employee motivation, and learning processes as they influence employee behavior and performance. How do these topics relate to organizational behavior? Organizations are made up of people with unique characteristics. A manager must recognize these variations because, as shall be seen, they affect organizational dynamics.

People are constantly being subjected to stimuli or cues from their environment, all of which compete for their attention. In the work place, these stimuli include supervisors' instructions, co-workers' comments, machine noises, people walking by, and posted signs and notices. Given the very large number of these stimuli, individuals are faced with the problem of how to make sense out of so many variables, how to organize and interpret the more relevant stimuli, and how to respond to them. The process by which this is done is *perception*.

In this chapter we will examine the following aspects of the perceptual process as they relate to organizational behavior: (1) basic perceptual processes; (2) perceptual selectivity; (3) social perception at work; (4) attribution theory; (5) perceptual differences between superiors and subordinates; and (6) barriers to accurate perception of others. We begin with a few words about why perception is pertinent to the management process.

IMPORTANCE OF TOPIC FOR MANAGERS

The nature of employee perception and the perceptual process is relevant for managers in a variety of ways. First of all, as noted by Lewin (1935) and others, people behave based on how they see the environment, and views of the world differ considerably among individuals. For instance, a management directive to work harder may be seen by an aspiring young manager as a way of moving up in the organization. This same directive, however, may be interpreted by a factory worker as another attempt by management to exploit the worker. It is important for managers to recognize that people perceive things differently and attempt to understand how perceptual processes work.

Perceptual processes also play an important role in the decisions managers make concerning employee selection, placement, and promotion. Most people have subtle biases that affect their decisions. In view of the significance of managerial decisions, both for the individuals involved and for the organization, it is important to understand as clearly as possible how these biases are formed and how they affect our attitudes and behavior.

In addition, perception plays a large part in the performance appraisal process. One of the most popular methods of evaluating employees is with the use of rating forms. These forms are subject to a wide variety of potential errors, many of which can be attributed to poor or inaccurate perception. An understanding of perceptual processes can therefore facilitate more accurate appraisal systems which, in turn, have the capability of more accurately tying rewards to behavior.

A knowledge of perception can improve a manager's ability to communicate—orally or in writing—with employees. The notion of perceptual selectivity, discussed in this chapter, acts to screen out or allow in various messages from the environment. A knowledge of what gets attention can aid us in getting our messages across to those we work with.

Finally, an understanding of the basic nature of perceptual processes can help us better understand ourselves and our reactions to our surroundings. For instance, many students of management—as well as many managers —perceive blue-collar workers as being basically lazy. Such generalizations about any occupational grouping are seldom accurate and hardly serve to improve the capacity to manage.

BASIC PERCEPTUAL PROCESSES

By *perception* we mean the process by which an individual screens, selects, organizes, and interprets stimuli so that they have meaning to the individual. It is a process of making sense out of one's environment so an appropriate behavioral response can be made. Perception does not necessarily lead to an accurate portrait of the environment, but rather, to a unique portrait, influenced by the needs, desires, values, and disposition of the perceiver. As described by Kretch et al. (1962, p. 20), an individual's perception of a given situation

> is not, then, a photographic representation of the physical world; it is, rather, a partial, personal construction in which certain objects, selected out by the individual for a major role, are perceived in an individual manner. Every perceiver is, as it were, to some degree a nonrepresentational artist, painting a picture of the world that expresses his individual view of reality.

The multitude of objects that vie for attention are first selected or screened by individuals. This process is called *perceptual selectivity*. Certain of these objects catch our attention, while others do not. Once individuals notice a particular object, they then attempt to make sense out of it by organizing or categorizing it according to their own unique frame of reference and their needs. This second process is termed *perceptual organization*. When meaning has been attached to an object, individuals are in a position to determine an appropriate response or reaction to it. Hence, if we clearly recognize and understand we are in danger from a falling rock or a car we can quickly move out of the way.

Because of the importance of perceptual selectivity for understanding the perceptual process in work situations, we will examine this concept in some detail before considering the topic of social perception.

PERCEPTUAL SELECTIVITY

As noted above, *perceptual selectivity* refers to the process by which certain objects in the environment are selected by individuals for attention. Without this ability to focus on one or a few stimuli instead of the hundreds of stimuli constantly surrounding us, individuals would be unable to process all the

EXHIBIT 4.1   THE PROCESS OF PERCEPTUAL SELECTIVITY

| Exposure | → | Attention | → | Perception | → | Retention |

relevant information necessary to initiate behavior. In essence, perceptual selectivity works as follows (see Exhibit 4.1). The individual is first exposed to an object or stimulus—a loud noise, a new car, a tall building, another person, etc. Next, the individual focuses attention on this one object or stimulus, as opposed to others, and concentrates his or her efforts on understanding or comprehending the stimulus. Once this has been achieved, the individual is more likely to retain an image of the object or stimulus in his or her memory.

Perceptual selectivity is enhanced by two related processes: (1) absolute thresholds of activation and (2) sensory adaptation. First, it is believed that all sense organs have *absolute thresholds of activation;* thus, many stimuli go unnoticed by individuals because they are not strong, bright, or loud enough to activate our senses. The use of camouflage by the military is an example of intentionally attempting to reduce the chance of sense (in this case, optical) activation. Choosing neutral colors like grey or beige for clothing is another example. *Sensory adaptation,* on the other hand, is a process by which individuals tune out certain objects or stimuli after continued exposure. The ticking of a clock, for instance, may appear to be very loud for an individual who has focused on this sound, but another individual may not even hear the ticking because the senses have adapted to it and nullified its impact on perception.

Hence, many objects or stimuli are removed from the perceptual field by the above two processes. Beyond this, all other stimuli must compete for our attention. A variety of factors influence which stimuli we notice and which we ignore. These various influences on selective attention can be divided into external influences and internal (personal) influences (see Exhibit 4.2).

External Influences on Selective Attention

External influences consist of the characteristics of the observed object or person that activate the senses. Most external influences affect selective attention because of either their physical properties or their dynamic properties.

Physical Properties. The physical properties of the objects themselves often affect which objects receive attention by the perceiver. Emphasis here is on the unique, different, and out of the ordinary. A particularly important physical

EXHIBIT 4.2   MAJOR INFLUENCES ON SELECTIVE ATTENTION

I. *External Influences*

Physical Properties
Size
Intensity
Contrast
Novelty or familiarity

Dynamic Properties
Motion
Repetition
Ordering

II. *Personal Influences*

Response salience
Response disposition
Attitudes and feelings toward object or person

property is *size.* Generally, larger objects receive more attention than smaller ones. Advertising companies use the largest signs and billboards allowed to capture the perceiver's attention. However, when most of the surrounding objects are large, a small object against a field of large objects may receive more attention. In either case, size represents an important variable in perception.

Brighter, louder, more colorful objects tend to attract more attention than objects of less *intensity.* For example, when a factory foreman yells an order at his or her subordinates, it will probably receive more notice (although it may not receive the desired response by workers). It must be remembered here, however, that intensity heightens activation only when compared to other comparable stimuli. If the foreman always yells, sensory adaptation may tune out the message.

Objects that *contrast* strongly with the background against which they are observed tend to receive more attention than less contrasting objects. An example of the contrast principle can be seen in the use of plant and highway safety signs. A terse message like DANGER is lettered in black against a yellow or orange background.

A final physical characteristic that can heighten perceptual awareness is the *novelty* or *unfamiliarity* of the object. Specifically, the unique or unexpected seen in a familiar setting (an executive of a conservative company who comes to work in bermuda shorts) or the familiar seen in an incongruous setting (someone in church holding a can of beer) will receive attention.

Dynamic Properties. The second set of external influences on selective attention concerns those properties which either change over time or derive their uniqueness from the order in which they are presented. The most obvious dynamic property is *motion.* We tend to pay attention to objects that move against a relatively static background. This principle has long been recognized by advertisers who often use signs with moving lights or moving objects to attract attention. In an organizational setting, a clear example is a rate-buster, who shows up his or her colleagues by working substantially faster, attracting more attention.

Another principle basic to advertising is *repetition* of a message or image. As noted by Morgan and King (1966, p. 343), "A stimulus that is repeated has a better chance of catching us during one of the periods when our attention to a task is waning. In addition, repetition increases our sensitivity or alertness to the stimulus." Work instructions that are repeated tend to be received better, particularly on a dull or boring task on which it is difficult to concentrate. This process is particularly effective in the area of plant safety. Most industrial accidents occur because of careless mistakes during monotonous activities. Repeating safety rules and procedures can often help keep workers alert to the possibilities of accidents.

A final external influence on selective attention is the *order* in which the objects or stimuli are presented (Secord and Backman, 1964). This principle is particularly important in interpersonal communications in organizational settings. Generally, research has shown that the order in which objects are presented to individuals can have a dramatic impact on what is noticed and what is not.

Two kinds of ordering effects have been found: primacy effects and recency effects. *Primacy effects* occur when the first stimulus or piece of information received from an object receives the greatest weight and colors subsequent information. *Recency effects,* on the other hand, occur when the last, or most recent, stimulus receives the greatest attention. Recency effects are often employed in both written and oral communications where the writer or speaker intentionally builds up to a major point by proceeding through several smaller, less important points. The initial points thus build and set the stage for the final (most recent) message. For instance, in a sales meeting the general sales manager may plod through sales statistics from the past ten years and finally, perhaps enthusiastically, present the present year's target. If this final stimulus is presented with enthusiasm and vigor, it may override earlier stimuli and create a heightened awareness of the need to increase sales *this* year.

Personal Influences on Selective Attention

In addition to a variety of external factors, several important personal factors are also capable of influencing the extent to which an individual pays attention to a particular stimuli or object in the environment. The three most important personal influences on perceptual readiness are: (1) response salience; (2) response disposition; and (3) attitudes and feelings toward an object or person.

Response Salience. This is a tendency to focus on objects that relate to our *immediate* needs or wants. Secord and Backman (1964, p.14) describe response salience as the influence of "the contemporary factors prevailing at the moment of perception. Certain current conditions, such as hunger, fatigue, or anxiety may affect what is perceived." As examples, a very nervous person may react intensely to sudden loud noises, or a person who is hungry may miss a stoplight in the haste to find a restaurant.

Response salience in the work environment is easily identified. A worker who is tired from many hours of work may be acutely sensitive to the number of hours or minutes until quitting time. Employees negotiating a new contract may know to the penny the hourly wage of workers doing similar jobs across town. Managers with a high need to achieve may be sensitive to opportunities for work achievement, success, and promotion. Finally, female managers may be more sensitive than many male managers to condescending male attitudes toward women.

Response salience, in turn, can distort the view of our surroundings. For example, as noted by Ruch (1967, p. 323):

> Time spent on monotonous work is usually overestimated. Time spent in interesting work is usually underestimated. . . . Judgment of time is related to feelings of success or failure. Subjects who are experiencing failure judge a given interval as longer than do subjects who are experiencing success. A given interval of time is also estimated as longer by subjects trying to get through a task in order to reach a desired goal than by subjects working without such motivation.

Response Disposition. Whereas response salience deals with immediate needs and concerns, *response disposition* is the tendency to recognize familiar objects more quickly than unfamiliar ones. The notion of response disposition carries with it a clear recognition of the importance of past learning on what we perceive in the present. For instance, in an early study, Bruner and Postman (1949) presented a group of individuals with a set of playing cards with the colors and symbols reversed: that is, hearts and diamonds were printed in black, and spades and clubs in red. Surprisingly, when subjects were presented with these cards for brief time periods, individuals consistently described the cards as they expected them to be (red hearts and diamonds, black spades and clubs) instead of how they really were. They were predisposed to see things as they always had been in the past.

Attitudes and Feelings Toward an Object or Person. The way people feel toward a particular object or person can also have a marked influence on how (or whether) the object or person is perceived. In general, research has found that objects about which we have strong feelings are more readily perceived than more neutral objects (Secord and Backman, 1964). For instance, in one experiment, subjects were given a questionnaire designed to identify which values were more important to them. Six categories of values were used: political, aesthetic, theoretical, economic, religious, and social. Words were then chosen from these various categories and shown briefly on a screen to the subjects. The experiment revealed that the greater the interest a person had in a particular value area, the more rapidly he or she recognized the words relevant to that area. For instance, words like money and bank were more readily perceived by those with strong economic interests, even though the words were presented so rapidly that many were below the threshold of recognition. Attitudes and values sensitize us so we more readily recognize stimuli or objects related to our strongest feelings.

The basic perceptual process is in reality a fairly complicated process. Several factors, including our own personal makeup and the environment, influence how we interpret and respond to the events we focus on. While the process itself may seem somewhat complicated, it in fact represents a shorthand to guide us in our everyday behavior. That is, without perceptual selectivity we would be immobilized by the millions of stimuli competing for our attention and action. The perceptual process allows us to focus our attention on the more salient events or objects and, in addition, allows us to categorize such events or objects so that they fit into our own conceptual map of the environment. The importance of perception should not be overlooked by managers interested in the study of people at work.

SOCIAL PERCEPTION IN ORGANIZATIONS

Up to this point, we have focused on an examination of basic perceptual processes—how we see objects or attend to various stimuli. Based on this discussion, we are now ready to examine a special case of the perceptual process; namely, social perception as it relates to the work place. Social perception consists of those processes by which we perceive other *people.* Particular emphasis in the study of social perception is placed on how we interpret other people, how we categorize them, and how we form impressions of them.

Clearly, the process of social perception is far more complex than the perception of inanimate objects like tables, chairs, signs, and buildings. This is true for at least two reasons. First, people are obviously far more complex and dynamic than tables and chairs. More careful attention must be paid in perceiving them so as not to miss important details. Second, an accurate perception of others is usually far more important to us personally than are our perceptions of inanimate objects. The consequences of misperceiving people are great. Failure to accurately perceive the location of a desk in a large room may mean we bump into it by mistake. Failure to accurately perceive a social situation (e.g., power relationships, status symbols, the attitudes of others) can have severe consequences in work situations. Social perception as it relates to the work situation deserves special attention.

We will concentrate now on the major influences on social perception. There are three basic categories of influence in the way we perceive other people: (1) the characteristics of the person being perceived; (2) the characteristics of the particular situation; and (3) the characteristics of the perceiver. When taken together, these three major influences are the dimensions of the environment in which we view other people. As such, it is important for

EXHIBIT 4.3   MAJOR INFLUENCES ON SOCIAL PERCEPTION IN ORGANIZATIONS

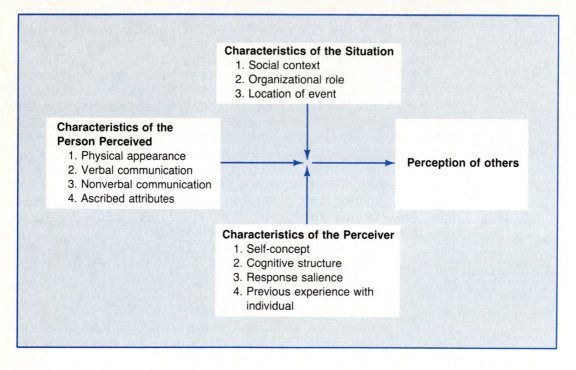

students of management to understand the way in which these sets of influences interact if perceptual accuracy is to be facilitated at work (see Exhibit 4.3).

Characteristics of the Person Perceived

The way in which people are perceived in social situations is greatly influenced by their characteristics. That is, our dress, talk, and gestures determine the kind of impressions people form of us. In particular, four characteristics of ourselves can be identified: (1) physical appearance; (2) verbal communication; (3) nonverbal communication; and (4) ascribed attributes.

Physical Appearance. A variety of physical attributes influence how we are seen by others. These include many of the obvious demographic characteristics like age, sex, race, height, and weight. A study by Mason (1957) found that most people agree on the physical attributes of a leader (i.e., what leaders *should* look like), even though these attributes were not found to be consistently held by actual leaders. However, when we see a person who appears to be assertive, goal-oriented, confident, and articulate, we infer that this person is a natural leader.

Another example of the potency of physical appearance in influencing perception is in the clothing we wear. People dressed in business suits are generally thought to be professionals, while people dressed in work clothes are assumed to be lower-level employees. The importance of these distinctions is that physical appearance, like clothing, influences how we respond to individuals; whether we are assertive or deferential, polite or gruff.

Verbal and Nonverbal Communication. What we say to others—as well as how we say it—can influence the impressions others form of us. Several aspects of verbal communication can be noted. First, the *precision* with which one uses language can influence impressions about cultural sophistication or education. An *accent* provides clues about a person's geographic background. The *tone of voice* used provides clues about whether people are happy, angry, or sad. Finally, the *topics* people choose to converse about provide clues about them.

Impressions are also influenced by nonverbal communication—how people behave. For instance, facial expressions often provide good clues in forming impressions of others. People who consistently smile are often thought to have positive attitudes (Secord, 1958). A whole field of study has recently emerged in *body language,* or the way in which we express our inner feelings subconsciously through physical actions: sitting up straight versus being relaxed; looking people straight in the eye versus looking away from people. These forms of expressive behavior provide information to the perceiver concerning such things as how approachable others are, how self-confident they are, or how sociable they are.

Ascribed Attributes. Finally, certain attributes are often ascribed before or at the beginning of an encounter, and these attributes can influence how we perceive others. Three ascribed attributes are status, occupation, and personal characteristics. *Status* is ascribed to someone when we are told that he or she is an executive, holds the greatest sales record, or has in some way achieved unusual fame or wealth. Research has consistently shown that people infer different motives to people they believe to be high or low in status, even though they may behave in an identical fashion (Thibaut and Riecker, 1955). For instance, high-status people are seen as having greater control over their behavior, as being more self-confident and competent, and are given greater influence in group decisions than low-status people. Moreover, high-status people are generally better liked than low-status people.

Occupations also play an important part in how we perceive people. Describing people as salespersons, accountants, teamsters, or research scientists conjures up distinct pictures of these various people before any first-hand encounters. In fact, these pictures may even determine whether there can be an encounter.

Other ascribed attributes involve presumed *personal characteristics.* For instance, research by Kelley (1950) found that when a man others were about to meet was described as warm, people made different judgments about him and behaved more cordially than when he was described as cold—even though this was the same person! Strickland (1958) found that supervisors who thought certain employees were more trustworthy than others (based on prior information) felt these employees needed less supervision, even though both sets of employees had similar performance records.

Characteristics of the Situation

The second major influence on how we perceive others is the situation in which the perceptual process occurs. Three situational influences can be identified: (1) the social context; (2) the organization and the employee's place in it; and (3) the location of the event (Zalkind and Costello, 1962).

Social Context. A great deal of research has focused on social influences on perception. Relating these findings to organizational behavior, several conclusions can be drawn. First, when people are given an opportunity to interact in a friendly and sociable work situation, they tend to see one another as similar to themselves (Rosenbaum, 1959). This environment is felt to be less threatening, allowing people to be more trusting and more willing to be open in their perceptions of others. Findings suggest that cooperative (rather than competitive) work situations are colored by less defensiveness and more trust (Cherrington, 1973). This environment would be particularly well-suited for a research laboratory, where creativity requires the right to be wrong.

In addition, findings by Exline (1960) suggest that when members of a group or committee are congenial, they tend to be more accurate in assessing the work motives and goals of their colleagues, although they are less accurate in assessing personal (as opposed to work-related) goals. These findings imply that committees or work groups composed of adversaries may devote more time and energy to personal clashes at the expense of group goals. The implications of this for personnel selection and placement are clear.

Organizational Role. An employee's place in the organizational hierarchy can also influence his or her perceptions. A classic study of managers by Dearborn and Simon (1958) emphasizes this point. In this study, executives from various departments (accounting, sales, production) were asked to read a detailed and factual case about a steel company. Next, each executive was asked to identify the major problem a new president of the company should address. The findings showed clearly that the executives' perceptions of the most important problems in the company were influenced by the departments in which they worked. Sales executives saw sales as the biggest problem, while production executives cited production issues. Industrial relations and public relations executives identified human relations as the primary problem in need of attention.

In addition to perceptual differences emerging horizontally across departments, such differences can also be found when we move vertically up or down the hierarchy. The most obvious difference here is seen between managers and union, where the former see profits, production, and sales as vital areas of concern for the company, while the latter places much greater emphasis on wages, working conditions, and job security. Indeed, our views of managers and workers are clearly influenced by the group to which we belong. Hence, the positions we occupy in organizations can easily color how we view our work world and those in it.

Location of Event. Finally, how we interpret events is also influenced by the location of the event. Behaviors that may be appropriate at home, like taking off one's shoes, may be inappropriate in the office. Acceptable customs vary from country to country. For instance, assertiveness may be a desirable trait for a sales representative in the United States, but may be seen as being brash or coarse in Japan or China.

Characteristics of the Perceiver

The third major influence on social perception is the perceiver. Several characteristics unique to our personalities can affect how we see others. These include: (1) self-concept; (2) cognitive structure; (3) response salience; and (4) previous experience with the individual.

Self-concept. Our self-concept represents a major influence on how we perceive others. This influence is manifested in several ways (Zalkind and Costello, 1962). First, when we understand ourselves (i.e., can accurately describe our own personal characteristics), we are better able to perceive others accurately (Norman, 1953). Second, when we accept ourselves (i.e., have a positive self-image), we are more likely to see favorable characteristics in others. Studies have shown that if we accept ourselves as we are, we broaden our view of others and are more likely to view people uncritically. Conversely, less secure people often find faults in others (Omwake, 1954). Third, our own personal characteristics influence the characteristics we are likely to see in others. For instance, people with authoritarian tendencies tend to view others in terms of power, while secure people tend to see others as warm rather than cold (Bossom & Maslow, 1957). From a management standpoint, these findings emphasize the importance for administrators to understand themselves. They also provide an argument for the kind of human relations training programs that are popular in many organizations today.

Cognitive Structure. Our cognitive structures also influence how we view people. People describe each other differently (Scott and Mitchell, 1976). Some use physical characteristics like tall or short, while others use central traits like deceitful, forceful, or meek. Still others have more complex cognitive structures and use multiple traits in their descriptions of others; hence, a person may be described as being aggressive, honest, friendly, *and* hardworking.

Ostensibly, the greater our cognitive complexity (i.e., our ability to differentiate between people using multiple criteria), the more accurate is our perception of others. People who tend to make more complex assessments of others also tend to be more positive in their appraisals (Frauenfelder, 1974). Research in this area highlights the importance of selecting managers who exhibit high degrees of cognitive complexity. These individuals should form more accurate perceptions of the strengths and weaknesses of their subordinates and be able to capitalize on their strengths while ignoring or working to overcome their weaknesses.

Response Salience. Response salience refers to our sensitivity to objects in the environment as influenced by our particular needs or desires. Response salience can play an important role in social perception because we have a tendency to see what we *want* to see. A company personnel manager who has a bias against women, minorities, or handicapped persons would tend to be adversely sensitive to them during an employment interview. This focus may cause the manager to look for other potentially negative traits in the candidate to confirm his biases. The influence of these arbitrary biases is an example of the halo effect. Another personnel manager without these biases would be much less inclined to be influenced by these characteristics when viewing prospective job candidates.

Previous Experience with Individual. Our previous experiences with others often will influence the way in which we view their current behavior. When an employee has consistently received poor performance evaluations, a marked improvement in performance may go unnoticed because the supervisor continues to think of the individual as a poor performer. Similarly, employees who begin their career with several successes develop a reputation as fast-track individuals and may continue to rise in the organization long after their performance has leveled off or even declined. The impact of previous experience on present perceptions should be respected and studied by students of management. For instance, when a previously poor performer earnestly tries to perform better, it is important for this improvement to be recognized early and properly rewarded. Otherwise, employees may feel that nothing they do will make any difference and give up.

Together, these three sets of factors—characteristics of the person perceived, the situation, and the perceiver—jointly determine the impressions we form of others (see Exhibit 4.3 on p. 100). With these impressions, we make conscious and unconscious decisions about how we intend to behave toward people. Our behavior toward others, in turn, influences the way they regard us. Consequently, the importance of understanding the perceptual process, as well as factors that contribute to it, is apparent for managers. A better understanding of ourselves and careful attention to others and to our particular situations leads to more accurate perceptions and, as a result, more appropriate actions.

PERCEPTION AND ATTRIBUTION

A major influence on how people behave is the way they interpret the events around them. People who feel they have control over what happens to them are more likely to accept responsibility for their actions than those who feel control of events is out of their hands. The cognitive process by which people interpret the reasons or causes for their behavior is an area of study known as *attribution theory* (Kelley, 1967; Heider, 1958; Weiner, 1974). Specifically, "attribution theory concerns the process by which an individual interprets events as being caused by a particular part of a relatively stable environment" (Kelley, 1967, p. 193).

Attribution theory is based largely on the work of Fritz Heider (1958). Heider argues that behavior is determined by a combination of internal forces (e.g., abilities or effort) and external forces (e.g., task difficulty or luck). Following the cognitive approach of Lewin and Tolman, he emphasizes that it is the *perceived* determinants, not the actual ones, that influence behavior. Hence, if employees perceive that their success is a function of their own abilities and efforts, they can be expected to behave differently than they would if they believed job success was due to chance.

The underlying assumption of attribution theory is that people are motivated to understand their environment and the *causes* of particular events. If individuals can understand the causes of events, they will then be in a better position to influence or control the sequence of future events. This process is diagrammed in Exhibit 4.4.

Specifically, attribution theory suggests that particular behavioral events (e.g., the receipt of a promotion) are analyzed by individuals to determine their causes. This cognitive interpretation process may lead to the conclusion that the promotion resulted from the individual's own effort or, alternatively, from some other cause, such as luck. Based on cognitive interpretations of events, individuals revise their cognitive (or causal) structures and rethink their assumptions about causal relationships. For instance, an individual may infer that performance does indeed lead to promotion. Based on this new structure, the individual makes choices about future behavior. In some cases, the individual may decide to continue exerting high levels of effort in the hope that it will lead to further promotions.

On the other hand, if an individual concludes that the promotion resulted primarily from chance and was largely unrelated to performance, a different cognitive structure might be created, and there might be little reason to continue exerting high levels of effort. In other words, the way in which we perceive and interpret events around us significantly affects our future behaviors.

Attributions in psychological research are typically measured by the concept of *locus of control* (Rotter, 1966). An *internal* locus of control is a feeling by employees that they can personally influence their own outcomes and behavior through their abilities, skills, and effort. An *external* locus of

EXHIBIT 4.4   SCHEMATIC REPRESENTATION OF THE ATTRIBUTION PROCESS

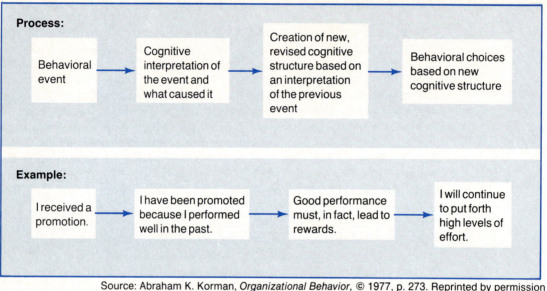

Source: Abraham K. Korman, *Organizational Behavior,* © 1977, p. 273. Reprinted by permission of Prentice-Hall, Inc., Englewood Cliffs, New Jersey.

control, on the other hand, is a feeling by employees that their outcomes or behavior is largely beyond their own control.

Research on attribution processes and locus of control has led to several interesting results. For example, in a series of experiments Weiner (1974) consistently found that when individuals perceive a high internal locus of control and seem to have control over their own behavior, successful performance on previous tasks leads to increased expectations of success on future tasks. Unsuccessful previous performance leads to reduced expectations for success on future tasks. As shown in Exhibit 4.5, success in one task for internals causes individuals to attribute the success to their own efforts, which augments the pride in accomplishment. This augmented pride in accomplishment, in turn, leads to increased expectations of success in future events. Failure on previous tasks for internals, in contrast, brings frustration, lack of confidence, and reduced future expectations. For persons perceiving an external locus of control, on the other hand, neither success nor failure on previous tasks would influence subsequent expectations. This is because individuals feel that behavior and performance are largely influenced by other people or events. Consequently, people feel there is little reason to try.

More research on locus of control has been summarized by Mitchell, Smyser, and Weed (1974). They found that people with a high internal locus of control (internals) were more satisfied with their work and were happier working under a participative-style manager. Externals, on the contrary, preferred a more directive style of management. Internals were more success-

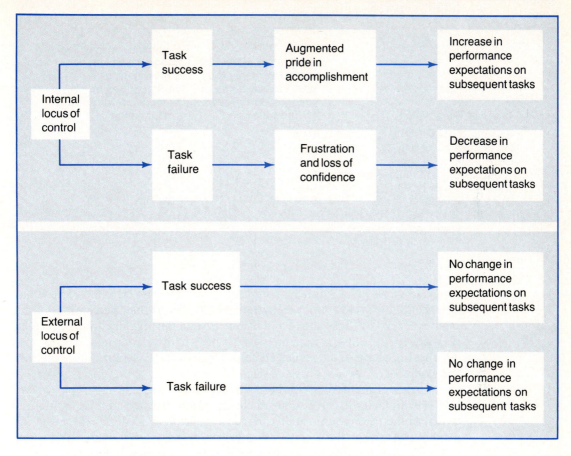

ful in their careers and were more often found in managerial positions (Valecha, 1972).

PERCEPTUAL DIFFERENCES BETWEEN SUPERIORS AND SUBORDINATES

So far, most of our discussion on social perception in organizations has focused on person-to-person perception, without much regard to rank or position in the hierarchy. Realistically, it is impossible to ignore the influence of position when examining major influences on social perception. It has been consistently found that superiors and subordinates tend to view situations somewhat differently, and these varying viewpoints influence how everyone behaves.

It was noted earlier that managers and union leaders tend to have

EXHIBIT 4.6　DIFFERENCES IN PERCEPTION BETWEEN SUPERVISORS AND SUBORDINATES

Types of Recognition	Frequency with which *supervisors* say they give various types of recognition for good performance	Frequency with which *subordinates* say supervisors give various types of recognition for good performance
Gives privileges	52%	14%
Gives more responsibility	48%	10%
Gives a pat on the back	82%	13%
Gives sincere and thorough praise	80%	14%
Trains for better jobs	64%	9%
Gives more interesting work	51%	5%

Source: Adapted from R. Likert, *New Patterns in Management* (New York: McGraw-Hill, 1961), p. 91. Used by permission.

distorted views of each others' competence and motives (Haire, 1955). It has also been shown that employees systematically distort their perceptions of the salaries earned by those above and below them in the organizational hierarchy (Lawler, 1971). The question we wish to pose here is what influence, if any, does position have in the perceived behavior of others? Several studies address this issue.

In one of the earliest studies of major importance on this topic, Likert (1961) examined the perceptions of superiors and subordinates in an attempt to determine the amounts and types of recognition subordinates received for good performance. Both superiors and subordinates were asked how often superiors gave rewards for good work. Results are shown in Exhibit 4.6.

As shown, superiors saw themselves as giving a wide variety of rewards for good performance fairly frequently. Subordinates, on the other hand, felt they received rewards from these same superiors much less frequently. In fact, the average percentage of time superiors felt they were giving such rewards was 63 percent, compared to 11 percent for subordinates. Hence, marked differences occur between superior and subordinate perceptions of the superiors' behavior.

Similar findings have been reported by Webber (1970) in superior-subordinate communications. Both superiors and subordinates in work organizations were asked how much time was spent by the superiors in initiating verbal communications with the subordinates. Superiors responded that they spent an average of 2.8 hours per week initiating such communications, while subordinates held that their superiors spent only about 1.6 hours. Again, superiors and subordinates looking at the same situation saw it differently.

Such discrepant findings raise questions about the accuracy of perceptions in work situations. Whose perception are we to believe? Haire (1976) argues persuasively that superiors probably are somewhat more accurate in

EXHIBIT 4.7   BARRIERS TO ACCURATE PERCEPTION OF OTHERS

Barrier	Definition
Stereotyping	A tendency to assign attributes to people solely on the basis of their class or category.
Halo effects	A tendency to allow the traits exhibited by people to influence our impressions of their other traits.
Implicit personality theory	A tendency to have an *a priori* picture of what other people are like that colors how we see them.
Selective perception	A process by which we systematically screen or discredit information we don't wish to hear and focus instead on more salient information.
Projection	A tendency to ascribe to others those negative characteristics or feelings we have about ourselves.
Temporal extension	A tendency to consider the first impressions we have of others to be their enduring characteristics.
Perceptual defense	A tendency to distort or ignore information that is either personally threatening or culturally unacceptable.

their perceptions of situations than subordinates for at least two reasons: (1) superiors tend to be more at the center of the communication network and hence have more information on which to base their judgments; and (2) superiors often achieve their leadership positions because of their ability to see situations clearly and act accordingly.

BARRIERS TO ACCURATE PERCEPTION OF OTHERS

In the perceptual process, at least seven barriers can be identified that inhibit our accuracy of perception. These barriers are: (1) stereotyping; (2) halo effects; (3) implicit personality theory; (4) selective perception; (5) projection; (6) temporal extension; and (7) perceptual defense. Each of these will be briefly considered as it relates to social perception in work situations (see Exhibit 4.7).

Stereotyping

One of the most common barriers in perceiving others at work is *stereotyping.* A stereotype is a widely held generalization about a group of people. It is a process in which attributes are assigned to people solely on the basis of their class or category. Stereotyping is particularly critical when meeting new people, since very little is known about them then. Based on a few prominent characteristics like sex, race, or age we tend to categorize them into a few general categories. We ascribe a series of traits to them based upon the attributes of the category we have put them in. We assume that an older person is old-fashioned, conservative, obstinate, and perhaps senile. Or, professors may be misjudged as absent-minded, impractical, idealistic, or eccentric.

One explanation for the existence of stereotypes has been suggested by Triandis (1971). He argues that stereotypes may be to some extent based upon fact. People tend to compare other groups with their own group, accentuating minor differences between groups to form a stereotype. For example, older people as a group may indeed be more conservative or more old-fashioned. These traits then become emphasized and attributed to *all* older people.

Stereotypes are not always dysfunctional for people. In fact, in many instances they can be quite helpful. In unfamiliar social situations, we need general guidelines to assist us in interpreting our environment. Stereotypes provide us with simple and quick ways of classifying people and reducing the ambiguity of our situations. They often protect us from making embarrassing social mistakes. Even so, while stereotypes have certain positive effects for the perceiver, they more often have detrimental effects for the person being perceived.

The power of stereotypes in organizational settings has been demonstrated in a variety of studies. Two particularly important studies are discussed here. The study in Close-Up 4.1 found that managers and union leaders have clear stereotypes concerning the characteristics and motives of each other (Haire, 1955). In Close-Up 4.2, a study revealed that men and women managers both tend to view a managerial career as predominantly male (Schein, 1973, 1975).

Several other relevant findings about sex-role stereotypes in work situations are worthy of note. In one study of business students, Bartol and Butterfield (1976) found that a manager's sex influenced the way in which people responded to variations in leadership style. Specifically, female managers were rated as being more effective when they emphasized interpersonal relations on the job, while male managers were seen as more effective when they emphasized task accomplishment.

Cohen and Bunker (1975) studied company recruiters and found that in the initial screening interview, female applicants were more often slotted into traditionally female jobs, while male applicants were more often directed into traditionally male jobs. Apparently, recruiters tended to typecast people according to sex and attribute certain work-related skills to them, depending upon whether they were male or female. Finally, Rosen and Jerdee (1974)

CLOSE-UP 4.1 UNION-MANAGEMENT STEREOTYPES

A classic study of social perception in work organizations was carried out by Mason Haire to examine the stereotypes business managers and union leaders had of each other. These stereotypes have obvious importance for such activities as contract negotiations and grievance handling.

Haire presented photographs of two men to samples of 108 industrial relations managers and 76 union leaders. Half the members of each group were told that the first man was a plant manager and that the second man was a labor official. The other half of both groups were given the same photographs but the descriptions were reversed. Subjects were then asked to describe the people in both pictures using a standardized list of adjectives.

As expected, Haire found that regardless of which picture was identified as a manager, the actual managers consistently described the person as more honest, dependable, and interpersonally competent than the labor official. Union leaders responded in the opposite fashion. In addition, managers felt that the manager was better able to appreciate labor's viewpoint than was the labor official capable of appreciating management's viewpoint. Again, opposite results occurred for actual union leaders.

This study has clear implications in the area of union-management relations. As noted by Stagner (1956, p. 35), "It is plain that unionists perceiving company officials in a stereotyped way are less efficient than would be desirable. Similarly, company executives who see all labor unions as identical are not showing good judgment or discrimination. To the extent that such stereotypes can be reduced, both managers and union leaders are in a better position to understand the other's point of view, to see the facts of a situation clearly, and to resolve differences with less stress, mistrust, and turmoil."

Source: M. Haire, "Role Perception in Labor-Management Relations: An Experimental Approach," *Industrial and Labor Relations Review* 8 (1955): 204–16.

found that sex-role stereotypes influenced the behavior of bank supervisors toward their subordinates. Supervisors tended to discriminate against women employees in personnel decisions involving promotion and development and against male employees in decisions involving leaves of absence for family reasons. Apparently the effects of sex-role stereotypes in work situations are fairly pervasive and represent a clear obstacle to managerial effectiveness.

Age stereotypes can also be found in organizations. A study by Rosen and Jerdee (1976) found that some business students have clear stereotypes of older employees. They are thought to be: (1) more resistant to organizational change; (2) less creative; (3) less likely to take calculated risks; (4) lower in physical capacity; (5) less interested in learning new techniques; and (6) less capable of learning new techniques. When asked to make personnel decisions concerning older people, the business students generally indicated several

CLOSE-UP 4.2 SEX-ROLE STEREOTYPES: A CONTINUING PROBLEM

Given the increasing number of women entering managerial ranks, it is important to understand how both men and women view the manager's job. If managerial jobs are viewed as being primarily masculine in nature, then negative reactions to women in management may inhibit women from either choosing or being chosen for managerial positions. In order to discover more about the possible effects of sex-role stereotypes on women in management, Virginia Schein carried out two related studies among male and female managers.

A questionnaire survey was administered to samples of 300 male and 167 female managers. The managers were asked to identify those traits that characterized men in general, women in general, and successful middle managers. It was hypothesized that both men *and women* managers would describe successful middle managers as possessing characteristics, attitudes, and temperaments more commonly ascribed to men than to women.

The results of the study clearly indicated that both men and women have strong male-oriented stereotypes of successful managers. That is, managers of both sexes described successful managers as exhibiting primarily masculine traits.

Several important implications for management result from this study, particularly in the area of employee selection, placement, and promotion. First, if a woman's self-image incorporates certain aspects of the stereotypical feminine role, she may be less inclined to pursue a managerial career because of an inconsistency between her (male-oriented) perceptions of the job and her own self-image. Moreover, if other male managers also view a managerial career as primarily a masculine one, they may attempt to dissuade or even block a woman from attempting it. Finally, a male sex-role stereotype of a manager's job may cause a sink-or-swim attitude among a new female manager's male peers. Without co-worker support, her chances of survival in a predominantly male world would obviously be diminished.

Source: V. E. Schein, "The Relationship Between Sex-Role Stereotypes and Requisite Management Characteristics," *Journal of Applied Psychology* 57 (1973): 95–100; and V. E. Schein, "Relationships Between Sex-Role Stereotypes and Requisite Management Characteristics Among Female Managers," *Journal of Applied Psychology* 60 (1975): 340–44.

trends. First, older people would receive lower consideration in promotion decisions. Older people would also receive less attention and fewer resources for training and development. Finally, older people would tend to be transferred to other departments instead of confronted by their superiors when a problem with their performance emerged.

As can be seen, stereotypes affect many segments of the working population: male and female, young and old, black and white, and union and management. The dysfunctional influence of stereotypes and the behaviors they prompt can only be imagined, but their impact on organizational behavior should not be minimized.

Halo Effects

A second important barrier to accurate social perception is the *halo effect*. A halo effect is a tendency to allow knowledge of one trait to influence impressions of an individual's other traits. Halo effects, which can be either positive or negative, act as a screen inhibiting perceivers from actually seeing the trait being judged (Zalkind and Costello, 1962).

Several examples of halo effects in social situations can be identified. For instance, one study found that people who were shown a photograph of a person who was smiling generally judged the person to be more honest than a person pictured as frowning, even though there is no reason to expect a strong connection between smiling and honesty. Moreover, in another study of halo effects, army officers who were well liked were also judged to be more intelligent than those who were disliked, in spite of equivalent intelligence test scores (Zalkind and Costello, 1962). Finally, a study by Asch (1946) found that when a stranger was described as warm, people described him as also being wise, imaginative, popular, and humorous. No such description was given of the *same* person when he was described as being cold.

These examples clearly demonstrate how one attribute can color people's impressions of other *unrelated* attributes of the same person. This finding has strong implications, particularly in the area of performance evaluation. Often, one positive attribute of an employee, like a consistent attendance record, can influence a supervisor's ratings of the employee's productivity or quality of work, regardless of the actual level of performance.

In addition to the area of performance evaluation, halo effects are also important in the way employees view the organization. Oftentimes, one negative attitude serves to nullify many positive aspects of the work situation. For instance, an early study by Grove and Kerr (1951) examined employee attitudes in a company that was in receivership. The company paid relatively high salaries, provided excellent working conditions, and had above-average supervision. Even so, the insecurity brought about by the financial exigency of the company led to a generalized negative attitude toward the company in all areas.

Three other points need to be made concerning halo effects. First, it has been found that negative information about people more strongly influences impressions of others than positive information (Hollman, 1972). Second, it appears that people place greater weight on social perception and information that comes from respected, trusted, or favored sources (Filley, House, and Kerr, 1976). Third, halo effects tend to be most severe under three conditions: (1) when the perceiver has little experience or knowledge in the area under evaluation; (2) when the evaluation concerns a person well known to the perceiver; and (3) when the traits have strong moral implications (Bruner and Tagiuri, 1954).

Implicit Personality Theory

Somewhat related to halo effects is the notion of *implicit personality theory.* Implicit personality theory is marked by a relatively fixed set of biases in judging others (Bruner and Tagiuri, 1954). Without knowing it, many people tend to have a theory about what others are like in general, and this theory influences perceptions.

For example, a person who is overly trusting tends to view others as honest, sincere, and kind. We are all familiar with the perpetual grouch who seems to have negative attitudes about everybody and everything. Such people have a theory or model that ascribes a host of attributes to people even before actual encounters.

The clearest approach to implicit personality theory in work organizations has been postulated by McGregor (1960) in his Theory X–Theory Y distinction. McGregor postulated that managers tend to have one of two views of employees. Theory X managers assume that the average worker is lazy and dislikes work. The employee must be coerced and closely controlled on the job and wants security instead of responsibility. Theory Y managers, on the other hand, assume that the average worker has the capacity to enjoy meaningful work and is self-directed, needing little supervision. He or she actively seeks responsibility and is capable of being imaginative and creative at work. Both of these oversimplified views of people represent implicit personality theories managers possess. The acceptance of either one in its entirety as a consistent picture of employees guarantees perceptual inaccuracies that will interfere with managerial effectiveness.

Two problems exist with implicit personality theory in social perception. The tendency to regard people as the same clearly ignores important individual differences. People are not the same and a generalized impression of others only distorts our understanding. Also, the related tendency to group or cluster several attributes to form one's own unique theory of personality assumes incorrectly that such attributes are consistently found together in people. This is not the case.

Selective Perception

Selective perception is the process by which we systematically screen out information we don't wish to hear, focusing instead on more salient information. Saliency here is obviously a function of our own experiences, needs, and orientations. The example of the Dearborn and Simon (1958) study of managers from various departments provides an excellent glimpse of selective perception. Production managers focused on production problems to the exclusion of other problems. Accountants, personnel specialists, and sales managers were similarly exclusive. Everyone saw his or her own specialty as more important in the company than other specialties (see Close-Up 4.3).

Another example of selective perception in groups and organizations is provided by Miner (1973). Miner summarizes a series of experiments dealing

In a classic study of conflicting role perceptions, Dearborn and Simon carried out a study among executives in various departments of a manufacturing firm. In all, twenty-three executives read a detailed case study from a business policy course. After reading the study, each executive was asked to identify what he or she considered to be the most important problem facing the firm to which a new incoming president should attend.

Results demonstrated that executives typically focused on their own functional area as the area requiring the primary attention of the new president. That is, five out of six people in marketing identified sales as the primary problem requiring attention, while four out of five production people saw organization and production problems as most important. People in public relations, industrial relations, and medicine identified human relations as the biggest problem.

The researchers concluded the data supported their hypothesis "that each executive will perceive those aspects of a situation that relate specifically to the activities and goals of his or her department" (p. 142). In view of the fact that all executives were instructed to examine the case on a company-wide rather than a departmental basis, the implications for organizational effectiveness are indeed troubling. If functional executives continue to examine problems from their own rather narrow vantage points, who then will consider the problem from an *organizational* perspective?

Source: D. C. Dearborn and H. A. Simon, "Selective Perception: A Note on the Departmental Identifications of Executives," *Sociometry 21* (1958): 140–44.

with groups competing with one another on problem-solving exercises. Consistently, the groups tended to evaluate their own solutions as better than the solutions proposed by others. Such findings resemble the not-invented-here syndrome found in many research organizations. There is a frequent tendency for scientists to view ideas or products originating outside their organization or department as inferior, and to judge other researchers as less competent and creative than themselves. Similar patterns of behavior can be found among managers, service workers, and secretaries.

Projection

Projection is a defense mechanism people use to protect their self-concept. In essence, people sometimes attribute or project onto others negative characteristics or feelings they have about themselves. Projection represents a barrier to accurate social perception because the perceiver sees certain self-related traits in ways that may not be accurate.

Several examples of projection in social perception can be cited. For instance, people who are fearful or anxious will often view others as being more aggressive and frightening than is warranted (Feshback and Singer,

1957). It has been demonstrated that people high in traits like stinginess, obstinacy, and disorderliness tend to rate others as being much higher on these traits than did the people who themselves were rated low on these same traits (Sears, 1936). The point here is that employees at all levels often ascribe to others characteristics they themselves possess, leading to misunderstanding, distrust, and decreased efficiency.

Temporal Extension

Temporal extension occurs when we observe a momentary characteristic of a person and consider it an enduring attribute (Secord and Backman, 1964). For instance, a smile often indicates that an individual is momentarily happy or is responding in a friendly way. Thus, if a person happens to smile when we first meet him, we may extend this attribute and continue to see the person as a happy or friendly person, long after the first encounter.

Temporal extensions are really first impressions in meeting people. They focus on unique and important characteristics that are observed. Several studies reveal that people tend to give undue emphasis to their first impressions of people and these first impressions tend to be enduring. As such, it is quite possible for different people to get very different impressions of a single individual, depending upon the circumstances of their first meeting.

Perceptual Defense

A final barrier to social perception is *perceptual defense.* As described by Secord and Backman (1964, pp. 26–27), perceptual defense is composed of three related processes:

1. Emotionally disturbing or threatening stimuli have a higher recognition threshold than neutral stimuli;
2. Such stimuli are likely to elicit substitute perceptions that are radically altered so as to prevent recognition of the presented stimuli;
3. These critical stimuli arouse emotional reactions even though the stimuli are not recognized.

In other words, through perceptual defense we tend to distort or ignore information that is either personally threatening or culturally unacceptable. Because emotionally disturbing stimuli have a higher recognition threshold, people are less likely to fully confront or acknowledge the threat. Instead, they may see entirely different or even erroneous stimuli that are safer. Even so, the presence of the critical stimuli often leads to heightened emotions despite its lack of recognition. For instance, suppose that during a contract negotiation for an assembly plant, word leaked out that because of declining profits the plant may have to close down permanently. Anxious workers might ignore this message and instead choose to believe the company management is only starting false rumors to increase their leverage during wage negotiations. Even if the leverage claim is accepted by the workers as truth, strong emotional reactions against the company can be expected.

One result of perceptual defense is to save us from squarely facing events that we either do not wish to handle or may even be incapable of handling. Perceptual defense helps us ignore these events. We dissipate our emotions by directing our attention to other (substitute) objects and hope the original event that distressed us will eventually disappear.

Perceptual defense is especially pronounced when people are presented with a situation that contradicts their long-held beliefs and attitudes. In a classic study of perceptual defense among college students, Haire and Grunes (1950) presented the students with descriptions of factory workers. Included in these descriptions was the word intelligent. Since the word was contrary to the students' beliefs concerning factory workers, they chose to reject the description by using perceptual defenses. Haire and Grunes (1950, pp. 407–11) describe four such defense mechanisms:

1. *Denial.* A few of the subjects denied the existence of intelligence in factory workers.
2. *Modification and distortion.* This was one of the most frequent forms of defense. The pattern was to explain away the perceptual conflict by joining intelligence with some other characteristic; for instance, "He is intelligent but doesn't possess initiative to rise above his group."
3. *Change in perception.* Many students changed their perception of the worker because of the intelligence characteristic. Most of the change, however, was very subtle, e.g., "cracks jokes" became "witty."
4. *Recognition, but refusal to change.* A very few students explicitly recognized the conflict between their perception of the worker and the characteristic of intelligence that was confronting them. For example, one subject stated, "The trait seems to be conflicting . . . most factory workers I have heard about aren't too intelligent."

Perceptual defense makes any situation in which conflict is likely to be present more difficult. It creates blind spots causing us to fail to hear and see events as they really are. The challenge for managers is to somehow reduce or minimize the perception of threat in a situation so these defenses are not immediately called into play. By reassuring people that things that are important to them will not be tampered with, or by accentuating the positive, this can be accomplished.

SUMMARY

In this chapter, we considered perceptual processes and how they relate to employee behavior at work. Perceptual selectivity was distinguished from perceptual organization. Major influences on perceptual processes in general were discussed as was the concept of social perception at work. A model of this process was presented. Next, attribution theory was introduced as one explanation of the relationship between behaviors and perception. Major differences were noted in the perceptions of managers and subordinates. Finally, barriers to accurate perceptions of others were identified, including stereotyping, halo effects, and selective perception. Throughout, emphasis was placed on gaining an understanding of how perception can affect our attitudes and behavior in the work place.

Managers face a variety of barriers to accurate perception of others in the work situation. These barriers may be either directed at the manager or held by the manager. Whatever the origin of these biases, it is important to recognize the existence of barriers and work to reduce or eliminate them. For example, stereotyping can be reduced if the persons being stereotyped continually draw attention to the problem. Women must often point out that all managers are not male. Halo effects in evaluating employees can be minimized by changing the ways in which employees are rated; this is discussed in Chapter Fifteen. Problems of selective perception and perceptual defense can be relieved through improved communications, as will be examined in Chapter Ten. Other examples could be cited here, but the point is that by recognizing the existence of perceptual problems, managers can take measures to remedy situations. First, however, they must be convinced of the importance of the problem.

KEY WORDS

absolute threshold of activation	primacy effects
attribution theory	projection
halo effect	recency effects
implicit personality theory	response disposition
locus of control	response salience
organizational role	selective perception
perception	self-concept
perceptual defense	sensory adaptation
perceptual organization	stereotyping
perceptual selectivity	temporal extension

FOR DISCUSSION

1. What is meant by perception?
2. Describe perceptual selectivity. How does it relate to absolute thresholds of activation and sensory adaptation?
3. Describe several major external influences on perceptual selectivity.
4. Describe the principle of ordering.
5. Discuss some major personal influences on perceptual selectivity as they relate to the work place.
6. Contrast response salience and response disposition.
7. Describe the major influences on social perception at work.
8. How does attribution theory work?

9. Explain the concept of locus of control.
10. Explain how superiors and subordinates may interpret the same facts or events differently.
11. Identify several barriers to accurate perception of others.
12. How does the implicit personality theory work?
13. What is meant by temporal extension?
14. How can a manager guard against halo effects?
15. Explain the concept of perceptual defense. How does it work?
16. What actions can managers take to reduce the barriers to accurate social perception at work?

EXERCISE
4.1

THE NEW PROFESSOR

Purpose

To examine the role of perception in problem solving.

Instructions

Divide into groups of about six persons each and read the case below. Then, as a group, discuss the point of view of each of the following: Liz Porter; Ned Martin; the other faculty members; and the department head. Focus on each of the four main characters' sides of the story, drawing from chapter information on perceptual processes to analyze the situation. Decide as a group what action the department head should take and compare recommendations with other groups in a class discussion.

Case: The Lesser of Two Evils

When Liz Porter arrived at State University, she had a one-year contract and was assigned to teach the introductory economics course. Since there were many sections, all instructors worked as a team in planning the course, making up exams, and so on.

Liz had trouble from the beginning. She was insecure, dominated the students, and failed to bring in relevant examples. In addition, she had trouble relating to colleagues as well as to students.

During the second semester, one of her teammates, Ned Martin, took over a section of a special elective and developed a strong following among students. Since this was the first time he had taught the course, he had to do a lot of extra work in addition to the time-consuming preparation for the introductory course he already taught. The special elective was in his area of expertise, however, and he did an outstanding job. As a result, he fully expected to be assigned to teach only the elective course the following semester. This would also mean moving up a bit in the hierarchy since teaching electives was

Exercise 4.1 adapted from D. T. Hall, D. D. Bowen, R. J. Lewicki, and F. S. Hall, *Experiences in Management and Organizational Behavior,* 2nd ed. (New York: Wiley, 1982), pp. 312–13. Copyright © 1982 by John Wiley & Sons, Inc. Reprinted by permission of John Wiley & Sons, Inc.

Exercise 4.1: The New Professor **119**

viewed as more desirable and higher status than teaching introductory courses.

Later in the semester the department head met with faculty members to discuss course assignments for the following year. The coordinator for the introductory course begged to have Liz Porter reassigned. Liz admitted that the experience had been an unhappy failure for her. Ned asked to teach the elective course again but didn't push the matter, assuming it was a natural assignment given his experience and expertise. Besides, he would be coming up for promotion soon and didn't want to appear too aggressive.

When the course assignments were posted, faculty members were shocked to learn that Liz would be teaching three sections of the special elective and Ned would teach only the intro course. Several professors went to the department head to voice their concerns. They argued that Liz had no knowledge of the elective area and that she had admitted she was scared to death to try to teach it. Ned, on the other hand, had worked hard to prepare to teach the elective and had had excellent results. In addition, Ned had seniority over Liz. It appeared that Liz was being "rewarded" for failing. Finally, the reputation of the course and the number of students enrolling would be adversely affected by putting a "bad" teacher in three sections out of four.

The department head explained his decision, stating that it was the "lesser of two evils." He believed it was important to support women and help them develop their competencies. He was proud that he had recruited another woman for the department, and he didn't want to let Liz go.

JOB PERCEPTIONS

Purpose
To consider how different people view different jobs.

Instructions
For each of the occupations listed below, identify (on a sheet of paper) what you believe to be the three best and three worst aspects of the job. Next, place an "X" beside any of the occupations in which *you* have worked. Your instructor will collect the papers and explain the next step. The occupations that you should evaluate are: (1) waiter or waitress; (2) sales clerk in a department store; (3) manager of a major corporation; (4) engineer; and (5) assembly line worker.

CHAPTER FIVE

INDIVIDUAL ABILITIES AND TRAITS

In this chapter, we continue our discussion of individual differences among employees and the role such differences play in job attitudes and behavior. In the last chapter, we examined perceptual processes. Here, we consider two additional factors: employee abilities and personal traits. Based on the information provided in these two chapters, we will proceed to discuss how people behave in work situations and how behavior can differ as a result of variations among individuals.

IMPORTANCE OF TOPIC FOR MANAGERS

A knowledge of employee abilities and traits is important. Employee abilities and traits represent those individual characteristics that determine an employee's *capacity* to contribute to the organization, in contrast to motivation, which determines an employee's *will* to contribute. If we expect actual performance to be a joint function of motivation *and* abilities and traits, a knowledge of these latter variables is certainly important.

A clear recognition of differences in employee abilities and traits allows managers to do a better job of selection and placement. People can be placed in jobs most suited to their individual talents and skills. However, individual characteristics and needs often conflict with organizational requirements. The nature of this conflict—as well as modes of conflict resolution—should be clearly understood by managers interested in optimizing both employee commitment and employee performance.

A good deal of research has been conducted over the years on the subject of employee differences and how they affect work behavior. It is an advantage for managers to be familiar with this literature. While these findings do not always provide clear answers to all personnel problems, an awareness of their scope can at least help managers better understand human behavior so personnel decisions can be made with as much available information as possible.

EMPLOYEE ABILITIES

Employee *abilities* are generally defined as those physical and intellectual characteristics of individuals that are relatively stable over time. Although such characteristics can in some instances change (e.g., through training or physical maturation), they are generally expected to be stable attributes of the individual. A detailed examination of the range of human abilities or their measurement is not the purpose of this discussion. Rather, it is to develop an appreciation of employee abilities as they influence job attitudes and performance.

Abilities are an important aspect of organizational behavior since they determine the extent to which an employee can perform adequately on the job. For instance, if a clerk typist simply cannot master typing skills, his or her performance would clearly be limited, no matter how much compensation was offered. Organizational effectiveness is enhanced to the extent that managers can hire and train individuals with sufficient job-related abilities.

There are many ways to categorize human abilities. Perhaps one of the most useful is to divide abilities into three areas: mental, mechanical, and psychomotor abilities (McCormick & Tiffin, 1976). Each of these plays a role in daily employee performance and behavior.

Mental abilities refer to an individual's intellectual capacities and are closely related to how people make decisions. Research has shown, for example, that managerial success is closely related to the level of one's intellectual capabilities (e.g., verbal comprehension, inductive reasoning, and memory). In fact, some have argued that the higher one reaches in the organizational hierarchy, the more important intellectual abilities are for managerial performance (Ghiselli, 1966).

Mechanical abilities focus on an individual's capacity to comprehend relationships between objects and to adequately perceive and manipulate spatial relations (the ability to visualize how parts fit together). Mechanical abilities are of central importance when considering an employee's capacity to respond.

Psychomotor abilities include a wide range of abilities, including manual dexterity, eye-hand coordination, and motor and manipulative ability. Psychomotor abilities describe various aspects of skilled muscular performance typically involving some degree of visual control.

All three of these abilities are important for understanding the nature of people at work and how they are better managed. The recognition of such abilities—and the recognition that people have *different* abilities—has clear implications in recruitment and selection decisions and emphasizes the importance of matching people to jobs. There are also clear implications for overly skilled personnel. Hiring highly skilled employees and then placing them on dull, repetitive jobs would not only stifle their performance potential but could also hasten their withdrawal from the organization.

PERSONAL TRAITS

The second individual difference characteristic to be discussed here is personal traits. When taken together, employee abilities and personal traits help considerably in developing portraits of various individuals in the work place. Information about these characteristics will prove useful as we consider a variety of topics throughout this book, including employee reactions to work design, stress, reward systems, and group dynamics. A major lesson to be learned here is that all individuals do not react similarly to the same stimuli or events.

We shall use the term *personal traits* instead of personality because of the various and often conflicting definitions of the concept of personality. Instead of engaging in debate over definitions, it is preferable to focus exclusively on identifying measurable traits that describe individuals and that are relevant to work place considerations. Specifically, a personal trait may be defined as a consistent predisposition or tendency to behave in a particular way (Brody, 1972). The primary focus in this definition is on observed and measurable behaviors or predispositions to behave. We shall be concerned with traits such as interpersonal style, emotional stability, and cognitive style rather than with the more esoteric self-concept or psychoanalytic processes. First, we will consider how personal traits are measured, followed by an examination of major influences in their development. In the next section, we will focus on several important work-related personal traits. Finally, we will look at a particular model that focuses on the interaction of the person and the organization.

The Measurement of Personal Traits

Personal traits can be assessed in organizations in at least three different ways: (1) inventories; (2) experimental procedures; and (3) independent ratings. (For a detailed discussion of the various techniques as well as a critique of each method, see Maier, 1973.)

By far the most popular technique used by industry is the self-report inventory. In this approach, individuals are asked a series of standardized questions and their responses are recorded using either a true-false format or a Likert-type scale, a scale where the respondent answers on a continuum from strongly agree to strongly disagree. Some of the more popular personality inventories include the California Psychological Inventory, the Minnesota Multiphasic Personality Inventory, and the Personality Research Form. These inventories are structured to provide percentile scores on a variety of personal traits or characteristics: for example, dogmatism, aggressiveness, and cognitive complexity. A major benefit of such inventories is that a large number of traits can be measured with little time or effort.

A second approach that is receiving increased attention in organizations is the use of experimental procedures. Individuals are placed in artificially created situations that attempt to simulate real life. The clearest industrial application of this procedure is the use of the assessment center, where personal characteristics are appraised through a series of simulated management exercises like role playing, in-basket techniques, or stress interviews (see Chapter Fifteen).

The third technique, independent ratings, makes use of either trained experts or peers to evaluate individuals on a set of predetermined traits. The most frequent use of independent ratings in industry are the recommendation forms many companies use for personnel selection and placement.

Major Influences on Individual Development

Early research on personality development focused on the issue of whether heredity or environment determined an individual's personality. While a few researchers are still concerned with this issue, most contemporary psychologists now feel this debate is fruitless. As noted long ago by Kluckhohn and Murray (1953):

the two sets of determinants can rarely be completely disentangled once the environment has begun to operate. The only pertinent questions therefore are: (1) which of the various genetic potentialities will be actualized as a consequence of a particular series of life-events in a given physical, social, and cultural environment? and (2) what limits to the development of this personality are set by genetic constitution?

In other words, if the individual is viewed from the whole-person perspective, the search for the determinants of personal traits focuses on both heredity and environment, as well as the interaction between the two over time. In this regard, five major categories of determinants of personal traits may be identified. They are: physiological, cultural, family and social group, role, and situational determinants.

Physiological determinants include factors such as stature, health, and sex that often act as constraints on personal growth and development. For instance, tall people often tend to become more domineering and self-confident than shorter people. Traditional sex-role stereotyping has served to channel males and females into different developmental patterns. For example, males were trained to be more assertive, females more passive.

Because of the central role of culture in the survival of a society, there is great emphasis on instilling cultural norms and values in children as they grow up. For instance, in capitalist societies, where individual responsibility is highly prized, emphasis is placed on developing achievement-oriented, independent, self-reliant people, while in socialistic societies, emphasis is placed on developing cooperative, group-oriented individuals who place the welfare of the whole society ahead of individual needs. *Cultural determinants* affect personal traits. As Mussen (1963, p. 62) notes, "the child's cultural group defines the range of experiments and situations he is likely to encounter and the values and personality characteristics that will be reinforced and hence learned." Consider, for example, how Japanese society develops its world-renowned work ethic (see Close-Up 5.1).

Perhaps the most important influences on personal development, however, are *family and social group determinants.* For instance, it has been found that children who grow up in democratic homes tend to be more stable, less argumentative, more socially successful, and more sensitive to praise or blame than those who grow up in authoritarian homes (Mussen, 1963). One's immediate family and peers contribute significantly to the socialization process, influencing how individuals think and behave through an intricate system of rewards and penalties.

People are assigned various roles very early in life, based on factors such as sex, socioeconomic background, and race. As one grows older, other factors like age and occupation influence the roles we are expected to play. Such *role determinants* often limit our personal growth and development as individuals and significantly control acceptable behavior patterns.

Finally, personal development can be influenced by *situational determinants.* These are unique factors that are often unpredictable, such as a divorce or death in the family. For instance, Abegglen (1958) studied twenty successful

How can a nation slightly smaller than the state of Montana continue year after year to generate tremendous trade surpluses with the United States? Why do we hear repeated reports about how hard the Japanese work? One answer to these questions lies in the personal characteristics of the Japanese people.

A foreign visitor notices early that offices in Tokyo's high-rise business district remain lit well into the night. Managers climbing the corporate ladder typically put in a day that begins in the early morning and lasts until past midnight. Work on Saturdays and Sundays is common, and employees seldom take all the vacation time to which they are entitled. After work, white-collar employees are expected to entertain clients or have dinner and drinks with co-workers in the interests of company spirit and loyalty.

The Japanese work ethic and demand for high performance are developed early. These traits are encouraged in the children, who in turn become desirable employees.

In this pursuit, many women with children have become what the Japanese call "education mothers." They are obsessed with pushing their children to excel in school so they can get into the best universities and, subsequently, get the best jobs. Japanese children go to school 5-½ days a week, 240 days a year—by the time they graduate from high school, they have attended the equivalent of four more years of school than their U.S. counterparts. Perhaps as a result, Japanese students score an average of 11 points higher than American students on IQ tests.

As Americans see their share of world and domestic markets shrinking, they are beginning to recognize the economic —if not personal—consequences of a rigorous work ethic learned early.

Source: Based on information in "Samurai Spirit Lives on in Japan's Economic Drive," *U.S. News & World Report,* November 19, 1984, pp. 47–48.

male executives who had risen from lower-class childhoods and discovered that in three-fourths of the cases these executives had experienced some form of severe separation trauma from their fathers. Their fathers (and role models) had either died, been seriously ill, or had serious financial setbacks. Abegglen hypothesized that the sons' negative identification with their fathers' plights represented a major motivational force for achievement and success.

PERSONAL TRAITS AND WORK BEHAVIOR

The concept of personal traits (and theories based on personal traits) has proven to be popular among investigators of employee behavior in organizations. There are several reasons for this. To begin, trait theories focus largely on the normal or healthy adult, in contrast to psychoanalytic and other personality theories that focus largely on abnormal behavior. Trait theories identify several specific characteristics that describe people. Allport (1961) insisted that our understanding of individual behavior could progress only by breaking behavior patterns down into a series of elements (traits). "The only thing you can do about a *total* personality is to send flowers to it," he once said. Hence, in the study of people at work, we may discuss an employee's dependability, or emotional stability, or cognitive complexity. These traits, when taken together, form a large mosaic that provides insight into individuals. Finally, a third reason for the popularity of trait theories in the study of organizational behavior is that the traits that are identified are measurable and tend to remain relatively stable over time. It is much easier to make comparisons among employees using these tangible qualities rather than the somewhat mystical psychoanalytic theories or the highly abstract and volatile self theories.

The number of traits people exhibit varies depending upon which theory one wishes to use. In an exhaustive search, Allport and Odbert (1936) were able to identify over 17,000 traits that describe people. However, such a large list makes it possible to develop a succinct model of human behavior. Efforts to reduce or cluster such traits have been welcome (see Cattell, 1965; Shaw, 1976). Building upon these earlier works, we will assess six relatively discrete clusters of personal traits (see Exhibit 5.1). They are: (1) interpersonal style; (2) social sensitivity; (3) ascendant tendencies; (4) dependability; (5) emotional stability; and (6) cognitive style. While no cluster of traits is ideal, these six identify important variables that have been shown to relate to organizational behavior.

Interpersonal Style

In the study of people at work, a major facet of individual characteristics is interpersonal style, or the way in which people typically behave in group settings. The importance of interpersonal style is perhaps best exemplified in the 1978 example of Henry Ford's firing of Ford president Lee Iacocca. Iacocca had developed a reputation for both efficiency and sales prowess and was personally responsible for many of the company's major successes. However, as a result of a long-smouldering feud between Iacocca and Henry Ford, the company chairman, Iacocca was summarily fired. Sources familiar with the discussions that preceded Iacocca's departure report that Iacocca said to Ford, "I've been with the company for thirty-two years. What did I do wrong?" Henry Ford reportedly replied, "I just don't like you." Iacocca subsequently went on to become the president of Chrysler Corporation, a major Ford competitor (*London Daily Telegraph,* July 15, 1978). Obviously, Iacocca has returned (see Close-Up 5.2).

Personal characteristics that fall into the interpersonal style cluster include the general tendency to trust (or not to trust) others, openness (or social distance), and one's orientation toward authority.

In particular, a great deal has been written about individual orientations

EXHIBIT 5.1   MAJOR CLUSTERS OF PERSONAL TRAITS

Personal Trait Cluster	Emphasis	Examples
Interpersonal style	The way individuals interact with others; how they behave in groups.	Trust, openness, authoritarian orientation
Social sensitivity	The way individuals perceive and respond to the needs, emotions, and preferences of others.	Empathy, social judgment, insight
Ascendant tendencies	Focuses on the extent to which individuals attempt to dominate or control others.	Assertiveness, dominance, prominence
Dependability	The level of consistency, responsibility, and predictability of individuals in group situations.	Self-reliance, responsibility, integrity
Emotional stability	Reflects the emotional and mental well-being of individuals.	Emotional control, defensiveness, anxiety, neuroticism
Cognitive style	Focuses on the way individuals process information and the judgments made based on these observations.	Dogmatism, risk taking, cognitive complexity

towards authority. Early work by Adorno and his associates (Adorno et al., 1950) found that this trait varies widely with people. An *authoritarian orientation* (or authoritarian personality) is characterized by several features all reflecting the notion that it is right and proper for there to be clear status and power differences between people. A high authoritarian is typically: demanding, directive, and controlling of subordinates; submissive and deferential to superiors; intellectually rigid; fearful of social change; highly judgmental and categorical in reactions to others; distrustful; and hostile in response to restraint. Nonauthoritarians, on the other hand, believe more firmly that status and power differences should be minimized, that social change can be constructive, and that people should be more accepting and less judgmental of others.

Studies of authoritarian personalities in groups and organizations are widespread. For instance, Vroom (1959) found that employees rated high in authoritarianism were more productive under autocratic supervision, while employees rated low in authoritarianism were more productive under partici-

CLOSE-UP 5.2   LEE IACOCCA

One of the best-known executives in the United States today is Lee Iacocca, president of Chrysler Corporation. To many people, Iacocca represents the ideal manager. He is an achievement-oriented, "take charge" executive who skillfully uses power to achieve institutional objectives. He is also a charismatic and articulate spokesman for corporate America, giving the impression that Lee Iacocca is devoted not just to Chrysler's success but to the success of the entire country.

Iacocca has achieved much as a manager. As president of Ford Motor Company, he introduced the enormously successful Mustang, along with several other cars. At Chrysler, he is credited with actually saving the company—and its 600,000 jobs. When asked the key to his excellent record, Iacocca replied, "Boys, there ain't no free lunches in this country. And don't go spending your whole life commiserating that you got the raw deals. You've got to say, 'I think that if I keep working at this and want it bad enough, I can have it.' It's called perseverance."

Iacocca's approach to life and corporate management helps explain the widespread respect he has earned as an executive. It also helps explain his success in starting—and finishing—projects others might shy away from.

Source: "Behind the Wheels," *Newsweek,* October 8, 1984, pp. 50–71.

pative or democratic supervisors. Shaw (1976) notes that high authoritarians strongly adhere to the rules and norms of groups to which they belong. They show greater conformity behavior in the face of group consensus than do nonauthoritarians.

Social Sensitivity

A second set of personal traits clusters around the extent to which individuals perceive and respond to the needs, emotions, and preferences of others. These traits include empathy, social judgment, and insight. Research studies have consistently shown a moderate relationship between these social skills and acceptance by group members, successful leadership attempts, amount of participation, and group performance effectiveness (Shaw, 1976). The lack of these skills is inversely related to friendliness and social interaction, as would be expected.

Ascendant Tendencies

People in any organization vary considerably in the extent to which they desire and attempt to be prominent, assertive, and domineering. Such an orientation reflects a strong desire by an individual to stand apart from the group, to be different or unique in a superior sort of way. People with ascendant tendencies are often self-assertive, creative, and popular. They frequently emerge as leaders and tend to be quite dissatisfied with the performance of *other* leaders (Shaw, 1976).

Dependability

People can also be differentiated with respect to their behavioral consistency and personal integrity. Individuals who are seen as self-reliant, responsible, consistent, and dependable are typically viewed by others as desirable colleagues or group members who will cooperate and work steadfastly toward group goals (Stogdill, 1948; Greer, 1955). Unconventional people, on the other hand, are often thought to lack dependability and commitment to group goals. As such, they are disrespected and rejected by other group members (Schachter, 1959). Consider the implications of these perceptions on hiring and promotion decisions.

Observers of international management have noted a key difference between North American managers and Japanese managers regarding both dependability and responsibility. Japanese managers are much more likely than managers from the United States and Canada to complete projects they have promised to finish. Moreover, consider what happens when something goes wrong. In Japan, there is a tradition called *inseki jishoku* (literally translated, "to take full responsibility and to resign one's position"). When a Japan Airlines (JAL) 747 crashed into a mountainside, killing all 500 on board, the president of JAL visited family members of all the victims to express regret. He then resigned as president, despite the fact that the crash was clearly attributed to an aircraft design flaw, not to the company. The president clearly felt he had to take public responsibility for the disaster. In the United States and Canada, such public accountability is rare indeed (Los Angeles *Times,* August 5, 1985).

Emotional Stability

Emotional stability refers to a class of personal traits that relate to the emotional and mental well-being of the individual. It includes the positive traits of emotional control and adjustment, as well as the negative traits of anxiety, defensiveness, depressive tendencies, and neuroticism.

Studies have revealed that one of the most important personal traits is *anxiety.* Anxiety, discussed in detail in Chapter Nineteen, is a general uneasiness or concern about some uncertain or future event. Anxious individuals experience a vague and uneasy feeling that is psychologically unpleasant and interferes with their responses to everyday life events. People who are highly anxious consistently have problems in developing rewarding interpersonal relationships, generally have low aspirations on task performance, conform easily to group norms, alter their judgments and opinions when confronted by differing opinions, and are highly dependent on others for clues to acceptable behavior (Shaw, 1976). Many recent attempts in organizations

to open communication and develop more interpersonal trust are intended to create a work climate where employees will experience less threat and anxiety and hence become more productive members of the organization.

Cognitive Style

Cognitive style refers to the way in which people process and organize information and arrive at judgments or conclusions based on their observations of situations. Three aspects of cognitive style are of particular importance for the study of people at work: (1) dogmatism; (2) risk-taking propensity; and (3) cognitive complexity.

Dogmatism. Dogmatism refers to a particular cognitive style that is characterized by closed-mindedness and inflexibility (Rokeach, 1960). This trait has received special attention in the area of managerial decision making. In particular, dogmatic managers tend to reach decisions quickly, following only a limited search for information, but are highly confident about the accuracy of the resulting decisions (Taylor and Dunnette, 1974).

There is also evidence that dogmatism interferes with efficient performance of duties. For instance, Esposito and Richards (1974) found that highly dogmatic individuals report large discrepancies between how they actually spent their time on the job and how they would ideally spend their time. Apparently, their inflexibility and rigidity of cognitive style interfere with their handling of work-related problems.

Risk-taking Propensity. Individuals also vary in their willingness to take risks in decision making (Kogan and Wallach, 1967). Research by Taylor and Dunnette (1974) among managers indicates that high risk takers, like those high in dogmatism, tend to make decisions more rapidly (with limited searching for relevant information) than do low risk takers. Such differences can be important for organizations, depending upon what type of jobs high and low risk takers are placed in. For instance, a high risk-taking propensity may be desirable for a sales representative who must act quickly to make a sale. On the other hand, such a propensity (accompanied by little search behavior) could be financially disastrous for a personnel manager negotiating a new labor contract.

Cognitive Complexity. This trait outlines a person's capacity to acquire and sort through various pieces of information from the environment and organize them in such a way that they make sense. People with a high cognitive complexity tend to use more information—and to see the relationships between this information—than people with low cognitive complexity. For example, if a manager was assigned a particular problem, would he have the capacity to break the problem down into its various facets and understand how these various facets relate to one another? A manager with low cognitive complexity would tend to see only one or two salient aspects of the problem, while a manager with a higher cognitive complexity would understand more of the nuances and subtleties of the problem as they relate to each other and to other problems.

People with *low* cognitive complexity typically exhibit the following characteristics (Ebert and Mitchell, 1975, p. 81):

1. They tend to be categorical and stereotypic. Cognitive structures that depend upon simple fixed rules of integration tend to reduce the possibility of thinking in terms of degrees.
2. Internal conflict appears to be minimized with simple structures. Since few alternative relationships are generated, closure is quick.
3. Behavior is apparently anchored in external conditions. There is less personal contribution in simple structures.
4. Fewer rules cover a wider range of phenomena. There is less distinction between separate situations.

On the other hand, people with *high* levels of cognitive complexity are typically characterized by the following (Ebert and Mitchell, 1975, p. 81):

1. Their cognitive system is less deterministic. Numerous alternative relationships are generated and considered.
2. The environment is tracked in numerous ways. There is less compartmentalization of the environment.
3. The individual utilizes more internal processes. The self as an individual operates on the process.

Research on cognitive complexity has focused on two important areas from a managerial standpoint: leadership style and decision making. In the area of leadership, it has been found that managers rated high on cognitive complexity are better able to handle complex situations, such as rapid changes in the external environment. Moreover, such managers also tend to use more resources and information when solving a problem and tend to be somewhat more considerate and consultative in their approach to managing their subordinates (Mitchell, 1970).

In the area of decision making, fairly consistent findings show that individuals with high cognitive complexity: (1) seek out more information for a decision; (2) actually process or use more information; (3) are better able to integrate discrepant information; (4) consider a greater number of possible solutions to the problem; and (5) employ more complex decision strategies than individuals with low cognitive complexity (Schroder, Driver, and Streufert, 1967).

It should be noted, however, that high cognitive complexity is not always an asset, particularly when it is combined in one individual with other traits such as dogmatism, lack of social sensitivity, or ascendant tendencies. In these cases, the highly capable and analytical (that is, cognitively complex) person may become impatient with his less intelligent co-workers, resulting in what has been called an abrasive personality. This abrasive personality and the problems it creates for management are discussed in Close-Up 5.3.

CLOSE-UP 5.3 THE ABRASIVE PERSONALITY AT THE OFFICE

A particularly annoying yet frequently encountered problem in work organizations is the abrasive personality. As described by Levinson, some men and women of high achievement work hard and contribute a great deal to the organization, yet in doing so rub people the wrong way. These people are often characterized by self-centeredness, isolation, perfectionism, condescending contempt, and a tendency to attack others. Yet at the same time they demonstrate a keen analytical capability necessary in management circles. Levinson (p. 78) describes one case:

> A couple of years ago, when Henry Weigl was abruptly relieved of all his operating responsibilities as chairman of Standard Brands, *Forbes* magazine carried this account: "Weigl's abrasive, authoritarian style drove potential successors from the company, even while he was building Standard Brands in the marketplace." Says a person close to the company: "There isn't a company in American industry with an executive turnover rate like that of Standard Brands." Another observer states: "Weigl had a way of publicly humiliating men at the executive level that no self-respecting person could stand."

Hence the problem: a high level of contribution to the company combined with a personality or interpersonal style unacceptable to others. Levinson notes that such people are relatively common in business firms and are not limited to the executive level.

The abrasive individual places considerable emphasis on control of himself and others. He is, to all appearances, emphatically right, self-confident, and self-assured. He stubbornly adheres to a position and considers compromise a lowering of standards. As a result, such individuals are often held back from promotions—or fired—despite the considerable expertise they can bring to problem solving.

Levinson suggests several useful strategies for dealing with abrasive personalities aimed at curbing such tendencies while simultaneously utilizing the individual's capabilities. He suggests that the supervisor should: (1) recognize the origins of such behavior—the vulnerable self-image, the hunger for affection, and the eagerness for perfection—and not become angry or provocative; (2) report observations concerning the individual's behavior uncritically and ask how he or she felt others would respond; (3) acknowledge his or her desire to achieve, but emphasize that the individual must take others into account if success is to be attained; (4) emphasize that goal attainment is usually a step-by-step process, that compromise is not necessarily second best, and that an all-or-nothing approach usually leads to failure; and (5) if all else fails, confront the individual's arrogance and point out clearly that such behavior is unsatisfactory.

Levinson notes that these techniques are not always successful but that they often work. He further notes that many managers are reluctant to address the problem squarely and develop internal hostilities toward the individual themselves as they suppress the problem. Such behavior by the supervisor only compounds the problem and often delays a satisfactory solution to the point where one party has to leave.

Source: H. Levinson, "The Abrasive Personality at the Office," *Psychology Today 11* (1978): 78–84.

EXHIBIT 5.2   DIFFERENCES IN SKILLS REQUIRED FOR SUCCESSFUL MANAGEMENT ACCORDING TO LEVEL IN THE HIERARCHY

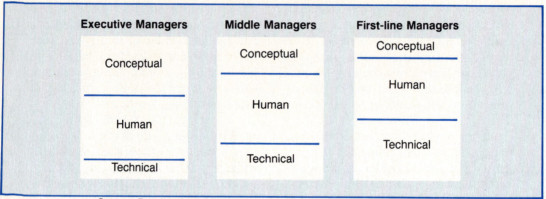

Source: Reprinted by permission of the *Harvard Business Review.* Exhibit from "Skills of an Effective Administrator" by Robert L. Katz (September-October 1974). Copyright © 1974 by the President and Fellows of Harvard College; all rights reserved.

MANAGEMENT SKILLS AND ABILITIES

Going one step further, we can ask what skills and abilities are best suited to management success. In one study, Katz (1974) pointed out that successful managers must exhibit three distinct types of skills:

Technical skills. Managers must have the ability to use the tools, procedures, and techniques of their special areas. An accountant should have expertise in accounting; a production manager must have mastered operations management techniques. These skills are the mechanics of the job.

Human skills. Human skills involve the ability to work with people and understand human motivation and group processes. These skills enable the manager to become involved with and lead his or her work group.

Conceptual skills. These skills represent the manager's ability to organize information to better understand or improve performance on the job. They include the manager's ability to see the organization as a whole and to understand how the various parts fit together to work as a well-integrated unit. Managers need these skills to coordinate the departments and divisions successfully so the organization can pull together.

Managers at different levels require these three managerial skills in different proportions. As shown in Exhibit 5.2, executive managers use primarily human and conceptual skills; technical skills are less important, though still necessary. In middle management, conceptual skills become less important, and the technical skills required for day-to-day operations become more significant. Finally, for first-line managers, technical skills are highly important, whereas conceptual skills diminish in importance considerably.

CLOSE-UP 5.4 WHAT CAUSES EXECUTIVE FAILURE?

In a recent study, two behavioral scientists attempted to identify personal abilities and traits that led to executive success and failure. They compared twenty successful and twenty unsuccessful executives and focused their analysis on how individuals get derailed en route to the top.

Among those who failed to get to the top, ten common personal characteristics emerged. In general, these people tended to be:

1. Insensitive to others; abrasive, intimidating, or bullying in style.
2. Cold, aloof, and arrogant.
3. Willing to betray trust.
4. Overly ambitious: for example, thinking of their next job or playing politics.
5. Unable to resolve specific performance problems within the business.
6. Unable to delegate responsibility.
7. Unable to staff effectively.
8. Unable to think strategically.
9. Unable to adapt to a boss with a different style.
10. Overdependent on an advocate or a mentor.

These attributes cause others to mistrust the manager's abilities and integrity, and as a result, the potential executive fails to perform well enough to reach top levels of management.

Source: Morgan McCall and Michael Lombardo, "What Makes a Top Executive?" *Psychology Today,* February 1983, pp. 26–31.

Note that the human skills of understanding and dealing with people are important on all managerial levels (see Close-Up 5.4).

Although this analysis is general and exceptions can easily be identified, the general model emphasizes that different skills may be necessary as a manager moves up the hierarchy. This fact becomes apparent in management education; junior-management courses tend to be technical in nature, whereas executive programs focus more on the development of conceptual skills. Both emphasize human relations skills.

PERSONALITY AND ORGANIZATION: A BASIC CONFLICT?

Most theories of personality stress that an individual's personality becomes complete only when it interacts with other people; growth and development do not occur in a vacuum. Or, as noted by Frank (in Argyris, 1957), human personalities are the individual expressions of our culture, and our culture and social order are the group expressions of individual personalities. This being the case, it is important to understand how work organizations influence the growth and development of the adult employee.

A model of person-organization relationships has been proposed by Chris Argyris (1957, 1973). This model, called the *basic incongruity thesis*, consists of three parts: what individuals want from organizations; what organizations want from individuals; and how these two potentially conflicting sets of desires are harmonized.

Argyris begins by examining how healthy individuals change as they mature. Based on previous work, Argyris suggests that as people grow to maturity, seven basic changes of needs and interests occur:

- People develop from a state of passivity as infants to a state of increasing activity as adults.
- People develop from a state of dependence upon others to a state of relative independence.
- People develop from having only a few ways of behaving to having many diverse ways of behaving.
- People develop from having shallow, casual, and erratic interests to having fewer but deeper interests.
- People develop from having a short time perspective (i.e., behavior is determined by present events) to having a longer time perspective (behavior is determined by a combination of past, present, and future events).
- People develop from subordinate to superordinate positions (from child to parent or from trainee to manager).
- People develop from a low understanding or awareness of themselves to a greater understanding of and control over themselves as adults.

While Argyris acknowledges that these developments may differ between individuals, the general tendencies from childhood to adulthood are believed to be fairly common.

Next, Argyris turns his attention to the defining characteristics of more traditional work organizations. In particular, he argues that in the pursuit of efficiency and effectiveness, organizations create work situations aimed more at getting the job done than at satisfying employees' personal goals. Examples include increased task specialization, unity of command, a rules orientation, and other things aimed at turning out a standardized product with standardized people. In the pursuit of this standardization, Argyris argues, organizations often create work situations characterized by the following:

- Employees are allowed minimal control over their work; control is often shifted to machines.
- They are expected to be passive, dependent, and subordinate.
- They are allowed only a short-term horizon in their work.
- They are placed on repetitive jobs that require only minimal skills and abilities.
- Based on the first four items, people are expected to produce under conditions leading to psychological failure.

EXHIBIT 5.3   BASIC CONFLICT BETWEEN EMPLOYEES AND ORGANIZATIONS

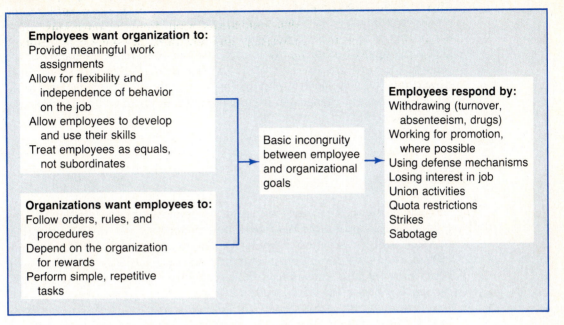

Employees want organization to:
Provide meaningful work
  assignments
Allow for flexibility and
  independence of behavior
  on the job
Allow employees to develop
  and use their skills
Treat employees as equals,
  not subordinates

Organizations want employees to:
Follow orders, rules, and
  procedures
Depend on the organization
  for rewards
Perform simple, repetitive
  tasks

Basic incongruity
between employee
and organizational
goals

Employees respond by:
Withdrawing (turnover,
  absenteeism, drugs)
Working for promotion,
  where possible
Using defense mechanisms
Losing interest in job
Union activities
Quota restrictions
Strikes
Sabotage

Hence, Argyris (1957) argues persuasively that many jobs in our technological society are structured in such a way that they conflict with the basic growth needs of a healthy personality. This conflict is represented in Exhibit 5.3. The magnitude of this conflict between personality and organization is a function of several factors. The strongest conflict can be expected under conditions where: employees are very mature; organizations are highly structured and rules and procedures are formalized; and jobs are fractionated and mechanized. Hence, we would expect the strongest conflict to be at the lower levels of the organization, among blue-collar and clerical workers. Managers tend to have jobs that are less mechanized and tend to be less subject to formalized rules and procedures.

Where strong conflicts between personalities and organizations exist or, more precisely, where strong conflicts exist between what employees and organizations want from each other, employees are faced with difficult choices. They may choose to leave the organization or to work hard to climb the ladder into the upper echelons of management. They may defend their self-concepts and adapt through the use of defense mechanisms. Disassociating themselves psychologically from the organization (e.g., losing interest in their work, lowering their work standards, etc.) and concentrating instead on the material rewards available from the organization is another possible response. Or, they may find allies in their fellow workers and, in concert, may further adapt *as a group* by such activities as quota restrictions, unionizing efforts, strikes, and sabotage.

Unfortunately, while such activities may help employees feel that they are getting back at the organization, they do not alleviate the basic situation that is causing the problem. To do this, one has to examine the nature of the job and the work climate. This we do in Chapter 18. Personality represents a powerful force in the determination of work behavior and must be recognized before meaningful change can be implemented by managers to improve the effectiveness of their organizations.

SUMMARY

This chapter continued the discussion of employee characteristics as they relate to work, examining the role of human abilities and various aspects of personal traits (also called personality). The measuring of such traits, major influences on trait development, and the traits themselves as they affect work behavior were also considered. Following this discussion, Argyris's basic incongruity thesis was introduced.

Together, this chapter and the previous one have presented a well-rounded introduction to the nature of individual differences in organizations. People differ in several dimensions, and these differences can have a substantial impact on how they view their jobs and can vary the extent to which they are capable of performing satisfactorily on the job. Such differences caution us against the traditional machine theory of employee behavior that assumes people are relatively homogeneous and therefore can be treated as interchangeable parts in the work place. Employees are not identical, and managers who ignore their differences risk creating a work environment that jeopardizes both performance and satisfaction.

Individual differences will continue to emerge as important factors as we discuss various aspects of organizational behavior in the chapters to come. For instance, in examining complex models of employee motivation, the role of personal characteristics will be seen as prominent. Hence, it is essential that managers recognize these differences and make attempts to accommodate them in their management practices.

KEY WORDS

abilities	cognitive style
anxiety	dependability
ascendant tendencies	dogmatism
authoritarian orientation	personal traits
basic incongruity thesis	social sensitivity
cognitive complexity	

FOR DISCUSSION

1. Discuss the role of human abilities in employee behavior and performance.
2. How do we measure personal traits?
3. Discuss some major influences on the development of personal traits.
4. Allport once remarked that "the only thing you can do about a total personality is to send flowers to it." What did he mean by this comment?
5. What is meant by an authoritarian orientation and what relation does it have to the work place?
6. What is meant by ascendant tendencies? Social sensitivity? Emotional stability?
7. What is the influence of emotional stability on employee behavior and performance?
8. What is meant by cognitive style? Describe the various aspects of cognitive style.
9. Discuss the major differences between high and low cognitive complexity in terms of their implications for work.
10. What is the basic incongruity thesis? Do you agree with this thesis? Why or why not?
11. Discuss the impact of the abrasive personality in the work place.
12. How might the skills required by managers differ across jobs and organizations? Explain.

CASE

5.1

HAROLD GENEEN AND ITT

Harold S. Geneen ran International Telephone and Telegraph for nearly two decades, and at the time of his retirement in 1979, his name was famous among U.S. executives. He was often described with words like genius, ambitious, tough, powerful, demanding, and successful. In many ways he was an archetype of a certain species of American boss. His success at meeting bottom-line goals was remarkable, and over two decades he fashioned ITT into precisely the kind of company that would meet those goals. But the costs to other people were considerable, and the company changed soon after his departure.

When Geneen became the chief executive officer in 1959, ITT was stagnating. Annual sales were $765 million, mostly from a world-wide communications-related business held at loose rein.

Source: Case 5.1 based on R. T. Pascale and A. G. Athos, *The Art of Japanese Management* (New York: Simon & Schuster, 1981). Copyright © 1981 by Richard Tanner Pascale and Anthony G. Athos. Reprinted by permission of Simon & Schuster, Inc.

Under Geneen's leadership, ITT diversified, acquiring over 150 companies. By the time Geneen retired in 1979, ITT was the world's largest conglomerate, with annual revenues in 1977 exceeding $11.8 billion and over a third of a million employees in ninety-three countries. Moreover, Geneen's nearly two decades of leadership were accompanied by dramatic improvements in the ratio of sales to assets: the sales-to-assets ratio increased from .82 in 1959 to 1.14 in 1979. In these terms, ITT gets more leverage than most companies in America. To a very great extent, these achievements are traceable to one man who not only increased the ITT empire tenfold, but welded it together as a coherent and efficient corporate enterprise.

Consider the primary elements of Geneen's approach to management. "Geneen, like General Patton, understood what it meant to wear two pistols," one ITT old-timer recounts. "When Geneen first took over this company, he needed to let people know he was the boss, that he was the man in charge. He did this by calling them up at odd hours, by asking someone about 'item 3' in his report, by demonstrating his total recall of facts and figures. In Europe he insisted that people at meetings address themselves by first names, even though the custom in Europe had always been to use last names. Phone calls in the middle of the night can really encourage people to do their homework —and the word gets around. And it should be remembered that Geneen does his homework more thoroughly than anyone else. He is really well prepared."

Geneen's behavior and the tension he created produced intense competitive pressures that drove the executives of his organization relentlessly. In some ways, his method of management was traditional. ITT developed a powerful central management group, semiautonomous divisions, and a highly refined sub-system of goals and controls. The head of each division was responsible in detail for all aspects of his operation, and was constantly scrutinized by top management. In Geneen's words, the system emphasized "comprehensive analysis covering (each division's) policies and plans as to sales, returns, and capital requirements for five years ahead." In addition, Geneen adds, "there are internal controls, monthly management reviews, constant pressures, and samplings to measure progress." It is the latter part of Geneen's formula that provided the thrust of his competitive approach.

Every month Geneen read all the monthly reports, which filled a book ten inches thick. Armed with this information, Geneen came well prepared to meetings, always probing for weak spots. Said one aide, "You spent endless time preparing for those meetings because you knew he would ask about the unexpected. If you floundered, he would pick it up." "Geneen's gift," comments one former subordinate, "wasn't just his capacity to review all elements of a business, but his knack for knowing *when* to pursue something and *how deep* to pursue it. Geneen seemed to have an automatic sensor which told him when he was getting flaky answers."

On those occasions when Geneen detected trouble, he moved in fast and demanded the details. "You could almost call it management by detail," one Geneen executive says. "There were more problems—some quite minor —solved at Geneen's level in ITT than in any other large company I know of." His questions went far beyond the balance sheet; he probed into marketing, research and development, etc.

Geneen's obsession for accurate facts fostered a variety of devices that ensured rigorous cross-checking. While Geneen recognized the interdependence of himself and his subordinates, he actively guarded against what he saw as overdependence by triangulating every piece of advice with independent data. "Geneen didn't mistrust people in a misanthropic sense," says one senior-level manager. "But he did mistrust a single source." Geneen disliked relying on one perspective as the means for giving him the whole picture. He believed that people have different viewpoints and that it is dangerous to listen to a small coterie. To effectively manage a conglomerate the size and complexity of ITT, Geneen believed a CEO needs multiple sources to know what's really going on.

The foundation of Geneen's system of checks and balances was designed into the organizational structure itself. Like many large firms, ITT was organized into a matrix design. But closer scrutiny reveals certain unique Geneen innovations. While the managers of ITT's subsidiaries reported up the line to Geneen, their controllers reported *directly* to the ITT chief controller in New York, and only in an advisory way to their own chief executives. Thus, if a subsidiary controller thought his boss's budget forecasts were not soundly conceived, he was required to disclose that to headquarters.

In addition, Geneen used intelligence squads called "task forces" or "action assignments." These teams cut across the entire company and were created whenever a problem or the suspicion of a problem arose. Sometimes two or three different task forces were established to study the same problem or to supply a solution. "Task forces were deadly," commented one highly successful ITT alumnus. "They could really hurt you. They intruded with all the power of the head office wrapped around them. Task forces usually had a charter and you could bet that their leader wasn't going to go back to New York empty-handed."

A central aspect of Geneen's approach to managing people can be seen in the meetings he chaired. In a locked room high up in the Manhattan headquarters of International Telephone and Telegraph Corporation, fifty executives sit around two long, felt-covered tables. There, from all over the world, they reported to Geneen who sat at the center of a table. "John," says Geneen, speaking to one of the executives, "what have you done about that problem?"

John speaks into the microphone in front of him. "Well, I called him, but I couldn't get him to make a decision."

"Do you want me to call him?"

"Gosh, that's a good idea. Would you mind?"

"I'll be glad to," says Geneen. "But it will cost you your paycheck."

"Never mind," says a flustered John. "I'll call him again myself."

Geneen and his top executives typically spent over three months each year in meetings. Why so many? Might not the same results have been achieved by reports? Not in Geneen's view, for it was the pressure-cooker atmosphere of the face-to-face sessions that sifted out the unshakable facts and distilled them into sound decisions for implementation.

Geneen's meetings were interrogatory, even adversarial, in nature. The general manager's report had already been written and everyone was assumed to have studied it. The meeting was really held to identify new problems and to update. And note the symbolism. Geneen's meetings employed a psychology

quite similar to the show trials that we have seen used increasingly in many countries in recent years. The use of the microphone and the formality of the "green felt" setting amplified a *personal* confrontation (which most bosses would handle privately with a subordinate) into public spectacle. As with show trials, Geneen was then able to exploit the leverage of example; he influenced the onlooker as powerfully as he did the individual in the hot seat. Fear of humiliation is a powerful motivator. After a few such drills, managers came to meetings well prepared, and they improved their performance on the job before they came if they possibly could. An essential aspect of Geneen's system, then, was fear. Fear of *individually* being caught uninformed, of being "humiliated" in meetings, of being "punished."

As a manager made his or her presentation, there was not only Geneen to be feared, but the staff as well. "For a guy in serious trouble," recalls one former ITT group executive, "it was like watching a wounded rooster in a barnyard being picked to death by the others. If Geneen zoomed in on a guy, that was the cue for the staff to follow suit. Then he would sit back and watch. It could get pretty rough sometimes."

Problems were not always resolved at the meetings, but when an unresolved question was raised and it was clear that something needed to be done, an "action assignment" was made. People were assigned specifically to work on a particular problem within a limited time. The action assignments drove the follow-ups of ITT's meetings.

Another intriguing aspect about Geneen was that he was extremely accessible. Any manager could get to the top; there was no palace guard. But Geneen's availability carried equal demands on his executives' time. "The first require-

ment of a senior executive," Geneen observed, "is instant availability. He must put his firm above his family; he must be prepared to go anywhere at any time, or simply to wait around in case he is needed." Geneen, who lived six blocks from his New York office, sometimes worked until midnight—and departed with three big briefcases of reading material. He returned again in midmorning, with the material read. "After a while," said one senior executive, "I just canceled my social life." Executives were expected to leave a phone number where they could be reached twenty-four hours a day, seven days a week.

Geneen worked different hours than most managers. He got to the office at 10:00 A.M. and stayed most often until ten or eleven o'clock at night. His top managers were expected pretty much to be around when he was. He came in on Saturdays and Sundays, and that was expected of other executives in the office of the president. Those who remained at ITT accepted this as the way the company worked. Geneen expected his subordinates to assign ITT matters their highest priority. Those who did not honor this fell by the wayside. Of one man, Geneen said, "He put himself above the company." Of another, "He moved to the suburbs,"—implying too much concern with family life. Geneen has said, "If I had enough arms and legs and time, I would do it all myself." He meant it. His subordinates were seen as less reliable extensions of himself.

As would be expected, ITT under Geneen developed the reputation for being a tough place to work. Turnover figures are hard to come by, but one former ITT executive who was present during the 1974 recession reported that ITT fired 400 of its 2500 managers. During a major shake-up of ITT's European subsidiaries in 1978 just prior to Geneen's retirement as chairman of the board, some former executives estimated that ITT had reduced its staff there by 40 percent. In fairness, it should also be added that many executives who stayed with ITT are proud of their company and proud of working for Geneen. One said, "Hire the right kind of aggressive managers who are dedicated to their work—and ITT's reward was the satisfaction one gets from working for one of the best-managed firms in America. True, the pressure keeps you on your toes—but for many of us there was something exhilarating in that. One wonders, in fact, if there weren't many outside ITT who wouldn't have gladly traded their boredom for high-pressure atmosphere that demanded excellence."

When he turned sixty-eight, under pressure from the board to relinquish operating control, Geneen appointed a successor as CEO. Geneen remained the chairman. Within twenty-eight months, Geneen replaced him with another man supposedly more to his liking.

Following Geneen's retirement in 1979, ITT's fortunes substantially de-clined: while it ranks eleventh in sales volume and twelfth in assets among the Fortune 500, it has dropped to 435th in terms of net income as a percentage of sales. ITT's return on stockholder equity in 1979 ranked even lower at 451. In its European operations, ITT incurred an $84 million dollar loss in 1979 and the liquidation of the firm's food, drug, and cosmetics operations. ITT has also shut down its consumer electronics appliance plants in France, Germany, and Britain.

CASE DISCUSSION QUESTIONS

1. Describe Geneen's abilities and traits as a manager.
2. To what do you attribute ITT's success? The economy? Geneen's abilities? Geneen's personal traits? Something else?
3. If you had the opportunity, would you have worked for Geneen? Why?
4. Why do you think ITT's position weakened after Geneen's departure?

CASE

PETERSEN ELECTRONICS

"Grow old along with me, the best is yet to be." When Robert Browning expressed this sentiment, he was not writing as a spokesman for business to promising young executives. Yet in the nineteenth century, while such poetry may have been out of place in business, the thought was very fitting.

In fact, until quite recently corporations have been able to reward capable employees with increased responsibilities and opportunities. Based on our

Source: Case 5.2 reprinted by permission of the *Harvard Business Review*. "Case of the Plateaued Performer" by E. K. Warren, T. P. Ference, and James A. F. Stoner (January/February 1975). Copyright © 1975 by the President and Fellows of Harvard College; all rights reserved.

recently completed research into nine companies, however, the more prevalent corporate sentiment might be, "Stay young along with me, or gone you well may be."

We found a large number of managers who, in the judgment of their organization, have "plateaued." That is, there is little or no likelihood that they will be promoted or receive substantial increases in duties and responsibilities. These long-service employees are being regarded with growing concern because plateauing is taking place more markedly, and frequently earlier, than in years past. Further, executives feel that plateauing is frequently accompanied by noticeable declines in both motivation and quality of performance.

While plateauing, like aging, is inevitable, in years past it was a more gradual process. For the most part, those who sought advancement in their managerial careers had ample opportunity to get it, within broad limits of ability, while those who did not desire advancement (including competent individuals content with more modest levels of achievement and success) could be bypassed by colleagues still on the way up.

Today the situation has changed. Declining rates of corporate growth and an ever-increasing number of candidates have heightened the competition for managerial positions. The top of the pyramid is expanding much more slowly than the middle, and the managers who advanced rapidly during the growth boom of the 1960s are now at or just below the top. Their rate of career progress has necessarily slowed, and yet they are still many years from normal retirement and with many productive years to go. As these managers continue in their positions, the queue of younger, aggressive aspirants just below them is likely to grow longer, with spillover effects

on opportunities and mobility rates throughout the organization.

This is precisely the dilemma confronting Benjamin Petersen, president and chairman of the board of Petersen Electronics.

Petersen founded the company in 1944, and it grew rapidly during the 1950s and 1960s, reaching sales of $200 million in 1968. Growth since then, though, has been uneven and at an average of less than 5 percent per year. However, 1974 was a good year, with sales and profits showing leaps of 12 percent and 18 percent respectively.

Despite the good year, Benjamin Petersen, now 61 years old, is concerned about the company as he nears retirement. His major problem involves George Briggs, 53, vice-president of marketing, and Thomas Evans, national sales manager, who is 34 years old and one of Briggs's four subordinates. Nor have the implications of the situation between Briggs and Evans been lost on Victor Perkins, 39, vice-president of personnel.

Petersen's View of the Predicament

"When we started, a handful of people worked very hard and very closely to build something bigger than any of us. One of these people was George Briggs. George has been with me from the start, as have almost all of my vice-presidents and many of my key department heads.

"For the first five years, I did almost all the inventing and engineering work. Tom Carroll ran the plant and George Briggs knocked on doors and sold dreams as well as products for the company.

"As the company grew, we added people, and Briggs slowly worked his way up the sales organization. Eight years ago, when our vice-president of marketing retired, I put George in the

job. He has market research, product management, sales service, and the field sales force (reporting through a national sales manager) under him, and he has really done a first-rate job all around.

"About ten years ago we began bringing in more bright young engineers and MBAs and moved them along as fast as we could. Turnover has been high and we have had some friction between our young Turks and the old guard.

"When business slowed in the early seventies, we also had a lot of competition among the newcomers. Those who stayed have continued to move up, and a few are now in or ready for top jobs. One of the best of this group is Tom Evans. He started with us nine years ago in the sales service area. Later, he spent three years in product management.

"George Briggs got him to move from head of the sales service department to assistant product manager. After one year, George Briggs named him manager of the product management group, and two years later, when the national sales manager retired, George named Evans to the post.

"That move both surprised and pleased me. I felt that Evans would make a good sales manager despite the fact that he had had little direct sales experience. I was afraid, however, that George would not want someone in that job who hadn't had years of field experience.

"I was even more surprised, though, when six months later (a month ago) George told me he was afraid Evans wasn't working out, and asked if I might be able to find a spot for him in the corporate personnel department. While I'm sure our recent upturn in sales is not solely Evan's doing, he certainly seems to be one of the keys. Despite his inexperience, he seems to have the field sales organization behind him. He spends

much of his time traveling with them, and from what I hear he has built a great team spirit.

"Despite this, George Briggs claims that he is in over his head and that it is just a matter of time before his inexperience gets him in trouble. I can't understand why George is so adamant. It's clearly not a personality clash, since they have always gotten along well in the past. In many ways, Briggs has been Evan's greatest booster until recently.

"Since George is going to need a replacement someday, I was hoping it would be Evans. If George doesn't retire before we have to move Evans again or lose him, I'd consider moving Evans to another area.

"When we were growing faster, I didn't worry about a new challenge opening up for our aggressive young managers—there were always new divisions, new lines—something to keep them stimulated and satisfied with their progress. Now I have less flexibility —my top people are several years from retirement. And yet I have some younger ones—like Evans, whom I would hate to lose—always pushing and expecting promotion.

"Evans is a good example of this; I could move him, but there are not that many *real* opportunities. He could go to personnel or engineering or even finance. Evans has the makings of a really fine general manager. But I'd hate to move him now. He really isn't ready for another shift—although he will be in a few years—and despite what George claims, I think he is stimulating teamwork and commitment in the sales organization as a result of his style.

"Finally, while I don't want to appear unduly critical of Briggs, I'm not sure he could get the job done in these competitive times without a bright young person like Evans to help him."

Briggs's Account of the Situation

"Before I say anything else, let me assure you there is nothing personal in my criticism of Evans.

"I like him. I have always liked him. I've done more for him than anyone else in the company. I've tried to coach him and bring him along just like a son.

"But the simple truth is that he's in way over his head and showing a side of his personality I've never seen before. I brought him along through sales service and product management and he was always eager to learn. While I couldn't give him a lot of help in those areas (frankly, there are aspects of them I don't yet fully understand), I still tried, and he paid attention and learned from others as well.

"The job of national sales manager, however, is a different story. In the other jobs Evans had—staff jobs—there was always time to consult, to consider, to get more data. In sales, however, all this participative stuff he uses takes too long. The national sales manager has to be able to make quick, intuitive decisions. What's more, like the captain of a ship, he has to inspire confidence in those below him. If the going gets rough, the only thing that keeps the sailors and junior officers from panicking is confidence in the skipper. I've been there and I know.

"Right now, with orders coming in strong, he can get away with all of his meetings and indecisiveness. The people in the field really like him and are trying to keep him out of trouble. In addition, I have been putting in 60 to 70 hours a week trying to do my job and also make sure he doesn't make any serious mistakes.

"I know he is feeling the pressure, too. Despite the fact that he has been his usual cheery self with others, when I call him in to question a decision he has made or is about to make, he gets very defensive. He was never that way with me before.

"I may have lost a little feel for what's going on in the field over the years, but I suspect I still know more about the customers and our sales people than Tom Evans will ever know. I've tried for the past seven months to get him to relax and let the old man help him, but it's no use. I'm convinced he's just not cut out for the job, and before we ruin him I want to transfer him somewhere else. He would probably make a fine personnel director someday. He's a very popular guy who seems genuinely interested in people and in helping them.

"I have talked with Ben Petersen about the move, and he has been stalling me. I understand his position. We have a lot of young comers like Evans in the company, and Ben has to worry about all of them. He told me that if anyone can bring Evans along I can, and he asked me to give it another try. I have, and things are getting worse.

"I hate to admit I made a mistake with Evans, but I plan on seeing Ben about this again tomorrow. We just can't keep putting it off. I'm sure he'll see it my way, and as soon as he approves the transfer, I'll have a heart-to-heart talk with Tom."

Evans's Side of the Story

"This has been a very hectic but rewarding period for me. I've never worked as hard in my life as I have during the last six months, but it's paying off. I'm learning more about sales each day, and more important, I'm building a first-rate sales team. My people are really enjoying the chance to share ideas and support each other.

"At first, particularly with our markets improving, it was hard to convince them to take time to meet with me and

their subordinates. Gradually they have come to accept these sessions as an investment in team building. According to them, we've come up with more good ideas and ways to help each other than ever before.

"Fortunately, I also have experience in product management and sales service. Someday I hope to bring representatives from this department and market research into the meetings with regional and branch people, but that will take time. This kind of direct coordination and interaction doesn't fit with the thinking of some of the old-timers. I ran into objections when I tried this while I was working in the other departments.

"But I'm certain that in a year or so I'll be able to show, by results, that we should have some direct contact across department levels.

"My boss, George Briggs, will be one of the ones I will have to convince. He comes from the old school and is slow to give up what he knows used to work well.

"George likes me, though, and has given me a tremendous amount of help in the past. I was amazed when he told me he was giving me this job. Frankly, I didn't think I was ready yet, but he assured me I could handle it. I've gotten a big promotion every few years and I really like that—being challenged to learn new skills and getting more responsibility. I guess I have a real future here, although George won't be retiring for some years and I've gone as high as I can go until then.

"George is a very demanding person, but extremely fair, and he is always trying to help. I only hope I can justify the confidence he has shown in me. He stuck his neck out by giving me this chance, and I'm going to do all I can to succeed.

"Recently we have had a few run-ins.

George Briggs works harder than anyone else around here, and perhaps the pressure of the last few years is getting to him. I wish he'd take a vacation this year and get away for a month or more and just relax. He hasn't taken more than a week off in the nine years I've been here, and for the last two years he hasn't taken any vacation.

"I can see the strain is taking its toll. Recently he has been on my back for all kinds of little things. He always was a worrier, but lately he has been testing me on numerous small issues. He keeps throwing out suggestions or second-guessing me on things that I've spent weeks working on with the field people.

"I try to assure him I'll be all right, and to please help me where I need it with the finance and production people who've had a tough time keeping up with our sales organization. It has been rough lately, but I'm sure it will work out. Sooner or later George will accept the fact that while I will never be able to run things the way he did, I can still get the job done for him."

Perkins's Opinions

"I feel that George Briggs is threatened by Evans's seeming success with the field sales people. I don't think he realizes it, but he is probably jealous of the speed with which Tom has taken charge. In all likelihood, he didn't expect Tom to be able to handle the field people as well as he has, as fast as he has.

"When George put Tom on the job, I have a feeling that he was looking forward to having him need much more help and advice from the old skipper. Tom does need help and advice, but he is getting most of what George would offer from his own subordinates and his peers. As a result, he has created a real team spirit below and around him, but he has upset George in the process.

"George not only has trouble seeing Tom depend so much on his subordinates, I feel that he resents Tom's unwillingness to let him show him how he used to run the sales force.

"I may be wrong about this, of course. I am sure that George honestly believes that Tom's style will get him in trouble sooner or later. George is no doddering old fool who has to relive his past success in lower-level jobs. In the past, I'm told, he has shown real insight and interest in the big-picture aspects of the company.

"The trouble is he knows he was an outstanding sales manager, but I am not sure he has the same confidence in his ability as vice-president. I have seen this time and again, particularly in recent years. When a person begins to doubt his future, he sometimes drops back and begins to protect his past. With more competition from younger subordinates and the new methods that they often bring in, many of our experienced people find that doing their job the way they used to just isn't good enough anymore.

"Some reach out and seek new responsibilities to prove their worth. Others, however, return to the things they used to excel in and try to show that theirs is still the best way to do things. They don't even seem to realize that this puts them in direct competition with their subordinates.

"What do we do about this? I wish I knew! At lower levels, where you have more room to shift people around, you have more options. When the company is growing rapidly, the problem often takes care of itself.

"In this case, I am not sure what I will recommend if Ben Petersen asks my advice. Moving Tom to personnel at this time not only won't help me (I really don't have a spot for him), but it won't help Briggs or Evans either. Moving Evans now would be wasteful of the time and effort we've invested in his development. It may also reverse some important trends Tom has begun in team building within the sales force.

"If Briggs were seven or eight years older, we could wait it out. If the company were growing faster, we might be able to shift people. As things stand, however, I see only one approach as a possibility. And I'm not entirely sure it will work.

"I would recommend that we get busy refocusing Briggs's attention on the vice-president's job and get him to see that there is where he has to put his time and efforts. Perhaps the best thing would be to send him to one of the longer programs for senior executives. Don't forget he is a very bright and experienced person who still has a great deal to offer the company if we can figure out how to help him."

What Would You Suggest?

Petersen has agreed to talk with Briggs about Evans tomorrow afternoon. As he thinks about the situation, he wonders what he can do that would be best for the company and everyone concerned. Should he go along with Briggs's recommendation that Evans be transferred to personnel? Or would it be preferable to do as Perkins has suggested and send Briggs to an executive program? As you consider the various perspectives, why do you think the impasse came to be and what do you think could be done to resolve it?

CASE DISCUSSION QUESTIONS

1. If you were Petersen, how would you respond to the questions noted above under "What Would You Suggest"?

2. In your opinion, what would be the effect of bringing Briggs and Evans together for a meeting to iron out their differences?

3. How does Argyris's basic incongruity hypothesis fit here?

4. How would you handle the problem of good employees having no opportunities to move up in the organization?

CHAPTER SIX

INDIVIDUAL NEEDS AND MOTIVATION

Knowledge of the behavioral sciences is readily applied to management practice. Managers can use their knowledge to improve their interpersonal abilities and enhance the likelihood of managerial success. For example, as discussed in the previous chapter, individual abilities and traits play a role in an employee's capacity to contribute to an organization. Managers who understand this role have more information with which to make personnel decisions and can use it to perform more effectively.

Also essential for good management is an understanding of the concept of motivation. In this chapter, basic motivational processes will be discussed. More complex models of motivation will be introduced in Chapter Seven, and Chapter Eight will explore the role of learning in motivation.

IMPORTANCE OF TOPIC FOR MANAGERS

The concept of individual differences and, more specifically, employee need strengths, and the related concept of motivation are important for several reasons. A knowledge of how employees differ can help the manager better understand his or her employees and, as a result, take actions aimed at facilitating employee need satisfaction. Consider, for instance, the implications for employee selection and placement. As we shall see, certain types of employees are likely to be more successful in sales positions, while others are likely to excel in staff positions (like personnel administration). Understanding these differences can be useful in decisions concerning who is placed in which positions.

The concept of needs also has clear implications for reward practices. Since employees respond differently to different rewards, an awareness of differences in needs can help the manager design reward systems appropriate to employee needs. The recognition that employees pursue different needs also helps the manager understand to some extent why different employees behave as they do. For instance, an employee with a high need for achievement is likely to pursue task-related activities with vigor, while an employee with a high need for affiliation may devote more attention to developing social relationships on the job.

Finally, on a general level, a thorough knowledge of basic motivational processes is essential to understand organizational dynamics. Why do people behave as they do? What causes good or bad performance? Why is absenteeism or turnover high? The answers to questions such as these rest squarely on comprehending what motivates the employee.

THE NATURE OF MOTIVATION

The word *motivation* derives from the ancient Latin *movere*, which means to move. As used in the study of employee motivation in work settings, however, this definition is clearly inadequate. A more comprehensive approach defines motivation as that which energizes, directs, and sustains human behavior.

This more complete definition emphasizes three distinct aspects of motivation that are important. First, motivation represents an energetic force that *drives* people to behave in particular ways. Second, this drive is directed *toward* something. In other words, motivation has strong goal-orientation. Third, the idea of motivation is best understood within a *systems* perspective. That is, to understand human motivation, it is necessary to examine the forces within individuals and their environments that provide them with feedback and reinforce their intensity and direction.

Basic Motivational Processes

Before considering the various models of employee motivation that are currently in use, we will examine the nature of the underlying motivational process. While the models of motivation may sometimes differ in certain aspects, they all tend to share basic assumptions about how behavior is energized, directed, and sustained through time.

A generalized model of basic motivational processes is shown in Exhibit 6.1. As can be seen in this exhibit, there are four basic components of the process (Dunnette and Kirchner, 1965): (1) needs or expectations; (2) behavior; (3) goals; and (4) feedback. At any point in time, individuals are seen as having a constellation of needs, desires, and expectations. For instance, one employee may have a strong need for achievement, a desire for monetary gain, and an expectation that doing his job well will, in fact, lead to the receipt of desired rewards. When such needs, desires, and expectations are present, individuals experience a state of inner disequilibrium. This disequilibrium, in turn, may cause behavior that is motivated toward specific goals. Having these goals facilitates a return to a state of homeostasis or balance. The resulting behavior activates a series of cues (either within the individuals or from the external environment) that feed messages back to the individuals concerning the impact of their behavior. This feedback may serve to reassure individuals that the behavior is correct (that is, it satisfies their needs), or it may tell them that their present course of action is incorrect and should be modified.

Consider the following example. A young salesperson has a high need for personal achievement. As such, she experiences an inner state of disequilibrium; a need exists that has not been met. Based on the strength or potency of this need, the salesperson attempts to engage in behavior that she feels will lead to feelings of personal accomplishment. For instance, she may attempt to outsell her colleagues, thereby receiving recognition for a job done well. Based on this goal-directed behavior, she receives feedback both from her own assessment of her behavior and from others. The feedback may tell her that she has indeed accomplished something important or worthwhile, returning her (at least temporarily) to a state of homeostasis with respect to this particular need.

While this simple model of motivation obviously does not take into account all influences on human motivation, it is illustrative of the basic nature of the process. Moreover, it emphasizes the cyclical nature of motivation. It shows that people are in a continual state of disequilibrium, constantly striving to satisfy a variety of needs. Once one need has been adequately met, another need or desire emerges to stimulate further action. In this way, people direct and redirect their energies as they attempt to adapt to changing needs and a changing environment.

EXHIBIT 6.1   A MODEL OF BASIC MOTIVATIONAL PROCESSES

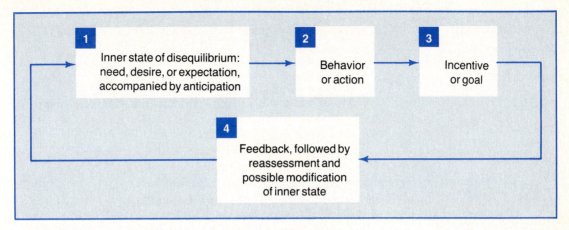

EARLY THEORIES OF MOTIVATION

The topic of motivation has long been of concern to both managers and psychologists. However, until recently, the emphasis and approach of these two divergent groups differed sharply. In order to gain a clearer understanding of how today's contemporary models evolved, it is necessary first to examine briefly the developmental sequences of both managerial and psychological models of motivation.

Managerial Approaches to Motivation

The evolution of management thought concerning employee motivation passed through three relatively distinct stages: traditional; human relations; and human resources (Miles, Porter, and Craft, 1966).

Traditional Model (1900–1930). With the emergence of the industrial revolution in the late 1800s, it became necessary to redefine both our conception of the nature of work and the social relationships between people in various levels in organizations. A need existed for a new philosophy of management that was consistent with the prevailing managerial beliefs of the times. These beliefs held that the average worker was basically lazy and was motivated almost entirely by money. Moreover, it was felt that few workers wanted or could handle a high degree of autonomy or self-direction on their jobs. These assumptions are summarized in Exhibit 6.2.

Based on these assumptions, it was felt that the best way to motivate employees was to pay them using a piece-rate system, then redesign their jobs so the average worker could maximize his or her output. This job redesign,

EXHIBIT 6.2   GENERAL PATTERNS OF MANAGERIAL APPROACHES TO MOTIVATION

Traditional model	Human relations model	Human resources model
Assumptions 1. Work is inherently distasteful to most people. 2. What they do is less important than what they earn for doing it. 3. Few want or can handle work that requires creativity, self-direction, or self-control.	**Assumptions** 1. People want to feel useful and important. 2. People desire to belong and to be recognized as individuals. 3. These needs are more important than money in motivating people to work.	**Assumptions** 1. Work is not inherently distasteful. People want to contribute to meaningful goals that they have helped establish. 2. Most people can exercise far more creative, responsible self-direction and self-control than their present jobs demand.
Policies 1. The manager's basic task is to closely supervise and control subordinates. 2. He or she must break tasks down into simple, repetitive, easily learned operations. 3. He or she must establish detailed work routines and procedures, and enforce these firmly but fairly.	**Policies** 1. The manager's basic task is to make each worker feel useful and important. 2. He or she should keep subordinates informed and listen to their objections to his or her plans. 3. The manager should allow subordinates to exercise some self-direction and self-control on routine matters.	**Policies** 1. The manager's basic task is to make use of "untapped" human resources. 2. He or she must create an environment in which all members may contribute to the limits of their ability. 3. He or she must encourage full participation on important matters, continually broadening subordinate self-direction and control.
Expectations 1. People can tolerate work if the pay is decent and the boss is fair. 2. If tasks are simple enough and people are closely controlled, they will produce up to standard.	**Expectations** 1. Sharing information with subordinates and involving them in routine decisions will satisfy their basic needs to belong and to feel important. 2. Satisfying these needs will improve morale and reduce resistance to formal authority —subordinates will "willingly cooperate."	**Expectations** 1. Expanding subordinate influence, self-direction, and self-control will lead to direct improvements in operating efficiency. 2. Work satisfaction may improve as a "by-product" of subordinates making full use of their resources.

Source: Adapted from R. E. Miles, L. W. Porter, and J. A. Craft, "Leadership Attitudes Among Public Health Officials," *American Journal of Public Health 56* (1966): 1990–2005.

which was at the heart of the *scientific management* movement, was aimed not at enrichment but at increased job simplification and fractionization. The simpler the task, it was reasoned, the greater the output. Far from being exploitative in nature, the original advocates of scientific management (like Frederick Taylor) saw this approach as being in the best interest of the worker since workers' pay increased with output. It was felt that, in exchange for increased income, workers would tolerate the fractionated and routinized jobs of the factory.

Human Relations Model (1930–1960). As the scientific management movement gained momentum, several problems began to emerge. First, it became increasingly apparent that factors other than money had motivating potential. This is not to say that money was unimportant—only that it was not the sole influence on employee effort. Second, managers became aware that many employees were self-starters and did not need to be closely supervised and controlled. Finally, some managers attempted to use the job simplification techniques of scientific management without tying resulting output to pay increases. This practice quickly led to employee distrust of management as wages fell behind productivity and as more workers were laid off because of increased efficiency. The result was often reduced effort by workers, accompanied by drives for unionization. Thus, managers learned that the human factor had to be taken into account if long-term productivity was to be maintained.

This emphasis on the human factor in employee performance, beginning around 1930, became known as the *human relations* movement. With this added perspective, the basic assumptions about the nature of people at work changed. It was now known that people wanted to feel useful and important at work; they wanted to be recognized as individuals. Such needs were seen to be as important as money (see Exhibit 6.2). Hence, managerial approaches to motivation were characterized by a strong *social* emphasis. Attention shifted away from the study of man-machine relations toward a better understanding of the nature of interpersonal and group relations on the job. The clearest example of this new emphasis was the Hawthorne studies (Roethlisberger and Dickson, 1939), where it was concluded that the failure to treat employees as human beings was largely responsible for the existence of problems such as low morale and poor performance.

In order to overcome these problems, managers were told to make employees feel important and involved. Morale surveys emerged as a popular index of employee discontent. Moreover, increased efforts were directed at opening new communication channels within organizations. Departmental meetings, company newspapers, and seminars on improving communications effectiveness all emerged to ensure that employees felt they were involved and were important to the organization. Finally, supervisory training programs were begun to train managers to understand the nature of group dynamics and how the forces that operate within them could be used for the benefit of the organization.

Two features carried through from the traditional theories of motivation. First, the basic goal of management under human relations was still to secure employee compliance with managerial authority; changed, however, were the strategies for accomplishing this. Second, throughout the human relations movement, almost no attention was given to changing the nature of the job itself. Instead, emphasis was placed on making employees more satisfied (and, it was hoped, more productive) primarily through interpersonal strategies.

Human Resources Model (1960–Present). Recently, it has become increasingly apparent that the assumptions underlying the human relations model represent an incomplete statement of human behavior at work. More contemporary models view motivation in more complex terms, assuming that *many* factors are capable of influencing behavior. These factors may include the nature of the incentive system, social influences, the nature of the job, supervisory style, employees' needs and values, and one's perceptions of the work environment.

These newer models also assume that different employees want different rewards from their jobs, that many employees sincerely want to truly contribute, and that employees by and large have the capacity to exercise a great deal of self-direction and self-control at work (see Exhibit 6.2). In short, many contemporary managerial views of motivation focus on employees as potential human *resources*. Given this assumption, it becomes management's responsibility to find ways to tap these resources such that both the employees' and the organization's needs and goals are facilitated.

Utilizing an organization's human resources can be accomplished in a variety of ways. First, attempts can be made to fit the person to the job so employees can most fully use their talents. Efforts can be made to integrate personal goals with organizational goals so employees can satisfy their own needs while working for organizational objectives. The popular practice of paying sales representatives a commission or bonus based on level of sales is a good example of such goal integration. In addition, some organizations have increasingly turned to various forms of participative decision making to better utilize the talents, ideas, and suggestions of their employees in solving organizational problems (Vroom and Yetton, 1973). Contemporary managerial approaches to employee motivation stress the importance of managers understanding basic motivational processes so as to better deal with their employees and their work environment and to facilitate the achievement of both high levels of performance and high levels of job satisfaction.

Psychological Approaches to Motivation

Just as there has been an evolutionary process in managerial approaches to motivation, so too has there been a similar developmental trend among psychologists interested in motivation. This trend passed through an evolution of four stages: (1) hedonism; (2) instinct theory; (3) reinforcement theory; (4) cognitive theory. As we shall see, while psychologists originally approached the topic of motivation from a quite different perspective than did management theorists, the contemporary positions of both groups have apparently converged to a considerable extent. This convergence is shown in Exhibit 6.3.

Hedonism. The first coherent documentation of the principle of *hedonism* dates from the time of the early Greeks. It later reemerged in the eighteenth and nineteenth centuries as a popular explanation of behavior among such philosophers as Locke, Bentham, and Mill. Briefly, the principle of hedonism implies that individuals will tend to seek pleasure and avoid pain. It is

EXHIBIT 6.3   HISTORICAL DEVELOPMENT OF APPROACHES TO MOTIVATION

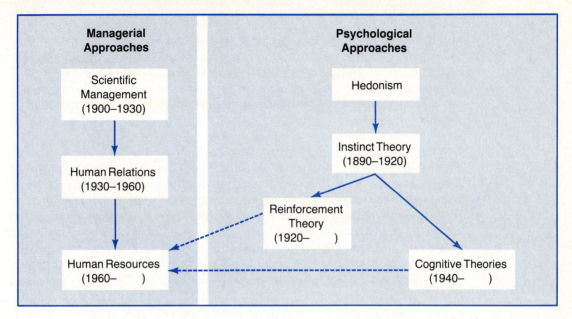

assumed that individuals are likely to do those things that bring them some kind of satisfaction and to avoid those that are less satisfying.

While the concept of hedonism is still pervasive throughout our current models of motivation, it is far too simplistic to represent a comprehensive explanation of motivated behavior. Moreover, it fails to account for those instances when people engage in various activities even though they may be unpleasant. Hence, more complete explanations of behavior were needed. The first such theory that evolved chronologically was instinct theory.

Instinct Theory (1890–1920). The first psychological *theory* of motivation emerged late in the last century as a result of the work of James, Freud, and McDougall. These theorists argued that a large portion of human behavior was not conscious and rational, as suggested by hedonism. Instead, behavior was thought to be largely influenced by instincts. An *instinct* was defined as an inherited biological tendency toward certain objects or actions (McDougall, 1908). Included in the list of instincts were locomotion, curiosity, love, fear, jealousy, and sympathy. These instincts were thought to be the primary determinants of behavior.

While instinct theory was fairly widely accepted during the first quarter of this century, beginning in the 1920s it came under increasing attack on several grounds (Hilgard and Atkinson, 1967). The list of instincts continued to grow, ultimately reaching almost 6000. With so many variables, it became exceedingly difficult to develop a cogent explanation of human behavior. There was no acceptable explanation concerning which of the many instincts would be stronger influences on performance. So, in the absence of a solid conceptual framework, it was difficult to predict behavior. Also, it was found in various research studies that only a very weak relationship existed between an instinct and subsequent behavior. Other factors were apparently also influencing behavior in addition to the instincts under study. Finally, it was argued by some psychologists that instincts were not inherited, but rather represented *learned* behavior. This last criticism was advanced by those who subsequently suggested a quite different theory of motivation: reinforcement theory.

Reinforcement Theory (1920–Present). Beginning with the early work of Thorndike, Woodworth, and Hull, reinforcement theory (also known as drive theory) emerged as a widely accepted, systematic explanation of behavior. Reinforcement theory assumes that people make decisions about their current behavior based on the consequences or rewards of past behavior. When past actions lead to positive consequences or rewards, individuals are likely to repeat such actions. On the other hand, when past actions lead to negative consequences or punishment, individuals are likely to avoid repeating them. This contention, known as the *law of effect* (Thorndike, 1911), emphasizes the role of learning on human behavior. Past learning and previous *stimulus-response* connections are viewed as the major cause of behavior. Today, reinforcement still remains a popular explanation of human behavior. This is discussed in the chapter on behavior modification, an application of reinforcement theory.

Cognitive Theory (1940–Present). The most recent psychological approach to understanding motivation is cognitive theory. In contrast to reinforcement theory, where emphasis is placed on the influence of past rewards and reinforcements, cognitive models emphasize future expectations and beliefs. That is, individuals are viewed as thinking, rational beings who make conscious decisions about their present and future behavior based on what they believe will happen (Lewin, 1938; Tolman, 1959). Past behavior influences these decisions only to the extent that the individual believes that past cause-effect relationships affect future events. Behavior is therefore seen as purposeful, goal-directed, and based on the conscious behavioral intentions of individuals. Significantly, it is this emphasis on reasoning and anticipation that sets cognitive models apart from other models of motivation.

The influence of the cognitive approach to understanding motivation is pervasive and can be seen in several models of employee effort and performance that are discussed in Chapter Seven. In particular, equity theory, goal-setting theory, and expectancy/valence theory all draw heavily from the basic cognitive model.

Before examining these complex models of employee motivation, it will be useful to review two somewhat simpler approaches to motivation. These two models, advanced by Maslow (1954) and Murray (1938), focus primarily on the interrelationship between individual motives or needs and subsequent behavior. Both of these *need theories* provide a useful foundation for understanding the more complex models that follow.

MASLOW'S NEED HIERARCHY THEORY

Perhaps the most widely known theory of individual needs and motivation is the need hierarchy proposed by Abraham Maslow. Maslow was a clinical psychologist who, in the 1940s, began his early developmental work on this theory among children with mental or emotional problems. Based on his observations, he attempted to develop a model of how the healthy personality grows and develops over time and how personality manifests itself in terms of motivated behavior. During the 1960s the theory was popularized among managers and organization analysts, primarily by the work of Douglas McGregor.

Basic Premises of the Need Hierarchy Model

The need hierarchy model consists of two basic premises. First, people are seen as being motivated by a desire to simultaneously satisfy several types of specific needs. Second, it is postulated that these needs are arranged in a hierarchical form and that people work their way through this hierarchy as their needs are satisfied.

Maslow (1968) argues that there are two basic kinds of needs: deficiency needs and growth needs. *Deficiency needs* are needs that must be satisfied if the individual is to be healthy and secure. "Needs for safety, the feeling of belonging, love and respect (from others) are all clearly deficits." (Maslow, 1954, p. 10). To the extent that these needs are not met, the individual will fail to develop a healthy personality. *Growth needs,* on the other hand, refer to those needs that relate to the development and achievement of one's potential. Maslow notes that the concept of growth needs is a vague one: "growth, individuation, autonomy, self-actualization, self-development, productiveness, self-realization, are all crudely synonymous, designating a vaguely perceived area rather than a sharply defined concept" (Maslow, 1968, p. 24).

Maslow goes further to suggest that people are motivated by five rather general needs and that these needs are arranged in a hierarchy. In their order of ascendance they are:

Deficiency Needs
- *Physiological needs.* These needs are thought to be the most basic needs and include the needs for food, water, and sex.
- *Safety needs.* The second level of needs centers around the need to provide a safe and secure physical and emotional environment, one that is free from threats to continued existence.

- *Belongingness needs.* The third level consists of those needs relating to one's desire to be accepted by one's peers, to have friendships, and to be loved.

Growth Needs

- *Esteem needs.* These needs focus on one's desire to have a worthy self-image and to receive recognition, attention, and appreciation from others for one's contributions.
- *Self-actualization needs.* The highest need category is the need for self-fulfillment. Here the individual is concerned with developing his or her full potential as an individual and becoming all that it is possible to become.

Individuals move up the hierarchy by a process of *deprivation* and *gratification.* That is, when a particular need is unfulfilled (i.e., deprived), this need will emerge to dominate the individual's consciousness. Hence, a person concerned about physical safety will ignore other higher-order needs and devote all of his or her efforts to securing a safer environment. Once this need is gratified, however, that need submerges in importance and the next need up the hierarchy is activated (in this case, belongingness needs). This dynamic cycle of alternating deprivation, domination, gratification, and activation continues throughout the various need levels until the individual reaches the self-actualization level.

Maslow in his later writings suggested that, unlike the other needs, gratification of the need for self-actualization tended to cause an *increase* in the potency of this need instead of a decline. In other words, self-actualization is a process of *becoming;* this process is intensified, as well as sustained, as one gradually approaches self-fulfillment.

While Maslow did not feel that growth needs could be defined precisely, he did suggest some characteristics exhibited by individuals manifesting such needs based on his clinical observations. These include (1968, p. 25):

1. Superior perception of reality
2. Increased acceptance of self, of others, and of nature
3. Increased spontaneity
4. Increase in problem-centering
5. Increased detachment and desire for privacy
6. Increased autonomy and resistance to enculturation
7. Greater freshness of appreciation and richness of emotional reaction
8. Higher frequency of peak experiences
9. Increased identification with the human species
10. Changed (the clinician would say, improved) interpersonal relations
11. More democratic character structure
12. Greatly increased creativeness
13. Certain changes in the value system

Parenthetically, it should also be noted that Maslow (1954) also discussed two other needs in his early work: these needs are thought to transcend the notion of the hierarchy and, as such, are not included in the hierarchy itself. The two needs are cognitive needs and aesthetic needs. *Cognitive* needs refer to the desire to know and understand one's environment. Examples include the need to satisfy curiosity and the desire to learn. *Aesthetic* needs include the desire for beauty, harmony, and order in nature. While the notion of aesthetic needs may have little relevance for the study of organizational behavior, such is not the case for cognitive needs. The importance of cognitive needs in organizations can be seen in attempts by employees to understand and relate to the tasks they perform and to be able to master tasks that are meaningful for them. In this sense, Maslow's cognitive needs are similar to Robert White's (1959) notion of the *competence motive.* White, like Maslow, argued that individuals have a strong need to develop mastery over their environment. The importance of such a need becomes apparent in the recent efforts to redesign employees' jobs so they are more challenging and meaning-ful. Job redesign experts hope that their redesign efforts will facilitate the feeling of mastery necessary to satisfy the cognitive and competence motives.

Implications for Management

Maslow's need hierarchy theory has proved to be particularly popular among managers, probably because of its simplicity as a conceptual framework in the discussion of motivation. When it is applied to organizations, clear recom-mendations for management emerge. The theory suggests that managers have a responsibility to create a work climate in which employees can satisfy their needs. Assuming that most employees have largely met their deficiency needs (i.e., they are free from hunger and threat and have established sufficient social relationships), managers can focus on creating a work climate that is aimed at satisfying growth needs. For instance, the proper climate may include oppor-tunities for greater variety, autonomy, and responsibility so that employees can more fully realize their potential. Failure to provide such a climate would logically lead to increased employee frustration, poorer performance, lower job satisfaction, and increased withdrawal from work activities (see Close-Up 6.1).

Research Evidence on Need Hierarchy Theory

Maslow's work has prompted a good deal of research into the utility of the theory in organizational settings. For instance, it has been found that managers in higher echelons of organizations are generally more able to satisfy their growth needs than lower-level managers (Porter, 1961). Such a finding follows from the fact that upper-level managers tend to have more challenging, autonomous jobs where it is possible to seriously pursue growth needs. Lower-level managers, on the other hand, tend to have more routine jobs, thus making it more difficult to satisfy these needs.

However, while it is possible to differentiate between jobs that facilitate growth need satisfaction and those that inhibit it, it is much more difficult to

CLOSE-UP 6.1 NEED HIERARCHY THEORY AT IBM

Need theorists argue that people are motivated primarily by whatever needs are most prominent at a given time. What happens, then, when a company changes its compensation system so that it fulfills security needs instead of growth needs? During the past decade, there has been a shift among companies away from commission payment for sales representatives and toward straight salary payment. The change represents an effort not so much to improve productivity as to protect employees from the variability of business cycles. As one observer puts it, "Today's salesman was raised in an affluent society. A guy is used to a particular standard of living, and he wants the security of a fixed salary. He doesn't want to assume much risk."

To some, offering such security is enlightened management. They argue that salaries encourage more professional marketing and help reps avoid foot-in-the-door pressure tactics. Others, however, feel that putting sales reps on straight salary (or salary with low commissions) destroys their motivation to produce. And in fact, recent studies show that building too much protection into pay plans tends to favor the least productive salespeople and provides little stimulus to put forth maximum effort.

Consider the case of IBM. In recent years, IBM has been reducing the commission portion of its sales compensation program, causing discord among its top sales performers. One high performer spent several months cultivating a new customer and landed a $2 million mainframe contract only to receive a commission for this effort of a mere $2,000. This sales rep no longer works for IBM.

This change in need levels creates a challenge for management. By implementing a compensation system for its sales force aimed at meeting security but not growth needs, an organization may end up with security-minded, not achievement-oriented, sales reps. But by ignoring or neglecting the security needs manifested by a new generation of salespeople, the company risks losing salespeople or failing to attract top candidates. The choice, to at least some degree, is up to the company.

Source: J. A. Byrne, "Motivating Willy Loman," *Forbes,* January 30, 1984, p. 91. Adapted by permission of *Forbes* magazine. © Forbes Inc., 1984.

establish the validity of the need hierarchy itself. In fact, after an extensive review of the research findings on the need hierarchy concept, Wahba and Bridwell (1976, p. 212) conclude: "Maslow's need hierarchy theory presents the student of work motivation with an interesting paradox: The theory is widely accepted, but there is little research evidence to support it."

Wahba and Bridwell examined three aspects of Maslow's model: (1) the existence of the hierarchy itself; (2) the proposition that deprivation of a need leads to domination of the individual by that need; and (3) the proposition that gratification of one need activates the next higher need. To examine the first issue, whether or not there is a five-level hierarchy of needs, seventeen studies were reviewed. These studies used either a factor analytic approach or a ranking approach to test the hypothesis. Based on this review, Wahba and Bridwell (1976, p. 224) conclude:

> Taken together, the results of the factor analytic studies and the ranking studies provide no consistent support for Maslow's need classification as a whole. There is no clear evidence that human needs are classified in five distinct categories, or that these categories are structured in a special hierarchy. There is some evidence for the existence of possibly two types of needs, deficiency and growth needs, although this categorization is not always operative.

The second of Maslow's propositions examined by Wahba and Bridwell was the deprivation/domination proposition. This proposition states that the higher the deprivation or deficiency of a given need, the higher will be its importance to the individual. Thus, if an employee feels highly deficient in his belongingness or social needs, these needs will become paramount in his motivated behavior to the exclusion of other needs. Only mixed results were found concerning this proposition, with some studies supporting the proposition and some failing to support it.

The final proposition is the gratification/activation proposition. Maslow's theory states that as one need is gratified it diminishes as a motivator and the next need up the hierarchy is activated. Hence, once an individual has sufficiently satisfied his esteem needs, he will focus his total energies toward self-actualization. Again, after reviewing the available evidence, Wahba and Bridwell (1976, p. 227) note that the progression from one need to another does not always follow the same pattern and that the trends in these patterns "are not in agreement with those proposed by Maslow as far as the progression of satisfaction."

These findings, when taken together, are not generally supportive of the need hierarchy theory as proposed by Maslow. However, in fairness, several limitations of the various studies reviewed above must be acknowledged. First, most tests of Maslow's theory were carried out among samples of working adults at one (or only a few) point(s) in time. In contrast, Maslow saw his theory as operating throughout one's lifetime. Hence, many of the studies purporting to examine Maslow's hypotheses are highly restrictive; they used only adults and they measured the needs at only one point in time (or at several points in time, but across only a few years). Hence, a true test of Maslow may be possible only by following people as they grow from childhood through adulthood—no easy task for any researcher.

Second, there are a variety of problems encountered when one attempts to measure needs. In fact, the imprecision of the need concept has led some to suggest that Maslow's theory is basically nontestable because of the difficulty of operationalizing the study variables.

Even so, the fairly consistent negative findings that have emerged raise doubts about the validity of the model as it now stands. The one conclusion that did appear to stand empirical testing is the notion of two distinct need levels, deficiency needs and growth needs. That is, people generally attempt to satisfy deficiency needs before attending to growth needs. Ultimately,

Maslow's need hierarchy model has proved useful in generating ideas about the basic nature of human motives and in providing a conceptual framework for understanding the diverse research findings about people at work (Miner and Dachler, 1973).

ERG Theory: A Reformulation

A modification of Maslow's original theory has been proposed by Clayton P. Alderfer (1969, 1972). Alderfer's reformulation was suggested largely in response to the failure of Maslow's five-level hierarchy to hold up to empirical validation. Instead of Maslow's five need levels, Alderfer reformulates them into three more general need levels:

- *Existence needs.* Those needs required to sustain human existence, including both physiological and safety needs.
- *Relatedness needs.* Those needs concerning how people relate to their surrounding social environment, including the need for meaningful social and interpersonal relationships.
- *Growth needs.* Those needs relating to the development of human potential, including the needs for self-esteem and self-actualization. Growth needs are thought to be the highest need category.

Alderfer's model is similar to Maslow's earlier formulation in that both models posit that individuals move up the hierarchy one step at a time. The model differs from Maslow's, however, in two important regards. First, according to Maslow, individuals progress up the hierarchy as a result of the satisfaction of the lower-order needs. In contrast, Alderfer's ERG theory suggests that in addition to this satisfaction-progression process, there is also a frustration-regression process (see Exhibit 6.4). Hence, when an individual is continually frustrated in his or her attempts to satisfy growth needs, related-ness needs will reemerge as a primary motivating force, and the individual is likely to redirect his or her efforts toward lower-level needs.

Second, while Maslow's model has individuals focusing on one need at a time, Alderfer's model suggests that more than one need may be operative (or activated) at the same time. As such, Alderfer's model is less rigid, allowing for greater flexibility in describing human behavior.

MURRAY'S MANIFEST NEEDS THEORY

Another need theory of motivation was developed by Henry A. Murray (1938) and is called the *manifest needs theory* (or the need-press model). While the initial formulations were developed by Murray in the 1930s and 1940s, the model has been considerably developed and extended by David McClelland and John Atkinson (Atkinson, 1964; McClelland et al., 1953).

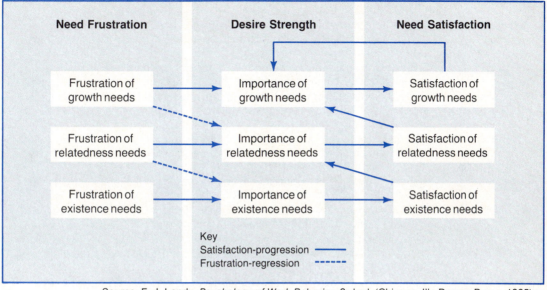

Source: F. J. Landy, *Psychology of Work Behavior,* 3rd ed. (Chicago, Ill.: Dorsey Press, 1985), p. 324.

Basic Premises of the Manifest Needs Model

Like Maslow, Murray felt that individuals could be classified according to the strengths of various needs. People were thought to possess at any one time a variety of divergent—and often conflicting—needs that influence behavior. A *need* was defined as a "recurrent concern for a goal state" (McClelland, 1971, p. 13). Each need was believed to be composed of two components: (1) a qualitative, or directional, component that includes the object toward which the need is directed; and (2) a quantitative, or energetic, component that consists of the strength or intensity of the need toward the object. Needs were thus viewed as the central motivating force for people in terms of both direction and intensity.

Overall, Murray posited that individuals possess about two dozen needs, including the needs for achievement, affiliation, power, and so forth. These needs and their definitions are shown in Exhibit 6.5. Murray believed that needs are mostly learned, rather than inherited, and are activated by cues from the external environment. For example, an employee who had a high need for achievement would only be expected to pursue that need (that is, to try to achieve something) when the environmental conditions were appropriate (e.g., when he was given a challenging task). Only then would the need become *manifest.* When the need was not cued, the need was said to be *latent,* or not activated.

EXHIBIT 6.5   MURRAY'S MANIFEST NEEDS

Need	Characteristics
Achievement	Aspires to accomplish difficult tasks; maintains high standards and is willing to work toward distant goals; responds positively to competition; willing to put forth effort to attain excellence.
Affiliation	Enjoys being with friends and people in general; accepts people readily; makes efforts to win friendships and maintain associations with people.
Aggression	Enjoys combat and argument; easily annoyed; sometimes willing to hurt people to get his or her way; may seek to "get even" with people perceived as having harmed him or her.
Autonomy	Tries to break away from restraints, confinement, or restrictions of any kind; enjoys being unattached, free, not tied to people, places, or obligations; may be rebellious when faced with restraints.
Exhibition	Wants to be the center of attention; enjoys having an audience; engages in behavior that wins the notice of others; may enjoy being dramatic or witty.
Harm avoidance	Does not enjoy exciting activities, especially if danger is involved; avoids risk of bodily harm; seems to maximize personal safety.
Nurturance	Gives sympathy and comfort; assists others whenever possible, interested in caring for children, the disabled, or the infirm; offers a "helping hand" to those in need; readily performs favors for others.
Order	Concerned with keeping personal effects and surroundings neat and organized; dislikes clutter, confusion, lack of organization; interested in developing methods for keeping materials methodically organized.
Power	Attempts to control the environment and to influence or direct other people; expresses opinions forcefully; enjoys the role of leader and may assume it spontaneously.
Succorance	Frequently seeks the sympathy, protection, love, advice, and reassurance of other people; may feel insecure or helpless without such support; confides difficulties readily to a receptive person.
Understanding	Wants to understand many areas of knowledge; values synthesis of ideas, verifiable generalization, logical thought, particularly when directed at satisfying intellectual curiosity.

Source: Adapted from the *Personality Research Form Manual,* published by Research Psychologists Press, Inc., P.O. Box 984, Port Huron, MI 48061-0984. Copyright © 1967, 1974, 1984, by Douglas N. Jackson. Reproduced by permission.

Maslow Versus Murray

The manifest needs theory resembles Maslow's model in that both theories identify a set of needs and goals toward which behavior is directed. The two models differ, however, in two important respects. First, Murray does not suggest that needs are arranged in hierarchical form as does Maslow. And, second, Murray's model allows for more flexibility in describing people. Maslow's need hierarchy model places individuals on one level at a time in the hierarchy (e.g., esteem needs). Using Murray's manifest needs model, on the other hand, we can describe an individual as having high needs for achievement and autonomy and low needs for affiliation and power—all at the same time. Hence, we are able to be more specific in describing people, instead of merely claiming they have "higher-order need strengths" as is the case with Maslow.

While the manifest needs model encompasses an entire set of needs, most research in organizational settings has focused on the four needs of achievement, affiliation, autonomy, and power. These four needs seem to be particularly important for understanding people at work. Therefore, we shall consider each of these needs as they relate to work settings.

Need for Achievement

Basic Concepts. By far the most prominent need from the standpoint of studying organizational behavior is the need for achievement (also known as *n Ach* or n Achievement). Need for achievement is defined as "behavior toward competition with a standard of excellence" (McClelland et al., 1953). High need for achievement is characterized by: a strong desire to assume personal responsibility for finding solutions to problems; a tendency to set moderately difficult achievement goals and take calculated risks; a strong desire for concrete feedback on task performance; and a single-minded preoccupation with task and task accomplishment. Low need for achievement, on the other hand, is typically characterized by a preference for low risk levels on tasks and for shared responsibility on tasks.

Need for achievement is an important motive in organizations because many managerial and entrepreneurial positions require such drive in order to be successful. This is clearly shown in the case of young entrepreneurs who start their own companies (see Close-Up 6.2). Thus, when a manager who has a high *n Ach* is placed on a difficult job, the challenging nature of the task serves to cue the achievement motive which, in turn, activates achievement-oriented behavior. However, it is important to point out that when high need achievers are placed on routine or nonchallenging jobs, the achievement motive will probably not be activated. Hence, there would be little reason to expect them to perform in a superior fashion under such conditions (McClelland, 1961; Steers and Spencer, 1977).

The concept of need for achievement is important, not only for understanding human behavior in its own right, but also for understanding how people respond to the work environment. As such, the concept has important implications for job design. Enriching an employee's job by providing greater amounts of variety, autonomy, and responsibility would probably enhance performance only for those employees who were challenged by such a job (that is, high need achievers). Low need achievers, on the other hand, may be frustrated by the increased personal responsibility for task accomplishment and, as such, may perform poorly or may even withdraw from the situation. We shall examine this phenomenon more in Chapter Fourteen when we explore job design.

CLOSE-UP 6.2 THE YOUNG ENTREPRENEURS

A characteristic trait of high need achievers is the strong desire to take risks and accomplish important goals. Nowhere is this better witnessed than in the behavior of young entrepreneurs. Consider the following examples:

At age 28 Nolan K. Bushnell created Pong, which became the first video game to invade the nation's amusement arcades, until then the preserve of pinball machines. To market his invention, he formed his own company, which he named Atari. Within five years he sold his interests in Atari for $28 million. Another young entrepreneur, Frederick W. Smith, sketched out plans for an air-delivery service while still a student at Yale. In his twenties he founded such a company, and by the time he was 37 this overnight service—Federal Express—was grossing almost $600 million. Similarly, Steven Jobs was barely into his twenties when, along with Stephen Wozniak, he developed and marketed the first Apple computer, which ushered in a technological revolution that has changed the way Americans work and live. By age 26 Jobs had amassed a personal fortune estimated at $149 million.

What is it that creates young entrepreneurs? Two researchers in the area, John Welsh and Jerry White, suggest that such risk takers typically exhibit strong self-confidence, a driving vision of what they want to accomplish, and a need to control their own destinies.

Most gain some experience in major firms, but soon leave these large organizations in order to pursue their own goals. Another researcher in the field, Patrick Liles, observes that the ideal period for beginning a new business venture comes between ages twenty-six and thirty-six: younger entrepreneurs may lack the confidence and experience they need, while older people are generally too constrained by their careers or their finances.

Interestingly, the Europeans and Japanese, who have posed a formidable challenge to established American industry, have been no match in terms of revolutionary new ventures. A Steven Jobs in Europe would probably find start-up capital unavailable, and in Japan would be expected to focus on the corporate needs of his employer. In such circumstances, a young entrepreneur's penchant for taking risks and making fast decisions would be discouraged.

The success of young entrepreneurs in the United States has implications far beyond the corporate halls. It has been estimated that small, emerging businesses accounted for three million new jobs over a ten-year period from the 1970s to the early 1980s, a time when employment in the one thousand largest U.S. companies stagnated. It seems that America's economic and social future may be tied closely to the rise of the young entrepreneurs.

Source: Based on information in "Striking It Rich," "The Seeds of Success," and "Sagas of Five Who Made It," *Time*, February 15, 1982, pp. 36–44.

Need for Achievement and Economic Development. McClelland (1961) has applied the notion of n Achievement to the study of economic development in underdeveloped countries. These studies are described in an interesting book entitled *The Achieving Society*.

As a result of several years of study, two general findings emerged. First, according to McClelland, there is a fairly consistent correlation between a country's current state of economic development and measurable mean levels of n Achievement in that country. Higher mean levels of *n Ach* are found in more prosperous nations, while lower levels are found in the less prosperous. Second, when McClelland examined the literature of ancient cultures for references to achievement-oriented aspirations and behaviors, he found some evidence that increases in the achievement motive preceded subsequent economic development in those civilizations.

Based on these findings, McClelland argues that economic development and prosperity at a national level can be influenced to some extent by the achievement strivings of a nation's people. Such findings have important implications for current efforts to assist underdeveloped nations because they suggest that, in addition to giving economic aid, there is a need to instill the achievement motive in the population in order to facilitate development.

Developing n Achievement. Need for achievement, like other needs, is apparently learned at an early age and is influenced largely by the independence training given children by their parents. As Sanford and Wrightsman (1970, p. 212) point out, "the relatively demanding parent who clearly instigates self-reliance in the child and who then rewards independent behavior is teaching the child a need for achievement."

Since it is estimated that only about ten percent of the population are high need achievers, questions are logically raised concerning how one becomes a high need achiever. McClelland's (1965) answer to this question is that achievement motivation can be taught to adults with moderate success. Achievement motivation training consists of four steps:

1. Teach participants how to think, talk, and act like a person with high need achievement.
2. Stimulate participants to set higher, but carefully planned and realistic, work goals for themselves.
3. Give the participants knowledge about themselves.
4. Create a group *esprit de corps* from learning about each others' hopes and fears and successes and failures, and from going through an emotional experience together.

To date, the evidence appears to support the usefulness of such training programs for increasing *n Ach*. With few exceptions, managers in various countries who attended such programs received more rapid promotions, made more money, and expanded their businesses more quickly after completing the course than did control groups. It is important to note here, however, that such managers were consistently chosen from entrepreneurial-type jobs thought to be most suited for high need achievers. The success of such programs on employees who perform routine, clerical, or automated tasks remains very doubtful because such jobs are not designed to activate the achievement motive.

Need for Affiliation

In contrast to the need for achievement, relatively little is known about the behavioral consequences of the need for affiliation, despite the fact that this need has been widely recognized since early in this century (Trotter, 1916). The need for affiliation *(n Aff)* may be defined as an "attraction to another organism in order to feel reassured from the other that the self is acceptable" (Birch and Veroff, 1966, p. 65). This need should not be confused with being sociable or popular; instead, it is the need for human companionship and reassurance.

People with a high need for affiliation are typified by the following: a strong desire for approval and reassurance from others; a tendency to conform to the wishes and norms of others when pressured by people whose friendship they value; and a sincere interest in the feelings of others. High *n Aff* individuals tend to take jobs characterized by a high amount of interpersonal contact, like sales, teaching, public relations, and counseling.

How does *n Aff* influence employee behavior? Some evidence suggests that individuals with a high need for affiliation have better attendance records than those with a low *n Aff* (Steers and Braunstein, 1976). Moreover, some research suggests that high *n Aff* employees perform somewhat better in situations where personal support and approval are tied to performance. Support for this position comes from French (1958), who found in a laboratory experiment that, while high *n Ach* individuals performed better when given *task-related* feedback, high *n Aff* individuals also performed better when given *supportive* feedback. In addition, effort and performance for those high in *n Aff* can be enhanced somewhat under a cooperative work norm where pressure for increased output is exerted by one's *friends* only (French, 1955; Atkinson and Raphelson, 1956; DeCharms, 1957). The implications of such findings for leadership or supervisory behavior are fairly clear. To the extent that supervisors can create a cooperative, supportive work environment where positive feedback is tied to task performance, we would expect high *n Aff* employees to be more productive. The reason for this is simple: Working harder in such an environment would lead to the kinds of need satisfaction desired by those high in *n Aff*.

Need for Autonomy

Need for autonomy *(n Aut)* is a desire for independence and for freedom from any kind of constraint. Individuals with a high need for autonomy prefer situations where they: work alone; control their own work pace; and are not hampered by excessive rules or procedures governing their work behavior (Birch and Veroff, 1966).

The effects of a high need for autonomy on employee behavior can be significant. For instance, it has been found that high *n Aut* individuals: tend not to react to external pressures for conformity to group norms (Kasl, Sampson, and French, 1964); tend to be poor performers unless they are allowed to participate in the determination of their tasks (Vroom, 1959); are not committed to the goals and objectives of the organization; and are typically found among craft and tradespeople and lower-echelon employees, not managers (Vroom, 1959). This last finding may be explained by the fact that managerial success is in large measure determined by a manager's ability to interact successfully with others, to cooperate, and to compromise. Individuals with a high need for autonomy typically refuse to do this.

Need for Power

A final need that has proved important for understanding organizational behavior is an individual's need for power (or dominance). Need for power represents a desire to influence others and to control one's environment. It has a strong social connotation, in contrast to n Autonomy, in that a high *n Pow* employee will try to control or lead those around him.

Interest in the power motive dates from the early work of Alfred Adler (1930), who believed that power was the major goal of all human activity. Adler saw human development as a process by which people learn to exert control over the forces that have power over them. Hence, a person's ultimate satisfaction comes with his or her ability to have influence over the environment. While the subsequent works of Murray (1938), McClelland (1975), and others do not see power as an all-consuming drive as Adler did, they nevertheless view it as an important need.

In summarizing the research on need for power, here's how Litwin and Stringer (1968, p. 18) describe individuals high in *n Pow*:

> They usually attempt to influence others directly—by making suggestions, by giving their opinions and evaluations, and by trying to talk others into things. They seek positions of leadership in group activities; whether they become leaders or are seen only as "dominating individuals" depends on other attributes such as ability and sociability. They are usually verbally fluent, often talkative, sometimes argumentative.

Additional recent research demonstrates that employees with high needs for power or dominance tend to be superior performers, have above-average attendance records, and tend to be in supervisory positions (Steers and Braunstein, 1976). Moreover, such individuals were rated by others as having good leadership abilities.

Two Faces of Power. McClelland (1976) notes that n Power can take two forms among managers: personal power and institutionalized power. Employees with a *personal-power* orientation strive for dominance almost for the sake of dominance. Personal conquest is very important to them. Moreover, such individuals tend to reject institutional responsibilities. McClelland likens personal-power types to conquistadors or feudal chieftains; that is, they attempt to inspire their subordinates to heroic performance but want their subordinates to be responsible to their leader, not to the organization.

CLOSE-UP 6.3   THE GAMESMAN

In the past twenty years, we have witnessed significant changes in the way organizations are managed. There are fewer autocratic managers, teamwork has often replaced the individual star, experiments in job satisfaction and the quality of working life are rampant, and flexible approaches to both working hours and division of labor are commonplace. As a result, organizations and their managers have had to adapt to a changing work environment and, all too often, the past keys to managerial success no longer work. New patterns of managerial behavior must be found.

A recent study made by Michael Maccoby focused on this problem by observing 250 middle and top managers from twelve major corporations. Maccoby began with the proposition that any strategy for social change must account for the personal characteristics of those responsible for change. "What mix of motives—ambition, greed, fascination with technology, scientific interest, security-seeking, or idealism —determined their actions?" (p. 1). As a result of his study, Maccoby identified four relatively distinct "corporate personalities" based on the motives of the individuals involved. These four types are:

- *The craftsman.* The goal of a craftsman is to perfect the work at hand. As such, the individual identifies only with his or her own job and often ignores larger corporate objectives. The craftsman's narrowness of view and obsession with perfection at the expense of production usually limit him or her to middle management.
- *The company man or woman.* This person identifies only with corporate goals and, in a real sense, the company is his or her life. This individual questions little and follows blindly. He or she is loyal, has limited vision, and often ends up as second in command.
- *The jungle fighter.* These managers are often useful in a crisis when strong and decisive (if autocratic) leadership is necessary in the short run. Maccoby differentiates here between lions, who have both strength and ability and lead naturally but ruthlessly, and foxes, who scheme and manipulate. Both are often dispensed with by the organization when the crisis is over and members want a return to normalcy.
- *The gamesman.* The gamesman is the ultimate careerist who recognizes both personal goals and those of the corporation and who devotes his or her life to reconciling the two.

The gamesman's main interest is in competitive activity, where he or she can prove to be a winner by taking moderate risks and motivating others to push themselves beyond their normal pace. The gamesman responds to work as a game. The contest energizes the individual and this energy is communicated to others. Emphasis is on new ideas, new techniques, and shortcuts. The main goal of such people is to be a winner, and talking about themselves invariably leads to a discussion of their tactics and strategies in the corporate contest.

Maccoby argues, based on his clinical observations, that the new corporate top executives combine many gamesman traits with aspects of the company man or woman. That is, successful top executives are team players who are committed to the organization and who feel personally responsible for its success. Career goals have merged with corporate goals and one's focus is on what is good for the company without separating that from what is good for the individual. Such individuals tend to be worriers and see people in terms of their use to the organization. Moreover, they generally succeed in submerging their own egos and gain strength from this exercise in self-control.

As Maccoby (p. 42) notes, "to function, the corporations need craftsmen, scientists, and company men (many could do without jungle fighters), but their future depends most of all on the gamesman's capacity for mature development."

Source: M. Maccoby, *The Gamesman* (New York: Simon & Schuster, 1976).

The *institutionalized-power* manager, on the other hand, is far more concerned with problems of the organization and what he or she can do to facilitate goal attainment. McClelland (1976) describes institutionalized-power types as follows: they are organization-minded and feel personal responsibility for building up the organization; they enjoy work and getting things done in an orderly fashion; they seem quite willing to sacrifice some of their own self-interest for the welfare of the organization; they have a strong sense of justice or equity; and they are more mature (i.e., they are less defensive and more willing to seek expert advice when necessary).

A recent study of managers and their motives carried out by Maccoby (1976) leads to the same conclusions as McClelland's work. The results are summarized in Close-Up 6.3. Although Maccoby uses different terms (e.g., the gamesman), his work rests largely on managers' need for power.

Manifest Needs and Managerial Effectiveness

Based on the foregoing discussion of various needs, questions are logically raised concerning the influence these manifest needs have on managerial behavior and effectiveness. Is it possible to build a profile of a successful manager based on these needs? Recent research by McClelland (1975, 1976) suggests that such a profile is possible on a very general level.

McClelland's (1976, p. 102) argument begins by asking what we mean by managerial success:

> Almost by definition, a good manager is one who, among other things, helps subordinates feel strong and responsible, who rewards them properly for good performance, and who sees that things are organized in such a way that subordinates feel they know what they should be doing. Above all, managers

should foster among subordinates a strong sense of team spirit, of pride in working as part of a particular team. If a manager creates and encourages this spirit, his subordinates certainly should perform better.

Based on this description, what type of manager is most suited to the tasks of managing? A manager with a high need for achievement? need for affiliation? need for power? McClelland argues persuasively that the best manager is one who has a high need for power! Let's examine why.

Managers who have a high need for *achievement* concentrate their efforts on personal accomplishment and improvement. They tend to be highly independent individuals who want to assume responsibility and credit for task accomplishment and who want short-term concrete feedback on their performance so they know how well they are doing. These characteristics are often closely associated with *entrepreneurial* success as shown in Close-Up 6.2. However, these same characteristics can be detrimental where the individual has to manage others. In complex organizations, managers obviously cannot perform all the tasks necessary for success; teamwork is necessary. Moreover, feedback on the group's effort and performance is often vague and delayed. Hence, the managerial environment is not totally suitable to stimulate the achievement motive in managers.

Managers who have a high need for *affiliation* fare no better. Affiliative managers have a strong need for group acceptance and, partly as a result of this, they often tend to be indecisive in decision making for fear of alienating one faction or another. Moreover, this concern for maintaining good interpersonal relationships often results in their attention being focused on keeping subordinates happy instead of on work performance. McClelland (1976, p. 104) summed up his research findings on the affiliative manager by noting:

> The manager who is concerned about being liked by people tends to have subordinates who feel that they have very little personal responsibility, that organizational procedures are not clear, and that they have little pride in their work groups.

In contrast, managers with a high need for *institutionalized* power were found in McClelland's (1976) study to supervise work groups that were both more productive and more satisfied than other managers. (McClelland also found that managers high in need for *personal* power were far less successful managers than those with a need for institutionalized power.) Several reasons exist for the success of the n Power manager. One explanation is suggested by Zaleznik (1970, p. 47):

> Whatever else organizations may be (problem-solving instruments, sociotechnical systems, reward systems, and so on), they are political structures. This means that organizations operate by distributing authority and setting a stage for the exercise of power. It is no wonder, therefore, that individuals who are highly motivated to secure and use power find a familiar and hospitable environment in business.

In other words, power-oriented managers, when truly concerned about the organization as a whole (instead of themselves), provide the structure, drive, and support necessary to facilitate goal-oriented group behavior. In this sense, they fit very nicely into the definition of managerial success noted above. However, as noted by McClelland (1976), a power-oriented manager pays a price in terms of personal health. He measured need for power among a group of Harvard graduates over twenty years ago. Twenty years later in a follow-up study, McClelland found that 58% of those rated high in power in the earlier study either had high blood pressure or had died of heart failure!

One final point needs to be discussed before leaving the topic of needs and managerial success. This concerns the *interactive* effects of the various needs on performance. In particular, a study by Andrews (1967) looked at both n Power and n Achievement in two Mexican companies. Company A was a dynamic and rapidly growing organization characterized by high employee morale and enthusiasm. Company B, on the other hand, had shown almost no growth despite large initial investments and a favorable market; moreover, Company B had serious problems of employee dissatisfaction and turnover. An assessment of the various need strengths among managers in both companies revealed several interesting findings. To begin with, the upper management of Company A (the more dynamic firm) rated much higher on n Achievement than did managers in Company B. The presidents of both companies were extremely high in n Power. However, in Company A, the president's n Power was combined with a moderately high n Achievement. This was not the case in the less successful Company B. Hence, based on these findings, it would appear that the most successful managers may be those who combine a power-orientation *with* an achievement-orientation.

SUMMARY

This chapter introduced the concept of motivation as it relates to individual employee needs. Motivation was defined as the force that energizes, directs, and sustains human behavior. Based on this, a simple model of the motivational process was presented.

Next, the development of management thought on employee motivation was reviewed and was compared to various developments in the study of motivation by psychologists.

Building on this discussion, two need theories of motivation were presented. The first, by Maslow, suggests that individual needs are arranged in a hierarchy and that people move from one level in the hierarchy to the next. On the other hand, the second, by Murray and McClelland, does not recognize the existence of such a hierarchy. Instead, focus is on describing various human needs such as achievement, affiliation, and power. To conclude, the implications for managerial effectiveness with regard to the various needs were discussed.

KEY WORDS

cognitive theory	manifest needs theory	need
hedonism	motivation	need hierarchy theory
human relations	n Achievement	reinforcement theory
human resources	n Affiliation	scientific management
instinct theory	n Autonomy	
law of effect	n Power	

FOR DISCUSSION

1. Define motivation.

2. Describe the basic motivational process.

3. Review the development of management thought concerning approaches to motivation. How does this compare to the development of psychological approaches to motivation?

4. What is the basic difference between the human relations approach to management and motivation and the human resources approach?

5. What is the law of effect?

6. Compare and contrast the reinforcement theory and the cognitive theory of motivation.

7. Compare and contrast Maslow's need hierarchy theory and Murray's manifest needs theory. Which model do you prefer as a manager?

8. Describe Maslow's deprivation/gratification cycle.

9. What changes did Alderfer's ERG theory make in Maslow's original formulation of the need hierarchy theory?

10. Review the research evidence on Maslow's need hierarchy theory.

11. Discuss the role of achievement motivation in economic development.

12. How is need for achievement developed?

13. What impact does need for affiliation have on employee performance?

14. Describe the two faces of power and the impact of each on organizational performance.

15. What are the basic characteristics of Maccoby's "gamesman"?

16. What kind of need set combination makes the best manager?

EXERCISE

6.1

ATTENDANCE AND PERFORMANCE: AN INTERVIEW EXERCISE

Purpose

To study attendance behavior and work motivation firsthand by interviewing employees in various work organizations.

Instructions

Students, either individually or in pairs, should contact and interview up to twenty employees who hold various kinds of jobs in different types of organi-

zations. It would be helpful if this sample includes both males and females, minorities, managers and workers, and public and private employees. For each employee, note his or her occupation and place of work and ask the following three questions:

1. What determines whether or not you will come to work on a particular day?
2. On the job, what determines how much effort you will put forth on a given day?

3. Think back to a time in the past few months when you felt really motivated to perform on the job. What caused this high motivation to occur?

Note the answers during each interview and summarize the results for presentation in class. When summarizing, pay attention not only to differences in answers but also to possible differences across sex, race, occupation, and type of organization.

CASE

HAWKINS' NOB HILL PLANT

6.1

Mr. Kiplinger is plant manager of the Nob City division of the Hawkins Company. He was originally transferred to Nob City in 1970 from the home office in Altoona (Pennsylvania). He, his wife, and their four children reside in Nob City. Reporting directly to Mr. Kiplinger are his key staff officers, the office manager, the personnel and safety manager, and the production manager. The line command includes foremen who report directly to the production manager.

The workers have a certain set of expectations concerning their own rights and privileges. Some of these "privileges" are obvious, while others are rather subtle. One of the more widely held values on the part of the workers is what they call "leniency." The workers know they have a job to do and expect

that, in the process of doing it, management will leave them alone. The main obligation they feel to the company is that of producing. Obedience to supervisors is displayed so long as it is directly related to a job to be done. Hostility is directed toward management when discipline or forced obedience is exerted as a means of asserting the will of management. Conversely, the workers commend management when given certain privileges or when flexibility is shown in discipline.

"Job-shifting" provides another route for circumventing formal supervisory authority, and is a type of vertical and horizontal mobility in the plant. Job-shifting is done by "bidding" for a vacancy in the plant, prompted either by desire for a job with higher status or as a means to escape an unpleasant foreman.

Case 6.1 reprinted with permission of Macmillan Publishing Company from *Organizational Behavior: Readings and Cases* by Theodore T. Herbert. Copyright © 1976 by Theodore T. Herbert. Adaptations and case discussion questions from *Management Fundamentals: Modern Principles & Practices*, 4th ed., by Gary Dessler, © 1985 by Reston Publishing Company, Inc.; reprinted by permission of Prentice Hall.

The foremen resent this practice, since they feel that they should have the prerogative of choosing their own subordinates—and not the other way around.

A third right includes the use of company material for home repairs. The workers expect that they should have access to the company's finished product, either without charge or at a very large discount, and that company equipment should be made available for use in repairing broken down machinery or household furnishings.

One day Skip Kiplinger received a call from the home office notifying him that he could expect about $2 million worth of new equipment to be added to his plant's equipment. Along with the equipment addition, the home office notified Skip that they were transferring Louis Hirtmann from the plastics division in Pottstown to replace the retiring Ed Patterson as production manager. Hirtmann was a former Army officer and had an outstanding industrial record too. It was hoped by the board of directors that the change of leadership and the addition of equipment would add considerably to Hawkins' profit margin.

One of Hirtmann's first moves was to stop the practice of allowing workers to have access to company equipment and to reduce the discount given on the purchase of company-made equipment. He was able to do this after showing Kiplinger that several thousands of dollars in sales had been lost from abuse of this particular privilege, in the last year alone; some workers had resold company equipment at considerable profits. Another move was to eliminate the job-shifting policy and to replace it with a new seniority system. The new system was roundly applauded by foremen and other supervisory personnel, but workers became noticeably irritable and frus-

trated. Hirtmann believed that once an order was given, it was to be followed without question. Generally he paid attention to employee grievances only when they reached critical proportions.

Hirtmann made rounds every hour to check on the progress of the work flow. In the course of six months he instituted many technical changes designed to speed up production and reduce labor costs. These improvements were reflected in the profit margin; but during this six-month period, dissension had been building up, almost unnoticed tensions in the plant ran high, and employees were becoming very defensive. Dissatisfaction over the installment of new machinery became a focal point of the disruption. If the company could afford two million dollars for machinery, workers grumbled, it could afford higher wages.

About the eighth month Hirtmann was notified by the home office that he would attend a month-long managerial seminar in Chicago. Mr. Kiplinger decided to leave Hirtmann's post vacant in his absence, and to have each shift foreman be responsible for his particular shift with no further supervision.

Kiplinger learned through the foremen that the women on the first shift wanted their rest room painted and, because the room was exposed to the afternoon sun, they also asked for some shades and a fan. Without hesitation Kiplinger told the maintenance crew to go to work on the job. In addition he told the foremen to feel free to handle such minor grievances and requests on their own authority until Hirtmann returned.

Within the next week another request was presented. This time the workers complained about working a six-day week. Kiplinger considered the point and proposed that if production reached

20,000 pounds per day (a 5,000 pound increase) he could then institute a short shift on Saturday running from 7:30 A.M. to noon. Within a few days production reached the level indicated. Unfortunately now Kiplinger was in a difficult position because the Altoona office demanded even more production to meet their orders. Kiplinger then had to go back to the workers and ask them to continue on the six-day schedule for another few days until the orders were filled. Although there was some grumbling, most of the workers continued to perform effectively. Within a week the press for more production was reduced so that it was possible to institute the promised short day on the following Saturday.

It had been the practice to blow a steam whistle in the plant at the beginning and end of the shift, as well as at five-minute rest periods and at lunch. One of the workers suggested that the company use the public address system instead. At first, employees ridiculed the new system but in a few days they took announcements as a matter of course; in one instance when the announcement was not made, the employees returned from lunch just the same. Later on in the month the announcements were dropped, yet the employees started and stopped work promptly.

Between the first and the last of the month the daily output of the plant had increased steadily from 25,000 pounds to about 33,000 pounds.

Kiplinger was puzzled. He could not understand why production was up with no production manager present.

CASE DISCUSSION QUESTIONS

1. Why do you think production was up by 32 percent with no production manager present?
2. How specifically do you think Hirtmann's actions influenced workers' "higher-order needs"?
3. Do you think Hirtmann's leadership style was appropriate for this situation?
4. What would you do now if you were Kiplinger?

CHAPTER SEVEN

COGNITIVE MODELS OF MOTIVATION AND PERFORMANCE

Employee needs, abilities, and traits, as well as perceptions, influence how people behave at work. Managers must not only recognize these various influences, but must also understand how they fit together to *jointly* determine human behavior. It is only through a systematic understanding of the major variables and how they affect one another that managers can take necessary actions to facilitate a performance-oriented and satisfying work environment.

In this chapter, a systematic framework is outlined by examining complex cognitive models of employee motivation. These models are labeled complex because they incorporate individual characteristics, job characteristics, and organization-wide characteristics. They incorporate many of the factors discussed earlier that have been shown to influence behavior and illustrate how these factors interact. The models are cognitive in that they reflect the thought processes of individuals making decisions about the extent of their involvement in work activities.

IMPORTANCE OF TOPIC FOR MANAGERS

The topic of employee motivation is clearly one of the most important topics for managers. One of the most persuasive arguments for studying motivation is advanced by Katz and Kahn (1978). They note that organizations have three *behavioral requirements* of the people who work in them. First, people must be attracted to join the organization and remain with it. Second, people must dependably perform the tasks for which they were hired. Third, people must transcend dependable role performance and engage in some form of creative, spontaneous, and innovative behavior at work. These three behavioral requirements deal squarely with motivation. Motivational techniques must be employed not only to encourage employees to join and remain with an organization, but also to perform in a dependable fashion and to think and take advantage of unique opportunities.

In addition, managers should never overlook the ever-present nature of motivational processes in organizations. Motivation affects and is affected by a multitude of factors in the work environment. A comprehensive understanding of the way in which organizations function and survive requires an in-depth knowledge of why people behave as they do on the job.

Because of ever-tightening constraints placed on organizations by unions, government agencies, and increased foreign and domestic competition, companies must find ways to improve their efficiency and effectiveness in the work place. Much of the organizational slack that was relied on in the past has diminished, requiring that all resources—including human resources—be utilized to their maximum. In recent years, increased attention has been devoted to developing employees as future resources—a sort of talent bank—from which organizations can draw as they grow and develop. Examples of these efforts can be seen in the increase in management development programs, manpower planning, and job redesign. Motivation is the foundation upon which these efforts are built.

From the individual's standpoint, motivation is a key to a productive and useful life. Work consumes a sizable portion of our waking hours. If this time is to be meaningful and contribute toward the development of a healthy personality, the individual must be willing to devote effort toward task accomplishment. Motivation plays a central role in this.

MOTIVATIONAL FACTORS IN LOW PRODUCTIVITY

To set the stage for a discussion of cognitive models of motivation and performance, first consider a major reason why such models have received so much attention in recent years. The reason is the problem of low productivity and the motivational factors inherent in it. The reasons for low productivity highlight the importance of understanding motivational processes in work organizations. In fact, a major aim of many contemporary motivational models is to diagnose and alleviate these kinds of problems.

Managers often complain that employees don't put forth as much effort on the job as they would like to see. We hear that employees are lazy or that they conspire to reduce output. Although many of these complaints are frequent, we seldom see managers attempt to identify the reasons behind such restriction of output. In fact, employees often feel, rightly or wrongly, that it is in their best interest to restrict productivity. At least five reasons for this behavior can be identified (Steers, 1977c).

As will be discussed later in this chapter, employees place different values on different outcomes. Some employees prize added income, for example, while others prefer to be given extra time off or an opportunity to enter a training program. But if employees find their *potential rewards are unappealing,* they are unlikely to increase their efforts. Employees must place a high value on the rewards available to them in order to justify increasing their performance. Rewards that are not valued will not merit special effort. An example of this is a situation in which some employees will continually take work home at night to maximize job performance, in hope of getting a raise or promotion. However, other employees elect to take home no work and instead spend the evening hours with their families, even when it slows their career progression.

Sometimes, the problem is not that the rewards themselves are unappealing, but that there is *weak performance-reward linkage.* Employees may fail to see a strong connection between increased performance and receipt of additional rewards. And the employees are not necessarily wrong: the failure to see a linkage is often because there is none. It is difficult to measure performance accurately, especially at the managerial level. As a result, opportunities for inequity emerge in the reward system and good performance may not be rewarded to the extent it should be. When employees fail to see a good relationship between performance and subsequent rewards, a major motivating force is lost. This point is demonstrated in Close-Up 7.1.

A third reason employees might restrict their productivity is their *distrust of management.* Workers may feel that increased performance can only result in increases in the quotas or production rates required. Such distrust, which can be particularly strong among blue-collar workers, tends to neutralize the incentive system. In addition, workers at times feel that increased performance will lead to a reduction in the work force (that is, they may work themselves out of a job). These fears lead to group pressures to maintain acceptable, moderate performance levels and to punish rate-busters as threats to the well-being of the group.

On an individual level, one cause of restricted output is the *desire to have control over one's job.* In order to resist being a cog in the wheel, employees often attempt to leave sufficient slack in their work schedule (by intentional underproduction) so they can vary their work methods. By doing so, they

CLOSE-UP 7.1 ARE EMPLOYEES CONCERNED ABOUT PRODUCTIVITY?

Is employee apathy toward productivity or restriction of output a problem in contemporary work organizations? Available evidence seems to suggest this is the case. One poll of over 4000 U.S. employees on various jobs carried out by the Opinion Research Corporation found that fifty-seven percent of those surveyed felt they could easily produce more on their jobs if they wanted to. The survey found that many people simply saw no reason to increase their output at work.

Or, take the recent example of a west coast plywood manufacturer. In the plywood industry, a typical spreader machine crew will produce from 65,000 to 90,000 core-line feet of plywood in an eight-hour shift. In an effort to determine how much plywood could be produced at maximum pace, one crew (running a high average of 108,020 core-line feet) attempted to set a new record for plywood production. The result: 214,720 core-line feet—an increase of almost 100 percent over their own average and almost 300 percent over the industry average. Or, from a qualitative standpoint, consider the plight of the U.S. automotive industry which in 1977 recalled more cars than they manufactured due to faulty design and workmanship.

In contrast, while many U.S. corporations are concerned about discovering ways to improve employee commitment to high productivity, many Japanese firms are concerned about workers pushing themselves too hard. A recent study found that a majority of Japanese workers take less than one-third of the time off they are entitled to and feel that utilizing all of their holiday time reflects disloyalty or lack of interest in their work. Things in Japan have reached such a state that the Japanese ministry of labor has begun a campaign aimed at encouraging workers to take full advantage of their vacation benefits. Moreover, some firms that have been unable to convince employees to take time off have been forced to shut down factories entirely so employees would be unable to come to work.

Sources: Opinion Research Corporation, "America's Growing Anti-business Mood," *Business Week,* June 17, 1972, p. 101; D. Wyant, "Plywood Crew Claims Production Record," *Eugene Register-Guard,* December 6, 1978; "Industry Recalls More Cars Than It Sold in Worst Year," *Eugene Register-Guard,* April 12, 1978; "Workaholics," *Parade,* December 24, 1978.

reassure themselves that they still have some mild degree of control over their own behavior and therefore count as people. It increases individuals' feelings of self-worth and independence by increasing their freedom of action.

Finally, a fifth reason for output restriction may be a *lack of job involvement* due simply to dislike of the job. If an employee is not interested in a job and would really prefer to do something else, he or she will find it difficult to concentrate and focus energy on the immediate task at hand. Employees may demonstrate their lack of involvement through absenteeism or other forms of withdrawal (such as alcoholism), thus reducing performance levels even further.

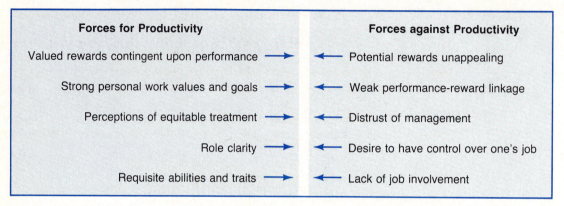

Forces for Productivity	Forces against Productivity
Valued rewards contingent upon performance →	← Potential rewards unappealing
Strong personal work values and goals →	← Weak performance-reward linkage
Perceptions of equitable treatment →	← Distrust of management
Role clarity →	← Desire to have control over one's job
Requisite abilities and traits →	← Lack of job involvement

One way to better understand how these factors influence or inhibit productivity is to use a *force field analysis.* A force field analysis is a technique developed by Kurt Lewin to pictorially represent forces or pressures to do something (in this case, pressures for productivity), as compared to forces *not* to do something (in this case, restriction of output). We can develop a fairly simple force field analysis of influences on productivity by comparing various factors that promote production with factors that may inhibit production, as shown in Exhibit 7.1.

At least five forces against productivity can be identified, as noted above. These are shown in the right half of Exhibit 7.1. Opposing these are a series of positive performance forces. These positive forces can include having valued rewards contingent upon performance, strong personal work values and goals, employee perceptions of equitable treatment by peers and management, role clarity, and employees who have the necessary abilities and traits to do the job. Of course, these are only a few examples of many of the forces in favor of productivity. However, these examples do illustrate how the employee weighs positive and negative forces to determine how much effort to devote to performance.

Problems resulting from poor motivation to work are commonplace in contemporary work organizations. If managers intend to remedy this situation, they must make an effort to understand the underlying influences on such behavior and how the nature of the job and the work environment affect it. One way is to develop more comprehensive models of employee motivation that focus on the way individuals react to the work situations. Examples of such complex models are discussed here. A review of three major cognitive models of motivation will shed light both on *why* employees do or do not produce and on *what* managers can do to facilitate employee performance and job satisfaction. First, let's look at the nature of cognitive models.

COGNITIVE VERSUS ACOGNITIVE MODELS OF MOTIVATION

There are now two basic schools of thought concerning employee motivation: the acognitive and the cognitive approaches. *Acognitive* models of motivation assert that it is possible to predict behavior without an understanding of internal thought processes. They stress instead the relationship between external stimuli and behavior and do not explore the effects of internal mechanisms. People are seen as being largely reactive to environmental stimuli, making it unnecessary, according to this view, to examine internal processes. Acognitive models will be discussed in Chapter Eight.

On the other hand, *cognitive* models of motivation, such as the models presented in this chapter, rest on the assumption that individuals often make conscious decisions about their behavior, and that this decision process must be clearly understood in order to understand human behavior. Cognitive theories emphasize the how and why of behavior by focusing on internal mechanisms. Individuals are seen as active organisms in their environment. They are proactive as well as reactive to environmental forces.

While these two basic approaches to understanding human behavior are not totally incompatible, they do represent distinct differences in emphasis and assumptions about the nature of people. This distinction should become clear as we examine three complex cognitive theories of employee motivation: equity theory, goal-setting theory, and expectancy/valence theory. Each theory rests on the assumption that people are reasoning (if not reasonable) creatures that make conscious choices from among alternative forms of behavior. (See Steers and Porter [1987] for a more detailed discussion of the three models.) All three models emerge from and are unified by the role of cognitions in human behavior.

EQUITY THEORY

Basic Premises of Equity Theory

One cognitive explanation of human behavior in work organizations is equity theory. Equity theory, as first advanced by Adams (1965) and Weick (1966), is the most popular in a series of *social comparison theories* of motivation (Goodman, 1977). Social comparison theories focus on individuals' feelings or perceptions of how fairly they are being treated as compared to others.

Equity theory rests on two basic assumptions about human behavior (Mowday, 1979). First, it is assumed that individuals engage in a process of evaluating their social relationships much like they would evaluate economic transactions in the marketplace. Social relationships are viewed as an exchange process in which individuals make contributions or investments and expect certain outcomes in return. March and Simon's (1958) inducements-contributions theory is one such early example. We expect individuals to have expectations about the outcomes they receive as a result of their contributions of time and effort.

Second, it is assumed that people do not assess the equity of an exchange in a vacuum. Instead, they compare their own situation with others to determine the relative balance. Determining the extent to which an exchange is satisfactory is influenced by what happens to oneself compared to what happens to others.

In this section, we shall examine the basic ingredients of equity theory, and follow this with a discussion of the consequences of inequity. Next, a brief summary of the research on equity theory will be presented, followed by a discussion of the managerial implications of the model. Throughout, be aware of the central role played by cognitions in the process.

Antecedents of Inequity

Social comparison processes, like those involved in equity theory, are typically based on the relationship between two variables: inputs and outcomes. *Inputs,* or investments, represent those things an individual contributes to an exchange. In a work situation, inputs include items like previous work experience, education, and level of effort on the job. *Outcomes* are items that an individual receives from the exchange. Outcomes include pay, fringe benefits, accrued status, seniority, and positive feedback.

In order for an input or outcome to be relevant in evaluating exchange relationships, two conditions must be met. First, the existence of an input or outcome must be recognized by one or both parties in the exchange. The major outcome from a particular job is irrelevant unless at least one of the parties involved considers it a major outcome. Second, an input or outcome must be considered relevant or have marginal utility to the exchange. Unless both conditions—recognition and relevancy—are met, potential inputs or outcomes will not be considered in determining the degree of equity in the exchange.

According to the theory, individuals assign weights to the various inputs and outcomes based on their perceived importance. This is not to say that people are highly precise in these weighting processes, but that they roughly differentiate between more important and less important inputs and outcomes. Intuitively, people arrive at a ratio of their outcomes to inputs *as compared to* the ratio of another individual's or group's outcomes to inputs. The other individual or group may be any of the following: people with whom we engage in direct exchanges; other individuals engaged in exchanges with a common third party; or persons in a previous or hypothetical work situation. This referent other becomes the point of comparison for people in determining the degree to which they feel equitably treated.

From this, a state of equity exists whenever the ratio of a person's outcomes to inputs is equal to the ratio of others' outcomes to inputs. This state can be represented where p represents the ratio of the person and o represents the ratio of the comparison other:

$$\frac{O_p}{I_p} = \frac{O_o}{I_o}$$

A state of inequity exists whenever these two ratios are unequal:

$$\frac{O_p}{I_p} < \frac{O_o}{I_o} \quad \text{or} \quad \frac{O_p}{I_p} > \frac{O_o}{I_o}$$

In this approach to the concept of equity in social exchange, several specific aspects of the model must be emphasized. To begin, the conditions necessary to produce a state of equity or inequity are based on a person's *perceptions* of inputs and outcomes. If an individual has a highly distorted view of the major factors involved in an exchange (e.g., he thought his co-workers were earning far more than they actually were), these distortions will be incorporated into the person's calculations of equity or inequity. Second, inequity is a *relative* phenomenon. That is, inequity does not necessarily exist simply because a person has high inputs and low outcomes, so long as the comparison other also has a similar ratio. Employees may be fairly satisfied with a job demanding high effort and offering low rewards if their frame of reference is in a similar situation.

Third, it is important to note that inequity occurs when people are relatively underpaid *or overpaid.* Available research suggests that the threshold for underpayment is lower than it is for overpayment (Mowday, 1979). People are more willing to accept overpayment in an exchange relationship than underpayment. Even so, both theory and research observe that people who experience overpayment will sometimes be motivated to reduce the exchange imbalance by working harder. The ways people strive to reduce inequities in exchange are discussed below.

Consequences of Inequity

The implications of equity theory in motivation follow from the hypothesized consequences of perceived inequity. As formulated by Adams (1965), the major postulates of the theory are as follows: (1) perceived inequity (underpayment or overpayment) creates tension within individuals; (2) the tension is proportionate to the magnitude of the inequity; (3) the tension experienced by individuals will motivate them to attempt to reduce it; and (4) the strength of the motivation or drive to reduce it is proportionate to the perceived inequity. This process is shown in Exhibit 7.2.

In this process, individuals are faced with the problem of *how* to reduce perceived inequity. Adams (1965) suggests six methods of resolution:

EXHIBIT 7.2   MOTIVATIONAL IMPLICATIONS OF PERCEIVED INEQUITY

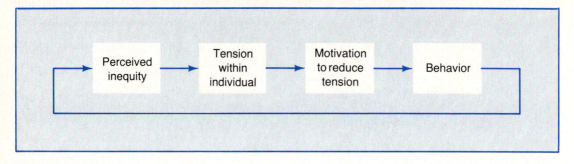

1. *People may alter their inputs.* People may increase or decrease their inputs depending upon whether the inequity is advantageous or disadvantageous. For instance, underpaid people may reduce their level of effort on the job or increase absenteeism, while overpaid people may increase effort (see Close-Up 7.2).

2. *People may alter their outcomes.* Similarly, it is possible for individuals to increase or decrease outcomes received on the job. One clear example of increasing outcomes can be seen in union efforts to improve wages, hours, and working conditions without parallel increases in employee effort (or input).

3. *People may distort their inputs or outcomes cognitively.* For instance, people who feel inequitably treated may artificially increase the status outcomes attached to their job ("This is really an important job") or may decrease perceived effort ("I really don't work that hard on this job"). By doing so, the input-outcome ratios become more favorable by comparison and people are more content.

4. *People may leave the field.* Simply put, individuals who feel inequitably treated may decide to leave the situation by transferring to another job or department or by quitting. In doing so, they apparently hope to find a more favorable balance of inputs to outcomes.

5. *People may distort the inputs or outcomes of others.* In the face of injustice, people may cognitively distort the ratio of the referent. For instance, people may come to believe that the referent other actually works harder than they do, and thereby deserves greater rewards. Or, they may reduce the perceived salary that the referent other makes and thereby reduce the other's outcomes.

6. *People may change objects of comparison.* Finally, people may decide that their referent other is not the most suitable point of comparison and may select another who will yield a more favorable balance in the social exchange process. For instance, if the other receives a salary increase while the person does not, he may decide that the other now belongs to a different level in the organization hierarchy, thereby justifying the need to select a more relevant other.

Equitable Life Assurance Company's revenues stood at more than $6 billion, and its earnings continued to rise faster than the industry standard. Even so, the company thought it could do better.

Under the leadership of Coy G. Eklund, Equitable Life initiated a "More Profitable Growth" (MPG) program. Its goal was to curb rising operating expenses and thereby make the firm more profitable. As part of the program, Eklund fired 550 of the company's 15,000 employees. The terminations occurred primarily in headquarters and affected personnel from file clerks to corporate vice-presidents.

The firings, which dramatically overturned Equitable's company tradition of lifetime employment for employees with acceptable levels of performance, had a devastating impact on employee morale. Equitable had often bragged about this policy, and then it suddenly changed the rules. As Eklund stated, "A policy of lifetime employment has clearly become an inconsistent one as we have moved in recent years to meet competition."

Although Eklund claimed that morale was not affected by the cutbacks, a *Business Week* survey of past and present employees found just the opposite. Said one employee, "The loyalty and dedication are gone. In the past, people always put out a little more than was expected of them, but not anymore."

While the layoffs themselves hurt morale, what really took its toll was the way in which they were done. Eklund simply told all departments to cut back the number of positions by ten percent, thereby eliminating what he termed all "nonessential" jobs. Many employees felt that what ensued was a popularity contest in which quality of performance or even tenure became less important than the good graces of one's supervisor. Even Eklund admits that many of those fired were "highly capable and were skilled and excellent in their performance."

What this move did at Equitable was call into question the company's commitment to equity towards its employees. Consistent with equity theory, the employees simply felt they were not being treated fairly. As a result, they decreased their effort. Performance fell, and turnover increased. Equitable's problems demonstrate something many American firms have found when they attempted to learn the secrets of successful Japanese management practices: there appear to be benefits in lifetime employment for suitably performing employees.

Source: "Why Equitable Life Looks Good But Feels Bad," *Business Week,* March 26, 1979, pp. 80–82.

Through these techniques, individuals attempt to cope with situations they believe are unfair. Their efforts and motivations are aimed at returning to a state of equity and reduced tension. Equity theory, like other cognitive theories of motivation, views individuals as existing in a constant state of flux. They continually try to understand their environment and to act on it in a way that satisfies their more pressing needs, desires, and expectations.

Research on Equity Theory

A great deal of research generated over the past decade focuses on the validity and utility of equity theory (Goodman, 1977; Mowday, 1979; Pritchard, 1969). From the standpoint of work-related behaviors, the most relevant research has focused on equity theory predictions of employee reactions to pay. These predictions generally distinguish between two conditions of pay inequity (underpayment and overpayment) and two methods of compensation (hourly and piece rate). The specific predictions of each interaction are shown in Exhibit 7.3.

Available evidence tends to support many equity theory predictions, particularly concerning underpayment, as they relate to expected behaviors under various compensation and equity conditions. The findings are not unanimous. Following a recent review, Mowday (1979, p. 134) concluded:

> In summary, predictions from Adams' theory about employee reactions to wage inequities have received some support in the research literature. Research support for the theory appears to be strongest for predictions about underpayment inequity. Although there are fewer studies of underpayment than of overpayment, results of research on underpayment are relatively consistent and subject to fewer alternative explanations. There are both theoretical and empirical grounds for being cautious in generalizing the results of research on overpayment inequity to employee behavior in work organizations. Where such studies have manipulated perceived inequity by challenging subject's qualifications for the job, observed differences in performance can be explained in ways that have little to do with inequity. Where other methods of inducing overpayment inequity are used, considerably less support is often found for the theory. Predicted differences in productivity and satisfaction due to overpayment inequity are often in the predicted direction but fail to reach acceptable levels of statistical significance.

Equity theory does make a contribution toward a better understanding of work behavior in organizations. Perceived states of equity affect our responses to the work environment as well as our intentions and behavior on the job. Although equity theory is not a complete statement of employee motivation, it does describe several important motivationally relevant processes that managers should understand. Now, let's consider some of the more salient managerial implications of the theory.

Managerial Implications of Equity Theory

From a managerial standpoint, perhaps the most obvious implication is the necessity for managers to be continually alert to social comparison processes in organizations and, as a consequence, to view motivation in dynamic and changing terms. For example, redesigning someone's job may not increase subsequent motivation and performance if the changes do not change the inputs-outcomes balance. If employees still think they are inequitably treated

EXHIBIT 7.3   EQUITY THEORY PREDICTIONS OF EMPLOYEE REACTIONS TO INEQUITABLE PAYMENT

	Underpayment	Overpayment
Hourly payment	Subjects underpaid by the hour produce less or poorer-quality output than equitably paid subjects.	Subjects overpaid by the hour produce more or higher-quality output than equitably paid subjects.
Piece-rate payment	Subjects underpaid by piece rate will produce a large number of low-quality units in comparison with equitably paid subjects.	Subjects overpaid by piece rate will produce fewer units of higher quality than equitably paid subjects.

Source: R. T. Mowday, "Equity Theory Predictions of Behavior in Organizations," in *Motivation and Work Behavior,* 2nd ed., ed. R. M. Steers and L. W. Porter (New York: McGraw-Hill, 1979). Reprinted by permission.

(perhaps they feel they are paid less than comparable others), there is little reason to expect increased effort. Hence, as much as possible, managers have a responsibility to insure that employees feel they are equitably treated.

Employers and managers must also recognize the importance of perception in employee motivation. If employees *perceive* that they are inequitably treated, they will act accordingly—even if they are in fact overcompensated for their level of effort. Managers view the workplace differently from workers and often fail to understand this critical point.

Equity theory attaches much importance to monetary rewards and the manner in which they are distributed. Money is one of the few rewards that people clearly see and measure. As a result, it often becomes a major focal point in employee assessments about their own equity.

Finally, equity theory requires managers to evaluate (and reevaluate) the bases on which they distribute available rewards. Leventhal (1976) identifies three general types of *distribution rules:* (1) distribution of rewards based on equity or contribution; (2) distribution of rewards based on feelings of social responsibility; and (3) distribution of rewards based on equality, with equal outcomes given to all participants. Managers tend to select one or more of these ways based on the nature of the situation and based on certain known factors at the time. It should be clear that the manager's choice of distribution rule in no small way affects employee's perceptions of their own state of equity and their willingness to respond and participate.

GOAL-SETTING THEORY

A second cognitive theory of motivation is *goal-setting theory.* The chief proponent of this model is Edwin A. Locke (1968). We will examine several

EXHIBIT 7.4   THE GOAL-SETTING MODEL OF MOTIVATION AND PERFORMANCE

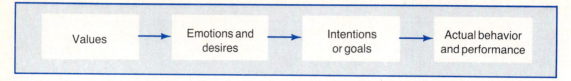

aspects of the model here. First, the basic premises are introduced. Next, the role of task-goal attributes in goal-setting success is examined, followed by a discussion of the effects of individual and situational factors on the model. Finally, we review managerial implications.

Basic Premises of Goal-Setting Theory

Locke's (1968) basic premise in support of goal-setting theory is that behavior is determined by two cognitions: values and intentions (or goals). As shown in Exhibit 7.4, values (or what one regards as conducive to welfare) are experienced by people in the form of emotions and desires. Our values cause us to want certain things that are consistent with our values. For instance, we may have a strong personal work ethic that causes us to have a desire to perform at high levels. As a result of these emotions and desires, we set goals. We may decide to put in longer hours on the job, for instance. These goals then represent the primary determinant of actual behavior. In other words, Locke's model emphasizes the role of conscious intentions in actual behavior. If we set out to accomplish something, these conscious intentions guide our effort and performance.

Much research supports the basic premises of a goal-setting model of motivation. People set goals concerning their future behaviors and these goals influence actual behaviors. If we are to understand more about the goal-setting process, however, it is necessary to look beyond the basic premise of the model and understand many of the complexities involved. To do this, we begin with an examination of the role of task-goal attributes in goal-setting and performance.

Task-Goal Attributes and Performance

Although Locke's goal-setting model implies a fairly refined sequence of events leading up to behavior and performance, the research on the topic has not been as systematic. Instead, much of what we know of the effects of goal-setting on performance comes from studies of the effects of several task-goal attributes.

A *task-goal attribute* may be defined as a characteristic or dimension of an employee's task goals (Steers and Porter, 1974). It is possible to identify six relatively distinct task-goal attributes that facilitate task performance in a

EXHIBIT 7.5   MAJOR INFLUENCES ON GOAL-SETTING AND PERFORMANCE

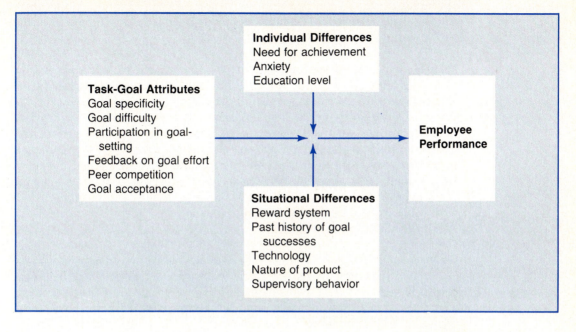

Individual Differences
Need for achievement
Anxiety
Education level

Task-Goal Attributes
Goal specificity
Goal difficulty
Participation in goal-
    setting
Feedback on goal effort
Peer competition
Goal acceptance

**Employee
Performance**

Situational Differences
Reward system
Past history of goal
    successes
Technology
Nature of product
Supervisory behavior

goal-setting environment: (1) goal specificity; (2) goal difficulty; (3) participation in goal-setting; (4) feedback on goal effort; (5) peer competition for goal attainment; and (6) goal acceptance. The relation of these to employee performance is summarized below and shown in Exhibit 7.5. See Steers and Porter (1974) and Tubbs (1986) for extensive reviews of the literature.

Goal Specificity. It has been consistently found that goal specificity is directly related to increased performance. When employees are given specific goals, they consistently perform at higher levels than when they are simply told to do their best or are given no instructions at all. The more specific the goals, the higher the performance (Locke, 1967). Such findings are not surprising. Increasing goal specificity on a task reduces role ambiguity and reduces the search for acceptable modes of behavior. The employee has a very clear idea of what is expected and can perform accordingly.

Goal Difficulty. A second tenet of goal-setting theory is that, up to a point, increasing the difficulty of employees' goals increases the perceived challenge of the task and increases the amount of effort expended for goal attainment. This is particularly true for high need achievers. Strong support is shown for this position. More difficult goals tend to lead to increased effort and performance (at least to the point such goals are still seen as feasible). However, serious exceptions to this trend can be noted. It has been found that difficult goals may lose their motivating potential when they are not properly reinforced. Past failures on previous goals may negate the effects of setting difficult future goals (Zander and Newcomb, 1967). Goals apparently must not be set at such a level that they are seldom, if ever, achieved. Under these conditions, employees may simply stop trying, leading to reduced effort and performance.

Participation in Goal-Setting. The virtues of participative decision making have long been described as a means not only of increasing organizational efficiency and effectiveness but also of increasing employee involvement and job satisfaction (Vroom, 1964). Unfortunately, available evidence suggests that, while increased participation in goal-setting may increase job satisfaction and attendance, its effects on job performance are mixed. While participation does not seem to detract from performance, it appears that the act of setting goals (goal specificity) is a far more powerful tool in influencing performance (Lawrence and Smith, 1955). This is made clear in Close-Up 7.3. A possible explanation for this finding is suggested when we consider the effects of individual differences.

Feedback on Goal Effort. Another influence on goal-setting effectiveness is the extent to which employees are given feedback on task-oriented behavior. Feedback serves at least two functions: (1) it acts as a directive, keeping a goal-directed behavior on target; and (2) it serves as an incentive, stimulating employees to greater effort (Payne and Hauty, 1955). When available evidence is considered, it must be concluded that no simple feedback-performance relationship exists. While feedback is obviously important in facilitating performance for some people, other factors like individuals' needs appear to moderate the relationship.

Peer Competition for Goal Attainment. Many managers feel that performance can be enhanced by placing employees in a competitive situation relative to their peers. Unfortunately, available evidence is again not too clear about the purported benefits of peer competition on performance. Several additional factors need to be taken into account in order to adequately explain this association. First, the relationship between peer competition and performance depends on how we define performance. We would expect competition to positively influence performance *only* when product quality either is not a consideration or is controlled by technology. This is because competition often leads to increased *quantity* of output at the expense of *quality*. If craftsmanship is a central concern, competition may be detrimental.

Second, the nature of job technology may influence the effects of competition. Under conditions of high task interdependence, such as those found on assembly lines where product manufacture depends on many people working together, we would not expect competition to lead to improved results. On the other hand, under conditions of task independence where people are responsible for their own product or component, competition is often useful.

Finally, competition among peers for goal attainment is also influenced by the nature of the reward system. Competition would be expected to be

CLOSE-UP 7.3 GOAL-SETTING AND PERFORMANCE AMONG TYPISTS

The Problem. Does goal-setting really work? And if so, which aspects of goal-setting are most pronounced in their influence on employee behavior? In order to answer this question, Gary Latham and Gary Yukl have carried out a series of studies relating different aspects of goal-setting programs to employee performance. One study focused on typists.

The Program. In this experiment forty-one typists from the word processing center of a major corporation were assigned to two groups. In the first group, productivity goals were assigned by the supervisor, while in the second group goals were participatively set by the typists and their supervisors. Goals were established each week and the previous week's performance was used in setting goals for the next week. Performance was measured using an index of the weighted sum of the number of lines typed each week divided by the number of hours worked. The weights were determined based upon the difficulty level of the material typed.

The Results. After ten weeks, *both* groups experienced significantly higher performance rates than before the experiment. Productivity increased 18 percent in the participative group and 15 percent in the assigned group. So, while level of goal difficulty and goal specificity (that is, whether or not goals were set at all) were both found to be important influences on performance, participation in setting goals did not emerge as an important influence in this study. The utility of goal-setting processes in facilitating employee performance, however, was clearly established.

Source: G. P. Latham and G. A. Yukl, "Effects of Assigned and Participative Goal-Setting on Performance and Job Satisfaction," *Journal of Applied Psychology* 61 (1976): 166–71.

strongly related to performance where a "zero-sum game" situation dictates rewards. There can be only one winner in a race, for example. Similarly, there can be only one best sales representative who wins a trip to Hawaii. On the other hand, where there can be many winners (that is, a non-zero-sum game), as would probably be the case in a majority of actual work situations, we would expect the effects of peer competition to be greatly diminished.

Goal Acceptance. Finally, Locke (1968) has noted that employee level of aspiration significantly affects motivation to perform. It is important to draw a clear distinction between externally assigned task goals (by a supervisor) and those goals that are set by employees. In fact, Locke's theory suggests that task goals will affect behavior only to the extent that they are accepted by employees in the form of personal aspiration levels:

. . . it is not enough to know that an order or request was made; one has to know whether or not the individual heard it and understood it, how he appraised it, and what he decided to do about it before its effects on his behavior can be predicted and explained (Locke, 1968, p. 174).

In other words, goal acceptance, defined as a congruence of assigned task goals and the personal aspiration levels on such goals, apparently represents an important influence on the relation between goals and performance. This fact is often overlooked by managers when they attempt to implement a goal-setting or MBO program in organizations. The fact that the managers accept the goals is clearly no reason to believe the employees will accept them. First, employees must understand why they should accept the goals and what benefits accrue to them for doing so. The failure of managers to understand this simple fact probably explains many of the failures of MBO programs in business today.

Additional Influences on Goal-Setting Success

It was noted that several aspects of the goal-setting environment (task-goal attributes) influence the extent to which goals are actually achieved. It was also noted that, in many cases, no direct relationship exists between these task-goal attributes and subsequent performance. Instead, two major moderators of the task-goal attribute-performance relationship can be identified (see Exhibit 7.5).

First, several *situational differences* must be taken into account. Variations in reward systems (zero-sum games vs. non-zero-sum games), past history of goal successes, technology (independent vs. interdependent), and the nature of the product (quantity vs. quality) all can influence performance under goal-setting conditions. Added to this is the nature of supervisory behavior. We might expect that attempts to allow employees greater participation in goal-setting would be facilitated by a considerate leadership style, rather than by a task-oriented one. Under these conditions, employees feel that their supervisor has a sincere interest in their opinions and inputs.

In addition, several *individual differences* can be identified. In particular, employee need for achievement can moderate the extent to which attributes influence performance. For instance, it has been found that high need achievers perform better when given high levels of feedback and very specific goals, while low need achievers perform better when allowed to participate in goal-setting (Steers, 1975; see also Ivancevich and McMahon, 1977). These findings are expected in view of the theory on the achievement motive. Other evidence suggests that anxiety or apprehension about being evaluated by one's supervisor against specific criteria facilitates performance (White, Mitchell, and Bell, 1977). Finally, it has been found that goal-setting techniques, particularly goal specificity, are more effective with less educated rather than highly educated employees (Latham and Yukl, 1975; Ivancevich and Mc-Mahon, 1977).

Clearly, the notion of goal-setting is more complex than was first believed. If goal-setting techniques are to be successfully implemented in organizations, managers must pay attention not only to the attributes of task goals but also to the personal characteristics of employees and the various situational characteristics.

The way managers do this—the way they translate their various findings into actual practice—is best characterized by the management-by-objectives programs that are now widely used in organizations. *Management-by-objectives* (MBO) is a process in which employees of complex organizations, working in conjunction with one another, identify common goals and coordinate their efforts toward achieving them (Tosi, Rizzo, and Carroll, 1970). It is future-oriented and focuses employee attention and effort on "where are we going" instead of "where have we been." While MBO is clearly not a panacea for poorly managed organizations, managers can make use of the technique to provide greater structure, clarity, and focus in otherwise ambiguous situations. Without proper attention to the nature of the goals and the people asked to work toward them, however, the naive assumption that MBO can solve management's problems will hardly bring about success.

Managerial Implications of Goal-Setting Theory

The concept of goal-setting and MBO is very rich in terms of the implications for management. For example, greater consideration can be given by managers to the precise nature of the task-goal attributes of each employee. Managers have a responsibility not simply to assign goals to their subordinates, but to see to it that these goals are specified in such a way that they have maximum motivational potential.

In addition, increased attention can be paid to how different types of employees react to their assigned goals. For instance, it has been found that high and low need achievers each perform better under different conditions. Such findings suggest that managers have a responsibility to tailor goals to individual needs as much as possible, and to create an optimal performance environment for each employee.

Increased attention can also be paid to how different situational variables influence performance effectiveness. Differences in leadership style, technology, and group structure often influence the impact of various task-goal attributes on performance.

Some awareness of the possible negative job attitudes that might result from certain aspects of MBO programs is necessary. Recent research has indicated that while goal-setting techniques often lead to improved performance, this performance is at times achieved at the expense of decreased job satisfaction. Where goals are seen by employees as being far too rigid, the credibility of the program itself may be jeopardized, leading to poor effort and performance. Care must be taken to insure that the general parameters of the program are widely accepted by program participants.

Where MBO programs are used, it is advisable to continuously monitor both performance and attitudes among employees as an early-warning system for possible trouble spots. Some research has indicated that MBO programs can lose their potency as a motivating force over time. Continuous monitoring systems can help identify trends and suggest remedies where needed.

Finally, consideration must be given to reinforcing contingencies, thereby improving the motivating potential of the program. Where employees can clearly see personal rewards to be gained from directing effort toward goal attainment, effort and performance should be enhanced.

In summary, available evidence on the effectiveness of goal-setting techniques clearly shows that the relative success of these techniques is largely a result of management's ability to assess problems comprehensively. Consideration must be given not only to the feasibility of task goals and their applicability to the larger issue of organizational objectives, but also to the role played by individual and situational differences as they relate to performance. When all of these factors are jointly considered, program effectiveness is enhanced and the rate of goal failure is diminished.

EXPECTANCY/VALENCE THEORY

The third cognitive model of employee motivation to be discussed here is *expectancy/valence theory*. Expectancy/valence theory (or simply expectancy theory) of work motivation dates from the early work of Kurt Lewin and Edward Tolman during the 1930s and 1940s. These early investigators rejected many of the notions of drive theory and instead argued that much of human behavior results from interaction between the characteristics of individuals (e.g., their personality traits, attitudes, needs, and values), and their perceived environment. This basic model was first applied to work settings by Georgopoulos, Mahoney, and Jones (1957) in their path-goal theory of motivation. (It should be noted that expectancy theory is known by many titles, including path-goal theory, instrumentality theory, and valence-instrumentality-expectancy theory.)

According to the basic model, individuals are seen as thinking, reasoning persons who make conscious choices about present and future behavior. People are not seen as inherently motivated or unmotivated, as many earlier models suggest. Instead, motivational level depends on the particular work environment people find themselves in. To the extent that this environment is compatible with their needs, goals, and expectations, they are motivated. This point will become clearer as we examine the major parts of the theory.

The first systematic, comprehensive formulation of expectancy theory as it relates to work situations was presented by Victor Vroom in his classic book *Work and Motivation* (1964). This was followed closely by extensions and refinements of the model by Galbraith and Cummings (1967), Porter and Lawler (1968), Graen (1969), and Campbell et al. (1970). Instead of presenting several variations of models that exist, we shall review a general expectancy model as it relates to the work situation. Following this, available research evidence will be discussed as it concerns the validity of the model. Finally,

some of the more important managerial implications of the model will be presented.

A useful way to review expectancy theory is to break it down into its various components. Expectancy theory attempts to answer two basic questions: (1) What causes motivation? and (2) What causes performance? Expectancy theory also has a third component—what causes job satisfaction?—discussed in Chapter Twelve. We shall deal with the first two questions here.

What Causes Motivation?

In expectancy theory, motivation is determined by expectancies and valences. An *expectancy* is a belief about the likelihood or probability that a particular behavioral act (such as working harder) will lead to a particular outcome (such as a pay raise). The degree of this belief can vary from 0, where an individual sees no chance that the behavior will lead to the outcome, to 1.0, where an individual is absolutely certain that the behavior will lead to the outcome. Of course, most expectancies fall somewhere in between these two extremes. *Valence* refers to the value an individual places on available outcomes or rewards. A valence can range from +1.0 to −1.0, depending upon whether the outcome is highly prized by the employee (money) or highly undesirable (being fired).

E→P **Expectancies.** Expectancies can be divided into two types: (1) *effort-performance* (or *E→P) expectancies* and (2) *performance-outcome* (or *P→O) expectancies* (Lawler, 1973). An *E→P* expectancy is an individual's belief that effort will, in fact, lead to performance. For example, an employee may feel that working overtime will lead to a higher level of output. Lawler has suggested several influences on the effort-performance expectancies we form about work. These include: level of self-esteem; past experiences in similar situations; and perception of the actual situation.

P→O **Expectancies.** A performance-outcome expectancy (or *P→O* expectancy), is the belief that if a person performs well in a given situation, certain desired outcomes will follow. For instance, an employee may believe that a higher level of output will result in a pay raise. Conversely, the same employee may also believe that increased performance might lead to a layoff as he works himself out of a job.

Performance-outcome expectancies are influenced by a variety of factors, including: (1) past experience in similar situations; (2) attractiveness of the various outcomes; (3) extent of one's internal locus of control and belief in an ability to control the environment; (4) *E→P* expectancies; and (5) perception of the actual situation.

Valence. Valence, as noted above, is the value individuals place on the available outcomes or rewards. If employees truly do not value the rewards offered by an organization, we do not expect them to be motivated to perform.

The valence attached to certain outcomes can vary widely. For instance, some employees do not want to be promoted into positions of increased responsibility and stress, while others welcome such opportunities. Hence, rewarding employees with a promotion is not always likely to be well received. (Consider the detrimental effects of the up-or-out promotional policies of many large companies.) On the other hand, some rewards like money are consistently valued in their own right or because of their instrumental value in leading to the acquisition of other outcomes.

Having identified the major variables that influence motivation in expectancy theory, we can consider how they fit together. As shown in Exhibit 7.6, these three variables are believed to influence an employee's motivational level in a multiplicative fashion. According to expectancy theory, employee motivation (not to be confused with actual performance) is a result of an employee's $E \rightarrow P$ expectancies *times* the $P \rightarrow O$ expectancies *times* the valences for the outcomes.

A simple example will illustrate how this process works. If a salesperson believes that the chances are good (say 8 out of 10, or .8) that increased effort in selling leads to higher sales, we say the person has a high $E \rightarrow P$ expectancy. Moreover, if this individual further believes (also at a .8 level of probability) that such sales increases would lead to a bonus or a pay raise, we say that he or she has a high $P \rightarrow O$ expectancy. Finally, let's assume the salesperson places a high value on this bonus or pay raise (say .9 on a scale from -1.0 to $+1.0$). When these three factors are combined in a multiplicative fashion ($.8 \times .8 \times .9 = .58$), it becomes clear that the salesperson has a high motivational force. On the other hand, if expectancies were high (.8 and .8, respectively), but the salesperson genuinely had little desire for money (say a valence of .1 instead of .9), the motivational force would be considerably lower ($.8 \times .8 \times .1 = .06$). Hence, for an employee to be highly motivated, *all three* factors must be high. In the absence of one of the factors, we do not expect to see high motivational levels.

What Causes Performance?

Although an understanding of the determinants of employee motivation is obviously important, the concepts of motivation and performance are not synonymous. Motivation represents an employee's desire to perform, or level of effort, while *performance* is the extent to which an individual can successfully accomplish a task or achieve a goal. Performance as a concept includes not only the production of certain tangible units of output but also less tangible outputs like effectively supervising others, thinking in a creative way, inventing a new product, resolving a conflict between others, or selling a good or service. In many ways, effective employee performance is the ultimate criterion by which managers are judged.

As can be seen in Exhibit 7.6, performance is influenced by several factors. Clearly, motivation is a central influence. But *in addition to motivation,* at least three ingredients are involved: (1) abilities and traits; (2) role

EXHIBIT 7.6   A MODEL OF EXPECTANCY/VALENCE THEORY OF MOTIVATION AND PERFORMANCE

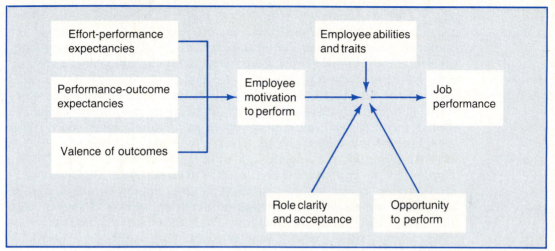

Source: Adapted from L. W. Porter and E. E. Lawler, *Managerial Attitudes and Performance* (Chicago, Ill.: Irwin, 1968).

clarity and acceptance; and (3) opportunity to perform (Porter and Lawler, 1968; Campbell and Pritchard, 1976).

Abilities and Traits. The abilities and traits that employees bring to the job largely determine their *capacity* to perform, as opposed to employee motivation, which is concerned with employees' *will* to perform. Abilities and traits are believed to be enduring and stable over time, although some changes are possible as a result of outside intervention, such as employee training.

Job performance can be influenced by employee abilities and traits in several ways. For example, it has been shown that managerial effectiveness is modestly related to intellectual capabilities such as verbal comprehension, inductive reasoning, and memory. Ghiselli (1966) suggested that these capabilities grow in importance as individuals move up the managerial hierarchy into increasingly responsible positions. Abilities and skills like typing or knowing a trade are also obviously important for the successful performance of clerical or blue-collar employees. Finally, several personal traits (such as cognitive complexity) have been shown to influence performance.

These findings have clear implications in the recruitment, selection, and placement of new employees *as long as* management is willing to fit individuals to jobs that match their skills. Placing highly intelligent employees who have high needs for achievement in jobs that lack challenge or interest would not only inhibit their level of motivation and performance, it would probably hasten their leaving the organization altogether. A major responsibility for managers is to ensure that they select employees who are suitable to the tasks to be done.

Role Clarity and Acceptance. Being motivated to perform and having the requisite abilities do not ensure good job performance. In addition, employees must understand and accept the requirements of the job (Porter and Lawler, 1968). Providing employees with greater role clarity increases the amount of energy that is directed specifically toward work goals and decreases the amount of energy that is wasted on other activities. For instance, if supervisors know that they bear primary responsibility for reducing shop floor accidents, they will be likely to devote effort to accomplishing this goal. On the other hand, if roles are unclarified, supervisors may take a "let the employee worry about it" attitude, with negative results. Role clarity has also been found to lead to increased goal commitment, work group cohesiveness, job involvement, and job satisfaction (Locke, 1976).

Opportunity to Perform. Finally, a point that is often overlooked in a consideration of employee motivation is that employees must have an *opportunity* to perform in order to achieve job success (Campbell and Pritchard, 1976). If a salesperson is asked to sell a product that nobody wants, such as buggy whips, or if a production manager is given an unrealistic deadline to produce a quantity of a certain product, the chances of successful job performance are low—even if the employee is motivated, has the requisite abilities, and has a clear picture of the task.

The inhibiting effects placed on the opportunity to perform can be seen in the problems personnel managers face when asked to develop programs to improve employee motivation *without* affecting production levels or changing jobs substantially or changing the compensation and reward system. Under such circumstances, it is not surprising that managers are unable to improve motivational levels substantially; they simply do not have the opportunity to perform.

Another example of the lack of opportunity to perform can be seen in assembly-line jobs where the pace of production is determined by machines. Where technology controls production, improved motivation can do little to increase quantity of output, although it may influence quality of output in some cases.

In summary, the model outlined in Exhibit 7.6 suggests four primary influences on job performance: (1) employee motivation; (2) employee abilities and skills; (3) role clarity and acceptance; and (4) opportunity to perform. These four factors together suggest that successful job performance is indeed determined jointly by individuals and their environment, as suggested by Kurt Lewin. Individuals can contribute to job performance through their motivation to perform and the skills and abilities they bring to the work place. Managers, on the other hand, can contribute to job performance by ensuring that reward systems encourage motivation and that job requirements are clear and precise. In addition, managers can attempt to create work assignments in which employees have opportunities to really perform. The more control employees have over their performance environment, the greater the impact of their motivation on subsequent job performance.

Research on Expectancy Theory

In recent years, numerous empirical studies have been done that examine various aspects of the expectancy model of employee motivation. Details of these findings are reviewed in Mitchell (1974) and Campbell and Pritchard (1976). While an in-depth review of the various problems in research on this topic is beyond the scope of this discussion, it is possible to summarize the current status of research on the model.

Each of the three components of the expectancy model, $E \rightarrow P$ expectancy, $P \rightarrow O$ expectancy, and valence, has been found to be moderately and independently related to effort and performance (Campbell and Pritchard, 1976). This relationship is particularly strong in $P \rightarrow O$ expectancies. In a number of studies, it has been found that modifying performance-outcome contingencies (so employees see a clear relationship between performance and subsequent rewards) consistently leads to improved levels of performance. Nowhere is this relationship more clearly demonstrated than in pay incentive systems where pay is based on performance rather than seniority or some other criteria. Under these conditions, employees see that their performance leads to receipt of desired rewards; thus performance levels are generally higher.

The predictive powers of the expectancy model are improved somewhat when the three basic variables are combined in a multiplicative fashion, instead of in an additive one (Campbell and Pritchard, 1976). This finding supports the idea that all three components must be present for motivational force to be high. If individuals value a reward and feel they can perform the task, but do not believe that performance will lead to the reward, they would probably not be highly motivated.

There is some disagreement about whether employee abilities are better predictors of performance than motivational force. Dunnette (1972) reviews several laboratory experiments which suggest that brief aptitude or general intelligence tests predict task performance better than does motivational level. Lawler and Suttle (1973) disagree, however, noting that it is very difficult to accurately measure motivational level. In fact, they suggest that "the theory has become so complex that it has exceeded the measures which exist to test it" (p. 502). In other words, available evidence, while oftentimes modest, suggests that "the heuristic value of the expectancy framework will remain as a powerful force in organizational psychology even though its empirical house is certainly not in order" (Campbell and Pritchard, 1976, p. 92).

Managerial Implications of Expectancy Theory

Given the somewhat complicated structure of expectancy theory, it might be thought that the model had little to say to managers concerned with real organizational problems. This is not the case, however. In fact, expectancy theory provides a rich conceptual framework for managers interested in understanding how motivation and performance can be improved. Included in these managerial implications are the following:

1. *Clarify E→P Expectancies.* Employees' beliefs that effort will lead to performance can be enhanced in several ways, including the use of training programs, coaching, supervisory support, guidance, and participation in job-related decisions. Through such assistance, employees will feel that high levels of performance are actually within reach.

2. *Clarify P→O Expectancies.* One of the most important functions of management is to design reward systems that are based on actual performance. Increasing performance-reward contingencies lets employees know exactly what they can expect in exchange for high levels of performance. Such contingencies add equity to the reward system (See Close-Up 7.4).

3. *Match Rewards to Employee Desires.* Different employees often want different rewards or outcomes from their jobs. While some employees may place a high valence on receiving additional income, others may prefer time off, either for vacation or for receiving additional training for a future promotion. Managers can improve motivational levels by offering a variety of rewards for employees. "Cafeteria" fringe benefit plans have been used successfully by organizations like TRW and the Educational Testing Service.

4. *Recognize Conscious Behavior.* A major tenet of expectancy theory is that individuals often make conscious decisions about their present and future behavior based on the outcomes they expect for the various behaviors. This is not to say that people make conscious decisions before every act. Instead, people periodically evaluate and reevaluate what they are doing and why they are doing it. For example, when a job applicant is confronted with two job offers, the applicant typically weighs the positive and negative aspects of each job to arrive at a decision of which job to accept. Once on the job, employees often reassess the jobs they hold in comparison to alternative options. In short, managers should acknowledge that employees often do not accept the status quo for very long, thus forcing situations and managers to change and adapt over time.

5. *Select People Who Are Equipped for the Job.* The role of employee abilities and traits in performance should not be minimized. All too often, employees are hired, promoted, transferred, or fired based on personality rather than ability.

6. *Clarify Role Expectations.* Sometimes, people are hired into ambiguous jobs and given little guidance about what is expected of them. We hear the comment that "I want to see what he can *make* out of the job." Such attitudes can lead to wasted efforts while employees search for answers. If managers instead spend the necessary time to clarify job objectives (as in management-by-objectives programs), less search behavior and more task-related behavior takes place.

CLOSE-UP 7.4 EXPECTANCY THEORY AND THE TWO-TIER WAGE SYSTEM

Expectancy/valance theory suggests that employees' effort and performance are heavily influenced by the beliefs they hold that their effort will lead to performance and performance will lead to valued rewards. The notion of equity, or what is a fair wage-effort bargain, is an important part of this. What happens when a company converts to a two-tier approach to compensation, in which employees hired after a certain date receive less money for the same job?

The two-tier wage systems have become popular in recent years as a compromise strategy to keep wages down and prevent layoffs in the face of poor economic conditions, protecting more senior employees. A company in need of financial savings goes to its union and says, in effect, that it will keep wages at current levels in exchange for an agreement to pay new hires substantially less. The company and current employees benefit, though subsequent hires clearly do not.

A major retail food chain, Kroger's, uses such a tiered system. In some Kroger's markets the hourly wage for clerks varies from $6.34 to $10.02, according to when the person was hired—even though all these clerks do the same job. As one manager puts it, "This is the only way we've been able to stay alive in an industry where there is strong . . . competition." The manager points out that the system is not a problem for the company. "It's a constant communication thing to show employees that it's in their best interest" to allow lower-paid jobs; otherwise, he contends, there would be no jobs at all.

The argument may be convincing except for the motivational effects such a system has on the newer, lower-paid employees. From an expectancy theory standpoint, the lower-paid employees would probably have the same beliefs, or expectancies, concerning their ability to do the job as the higher-paid people. If they put forth the effort, they will succeed. However, if they do succeed, what happens? They are still paid substantially less than the person standing next to them. Should they be motivated to perform? Probably not. Should they be motivated to stay? Probably not, if they can find another job. The situation is clearly inequitable from the employees' standpoint. In addition, knowing that senior colleagues "sold them out" cannot help new hires' feelings of unfair treatment. Hence, while such tiered compensation systems are probably born of necessity, they clearly do not enhance employee motivation.

Source: "The Double Standard That's Setting Worker Against Worker," *Business Week,* April 8, 1985, pp. 70–71.

7. *Provide Opportunities to Perform.* If employees are placed on impossible jobs or in situations where probability of success is small, they will see little reason to perform. An example of this problem can be seen in the frustration experienced by local branch managers in banks. Although they are held accountable for improving such performance indicators as deposits on account, these indicators are often more a function of the location of the branch than of the manager's effort. An encyclopedia salesperson in a poor neighborhood experiences similar frustration from learning that no one there can afford the product. If we want people to perform, they must be placed in situations where high performance is possible.

The expectancy model of motivation points to several concrete guidelines for managers seeking to increase performance. The majority of these suggestions are not simply ways to manipulate employees. Instead, they often lead to improved situations for employees. In this sense, the implications suggested here represent a strategy for integrating employee needs, desires, and goals with those of the organization.

COMPARISON OF MODELS OF MOTIVATION

Having reviewed three contemporary models of employee motivation, it is useful now to pause and consider how these models compare. There are obvious differences in the various implications each model suggests for management. As noted in earlier discussions, the three models emphasize quite different aspects of persons and work situations as primary motivators.

In addition to differences in application, distinct differences can also be noted in theory. For instance, equity theory suggests that people make motivational decisions almost exclusively by comparing their own situations to others. Expectancy theory, on the other hand, recognizes the importance of peer influence but allows for situations where individuals make decisions irrespective of others. Expectancy theory is more of an individual-oriented theory.

While equity theory and expectancy theory both emphasize the role of future rewards in motivation and behavior, goal-setting theory focuses on the nature of task-goals (and whether they are accepted) and is relatively silent about the role of rewards. Even so, goal-setting theory possibly has clearer applications for managers than the other two models.

Several similarities across the three models should also be recognized. To begin, all three models recognize individual and situational differences, although this recognition is more pronounced in expectancy theory and goal-setting theory. All three models focus on the motivational *process,* the steps leading up to behavior. This is important in order to better understand employee behavior at work. Finally, the models are in agreement in their predictions of human behavior. In fact, it has been argued by Campbell and Pritchard (1976) that equity considerations and goal-setting processes could be subsumed under the more general expectancy theory framework.

Which is the best theory of motivation? This question is basically unanswerable since each theory may at some time be most appropriate, depending upon the situation and the people involved. Rather than attempting to select the one best model, it is probably far more useful to ask what managers can learn from a review of cognitive models of motivation in general. In this we can be much more specific. Several useful lessons can be learned from a review (Steers and Porter, 1987).

Perhaps most important, managers must understand that if they are truly concerned with improving performance and work attitudes, they must take an active role in *managing* motivational processes on the job. Managing motivation represents a conscious attempt by managers to actively participate in creating proper work environments and matching people to jobs. Managers cannot sit back and simply complain about unmotivated workers; motivating employees requires work.

Efforts by managers to improve employee motivation and performance should be preceded by self-examination of their own strengths and weaknesses. Do they really understand their own needs, aspirations, and expectations? Are their self-perceptions consistent with the perceptions others have of them? Failure to understand oneself does not facilitate motivation in others.

The need to recognize and deal with individual differences in the work environment has emerged consistently throughout our discussion of motivational processes. Managers must recognize that employees possess different abilities, expectations, and valences. An awareness of these differences allows managers to utilize more effectively the diversity of talent among subordinates and, within policy limitations, acknowledge good performance with rewards most valued by employees.

It is important for managers to establish clear performance-reward contingencies. Managers need to know their subordinates well enough to recognize good performance when it occurs (and not be unduly influenced by stereotypes or halo effects). Once such performance occurs, rewards should be forthcoming in a way clearly recognized by employees as resulting from performance. This contention argues against compensation systems that fail to recognize individual merit.

Questions of motivation ultimately come to rest on the nature of the job or task that we ask employees to perform. While the issue of job design is reserved for Chapter Fourteen, we can point out here the obvious need to design jobs, when possible, in a way that employees find meaningful and personally satisfying. When this cannot be done, greater management creativity is called for to compensate for less desirable jobs with other rewards.

Managers should give attention to improving the overall quality of the work environment. What effects do group processes, supervisory style, or working conditions have on employee morale and the desire to participate actively in organizational activities?

Efforts can be made to monitor employee attitudes periodically and discover general trends. When attitudes begin to decline, managers are alerted to potential problems that can be solved before they adversely affect employee performance or retention.

Finally, managers can recognize the simple fact that, without employee cooperation and support, a great deal of managerial energy can be wasted. It is important to involve employees as much as possible in decisions and problems affecting their jobs. Employees have a major stake in what happens to an organization and are often willing to contribute beyond what is asked (or allowed) of them. In short, managers can recognize that employees represent a human resource for which they are responsible. A major criterion for evaluating managerial effectiveness is the extent to which managers efficiently make use of these resources.

SUMMARY

We have presented three widely accepted cognitive theories of work motivation. Cognitive and acognitive motivational models were distinguished. Acognitive models assume that it is possible to predict behavior without an understanding of internal thought processes. The cognitive models presented are based on the assumptions that much human behavior is planned and that people often make conscious decisions about their behavior. This is not to say that people always do so, only that much behavior is thought out in advance.

Throughout the discussion of the three cognitive models—equity theory, goal-setting theory, and expectancy/valence theory—managerial implications were stressed. These models should not be seen as abstract or irrelevant for managers. Indeed, each model provides insight to practicing managers about how to structure work situations and reward contingencies so employees and organizations benefit from increased performance. To do this, managers must clearly be interested in the welfare of employees and not simply in pursuing profit in a short-sighted manner. Managers must understand the needs, goals, and abilities of their subordinates and incorporate them into work design. Employees will then be more likely to respond by providing individual service in support of organizational performance. In this way, both benefit.

KEY WORDS

behavioral requirements
E→P expectancy
equity theory
expectancy/valence theory
force field analysis
goal-setting theory

management-by-objectives
P→O expectancy
task-goal attributes
two-tier wage system
valence

FOR DISCUSSION

1. What do Katz and Kahn mean when they argue that every organization must meet three behavioral requirements?
2. Discuss several reasons for employee restriction of output.
3. In Close-Up 7.1 major differences are noted between performance levels among U.S. and Japanese employees. What differences account for this diversity?

4. Contrast cognitive and acognitive theories of employee motivation.
5. What are the basic premises of equity theory? How do these premises differ from goal-setting theory and expectancy/valence theory?
6. Describe the process by which perceptions of equity or inequity result.
7. How can an employee resolve feelings of inequity on the job?
8. Does existing research support equity theory?
9. Describe how the various task-goal attributes influence performance under goal-setting conditions. Which task-goal attributes are most powerful in determining performance?
10. What individual and situational influences serve to moderate the influence of task-goal attributes on performance?
11. According to expectancy theory, what causes motivation? What causes performance?
12. Compare and contrast the various managerial implications of the three theories of motivation.

EXERCISE

MONEY MOTIVATES EMPLOYEE PERFORMANCE: A DEBATE

7.1

Purpose

To consider the role money plays in motivating work behavior and performance and to examine the role of money in the various models of employee motivation.

Instructions

Select two teams of five persons each from the class. The teams should meet for twenty minutes to develop arguments in favor of (Team #1) and opposed to (Team #2) the proposition that money is a prime motivator of performance. During this time, the rest of the class, who will act as judges, will discuss criteria for evaluating the merits of the two presentations.

After twenty minutes of preparation, each team should be given five minutes to present its case, followed by one minute each for rebuttals. The judges then discuss the presentations and vote to determine a winner. To close, the class should discuss the results in terms of a theory of work motivation and in terms of managerial implications.

CASE

PAMELA JONES

7.1

Pamela Jones enjoyed banking. She had taken a battery of personal aptitude and interest tests that suggested that she might like and do well in either banking

or librarianship. Since the job market for librarians was poor, she applied for employment with a large chartered bank, the Bank of Winnipeg, and was quickly accepted.

Her early experiences in banking were almost always challenging and rewarding. She was enrolled in the bank's management development program because of her education (a B.A. in languages and some postgraduate training in business administration), her previous job experience, and her obvious intelligence and drive.

During her first year in the training program, Pamela attended classes on banking procedures and policies, and worked her way through a series of low level positions in her branch. She was repeatedly told by her manager that her work was above average. Similarly, the training officer who worked out of the main office and coordinated the development of junior officers in the program frequently told Pamela that she was "among the best three" of her cohort of twenty trainees.

Although she worked hard and frequently encountered discrimination from senior bank personnel (as well as customers) because of her sex, Pamela developed a deep-seated attachment to banking in general, and to her bank and branch, in particular. She was proud to be a banker and proud to be a member of the Bank of Winnipeg.

After one year in the management development program however, Pamela found she was not learning anything new about banking or the B. of W. She was shuffled from one job to another at her own branch, cycling back over many positions several times to help meet temporary problems caused by absences, overloads, and turnover. Turnover—a rampant problem in banking—amazed Pamela. She couldn't understand, for many months, why so many people started careers "in the service" of banking, only to leave after one or two years.

After her first year, the repeated promises of moving into her own position at another branch started to sound hollow to Pamela. The training officer claimed that there were no openings suitable for her at other branches. On two occasions when openings did occur, the manager of each of the branches in question rejected Pamela, sight unseen, presumably because she hadn't been in banking long enough.

Pamela was not the only unhappy person at her branch. Her immediate supervisor, George Burns, complained that because of the bank's economy drive, vacated customer service positions were left unfilled. As branch accountant, Burns was responsible for day-to-day customer service. As a result, he was unable to perform the duties of his own job. The manager told Burns several times that customer service was critical, but that Burns would have to improve his performance on his own job. Eventually, George Burns left the bank to work for a trust company, earning seventy dollars a month more for work similar to that he had been performing at the B. of W. This left Pamela in the position of having to supervise the same tellers who had trained her only a few months earlier. Pamela was amazed at all the mistakes the tellers made but found it difficult to do much to correct their poor work habits. All disciplinary procedures had to be administered with the approval of Head Office.

After several calls to her training officer, Pamela was finally transferred to

her first "real" position in her own branch. Still keen and dedicated, Pamela was soon to lose her enthusiasm.

At her new branch, Pamela was made "assistant accountant." Her duties included the supervision of the seven tellers, some customer service and a great deal of paper work. The same economy drive that she had witnessed at her training branch resulted in the failure to replace customer service personnel. Pamela was expected to "pick up the slack" at the front desk, neglecting her own work. Her tellers seldom balanced their own cash, so Pamela stayed late almost every night to find their errors. To save on overtime, the manager sent the tellers home while Pamela stayed late, first to correct the teller's imbalances, then to finish her own paper work. He told Pamela that as an officer of the bank, she was expected to stay until the work of her subordinates, and her own work, were satisfactorily completed. Pamela realized that most of her counterparts in other B. of W. branches were willing to give this sort of dedication; therefore, so should she. This situation lasted six months with little sign of change in sight.

One day, Pamela learned from a phone conversation with a friend at another branch that she would be transferred to Hope, B.C. to fill an opening that had arisen. Pamela's husband was a professional, employed by a large corporation in Vancouver. His company did not have an office in Hope; moreover, his training was very specialized, and he could probably find employment only in large cities anyway.

Accepting transfers was expected of junior officers who wanted to get ahead. Pamela inquired at Head Office and learned that the rumor was true. Her training officer told her, however, that Pamela could decline the transfer if she wished, but he couldn't say how soon her next promotion opportunity would come about.

Depressed, annoyed, disappointed and frustrated, Pamela quit the bank.

CASE DISCUSSION QUESTIONS

1. Analyze this case from the point of view of the frustration model presented in Chapter Four, identifying Pamela's most salient work-related needs, goals, and the nature of the "barriers" that caused her frustration.
2. Describe Pamela's behavior in terms of expectancy theory. Why did she eventually elect to leave the bank?
3. Use the operant conditioning approach to explain Pamela's situation. How does your analysis differ from that suggested by expectancy theory?
4. Does equity theory help explain Pamela's behavior? How?
5. What suggestions might you offer the personnel department at the B. of W. on the basis of Pamela's experience? (Be sure to let relevant theories guide your counsel.)

Source: C. C. Pinder, *Work Motivation: Theory, Issues, and Applications* (Glenview, Ill.: Scott, Foresman and Company, 1984), pp. 317–318. Reprinted by permission of Scott, Foresman and Company.

JIM PRESTON

Ever since the Atlas Electrical Supply Co. was bought out by Carey and Co., Jim Preston had been in a sales slump. A leading salesman for Atlas for the past twenty-eight years, Preston made a regular practice of enjoying handsome monthly bonuses in response to the company's incentive pay system. He had always been proud of the extra money, both as a symbol of his value to the company and for the practical uses to which he had applied it. He often boasted about how the bonuses had helped him complete his mortgage several years early as well as finance his daughter's education at the University of Toronto. In the four months since the new management took over, however, Jim's sales had fallen off sharply, along with his enthusiasm and company spirit, even though the bonus system was still being used. In fact, he had not collected a bonus in months. Sarah Powell, Jim's new supervisor since the takeover, was concerned. She held a series of informal discussions with Jim and several other sales personnel to try to get to the bottom of Jim's problems.

Mrs. Powell learned from her meetings that Jim resented being supervised by a woman who was younger than his own daughter—now a college graduate. He blew up at her during one of their meetings, yelling, "All of you new brass are the same—always trying to squeeze more out of the little guy. You think you know everything about selling! I was selling electrical parts and supplies before you or any of the other Carey super-

visors were old enough to know what they are. Now you're telling me how to do my job. Why don't you get off my back? It's my business if I don't earn any bonuses!"

Sarah was startled by Preston's outburst, and concerned by his apparent resentment and hostility toward her. She learned that several of Preston's fellow salesmen, who were mostly younger than him, also resented him because of his resistance to the recent attempt to unionize the office staff. Several of them claimed that he was "a real company man," even though his sales figures didn't reflect it. She also learned that Jim was periodically receiving sales directives from Stan Campbell, Jim's former boss who had been moved laterally at the time of the takeover. Jim claimed he was never told clearly who his new supervisor was, now that the companies had merged.

After attending a luncheon meeting on job redesign, Sarah tried to "motivate" higher sales from Jim by adding to the product lines he carried, giving him a larger district to cover, and letting him move upstairs into a slightly larger office. She hoped that the changes would arouse new energy in Preston who, to her added frustration, seemed increasingly more preoccupied with his imminent retirement to a country town. Finally, Sarah asked Jim if he would like to retire early. He declined the offer, but Sarah recommended to her boss that they give old Jim "the golden handshake." Nothing else had worked.

CASE DISCUSSION QUESTIONS

1. Approach this case using the same questions that appear following the Pamela Jones case. Then, in addition, consider the following:
2. How does the reward system in the Carey Company differ from that of the Bank of Winnipeg, particularly with regard to concerns that might arise from equity theory and expectancy theory?

3. Contrast Jim Preston's salient needs with those of Pamela Jones. How do you explain any differences you find between them?
4. What would you have recommended to Sarah Powell, Jim's boss?

Source: C. C. Pinder, *Work Motivation: Theory, Issues, and Applications* (Glenview, Ill.: Scott, Foresman and Company, 1984). Reprinted by permission of Scott, Foresman and Company.

CHAPTER EIGHT

LEARNING PROCESSES AND BEHAVIOR MODIFICATION

The role of learning in organizations has received quite a lot of attention recently. Why? Managers have come to realize that their understanding of the learning process is helpful in improving employee motivation and performance.

This chapter closely examines learning processes and behavior modification —a popular motivation strategy for closely tying rewards to performance and attendance. Beginning with a definition of learning, the discussion focuses on several basic learning models and major influences on learning. The relationship of reinforcement to motivation and performance is explored next. Lastly, behavior modification techniques used in industry are examined, as well as criticisms leveled against such practices.

IMPORTANCE OF TOPIC FOR MANAGERS

Why are learning processes important to students of management? We know that learning is a prerequisite to most forms of behavior, both on the job and off. Managers, skilled craftspeople—*every* employee—must learn certain skills that are necessary for good job performance. Understanding how learning takes place and how it influences subsequent behavior is extremely useful. Thus, many companies spend considerable sums on training and developing their employees. To the extent that such efforts are based on a sound understanding of the principles of learning, their chances for success are enhanced.

Just as personality and motivation are related, so too are learning and motivation. A knowledge of learning processes is helpful in understanding employee motivation at work. This connection is particularly evident in recent efforts to use behavior modification techniques in organizations. Behavior modification, an application of learning theory, is gaining popularity among managers as a strategy for improving employee performance. Without a thorough understanding of the mechanisms underlying behavior modification, managers run the risk of inappropriately applying the technique to the detriment of performance and organizational effectiveness.

Finally, a major responsibility of managers is to evaluate and reward their subordinates. Such reward practices rest on the principle of reinforcement. If managers are to maximize the impact of available (and often limited) rewards, a thorough knowledge of reinforcement techniques is essential.

BASIC MODELS OF LEARNING

Learning may be defined for our purposes here as a relatively permanent change in behavior that occurs as a result of experience. That is, someone is said to have learned something when he or she consistently exhibits a new behavior over time. Several aspects of this definition are noteworthy (Kimble and Garmezy, 1963).

First, learning involves a change in an attitude or behavior. This change does not necessarily have to be an improvement, however, and can include things like learning bad habits or forming prejudices. In order for learning to occur, the change that takes place must be relatively permanent. So, changes in behavior that result from fatigue or temporary adaptations to a unique situation would not be considered as examples of learning.

Learning typically involves some form of practice or experience. Thus, the change that results from physical maturation, as when a baby develops the physical *strength* to walk, is in itself not considered learning. This practice or experience must be reinforced over time for learning to take place. Where such reinforcement does not follow practice or experience, the behavior would eventually diminish and disappear.

Finally, learning is an inferred process; it is not possible to directly observe learning. Instead, we must infer the existence of learning from observing changes in overt behavior.

Scientific interest in learning dates from the early experiments of Pavlov at the turn of the century. Much of this early work and, indeed, much of the current research results from laboratory experiments using animals. While these techniques may help to enlighten our understanding of the most basic forms of human learning, it is necessary to study more complex learning processes in the field, as we shall see later in this chapter.

To date, three major theories of learning can be identified: (1) classical conditioning; (2) operant conditioning; and (3) cognitive learning theory. The first two models, classical and operant conditioning, both focus on the stimulus-response (S-R) connection as the basic unit of analysis in learning processes, although each suggests alternative explanations about how these bonds are established. The third model, cognitive learning theory, represents a significant departure from the other two models. We will briefly examine each of these models.

Classical Conditioning

Classical conditioning focuses on the process whereby a stimulus-response bond is developed between a conditioned stimulus and a conditioned response through the repeated linking of a conditioned stimulus with an *un*conditioned stimulus. This process is shown in Exhibit 8.1.

The classical example of Pavlov's experiments performed around the turn of the century should serve to explain the process. Pavlov was interested in the question of whether animals could be trained to draw a causal relationship between previously unconnected factors. Specifically, using dogs as subjects, he wished to know whether they could *learn* to associate the ringing of a bell with the act of salivation. The experiment began with unlearned, or *unconditioned,* stimulus-response relationships. When a dog was presented with meat (unconditioned stimulus), the dog salivated (unconditioned response). No learning was necessary here as this relationship represented a natural physiological process.

Next, Pavlov paired the unconditioned stimulus (meat) with a *conditioned* stimulus (the ringing of a bell). The ringing of the bell by itself would not be expected to elicit salivation. However, over time, a learned linkage developed for the dog between the bell and meat, ultimately resulting in an S-R bond between the conditioned stimulus (the bell) and the response (salivation) without the presence of the unconditioned stimulus (the meat). Evidence emerged that learning had occurred and that this learning resulted

EXHIBIT 8.1   CLASSICAL VERSUS OPERANT CONDITIONING

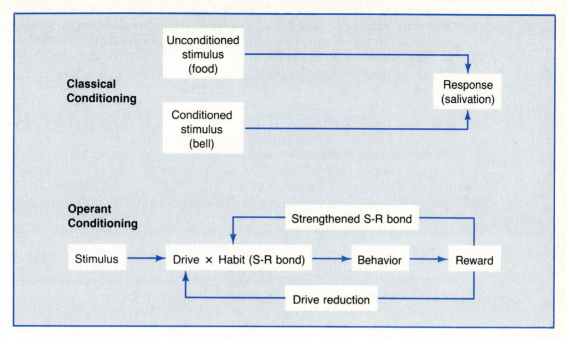

from conditioning the dogs to associate two normally unrelated objects, the bell and the salivation.

Although Pavlov's experiments are widely cited as evidence of the existence of classical conditioning, it is necessary from the perspective of organizational behavior to ask how this process relates to people at work. Ivancevich, Szilagyi, and Wallace (1983, p. 80) provide one such work-related example of classical conditioning:

> An illustration of classical conditioning in a work setting would be an airplane pilot learning how to use a newly installed warning system. In this case the behavior to be learned is to respond to a warning light that indicates that the plane has dropped below a critical altitude on an assigned glide path. The proper response is to increase the plane's altitude. The pilot already knows how to appropriately respond to the trainer's warning to increase altitude (in this case we would say the trainer's warning is an unconditioned stimulus and the corrective action of increasing altitude is an unconditioned response). The training session consists of the trainer warning the pilot to increase altitude every time the warning light goes on. Through repeated pairings of the warning light with the trainer's warning, the pilot eventually learns to adjust the plane's altitude in response to the warning light even though the trainer is not present. Again, the unit of learning is a new S-R connection or habit.

Although classical conditioning clearly has applications to work situations, particularly in the area of training and development, it has been criticized as explaining only a limited part of total human learning. Skinner (1963) argues that classical conditioning focuses on respondent, or reflexive, behaviors; that is, it concentrates on explaining largely involuntary responses that result from stimuli. More complex learning cannot be explained solely by classical conditioning. As an alternative explanation, Skinner and others have proposed the operant conditioning model of learning.

Operant Conditioning

The major focus of operant conditioning is on the effects of reinforcements or rewards on desired behaviors. One of the first psychologists to examine such processes was Watson (1914), a contemporary of Pavlov, who argued that behavior was largely influenced by the rewards one received as a result of actions. This notion is best summarized in Thorndike's (1911) *Law of effect.* This law states that:

> of several responses made to the same situation, those which are accompanied or closely followed by satisfaction [reinforcement] . . . will be more likely to occur; those which are accompanied or closely followed by discomfort [punishment] . . . will be less likely to occur (Thorndike, 1911, p. 244).

In other words, Thorndike's law of effect posits that behavior that leads to positive or pleasurable outcomes tends to be repeated, while behavior that leads to negative outcomes or punishment tends to be avoided. In this manner, individuals learn appropriate, acceptable responses to their environment. For example, by repeatedly docking the pay of an employee who is habitually tardy, we would expect that employee to learn to arrive early enough to receive a full day's pay.

A basic operant model of learning is presented in Exhibit 8.1. There are three important concepts of this model:

- *Drive.* A drive is an internal state of disequilibrium; it is a felt need. It is generally believed that drive increases with the strength of deprivation. A drive or desire to learn must be present for learning to take place.
- *Habit.* A habit is the experienced bond or connection between stimulus and response. For example, if a person learns over time that eating satisfies hunger, a strong stimulus-response (hunger-eating) bond would develop. Habits thus determine the behaviors or courses of action we choose.
- *Reinforcement or reward.* This represents the feedback individuals receive as a result of action.

A stimulus activates an individual's motivation through its impact on drive and habit. The stronger the drive and habit (S-R bond), the stronger the motivation to behave in a certain way. As a result of this behavior, two things happen. First, the individual receives feedback that reduces the original drive. Second, the individual strengthens his or her belief in the veracity of the S-R bond to the extent that it proved successful. That is, if one's response to the stimulus satisfied one's drive or need, the individual would come to believe more strongly in the appropriateness of the particular S-R connection and would respond in the same way under similar circumstances.

An example will clarify this point. Several recent attempts to train chronically unemployed workers have used a daily pay system instead of weekly or monthly systems. The primary reason for this is that the workers, who do not have a history of working, can more quickly see the relationship between coming to work and receiving pay. An S-R bond develops more quickly because of the frequency of the reinforcement or reward.

Operant Versus Classical Conditioning. Operant conditioning can be distinguished from classical conditioning in at least two ways (Luthans, 1977). First, the two approaches differ in what is believed to cause changes in behavior. In classical conditioning, changes in behavior are thought to arise through changes in stimuli, that is, a change from an unconditioned stimulus to a conditioned stimulus. In operant conditioning, on the other hand, changes in behavior are thought to result from the *consequences* of previous behavior. When behavior has been rewarded, we would expect it to be repeated; when behavior has not been rewarded, or has been punished, we would not expect it to be repeated.

Second, the two approaches differ about the role and frequency of rewards. In classical conditioning, the unconditioned stimulus, acting as a sort of reward, is administered during every trial. In contrast, in operant conditioning the reward results only when individuals choose the correct response. That is, in operant conditioning, individuals must correctly operate on their environment before a reward is received. Thus, the response is instrumental in obtaining the desired reward.

Guidelines for Using Operant Conditioning. In the use of operant conditioning to shape employee behavior, several important guidelines should be kept in mind (Hamner and Hamner, 1976). To begin, don't give the same level of reward to all. Failure to respond to behavior has reinforcing consequences: Superiors are bound to shape the behavior of the subordinates by the way in which they utilize the rewards at their disposal. Therefore, managers must be careful that they examine the consequences on performance of their non-actions as well as their actions. Tell a person what behavior gets reinforced. Tell a person what he or she is doing wrong. Don't punish in front of others. Make the consequences equal to the behavior. In other words, don't cheat the worker out of his or her just rewards.

Cognitive Learning Theory

Cognitive theories were discussed in Chapter Seven. It should be noted here, however, that cognitive theorists have long been interested in learning processes. Without rejecting traditional stimulus-response approaches to the study of learning, cognitive theorists like Edward Tolman believe that much learning takes place outside of the S-R bond. That is, learning is viewed as a process that requires an individual's entire personality. As such, the learning process is seen as being far more complex than simple S-R connections.

Cognitive learning theorists believe that much learning results from simply thinking about a problem, from insight, and from piecing together known facts. Thus, "the significant process in learning is the acquisition of information (including abstract concepts and generalizations) rather than of specific responses" (Zimbardo and Ruch, 1979, p. 110). As a result, the cognitive approach to understanding learning processes emphasizes an individual's reasoning and analytical, perceptual, and problem-solving abilities. This approach also places significance on an individual's purposiveness and goal-orientation, assuming that the individual is motivated and desires to learn. It starkly contrasts with the two earlier conditioning models that rely on S-R bonds developed over time.

MAJOR INFLUENCES ON LEARNING

While classical or operant conditioning may be successful for learning simple or repetitive tasks, complex learning of more sophisticated material requires the proper learning environment if it is to be highly successful. An individual's desire to learn, his or her background knowledge of a subject, and the length of the learning period are examples of some of the components of a learning environment. Filley, House, and Kerr (1975) identify five major influences on learning effectiveness.

Drawing largely from cognitive theory, substantial research evidence indicates that learning effectiveness is increased considerably when individuals have high *motivation to learn.* We sometimes encounter students who work day and night to complete a term paper that is of interest to them. Writing of uninteresting term papers, on the other hand, may be postponed until the last possible minute. Maximum transfer of knowledge is achieved when a student or employee is motivated to learn by a high need to know.

Considerable evidence also demonstrates that learning is facilitated by providing individuals with feedback on their performance. *A knowledge of results* serves a gyroscopic function, showing individuals where they are correct or incorrect, furnishing them with the perspective to improve. Feedback also serves as an important positive reinforcer that can enhance an individual's willingness or desire to learn.

In many cases, *prior learning* can increase the ability to learn new materials or tasks by providing needed background or foundation materials. These beneficial effects of prior learning on present learning tend to be greatest when the prior tasks and the present tasks exhibit similar stimulus-response connections. For instance, most of the astronauts selected for the space program have had years of previous experience flying airplanes. It is assumed that their prior experience and developed skill will facilitate learning to fly the highly technical, though somewhat similar, vehicles.

Another influence on learning concerns whether the materials to be learned are presented in their entirety or in parts—*whole versus part learning.* Available evidence (McCormick and Tiffin, 1976) suggests that when a task consists of several distinct and unrelated duties, part learning is more effective. Each task should be learned separately. However, when a task consists of several *integrated* and related parts (like learning the components of a small machine), whole learning is more appropriate because it ensures that major interrelationships between parts, as well as proper sequencing of parts, is not overlooked or underemphasized.

The final major influence on learning highlights the advantages and disadvantages of concentrated as opposed to distributed training sessions. Evidence reviewed in Bass and Vaughn (1966) indicates that *distribution of practice,* or short learning periods at set intervals, are more effective for learning motor skills than for learning verbal or cognitive skills. Distributed practice also seems to facilitate learning of very difficult, voluminous, or tedious material. It should be noted, however, that concentrated practice appears to work well where insight is required for task completion. Apparently, concentrated effort over short durations provides a more synergistic approach to problem solving.

While there is general agreement that these influences are important (and are under the control of management in many cases), they cannot substitute for the lack of an adequate reinforcement system. In fact, reinforcement is widely recognized as the key to effective learning. If managers are concerned with eliciting desired behaviors from their subordinates, a knowledge of reinforcement techniques is essential. It is to this that we now turn.

REINFORCEMENT AND BEHAVIORAL CHANGE

A central feature of both operant learning theory and behavior modification is the concept of reinforcement. This concept dates from Thorndike's law of effect which, as mentioned earlier, states that behavior that is positively reinforced tends to be repeated while behavior that is not reinforced will tend not to be repeated. Hence, *reinforcement* can be defined in terms of anything that causes a certain behavior to be repeated or inhibited.

Reinforcement Versus Motivation

It is important to differentiate reinforcement from the concept of employee motivation. Motivation, as described in an earlier chapter, represents a primary psychological process that is largely cognitive in nature. Thus, motivation is largely internal; it is *experienced* by the employee and we can see only subsequent manifestations of it in actual behavior. Reinforcement, on the other hand, is typically observable and most often externally administered. A supervisor may reinforce what he or she considers desirable behavior without knowing anything about the underlying motives that prompted it. This distinction should be kept in mind when examining behavior modification later in this chapter.

Strategies for Behavioral Change

From a managerial standpoint, several strategies for behavioral change are available to facilitate learning in organizational settings. Rachlin (1970) has identified four basic types: (1) positive reinforcement; (2) avoidance learning or negative reinforcement; (3) extinction; and (4) punishment. Each type plays a different role in both the manner and extent to which learning occurs. Each will be considered separately here.

Positive Reinforcement. Positive reinforcement consists of presenting someone with an attractive outcome following a desired behavior. As noted by Skinner (1953, p. 73), "a positive reinforcer is a stimulus which, when added to a situation, strengthens the probability of an operant response." A simple example of positive reinforcement is when a supervisor praises subordinates when they perform well in a certain situation. For example, a supervisor may praise an employee for being consistently punctual in attendance, as shown in Exhibit 8.2. This behavior-praise pattern may encourage the subordinate to be on time in the future in the hope of receiving additional praise.

In order for a positive reinforcement to be effective in facilitating the repetition of desired behavior, several conditions must be met. First, the reinforcer itself (praise) must be valued by the employee. It would prove ineffective in shaping behavior if employees were indifferent to it. Second, the reinforcer must be strongly tied to the desired behavior. Receipt of the reinforcer by the employee must be directly contingent upon performing the desired behavior. "Rewards must result from performance, and the greater the degree of performance by an employee, the greater should be his reward" (Hamner, 1977, p. 98). It is important to keep in mind here that "desired behavior" represents behavior defined by the supervisor, not the employee. Third, there must be ample occasion for the reinforcer to be administered following desired behavior. If the reinforcer is tied to certain behavior that seldom occurs, such as *very* high performance, then individuals will seldom be reinforced and will probably not associate this behavior with a reward. It is important that the performance-reward contingencies be structured so that they are easily attainable.

Avoidance Learning. A second method of reinforcement is avoidance learning, or negative reinforcement. Avoidance learning is the seeking to avoid an unpleasant condition or outcome by following a desired behavior. Employees learn to avoid unpleasant situations by behaving in certain ways. If an

EXHIBIT 8.2   STRATEGIES FOR BEHAVIORAL CHANGE

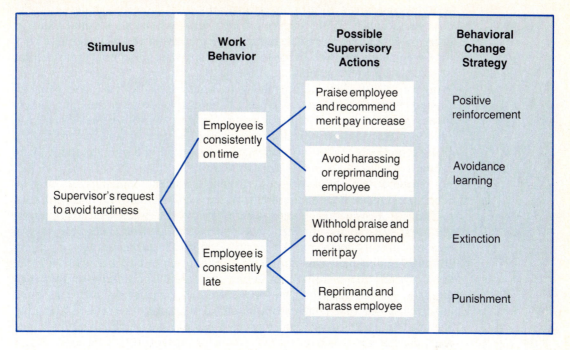

employee correctly performs a task, or is continually prompt in coming to work (see Exhibit 8.2), the supervisor may refrain from harassing, reprimanding, or otherwise embarrassing the employee. Presumably, the employee learns over time that engaging in correct behavior diminishes admonishing from the supervisor. In order to maintain this condition the employee continues to behave as desired.

Extinction. The principle of extinction suggests that undesired behavior will decline as a result of a lack of positive reinforcement. If the perpetually tardy employee in the example in Exhibit 8.2 consistently fails to receive supervisory praise and is not recommended for a pay raise, we would expect this nonreinforcement to lead to an "extinction" of the tardiness. The employee may realize—albeit subtly—that being late is not leading to desired outcomes and may try being on time for work.

Punishment. Finally, a fourth strategy for behavior change used by managers and supervisors is punishment. Punishment is the administration of unpleasant or adverse outcomes as a result of undesired behavior. An example of the application of punishment is for a supervisor to publicly reprimand or harass an employee who is habitually tardy (see Exhibit 8.2). Presumably, the employee would refrain from being tardy in the future in order to avoid such an undesirable outcome. The use of punishment is indeed one of the most controversial issues of behavior modification.

In summary, positive reinforcement and avoidance learning focus on bringing about the *desired* response from the employee. With positive reinforcement the employee behaves in a certain way in order to gain desired rewards, while with avoidance learning the employee behaves in order to avoid certain unpleasant outcomes. In both cases, however, the behavior desired by the supervisor is enhanced. In contrast, extinction and punishment focus on supervisory attempts to reduce the incidence of *undesired* behavior. That is, extinction and punishment are typically used to get someone to stop doing something. It does not necessarily follow that the individual will begin acting in the most desired, or correct, manner.

From a managerial perspective, questions arise about which strategy of behavioral change is most effective. Advocates of behavior modification, such as Skinner, answer that positive reinforcement combined with extinction is the most suitable way to bring about desired behavior. There are several reasons for this focus on the positive approach to reinforcement. First, although punishment can inhibit or eliminate undesired behavior, it often does not provide information to the individual about how or in which direction to change. Also, the application of punishment may cause the individual to become alienated from the work situation, thereby reducing the chances that useful change can be effected. Similarly, avoidance learning tends to emphasize the negative; that is, people are taught to stay clear of certain behaviors, like tardiness, for fear of the repercussions. In contrast, it is felt that combining positive reinforcement with the use of extinction has the least undesirable side effects and allows individuals to receive the rewards they desire. A positive approach to reinforcement is believed by some to be the most effective tool management has to bring about favorable changes in organizations.

Schedules of Reinforcement

Having examined four distinct strategies for behavioral change that can be used to elicit desired behavior, we now turn to an examination of the various ways, or *schedules,* of administering these techniques. As noted by Costello and Zalkind (1963, p. 193), "The speed with which learning takes place and also how lasting its effects will be is determined by the timing of reinforcement." Thus, a knowledge of various schedules of reinforcement is essential to managers if they are to know how to choose rewards that will have maximum impact on employee performance.

Although there are a variety of ways in which rewards can be administered, most approaches can be categorized into two groups: continuous and partial reinforcement schedules. A *continuous* reinforcement schedule rewards desired behavior every time it occurs. For example, a manager could praise (or pay) employees every time they perform properly. With the time and resource constraints most managers work under, this is often difficult, if

EXHIBIT 8.3   SCHEDULES OF PARTIAL REINFORCEMENT

Schedule of Reinforcement	Nature of Reinforcement	Effects on Behavior when Applied	Effects on Behavior when Terminated	Example
Fixed interval	Reward on fixed time basis	Leads to average and irregular performance	Quick extinction of behavior	Weekly paycheck
Fixed ratio	Reward consistently tied to output	Leads quickly to very high and stable performance	Quick extinction of behavior	Piece-rate pay system
Variable interval	Reward given at variable intervals around some average time	Leads to moderately high and stable performance	Slow extinction of behavior	Monthly performance appraisal and reward at random times each month
Variable ratio	Reward given at variable output levels around some average output	Leads to very high performance	Slow extinction of behavior	Sales bonus tied to selling X accounts, but X constantly changes around some mean

not impossible. So, most managerial reward strategies operate on a partial schedule. A *partial* reinforcement schedule rewards desired behavior at specific intervals—not every time desired behavior is exhibited. Compared to continuous schedules, partial reinforcement schedules lead to slower learning but stronger retention. Thus, learning is generally more permanent. Four kinds of partial reinforcement schedules can be identified: (1) fixed interval; (2) fixed ratio; (3) variable interval; and (4) variable ratio (see Exhibit 8.3).

Fixed Interval Schedule. A fixed interval reinforcement schedule rewards individuals at prespecified intervals for their performance. If employees perform even minimally, they are paid. This technique generally does not result in high or sustained levels of performance, since employees know that marginal performance usually leads to the same level of rewards as high performance. Thus, there is little incentive for high effort and performance. Also, when rewards are withheld or suspended, extinction of desired behavior occurs quickly. Many of the recent job redesign efforts in organizations were prompted by recognition of the need for alternate strategies of motivation rather than pay on fixed interval schedules.

Fixed Ratio Schedule. The second fixed schedule is the fixed ratio schedule. Here the reward is administered only upon the completion of a given number of desired responses. In other words, rewards are tied to performance in a ratio of rewards to results. For every so many results, employees receive a reward. A common example of the fixed ratio schedule is a piece-rate pay system, where employees are paid for each unit of output they produce. Under this system, performance rapidly reaches high levels. In fact, according to Hamner (1977, p. 105), "the response level here is significantly higher than that obtained under any of the interval (or time-based) schedules." On the negative side, however, performance declines sharply upon the cessation of the receipt of the reward, as with fixed interval schedules.

Variable Interval Schedule. Using variable reinforcement schedules, both variable interval and variable ratio reinforcement are administered at random times that cannot be predicted by the employee. The employee is generally not aware of when the next evaluation and reward period will be. Under a variable interval schedule, rewards are administered at intervals of time that are based on an average. For example, an employee may know that *on the average* his or her performance is evaluated and rewarded about once a month, but he or she does not know when this event will occur. He or she does know, however, that it will occur sometime during the interval of a month. Under this schedule, effort and performance will generally be high and fairly stable over time because employees never know when the evaluation will take place.

Variable Ratio Schedule. Finally, a variable ratio schedule is one in which rewards are administered only after an employee has performed the desired behavior a number of times, with the number changing from the administration of one reward to the next but averaging over time to a certain *ratio* of number of performances to rewards. For example, a manager may determine that a salesperson will receive a bonus for every fifteen new accounts sold. However, instead of administering the bonus every fifteenth sale (as in a fixed interval schedule), the manager may vary the number of sales that is necessary for the bonus, from perhaps ten sales for the first bonus to twenty for the second. On the average, however, the 15:1 ratio prevails. As with the variable interval, the variable ratio schedule typically leads to high and stable performance. Moreover, extinction of desired behavior is slow.

Which of these four schedules of reinforcement is superior? In a review of several studies comparing the various techniques, Hamner (1977, p. 105) concluded:

> The necessity for arranging appropriate reinforcement contingencies is dramatically illustrated by several studies in which rewards were shifted from a response-contingent (ratio) to a time-contingent basis (interval). During the period in which rewards were made conditional upon occurrence of the desired behavior, the appropriate response patterns were exhibited at a consistently high level. When the same rewards were given based on time and independent of the worker's behavior, there was a marked drop in the desired behavior. The reinstatements of the performance-contingent reward schedule promptly restored the high level of responsiveness.

In other words, the performance-contingent (or ratio) reward schedules generally lead to better performance than the time-contingent (or interval) schedules, regardless of whether such schedules are fixed or variable. We will return to this point in a subsequent chapter on performance appraisal and reward systems.

BEHAVIOR MODIFICATION IN ORGANIZATIONS

The application of learning theory and reinforcement principles to organizational situations is seen in *behavior modification* programs. Behavior modification is the use of operant conditioning principles to shape human behavior to conform to desired standards defined by superiors.

In recent years, behavior modification has been applied in a wide variety of organizations. In most cases, positive results are claimed. For example, at Emery Air Freight, the implementation of behavior modification purportedly led to a cut in operating costs of $2 million during its first three years of operation. The 3M Company estimated that the technique saved them $3.5 million in one year alone. In the accounting department of Collins Foods International, behavior modification led to a reduction in the error rate in accounts payable from 8 percent to 0.2 percent *(Business Week,* 1978). Examples such as these stimulate interest in the technique as a management tool to improve performance and reduce costs.

Because of its emphasis on shaping behavior, it is more appropriate to think of behavior modification as a *technique* for motivating employees, rather than as a *theory* of work motivation. It does not attempt to provide a comprehensive model of the various personal and job-related variables that contribute to motivation. Instead, its managerial thrust is *how* to motivate and it is probably this emphasis that has led to its current popularity among managers. Even so, we should be cautioned against the unquestioned acceptance of any technique until we understand the assumptions underlying the model. If the underlying assumptions of a model appear to be uncertain or inappropriate in a particular situation or organization, its use is clearly questionable.

Assumptions of Behavior Modification

The foundation of behavior modification as a theory of management rests on three ideas (Skinner, 1971). First, advocates of behavior modification believe that individuals are basically passive and reactive (instead of proactive). They respond to stimuli in their environment rather than assuming personal responsibility in initiating behavior. This assertion is in direct contrast to cognitive theories of motivation (such as expectancy theory) that hold that individuals make conscious decisions about their present and future behaviors and take an active role in shaping their environment.

Second, advocates of behavior modification focus on behavior itself—on observable and measurable behaviors, instead of nonobservable needs, attitudes, goals, or motivational levels. In contrast, cognitive theories focus on both observable and unobservable factors as they relate to motivation.

Third, behavior modification stresses that permanent changes can be brought about only as a result of reinforcement. Behaviors that are positively reinforced will be repeated (learned) while behaviors not so reinforced will diminish (law of effect).

Designing a Behavior Modification Program

If behavior modification techniques are to work, their application must be well thought out and systematically applied. Systematic attempts to implement these programs typically go through five phases (see Exhibit 8.4).

First, management attempts to define and clearly specify the behavioral aspects of acceptable performance. Management must be able to clearly designate what constitutes acceptable behavior, and this specification must be in objective, measurable terms. Examples of *behavioral criteria* are good attendance, promptness in arriving for work, and completing tasks on schedule. Sometimes it is difficult to determine suitable objective indicators of successful performance. For instance, as a training director of a major airline asks, "How do you quantify what a flight attendant does?"

Second, once behavioral criteria have been specified, a *performance audit* can be done. Because management is concerned about the extent to which employees are successfully meeting behavioral criteria, the audit is aimed at pinpointing trouble spots where desired behaviors are not being carried out. For instance, a review of attendance records of various departments may reveal a department where absenteeism is unusually high. Action can then be taken to focus on the problem area.

Third, *specific behavioral goals* must be set for each employee. As noted by Hamner and Hamner (1976), failure to specify concrete behavioral goals is a primary reason for the failure of many behavioral modification programs. Examples of goals are to decrease absenteeism and meet production schedules. The goals should be both reasonably achievable by the employees and acceptable to them (Meyer, Kay, and French, 1965).

Fourth, employees are asked to *keep a record* of their own work. This record provides them with continuous feedback concerning the extent to which they are on target in meeting their goals.

Fifth, supervisors examine the employees' records, as well as other available performance indicators, and *praise* the positive aspects of their work performance. Such praise is designed to strengthen desired performance by the employee (positive reinforcement). The withholding of praise for less than adequate performance, below established goals, supposedly causes employees to change inappropriate behavior (extinction). It is this fifth step in the

EXHIBIT 8.4   STEPS IN IMPLEMENTING A BEHAVIOR MODIFICATION PROGRAM

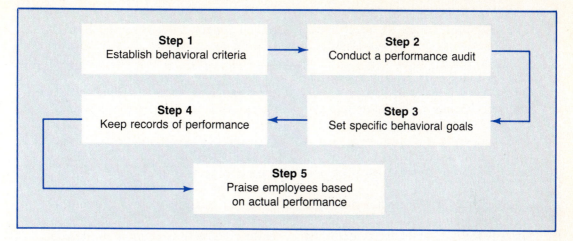

program (the use of praise and the absence of punishment) that advocates of behavior modification suggest differentiates it from other motivational strategies.

Examples of Behavior Modification in Organizations

While many of the principles of operant conditioning and behavior modification have been used by organizations for years, systematic attempts to apply behavior modification programs were rare prior to the last decade. In fact, as late as 1973, one researcher concluded: "There is little objective evidence available [that behavior modification works], and what evidence there is abounds in caveats—the technique will work under the proper circumstances, the parameters of which are usually not easily apparent" (Organizational Dynamics, Winter 1973, p. 49).

The earliest experiments in behavior modification, most notably Emery Air Freight (as shown in Close-Up 8.1), were hailed by some as a clear demonstration of the usefulness of these techniques for motivating employee behavior and facilitating organizational effectiveness. Concern soon arose, however, over the long-term effects of the techniques. As a result of this concern, Hamner and Hamner (1976) surveyed companies that had used positive reinforcement and behavior modification to determine the effects that resulted from the program. Some of these results are summarized in Exhibit 8.5 (pages 232–233).

The exhibit communicates several interesting points. First, it should be noted that most behavior modification programs have been carried out among blue-collar workers, possibly because the tasks performed by these employees are usually somewhat routine and lend themselves to goal-setting techniques. Second, most of the goals set by the organizations deal with improving

CLOSE-UP 8.1 THE CASE OF EMERY AIR FREIGHT

The program. Perhaps the most widely known example of the application of behavior modification in industry is that of Emery Air Freight. Under the direction of Edward J. Feeney, Emery selected behavior modification as a simple answer to the persistent problems of inefficiency and low productivity. In an air freight firm, rapid processing of parcels is important to corporate profitability.

Emery Air Freight began with a performance audit, which attempted to identify the kind of job behaviors which had the greatest impact on profit and the extent to which these behaviors were shown in the company. One area of special concern was the use of containers. Emery loses money if shipping containers are not fully loaded when shipped. Hence, one goal was to ensure that empty container space was minimized. Before the program was implemented, workers reported that they believed they were filling the containers about 90 percent of the time. However, the performance audit revealed that this was really so only about 45 percent of the time. In other words, over half of the containers were shipped unfilled.

The results. Through the use of feedback (in the form of self-report checklists provided to each worker) and positive reinforcement (praise), the percentage of full containers rose swiftly from 45 percent to 95 percent. Cost reductions for the first year alone exceeded $500,000, and rose to $2 million during the first three years. In other words, when workers were given consistent feedback and kept informed of their performance, output increased rapidly. As a result of this initial success, similar programs were initiated at Emery, including the setting of performance standards for handling customer problems on the telephone and for accurately estimating the container sizes needed for shipment of lightweight packages. Again, positive results were claimed.

The aftermath. While the use of praise as a reinforcer proved initially to be a successful and inexpensive reinforcer, its effects diminished over time as it became repetitious. As a result, Emery had to seek other reinforcers. These included invitations to business luncheons, formal recognition such as a public letter or a letter home, being given a more enjoyable task after completing a less desirable one, delegating responsibility and decision making, and allowing special time off from the job. Hence, the use of praise alone does not appear to have sustained effects and managers had to continually turn to new reinforcers to keep the program in operation.

Source: W. C. Hamner and E. P. Hamner, "Behavior Modification on the Bottom Line," *Organizational Dynamics 4* (4) (1976): 8–21.

performance and attendance. Third, feedback provided on goal-directed effort is typically given either on a daily or weekly basis; thus, employees receive a good deal of immediate feedback on performance. It appears that the frequency of feedback declines as higher-level employees become involved in the program. Fourth, the most typical reinforcers used are praise, recognition, and positive feedback. Monetary reinforcers were used in only two of the ten programs surveyed. Finally, the results of the programs were consistently described as successful (from the company's standpoint). Typical results included cost savings, increased production, and increased attendance. In only one of the ten cases was the program discontinued because of lack of success. In other words, this survey by Hamner and Hamner (1976) suggests that behavior modification techniques can be successfully used in organizational settings and can lead to specific desired outcomes at little cost to the organization.

Much of the success of these programs can be attributed to a combination of goal-setting, accurate and timely feedback, and adequate rewards for task accomplishment. As the general manager of Michigan Bell–Operator Services observed (quoted in Hamner and Organ, 1978, p. 253):

> We have found through experience that when standards and feedback are not provided, workers generally feel their performance is at about the 95 percent level. When the performance is then compared with clearly defined standards, it is usually found to meet only the 50th percentile in performance. It has been our experience, over the past ten years, that when standards are set and feedback provided in a positive manner, performance will reach very high levels—perhaps in the upper 90th percentile in a very short period of time. . . . We have also found that when positive reinforcement is discontinued, performance returns to levels that existed prior to the establishment of feedback.

Advocates of behavior modification can point to a series of successful applications of the technique. This success has emerged using objective indicators like attendance and increased output that clearly relate to organizational effectiveness. Even so, behavior modification has been criticized on several grounds.

Criticisms of Behavior Modification

At least five criticisms have been leveled against behavior modification in work situations. None of these criticisms is clear-cut; for each point there is a counterpoint in the continuing controversy over reinforcement techniques. We shall examine each criticism as well as a possible response to each.

Behavior modification ignores individual differences. A consistent complaint against the use of operant techniques in work situations is that they ignore the fact that people are different and have differing needs, desires, values, abilities, and so forth (Locke, 1977). For instance, when we set up a positive reinforcement system that gives praise for desired behaviors, we assume that all individuals value praise and that all individuals have the requisite skills and abilities to carry out the desired behaviors. Often, this is not the case.

This problem of individual differences is recognized by advocates of behavior modification. For instance, Hamner and Organ (1978, p. 61) note,

EXHIBIT 8.5   RESULTS OF POSITIVE REINFORCEMENT AND SIMILAR BEHAVIOR MODIFICATION PROGRAMS IN ORGANIZATIONS

Organization Surveyed	Type of Employees	Specific Goals	Frequency of Feedback	Reinforcers Used	Results
Michigan Bell Operator Services	Employees at all levels in operator services	(a) Decrease turnover and absenteeism (b) Increase productivity (c) Improve union-management relations	(a) Lower level— weekly and daily (b) Higher level— monthly and quarterly	(a) Praise and recognition (b) Opportunity to see oneself become better	(a) Attendance performance has improved by 50% (b) Productivity and efficiency have continued to be above standard in areas where positive reinforcement (PR) is used
City of Detroit Garbage Collectors	Garbage collectors	(a) Reduction in paid man-hour per ton (b) Reduction on overtime (c) 90% of routes completed by standard (d) Effectiveness (quality)	Daily and quarterly based on formula negotiated by city and sanitation union	Bonus (profit sharing) and praise	(a) Citizen complaints declined significantly (b) City saved $1,654,000 first year after bonus paid (c) Worker bonus = $307,000 first year or $350 annually per man (d) Union somewhat dissatisfied with productivity measure and is pushing for more bonus to employee

Organization Surveyed	Type of Employees	Specific Goals	Frequency of Feedback	Reinforcers Used	Results
B. F. Goodrich Chemical Co.	Manufacturing employees at all levels	(a) Better meeting of schedules (b) Increase productivity	Weekly	Praise and recognition; freedom to choose one's own activity	Production has increased over 300%
ACDC Electronics Division of Emerson Electronics	All levels	(a) 96% attendance (b) 90% engineering specifications met (c) Daily production objectives met 95% of time (d) Cost reduced by 10%	Daily and weekly feedback from foreman to company president	Positive feedback	(a) Profit up 25% over forecast (b) $550,000 cost reduction to $10 M sales (c) Return of 1900% on investment including consultant fees (d) Turnaround time on repairs went from 30 to 10 days (e) Attendance is now 98.2% (from 93.5%)

Source: Reprinted, by permission of the publisher, from "Behavior Modification on the Bottom Line," by W. C. Hamner and E. P. Hamner, *Organizational Dynamics 4* (4) (1976), pp. 12–14, © 1976 American Management Association, New York. All rights reserved.

233

"What is reinforcing to one person may not be reinforcing to another person because of the latter's past history of satiation, deprivation, and conditioning operations." Even so, it is suggested that managers can account for these differences in at least two ways in their application of operant techniques. First, managers can attempt to select and hire employees who value the rewards offered by the organization. Efforts can be made to match employee values (insofar as rewards are concerned) with organizational values. To the extent that this approach is successful, it might lead to the hiring of employees with high needs for achievement, since these employees typically desire frequent feedback on performance. However, attempts by managers to adequately screen applicants for appropriate values is no easy task. Also, this solution does nothing for the majority of employees—those already employed.

The second technique managers may use to attempt to overcome the problem of individual differences is to allow greater employee participation in the determination of rewards. Thus, if the present rewards or performance-reward contingencies are ineffective, employee advice may be sought about ways to improve the situation. This solution gives employees a greater voice in the design of their work environment and, as Vroom (1960) has noted, such actions should lead to greater employee ego involvement in seeing that the solution arrived at is successful. However, the success of such an apporach assumes that managers have a genuine concern for the welfare of the employees. If behavior modification is used simply to exploit employees, employees will find suitable ways to nullify the impact of the technique on performance results.

Behavior modification ignores prevailing work-group norms. It is often the case in work situations that employees feel that management has consistently tried to exploit them. Where these feelings exist, group norms often emerge that aim to control the degree of employee cooperation with management. This control typically takes the form of employee restriction of output. Where this situation prevails, the implementation of a behavior modification program (particularly one that relies on praise for increased performance) is likely to be met with stiff resistance from the work group. Group members feel there is little reason to cooperate with management since outcomes may have detrimental effects like an increase in output without a corresponding raise in pay.

The power of work-group norms to reduce the effectiveness of reward systems is possible in all types of reward systems, not just behavior modification. Even so, these influences should not be overlooked by managers contemplating implementing such techniques. Where an organization has a history of distrust between managers and employees, behavior modification is not likely to improve performance. It is first necessary to develop a suitable work climate and improve the degree of perceived organizational concern and dependability. Once that is accomplished and the employees do not feel they are being exploited, operant techniques stand a better chance of success.

Behavior modification ignores the fact that employees can be intrinsically motivated. As a strategy of employee motivation, behavior modification relies on the use of *extrinsic* (that is, externally administered) rewards, such as praise, positive feedback, and money. Opponents of this technique point out that, in many cases, the nature of the job itself may represent an *intrinsic* source of motivation, often making operant techniques unnecessary. It is argued that behavior modification relies too heavily on satisfying lower-order needs while ignoring higher-order needs (see Chapter Six). Instead, opponents such as Deci (1972) suggest deemphasizing contingent reward systems like the piece-rate system and substituting noncontingent systems such as salaries. Such noncontingent systems will provide sufficient income to employees for their lower-order needs to be met. Then, managers can concentrate on redesigning jobs to be intrinsically motivating and appeal more to employees' higher-order needs.

This criticism of behavior modification may be misdirected since proponents of the technique are supportive of job redesign efforts (Skinner, 1969). As Skinner (p. 18) notes:

> It has often been pointed out that the attitude of the production-line worker toward his work differs conspicuously from that of the craftsman, who is envied by workers and industrial managers alike. One explanation is that the craftsman is reinforced by more than monetary consequences, but another important difference is that when a craftsman spends a week completing a given set object, each of the parts produced during the week is likely to be automatically reinforcing because of its place in the completed object.

So, there appears to be no disagreement over the advantages of enriched jobs, although there is some disagreement over why such jobs motivate as they do. Whereas Deci (1972) argues that enriched jobs motivate because of their intrinsic appeal to higher-order needs, Skinner suggests that they motivate because they offer a wide array of positive reinforcers.

Thus, while advocates of behavior modification and operant techniques may focus their attention on extrinsic reward systems and not as fully discuss intrinsic reward systems, it does not follow that they reject them. They do, however, reject the use of noncontingent reward systems where pay is not linked to performance. In this sense, they are in agreement with most theories of work motivation.

Behavior modification assumes incorrectly that all behaviors must be externally reinforced in order to be learned. Advocates of operant techniques assume that most behavior can be controlled by reinforcements given to individuals. This assumption ignores the fact that people can learn new responses by observing other people getting reinforced for the same response. This process is called *vicarious reinforcement* (Kanfer, 1965). In addition, people often learn something by imitating others who are *not* reinforced for their behavior; this is called *vicarious learning* (Marlatt, 1970). Finally, some people learn to behave in certain ways through *self-reinforcement;* that is, they evaluate their own behavior and decide to change some aspect of it without external interference (Kanfer and Karoly, 1972). Given the existence of such practices, it would seem that behavior modification and operant techniques have a limited range of application.

In cases where junior managers observe and imitate the behavior of their senior counterparts, learning can easily take place without the need for overt reinforcements from the organization. In fact, a major organizational benefit of the use of managerial assistants (for example, Assistant to the Controller) is that they learn by imitation to perform desired behaviors. Assuming that lower-level employees wish to rise through the ranks of an organization, it is only natural that they want to prepare for this, and a major part of their preparation is imitating those who rank above them.

Behavior modification is not a new technique for motivating employees. Finally, several people have pointed out that the techniques advocated by behavior modification are not new. In discussing Feeney's widely-cited behavior modification effort at Emery Air Freight, Locke (1977, p. 549) notes:

> There is little difference between Feeney's ideas and some key elements of Scientific Management presented more than 60 years ago by Taylor. Taylor's central concept, the task, which consisted of an assigned work goal (with the work methods also specified), is virtually identical in meaning to Feeney's concept of a "performance standard," a term which also was used by advocates of Scientific Management. Similarly, Taylor argued that work should be measured continually and the results fed back to employees so that they could correct errors and improve or maintain their quality of output. . . . Two additional concepts occasionally used by Feeney are praise and participation. Both are taken directly from the Human Relations school of management.

Locke (1977) goes on to argue that many so-called successful applications of behavior modification may not be attributed to the use of operant techniques but instead may have resulted simply through job redefinition. For example, in the Emery Air Freight experiment, it was claimed that behavior modification caused performance to leap from thirty percent of standard to ninety-five percent in a single day in the customer service offices. In the container departments, container use jumped from forty-five percent to ninety-five percent in a single day. As Locke (1977, p. 548) points out, "Since genuine conditioning is asserted to be a gradual process, the very speed of these improvements mitigates against a conditioning explanation of the results. More likely what occurred was a conscious *redefinition of the job* resulting from the new standards and the more accurate feedback regarding performance in relation to those standards."

Perhaps the most serious criticism of behavior modification is that it is simply a return to closer supervision, tighter job specifications, and more frequent evaluation and feedback on performance. This is not to say that the technique is inappropriate, only that such techniques have been around since the emergence of scientific management. Recent studies clearly show that behavior modification does improve performance. Whether credit for this goes to Skinner's theory and techniques or simply to closer supervision and increased task specification will be debated for some time. The techniques have generally proven successful in improving performance and attendance, if not job attitudes.

SUMMARY

In this chapter, learning processes were shown to be an important facet of employee behavior. Basic models of learning were introduced and compared. Following this, several influences on learning were examined.

Next, the concept of reinforcement was discussed at length, including consideration of various types of reinforcement and schedules of reinforcement. Behavior modification was reviewed as it relates to work organizations, and examples of behavior modification programs and their basic design were given. Also included was a review of several major criticisms of behavior modification with rebuttals by advocates of the technique.

KEY WORDS

avoidance learning
behavioral criteria
behavior modification
classical conditioning
cognitive learning theory
drive
extinction
fixed interval schedule
fixed ratio schedule
habit
law of effect

learning
operant conditioning
performance audit
punishment
reinforcement
self-reinforcement
variable interval schedule
variable ratio schedule
vicarious learning
vicarious reinforcement

FOR DISCUSSION

1. Explain what is meant by learning.
2. Compare and contrast classical conditioning and operant conditioning. Compare both of these to cognitive learning theory.
3. According to Hamner and Hamner, what are some of the rules for using operant conditioning?
4. Discuss several major influences on learning.
5. What is the difference between reinforcement and motivation?
6. Identify the various types of reinforcement.
7. What are some schedules of reinforcement? Which ones are more effective in motivating performance?
8. Describe the various assumptions underlying behavior modification. Do you agree with these assumptions? Why or why not?
9. Review the design of a typical behavior modification program.
10. Discuss several criticisms that have been advanced against behavior modification.

THE DISTRICT TRAFFIC MANAGER'S PROBLEM

Purpose

To consider how various approaches to employee motivation apply to specific work-related problems.

Instructions

Before starting this exercise, students should have a solid understanding of the various theories of motivation, including need theory, equity theory, goal-setting theory, expectancy theory, and behavior modification.

Divide into groups of five or six students and diagnose the problem below in terms of the five motivation models identified above. Specifically, what is causing the problem according to *each* of the theories? Second, what solution to the problem emerges from each of the motivation theories? That is, what are the implications for management for each model?

Following the group analysis, share the group results as a class. Pay particular attention to which motivation theory or theories provide(s) the most insight into the problem and which theory or theories has (have) the best recommendations for management.

The Problem*

You are consultants to the district traffic manager of a telephone company. The traffic department is responsible for information service, long distance calls, and certain customer inquiries. Most of your employees are operators, both directory assistance (information) and long distance. About eighty-five percent are women, and most are in their late teens and early twenties.

Tardiness and absenteeism have been big problems in this district. As a result, the traffic manager has had to schedule twenty percent more operators than she needs for each shift in order to have fully staffed boards. The personnel costs of this overstaffing are not acceptable. Remedial action must be taken. If each operator would just arrive for work each day at the appointed time, personnel costs would drop back to their budgeted level.

*Source: Case example adapted from D. T. Hall, D. D. Bowen, R. J. Lewicki, and F. S. Hall, *Experiences in Management and Organizational Behavior,* 2nd ed. (New York: Wiley, 1982), p. 82. Copyright © 1982 by John Wiley & Sons, Inc. Reprinted by permission of John Wiley & Sons, Inc.

BEHAVIOR MODIFICATION IN AN INDUSTRIAL PLANT

Because of the newness of O.B. Mod [organizational behavior modification], only a few empirically based research studies have been conducted to date. This case reports one of them. It represents a viable approach to building a

meaningful body of knowledge about O. B. Mod. The firm in this study is a medium-sized industrial plant engaged in light manufacturing. Two groups of nine first-line supervisors from the production division participated in the study. One of the groups went through a training program and served as the experimental group. The other group, which was matched with the experimental group on the basis of age, education, experience as foremen, and mental test score, did not undergo any training and served as the control group. Spans of control for the supervisors ranged from ten to thirty. All have worked their way up from operative positions in the plant. For the most part, each had gained his managerial knowledge from the "school of hard knocks" rather than from formal education or supervisory training.

Behavior Contingency Management Training

O. B. Mod was applied by training the first-line supervisors how to use BCM [behavior control management]. The training sessions were held in the plant's training room for ten ninety-minute sessions spread over ten consecutive weeks. A process rather than content training approach was used. This approach replaced the traditional lecture format, where the trainer has a dominant role, with a relatively free give-and-take discussion format, where the trainees themselves dominate.

In general, the content of the sessions was preplanned and sequenced, but not rigidly structured during the session itself. Some of the assumptions made by the trainers included: it is easier to change the trainees' behavior first and overall style later than the reverse; appropriate trainee responses must be reinforced immediately and frequently; complex trainee behaviors must be grad-

ually shaped; and allowances must be made for individual differences in learning speed.

The process approach resulted in an informal and relaxed learning environment. Importantly, the trainers served as models of what they were teaching by first cueing and then contingently reinforcing appropriate trainee behavior. Among the reinforced trainee behaviors were attendance, contributions to discussion, and data presentation and analysis. In effect, the BCM approach was taught to the trainees through the use of BCM.

The steps of BCM as taught to the trainees were as follows:

1. *Identifying target behavior.* The focus was on objective behavior rather than on internal states. Initial reliance upon internal explanations such as "Joe has a bad attitude" was eventually replaced in the training sessions and on the job by an attention to observable behavior. Identification of *performance-related* behavior was stressed. The trainees in the study identified behavior such as work-assignment completions, absences, rejects, quality-control problems, complaints, excessive breaks, leaving the work area, and scrap rates.
2. *Measuring the frequency of behavior.* After learning the measuring techniques, the trainees charted real behavioral data on the job and discussed it during the training sessions. The resulting frequency charts provided both training session data and feedback for the trainees on their progress with implementing the BCM approach.
3. *Functionally analyzing behavior.* The trainees were taught to identify the three elements in the behavior con-

tingency (antecedent→behavior→ consequence). By analyzing antecedents and especially contingent consequences, the supervisors began to see for themselves how target behavior could be predicted and controlled. Emphasis was placed on managing contingent consequences to change on-the-job behavior.

4. *Developing intervention strategies.* Strengthening desirable performance behavior and weakening undesirable behavior was the goal of the intervention. Shaping, modeling, and reinforcement were discussed in terms of strengthening behavior. Extinction, reinforcement of incompatible behavior, and, in exceptional cases, punishment were examined as strategies for reducing the frequency of unproductive or counterproductive behavior. Because of the difficulty of identifying reinforcers ahead of time, methods of selecting and establishing effective reinforcers were given a great deal of attention. Potential reinforcers that were proposed and used included attention, work scheduling, positive feedback on performance, approval, recognition, praise, responsibility, and contingent assignment to favorite tasks.

5. *Evaluating results.* The supervisors continually monitored their interventions through measurement to see whether the intended effects were in fact taking place. The goal of the evaluations was to determine if performance improvement was occurring.

Importantly, emphasis throughout the entire ten-week training program was on getting the supervisors to identify and solve behavioral problems on their own. As much as possible, the trainers resisted offering any direct prescriptions. Oc-

casionally in the sessions a problem would be brought up by trainees and solutions suggested by the trainers, but mainly the trainees became problem-solving behavior contingency managers.

Results were measured on two levels to evaluate the overall effectiveness of the BCM training program. First, individual and group performance of the trainees' workers was analyzed to determine the trainees' ability to put the BCM approach into actual practice. Second, since performance improvement is the ultimate test, a comparison was made between the experimental and control groups in terms of the overall, "bottom-line" performance to determine if the training had a significant impact on improving the performance of the experimental group's respective departments. These results are discussed below.

Changes in Specific On-the-Job Behavior

Frequency of response was the dependent variable and the intervention strategy was the independent variable in measuring on-the-job behavioral changes. The supervisors/trainees measured the frequency of a target behavior of an individual subordinate or a group of subordinates during a baseline period and subsequently during the intervention period. Thus, the data for the behavioral change analysis were contained on response frequency charts. Four representative illustrations of these behavioral change problems are discussed in the following sections. They involve both individual and group problems and different types of intervention strategies.

The Disruptive Complainer.
A particularly disruptive female machine operator was selected as a target for BCM by one supervisor/trainee in the program. She often complained bitterly about the

EXHIBIT 1　　FREQUENCY OF COMPLAINTS

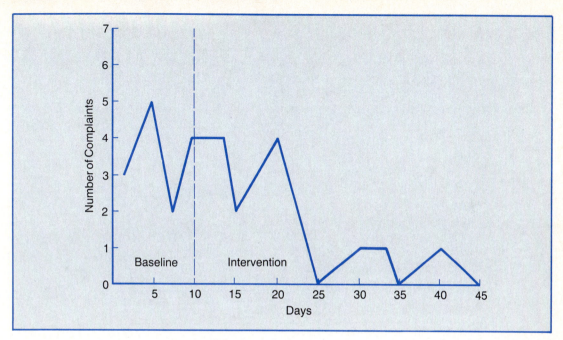

production standards to the supervisor. In addition, she seemed to adversely affect the productivity of her co-workers by talking to them about their rates and production sheets. According to her, everyone else in the plant had an easier job. Close review of her case revealed that her complaints were unfounded.

After identifying the complaining behavior, the supervisor gathered baseline data on this behavior during a ten-day period. No new contingencies were introduced during this "before" baseline measure. In conducting a functional analysis of the target response during the baseline period, the supervisor determined that he was probably serving as a reinforcing consequence by paying attention to the complaints.

Armed with the baseline data and information gathered in the functional analysis, the supervisor decided to use a combination extinction/positive reinforcement intervention strategy. Extinction took the form of his withholding attention when she complained. Satisfactory production and constructive suggestions were socially reinforced by praise in an effort to strengthen the compatible behavior. In addition, her constructive suggestions were implemented whenever possible.

The supervisor's chart, shown in Exhibit 1, illustrates that the combination intervention strategy did in fact have the desired effect. The complaining behavior decreased in frequency. The chart shows that a time-sampling technique was used. Rather than carrying out time-consuming measures every day, the target response was charted on randomly selected days (the 1st, 5th, 7th, 10th, 13th, etc.). Implementing constructive suggestions turned out to be

EXHIBIT 2   GROUP SCRAP RATE

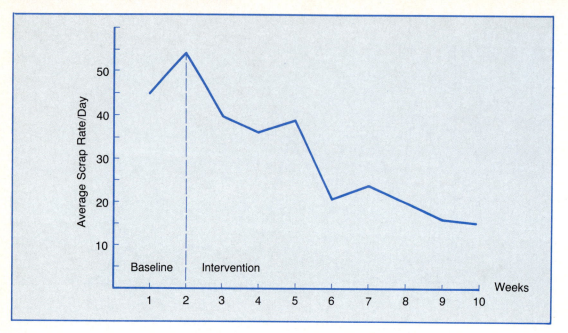

especially reinforcing in this case. The supervisor noted to the trainers that the rapid reduction in frequency of complaints was amazing because it had been such a long-standing problem.

Group Scrap Rate. Another supervisor/trainee identified group scrap rate as a growing performance problem in his department. Attempts at reducing the scrap by posting equipment maintenance rules and giving frequent reminders to his workers had not produced any noticeable improvement. The specific target response to be strengthened was identified as stopping the stamping mill when a defective piece was sighted and sharpening and realigning the dies.

During a two-week baseline period the supervisor kept a careful record of the group's scrap rate. Importantly, no new contingencies were introduced during this baseline period. The extent of the problem had to be determined before any intervention was attempted. After conducting a functional analysis, the supervisor decided to install a feedback system to inform the group of their scrap rate. This was accompanied by measuring, charting, and posting in the department work area the group scrap rate. The supervisor then actively solicited ideas from his workers on how to improve the scrap rate. Providing the feedback and implementing the suggestions turned out to be potent reinforcers.

Exhibit 2 shows the results of the intervention. In this case, group, not individual, behavior was charted. In addition to the improved scrap rate, the supervisor noted an increase in interaction between himself and his workers and among the workers themselves. A number of social reinforcers were discovered.

EXHIBIT 3   FREQUENCY OF OVERLOOKED DEFECTIVE PIECES

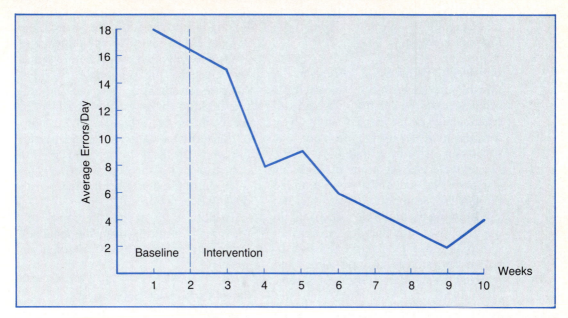

Group Quality Control. A third supervisor/trainee identified quality control in the paint line as a major performance problem in his department. The paint-line attendants' job consisted of hanging pieces on a paint-line conveyor, removing the painted pieces, and inspecting them for acceptance or rejection. "Getting on the men's backs" by the supervisor typically produced only temporary improvement in quality control. Soon after the supervisor reprimanded the men, the defective pieces would again pass unnoticed. As defined by the supervisor, a desirable target response consisted of identifying and removing defective pieces from the paint line. An undesirable response involved overlooking a defective piece.

During the two-week baseline period the average daily number of overlooked defective pieces was recorded for the entire work group. Figures were charted weekly during both the baseline period,

when contingencies remained unchanged, and the intervention period. The supervisor noted to the trainers that after conducting a functional analysis he had concluded that he had a group of "clock watchers" on his hands, particularly around break time, lunch time, and quitting time.

The supervisor developed his intervention strategy during a discussion session with his work group. It was decided that a group rate of eight or less overlooked defective pieces a day would qualify the group for an extra five minutes for each of two breaks the next day. To increase the value of the potential reinforcer, the paint-line attendants were told each morning if they had qualified for the extended breaks.

Exhibit 3 shows that the extra time off in the form of extended coffee breaks did in fact prove to be reinforcing. Contingency contracting had been effectively used. With the average daily rate of defectives down around two or three, the supervisor confided to the trainers that he couldn't see much more room for improvement.

Individual Performance Problem. A fourth supervisor/trainee was having a problem with the quality of assembled components in his department. Upon detailed analysis of the problem, the supervisor discovered that most of the rejects were coming from a single assembler. The assembly work entailed the precise manipulation of intricate subcomponents and the individual in question had satisfactory scores on screening tests for dexterity and coordination. In addition, this assembler had received the standard training in assembly and checking. After initial consideration, the supervisor rejected the alternative of running the assembler through more training. In his previous experience with similar cases, more training had failed to improve poor performance. Thus, he decided to use the BCM approach on this particular employee.

The supervisor specifically identified undesirable behavior as more than two rejects per one hundred assembled components and desirable behavior as two or less. Without changing the existing contingencies, the supervisor obtained a two-week baseline measure. To facilitate measuring, boxes of assembled components were randomly sampled and the per-box average recorded weekly. After a functional analysis, the supervisor decided that feedback on performance and compliments and praise for desirable behavior would be an appropriate positive reinforcement intervention strategy.

Beginning a shaping process at five or fewer errors, the supervisor contingently praised the assembler for any improved quality. As the reject level began to drop, the reinforcement schedule was gradually stretched. In other words, the worker had to have four, then three, and eventually only two rejects before praise was given by the supervisor. Summarized reject statistics were charted and presented to the assembler as a form of feedback on performance. Discussions of this feedback data between the assembler and the supervisor provided the opportunity for the supervisor to reinforce desirable behavior and ignore undesirable behavior.

Exhibit 4 illustrates the rapid improvement resulting from the feedback and positive reinforcement intervention strategy.

Overall Performance Improvement

The supervisors' ability to modify specific on-the-job individual and group behavior represents only one level of evaluation in BCM. Of more importance is overall performance improvement. The supervisors worked on the specific problems discussed above during the training program, but the trainers' ultimate objective was to have BCM generalize to the supervisors' total method of managing their human resources. To evaluate the effectiveness of BCM as an overall method of managing, direct labor effectiveness (a ratio of actual to standard hours stated as a percent) was measured for each of the supervisors' departments both in the experimental group (those who received BCM training) and in the control group (those who received no training).

Exhibit 5 shows the results of the overall performance evaluation. The figure shows the experimental group's and the control group's mean direct labor effectiveness curves over a six-month period subsequent to the start of the training program at the end of Septem-

EXHIBIT 4   ASSEMBLY REJECT RATE

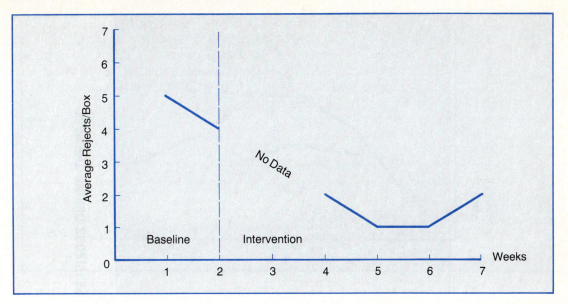

ber. The training program itself lasted ten weeks (until the middle of December). The figure clearly shows that the overall performance of the control group remained relatively stable over the six-month period, but the performance of the experimental group significantly improved and seemed to be maintained even after the training period was over. This evaluation demonstrated that the BCM training had paid off in terms of overall performance improvement.

Although not all the supervisors were able to obtain as clear-cut results of behavioral change as the four reported above, the overall performance was impressive. . . . Some of the significant features of this production case are:

1. Specific performance-related problems were identified by supervisors and reduced to desirable/undesirable behavioral events.
2. Baseline measures were obtained on target behavior. The frequency

measures were accomplished with little difficulty.
3. A functional analysis was performed by supervisors that determined actual and potential contingent consequences for positive control.
4. Making use of the functional analysis, supervisors were able to design and generally successfully implement intervention strategies. Natural positive reinforcers were readily identified and contingently applied by the supervisors.
5. Both behavioral change and significant overall, "bottom-line" results were achieved by first-line supervisors using a BCM approach.

CASE DISCUSSION QUESTIONS

1. Compare the BCM training received by supervisors in the case to the steps outlined in Chapter Eight

EXHIBIT 5   **INTERGROUP COMPARISON OF OVERALL PERFORMANCE USING BCM**

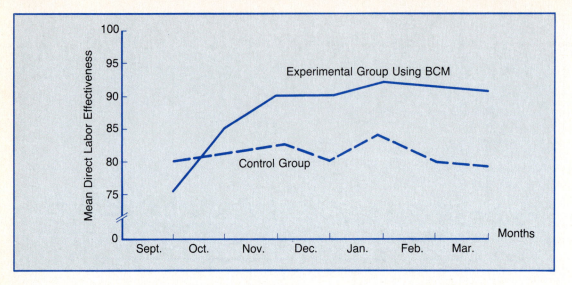

for designing a behavior modification program.

2. Why do you think the four examples of behavior modification application in the case received such positive results? Discuss types of behaviors involved and reinforcers used.

3. Figures 3 and 4 show that in the third and fourth examples, after an initial dramatic improvement in behavior, undesirable behavior started to reappear to some degree. Why do you think this might happen? Do you think that the positive results obtained in these examples will be prolonged?

4. Identify some situations in which behavior modification may not be as effectively used.

Source: F. Luthans and R. Kreitner, *Organizational Behavior Modification* (Glenview, Ill.: Scott, Foresman and Company, 1975), pp. 150–59. Reprinted by permission of Robert Otteman.

CHAPTER NINE

APPRAISING AND REWARDING PERFORMANCE

One of the most important responsibilities managers have is to evaluate and reward the performance of their subordinates. Where employee efforts fall short of acceptable standards, managers must devise mechanisms to improve performance. How does a manager assess the quality of a subordinate's work? In most organizations, evaluation is done through a performance appraisal system. In fact, one survey found that ninety percent of the organizations contacted had some form of performance appraisal system.

Because performance appraisal and reward systems are vital for employee development and organizational strength, various aspects of each will be examined here. First, the focus will be on general characteristics of appraisal systems, including their associated problems. Specific appraisal techniques will also be examined. The purpose of reward systems in organizations will be considered next, followed by a discussion of various incentive plans. To conclude, several new developments in reward systems will be explored.

IMPORTANCE OF TOPIC FOR MANAGERS

Why are appraisal and reward systems so important to managers? Performance appraisal systems provide a means of systematically evaluating employees across various performance dimensions to ensure that organizations are getting what they pay for. They provide valuable feedback to employees and managers and may assist in identifying promotable people as well as problem areas.

Reward systems represent a powerful motivational force in organizations, but this is true only when the system is fair and tied to performance. Since a variety of approaches to appraising performance exists, managers should be aware of the advantages and disadvantages of each. In turn, an understanding of reward systems will help managers select the system best suited to the needs and goals of the organization.

Performance appraisal systems serve a variety of functions of central importance to employees. Appraisal techniques practiced today are not without problems, though. Thus, managers should keep abreast of recent developments in compensation and reward systems so they can modify existing systems when more appropriate alternatives become available.

PERFORMANCE APPRAISAL SYSTEMS

We begin by examining three aspects of performance appraisal systems: various functions; associated problems; and methods for reducing appraisal system errors. This overview will provide a foundation for studying specific techniques of performance appraisal. Those interested in more detailed information on performance appraisal systems may wish to consult books on personnel administration or compensation.

Functions of Performance Appraisals

In most work organizations, there are many reasons why performance appraisals are used. These reasons range from improving various aspects of employees' output to developing the employees themselves. This diversity of uses is well documented in a survey of 216 organizations that sought to determine the uses for appraisals (Locher and Teel, 1977). As shown in Exhibit 9.1, compensation and performance improvement were the most prominent reasons organizations used performance appraisals.

Summarizing this information, it is possible to identify some major

EXHIBIT 9.1   PRIMARY USES OF APPRAISALS

Use	Small Organizations (Percent)	Large Organizations (Percent)
Compensation	80.6	62.2
Performance improvement	49.7	60.6
Feedback	20.6	37.8
Promotion	29.1	21.1
Documentation	11.4	10.0
Training	8.0	9.4
Transfer	7.4	8.3
Manpower planning	6.3	6.1
Discharge	2.3	2.2
Research	2.9	0.0
Layoff	0.6	0.0

Source: Alan H. Locher and Kenneth S. Teel, "Performance Appraisal—A Survey of Current Practices," *Personnel Journal,* May, 1977. Reprinted with the permission of *Personnel Journal,* Inc., Costa Mesa, California; all rights reserved. Copyright May, 1977.

functions of performance appraisals. Performance appraisals provide *feedback* to employees about quantity and quality of job performance. Without this information, employees have little knowledge of how well they are doing their jobs and how they might improve their work. Performance appraisals can also be *self-development* indicators. Individuals learn about their strengths and weaknesses as seen by other people. In addition, appraisals may form the basis of organizational *reward systems*—particularly merit-based compensation plans.

Performance appraisals serve personnel-related functions as well. In making *personnel decisions,* such as those relating to promotions, transfers, and terminations, performance appraisals are useful. Employers can make choices based on appraisal information about individual talents and shortcomings. In addition, appraisal systems help the organization to evaluate the effectiveness of its *selection and placement decisions.* If newly hired employees consistently perform poorly, managers should consider whether the right kind of people are being hired in the first place. However, poor performance may be due to inadequate employee *training and development.* Appraisal systems highlight areas for which training programs should be developed or improved.

It is apparent that performance appraisal systems serve a variety of functions in organizations. In light of the importance of these functions, it is imperative that methods of evaluation be selected that attempt to maximize the accuracy and fairness of the appraisal. Many such methods of performance appraisal exist. The job for the manager, as we shall soon see, is to select that technique or combination of techniques that best serves the particular needs (and constraints) of the organization. Before considering these various techniques, however, several of the more prominent sources of error, or problems, in performance appraisals will be examined.

Problems with Performance Appraisals

A number of problems can be identified that pose a threat to the usefulness of performance appraisal techniques. Most of these problems deal with the related issues of validity and reliability. *Validity* is the extent to which an instrument actually measures what it intends to measure; *reliability* is the extent to which the instrument consistently yields the same results each time it is used. Ideally, a good performance appraisal system will exhibit high levels of both validity and reliability. If not, serious questions must be raised concerning the utility (and possibly the legality) of the system.

It is possible to identify several common sources of error, or problems, found in performance appraisal systems that can jeopardize validity and reliability. These include: (1) central tendency error; (2) strictness or leniency error; (3) halo effect; (4) recency error; and (5) personal biases.

Central Tendency Error. It has often been found that supervisors rate most of their employees within a narrow range (Glueck, 1979). Regardless of how people actually perform, the rater fails to distinguish significant differences between group members and lumps everyone together in an average or above-average category. This central tendency error is shown in Exhibit 9.2. In short, the central tendency error is the failure to recognize both very good and very poor performers.

Strictness or Leniency Error. A related rating problem exists when a supervisor is overly strict or overly lenient in evaluations (see Exhibit 9.2). In college classrooms, we hear of professors who are "tough graders" or, conversely, "easy A's." Similar situations exist in the work place where some supervisors see most subordinates as not measuring up to their high standards, while others see most subordinates as deserving of a high rating. As with central tendency error, strictness and leniency errors fail to adequately distinguish between good and bad performers, and instead relegate almost everyone to the same or related categories.

Halo Effect. The halo effect was discussed earlier in Chapter Four on perceptual biases. Halo effect exists where a rater assigns the same rating to each factor being evaluated for an individual. An employee rated "above average" on quantity of performance may also be rated "above average" on quality of performance, interpersonal competence, attendance, and promotion readiness. Such a practice fails to differentiate strong points from weak and tells the employee that the supervisor cannot differentiate across presumably distinct categories of behavior.

A good example of the halo effect in operation can be seen in a description of performance appraisal systems at General Motors (Wright, 1979, pp. 251–52). A former GM executive claims that so much emphasis was placed on cost cutting in the company that other important areas of managerial accountability went almost unnoticed in evaluations. For instance, the Tarrytown, New York, assembly division once had the dubious distinction of

EXHIBIT 9.2   EXAMPLES OF STRICTNESS, CENTRAL TENDENCY, AND LENIENCY ERRORS

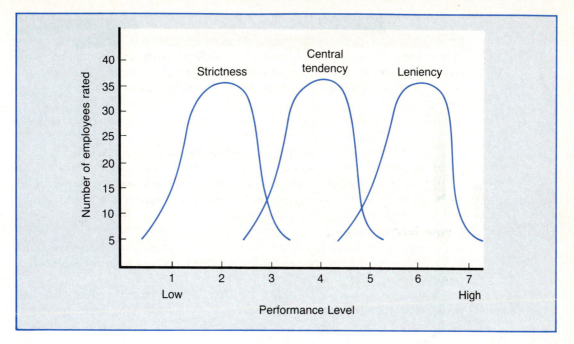

producing the poorest quality cars of all twenty-two U.S. GM plants. (Note: Tarrytown no longer has this reputation. Indeed, recent work redesign efforts have dramatically improved product quality.) During this time, some cars were so poorly built that dealers refused to accept them. Even so, the plant had the lowest manufacturing costs in GM. As a result, the plant manager at Tarrytown received one of the largest bonuses of all the assembly divisions while building the worst cars in the company. Clearly, the manager's evaluation concerning costs overshadowed considerations of product quality.

Recency Error. Oftentimes, evaluators focus on an employee's most recent behavior in the evaluation process. That is, in an annual evaluation, a supervisor may give undue emphasis to performance during the past two or three months and ignore performance levels prior to this. This practice, if known to employees, leads to a situation where employees float for the initial months of the evaluation period and then overexert themselves in the last few months prior to evaluation. This practice leads to uneven performance, as well as contributing to the attitude of "playing the game."

Personal Biases. Finally, several studies have revealed that supervisors often allow their own personal biases to influence their appraisals (Jones, 1973). Biases include like or dislike for someone, as well as racial and sexual biases. Personal biases can interfere with the fairness and accuracy of an evaluation.

Reducing Errors in Performance Appraisals

A number of suggestions have been advanced recently to minimize the effects of various biases and errors on the performance appraisal process (Bernardin and Walter, 1977; Lawler, Mohrman, and Resnick, 1983). When errors are reduced, more accurate information is available for personnel decisions and personal development. These methods for reducing error include:

- Ensure that each dimension or factor on a performance appraisal form represents a single job activity instead of a group of job activities.
- Avoid terms like "average," since different evaluators react differently to the term.
- Ensure that raters observe subordinates on a regular basis throughout the evaluation period. It is even helpful if the rater takes notes for future reference.
- Keep the number of persons evaluated by one rater to a reasonable number. When one person must evaluate many subordinates, it becomes difficult to discriminate. Rating fatigue increases with the number of ratees.
- Ensure that the dimensions used are clearly stated, meaningful, and relevant to good job performance.
- Train raters so they can recognize various sources of error and understand the rationale underlying the evaluation process.

Using mechanisms like these, rating that has greater meaning both for the individual and the organization should result.

TECHNIQUES OF PERFORMANCE APPRAISAL

Organizations use numerous methods to evaluate personnel. We will summarize several popular techniques. While countless variations on these themes can be found, the basic methods presented provide a good summary of the commonly available techniques. Following this review, we will consider the various strengths and weaknesses of each technique. Six techniques are reviewed here: (1) graphic rating scales; (2) critical incident technique; (3) behaviorally anchored rating scales; (4) behavioral observation scales; (5) management-by-objectives; and (6) assessment centers.

Graphic Rating Scales

Certainly the most popular method of evaluation used in organizations today is the *graphic rating scale.* Locher and Teel (1977) found that fifty-seven percent of the organizations they surveyed used rating scales. While this

EXHIBIT 9.3   TYPICAL GRAPHIC RATING SCALE

Name _____ Dept. _____ Date _____

	Outstanding	Good	Satisfactory	Fair	Unsatisfactory
Quantity of work Volume of acceptable work under normal conditions Comments:	☐	☐	☐	☐	☐
Quality of work Thoroughness, neatness, and accuracy of work Comments:	☐	☐	☐	☐	☐
Knowledge of job Clear understanding of the facts or factors pertinent to the job Comments:	☐	☐	☐	☐	☐
Personal qualities Personality, appearance, sociability, leadership, integrity Comments:	☐	☐	☐	☐	☐
Cooperation Ability and willingness to work with associates, supervisors, and subordinates toward common goals Comments:	☐	☐	☐	☐	☐
Dependability Conscientious, thorough, accurate, reliable with respect to attendance, lunch periods, reliefs, etc. Comments:	☐	☐	☐	☐	☐
Initiative Earnestness in seeking increased responsibilities. Self-starting, unafraid to proceed alone Comments:	☐	☐	☐	☐	☐

Source: William Glueck, *Personnel: A Diagnostic Approach,* 3rd ed. (Dallas, Texas: Business Publications, 1982).

method appears in many formats, the rater is typically presented with a printed form that contains both the employee's name and several evaluation dimensions (quantity of work, quality of work, knowledge of job). The rater is then asked to rate the employee by assigning a number, or rating, on each of the dimensions. An example of the graphic rating scale is shown in Exhibit 9.3.

By using this method—and assuming that evaluator biases can be minimized—it is possible to compare employees in terms of who received the best and poorest ratings. It is also possible to examine the relative strengths and weaknesses of a single employee by comparing scores on the various dimensions.

However, one of the most serious drawbacks of this technique is its openness to central tendency, strictness, and leniency error. It is possible to rate almost everyone in the middle of the scale or, conversely, at one end of the scale. In order to control for this, some companies have assigned required percentage distributions to the various scale points. Supervisors may be allowed to rate only ten percent of their people outstanding and must rate ten percent unsatisfactory, perhaps assigning twenty percent, forty percent, and twenty percent to the remaining middle categories. By doing this, a distribution is forced within each department. However, this procedure may penalize a group of truly outstanding performers or reward a group of poor ones.

Critical Incident Technique

With the *critical incident* method of performance appraisal, supervisors record incidents in each subordinate's behavior that led to either unusual success or unusual failure on some aspect of the job. These incidents are recorded in a daily or weekly log under predesignated categories (planning, decision making, interpersonal relations, report writing). The final rating consists of a series of descriptive paragraphs or notes about various aspects of an employee's performance (see Exhibit 9.4).

The critical incident method provides useful information for appraisal interviews, and managers and subordinates can discuss specific incidents. Good qualitative data are generated. However, since no quantitative data emerge, it is difficult to use this technique for promotion or salary decisions. The qualitative output here has led some companies to combine the critical incident technique with one of the quantitative techniques, such as rating scales, to provide different kinds of feedback to the employees.

Behaviorally Anchored Rating Scales

An appraisal system that has received increasing attention in recent years is the *behaviorally anchored rating scale* (or BARS). This system requires considerable work prior to evaluation but, if the work is carefully done, can lead to highly accurate ratings with high inter-rater reliability. Specifically, the BARS technique begins by selecting a job that can be described in observable behaviors. Managers and personnel specialists then identify these behaviors as they relate to superior or inferior performance.

An example of this is shown in Exhibit 9.5, where the BARS technique has been applied to the job of grocery clerk. As shown, as one moves from extremely poor performance to extremely good performance, the performance descriptions, or behavioral anchors, increase. Oftentimes, six-to-ten scales are used to describe performance on the job. Exhibit 9.5 evaluates judgment and

EXHIBIT 9.4 AN EXAMPLE OF CRITICAL INCIDENT EVALUATION

The following performance areas are designed to assist you in preparing this appraisal and in discussing an individual's performance with him. It is suggested that areas of performance that you feel are significantly good or poor be documented below with specific examples or actions. The points listed are suggested as typical and are by no means all-inclusive. Examples related to these points may be viewed from either a positive or negative standpoint.

1. Performance on Technology of the Job

    A. Safety Effectiveness—possible considerations:
        1. Sets an excellent safety example for others in the department by words and action.
        2. Trains his people well in safety areas.
        3. Gains the cooperation and participation of his people in safety.
        4. Insists that safety be designed into procedure and processes.
        5. Is instrumental in initiating departmental safety program.
        6. Accepts safety as a fundamental job responsibility.

Item   Related Examples

    B. Job Knowledge—Technical and/or Specialized—possible considerations:
        1. Shows exceptional knowledge in methods, materials, and techniques; and applies in a resourceful and practical manner.
        2. Stays abreast of development in field and applies to job.
        3. "Keeps up" on latest material in his special field.
        4. Participates in professional or technical organizations pertinent to his activities.

Item   Related Examples

2. Performance on Human Relations

    A. Ability to Communicate—possible considerations:
        1. Gives logical, clear-cut, understandable instructions on complex problems.
        2. Uses clear and direct language in written and oral reporting.
        3. Organizes presentations in logical order and in order of importance.
        4. Provides supervisor and subordinates with pertinent and adequate information.
        5. Tailors communications approach to group or individual.
        6. Keeps informed on how subordinates think and feel about things.

Item   Related Examples

    B. Results Achieved Through Others—possible considerations:
        1. Develops enthusiasm in others that gets the job done.
        2. Has respect and confidence of others.
        3. Recognizes and credits skills of others.
        4. Coordinates well with other involved groups to get the job done.

Item   Related Examples

3. Performance on Conceptualizing

    A. Originality—possible considerations:
        1. Originates new approaches to problems.
        2. Improvises effectively in developing unique solutions to unforeseen changes and problems.
        3. Has ability to think abstractly or theoretically and relate to the concrete.
        4. Has ability to innovate for needed improvement.

Item   Related Examples

    B. Ability to Use New Methods—Ideas—Technology—possible considerations:
        1. Searches out best sources of information, I.E.: associates, specialists, and literature.
        2. Relates to and adopts newest technology available.
        3. Creates a climate conducive to innovation and improvements.

Item   Related Examples

Source: R. Daft and R. Steers, *Organizations: A Micro/Macro Approach* (Glenview, Ill.: Scott, Foresman and Company, 1986), p. 129.

EXHIBIT 9.5 BEHAVIORALLY ANCHORED RATING SCALE FOR EVALUATING JUDGMENT AND KNOWLEDGE OF GROCERY CLERKS

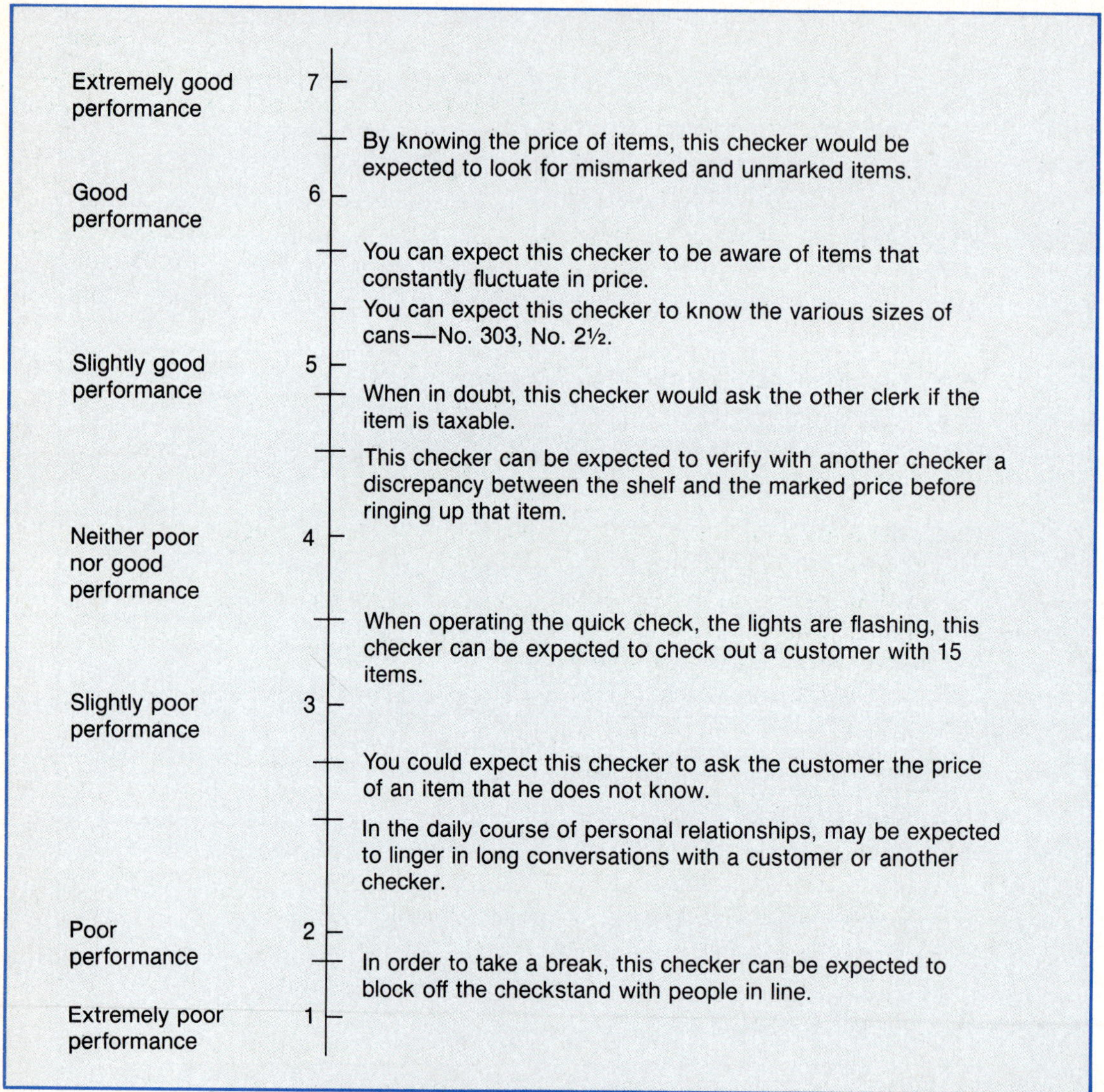

Extremely good performance — 7

By knowing the price of items, this checker would be expected to look for mismarked and unmarked items.

Good performance — 6

You can expect this checker to be aware of items that constantly fluctuate in price.

You can expect this checker to know the various sizes of cans—No. 303, No. 2½.

Slightly good performance — 5

When in doubt, this checker would ask the other clerk if the item is taxable.

This checker can be expected to verify with another checker a discrepancy between the shelf and the marked price before ringing up that item.

Neither poor nor good performance — 4

When operating the quick check, the lights are flashing, this checker can be expected to check out a customer with 15 items.

Slightly poor performance — 3

You could expect this checker to ask the customer the price of an item that he does not know.

In the daily course of personal relationships, may be expected to linger in long conversations with a customer or another checker.

Poor performance — 2

In order to take a break, this checker can be expected to block off the checkstand with people in line.

Extremely poor performance — 1

Source: L. Fogli, C. L. Hulin, and M. R. Blood, "Development of First-level Behavioral Job Criteria," *Journal of Applied Psychology* 55 (1971): 3–8. Copyright 1971 by the American Psychological Association. Reprinted by permission of the publisher and authors.

knowledge on the job. Other scales could relate to customer relations, promptness, attendance, and innovation. Once these scales are determined, managers have only to check the category that describes what they observe on the job, and the employee's rating is simultaneously determined.

The BARS technique has several purported advantages. In particular, many of the sources of error discussed earlier (central tendency, leniency, halo) should be significantly reduced since raters are considering verbal descriptions of specific behaviors instead of general categories of behaviors like those used in graphic rating scales. The technique focuses on job-related behavior and does not consider less relevant issues like a subordinate's personality. Also, in the performance appraisal interview, emphasis is placed on these actual behaviors, not the person; hence, employees should be less defensive in the review process. Finally, BARS can aid in employee training and development by identifying those performance domains needing most attention.

On the negative side, as noted above, considerable time and effort in designing the forms are required before the actual rating. Because a separate BARS is required for each job, it is only cost-efficient on common jobs. Finally, since the technique relies on observable behavior, it may have little applicability for a job such as research scientist, where much of the work is mental and relevant observable behaviors are hard to obtain.

Behavioral Observation Scales

The *behavioral observation scale* (BOS) is similar to BARS in that both focus on identifying observable behaviors as they relate to performance. A major difference in BOS, however, is the task facing the evaluator. Typically, the evaluator is asked to rate each behavior on a scale from 1 to 5 to indicate the frequency with which employees exhibit that behavior. Evaluation of an employee's performance on a particular dimension is derived by summing the frequency ratings for the behaviors in each dimension.

An example of this technique is shown in Exhibit 9.6, which is a form designed to evaluate a manager's ability to overcome resistance to change. The rater has simply to circle the appropriate numbers describing observed behaviors and get the summary rating by adding the results.

This technique is easier to construct than the BARS technique and makes the evaluator's job somewhat simpler. Even so, this is a relatively new technique that is only now receiving some support in industry.

Management-by-Objectives

Another popular technique for appraising employees is *management-by-objectives* (MBO). Although the concept of MBO is really broader than the appraisal itself (incorporating an organization-wide motivation, performance, and control system), we will focus here on its narrower role in the evaluation process (see Tosi and Caroll, 1973). MBO is closely related to goal-setting theory of motivation, as discussed in Chapter Seven.

Under MBO, individual employees or groups work with their supervisor to establish goals and objectives for the coming year. These goals are stated in clear language and relate to tasks that are within the domain of the employee. An example of these goals for a salesperson is shown in Exhibit 9.7. Following a specified period of time (usually one year), employees' performances are

EXHIBIT 9.6   AN EXAMPLE OF A BEHAVIORAL OBSERVATION SCALE

Overcoming resistance to change

1. Describes the details of the change to subordinates.

   Almost never   1   2   3   4   5   Almost always

2. Explains why the change is necessary.

   Almost never   1   2   3   4   5   Almost always

3. Discusses how the change will affect the employee.

   Almost never   1   2   3   4   5   Almost always

4. Listens to the employee's concerns.

   Almost never   1   2   3   4   5   Almost always

5. Asks the employee for help in making the change work.

   Almost never   1   2   3   4   5   Almost always

6. If necessary, specifies the date for a follow-up meeting to respond to employee's concerns.

   Almost never   1   2   3   4   5   Almost always

Total = _____

Below adequate 6–10	Adequate 11–15	Full 16–20	Excellent 21–25	Superior 26–30

Source: G. Latham and K. Wexley, *Increasing Productivity Through Performance Appraisal,* Figure 3.8, p. 56, © 1981, Addison-Wesley Publishing Company, Inc., Reading, Massachusetts. Reprinted with permission.

compared to the goals to determine the extent to which the goals have been met or exceeded.

Several advantages of MBO have been observed. As noted by Gibson et al. (1979, p. 367), "the assumed benefits include better planning, improved motivation because of knowledge of results, basing evaluation decisions on results instead of on personality or personal traits, improving commitment through participation, and improving supervisory skills in such areas as listening, counseling, and evaluating."

On the negative side, MBO has been criticized because it emphasizes quantitative goals at the expense of qualitative goals and often creates too much paperwork. It is difficult to compare performance levels among employees, since most are responsible for different goals. Finally, in order to succeed, MBO must have constant attention and support from management; it does not run itself. In the absence of this support, the technique loses legitimacy and often falls into disrepair.

Assessment Centers

A relatively new method of evaluation is the *assessment center*. Assessment centers are unique among appraisal techniques in that they focus more on

EXHIBIT 9.7   MBO EVALUATION REPORT FOR SALESPERSON

Objectives Set	Period Objective	Accomplishments	Variance
1. Number of sales calls	100	104	104%
2. Number of new customers contacted	20	18	90
3. Number of wholesalers stocking new product 117	30	30	100
4. Sales of product 12	10,000	9,750	92.5
5. Sales of product 17	17,000	18,700	110
6. Customer complaints/service calls	35	11	32
7. Number of sales correspondence courses successfully completed	4	2	50
8. Number of sales reports in home office within 1 day of end of month	12	10	80

Source: William Glueck, *Personnel: A Diagnostic Approach,* 3rd ed. (Dallas, Texas: Business Publications, 1982).

evaluating employee long-range potential to an organization instead of on performance over the past year. They are also unique in that they are used almost exclusively among managerial personnel.

An assessment center consists of a series of standardized evaluations of behavior based on multiple inputs (Bray and Moss, 1972). Over a two- or three-day period (away from the job) trained observers make judgments on managers' behavior as a result of specially developed exercises. These exercises may consist of in-basket exercises, role playing, and case analyses, as well as personal interviews and psychological tests. An example of an assessment center program is shown in Exhibit 9.8.

As a result of these exercises, the trained observers make judgments on employees' potential for future managerial assignments in the organization. More specifically, information is obtained concerning employees' interpersonal skills, communication ability, creativity, problem-solving skills, tolerance for stress and ambiguity, and planning ability. This technique has been used successfully by some of the largest corporations in the U.S., including AT&T; Sears, Roebuck and Company; J.C. Penney; IBM; and General Electric.

Results from a series of assessment center programs appear promising, and the technique is growing in popularity as a means of identifying future managerial potential. Even so, some problems with the technique have been noted (Klimoski and Strictland, 1977; Norton, 1977). In particular, owing to the highly stressful environment created in assessment centers, many otherwise good managers may simply not perform up to their potential. The results of a poor evaluation in an assessment center may be far-reaching; individuals may receive a "loser" image that will follow them for a long time. Finally, there is some question concerning exactly how valid and reliable assessment centers really are in predicting future managerial success. While some initial

EXHIBIT 9.8   EXAMPLE OF TWO-DAY ASSESSMENT CENTER

Day #1		Day #2	
8:00– 9:00 AM	Orientation session	8:00–10:30 AM	In-basket exercise
9:00–10:30 AM	Psychological testing	10:30–10:45 AM	Coffee break
10:30–10:45 AM	Coffee break	10:45–12:30 PM	Role-playing exercise
10:45–12:30 PM	Management simulation game	12:30– 1:30 PM	Lunch
12:30– 1:30 PM	Lunch	1:30– 3:15 PM	Group problem-solving exercise
1:30– 3:15 PM	Individual decision-making exercise	3:15– 3:30 PM	Coffee break
		3:30– 4:30 PM	Debriefing by raters
3:15– 3:30 PM	Coffee break		
3:30– 4:30 PM	Interview with raters		

successes have been noted, more research is needed to evaluate the true potential of the technique.

Comparison of Appraisal Techniques

From a managerial standpoint, questions are raised about which appraisal technique or set of techniques is most appropriate for a given situation. Although there is no simple answer to this question, we can consider the various strengths and weaknesses of each technique. This is done in Exhibit 9.9.

As would be expected, the easiest and least expensive techniques are also the least accurate. They are also the least useful for purposes of personnel decisions and employee development. Once again, it appears that managers and organizations get what they pay for. If performance appraisals represent an important aspect of organizational life, clearly the more sophisticated —and more time-consuming—techniques offer more useful information. If, on the other hand, it is necessary to evaluate employees quickly and with few resources, techniques like the graphic rating scale may be more appropriate. Managers must make cost-benefit decisions about the price (of time and money) they are willing to pay for a quality performance appraisal system.

REWARD SYSTEMS IN ORGANIZATIONS

After an organization has implemented and conducted a systematic performance appraisal, the next step is to consider how to tie rewards to the outcomes of the appraisal. Behavioral research consistently demonstrates that performance levels are highest when rewards are contingent upon performance. So, in this section, we will examine five aspects of reward systems in

EXHIBIT 9.9 **MAJOR STRENGTHS AND WEAKNESSES OF APPRAISAL TECHNIQUES**

	Rating Scales	Critical Incidents	BARS	BOS	MBO	Assessment Centers
Meaningful dimensions	Sometimes	Sometimes	Usually	Usually	Usually	Usually
Amount of time required	Low	Medium	High	Medium	High	High
Developmental costs	Low	Low	High	Medium	Medium	High
Potential for rating errors	High	Medium	Low	Low	Low	Low
Acceptability to subordinates	Low	Medium	High	High	High	High
Acceptability to superiors	Low	Medium	High	High	High	High
Usefulness for allocating rewards	Poor	Fair	Good	Good	Good	Fair
Usefulness for employee counseling	Poor	Fair	Good	Good	Good	Good
Usefulness for identifying promotion potential	Poor	Fair	Fair	Fair	Fair	Good

organizations: (1) types of rewards; (2) functions of reward systems; (3) bases for reward distribution; (4) money and motivation; and (5) management compensation around the world.

Types of Rewards: Extrinsic and Intrinsic

The variety of rewards that employees can receive in exchange for their contribution of time and effort can be classified into extrinsic and intrinsic rewards. *Extrinsic rewards* are those rewards external to the work itself. They are administered externally—that is, by someone else. Examples of extrinsic rewards include wages and salary, fringe benefits, promotions, and recognition and praise from others.

On the other hand, *intrinsic rewards* represent those rewards that are related directly to performing the job. In this sense, they are often described as self-administered rewards since engaging in the task itself leads to their receipt. Examples of intrinsic rewards include feelings of task accomplishment, autonomy, and personal growth.

Functions of Reward Systems

Reward systems in organizations are used for a variety of reasons. It is generally agreed that reward systems influence the following:

- *Performance.* Both intrinsic and extrinsic rewards can be used to motivate performance. Following expectancy theory, employees' effort and performance would be expected to increase when they felt that rewards were contingent upon good performance. Hence, reward systems serve a very basic motivational function (Porter and Lawler, 1968).
- *Attendance and Retention.* Reward systems have also been shown to influence an employee's decision to come to work or to remain with the organization (Mowday, Porter, and Steers, 1982).
- *Organizational Commitment.* In brief, it has been found that reward systems in no small way influence commitment to the organization, primarily through the exchange process (Mowday et al., 1982; Salancik, 1977).
- *Job Satisfaction.* Job satisfaction has also been shown to be related to rewards. Lawler (1976) has summarized available evidence on satisfaction as follows: (1) satisfaction with a reward is a function of both how much is received and how much the individual feels should be received; (2) satisfaction is influenced by comparisons with what happens to others; (3) people differ with respect to the rewards they value; and (4) some extrinsic rewards are satisfying because they lead to other rewards.
- *Occupational and Organizational Choice.* Finally, selection of an occupation by an individual, as well as the decision to join a particular organization within that occupation, is influenced by the rewards that are thought to be available in the occupation or organization.

Reward systems in organizations have far-reaching consequences for both individual satisfaction and organizational effectiveness. Unfortunately, cases can easily be cited where reward systems have been distorted to punish good performance or inhibit creativity. Consider, for example, the Greyhound Bus Company driver who was suspended for ten days without pay for breaking a company rule against using a CB radio on his bus. The bus driver had used the radio to alert police that his bus, with thirty-two passengers on board, was being hijacked by an armed man. The police arrested the hijacker, and the bus driver was suspended for breaking company rules (Eugene *Register-Guard,* July 15, 1980). Further evidence of good performance being punished can be seen in a series of examples where U.S. government bureaucracies punished whistle blowers in their own agencies, as described in Close-Up 9.1. These incidents hardly encourage employees to focus on efforts to perform well.

In theory, rewards should be tied to performance. In this way, employees who are highly committed to the organization and who exhibit exceptional performance receive compensation to justify their efforts. In reality, however, there are many situations in which employees are actually *penalized* for high performance—particularly when their supervisors consider this high performance "rocking the boat."

Consider the case of Ernest Fitzgerald. Fitzgerald was a civilian employee in the U.S. Air Force in charge of cost controls. In the course of carrying out his job, he discovered and reported to the Joint Congressional Economic Committee in 1968 that the Air Force was incurring a $2.5 billion cost overrun on the C-5A transport plane. Shortly after this whistle blowing, the Air Force laid off Fitzgerald in an "economy move."

Or consider the case of Oscar Hoffman, a government inspector of pipe welds on combat ships being built for the U.S. Navy. In the course of his inspections, he discovered many defects in welds, which he reported to his superiors. His superiors ignored the reports and threatened him with reprimand if he persisted in reporting the defects. When Hoffman filed a grievance against this threat, he was reprimanded and transferred from Seattle to Tacoma, Washington. Soon after his transfer, the Navy laid him off (in 1970) because his services were "no longer needed." Ironically, a series of accidents involving faulty welds have occurred on many of the ships identified by Hoffman. What has since happened to Hoffman? Although his superior has been promoted, Hoffman has been unable to secure another job as a government inspector.

Numerous other examples could be cited. The point here is that in at least two major government bureaucracies, effective means have been found to stifle or eliminate those who take their jobs too seriously. One can easily imagine the effects of these layoffs on other employees concerned with facilitating organizational effectiveness.

Source: R. Vaughn, *The Spoiled System* (New York: Charterhouse Books, 1975).

Bases for Reward Distribution

A common reality in many contemporary work organizations is the inequity that exists in the distribution of available rewards. One often sees little correlation between those who perform well and those who receive the greatest rewards. At the extreme, it is hard to understand how one company could pay its president over $1 million per year (as many large corporations do) while it pays its secretaries or clerks less than $10,000. Both work approximately forty hours per week; both are important for organizational performance. Is it really possible that the president is 100 times as important as the secretary, as the salary differential suggests?

How do organizations decide on the distribution of available rewards? At least four mechanisms can be identified. In more cases than we choose to admit, rewards go to those with the greatest *power.* In many of the corporations whose presidents earn seven-figure incomes, we find that these same people are major shareholders in the company. Indeed, the threat to resign by an important or high-performing manager often leads to increased rewards.

A second base for reward distribution is *equality.* Here, all individuals within one job classification receive the same rewards. The most common example is many labor union contracts, where pay rates are established and standardized with no reference to performance level. These systems often recognize seniority, however.

The basis for the social welfare reward system in this country is *need.* In large part, the greater the need, the greater the level of support. It is not uncommon to see situations in business firms where need is taken into account in layoff situations, where an employee is not laid off because he or she is the sole basis for the support of a family.

A fourth mechanism used by organizations in allocating rewards is *distributive justice.* Under this system, employees receive (at least a portion of) their rewards as a function of their level of contribution. The greater the contribution, the greater the rewards. This mechanism is most prominent in merit-based incentive programs where pay and perhaps bonuses are determined by performance levels.

Money and Motivation

A recurring debate among managers focuses on the issue of whether or not money is a primary motivator. Opsahl and Dunnette (1966) suggest that money serves several functions in work settings. These include: (1) money as a goal or incentive; (2) money as a source of satisfaction; (3) money as an instrument for gaining other desired outcomes; (4) money as a standard of comparison for determining relative standing or worth; and (5) money as a conditional reinforcer where its receipt is contingent upon a certain level of performance.

Even so, experience tells us that the effectiveness of pay as a motivator varies considerably. At times there seems to be almost a direct relationship between pay and effort, while at other times no such relationship is found. Why? Lawler (1971) suggests that certain conditions must be present in order for pay to act as a strong motivator:

- Trust level between managers and subordinates is high.
- Individual performance can be accurately measured.
- Pay rewards to high performers are substantially higher than those to poor performers.
- Few perceived negative consequences of good performance exist.

Under these conditions, a climate is created where employees have reason to believe that significant performance-reward contingencies truly

Reward systems are designed to reward good performance. But consider the following example. In 1981 the head of the U.S. Forest Service was earning $50,112.50 per year. In the same year, the Forest Service's five deputy chiefs and eight associate deputy chiefs earned exactly the same amount. Indeed, a total of 177 Forest Service employees earned precisely that salary.

Why? The wage congestion originated when Congress passed a law in 1978 to limit the salaries of career bureaucrats. Within two years after this action, 6000 senior managers were earning no more than about 30,000 of their subordinates. The subordinates had received cost-of-living raises, but the supervisors —already at the peak of the pay scale —were fixed in place.

As a result, turnover among highly competent government executives skyrocketed. Before the 1978 ceiling went into effect, only about 15 percent of the senior executives took early retirement (usually at age fifty-five). In 1980, however, after the imposition of the ceiling, 95 percent opted for early retirement. Of course many bureaucrats remaining in the government complained that the system was unfair, discouraging, and absurd.

In such a case, questions must be raised about the effectiveness of the government's cost reduction efforts. If pay is not related to performance, why should employees have reason to perform? Moreover, if the system causes massive turnover, where does the organization get its experienced managerial talent to handle operations effectively?

Source: Based on information in "Federal Pay Jam," *Time,* September 7, 1981, p. 17.

exist. Under this perception (and assuming the reward is valued), we would expect performance to be increased (see Hamner, 1975). A situation in which the opposite results occurred is illustrated in Close-Up 9.2—the problem of pay raises in the federal government.

Management Compensation Around the World

We often do not realize that compensation systems and amounts vary considerably from country to country. For example, an entry-level manager in the United States often earns between $25,000 and $45,000 per year, while his or her counterpart in the People's Republic of China earns about $300 per year! A recent survey by the Japan Economic Institute found that whereas American companies try to base a manager's salary on his or her ability to produce profits for the firm, most Japanese companies prefer to balance pay more closely between managers and workers, avoiding a wide pay gap between the two. Consequently, salaries of Japanese chairpersons and presidents, which range between $50,000 and $250,000, are well below comparable U.S. salaries for CEOs (Mesdag, 1984). Such differences can be seen in a recent

EXHIBIT 9.10   **SALARIES FOR MIDDLE MANAGERS FROM SELECTED COUNTRIES**

Country	Annual Salary (U.S. Dollars)
Australia	38,600
Brazil	40,900
Canada	48,600
France	49,000
Italy	40,100
Japan	29,600
Mexico	28,600
Spain	33,900
United Kingdom	33,200
United States	65,000
West Germany	58,000

Source: Data summarized from L. M. Mesdag, "Are You Underpaid?" *Fortune,* March 19, 1984, pp. 20–25.

survey of average salaries for middle managers in various countries (see Exhibit 9.10).

In countries outside the United States, particularly countries that have confiscatory tax rates, companies provide less cash and more perks. These perks can include cars, chauffeurs, housing allowances, access to private resorts, and so on. Hence executives living in Holland, Germany, or Japan may, in fact, live at the same level as their American counterparts, even though their official salaries are far less.

INDIVIDUAL AND GROUP INCENTIVE PLANS

We turn now to an examination of various employee incentive programs used by organizations. Managers have choices among various alternative plans and must make decisions about which plan is most effective for the particular organization and work force. Incentive systems in organizations are usually divided into two categories, based on whether the unit of analysis—and the recipient of the reward—is the individual or the group (or organization).

Individual Incentives

Several individual incentive plans can be identified. Each assumes that the most effective method of motivating employee performance is by tying rewards to individual initiative and effort. These plans include the following:

- *Merit-based Compensation Plan.* When a major portion of employee salary is determined by performance level, individuals have increased control over their output. In most organizations using these plans, all employees receive a base (cost-of-living) pay raise and then merit pay is added to this as a function of rated performance.
- *Piece-rate Plan.* On many blue-collar production jobs, employees are paid based on each unit of output they produce. The most common variation on this plan is when employees are guaranteed an hourly rate for performing at a minimum level of output (the standard). Production over and above this standard is then rewarded based on pay for each unit of output.
- *Bonus Plans.* A variety of bonus plans can be found in organizations, particularly among upper managers in private firms (not public organizations). Under this plan, individuals receive a bonus that is usually a percentage of some figure. Senior auto executives, for example, receive a bonus based on car sales volume above certain levels.
- *Commissions.* Commissions are typically found among sales personnel where part or all of their salary is tied to their level of sales.

Although individual incentive systems in many cases lead to improved performance, some reservations have been noted. In particular, these programs may at times lead to employees competing with one another with undesirable results. For instance, department-store salespeople on commission may fight over customers. Second, these plans typically are resisted by unions, who prefer compensation to be based on seniority or job classification. Third, where quality control systems are lax, individual incentives such as piece-rates may lead employees to maximize units of output, sacrificing quality. Finally, in order for these programs to be successful, an atmosphere of trust and cooperation between employees and managers is necessary. In order to overcome some of these shortcomings, many organizations have turned to group or organizational incentive plans.

Group and Organizational Incentives

Several frequently used incentive systems can be identified in which employees as a group benefit from improved performance, reduced costs, or increased profits. Three of the major plans are:

- *Profit-sharing Plans.* Basically, profit-sharing plans pay company employees a certain percentage of profits each year (Lawler, 1983). At least 100,000 corporations currently have these plans. The basic rationale is that by contributing to company profitability, all employees benefit.
- *Employee Stock Option Plans.* This plan, known as ESOP, is designed to give employees some ownership in the organization. Typically, a block of stock is set aside each year for distribution to employees based on tenure, performance level, or salary. Employees usually pay for the stocks at

reduced rates. ESOPs are probably more useful in developing commitments among employees and reducing turnover than in improving performance (Rosen, Klein, and Young, 1986).

- *Company Incentive Plans.* A wide variety of organization-wide incentive plans are currently in use. Two of the most publicized plans are the Lincoln Electric Plan and the Scanlon Plan. While a detailed description of these plans goes beyond the scope of this chapter, these plans typically reward employees based on cost savings or production increases that have been achieved during the past year or quarter.

Guidelines for Effective Incentive Programs

Whatever incentive plan is selected, care must be taken to ensure that the plan is appropriate for the particular organization and work force. Mathis and Jackson (1979) note five guidelines for effective incentive programs. First, they point out that the plan should be tied as closely as possible to performance. This point was discussed earlier in the chapter.

Second, if possible, incentive programs should allow for individual differences. They should recognize that different people want different outcomes from a job. Cafeteria-style plans, discussed later, do this.

Third, incentive programs should reflect the type of work that is done and the structure of the organization. This simply means that the program should be tailored to the particular needs, goals, and structures of a given organization. Individual incentive programs, for example, would probably be less successful among unionized personnel than would group programs like the Scanlon plan.

This point has been clearly demonstrated in the recent work of Edward Lawler (1983), who points out that organizations employing more traditional (Theory X) management may be more effective by approaching reward systems quite differently than organizations with more participative (Theory Y) management. As shown in Exhibit 9.11, both types of companies can be effective as long as their reward systems are congruent with their overall approach to management.

Fourth, the incentive program should be consistent with the climate and constraints of the organization. Where trust levels are low, for example, it may take considerable effort to get any program to work. In an industry already characterized by high levels of efficiency, basing an incentive system on increasing efficiency even further may have little effect since employees may see the task as nearly impossible.

Finally, incentive programs should be carefully monitored over time to ensure that they are being fairly administered and accurately reflect current technological and organizational conditions. For instance, it may be more appropriate to offer sales clerks in a department store an incentive to sell outdated merchandise than to offer an incentive to sell current fashion items that sell themselves.

Responsibility falls on managers not to select the incentive program that

EXHIBIT 9.11   MATCHING REWARD SYSTEMS TO MANAGEMENT STYLE

Reward System	Traditional (Theory X)	Participative (Theory Y)
Fringe benefits	Vary according to organizational level	Cafeteria—same for all levels
Promotion	All decisions made by top management	Open posting for all jobs; peer group involvement in decision process
Status symbols	A great many, carefully allocated on the basis of job position	Few present, low emphasis on organization level
Pay type	Hourly and salary	All salary
Base rate	Based on job performed; high enough to attract job applicants	Based on skills; high enough to provide security and attract applicants
Incentive plan	Piece-rate	Group and organization-wide bonus, lump sum increase
Communication policy	Very restricted distribution of information	Individual rates, salary survey data, all other information made public
Decision-making locus	Top management	Close to location of person whose pay is being set

Source: E. E. Lawler, *The Design of Effective Reward Systems,* Technical Report (Los Angeles: University of Southern California, 1983), p. 52.

is in vogue or used "next door," but rather to consider the unique situation and needs of their own organization. Then, with this understanding, a program can be developed and implemented that will facilitate goal-oriented performance.

RECENT DEVELOPMENTS IN REWARD SYSTEMS

Recently, we have seen organizations become increasingly willing to experiment with new methods of compensation and reward systems. This develop-

EXHIBIT 9.12   SUMMARY OF NEW PAY PRACTICES

	Major Advantages	Major Disadvantages	Favorable Situational Factors
Cafeteria-style fringe benefits	Increased satisfaction with pay and benefits	Cost of administration	Well-educated, heterogeneous work force
Lump sum salary increases	Increased satisfaction with pay; greater visibility of pay increases	Cost of administration	Fair pay rates
Skills-based evaluation	More flexible and skilled work force; increased satisfaction	Cost of training and higher salaries	Employees who want to develop themselves; jobs that are interdependent
Open salary information	Increased satisfaction with pay; greater trust and motivation; better salary administration	Pressure to pay all employees the same; complaints about pay rates	Open climate, fair pay rates, pay based on performance
Participative pay decisions	Better pay decisions; increased satisfaction, motivation, and trust	Time consumed	Democratic management climate; work force that wants to participate and that is concerned about organizational goals

Source: Reprinted, by permission of the publisher, from "New Approaches to Pay: Innovations That Work," by E. E. Lawler, *Personnel,* September–October 1976, p. 20, © 1976 American Management Association, New York. All rights reserved.

ment accompanies the quality-of-working-life movement and represents one aspect of managerial efforts to improve the work situation to the benefit of both individuals and organizations. At least five new developments in reward systems can be identified. Exhibit 9.12 summarizes these new developments.

Cafeteria-Style Fringe Benefits

A typical fringe-benefit package provides the same benefits—and the same *amount* of benefits—to all employees. As a result, individual differences or preferences are largely ignored. Studies by Lawler (1976) indicate that different employees prefer variations in the benefits they receive. For instance, young unmarried men prefer more vacation time, while young married men prefer to give up vacation time for higher pay. Older employees want more retirement benefits, while younger employees prefer greater income.

Through a cafeteria-style compensation program, employees are allowed some discretion in the determination of their own package and can make trade-offs up to certain limits. Organizations like TRW and the Educational Testing Service already use such programs. While certain problems of administration exist with the programs, efforts in this direction can lead to increased need satisfaction among employees.

Lump Sum Salary Increases

Another technique that has received some attention is to allow employees to decide how (that is, in what amounts) they wish to receive their pay raise for the coming year. Under the traditional program, pay raises are paid in equal amounts in each paycheck over the year. Under this plan, employees can elect to receive equal amounts during the year or they can choose to take the entire raise in one lump sum.

This plan allows employees greater discretion over their own financial matters. If an employee wants to use the entire pay raise for a vacation, it can be paid in a lump sum in June. Then, if the employee quits before the end of the year, the unearned part of the pay raise is subtracted from the final paycheck.

This plan increases the visibility of the reward to the employee. That is, the employee receives a $600 pay raise (a rather sizable amount) instead of twelve $50 monthly pay raises. As with the cafeteria-style plan, however, the administration costs of the lump sum plan are greater than those of the traditional method.

Skills-Based Evaluation

Typically, compensation programs are tied to job evaluations in which jobs are first analyzed to assess their characteristics and then salary levels are assigned to each job based on factors like job difficulty and labor market scarcity. In other words, pay levels are set based on the job, not the individual. This approach fails to encourage employees to continue learning new skills on the job since there is no reward for the learning. This thinking also keeps all employees in their places and minimizes the possibility of inter-job transfers.

Under the skills-based evaluation program, employees are paid according to their skills level (that is, the number of jobs they can perform), regardless of the actual tasks they are allowed to perform. This approach has proven successful in organizations like Procter and Gamble and General Foods. Employees are encouraged to learn additional skills and are appropriately rewarded. The organization is provided with a more highly trained and more flexible work force. By the same token, however, training and compensation costs are necessarily increased. So, the program is appropriate only in some situations. The technique is most often seen as part of a larger quality-of-working-life program where it is associated with job redesign efforts.

Open Salary Information

Secrecy about pay rates seems to be a widely accepted practice in work organizations, particularly among managerial personnel. It is argued that salary is a personal matter and we should not invade another's privacy. Evidence compiled during the past decade, however, suggests that pay secrecy may have several negative side effects.

To begin, it has been consistently found that in an absence of actual knowledge people have a tendency to overestimate the pay of co-workers and those above in the hierarchy. As a result, much of the motivational potential of a differential reward system is eliminated (Lawler, 1971). Even if an employee receives a relatively sizable salary increase, the individual may still perceive that he or she is receiving less than is due.

This problem is highlighted in the results of a study by Lawler (1971, p. 174). In considering the effects of pay secrecy on motivation, Lawler noted:

> Almost regardless of how well the individual manager was performing, he felt he was getting less than the average raise. This problem was particularly severe among high performers, since they believed that they were doing well yet received minimal reward. They did not believe that pay was in fact based upon merit. This was ironical, since their pay did reflect performance. . . . Thus, even though pay was tied to performance, these managers were not motivated because they could not see the connection.

Pay secrecy also affects motivation via feedback. Several studies have shown the value of feedback in motivating performance. The problem is that, for managers, money represents one of the most meaningful forms of feedback. Pay secrecy eliminates the feedback.

When salary information is open, employees are generally provided with more recognition for satisfactory performance and are often more motivated to perform on subsequent tasks. It is easier to establish feelings of pay equity and trust in the salary administration system. On the other hand, publicizing pay rates and pay raises can cause jealousy among employees and create pressures on managers to reduce perceived inequities in the system. There is no correct position concerning whether pay rates should be secret or open. The point is that managers should not assume *a priori* that pay secrecy—or pay openness—is a good thing. Instead, careful consideration should be given to the possible consequences of either approach in view of the particular situation in the organization at the time.

Participative Pay Decisions

Finally, a question of concern to many managers deals with the extent to which employees should be involved in decisions over pay raises. Recently several organizations have been experimenting with involving employees in pay-raise decisions and the results seem to be quite positive. By allowing employees to participate either in the design of the reward system or in actual

EXHIBIT 9.13 GUIDE TO CHOOSING AMONG THE NEW APPROACHES TO PAY ADMINISTRATION

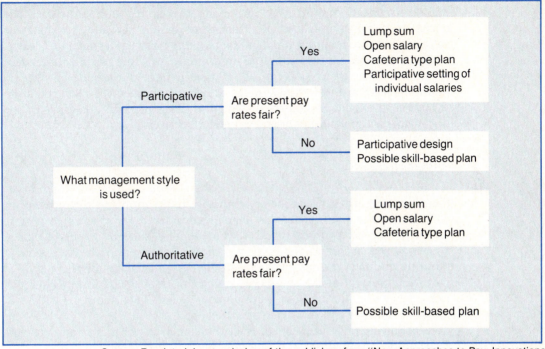

pay-raise decisions (perhaps through a committee), it is argued that decisions of higher quality are made based on greater information. Also, employees then have greater reason to place confidence in the fairness of the decisions. On the negative side, this approach requires considerably more time for both the manager and for the participating subordinates. Costs must be weighed against the benefits to determine which approach is most suitable for the particular organization and its goals.

In deciding which, if any, of these new approaches to implement, Lawler (1976) suggests that two principal issues are of concern: the management style of the organization and the condition of the present-day system (see Exhibit 9.13). If a participative style is preferred, a different approach may be in order than if an authoritative or top-down style is desired.

Beyond this, concern must be raised about the degree of fairness in the present system. As noted in Exhibit 9.13, most of the newer techniques require fairness in order to succeed. While this diagram is meant only to be illustrative, it does suggest some of the more relevant management concerns when deciding on changes in compensation and reward systems.

It must be remembered that allowing employees to participate in pay decisions, as well as the other techniques described above, is relatively new and in many cases largely untested. This is not to suggest that these new developments are without merit. On the contrary, many of these procedures hold considerable promise for improving the equity and fairness of pay decisions and pay practices. But managers should carefully consider the suitability of the techniques in their own unique work environments. Clearly, many of these techniques are more appropriate for some organizations than for others. Thus, the important role of management is to decide how (or if) the compensation and reward systems should be modified. Whatever solution is chosen, it should be consistent with the larger purpose and goals of the organization and facilitate organizational objectives.

SUMMARY

Based on our earlier discussions of employee motivation and performance in various work environments, this chapter considered ways in which performance could be appraised and rewarded. The concept of performance appraisal was introduced and it was noted that appraisals have several purposes and that various problems are inherent in the appraisals.

Next, several of the commonly used performance appraisal techniques were reviewed. The methods were compared with one another to identify major advantages and disadvantages of each.

Following this, functions of reward systems, as well as bases for reward distribution, were considered. The relation between money and motivation was also examined. Finally, various reward systems were introduced and compared, and new developments in this field were discussed.

KEY WORDS

assessment center
behaviorally anchored rating scale
behavioral observation scale
cafeteria-style fringe benefits
central tendency error
critical incident
distributive justice
extrinsic rewards
graphic rating scale
halo effect

intrinsic rewards
leniency error
management-by-objectives
performance appraisal
recency error
reliability
skills-based evaluation
strictness error
validity

FOR DISCUSSION

1. Identify the various functions of performance appraisal. How are appraisals used in most work organizations?

2. What are some of the problems associated with performance appraisals?
3. What is meant by validity and reliability? Why are these two concepts important from a managerial standpoint?
4. Suggest several ways in which errors in appraisal systems can be reduced.
5. Critically evaluate the advantages and disadvantages of the various techniques of performance appraisal.
6. Differentiate between intrinsic and extrinsic rewards.
7. What are the main functions of reward systems?
8. Identify the major bases for reward distribution.
9. How does money influence employee motivation?
10. Discuss the relative merits of individual versus group incentive plans.
11. What are some potential problems and benefits of many of the new developments in reward systems?

MOTIVATION THROUGH MERIT PAY INCREASES

Purpose

To examine the application of motivation theories to the problem of merit pay increases. To understand the relationship between motivation and performance. To consider the impact of multiple performance criteria in managerial decision making.

Instructions

Set up groups of four to eight students for the forty-five to sixty minute exercise. The groups should be separated from each other and asked to converse only with members of their own group. The participants should then read the following:

The Gordon Manufacturing Corporation is a small manufacturing company located in San Diego, California. The company is nonunionized and manufactures laboratory analysis equipment for hospitals.

Approximately one year ago, the manager of the Component Assembly Department established three manufacturing goals for the department. The goals were: (1) reduce raw material storage costs by ten percent; (2) reduce variable labor costs (i.e., overtime) by twelve percent; and (3) decrease the number of quality rejects by fifteen percent. The department manager stated to the six unit supervisors that the degree to which each supervisor met, or exceeded, these goals would be one of the major inputs into their merit pay increases for the year. In previous years, merit increases were based on seniority and an informal evaluation by the department manager.

The six department supervisors worked on separate but similar production lines. A profile of each supervisor is as follows:

- *Freddie McNutt:* white; twenty-four; married with no children; one year with the company after graduating from a local college. First full-time job since graduation from college. He is well-liked by all employees and has exhibited a high level of enthusiasm for his work.

- *Sara Morton:* white; twenty-eight; single; three years with the company after receiving her degree from the state university. Has a job offer from another company for a similar job that provides a substantial pay increase over her present salary (fifteen percent). Gordon does not want to lose Sara because her overall performance has been excellent. The job offer would require her to move to another state, which she views unfavorably; Gordon can keep her if it can come close to matching her salary offer.

- *Jackson Smith:* black; thirty-two; married with three children; three years with the company; high-school education. One of the most stable and steady supervisors. However, he supervises a group of workers who are known to be unfriendly and uncooperative with him and other employees.

- *Lazlo Nagy:* white; thirty-four; married with four children; high-school equivalent learning; one year with the company. Immigrated to this country six years ago and has recently become a U.S. citizen. A steady worker, well-liked by his co-workers, but has had difficulty learning English. As a result, certain problems of communication within his group and with other groups have developed in the past.

- *Karen Doolittle:* white; twenty-nine; divorced with three children; two years with the company; high-school education. Since her divorce one year ago, her performance has begun to improve. Prior to that, her performance was very erratic, with frequent absences. She is the sole support for her three children.

- *Vinnie Sareno:* white; twenty-seven; single; two years with the company; college graduate. One of the best-liked employees at Gordon. However, he has shown a lack of initiative and ambition on the job. Appears to be preoccupied with his social life, particularly around his recently purchased beach home.

Exhibit 9.1 presents summary data on the performance of the six supervisors during the past year. The presented data include the current annual salary, the performance level on the three goals, and an overall evaluation by the department manager.

The new budget for the upcoming year has allocated a total of $79,200 for supervisory salaries in the Component Assembly Department, a $7200 increase from last year. Top management has indicated that salary increases should range from five percent to twelve percent of the supervisors' current salaries and should be tied as closely as possible to their performance.

In making the merit pay increase decisions, the following points should be considered:

1. The decisions will likely set a precedent for future salary and merit increase considerations.
2. Salary increases should not be excessive, but should be representative of the supervisor's performance during the past year. It is hoped that the supervisors develop a clear perception that performance will lead to monetary rewards and that this will serve to motivate them to even better performance.
3. The decisions should be concerned with equity; that is, they ought to be consistent with each other.
4. The company does not want to lose these experienced supervisors to

EXHIBIT 1   INDIVIDUAL PERFORMANCE FOR THE SIX SUPERVISORS DURING THE PAST YEAR

| Supervisor | Current Salary (thousands) | Goal Attainment[a] | | | Manager's Evaluation[b] | | | | |
		Storage Costs (10%)	Labor Costs (12%)	Quality Rejects (15%)	Effort	Cooperativeness	Ability to Work Independently	Knowledge of Job
Freddie McNutt	$11.5	12%	12%	17%	Excellent	Excellent	Good	Good
Sara Morton	$12.5	12%	13%	16%	Excellent	Excellent	Excellent	Excellent
Jackson Smith	$12.5	6%	2%	3%	Good	Excellent	Good	Good
Lazlo Nagy	$11.5	4%	4%	12%	Excellent	Good	Fair	Fair
Karen Doolittle	$12.0	11%	10%	10%	Fair	Fair	Fair	Good
Vinnie Sareno	$12.0	8%	10%	3%	Fair	Fair	Fair	Fair

[a]Numbers designate actual cost and quality-reject reduction.
[b]The possible ratings are poor, fair, good, and excellent.

other firms. Management of this company not only wants the supervisors to be satisfied with their salary increases, but also wants to further develop the feeling that Gordon Manufacturing is a good company for advancement, growth, and career development.

Assignment

1. Each person in the class should *individually* determine the *dollar amount* and *percentage increase* in salary for each of the six supervisors. Individual decisions should be justified by a rationale or decision rule.
2. After each individual has reached a decision, the group will convene and make the same decision as noted in (1) above.
3. After each group has reached a decision, a spokesperson for each group will present the following information to the full class: (a) the group's decision concerning merit pay increase for each supervisor (dollar and percentage); (b) the high, low, and average individual decisions in the group; and (c) a rationale for the group's decision.

Source: A. D. Szilagyi and M. J. Wallace, *Organizational Behavior and Performance,* 2nd ed. (Glenview, Ill.: Scott, Foresman and Company, 1980), pp. 517–19. Reprinted by permission of Scott, Foresman and Company.

CASE

9.1

PERFORMANCE APPRAISAL AT INDSCO

Secrecy about salaries may be one reflection of the general uncertainty about the fairness of the distribution of rewards in large corporations. Uncertainty of merit criteria or patent unfairness of income differentials may result in deliberate concealment or obfuscation of the factors in the judgment of individual cases. There is also, of course, the problem of direct comparison of performance across functions. Indsco kept salary information secret, revealing the range for a grade only if a person requested it, and never revealing individual salaries. No one was supposed to have access to the overall salary picture, except those who administered it and decision makers at the top. Lower-level managers often received clues by accident: "I asked for something for one of my people and was told, 'You can't get that.' That's how I found out what the range was. There are so many things we're not supposed to know. . . ." To the question of the basis for income differentials within the managerial ranks could be added, of course, the more serious question of the basis for the wide gaps in reward between managers and operating workers.[1]

Uncertainty of criteria for management evaluation was a major issue at Indsco. There were definite variations in the extent to which functions could measure and reward for performance in general, let alone the work of managers, variations corresponding to the ex-

Source: Case 9.1 from *Men and Women of the Corporation,* by Rosabeth Moss Kanter, pp. 59–62. Copyright © 1977 by Rosabeth Moss Kanter. Reprinted by permission of Basic Books, Inc., Publishers.

tent to which the function remained nonroutinized and discretionary. The highest-ranking salary administrator concluded after a long review that engineering and R & D did the best job of rewarding for performance. In these areas, of course, performance in general was easiest to measure, since workers did roughly the same thing in centralized locations, and the exercise of managerial discretion was minimal compared to functions like sales or marketing. But when the administrator looked at the extent to which previous performance ratings had predicted who did well as officers during a five-year period (something for which he felt there should be about seventy-five percent accuracy), he found little correlation between ratings of "potential," "performance," and "growth," and actual behavior.

Managers themselves experienced uncertainties about evaluation. Said a sales manager, "It's hard as a manager to know when you're doing well. You can't *really* take credit for improvements in sales." The further away they were from first-line involvement with operating tasks, the more managers seemed to be aware of the increasingly vague performance criteria. When the new Indsco management system was introduced, everyone above grade five generated a position charter and wrote, in conjunction with his or her boss, a statement of objectives and performance standards. It was hard to prevent generalities from creeping in. A manager in one field office heard that the corporation president wrote as one of his performance standards: "The Chairman of the Board thinks I'm doing a good job." So the manager tried to put in his: "My boss thinks I'm doing a good job." That was the best and most precise measure he felt he could develop. (His boss did not accept this, but the problem

was made clear to everyone concerned.)

There were other examples of the difficulty in pinning down what made a good manager. An executive personnel committee generated a list of characteristics that would make a person "officer material" (although they also denied that such a list existed). The traits were so vague as to be almost meaningless, and they included a large number of elements subject to social interpretation: "empathy; integrity; acceptance of accountability; ambition; makes decisions; intelligent; takes appropriate risks; smart; uses the organization through trust and delegation; a good communicator; a good track record." A group of junior managers also made a list, as part of a training activity, and it did not succeed in being any more specific. If anything, the young managers' list increased the judgmental, interpretive social components: "good communicator; well organized; good interpersonal skills; a successful performer; high peer acceptance; a risk-taker; highly visible to other managers; able to recognize opportunities; results-oriented; and possessing the requisite amount of prior experience in the company and in the function."

Although the characteristics of a good manager were far from easily or directly measurable, there was agreement that being a good team player who fit into the organization and had strong "peer acceptance" was essential for moving into the managerial ranks in the first place. "Individual performers" who did a job unusually well but were not organization men could be rewarded by raises but not by promotions. Respondents to a sales force survey were asked to rank order twelve possible factors in both managerial promotions and salary increases. As Exhibit 1 shows, the factors contributing to both promotions and

Order of Factors in Promotion* (N = 162)	Order of Factors in Salary Increase* (N = 155)
Item (mean rank)	**Item (mean rank)**
1. Overall performance record (2.41)	1. Overall performance record (2.06)
2. Organizational, managerial ability (4.07)	2. Occasional spectacular sales performance (3.91)
3. Reliability, dependability (4.09)	3. Reliability, dependability (4.49)
4. Skill with people (4.58)	4. Organizational, managerial ability (5.03)
5. Seniority (5.14)	5. Seniority (5.26)
6. Occasional spectacular sales performance (5.48)	6. Skill with people (5.64)
7. Amount of education, special training (6.84)	7. Routine action—time scheduled to happen (6.36)
8. An "in" with management (6.89)	8. Amount of education, special training (7.28)
9. Reports from customers (8.10)	9. An "in" with management (7.42)
10. Routine action—time scheduled to happen (8.11)	10. Reports from customers (8.18)
11. Luck, good fortune (8.12)	11. Personal need (8.78)
12. Personal need (9.53)	12. Luck, good fortune (8.97)

*The rank orders were computed from the mean score given each item (taking a rank of 1 as a score of 1, a rank of 12 as a score of 12, etc.). There were no ties. Degree of agreement over all respondents ranged from .47 to .88, with a mean degree of agreement of .69. The greatest agreement and smallest standard deviation occurred for the item ranked #1 on both lists; the largest spread was around the items on an "in" with management, routine action, and education.

raises were given approximately the same rank—except in the case of the item reflecting exceptional performance of the job content. This was seen as very important for a raise (ranked second) but much less important for promotion (ranked sixth). For promotion, such factors as reliability and dependability, skill with people, and seniority were considered more important. Fitting in socially was a requisite for the transition to managerial status.

Furthermore, in the absence of clear and objective measures, organizations can fall back on a routinized system, in which advancement proceeds automatically when it is scheduled to happen —something the Indsco sample felt

was very *unimportant* in managerial promotions—or social, "nonability" factors can enter into career decisions. "Social credentials" are common substitutes for ability measures in management positions. A University of Michigan team identified a number of forms of "nonability" traits and social credentials that were important in executive selection in industrial firms in the Midwest: having the right social background; living in a good section of town; belonging to the right club or lodge; being white; graduating from a high-prestige college; being native born; having "solid respectability"; getting along with co-workers; and having superficial presentability. Indeed, the vagueness of the line between job-relevant and private conduct gave organizations the right to generate norms for the appropriate out-of-work behavior of higher-ranking members, and it gave management incumbents a rationale for distinguishing between candidates on the grounds of social acceptability. Indsco clearly prided itself on not going as far in this respect as other companies. (Managers liked to contrast Indsco with a competitor, headquartered in a company town, that told recruits what residential sections of town were appropriate for their status, what clubs they should join, and where to send their children to school.) But the similarity in manner and style among management people and the Anglo-Saxon flavor of the place led one young man with a very Italian name to legally change his name in order to take his wife's decidedly British name. And "peer acceptance," as we have seen, was considered essential to managerial success.

Note

1. Although the names have been disguised, this case is based on a study of a real organization.

CASE DISCUSSION QUESTIONS

1. Why do you suppose Indsco executives chose to keep salary information from even the lower-level managers?
2. What were some of the consequences of pay secrecy?
3. What problems did Indsco encounter when trying to establish performance evaluation criteria?
4. What happened at Indsco— and what happens in other organizations—when evaluation criteria are vague?
5. What would you have done to reduce the uncertainty surrounding evaluations at Indsco?

JOB ATTITUDES AND BEHAVIOR

One of the most widely discussed aspects of organizational life is job attitudes. We continually hear references to how satisfied—or dissatisfied —employees are on the job. Most managers have their own pet theories on how to improve satisfaction. However, while the importance of job attitudes has been recognized for many years, it is only recently that serious study of the actual determinants of attitudes in organizational settings and their consequences for organizational well-being has begun. In this chapter, we will examine the role of job attitudes in organizational behavior.

CHAPTER TEN

IMPORTANCE OF TOPIC FOR MANAGERS

An understanding of attitudes, attitude formation, and attitude change is important. Attitudes are inherent in every aspect of work life. People have attitudes about most things that happen to them, as well as about almost everyone they meet. In view of this universal characteristic of attitudes, an understanding of their nature is essential for managers.

Attitudes influence behavior. Much of how we behave at work is governed by how we feel about things. Therefore, an awareness of attitudes can assist managers in understanding human behavior at work. Changes in employee behavior can be expected to the extent that managers can change employee attitudes.

Understanding the influence of attitudes on employee behavior not only helps a manager be more effective, it can save an organization money as well. Bad attitudes on the job cost money. Poor job attitudes can be reflected in a variety of ways—subsequent poor performance, turnover, and absenteeism —all of which result in direct costs to the organization.

THE NATURE OF JOB ATTITUDES

This chapter examines several aspects of job attitudes. We begin with a discussion of the general nature of job attitudes, followed by a look at how attitudes are changed (or not changed) over time.

Attitude Defined

Although there are various definitions for the concept of attitude (Allport, 1935), several common threads can be found. For our purposes here, an *attitude* may be defined as a predisposition to respond in a favorable or unfavorable way to objects or persons in one's environment. When we like or dislike something, we are, in effect, expressing our attitude toward the person or object. An attitude reflects our feelings toward other objects and people.

Three important assumptions underlie this definition of attitudes. First, an attitude is a hypothetical construct; that is, while the consequences of an attitude may be observed, the attitude itself cannot. We do not see attitudes —we observe the resulting behavior. We only assume that attitudes exist inside people.

Second, an attitude is a unidimensional variable. That is, an attitude toward a particular person or object ranges on a continuum from very favorable to very unfavorable. We like something or we dislike something.

Something is pleasurable or unpleasurable. In all cases, the attitude can be measured along an evaluative continuum.

Third, attitudes are believed to be related to subsequent behavior. The text's definition of attitude implies that people behave based on how they feel. For instance, research has consistently shown that low job satisfaction (a negative attitude) is moderately related to employee absenteeism and turnover (a behavior). As we shall see later, the relationship between attitudes and behavior is not a perfect one. Other factors, like personality, external controls and conditions, etc., weaken the impact of attitudes on behavior.

A Model of Job Attitudes

One approach to gaining a clearer understanding of attitudes is to examine the antecedents and consequences of attitudes in a work situation. Some researchers suggest that the attitude construct be divided into three components: (1) a *cognitive* component, dealing with beliefs and ideas a person has about a certain person or object; (2) an *affective* component, dealing with the person's feelings toward the person or object; and (3) a *behavioral intention* component, dealing with the behavioral intentions a person has toward the person or object as a result of affective responses (Triandis, 1971). However, more recently Fishbein and Ajzen (1975) argued that the notion of attitudes is easier to understand if we separate these three components and define attitudes simply as affective responses, treating the cognitive and behavioral intention components as antecedents and outcomes of the attitude itself. This represents a more specific description of attitudes. While this model uses the same three basic components of earlier models, it clearly suggests how the components fit together and is helpful for measurement purposes.

This model, shown in Exhibit 10.1, has four basic components: beliefs (cognitions), attitudes (affects), behavioral intentions, and actual behavior. *Beliefs* represent the information a person holds about an object. For instance, an employee may describe his or her job as exciting or dull, dirty or clean, independent or dependent. These descriptions represent beliefs the individual has about the job. It is important to note that these beliefs may or may not be factual. An exciting job to one person may be dull to another. Regardless, beliefs are thought to be factual by the individual.

These beliefs, then, influence the *attitudes,* or affective responses, formed by employees. For instance, a person who believes his job is dull, dirty, and dependent may develop a negative attitude toward the job and be dissatisfied. This dissatisfaction with the job situation may, in turn, lead him to choose undesirable forms of behavior. For instance, he may decide to seek another job or to reduce his level of effort. This conscious decision to seek alternative employment is the *behavioral intention.* Finally, it is suggested by Fishbein and Ajzen (1975) that these behavioral intentions become translated into *actual job behavior* (such as high turnover, absenteeism, and lower performance).

This model clearly suggests that actual behavior is not determined by a

EXHIBIT 10.1   A CONCEPTUAL MODEL OF JOB ATTITUDES

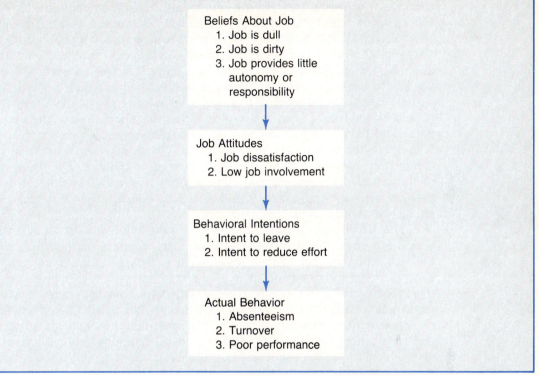

Beliefs About Job
1. Job is dull
2. Job is dirty
3. Job provides little autonomy or responsibility

Job Attitudes
1. Job dissatisfaction
2. Low job involvement

Behavioral Intentions
1. Intent to leave
2. Intent to reduce effort

Actual Behavior
1. Absenteeism
2. Turnover
3. Poor performance

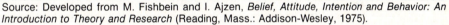

Source: Developed from M. Fishbein and I. Ajzen, *Belief, Attitude, Intention and Behavior: An Introduction to Theory and Research* (Reading, Mass.: Addison-Wesley, 1975).

person's attitudes. Instead, it argues that behavioral intentions represent a primary influence on behavior. Thus, individuals dissatisfied with their jobs would quit or reduce performance level only after consciously deciding to do so (behavioral intention). This concept is closely related to Locke's (1968) theory of goal-setting.

Belief and Attitude Formation

It was suggested above that attitudes are influenced by the beliefs we hold about people, objects, and events. We are now in a position to take a closer look at how attitudes are formed. To do this, we will examine beliefs, the process by which beliefs are formed, and what types of factors influence beliefs and attitudes.

Beliefs. A knowledge of beliefs is important in the study of attitudes for several reasons. To begin, beliefs represent a major influence on attitudes. Changing beliefs can change attitudes. As noted by Scheibe (1970, p. 26), "beliefs about future occurrences are often important determinants of those occurrences, for they influence the choices that are made, the chances that are taken, and the hypotheses that are adopted as working assumptions."

A *belief* may be defined as a perceived relationship between people, objects, and events. Beliefs are what individuals consider true about themselves and their environment. Beliefs differ from *values* in that beliefs are seen as having factual referents (Ebert and Mitchell, 1975). While beliefs may not actually be correct or accurate, the individual is convinced that they are true. Values, on the other hand, are closely held normative standards that are chosen on the basis of personal preference among alternatives. Values carry with them the notion of "should." For example, one employee may place a high value on getting ahead in a company and may work overtime to demonstrate dedication. Another employee may place a high value on recreation and free time and may prefer a job that is less demanding. Neither value is right or wrong in the factual sense, although people may feel very strongly about the values they hold.

How are beliefs formed? This question is difficult to answer. Apparently, beliefs are formed as a result of at least four processes (Sarbin, Taft, and Bailey, 1960). First, beliefs are often based on past experiences. Over time, we observe events and draw inferences about an important issue. For instance, a manager may observe that one of his employees is constantly late for work, leaves early, and spends much of the day in idle gossip. Based on this observation, the manager may develop the belief that the employee is lazy or lacks dedication. Second, beliefs may be constructed by individuals based on available information about a particular issue. For example, since some women stay home with children or quit their jobs because of family responsibilities, we may develop the belief that many women really don't want jobs outside the home. Depending on the individual, of course, such a belief may or may not be true.

Oftentimes, beliefs are developed as a result of generalizing from similar situations, events, or objects. For instance, a manager who is transferred from one location to another may take with him his beliefs about line-staff relationships, union militancy, or status symbols, assuming that the new location will be identical to the previous one. Finally, a fourth process involved in forming beliefs is the influencing effect of individuals in whom we have confidence. For instance, the first astronauts assumed that the engineers and scientists knew what they were doing when they built the spacecraft. Thus, the beliefs we have are shaped by a variety of events, including past experience, trust in others, and our own imagination and inductive reasoning.

Influences on Attitude Formation. Perhaps the most important thing to note about the formation of attitudes is that they are *learned*. People learn from their environment and from prior experiences which beliefs and attitudes are acceptable.

At least four major influences on attitude learning can be identified. First, many of our general attitudes are learned as a result of *cultural influences*. For instance, our attitudes toward allowing lower-level employees

EXHIBIT 10.2　FUNCTIONS OF WORK ATTITUDES

Functions	Definition	Example
Adjustment to work	To help individuals adjust to the necessity of work and to membership in an organization.	"This company is an okay place to work, since I have to have a job."
Ego-defense	To defend individuals from adverse truths about themselves.	"Why is management always acting so stuck up just because we workers don't have as much education or status?"
Value expression	To provide individuals with a vehicle for expressing values and opinions.	"What's good for General Motors is good for the country."
Knowledge	To help individuals explain and organize an otherwise chaotic world; to serve as a frame of reference.	"Workers should never trust management because, in the past, they have always tried to exploit us."

to have a major voice in the operations and decisions of a business firm are generally culturally based (Rokeach, 1973). Second, attitudes are influenced by *group memberships.* The study by Haire (1955) cited earlier demonstrated how managers and union members held different opinions of each other as a function of group membership. Third, the *family* can influence attitudes. Many attitudes toward members of other races and economic classes are formed here (Costello and Zalkind, 1963). Finally, *prior work experiences* influence our beliefs and attitudes about specific aspects of the job. For example, opinions of how much effort represents a fair day's work, what constitutes a fair day's pay, and how employees should be treated can be influenced by prior experience.

Functions of Attitudes

Before examining the nature of work attitudes in any detail it is useful to know why attitudes are important for individuals. Katz (1960) has suggested that attitudes serve four important *functions* for individuals (see Exhibit 10.2).

The Adjustment Function. Attitudes often help people adjust to their work environment. They facilitate need satisfaction. We tend to develop favorable attitudes toward objects or people that are associated with providing positive rewards and benefits, and negative attitudes toward those that are associated with negative sanctions and penalties. In this way, our attitudes and experiences become relatively congruent. They provide a cognitive map of what is good and bad. This adjustment function is illustrated in the attitudes employees have toward political parties. Blue-collar workers tend to have favorable attitudes toward more liberal politicians because they are seen as supportive of their causes, while executives and entrepreneurs tend to have favorable attitudes toward more conservative politicians for the same reason.

The adjustment function of attitudes is also clearly seen in Bem's (1972) *self-perception theory.* According to this theory, people form attitudes as a result of their behaviors (instead of behaviors resulting from attitudes). Their attitudes are formed as a defense or rationale for their behaviors. For example, an employee may say, "I continue to work here (behavior) so I must enjoy the job (attitude)." Here, the attitude helps the employee adjust to the work situation and, quite frankly, makes life easier for the employee.

Management often attempts to capitalize on this adjustment function as a vehicle for improving performance. In many instances, companies provide generous fringe benefits or recreational facilities in the hope of making workers more committed to the organization (form more positive attitudes toward it) and desirous of performing at higher levels. However, as Katz (1960) notes, while these activities may serve to make the organization seem more attractive as a place to work, there is little reason to believe that performance itself will improve. The provision of universal rewards such as fringe benefits may make the work place more attractive, but the absence of a performance-reward contingency fails to create a motivating environment. While people may be motivated to join and remain with an organization, there is little reason to expect them to perform.

The Ego-defensive Function. Attitudes can also protect individuals from acknowledging basic truths about themselves or the harsh realities of their external environments. In this way, attitudes protect a person's ego from internal or external threat. An employee who consistently has a negative attitude toward co-workers or who is persistently argumentative may, in fact, be acting out internal conflicts and thus may be relieving emotional tensions. This behavior does not, however, solve the problem of adjusting to the work situation.

Many attitudes in the work situation function in the defense of a self-image. For instance, at least part of the negative attitudes workers have toward their supervisors can be traced to feelings of inferiority due to lack of education or lack of advancement. Similarly, the negative attitude managers often have toward workers can be explained in part by inner feelings of inferiority and an experienced need to feel superior. When people cannot admit to themselves that they have deep feelings of inferiority, these feelings can be easily projected onto a convenient group (managers, workers, minorities) to bolster their own attitude of superiority.

The Value-expressive Function. Although many attitudes prevent individuals from revealing their true nature to themselves or those around them, other attitudes provide a vehicle for positive expression of central values. They allow individuals to demonstrate to others the type of person they think they are, and thus establish or reinforce self-identity.

The value-expressive function of attitudes can be readily seen in spontaneous political discussions at social gatherings. By clearly and forcefully stating political views, individuals are establishing a clear view of who they are and what they stand for. Similarly, many managers seem to be outspoken about "my company, right or wrong" in an effort to clearly portray their perceived role in the organization and society. Charlie Wilson, when he was president of General Motors, once stated that "what is good for General Motors is good for the country." Such statements represent clear value-expressive attitudes in that they convey strong feelings.

The Knowledge Function. Finally, attitudes help explain and organize an otherwise chaotic world. As Katz (1960) notes, people need standards or frames of reference for understanding and interpreting people and events around them. Attitudes help supply these standards. In Lippman's (1972) classic study of opinions and attitudes, it was pointed out that stereotypes (a form of attitude) provide order and clarity for a bewildering set of complexities that face individuals.

ATTITUDE CHANGE

One of the more difficult tasks of management is to create a work environment where employees have positive attitudes about their jobs and their place of work. If attitudes do, in fact, influence behavior, then creating positive attitudes toward the job is of critical importance. Two aspects of attitude change are worthy of note. First, we should understand two prominent barriers to attitude change. Second, we should know a few widely recognized techniques used in attitude change.

Barriers to Attitude Change

There are at least two primary barriers that can inhibit the extent to which employees change their attitudes. These are: (1) insufficient justification and (2) prior commitments.

Insufficient Justification. First, employees may see no reason to change their beliefs or attitudes. As Costello and Zalkind (1963, p. 275) note, just "because you [the manager] are dissatisfied with an individual's attitude is not a reason for him to want to change. His attitudes may be displeasing to you but satisfying to him." For example, a manager may want employees to develop more favorable attitudes toward and trust in management. However, those employees who feel that in the past, management treated them unfairly may see management's new overtures as somewhat hollow. In other words, such attitudes are serving an adjustment function. In the absence of a felt need to change, there is little reason to expect those employees to change their attitudes simply because management thinks it desirable.

Prior Commitments. A second barrier to attitude change is prior commitments. This is the ego-defensive function of attitudes. As Staw (1976) found, people who feel personally responsible for a bad choice—one that led to negative consequences—tend to commit additional resources to the previously chosen course of action. Instead of admitting their mistake, individuals often cognitively distort the negative consequences into positive consequences in order to rationalize their previous decision, or to defend themselves psychologically against adverse outcomes. One way to do this is to redouble the resolve to the previously chosen course of action, to "dig one's feet in" and selectively screen out, reject, or distort contradictory information. Thus, when a manager thinks about changing attitudes, he or she must remember that prior behavioral commitments made by others could represent significant barriers.

Mechanisms of Attitude Change

In view of these barriers, how are attitudes changed? Several mechanisms for change can be identified: (1) providing new information; (2) fear arousal and reduction; (3) dissonance arousal; (4) position discrepancy; and (5) participation in decision making.

Providing New Information. One of the most common methods of changing attitudes (and possibly subsequent behavior) is by providing individuals with new information that changes their set of beliefs. As discussed earlier, Fishbein (Fishbein and Ajzen, 1975) argues that beliefs cause attitudes. Hence, if we can alter belief structures, subsequent attitude changes can be expected. For example, in a study by Lieberman (1956) of unionized manufacturing workers, it was found that union workers held very strong beliefs on issues such as management concern for workers and labor standards. Subsequently, however, a subsample from the original group was promoted into managerial ranks. This subsample was exposed to new (though not necessarily more accurate) information that changed members' belief structures about the activities of management. As a result, the group receiving promotions altered their attitudes so they were substantially more pro-management and anti-union. In other words, being placed in a new situation with new information changed employee beliefs which, in turn, changed attitudes.

An important point relating to the provision of new information should be noted. In order for new information to affect beliefs and attitudes, it must come from what is perceived to be a credible or accurate source. If a supervisor announces that henceforth, instead of rewarding employees on a seniority basis, rewards (pay, promotion) will be closely tied to employee job performance, we would expect employees to try harder on the job if they believe the supervisor and value the rewards. Exhorting employees to work harder and promising unrealistic or nonexistent rewards should only lead to increased alienation, not increased effort. In the Lieberman study, it can be assumed that the employees who were promoted to managerial positions, and who subsequently altered their attitudes toward management and union, believed they were receiving new information that justified a modification in beliefs and attitudes.

Fear Arousal and Reduction. Two related aspects of attitude change center around the notion of fear. It is somewhat ironic that attitude change can be facilitated, depending upon the circumstances, both by arousing fear and by reducing fear. Let us see how this works.

Several studies have shown that *arousing* an individual's fear of an object or event can cause the individual to modify his or her position regarding that object or event (Triandis, 1971). Efforts to arouse employee fear are made by both unions and management just prior to a strike, for instance. However, the fear-arousal–attitude-change relationship is somewhat more complex than this. Specifically, it appears that the relationship between fear and attitude change is characterized by an inverted U-curve. At very low levels of fear arousal, the message may not be received or given much attention; it may not be sufficiently threatening to stimulate change. At moderate levels of fear arousal, however, reception of the message is likely to increase and attitude change is expected. Finally, when extremely high fear levels are aroused, it has been found that reception of the message actually decreases as individuals begin to defend themselves against highly objectionable stimuli. Under situations of extremely high fear arousal, attitudes do *not* tend to change because the message is rejected by individuals (McGuire, 1968).

An example will clarify this point. Consider a white manager working for a company that is under considerable affirmative action pressure from the government to hire minorities. Initially, this manager may not have strong opinions about minorities as managers. If a rumor is circulated throughout the organization that it is necessary to hire a few minority managers to "keep the government off our backs" (low fear arousal), there is little reason to believe that this manager would feel threatened or that he would modify his attitude toward the managerial capabilities of minorities. However, if a rumor is circulated that, given tremendous pressure, a disproportionate share of the new hires and promotions will be given to minorities (moderate fear arousal), it is highly conceivable that the white manager might feel threatened and develop negative (defensive) attitudes toward minorities. Finally, if a rumor is circulated that every new hire and every promotion must go to a minority and that perhaps many whites will be laid off to accommodate the minorities (high fear arousal), there is a good likelihood that the message will be rejected as either too extreme to be correct or too threatening to be acknowledged. In this circumstance, we would not expect much attitude change because the individual would either ignore or discount the message.

On the other hand, as noted by Katz (1960), there are times when fear *reduction* is more appropriate for changing attitudes than fear arousal. Specifically, when a particular attitude (e.g., a negative attitude toward management) protects the individual from internal conflicts or external threats (ego-defensive attitude), the use of threats to alter attitudes would only heighten fears, and thereby increase resistance to change. For instance, the installation of a new computer system is often met with stiff resistance by employees who fear such changes. In these situations, efforts by management to reduce fear (and, it is hoped, reduce threats to self-image and self-esteem) may create an atmosphere where changes receive a fair chance and where employees may even be receptive to them.

Dissonance Arousal. Much research has been conducted on the manner in which people accommodate discrepancies between behavior and attitudes. While several theories exist, the most widely received is Festinger's (1957) theory of *cognitive dissonance.* This theory states that when people find themselves behaving in a manner that is inconsistent with their attitudes, they experience tension and will attempt to reduce this tension.

For example, an employee may have negative attitudes toward her job but be required to work long hours. Here she is faced with a clear discrepancy between attitude and behavior and she will probably experience cognitive dissonance. In order to become *cognitively consistent,* the employee can do one of two things. First, she can change her behavior and work fewer hours. However, this may not be possible. Second, the employee can change her attitudes toward work so they are more consistent with her behavior. She may convince herself that the job really is not as bad as she envisioned and that the long hours may help her toward rapid promotion. In doing so, the employee achieves a state of cognitive consistency and the tension is reduced.

The potency of cognitive dissonance in attitude change can be seen in several studies of job choice behavior among business students (Lawler, Kuleck, Rhode, and Sorenson, 1975; Vroom and Deci, 1971). In these studies, graduating students were asked to rate the attractiveness (that is, favorableness of attitude) of several firms for which they could work. Students generally chose those firms that seemed to have greatest attractiveness. However, after the students actually began working for their selected firms, it was found that they lowered their attitudes toward the other firms (the firms they did *not* go to work for) and increased their attitudes toward the selected firms. In other words, the dissonance created by having to choose one firm was reduced by cognitively distorting (reducing) the attractiveness of the other firms. Thus, the students felt more secure that they had made the correct job choice decision.

Position Discrepancy. A fourth technique by which attitude change can be brought about concerns the difference between an individual's present position toward something and the position advocated by others. We are concerned here with the discrepancy between the two positions and their effects on change. Sometimes, an issue is not especially important to an individual, or does not particularly involve him. When this is the case, research shows that the greater the discrepancy between the individual's own position and the position advocated by others, the more the individual will move toward the position held by others. Hence, if someone told you that Fords were far superior to Chevrolets—and you did not drive—you would probably develop a more positive attitude toward Fords and a less positive attitude toward Chevrolets.

However, when the issue involved is of personal importance to you, findings show that moderate position discrepancy produces more change than extreme discrepancy. So, if you were a traveling salesperson who used your car extensively, and you had just spent much time and money choosing a new Chevrolet (high personal involvement), you would probably consider the individual advocating the extreme position on Fords biased or uninformed. Hence, a moderate approach is more suitable for producing change.

Participation in Decision Making. A final way of effecting attitude change is to involve target individuals in the process by which decisions are made. Early experiments by Kurt Lewin during World War II showed that when housewives were involved in discussions over the value of buying less desirable meat, they were more inclined to make purchases than when simply asked to do so. Similar examples can be found in organizational settings. In fact, a primary rationale behind the participative management movement is that the act of involving lower-level employees in decisions affecting their jobs creates more positive job attitudes. As noted by Vroom (1960), when employees are allowed to participate in decisions, they become more ego-involved in the outcomes and tend to identify more with the actual issues involved and with the organization.

One mechanism of facilitating employee participation is the use of attitude surveys. As noted in Close-Up 10.1, these surveys represent a potentially powerful mechanism for attitude change.

In summary, there are several ways in which attitudes can be changed. Most of these techniques involve changing the beliefs held by individuals which, in turn, affect attitude formation (Fishbein and Ajzen, 1975). To the extent that beliefs and attitudes can be changed, we would expect some changes in subsequent behavior.

JOB SATISFACTION

When the concept of attitudes is applied to work settings, it is necessary to be specific about which attitude we are concerned with. While a variety of work-related job attitudes can be mentioned, it appears that attitudes relating to job satisfaction are particularly important from the standpoint of management. The notion of job satisfaction is one of the most widely studied variables in organizational behavior. We will examine this concept in detail as it relates to the management of people at work.

CLOSE-UP 10.1 ATTITUDE SURVEYS IN ORGANIZATIONS

For many years companies have taken annual attitude (or morale) surveys to assess the general level of satisfaction among employees. In recent years, however, these surveys have become more important for at least two reasons: (1) attitude surveys now focus on a wider range of organizational activities and provide more information to management about possible trouble spots; and (2) companies have begun to take attitude surveys more seriously and actually implement changes based on results.

Here are three examples of successful applications of attitude surveys:

General Electric Company. In a survey of more than 20,000 employees, G.E. found that over one-half of the respondents were dissatisfied with the information and recognition they received and with their opportunities for advancement. As a result, management instituted regular monthly meetings, brought in experts to answer questions, and initiated a newsletter. One year later, a follow-up survey found that the number of employees dissatisfied with the information they received dropped from fifty percent to none, while the number dissatisfied with promotional opportunities fell from fifty percent to twenty percent.

Geosource, Incorporated. This Houston-based company found that its welders were extremely dissatisfied with pay levels, despite the competitive wage paid there. In a survey feedback session, management discovered that welders were reading want ads offering "up to $7.84 per hour" for welders. When it was pointed out that no company hires at the maximum wage the discontent subsided.

American Can Company. A survey found employees concerned about a lack of career opportunities. As a result, the company initiated a job information center where employees could discuss their qualifications, ambitions, and training needs, and a weekly thirty-minute job seminar where senior executives would talk about career opportunities in their areas.

Two factors seem to influence the success of these attitude surveys. First, it is important that results are fed back to all employees, not just to top management. There must be ready access to all information. Second, successful programs are marked by a commitment from top management to initiate changes where needed. Quick action by management, as noted in the three examples above, reassures employees that the company is concerned about creating a suitable work environment and about what employees' opinions are of such an environment.

Source: "A Productive Way to Vent Employee Gripes," *Business Week,* October 16, 1978, pp. 168–71.

The Concept of Job Satisfaction

Job satisfaction may be defined as "a pleasurable or positive emotional state resulting from the appraisal of one's job or job experience" (Locke, 1976, p.

1300). It results from the perception that an employee's job actually provides what an employee values in the work situation.

Several characteristics of the concept of job satisfaction follow from this definition. First, satisfaction is an emotional response to a job situation. It can be fully understood only by introspection. As with any attitude, we cannot observe satisfaction; we must infer its existence and quality either from an employee's behavior or verbal statements.

Second, job satisfaction is perhaps best understood as a discrepancy. Several writers have pointed to the concept of job satisfaction as being a result of how much a person wants or expects from the job *compared to* how much he or she actually receives (Locke, 1969; Katzell, 1964; Porter and Steers, 1973). People come to work with varying levels of job expectations. These expectations may vary not only in quality (different people may value different things in a job), but also in intensity. Based on work experiences, people receive outcomes, or rewards, from the job. These outcomes include not only extrinsic rewards like pay and promotion, but also a variety of intrinsic rewards, such as satisfying co-worker relations and meaningful work. To the extent that the outcomes received by an employee meet or exceed expectations, we would expect the employee to be satisfied with the job and wish to remain. On those occasions when outcomes actually surpass expectations, we would expect employees to reevaluate their expectations and probably raise them to meet available outcomes. However, when outcomes do not meet expectations, employees are dissatisfied and may prefer to seek alternative sources of satisfaction, either by changing jobs or by placing greater value on other life activities, such as outside recreation.

Dimensions of Job Satisfaction

It has been argued by several investigators (Smith, Kendall, and Hulin, 1969) that job satisfaction actually represents several related attitudes. So, when we speak of satisfaction, we must specify "satisfaction with what?" Smith et al. have suggested that five job dimensions represent the most salient characteristics of a job about which people have affective responses. These five are:

- *Work itself.* The extent to which tasks performed by employees are interesting and provide opportunities for learning and for accepting responsibility.
- *Pay.* The amount of pay received, the perceived equity of the pay, and the method of payment.
- *Promotional opportunities.* The availability of realistic opportunities for advancement.
- *Supervision.* The technical and managerial abilities of supervisors, the extent to which supervisors demonstrate consideration for and interest in employees.
- *Co-workers.* The extent to which co-workers are friendly, technically competent, and supportive.

While other dimensions of job satisfaction have been identified (satisfaction with company policies, fringe benefits), these five dimensions are employed most often when examining aspects of job attitudes at work.

Measurement of Job Satisfaction

Probably the most common survey that managers carry out among employees is the measurement of job satisfaction. Satisfaction is felt by many managers to be an important indicator of organizational effectiveness and, as such, necessitates continual monitoring of attitudes to assess employee feelings toward their jobs and the organization.

There are many ways in which job satisfaction can be measured (Locke, 1976). We will identify five: (1) rating scales; (2) critical incidents; (3) interviews; (4) overt behavior; and (5) action tendencies.

Rating Scales. The most popular technique for assessing job satisfaction is the use of *rating scales.* Rating scales are direct verbal self-reports and have been used since the 1930s (Hoppock, 1935). Several job satisfaction scales exist (Smith et al., 1969; Lofquist and Dawis, 1969). One scale that has been used in a variety of studies is the Minnesota Satisfaction Questionnaire (Lofquist and Dawis, 1969). This instrument uses a Likert-response format to generate satisfaction scores on twenty-six scales. Examples of MSQ questions are shown in Exhibit 10.3.

Another widely used scale is the Job Descriptive Index (Smith et al., 1969). The JDI, also partially shown in Exhibit 10.3, presents employees with a series of adjectives that may or may not describe five aspects of their job (work itself, pay, promotion, supervision, and co-workers). Employees are asked to answer each item with yes (Y), no (N), or don't know (?) to indicate the extent each adjective applies to their job.

The MSQ, the JDI, and similar rating scales have several advantages for evaluating levels of job satisfaction. First, they are relatively short and simple and can be completed by large numbers of employees quickly. Second, because of the generalized wording of the various terms, the instruments can be administered to a wide range of employees in various jobs. It is not necessary to alter the questionnaire for each job classification. Finally, the JDI has extensive normative data (or norms) available. These norms include summaries of the scores of thousands of people who have completed the JDI (see Smith et al., 1969). Hence, it is possible for employers in other organizations to determine relative standings.

However, while rating scales have many virtues compared to other techniques, at least two drawbacks must be recognized (Locke, 1976). First, as with any self-report inventory, it is assumed that respondents are both willing and able to accurately describe their feelings. As noted by several researchers (Staw, 1976; Vroom, 1964), people often consciously or unconsciously distort information that they feel is damaging and enhance information that they feel is beneficial. For example, it is possible that employees who think their

EXHIBIT 10.3   EXAMPLES OF TWO JOB SATISFACTION MEASURES

A. Examples from the *Minnesota Satisfaction Questionnaire*

On my present job, this is how I feel about . . .	Not Satisfied	Only Slightly Satisfied	Satisfied	Very Satisfied	Extremely Satisfied
1. the chance to be active much of the time	1	2	3	4	5
2. the variety in my work	1	2	3	4	5
3. the policies and practices toward employees of this company	1	2	3	4	5
4. the chance to be responsible for planning my work	1	2	3	4	5
5. the opportunities for advancement on this job	1	2	3	4	5

Source: University of Minnesota Industrial Relations Center, Minneapolis, Minnesota.

B. Sample Items from the Job Descriptive Index (Revised, 1985) (each scale is presented on a separate page)

Think of the pay you get now. How well does each of the following words or phrases describe your present pay? In the blank beside each word, write

__Y__ for "Yes" if it describes your pay
__N__ for "No" if it does NOT describe it
__?__ if you cannot decide

Present Pay
_____ Income adequate for normal expenses
_____ Insecure
_____ Less than I deserve
_____ Well paid

Think of the opportunities for promotion that you have now. How well does each of the following words describe these? In the blank beside each word, put

__Y__ for "Yes" if it describes your opportunities for promotion
__N__ for "No" if it does NOT describe them
__?__ if you cannot decide

Opportunities for Promotion
_____ Promotion on ability
_____ Dead-end job
_____ Unfair promotion policy
_____ Regular promotions

Source: The Job Descriptive Index is copyrighted by Bowling Green State University. The complete forms, scoring key, instructions, and norms can be obtained from Dr. Patricia C. Smith, Department of Psychology, Bowling Green State University, Bowling Green, Ohio 43403.

supervisors may see the results of their questionnaire may report overly favorable job attitudes.

A second problem with rating scales is the underlying assumption that questionnaire items mean the same thing to all people. There may, in fact, not be a common agreement of meaning across individuals. For instance, the JDI (see Exhibit 10.3) uses adjectives like adequate and dead-end to describe the job. However, these adjectives may have different meanings for various employees based on their abilities, expectations, needs, and previous experiences. Even so, rating scales have proved to be helpful in assessing satisfaction in various aspects of the job situation.

Critical Incidents. The use of the *critical incident* technique for assessing job satisfaction was first popularized by Herzberg (Herzberg et al., 1959). In a study of job attitudes, employees were asked to describe incidents on their jobs that were particularly satisfying and incidents that were particularly dissatisfying. These incidents were then content analyzed to determine which aspects of the work situation (work itself, supervision, pay and promotion, etc.) were most closely related to affective responses. In contrast to rating scales, this technique focuses on qualitative data rather than quantitative data.

A primary advantage of the critical incident technique is that it is typically nondirective. Employees are simply asked to describe a satisfying event. Thus, they are not biased by being given predetermined topics or categories. Even so, several drawbacks of this technique must be noted. First, it is time-consuming, both to collect the data and then to content analyze them. It is also open to bias in that the researcher or manager may distort incidents during the process of analyzing the content of the responses. Finally, it is highly likely that the employees themselves may distort their responses (Vroom, 1964). Employees may attribute a negative event to some fault of the supervisor, while attributing a positive event to their own abilities.

Interviews. A third way to assess employee satisfaction is *personal interviews.* Interviews may be structured (where predetermined and standardized questions are asked) or unstructured (open-ended). Interviews have several advantages in the assessment of job attitudes. First, interviews allow for in-depth explorations of those aspects of the job that are not possible to assess in rating scales. In addition, interviews are often useful when studying people with lower educational levels or language barriers who may not otherwise understand the terminology used on a printed questionnaire. Third, interviews allow a closer examination of the true meaning of the responses. What *exactly* did an employee like about the job?

On the other hand, at least three problems with the interview technique can be identified. First, there is a problem of objectivity; people may distort their responses. Second, there are often differences among interviewers that bias the results. The manner in which the interviewer asks questions and the types of information the interviewer chooses to record can affect the outcomes. Finally, there is a problem of time; interviews of large numbers of employees simply consume too many hours to be practical in many cases.

One strategy that has proven useful in the study of job attitudes is to combine rating scales with personal interviews. This strategy combines the highly quantitative data from rating scales with the important in-depth qualitative data from interviews. Often, a small subsample is selected for the interviews because of the time-consuming nature of this technique. By combining these two techniques, better cross-validated information is available for examination and decision making.

EXHIBIT 10.4 SAMPLE ITEMS FOR AN ACTION TENDENCY SCHEDULE FOR JOB SATISFACTION

1. When you wake up in the morning, do you feel reluctant to go to work?
2. Do you ever feel reluctant to go home from work at night because of the enjoyment you are getting from the job?
3. Do you often feel like going to lunch at work sooner than you do?
4. Do you feel like taking a coffee break more often than you should?
5. Do you ever wish you could work at your job on evenings or weekends?
6. Are you sometimes reluctant to leave your job to go on vacation?
7. When you are on vacation, do you ever look forward to getting back to work?
8. Do you ever wake up at night with the urge to go to work right then and there?
9. Do you ever wish holidays or weekends would get over with so that you could go back to work?
10. If you were starting over in your working career, would you lean toward taking the same type of job you have now?
11. Would you be tempted to recommend your present job to a friend with the same interests and education as yours?

Source: Edwin A. Locke, "Nature and Causes of Job Satisfaction," in M. D. Dunnette (ed.), *Handbook of Industrial and Organizational Behavior* (New York: John Wiley & Sons, 1976), Table 7, p. 1336. Copyright © 1976 by John Wiley & Sons, Inc. Reprinted by permission of John Wiley & Sons, Inc.

Overt Behaviors. A fourth technique often used by managers is to observe *overt* (or actual) *employee behaviors* (poor performance, absenteeism, turnover) as surrogate measures of dissatisfaction. As Locke (1976) notes, there are three reasons why this technique is questionable as a measure of job attitudes:

> This approach is clearly inadequate because there is no known behavior which would satisfy the minimal criteria needed to justify it, namely: (1) the behavior inevitably follows the experience of satisfaction; that is, satisfaction is always expressed in this particular way; (2) the behavior occurs with a frequency or intensity that is directly proportional to the intensity of the attitude experienced; and (3) no causal factors other than satisfaction influence the behavior, or if so, their influence can be precisely calculated (Locke, 1976, p. 1335).

Action Tendencies. Closely related to the notion of behavioral intentions discussed earlier is the concept of *action tendencies.* Action tendencies are the inclinations people have to approach or avoid certain things. Given these tendencies, and their relationship to behavioral intentions, another way to assess job attitudes is to ask people which action tendencies they experience with respect to their jobs. Instead of asking employees how they *feel* about their jobs, we can ask them how they feel like *acting* (other things equal) with respect to their jobs. Examples of action tendencies are shown in Exhibit 10.4.

Several advantages can be noted about the use of action tendencies. First, while some self-insight by the individual is necessary, this technique apparently requires less self-insight than rating scales. Second, action tendency questions have more of an absolute frame of reference than do evaluative questions. So, fewer distortions are incurred. In fact, in a study of blue-collar workers by Kornhauser (1965), it was found that by asking employees action tendency questions ("If you could start all over again, would you choose the same type of work?"), substantially lower levels of satisfaction were noted than by using more traditional rating scales. To date, little use has been made of the action tendency technique. It is believed, however, that it will be used more often in the future.

How Satisfied Are Employees?

Presumably, a major reason for studying the concept of job satisfaction is to learn ways to improve satisfaction levels in the work place. Given this goal, it is important to consider just how satisfied people are with their jobs. Many people think that most workers are very dissatisfied. The available evidence, however, contradicts that. In view of this contradiction, the reader must carefully study the evidence that is available and look behind the seemingly obvious conclusions.

First, consider the results of a series of job attitude surveys carried out by the University of Michigan, the University of California, and the National Opinion Research Center (Gallup). These results are summarized in a report released by the U.S. Department of Labor (1974), and clearly suggest that workers by and large are satisfied with their jobs based on self-report data. More specifically, between eighty percent and ninety percent of employees on various jobs and working in a wide range of organizations *consistently* report that they are satisfied with their jobs.

Based on these findings, one may conclude that employee job satisfaction does not need to be an area of management concern. However, several disturbing questions remain. If employees are so satisfied, why do many report that they wish to change jobs and occupations (Kahn, 1972)? Why are absenteeism, turnover, and work stoppages so prevalent? According to Kahn (1972), the results reported in these surveys may be greatly distorted. He criticizes the use of the direct question "How satisfied are you with your job?" because the question threatens self-esteem. As Kahn (1972) notes, asking the question of employees in this way poses:

> a choice between no work connection (usually with severe attendant economic penalties and a conspicuous lack of meaningful alternative activities) and a work connection which is burdened with negative qualities (routine, compulsory scheduling, dependency, etc.). In these circumstances, the individual has no difficulty with choice; he chooses work, pronounces himself moderately satisfied, and tells us more only if the questions become more searching. Then we learn that he can order jobs clearly in terms of their status or desirability, wants his son to be employed differently from himself, and if given a choice, would seek a different occupation.

Support for Kahn's argument can be found when we examine the results of an action tendency questionnaire instead of a rating scale. (Remember that Locke [1976] argues that action tendency questionnaires are superior to

EXHIBIT 10.5   PERCENTAGES IN OCCUPATIONAL GROUPS WHO WOULD CHOOSE SIMILAR WORK AGAIN

Professional and White-Collar Occupations	%	Working Class Occupations	%
Urban university professors	93	Skilled printers	52
Mathematicians	91	Paper workers	42
Physicists	89	Skilled autoworkers	41
Biologists	89	Skilled steelworkers	41
Chemists	86	Textile workers	31
Firm lawyers	85	Unskilled steelworkers	21
Lawyers	83	Unskilled autoworkers	16
Journalists (Washington correspondents)	82	*Blue-collar workers, cross section*	24
Church university professors	77		
Lawyers in private practice	75		
White-collar workers, cross section	43		

Source: Adapted from "The Meaning of Work: Interpretations and Proposals for Measurement," by Robert L. Kahn, from *The Human Meaning of Social Change*, edited by Angus Campbell and Phillip E. Converse. Copyright © 1972 by Russell Sage Foundation. Reprinted by permission of Basic Books, Inc., Publishers.

evaluative rating scales.) In a large survey of employees, respondents were asked, "What type of work would you try to get into if you could start all over again?" Results are shown in Exhibit 10.5.

As the exhibit shows, results are markedly lower than comparable results gathered through evaluative ratings. For instance, on the average, only forty-one percent of white-collar workers (including professionals) would again choose the same occupation, while only twenty-four percent of blue-collar workers would again choose the same occupation.

Similarly, in a separate study, a sampling of employees was asked, "What would you do with the extra two hours if you had a twenty-six-hour day?" Sixty-six percent of the university professors and twenty-five percent of the lawyers responded that they would use the extra two hours in work-related activities. By contrast, only five percent of nonprofessionals gave the same response (Wilensky, 1966). In short, if we look at what people *want* to do as an index of how well they enjoy their jobs, it becomes clear that most people —particularly blue-collar workers—are largely dissatisfied with their jobs. Thus, job satisfaction is indeed an important area for management concern and action.

INFLUENCES ON JOB SATISFACTION

Investigators have long sought to determine the major causes of job satisfaction in work organizations. To date, while we have been able to identify a variety of factors that are consistently related to satisfaction, we have yet to

EXHIBIT 10.6   PRIMARY FACTORS INFLUENCING OVERALL JOB SATISFACTION

Organization-wide Factors	Immediate Work Environment Factors	Job Content Factors	Personal Factors
Pay system	Supervisory style	Job scope	Age
Promotional opportunities	Participation in decision making	Role clarity and conflict	Tenure
Company policies and procedures	Work group size		Personality
Organization structure	Co-worker relations		
	Working conditions		

attain a comprehensive empirically validated model of satisfaction, although some useful attempts have been made (Lawler, 1973). We can, however, review briefly several of the more important factors found to be associated with it. It has been suggested by Porter and Steers (1973) that influences on employee attitudes and behavior can be grouped into four relatively discrete categories, representing four levels in the organization. These four levels are: (1) organization-wide factors, those variables widely available or applied to most employees; (2) immediate work environment factors, those variables that make up the work group; (3) job content factors, or the actual job activities; and (4) personal factors, those characteristics that differentiate one person from another. Influences on employee satisfaction can be found in all four levels (see Exhibit 10.6).

Organization-wide Factors

With respect to job satisfaction, the *pay* and *promotional opportunities* used by organizations are prominent factors. Substantial evidence points to pay as a primary determinant of satisfaction, especially when the pay received is seen as equitable; that is, when it is viewed as fair compared to level of effort and what others receive (Lawler, 1971; Locke, 1976). To the extent that employees feel that pay meets their expectations and is fair given their level of effort, they will tend to be satisfied. Likewise, individuals' perceptions of the rate and equity of their promotions also tend to influence their satisfaction (Locke, 1976).

In addition, *company policies and procedures* play a role in the determination of overall job satisfaction. Policies often govern or restrict employee behavior and can generate either positive or negative feelings toward the organization. For instance, company practices like the use of time clocks, reserved parking spaces for managers, and titles (Mr. Smith versus Joe) can influence employee perceptions of personal freedom on the job as well as status or place in the organization. Employees who feel unduly constrained or who feel like second-class citizens probably would not enjoy the work environment to the extent that others do.

Finally, a recent survey has found that *organization structure* often influences satisfaction (Cummings and Berger, 1976). In particular, available evidence suggests that increased job satisfaction is often associated with: (1) higher levels in the organizational hierarchy; and (2) increased decentralization in decision-making authority. Variations in organization size, span of control, or line-staff differences had no consistent or perceptible influence on satisfaction levels.

Immediate Work Environment Factors

The immediate work environment can also influence satisfaction in a variety of ways. One of these is *supervisory style.* Several studies have demonstrated that more considerate supervision leads to higher levels of satisfaction (Vroom, 1964; Stogdill, 1974). This is not to imply that considerate supervision leads necessarily to greater productivity—only satisfaction. Caution is in order in interpreting these results, however. Because of the correlational nature of the studies, direction of causality in the supervision-satisfaction relationship cannot be determined with any degree of certainty. It is possible that satisfied employees themselves create an environment that is more conducive to considerate supervisory behavior.

Related to supervisory consideration is the extent to which employees are allowed to participate in decisions affecting their jobs. *Participative decision making* has been found to lead to increased satisfaction, especially when the decisions involved are important to employees' jobs and when employee participation is authentic (Scott and Mitchell, 1976).

Several studies have also found a consistent relationship between *work group size* and satisfaction, where larger work groups lead to lower satisfaction levels (Porter and Lawler, 1965). It is believed that larger work groups lead to greater task specialization, poorer interpersonal communication, and reduced feelings of group cohesiveness. These factors, in turn, create conditions that reduce satisfaction.

The quality of *co-worker relations* has also been consistently found to be related to satisfaction (Smith et al., 1969). As noted by Locke (1976), people are generally attracted to and feel more comfortable with co-workers who exhibit characteristics, interests, and beliefs similar to their own. Where compatibility exists, we expect the affective response to the work environment to increase.

Finally, some evidence suggests that general *working conditions* can also have an impact on employee attitudes. People value having a clean and orderly work place, adequate equipment for the job, and acceptable levels of environmental quality (temperature, humidity, noise). Most employees prefer a location close to their home (Barnowe, Mangione, and Quinn, 1972). However, as noted by Chadwick-Jones (1969), these working conditions apparently only become salient for job attitudes when they are present (or absent) in the extreme or when employees have clear standards for comparison (perhaps based on earlier jobs). Otherwise, these factors may be ignored or overlooked by employees.

Job Content Factors

Two aspects of the job itself have been found to represent especially strong influences on satisfaction: job scope and role clarity. *Job scope* refers to those attributes that characterize a job, such as the amount of variety, autonomy, responsibility, and feedback provided (see Chapter Eighteen for a more detailed discussion of job design). The more these attributes are present, the higher the job scope. Much research has been done on the effects of job scope on employee attitudes. It has generally been found that increased job scope is related to increased satisfaction (Stone, 1978; Hackman and Lawler, 1971; Brief and Aldag, 1975). For a few employees, however, such as those who have low needs for achievement, providing a challenging job may lead not to satisfaction but to increased anxiety and frustration because of either an unwillingness or an inability to respond to the challenge (Steers, 1976; Hackman and Lawler, 1971; Hackman and Oldham, 1976). Even so, most evidence suggests that enriching employees' jobs typically increases their level of job satisfaction (if not their performance).

In addition, *role ambiguity* and *role conflict* have both been found to lead to increased stress and reduced job satisfaction for many people (Miles and Perreault, 1976; Morris, 1976). Apparently, employees feel more secure and prefer situations in which they know what is expected of them and where they have clear task goals.

Personal Factors

The fourth category of influences on job satisfaction is the attributes of individual employees. A good deal of research has shown that *age* and *tenure* are positively associated with favorable job attitudes (Herman, Dunham, and Hulin, 1975; O'Reilly and Roberts, 1975; Porter and Steers, 1973). Several explanations might account for this relationship. As people get older and acquire seniority, they typically move into more responsible (and perhaps challenging) positions. These individuals often receive at least some organizational rewards just for remaining with the organization. Finally, it may be that older employees have simply adjusted their expectations to more realistic levels based on experience and are therefore more satisfied with available rewards (Wanous, 1973).

A final factor often associated with satisfaction—albeit very modestly —is *personality*. O'Reilly and Roberts (1975) found, for example, that several personality variables (self-assurance, decisiveness, and maturity) were related to increased job satisfaction. Steers and Braunstein (1976) found that individuals manifesting higher needs for achievement and dominance were more satisfied, while individuals with high needs for autonomy tended to be less satisfied. Finally, Korman (1977) has suggested that individuals with high self-esteem also tend to be more satisfied with the work situation and take more pleasure (and reinforcement) from a job well done.

In conclusion, it can be seen that a multitude of factors—both within organizations and within individuals—are capable of influencing job satisfaction. The question that remains is *which* factors are more important for satisfaction? This question is difficult to answer. The available evidence to date suggests that personal factors are far *less* important in determining job satisfaction than are those factors that characterize the work place (O'Reilly and Roberts, 1975; Herman et al., 1975; Newman, 1975). In this regard, Locke (1976, p. 1328) has summarized what he feels are the most salient factors influencing satisfaction:

> Among the most important values or conditions conducive to job satisfaction are: (1) mentally challenging work with which the individual can cope successfully; (2) personal interest in the work itself; (3) work which is not too physically tiring; (4) rewards for performance which are just, informative, and in line with the individual's personal aspirations; (5) working conditions which are compatible with the individual's physical needs and which facilitate the accomplishment of his work goals; (6) high self-esteem on the part of the employee; (7) agents in the work place who help the employee attain job values such as interesting work, pay, and promotions, and whose basic values are similar to his own, and who minimize role conflict and ambiguity.

CONSEQUENCES OF JOB SATISFACTION

An awareness of the salient consequences of job satisfaction is equally important as understanding what causes job satisfaction in the first place. Since most of these factors are discussed more fully later in the book, they will be mentioned only briefly here as they relate to employee job satisfaction or dissatisfaction.

Satisfaction and Turnover

Consistently, satisfaction and employee turnover have been found to be moderately related. In an early review of the literature, Vroom (1964) found that correlations between the two variables ranged from $r = -.13$ to $r = -.42$ across various studies. More recently, Porter and Steers (1973) reviewed fifteen studies and found a median correlation of $r = -.25$ between satisfaction and turnover (see also Mobley, 1982). Thus, while the modest magnitude of the relationships suggests that several other factors influence turnover, job satisfaction is clearly an important influence. In addition, this influence translates into a direct financial loss for the organization. The nature and causes of employee turnover will be discussed in greater detail in Chapter Nineteen.

EXHIBIT 10.7   RELATIONSHIP OF JOB PERFORMANCE TO JOB SATISFACTION

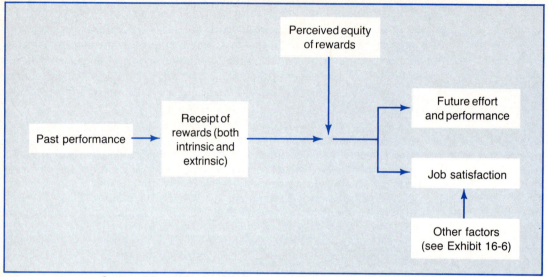

Source: Adapted from L. W. Porter and E. E. Lawler, *Managerial Attitudes and Performance* (Chicago, Ill.: Irwin, 1968).

Satisfaction and Absenteeism

While much less has been done with respect to absenteeism, available evidence again suggests the existence of a moderate inverse relationship between satisfaction and employee absenteeism. Vroom's (1964) review of several studies found correlations that ranged from $r = -.14$ to $r = -.38$. Porter and Steers (1973), Muchinsky (1977), and Steers and Rhodes (1978) found similar results. Muchinsky notes, "of all the variables that have been related to absenteeism, the most consistent results have occurred with attitudinal predictors" (p.322). Even so, other important influences on absenteeism must also be acknowledged.

Satisfaction and Performance

One of the most controversial issues encountered in the study of job satisfaction is its relationship to job performance. Three competing theories have been advanced: (1) satisfaction causes performance; (2) performance causes satisfaction; (3) rewards intervene between performance and satisfaction (Porter and Lawler, 1968; Schwab and Cummings, 1970; Greene, 1972).

The first two theories find only weak support. For instance, Vroom (1964) reviewed twenty studies dealing with the performance-satisfaction relationship and found a median correlation of only $r = .14$. More recent studies arrived at similar conclusions (Greene, 1972). Both of the first two theories can be rejected on theoretical grounds. That is, the fact that workers are satisfied does not mean they will necessarily produce more—only that they are satisfied. There is no compelling argument that performance must necessarily cause satisfaction, particularly if performance goes unrewarded.

The third theory, that rewards mediate the performance-satisfaction relationship, receives considerable support in the literature. This model, shown in Exhibit 10.7, was first suggested by Porter and Lawler (1968) and has received fairly consistent support in subsequent studies (Schwab and Cummings, 1970; Greene, 1972).

As shown in the exhibit, past performance of an employee leads to the receipt of rewards. These rewards can be both intrinsic (a feeling of personal accomplishment) and extrinsic (pay, promotion). To the extent that these rewards are perceived by the individual to be equitable (fair when compared to level of effort and to what other employees receive), the individual is satisfied. The receipt of perceived equitable rewards should also tend to create strong performance-reward contingencies in the minds of employees, leading to future effort and performance.

In other words, performance is really not a consequence of satisfaction at all! Instead, the two variables *by themselves* are virtually unrelated. It is only when the role of rewards and reward contingencies is also considered that a substantial relationship emerges.

Satisfaction and Organizational Effectiveness

The impact of job attitudes on organizational effectiveness, while admittedly an indirect one, is nonetheless important. It has been noted that one of the most popular indicators used by analysts and investigators to assess organizational effectiveness is job satisfaction (Steers, 1977c). Moreover, job attitudes affect organizational effectiveness to the extent that they influence turnover and absenteeism. Many years ago, Lawler (1973) noted that the cost of one turnover among lower-level jobs could easily surpass $2000, while the cost of one turnover among the managerial ranks could be five to ten times that amount. Today, the figure is probably twice this high. From the standpoint of the effective functioning of the organization, managers have a responsibility to consider seriously the impact of job attitudes and to attempt to discover ways of improving them (see Close-Up 10.2).

Additional Consequences of Job Satisfaction

In addition, job satisfaction has been found to be related to several other dysfunctional consequences. Highly satisfied employees tend to file fewer grievances (Fleishman and Harris, 1962), live longer (Palmore, 1969), exhibit better mental and physical health (Burke, 1969; Chadwick-Jones, 1969; Kornhauser, 1965), learn new job-related tasks more quickly (Wyatt et al., 1937), and have fewer on-the-job accidents (Vroom, 1964).

In short, job satisfaction brings with it a variety of positive consequenc-

At the Ford Motor Company plant in Edison, New Jersey, "workers on the assembly line move back and forth between storage bins and the conveyor, picking up parts and installing them on freshly painted body shells that soon will become Escorts and Lynxes. Each worker has about a minute to do his job. . . . Repetition dulls the senses, and the setting is perfect for the old, bull-of-the-woods foreman who stalks up and down the line, berating workers for omitting a bolt or failing to tighten a screw." But, in fact, the foremen rarely behave like that at the Edison plant.

Instead, says *Business Week,* the typical foreman now "chats with the workers, solicits their ideas, and even encourages them to use recently installed buttons to stop the line if a defect prevents them from correctly doing their jobs. . . . This 'stop concept' is one aspect of a worker participation program that has improved quality, reduced absenteeism, and lessened hostility between bosses and workers."

At the heart of this turnaround is Ford's Employee Involvement Program, which consists of thirteen problem-solving groups that meet once every two weeks to discuss production and quality problems. The stop concept resulted from one such meeting. When a worker stops the line, the foreman and worker together look at what has gone wrong and decide how to fix it. "This puts pressure on the foreman but also results in many fewer defective cars reaching the streets."

Commenting on the Employee Involvement Program, one supervisor admitted some initial difficulty accepting the fact that line workers might know more than he did. Now, he explains, "if any hourly guy brings something to me, I'll go and try it. It's surprising how much an employee can see that's wrong with a job."

What Ford has done is increase the responsibility employees feel to perform well. Such a move is designed to lead to improved performance and work attitudes. As a union official noted, "Ford has discovered that to build a good car, they've got to have harmony. Now, it's like we're all one family."

Source: "The Old Foreman Is on the Way Out, and the New One Will Be More Important," *Business Week,* April 25, 1983, pp. 74–75.

es, both from individual and organizational standpoints. It influences how an employee feels about the organization and contributes to the desire to maintain membership in it. It spills over to affect an employee's home life and general outlook toward living. Moreover, job satisfaction significantly influences how people approach their jobs, their levels of effort and commitment, and their contributions to organizational effectiveness.

SUMMARY

In this chapter, the concept of work attitudes was introduced and a model of these attitudes was presented. It was noted that attitudes serve a variety of functions for individuals. Next, the way in which attitudes change was discussed. Barriers to attitude change and mechanisms for overcoming barriers were examined. Following this discussion, the specific attitude of job satisfaction was considered, including its various dimensions and its measurement. Major influences on job satisfaction and the primary consequences of job satisfaction (or dissatisfaction) were also explored. Included were the effects of job satisfaction on turnover, absenteeism, and organizational effectiveness.

When discussing job attitudes there is an inclination to assume that everything possible must be done to facilitate job satisfaction. Unfortunately, there are many situations in which managers must confront a basic conflict between improving job satisfaction and improving performance. For instance, job satisfaction may be increased by allowing employees more time off from the job, but this also has the effect of potentially reducing productive hours. Production may be increased if a manager presses vigorously for maximum output at almost any cost, but this may also reduce employee job satisfaction. Thus, the manager must make difficult trade-offs, based on what appears to be a conflict in basic goals.

There is no easy resolution to this conflict. In some situations, it may be possible to pursue both goals by recognizing that improved job attitudes may lead to at least some increase in performance. Through employee participation, perhaps increased employee involvement in the task will also come about. On the other hand, managers also face situations where no compromise is possible and decisions must be made among equally attractive (or unattractive) outcomes. Then, managers are presented with the traditional conflict between concern for production and concern for people. Although compromises can sometimes be found, it would be misleading not to recognize that in some situations a clear choice must be made. In these cases, managers face a losing situation, but must nevertheless carry out their responsibilities.

KEY WORDS

action tendencies

attitude

belief

cognitive consistency

cognitive dissonance

critical incident

job satisfaction

self-perception theory

value

FOR DISCUSSION

1. What are the various components of an attitude? How are these components related?
2. How are beliefs formed? What is the relation between beliefs and attitudes?
3. What influences attitude formation?

4. What functions do attitudes serve?
5. Describe how self-perception theory works.
6. Identify some barriers to attitude change. How can these barriers be overcome?
7. What are the most commonly used dimensions of job satisfaction?
8. Discuss the various ways in which job satisfaction can be measured. What are the advantages and disadvantages of each?
9. Based on available evidence, how satisfied are most employees today?
10. Identify the major influences on job satisfaction.
11. Discuss the major consequences of job dissatisfaction.

EXERCISE

10.1

DETERMINANTS OF JOB ATTITUDES AND MOTIVATION

Purpose

To consider which factors motivate workers to perform on the job, and to compare the opinions of union leaders and executives with respect to the relative importance of such motivating factors.

Instructions

1. On the sheet below, rank the ten factors that relate to job attitudes and motivation in terms of how important each factor would be: (1) to union leaders; and (2) to business executives.

2. When you have finished, your instructor will distribute the results of a national survey of union leaders and business executives so you can compare your results against those of the national survey.

"In your organization at this time, how useful would each of the following be in improving employee attitudes and motivation?"

Rank Order (1 = most important)	Union Leaders		Business Executives	
	My Ranking	National Survey	My Ranking	National Survey
Better communication from management	_____	_____	_____	_____
Giving employees greater job security	_____	_____	_____	_____
Better treatment by supervisors	_____	_____	_____	_____
Sharing of profits or productivity gains	_____	_____	_____	_____
Higher pay	_____	_____	_____	_____
Improved work conditions	_____	_____	_____	_____
More feedback to employees	_____	_____	_____	_____
More opportunities for advancement	_____	_____	_____	_____
Better training programs	_____	_____	_____	_____
Building loyalty to the organization	_____	_____	_____	_____

IN THE SANDING BOOTH AT FORD

It's a cold, windy morning in January 1974. The recession is getting worse, and manufacturing plants all over the San Francisco Bay area are laying off. A steel plant has closed. International Harvester and Raytheon have laid off a shift. But the Milpitas Ford plant is hiring a swing shift to make more Pintos and Mustangs. It is the only plant in the United States actively hiring.

I'm twenty-four, unemployed, and trying to avoid going to law school. At 6:30 there are already twenty people in line. By the time the office opens at 8:00, the line has tripled in size. Most of the applicants are black or Chicano and half are women.

It is the same mix you see in unemployment offices. Men in platform shoes and construction boots, Coors beer tank tops and neatly ironed, flowered shirts. The only difference is that all the women wear pants, as if to point out that they are ready for manual labor. Everyone waits patiently. Already there are six applications for every place. The pay is over $5 an hour (by 1976 it will be over $6). No one talks.

At 9:00 I am sitting across from my interviewer, a black in his middle thirties. I notice his Boalt Law School ring and then look into his eyes. I promise myself I won't look down until he does. We stare at each other through the whole interview. I point out that I will do anything to get the job; stand in line again, fill out another application. He is impressed by my enthusiasm and assures me that one application is enough.

"Usually, we like people to stand out-side longer," he confides, adjusting his tie. "If it rains and people stay in line, we think that's a good sign. Shows they really want the job." For the first and only time, I look away and then back to see if he is serious. He is.

Three months later, I take a physical and am ready to work. Another fourteen days and I am sitting at a seminar table with twenty other new hires. Five are women. Our group leader from Labor Relations, who looks like Rocky Marciano, is passing out forms: medical insurance forms for Detroit and the union local. He advises that we take Blue Cross instead of Kaiser health insurance. All twenty of us dutifully follow his advice.

I look around the table. Most of the women are big, and everybody is healthy. There is none of the fat that would distinguish twenty randomly chosen Americans. I am one of the few who is not married. There is only one man over thirty. He has worked previously making Mack trucks.

We watch a movie, "Don't Paint It Like Disneyland." The film consists of interviews with Ford workers at River Rouge. The message is clear: the work is hard but the pay is good. Our group leader turns off the projector and announces that he worked on the line for ten years.

"If you don't have any guts, you'll quit the first day. I almost did. And you'll want to quit, I promise you that." I became convinced that if this behemoth almost quit, I'll never last five minutes.

"You're going to hate that job so bad during the first few weeks. You're going to hate Ford, this plant, your foreman. If you get through the first week, you have a chance."

He pauses and drops his voice. "But folks, let's face it. There's no place in the country, no place in the world, that's going to hire people like you, without any skills, and pay them over $5 an hour." I look at the man next to me, a young Chicano in an army jacket with Sanchez stenciled over the left pocket. He raises his eyes in an expression of resignation and agreement.

Carefully we put on our safety glasses, file out of the room, and walk through a door that says "Safety Equipment Required Beyond This Point." Moving from the quiet of the office, we are assaulted by a noise level like that of an airport runway. Everywhere there are cars of all different colors, lines of cars moving in different directions. Cars extend as far as can be seen.

We follow the group leader through the plant, respectful and wide-eyed as if in a cathedral for the first time. Conveyor belts hanging from the ceiling carry tires and parts. People hurry by in blue overalls or aprons. The foremen's neat shirts, ties, and slacks are a stark contrast. Everyone wears a watch.

Within the confusion I notice a few specific jobs. A young woman with a huge afro jams gas nozzles into cars as they pass by. Two men grab tires off a rack, bounce them on the floor, deftly catch them, secure them to each car, and bolt them tight.

As we walk workers stare at us and grin. Many are yelling. My ears gradually adjust to the din. "Don't do it," the workers are yelling. "You'll be sorry." I grin at the people pointing at us and realize that we new hires are the only ones wearing safety glasses.

Eight hours later, I drive home despondent. My hands are bleeding and I feel like an idiot. I am supposed to be a block sander: Unfortunately, I am only able to do about one-fifth of the work assigned me. Lew, who is teaching me the job, assures me that it is all right. "You'll learn," he says, "Don't worry. At least you hustle. As long as you kill yourself for them, they'll keep you." I arrive home, drink two beers, eat a steak, and go to bed four hours early.

The Closer You Look . . .

Within a few weeks, everything is more familiar. I drive to work with Denny, a block sander who was hired on the same day I was. We pass by alternating orchards, factories, trailer parks, and billboards. WHAT IS A BULLFROG? asks one. The answer is Smirnoff and lime. Just before you get to the plant, the Galaxy bar is full of people trying out bullfrogs before work. Similarly, the liquor stores do a rush business on beer. Many cars pulling into the plant parking lot give off the odor of marijuana.

The executive parking lot is uniformly populated by late model Fords. The employees' lot is crowded with '56 Chevies, Toyotas, Datsuns, and some exquisite, hand-painted motorcycles. People who have worked at both GM and Ford say that GM puts a little extra time into building its cars.

A huge banner over the employees' entrance proclaims, "The closer you look, the better we look."

Before work I walk slowly toward the time clock, relishing the few moments of freedom. If there's time, I wander around the plant. Under one roof, it has a floor space of ten football fields. The roof is two stories high. In some places

the assembly line goes up in the air or crisscrosses over itself. A private railroad brings in parts from the Midwest and divides the plant in half. On the west side, cars are made. On the east, small pickup trucks.

A few minutes before 4:30, I clock in, drink two cartons of chocolate milk for energy, go to the bathroom (no chance again until break), hop over two lines, and walk into the booth. I work in the paint department in an enclosed booth. The cars enter and exit through a narrow opening at either end. Our job is to sand the car smooth before it receives its final coat of colored paint.

The booth is hazy with dust from the shift before. The primer coat is lead-based and I wear a surgeon's mask that I bought in San Francisco. Ford provides masks, but they are uncomfortable. Art, who works across from me, uses the mask I give him. Denny, next to me, doesn't; it makes it too hard to breathe.

I hold a ten-pound air sander in my right hand and a handful of sandpaper in my left. My responsibility is the right-hand half of the trunk, roof, and hood. I open the passenger door and sand quickly inside with the sandpaper in my left hand. Then I sand the whole surface area with the air sander. Any large metal burrs or blobs of paint have to be removed with a scraper I carry in my apron pocket. The many paint runs, grease spots, or specks of dirt have to be ground down to bare metal and smoothed out. Also, the small grill in front of the windshield has to be sanded over three times. Since the line speed is usually between 55 and 58 cars per hour, I have to perform my job within 67 seconds.

After a few months, the work is routine. I've learned which parts of the job I can skip when I get tired. One day, however, a Frederick Taylor efficiency expert appears with a stopwatch and lurks behind pillars hoping we won't notice him. Even the foreman, Stan, hates him. If the expert thinks fewer workers are needed, the responsibility for enforcing an increased workload falls on Stan.

The word is quickly spread and the whole line slows down. Jobs that a worker used to be able to finish with a few seconds to spare suddenly become unbearable. In our case the acting is to no avail. Two people are taken out of the booth and the four remaining are given extra work. In addition to my normal job, I now have to sand around the tail and headlights, and help Denny, in front of me, with the sides.

Coping

The four of us adjust. The work is always physically exhausting, like playing a game of football or soccer. But the real punishment is the inevitability of the line. I want to take a walk, go to the bathroom, have a Mr. Goodbar. It doesn't matter. There's always another car.

Someone shows me a *Newsweek* article with a picture of an autoworker playing a guitar while the line rolls by. The implication is that the work is so easy it's possible to take time off to play a little blues. I have to plan ahead to get a drink of water: five seconds to the fountain, five seconds for the drink, five seconds back into the booth.

The monotony of the line binds us together. Small gaps, usually a few car lengths, happen almost every day. We constantly peer down the line to see if any are coming. The big hope is that a gap won't appear during your break.

Occasionally, the line breaks down. This is what we all wait for. The plant is turned upside down. Foremen in ties appear from nowhere and furiously try to figure out what has happened. It is the only time they do physical work. At the same time, we stand around grinning and give specious advice. For once, Ford is paying us to do nothing.

Yet, such moments are rare. Within the booth, we rely on each other for entertainment. We yell at each other or speculate about whether we'll go home early. Ron and Denny trade statistics from the *Guinness Book of World Records.* We invent a form of basketball using a trashcan as a basket and play fast games during gaps. The other three constantly exchange cigarettes. We tell each other about our lives before we joined Ford.

The booth is our world. Because we have to see any spots on the paint, the booth is white and brightly lit by neon lights. It is three car lengths long and 15 feet wide. The booth is enclosed to prevent the dust from escaping. There is a coating of dust on everything. The noise of the sanders makes it necessary to shout to be heard.

While working, although we may be immersed in our own thoughts, there is always an unconscious awareness of the other three. Unused to repetitive work, I am the most absentminded. Once, I find my foot caught on the line. The next car is proceeding normally and will run over my foot in a few seconds. I scream. Instantaneously, without need for explanation, Ron, Denny, and Art snap out of their private thoughts. They push the moving car back up the line and then free my foot. The whole incident takes five seconds.

I also have the least capacity to en-

dure the frustration. One day, hating myself and hating Ford, I smash my $150 sander into a hunk of twisted metal. I look up at my friends. They are amazed. To steal from Ford or to sabotage a car is understandable. But to destroy a tool is simply childish.

Our reliefman, who studied four years to be a Jesuit, gives me another sander. He switches parts among old sanders and is able to disguise the fact that my sander was ever destroyed. What I have done is no big deal, just odd.

You Die in Little Ways

Sabotage against the cars themselves is common. As a matter of course, we used to force the trunks closed in a way that ensured the cars couldn't be painted properly. But most sabotage takes place in the trim department, where dashboards, mirrors, inside panels, windows, and extras are installed. Because so many items are installed in this section, it is difficult to trace the saboteur. Every day, mirrors are smashed and quarter panels are ripped. The art lies in sabotaging in a way that is not immediately discovered. As work is done further down the line, it becomes progressively more difficult to repair the original problem. Another form of sabotage is to ignore work. There is a legendary trim worker whose job is to install six screws. He never puts in more than four.

Sometimes the results are artistic. For a week, cars would periodically come down our line with a huge, sculpted penis where the gear shift was to be installed. Workers came from all over the plant to look at these wonders. Gradually they grew larger and larger until the last was at least four feet long. Then they mysteriously ceased.

Usually the day passes with few such diversions. After conversation has lost its appeal, one slips inevitably, reluctantly, into daydreams. Ron mostly dreams about sex. Art hears music. Denny builds and rebuilds fantasy motorcycles or thinks of his ex-girlfriend and their little girl. I imagine going to South America and learning Spanish.

The fantasies on the line are replaced by nightmares of the line slowly devouring them or of falling further and further behind. One friend installs dream quarter panels into his girlfriend's back. She wakes him up, but the minute he falls asleep, he starts all over again.

Faced with the daytime prospect of working on 400 cars, it's nice to have a little artificial energy. The plant seems to be fueled by "crossroads"—little white benzedrine pills with a cross imprinted on them.

Speed is sold openly, when it's available. Dealers walk through the plant on a half-hour break and sell 20 bags. Sections of the line buy a couple of $5 or $10 bags and split them up over a week. However, there is never enough to fill the demand.

One day the painters in the booth next to us drop acid. Luis, who has two kids and a condominium on time, paints sitting down, can't talk, and skips lunch. The pass rate on their paint jobs is normal.

Drugs, no matter how strong, provide no anesthesia for certain conditions. The ventilation in the paint booth never seems to work too well. The painters complain of being unable to breathe and of getting headaches. One day they carry Luis out of their booth unconscious. He has been overcome by the paint fumes.

Another time, Denny comes back from his break and announces a big gap coming up. Half an hour later, when the gap arrives, we hear there has been a walkout in the arc welding booth. "Just a little labor problem," mutters our foreman. "I don't know any more about it than you do." I start to walk over to Body. "Got to keep to the area, Rick," Stan tells me. "General foreman wants it that way."

A taper comes back from break and says the welders are back at work. It was something about gloves and safety equipment, but she isn't sure. Three hours later, another rumor arrives. This time the welders have walked out of the plant. The four of us in the booth look at each other. We let two cars go by.

What was happening? Why had they walked out? If we joined them, would we be the only ones leaving the plant? "I'll do it if you do it." "I'll do it if you do it." Ron's wife has just had a baby. Art is getting married in a week. We start working again. You die in little ways.

Why the Welders Walked Out

The arc welders who walked out had been trained together in a federally financed manpower program in San Jose. They had been hired directly from the program. By the time they got to Ford, they already knew and trusted each other. Arc welding is one of the dirtiest, most painful jobs in the plant. The torches and general heat in Body Section combine to make the area like an oven. At the same time, the welders have to wear bulky protective clothing. Despite protective gloves, welders' arms are crisscrossed with scars from the sparks thrown up by their torches.

Their foreman, Becker, had been brought from St. Louis, where a Mer-

cury shift had been laid off. Discipline in the St. Louis plant is reputed to be the tightest in the Ford organization. In the summer it gets so hot that workers have to tie wet towels around their heads to keep from overheating. One time, St. Louis workers stayed on the line with a foot of water on the floor. California employees shake their heads in disbelief when they hear such stories.

Becker thought his young California workers were chicken. They kept asking for replacements of the long gloves that protected their arms. He wouldn't provide them; they're expensive and he wanted to make them last longer. The welders called their union rep. He told them things would be all right.

Becker continued to supervise their work. They asked for the gloves again. "They're coming." Everybody knows that safety equipment is kept in lockers close to the work area. Becker was playing with them. They stopped work.

Instantly, they were surrounded by UAW representatives, Labor Relations department bigwigs, and foremen. They demanded that the foreman be transferred and that they get their gloves. The gloves were produced. It was promised that the foreman would be replaced during lunch.

When the welders came back from lunch, the foreman was still there. One welder put down his tools and started walking out. Another later told me, "Hell, I didn't want to walk out right then. But when he's walking out of the plant, what can you do?" They all walked out.

Ten welders and two other workers left the plant. They were all fired. The UAW assured them that the problem was being handled. But nothing happened. Some of the welders appeared at the plant gates and passed out leaflets asking people to come to the next union meeting. A few days later, the company rehired three of the welders who were not considered "ringleaders." Anybody passing out leaflets was, of course, a ringleader.

At the union meeting it took two of the three hours and a challenge to the chair to bring up the question of the arc welders. A member of the International happened to be at the meeting and counseled against any type of action. Someone was finally able to move that the Union put out an information leaflet about the incident. Union official after union official warned that a leaflet would upset the delicate balance of negotiations. When asked what negotiations, they replied that they could not say.

People who supported the welders were baited as college agitators (as indeed some were). When it came to a vote, all the workers from the line voted unsuccessfully for the welders. Almost all the UAW officials voted against them.

United Against Workers

Ford won the battle of attrition. Without the support of the union, unable to muster a significant following inside the plant, the welders became increasingly discouraged. Gradually, Ford hired back the welders who had lost heart, the ones who stopped passing out leaflets at the plant gates. In the end, only the two or three most militant welders kept passing out leaflets and trying to organize legal help. They were never rehired.

What makes the assembly line work efficiently is fear, not engineering. There have been no significant technological breakthroughs since Henry Ford first designed the line. The system is based

on forcing men and women to produce as much per minute as possible. Once inside the factory, the fear system is immediately apparent. Every problem becomes a crisis, because it threatens to disrupt the smooth flow of the line.

Each department (Body, Paint, Trim, Chassis, and Pre-Delivery) has a quota to meet. In Paint, for example, seventy-five percent of the cars are supposed to pass inspection. Because the departments are competitive, there is a reluctance to admit mistakes. When a department supervisor has a problem he can't solve, he often just hides it.

Before the cars come to us to be sanded, they are dipped in an ionized paint solution called "E" coat. This coat of paint actually penetrates the metal and prevents rust. One day we noticed there was no E coat on the cars. We called Stan and he went to talk to the department supervisor.

A few minutes later Stan returned and told us to keep sanding. I counted at least seventy-five cars that passed without any E coat. The supervisor made sure they were duly inspected and passed. Once outside the paint section, the paint job would never be inspected again. Most people on the line estimated that the cars would rust out within a year. "They'll ship 'em to Boston and blame it on the rock salt," was the general prognosis.

If the department supervisor is displeased with a foreman under him, he will do anything to frighten him into performing better. Brutal tonguelashing is common. Foremen work under the constant threat of being returned to the line (foremen cannot be fired, they have the opportunity to start over as workers). While ulcers are a common problem among foremen, heart attacks are also frequent. Many new foremen quit in disgust and go back to the line.

The ones who remain are the most brutal and competitive. Strangely enough, their drive to extract the utmost from the workers carries over to the machines, which are used until they break. Obviously, it would be cheaper to replace them as they wear out, but the mentality doesn't allow it.

If management is harsh, at least it doesn't pretend to help you. But the union does, and some of the worst contempt is reserved for union officials. UAW stands for United Against Workers, a friend tells me.

Typically, union officials seem more at home with Labor Relations executives than with workers. The atmosphere is one of smoke-filled back rooms and secret bargains. It is hard to find a union official in the plant. When you have a problem, you have to telephone and then wait for your representative. Sometimes he comes and sometimes he doesn't.

Of course, all locals are different. Local 560 can be characterized by my own representative, who spent ten minutes one day delineating the problems of the auto industry to me. The root of the problem, he explained, is that workers are lazy. If people would just come to work faithfully and work a little harder, we'd all be better off.

A few years ago, someone was killed in Body Section. A piece of machinery fell on him. The story is that the chairman of the Health and Safety Committee presented his regular report at the next meeting a few weeks later. He didn't mention the dead man. When asked why not, he pointed out that the man hadn't filed a grievance. Consequently, he couldn't investigate the problem.

Staying Human

From what I've said, working at Ford must seem like a circle in Hell. That's mostly the way I remember it. The work is trivial and the conditions poor. Intense discipline is combined with poor planning. The UAW, one of the most liberal unions in the country, constantly proves itself unresponsive to workers' needs. Aside from a few isolated ex-student revolutionaries, there are no political movements.

Each worker seemingly stands alone. Some want to work for a few years and then go to school. Most want to last thirty years and retire with a full pension. As Jerry, our reliefman, says, "I may have been born here, but I'm not going to die here."

But the atmosphere is not one of total defeat. Among workers there is a strong, unstated feeling of trust. It manifests itself in little ways. On a break, a complete stranger will tell you about his deepest marital problems or his feelings of despair, simply because you too are wearing overalls. After five minutes, he'll look at his watch, wave goodbye, and rush back to the job.

Although opposition to Ford is not organized, it is constant. Militancy on an individual level is high. Overly tough foremen find their work sabotaged and are subject to continual verbal harassment. Efficiency experts are forced to hide while doing their inspections. Workers are united in one thing —hating Ford.

Still, thirty years is a very long time. Sabotage helps relieve frustration, but without some type of political context it becomes an empty gesture. So, the worker settles into a slow, cynical wait for retirement. After all, it's a steady job.

During the wait, there remains the dignity of not joining management. There is a clear distinction between exploiter and exploited. The refusal to become one of the exploiters is the constant, steadfast expression of humanity in the face of Ford's regime.

One of my clearest memories of Ford is walking down the chassis line one afternoon. One part of the line runs above the workers who assemble the undercarriage. All day they stand in a narrow concrete trench working on the cars passing over their heads. They have no room to move around and can't see anything.

I hear a strange noise suddenly, like the beat of jungle drums in a Tarzan movie. It gathers force and grows louder, drowning out the sound of the rest of the plant.

Every worker beneath the line is beating on the bottom of the cars with his wrenches. All around, above ground, people laugh and walk in rhythm to the percussion.

Sometimes, on the line, I fantasize about that sound, and the rhythm spreads and spreads.

CASE DISCUSSION QUESTIONS

1. Using the conceptual model of job attitudes (Exhibit 10.1), how would you describe the experiences of the case writer?
2. Exhibit 10.6 outlines a number of factors that influence overall job satisfaction. Consider these factors in view of the information presented in the case. How would you assess the satisfaction level of most production workers at the Ford plant?

3. Identify the primary consequences related to the negative job attitudes displayed at the plant. What would you do as a manager to overcome these problems?

Source: "In the Sanding Booth at Ford" by Rick King in *The Washington Monthly,* January 1976. Copyright © 1976 by The Washington Monthly Company, 1711 Connecticut Ave. N.W., Washington, D.C. 20009. Reprinted with permission.

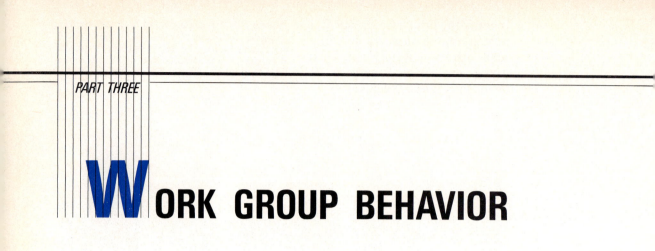

PART THREE

WORK GROUP BEHAVIOR

GROUP PROCESSES IN ORGANIZATIONS

Up to this point, the focus of the text has been on individuals. Having examined personality, perception, learning, and motivation, we have an understanding of the behavior of individuals in organizations. However, because most work in organizations is performed by groups or is the result of group effort, it is necessary to study individuals together in groups as well.

In this chapter, two general topics will be discussed—groups and group structure. This will provide a foundation in the chapters that follow for discussions of group processes, including communication, decision making, power and politics, and leadership. Throughout, we will see how group dynamics influence behavior and attitudes in work settings and how managers can intervene in the process to promote greater individual need satisfaction and organizational effectiveness.

IMPORTANCE OF TOPIC FOR MANAGERS

Why should managers know something about group dynamics? Groups are a fact of organizational life. They are the building blocks of organizations. A knowledge of organizational behavior would be incomplete without a thorough understanding of basic group processes.

In every organization there are various groups, each pursuing different goals and composed of different employees. People join groups for different reasons. A knowledge of the various types of groups and the reasons why people are drawn to become members enables managers to recognize diversity of purpose and to deal with it. For example, why do some employees unionize while others do not?

Groups structure themselves in a variety of ways. In designing a work group or assigning employees to various tasks in work groups, how does group size influence behavior and attitudes? How does managerial behavior influence the development of group norms and roles? How do these norms and roles, in turn, constrain behavior? The answers to these questions can help managers who are interested in facilitating task accomplishment.

Finally, power relationships within and between groups influence who does what for whom. Status relationships determine one's standing in a particular group or organization. Group cohesiveness also represents an important factor in determining level of group effort and performance. How can a manager work with group cohesiveness instead of against it? Under what conditions will cohesive groups facilitate organizational goal attainment?

Certainly, the answers to these questions are of interest to managers. This chapter examines the issues cited here, and the following chapters treat more serious problems involving groups at work. We begin by examining the anatomy of work groups.

THE NATURE OF WORK GROUPS

Available research on group dynamics demonstrates rather conclusively that individual behavior is highly influenced by co-workers in a work group. For instance, we see many examples of individuals who when working in groups intentionally set limits on their own income so they earn less than they otherwise would if they were working alone. We see other situations where individuals choose to remain on undesirable jobs because of their friends in the plant, even though more preferable jobs are available elsewhere. In summarizing much research on the topic, Hackman and Morris (1975, p. 49) concluded the following.

> There is substantial agreement among researchers and observers of small task groups that something important happens in group interaction which can affect performance outcomes. There is little agreement about just what that "something" is—whether it is more likely to enhance or depress group effectiveness, and how it can be monitored, analyzed, and altered.

In order to gain a clearer understanding of this something, we must first consider in detail what we mean by a group, how groups are formed, and how various groups differ.

Definition of a Group

The literature of group dynamics is a very rich field of study (Shaw, 1976; Katz and Kahn, 1978: Cartwright and Zander, 1968), and includes many definitions of work groups. We might conceive of a group in terms of *perceptions;* that is, if individuals see themselves as a group, then a group exists (Bales, 1950). Or, we can view a group in *structural* terms. For instance, McDavid and Harari (1968, p. 237) define a group as "an organized system of two or more individuals who are interrelated so that the system performs some function, has a standard set of role relationships among its members, and has a set of norms that regulate the function of the group and each of its members." Groups can also be defined in *motivational* terms as "a collection of individuals whose existence as a collection is rewarding to the individuals" (Bass, 1960, p. 39). Finally, a group can be viewed with regard to *interpersonal interaction,* the degree to which members communicate and interact with one another over time (Homans, 1950).

By integrating these various approaches to defining groups, we may conclude for our purposes here that a *group* is a collection of individuals who share a common set of norms, who generally have differentiated roles among themselves, and who interact with one another to jointly pursue common goals. This definition assumes a dynamic perspective and leads us to focus on two major aspects of groups: group structure and group processes. We must first learn something about how groups are put together and structure themselves for protection and task accomplishment. Next, we need to learn something about the dynamics of groups as they pursue task accomplishment. In this chapter, we will examine group structure.

Types of Groups

There are two primary types of groups: formal and informal. *Formal* groups are work units that are prescribed by the organization. Examples of formal groups include sections of departments (like the accounts receivable section of the accounting department), committees, or special project task forces. These groups are set up by management either on a temporary or permanent basis to accomplish prescribed tasks.

In addition, all organizations have a myriad of *informal* groups. These groups evolve naturally as a result of individual and collective self-interest among the members of an organization and are not the result of deliberate organizational design. People join informal groups because of common interest, social needs, or simply friendship. Informal groups typically develop their own norms and roles and establish unwritten rules for their members. Studies in social psychology have clearly documented the important role of these informal groups in facilitating (or inhibiting) performance and organizational effectiveness (Roethlisberger and Dickson, 1939; Shaw, 1976).

One of the more interesting aspects of group processes in organizations is the way in which informal groups work with—or against—formal groups. Both groups establish norms and roles, goals and objectives, and demand loyalty from their members. When an individual is a member of many groups—both formal and informal—a wide array of potentially conflicting situations emerge that have an impact upon behavior in organizations. We shall focus on this interplay throughout the next few chapters.

Reasons for Joining Groups

People join groups for many reasons (Kemp, 1970). They have a basic need for protection from external threats, real or imagined. These threats include the possibility of being fired or intimidated by the boss, the possibility of being embarrassed in a new situation, or simply the anxiety of being alone. Groups are a primary source of *security*. We have often heard that there is "security in numbers."

In addition, basic theories of personality and motivation emphasize that most individuals have relatively strong *social needs*. They need to interact with other people and develop meaningful relationships. People are clearly social creatures. Groups provide structured environments in which individuals can pursue friendships.

Similarly, membership in groups can assist individuals in developing *self-esteem*. People often take pride in being associated with prestigious groups, such as professors elected to membership in the National Academy of Sciences or salespersons who qualify for a million dollar club as a reward for sales performance.

People often associate with groups to pursue their own *economic* self-interest. Labor unions are a prime example as are various professional and accrediting agencies, such as the American Bar Association. These organizations often attempt to limit the supply of tradespeople or professionals in order to maintain employment and salaries.

Some groups are formed to pursue goals that are of interest to group members. Included here are bridge clubs, company-sponsored baseball teams, and literary clubs. By joining together, individuals can pursue *group goals* that are typically not feasible alone.

Finally, many groups form simply as a result of people being located in close *proximity* to one another. An example of this is the social relationships that develop between members of a typing pool.

As can be seen, there are many reasons individuals join groups. Often, joining one group can simultaneously satisfy several needs: that is, joining a company-sponsored baseball team can satisfy social needs, esteem needs, and group goals.

Stages in Group Development

Before beginning a rather comprehensive examination of the characteristics of groups, consider briefly the stages of group development. How do groups grow and develop over time? Tuckman (1965) has proposed one model of group development that consists of four stages through which groups generally proceed.

In the first stage of development, group members are engaged in *testing and forming dependence (forming)*. They are attempting to discover which interpersonal behaviors are acceptable or unacceptable in the group. In this process of sensing out the environment, a new member is heavily dependent upon others for providing cues to acceptable behavior.

In the next stages of group development, a high degree of *intragroup conflict (storming)* can be expected among group members as they attempt to develop a place for themselves and to influence the development of group norms and roles. Over time, *development of group cohesion (norming)* occurs. Group members come to accept fellow members and develop a unity of purpose that binds them.

Once group members agree on basic purposes, they set about developing separate roles for the various members. This final stage is labeled the *functional role-relatedness (performing)* stage. The role differentiation takes advantage of task specialization in order to facilitate goal attainment.

It should be emphasized that Tuckman does not claim that all groups proceed through this sequence of stages. Rather, this model provides a generalized conceptual scheme to help in understanding the processes by which groups form and develop over time.

Framework for Analyzing Groups in Organizations

Exhibit 11.1 depicts a five-part general framework for analyzing groups in organizations (after Mitchell, 1978). Group structure is seen as being affected by two primary influences. The first, *personal factors,* includes the attitudes and abilities individuals bring to the work situation, as well as their individual motives. Personality and other background factors can also be included here. These variables were discussed in detail in Part Two of this book. Simply put, it can be expected that the manner in which groups structure themselves is a function of these personal factors.

In addition to personal factors, a second primary influence on group

EXHIBIT 11.1   A GENERAL FRAMEWORK FOR ANALYZING GROUPS IN ORGANIZATIONS

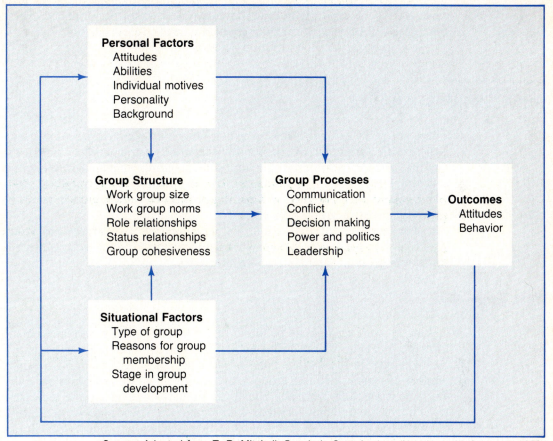

Source: Adapted from T. R. Mitchell, *People in Organizations* (New York: McGraw-Hill, 1978).
Used with permission.

structure is the variety of *situational factors* that must also be taken into
account. Situational factors include the type of group under consideration, the
reasons people chose to join the group, the motives or objectives of the group,
and the stage of group development. These factors set the conditions under
which many aspects of group structure can form, although other factors clearly
influence group structure.

The remainder of this chapter will be devoted to a consideration of *group
structure*—the way in which group members organize themselves for task
accomplishment and with groups' defining characteristics. The subject discussed in the next several chapters will be *group processes;* that is, what groups
actually do. Topics included will be communication, conflict, decision making, power and politics, and leadership. According to our model, these group
processes are influenced by at least three factors: personal factors, situational
factors, and group structure.

Finally, most groups have tangible *outcomes* that result from the existence of the group. The outcomes may include individual attitudes resulting from group processes, as well as individual and group performance. These outcomes will be referred to throughout the next several chapters.

WORK GROUP STRUCTURE

There are many different ways in which one could characterize work group structure. Our approach will be to simply examine several of those characteristics that are useful in describing and understanding what makes one group different from another. We shall attempt to describe a matrix of variables which, when taken together, will paint a portrait of work groups in terms of relatively enduring group properties.

For purposes of discussion, we will consider five aspects of group structure: (1) work group size; (2) work group norms; (3) role relationships; (4) status relationships; and (5) group cohesiveness.

Work Group Size

Obviously, work groups can be found in various sizes. Classical management theorists spent considerable time and effort to no avail attempting to identify the right size for the various types of work groups. There is simply no right number of people for most group activities. Even so, we can summarize the available research and indicate, roughly, what happens as group size increases. At least five size-outcome relationships are relevant. These involve the relation of group size to: group interaction patterns; satisfaction; productivity; absenteeism; and turnover (see Porter and Lawler, 1965; Cummings and Berger, 1976). These results are summarized in Exhibit 11.2.

Group Interaction Patterns. A series of classic studies begun by Bales and Borgatta (1956) examined the variations in group interaction patterns as a result of changes in group size. Using a technique called *interaction process analysis,* which records who says what to whom, Bales and his colleagues found that smaller groups (2–4 persons) typically exhibited greater tension, agreement, and opinion seeking, while larger groups (5–7 persons) showed more tension release and giving of suggestions and information. It was argued that harmony was crucial in smaller groups, and that people had more time to develop their thoughts and opinions. On the other hand, individuals in larger groups must be more direct because of the increased competition for attention.

Satisfaction. In a comprehensive review of the early research on the topic, Porter and Lawler (1965) found increases in work group size to be inversely related to satisfaction, although the relationship was not overly strong. That is,

EXHIBIT 11.2   EFFECTS OF INCREASES IN WORK GROUP SIZE ON VARIOUS OUTCOMES

Variable	Result of Increase in Size
Group interaction ⟶	Greater tension release and provides more direct information
Satisfaction ⟶	Decreased satisfaction
Productivity ⟶	No direct effect on productivity
Absenteeism ⟶	Increased absenteeism
Turnover ⟶	Increased turnover

people working in smaller work units or departments reported higher levels of satisfaction than those in larger units. This finding is not surprising in view of the greater attention one received in smaller groups and the greater importance group members typically experience.

Productivity. No clear relationship has been found between increases in group size and productivity (Porter and Lawler, 1965; Cummings and Berger, 1976). There is probably good reason for this. Unless we take into consideration the type of task that is being performed, we really cannot expect a clear or direct relationship. Mitchell (1978, p. 188) explains it as follows:

> Think of a task where each new member adds a new independent amount of productivity (certain piece-rate jobs might fit here). If we add more people, we will add more productivity. . . . On the other hand, there are tasks where everyone works together and pools their resources. With each new person the added increment of new skills or knowledge decreases. After a while increases in size will fail to add much to the group except coordination and motivation problems. Large groups will perform less well than small groups. The relationship between group size and productivity will therefore depend on the type of task that needs to be done.

Absenteeism. Available research indicates that increases in work group size and absenteeism are moderately related among blue-collar workers, while no such relationship exists for white-collar workers (Steers and Rhodes, 1978). One explanation for these findings is that increased work group size leads to lower group cohesiveness, higher task specialization, and poorer communication (Porter and Lawler, 1965). As a result, it becomes more difficult to satisfy higher-order needs on the job and job attendance becomes less appealing. In view of the increased job autonomy and control of white-collar workers compared to blue-collar, this explanation tends to be more relevant for the latter group. White-collar workers typically have more avenues available to them for need satisfaction.

Turnover. Similar findings exist for employee turnover. Turnover rates are higher in larger groups (Porter and Steers, 1973). Again, it can be hypothesized that since larger groups make need satisfaction more difficult, there is less reason for individuals to remain with the organization. The topics of turnover and absenteeism are considered in greater detail in Chapter Nineteen.

Work Group Norms

The idea of work group norms is a complex one with a history of social psychological research dating back several decades. In this section we will highlight several of the essential aspects of norms and how they relate to people at work. We shall consider: (1) characteristics of work group norms; (2) pattern and intensity of group norms; (3) conformity with and deviance from group norms; and (4) behavioral consequences of group norms.

Characteristics of Work Group Norms. A *norm* may be defined as a standard that is shared by group members and that regulates member behavior. McGrath (1964) notes that group norms include: (1) a frame of reference for viewing relevant objects in the environment; (2) prescribed correct attitudes and behaviors toward those objects; (3) feelings about the correctness of the attitudes and about tolerance for violators of norms; and (4) positive and negative sanctions by which acceptable behavior is rewarded and unacceptable behavior is punished by group members.

An example of a norm can be seen in a typical classroom situation when students develop a norm against speaking up in class too often. It is believed that such highly visible students improve their grades at the expense of others. Hence, a norm is created that attempts to govern acceptable classroom behavior.

Why do norms develop in groups? Festinger (1950) has suggested two principal reasons. First, norms provide group members with an easy frame of reference for understanding the complicated world of work. They provide readily apparent cues to what is right and what is wrong. Union members are often cautioned not to cooperate with management, for example, because of questionable motives attributed to management. Secondly, norms provide uniformity of action necessary if the group is to survive and reach its goals. When all members behave in a like manner (toward a supervisor, for example), group cohesiveness is enhanced and group goals are facilitated.

After reviewing available research on group norms in work settings, Hackman (1976) suggested that norms were characterized by five major characteristics:

1. Norms are structural characteristics of groups that summarize and simplify group influence processes. They denote the processes by which groups regulate and regularize member behavior.
2. Norms apply only to behavior, not to private thoughts and feelings. Although norms may be based on thoughts and feelings, the norms

themselves do not govern them. That is, private acceptance of group norms is unnecessary, only public compliance.

3. Norms are generally developed only for behaviors that are viewed as important by most group members.

4. Norms usually develop gradually, but the process can be quickened if members wish. Norms usually are developed by group members when the occasion arises, such as when a situation occurs that requires new ground rules for members in order to protect group integrity. Sometimes, however, these norms are prescribed by the group in an immediate fashion when the need arises.

5. All norms don't apply to all members. Some norms, for example, apply only to young initiates (like getting the coffee), while others are based on seniority, sex, race, or economic class.

Pattern and Intensity of Group Norms. A clearer understanding of group norms in organizations can be achieved by considering two factors that distinguish various norms. These are pattern and intensity. *Pattern* refers to behaviors that are acceptable or unacceptable (speaking up in class), while *intensity* refers to the extent or degree to which these behaviors are approved or disapproved. Pattern and intensity are incorporated into Jackson's (1965) *Return Potential Model* (RPM) of group norms.

An example will clarify the RPM model. Consider the expectations that students may have about student participation in classroom discussions. There may exist a norm that all students should speak up in class once in a while, but should not show off by talking incessantly. A schematic representation of this norm is shown in Exhibit 11.3. The number of times a student should speak in class according to the norm in our example is shown on the horizontal *x*-axis, ranging from 1 to 10 times. This is the pattern. The vertical *y*-axis shows the intensity, ranging from highly approve to highly disapprove. In this example it can be seen that the norm (the most highly approved behavior) for number of times a student should speak up in class is around 6 times (point a), with an approved range from 3 to 7 times (b). Less than 3 times or more than 7 times is disapproved by group members. Also note that overspeaking is more highly disapproved of than underspeaking.

The RPM model has many applications in organizational settings. Recently, Spencer (1979) used the model to measure the norms people have among their friends and co-workers about turnover. That is, to what extent would one's friends and co-workers approve or disapprove of one's leaving the organization? Using the RPM model allows us not only to examine or measure a norm but also to consider its pattern and intensity. By doing so, a clearer understanding can be achieved about how norms affect member behavior in organizations.

Conformity and Deviance. Managers often wonder why employees comply with the norms and dictates of their work group even when they seemingly work against their best interests. This concern is particularly strong when workers intentionally withhold productivity that could lead to higher incomes.

EXHIBIT 11.3   RETURN POTENTIAL MODEL OF GROUP NORMS

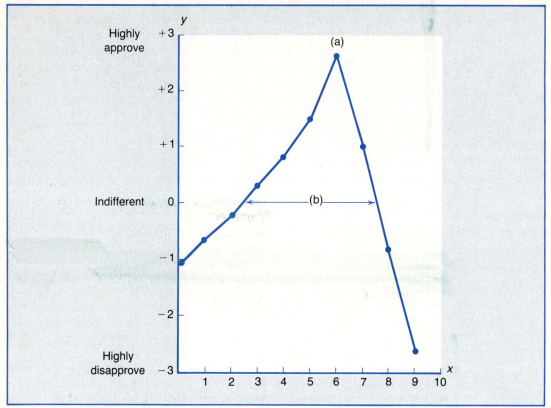

Source: Adapted from J. M. Jackson, "Structural Characteristics of Norms," in Nelson B. Henry (ed.), *The Dynamics of Instructional Groups,* Fifty-ninth Yearbook of the National Society for the Study of Education, Part 2 (Chicago, 1960), Figure 1, p. 139. This adaptation, which differs in several ways from Jackson's original diagram, is used by permission of the National Society for the Study of Education.

What causes such conformity to group norms and under what conditions will an individual deviate from these norms?

Conformity to group norms is believed to be caused by at least four factors (Reitan and Shaw, 1964). First, personality plays a major role. For instance, negative correlations have been found between conformity and intelligence, tolerance, and ego-strength, while authoritarianism was found to be positively related (Crutchfield, 1955).

Second, the initial stimulus that evokes responses can influence conformity. The more ambiguous the stimulus (e.g., a new and confusing order from top management), the greater the propensity to conform to group norms (e.g., continue what you were doing prior to the new order). In this sense, conformity provides a sense of protection and security in a new and perhaps threatening situation.

Third, a variety of situational factors can affect the degree of conformity.

CLOSE-UP 11.1 GROUP PRESSURE AND INDIVIDUAL JUDGMENT

In a classic study of individual conformity to group pressures, Solomon Asch created a laboratory situation in which a naive subject was placed in a room with several confederates. Each person in the room was asked to match the length of a given line (X) with one of three unequal lines, as shown below:

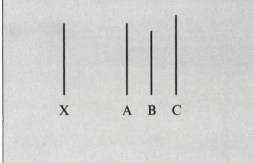

X   A   B   C

Confederates, who spoke first, were all instructed prior to the experiment to identify line C as the line closest to X in length, even though line A was in fact clearly the correct answer. In over one-third of the trials in this experiment, the naive subjects who accurately perceived the correct answer (A) denied the evidence of their own senses and agreed with the answers given by the unknown confederates (C). In other words, when confronted by a unanimous answer to a question by others in the group, a large percentage of individuals chose to go along with the group rather than express a conflicting opinion, even though the individuals were sure their own answer was correct.

Source: S. Asch, "Studies of Independence and Conformity: A Minority of One Against a Unanimous Majority," *Psychological Monographs 20* (1955), Whole No. 416.

As Asch (1955) found (see Close-Up 11.1), conformity to false answers increased with group size up to four members and then leveled off. He found that conformity was higher when there was unanimity among group members.

Finally, group characteristics themselves can influence conformity to group norms. Factors like the extent of pressure exerted on group members to conform, the extent to which a member identifies with the group, and the extent to which the group has been successful in achieving previous goals can influence conformity.

What happens when someone deviates from group norms? Research indicates that groups often respond by increasing the amount of communication directed toward the deviant member (Schachter, 1951). This communication is aimed at bringing the deviant back into the acceptable bounds set by the group. A good example of this process can be seen in Janis' (1972) classic study of the group processes leading up to the abortive Bay of Pigs invasion in Cuba. At one meeting Arthur Schlesinger, an advisor to President Kennedy, expressed opposition to the plan even though no one else expressed similar doubts. After listening to his opposition for a while, Robert Kennedy took Schlesinger aside and said, "You may be right or you may be wrong, but the President has his mind made up. Don't push it any further. Now is the time for everyone to help him all they can" (Janis, 1972, Ch. 2).

When a deviant member refuses to heed the communications and persists in breaking group norms, group members often respond by rejecting or isolating the deviant. They tell the deviant, in essence, that they will no longer tolerate such behavior and prefer to reconstitute the group. If the deviant is not expelled, the group must continually confront behavior that conflicts with what it holds to be true. Rather than question or reexamine its beliefs, it is simpler—and safer—to rid the group of dangerous influence.

Behavioral Consequences of Group Norms. One aspect of the effects of group norms on individual behavior was already discussed in the experiment by Asch. In addition, however, we know that group norms affect employee behavior in a number of ways. For example, when a group establishes a norm concerning a reasonable level of output on a job, serious performance side effects can be felt by the organization. This is especially true when groups are highly cohesive and exert strong social pressures to conform. From the managerial perspective, group norms represent a force to be acknowledged when seeking to optimize motivation and performance at work.

Role Relationships

In order to accomplish its goals and maintain its norms, groups of necessity differentiate the work activities of their members. One or more members assume leadership positions, others carry out the major work of the group, and still others serve as "go-fers." This specialization of activities is commonly referred to as role differentiation. More specifically, a *role* is an expected behavior pattern assigned or attributed to a particular position. It defines individuals' responsibilities on behalf of the group.

Perhaps the best way to understand the nature of roles is to examine a *role episode.* A role episode attempts to explain how a particular role is learned and acted upon (Katz and Kahn, 1978). As can be seen in Exhibit 11.4, a role episode begins with group members having expectations about what one person should be doing in a particular position (Stage 1). These expectations are then communicated to the individual (Stage 2), causing the individual to perceive the expectations about the expected role (Stage 3). Finally, the individual decides to act upon the role in terms of actual role-related behavior (Stage 4). In other words, Stages 1 and 2 deal with the *expected* role, while Stage 3 focuses on the *perceived* role, and Stage 4 focuses on the *enacted* role.

Consider the following simple example. A group may determine that its newest member is responsible for getting coffee for group members during breaks (Stage 1). This role is then explained to the incoming member (Stage 2), who becomes aware of his or her expected role (Stage 3). Based on these perceptions (and probably reinforced by group norms), the individual then would probably accept the assigned role (Stage 4).

Several aspects of this model of a role episode should be noted. First, Stages 1 and 2 are initiated by the group and are aimed at the individual. Stages 3 and 4, on the other hand, represent thoughts and actions of the individual receiving the stimuli. In addition, Stages 1 and 3 represent cognitive

EXHIBIT 11.4   A SIMPLIFIED MODEL OF A ROLE EPISODE

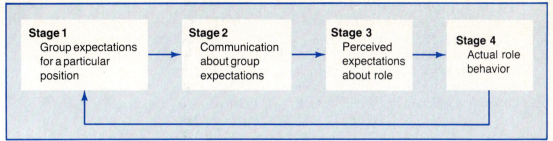

Stage 1
Group expectations
for a particular
position

Stage 2
Communication
about group
expectations

Stage 3
Perceived
expectations
about role

Stage 4
Actual role
behavior

Source: Developed from D. Katz and R. Kahn, *The Social Psychology of Organizations*, 2nd ed.
(New York: Wiley, 1978).

and perceptual evaluations, while Stages 2 and 4 represent actual behaviors.
The sum total of all the roles assigned to one individual is called the *role set*.

Although the role episode presented here seems straightforward, in
reality we know that it is far more complicated. For instance, individuals
typically receive multiple messages from various groups, all attempting to
assign them a particular role. This can easily lead to *role conflict*. Messages
sent to an individual may sometimes be unclear, leading to *role ambiguity*.
Finally, individuals may simply receive too many role-related messages,
contributing to *role overload*. Discussion of these topics is reserved for
Chapter Seventeen, where we will examine several important aspects of
psychological adjustment to work.

Status Relationships

Another characteristic or structural property of work groups is the emergence
of status systems. *Status systems* serve to differentiate individuals from each
other based on some criterion or set of criteria. Parsons (1949) identifies five
bases on which status differentiations are made: birth, personal characteristics, achievement, possessions, and formal authority.

All five bases can be seen in establishing status in work groups. An
employee may achieve high status because he is the boss's son (birth), or the
brightest or strongest member of the group (personal characteristics), the best
performer (achievement), the richest or highest paid (possessions), or the
foreman or supervisor (formal authority).

Status systems can be seen throughout all organizations (see Close-Up
11.2). We differentiate between blue-collar and white-collar employees, skilled
tradespersons and unskilled workers, senior and junior employees, high
achievers and low achievers, and popular and less popular. Why do we do this?
Scott (1967) suggests that status differentiation (and concomitant status
symbols) serves four purposes:

In Japan, etiquette is not simply a prescription for appropriate social responses—it is a complete guide to how one should conduct oneself in all social interactions. At the root of this system of social interaction lies status in society.

When two Japanese businesspeople meet for the first time they exchange business cards, which note their managerial rank (section manager, division manager, deputy president, and so) with considerable precision. They then know how they should relate to one another and who should defer to whom. Or consider what happens when three managers get into a car. Status determines who will sit where: the most honored (highest-status manager) will sit behind the driver; the next most honored manager will sit in the back seat across from the driver; the lowest-status person will sit in front. Similarly prescribed positions exist for such situations as sitting in a conference room and even standing in an elevator.

Though such prescriptive behavior based on status seems strange to many westerners, it is quite natural in Japan. In fact, many Japanese feel such guidelines are helpful and convenient in defining social relationships and avoiding awkward situations, making business more convenient and productive. Whether or not this perception is accurate, it is a fact of life that must be recognized by Western managers doing business in the Far East. Failure to understand such social patterns puts the American or Canadian manager at a distinct disadvantage when attempting to do business abroad.

Source: M. Yazinuma and R. Kennedy, "Life Is So Simple When You Know Your Place," *Intersect,* May 1986, pp. 35–39.

- *Motivation.* We ascribe status to persons as rewards or incentives for performance and achievement. If high achievement is recognized as positive behavior by an organization, individuals are more willing to exert effort.
- *Identification.* Status and status symbols provide useful cues to acceptable behavior in new situations. In the military, for example, badges of rank quickly tell members who has authority and who is to be obeyed. Similarly, in business, titles serve the same purpose.
- *Dignification.* People are often ascribed status as a means of signifying respect that is due them. A clergyman's attire, for instance, identifies a representative of the church.
- *Stabilization.* Finally, status systems and symbols facilitate stabilization in an otherwise turbulent environment by providing a force for continuity. Authority patterns, role relationships, and interpersonal interactions are all affected and indeed defined by the status system in effect. As a result, much ambiguity in the work situation is reduced.

Status can be conferred on an individual in many different ways. One way common in organizations is through the assignment and decoration of offices. John Dean (1976), counsel to President Nixon, provides the following account concerning status in the White House:

> Everyone [on the White House Staff] jockeyed for a position close to the President's ear, and even an unseasoned observer could sense minute changes in status. Success and failure could be seen in the size, decor, and location of offices. Anyone who moved into a smaller office was on the way down. If a carpenter, cabinetmaker, or wallpaper hanger was busy in someone's office, this was the sure sign he was on the rise. Every day, workmen crawled over the White House complex like ants. Movers busied themselves with the continuous shuffling of furniture from one office to another as people moved in, up, down, or out. We learned to read office changes as an index of the internal bureaucratic power struggles. The expense was irrelevant to Haldeman. . . . He once retorted when we discussed whether we should reveal such expense, "This place is a national monument, and I can't help it if the last three Presidents let it go to hell." Actually, the costs had less to do with the fitness of the White House than with the need of its occupants to see tangible evidence of their prestige.

An interesting aspect of status systems in organizations is the notion of *status incongruence*. This situation exists when a person is high on certain valued dimensions but low on others, or when a person's characteristics seem inappropriate for a particular job. Examples of status incongruence include a college student who takes a janitorial job during the summer (the college kid), the president's son who works his way up through the organizational hierarchy (at an accelerated rate, needless to say), or a young fast-track manager who is promoted to a level typically held by older employees.

Status incongruence presents problems for everyone involved. For the individual, hostility and jealousy are often experienced by co-workers who feel the individual has risen above his or her station. For co-workers, their own lack of success or achievement must be clearly acknowledged. One might ask, for example, "Why has this youngster been promoted over me when I have more seniority?" As noted by Mitchell (1978), at least two remedies for this conflict appear: (1) an organization can select or promote only those individuals whose characteristics are congruent with the job and work group; (2) an organization can attempt to change the values of the group. Neither of these possibilities seems realistic or fair. Hence, dynamic organizations that truly reward high achievement (instead of seniority) must accept some level of conflict resulting from status incongruence.

Group Cohesiveness

We have all come in contact with groups whose members feel a high degree of camaraderie, group spirit, and sense of oneness. In these groups, individuals seem to be concerned about the welfare of other group members, as well as that of the group as a whole. There is a feeling of "us against them" that creates a closeness among them. This phenomenon is called group cohesiveness.

More specifically, *group cohesiveness* may be defined as the extent to which individual members of a group are motivated to remain in the group. According to Shaw (1976, p. 197), "Members of highly cohesive groups are more energetic in group activities, they are less likely to be absent from group meetings, they are happy when the group succeeds and sad when it fails, etc., whereas members of less cohesive groups are less concerned about the group's activities."

Determinants of Group Cohesiveness. What causes people to join groups and develop a high degree of group cohesiveness? Cartwright and Zander (1968) have attempted to answer this question in their model of group cohesiveness (see Exhibit 11.5). It is suggested that at least four factors influence the extent to which this cohesiveness develops:

- *Motive base for attraction.* A primary influence on group cohesiveness is individual needs and motives. These motives include the needs for affiliation, recognition, security, and other needs that can be met by the group.
- *Incentive properties of the group.* This consists of the goals, programs, and characteristics of the group members, style of operation, prestige, and other significant properties of their motive base.
- *Expectancy about outcomes.* This concerns the extent to which employees feel that group membership and involvement will, in fact, be instrumental in achieving personal goals.
- *Comparison level.* Finally, employees are seen as comparing the cost-benefit ratio of membership and involvement in one group against alternative paths to goal attainment. This factor follows equity theory.

Several interesting implications arise from this information. For instance, Cartwright and Zander (1968, p. 96) suggest the following:

If, for example, a person joins a group with the expectation of fulfilling certain personal needs, but these change while he is a member, the attractiveness of the group will decrease for him unless the group is able to fulfill the new needs equally well or better. It is possible, of course, for an individual's needs to be modified through experience in the group. Indeed, some groups deliberately attempt to change the needs of their members. Sometimes such groups "lure" members into joining, by promising certain inducements, and then work on the members to develop other needs and interests that are considered more important to the group.

The precise manner in which these processes occur is not known. Even so, managers must recognize the existence of certain forces of group cohesive-

EXHIBIT 11.5 DETERMINANTS AND CONSEQUENCES OF GROUP COHESIVENESS

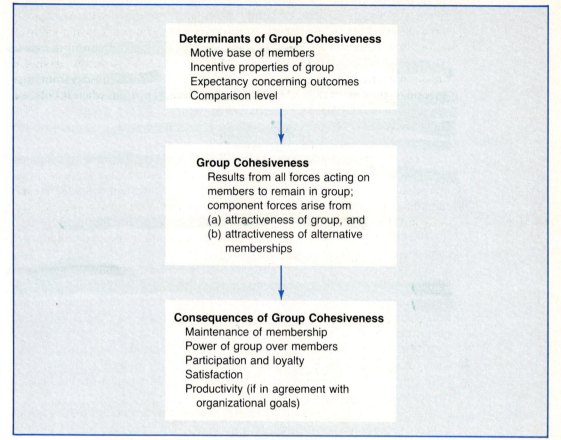

Determinants of Group Cohesiveness
Motive base of members
Incentive properties of group
Expectancy concerning outcomes
Comparison level

Group Cohesiveness
Results from all forces acting on members to remain in group; component forces arise from (a) attractiveness of group, and (b) attractiveness of alternative memberships

Consequences of Group Cohesiveness
Maintenance of membership
Power of group over members
Participation and loyalty
Satisfaction
Productivity (if in agreement with organizational goals)

Source: Developed from D. Cartwright and A. Zander, *Group Dynamics: Research and Theory*, 3rd ed. (New York: Harper & Row, 1968).

ness if they are to understand the nature of group dynamics in organizations. The second aspect of group cohesiveness that must be understood by managers relates to their consequences.

Consequences of Group Cohesiveness. As shown in Exhibit 11.5, several consequences can be identified. The first and most obvious consequence is *maintenance of membership.* If the attractiveness of the group is sufficiently stronger than the attractiveness to alternative groups, then we would not expect the individual to want to voluntarily leave the group. Hence, turnover rates should be low.

In addition, high group cohesiveness typically provides the group with considerable *power over group members.* Several explanations for this finding exist. According to Thibaut and Kelley (1959), the power of a group over members depends upon the level of outcomes members expect to receive from the group compared to what they could receive through alternate means. When the group is seen as being highly instrumental to personal goals, individuals will typically submit to the will of the group.

Third, members of highly cohesive groups tend to exhibit greater *participation and loyalty* (Cartwright and Zander, 1968). A variety of studies has shown that as cohesiveness increases there is more frequent communication among members, a greater degree of participation in group activities, and less absenteeism. Moreover, members of highly cohesive groups tend to be more cooperative and friendly, and generally behave in ways designed to promote integration among members (Shaw, 1976).

Fourth, members of highly cohesive groups generally report high levels of *satisfaction* (Shaw, 1976). In fact, the concept of group cohesiveness almost demands all this be the case since it is unlikely that members will feel like remaining with a group with which they are dissatisfied.

Finally, what is the effect of group cohesiveness on *productivity?* No clear relationship exists here. Instead, research shows that the extent to which cohesiveness and productivity are related is moderated by the extent to which group members accept organizational goals. Specifically, when cohesiveness is high and acceptance of organizational goals is high, performance will probably be high. Similar results would be expected for low cohesiveness and high goal acceptance, although results may not be as strong. On the other hand, performance would not be expected to be high when cohesiveness is high and goal acceptance is low. In this case, group effort will probably be directed away from organizational goals and toward goals valued by the group. Finally, when both cohesiveness and goal acceptance are low, effort will probably become dissipated, leading to low productivity.

The effects of group cohesiveness on performance and attitudes can be seen in two studies performed decades apart. The first, shown in Close-Up 11.3, reviews the classic Trist and Bamforth (1951) study among British coal miners. The second study, shown in Close-Up 11.4, reviews how simple participation by workers in a Swedish truck factory led to several desirable consequences. In both studies, it can be seen that the cohesiveness and oneness experienced by group members had a significant impact on performance outcomes. In the British coal-mining study, members reacted to threats to group solidarity by inhibiting company efforts to improve output through mechanization. It was only after modifications were made that allowed a sufficient degree of group interaction that the miners "allowed" the company to implement changes.

A similar phenomenon can be seen in the Saab-Scania experiment. By allowing employees greater input in decision making—and hence greater responsibility for decision outcome—members of the group identified more strongly with group goals and demonstrated a greater willingness to work with company officials to improve productivity. The rather dramatic results emphasize the important role of teamwork and group cohesiveness in facilitating overall organizational effectiveness.

CLOSE-UP 11.3 THE BRITISH COAL-MINING STUDY

A classic study of the effects of group cohesiveness on productivity has been carried out by Trist and Bamforth among British coal miners.

Prior to mechanization in the mines under study, coal was gathered by six-man teams who worked together and shared various coal gathering functions in the mines. With the mechanization that emerged shortly after World War II, increased task specialization was implemented and each worker was given specific required tasks. This new system, called the conventional long-wall method, was based on using a long face conveyor belt that allowed the company to fractionalize various tasks to increase efficiency and reduce training costs. Work teams were no longer needed since every miner now performed specialized tasks individually.

The conventional long-wall method of mining failed to yield desired economic returns. Social and technical problems became rampant, leading to increased inefficiency and labor strife. In an effort to discover the nature of the problem, a team of social scientists led by Eric Trist was called in to analyze the situation.

In their investigation, the researchers found that for many mines, the fractionated jobs destroyed group cohesiveness, and productivity suffered because of a lack of clear performance norms among group members. In other mines, however, workers had evolved into a new work system, called the composite long-wall method. There the miners themselves rejected the conventional method and adapted it to suit their own needs. This new method combined the technological advantages of the conventional long-wall method with the social system benefits of the earlier method. In essence, work group cohesiveness was rekindled as teams of miners worked together and made the new technology work for them instead of working for it.

Group cohesiveness in the new composite method was enhanced by having the groups select their own members, allocating work responsibilities to individual miners, and receiving payment based on group performance instead of individual effort.

As a result of increased group cohesiveness, several results emerged in the composite groups: (1) members were more sensitive to the work needs of co-workers and helped each other more; (2) greater task variety; (3) roughly one-half the absenteeism of that experienced in the conventional groups; (4) an average productivity rating of 95 percent compared to 78 percent in the conventional groups; and (5) fewer conflicts and labor disputes than in the conventional groups.

Trist and Bamforth concluded that social systems manifested in group cohesiveness cannot be ignored in carrying out technological innovations in the work place. Instead, both social and technical aspects of the job must be considered and integrated if changes are to be successful. This conclusion, resulting from the Trist and Bamforth study, formed the basis for the sociotechnical movement prevalent today.

Source: E. Trist and K. Bamforth, "Some Social and Psychological Consequences of the Long-wall Method of Coal-getting," *Human Relations* 4 (1951): 1–38.

The recent Swedish experiments in job redesign have received considerable positive publicity. One is often left with the impression that job redesign can work miracles for organizations. However, an often overlooked fact is that the most successful aspects of the Saab-Scania experiment occurred *before* the jobs were technologically redesigned.

In 1969 when the engine plant of Saab-Scania (a truck manufacturer) initiated its Quality of Working Life experiments, phase one addressed itself to building highly cohesive, well-integrated work teams. (This was before changes in the assembly line were begun). In two experimental groups, employees were brought into the decision-making process and asked to help the company solve its productivity and morale problems. Technical help was offered to group members when requested, but work groups were largely responsible for solving their own problems.

The results of phase one—before any technical redesign of jobs—were significant. Between 1969 and 1972, unplanned work stoppages dropped from six percent to two percent of total time; extra work and adjustment needed to correct omissions and errors in the finished products dropped by one-third; and turnover dropped from an average of fifty-five percent to twenty percent per year.

Clearly, allowing employees greater involvement in problem-solving leads to increased cohesiveness among group members and greater commitment to group goals which, in this case, were largely compatible with those of the organization. The second phase at Saab-Scania, involving redesigning the assembly techniques themselves, has yet to produce such significant results.

Source: Based on D. Katz and R. Kahn, *The Social Psychology of Organizations,* 2nd ed. (New York: Wiley, 1978), pp. 722–28.

MANAGING EFFECTIVE WORK GROUPS

We have examined in detail the nature and structure of work groups, noting that work groups differ along various dimensions such as size, norms, and roles. Despite these differences, however, there are several actions managers can take in order to encourage groups to be more effective.

To begin, managers can make themselves more aware of the nature of groups and the functions groups perform for individuals. By understanding why individuals join groups, for example, managers should be able to better understand the motivational implications of group dynamics. Is high group cohesiveness in a particular group a result of high commitment to the organization and its goals, or is it a result of alienation from the organization?

Managers can be sensitive to group norms and the extent to which they facilitate or inhibit group and organizational performance. The potency of group norms has been clearly established. It has also been shown that company actions can increase the likelihood that norms will work to the benefit of the organization, as in the Saab-Scania example, or decrease this likelihood, as in the British coal mining example. Much of the thrust of current organizational development efforts is to use process consultation techniques to develop group norms that are compatible with company goals.

Much has been said in the research literature about the effects of groups on individual conformity and deviance. Groups often place significant pressures on individuals to conform and punish deviants by means such as ostracism. From a managerial standpoint, conformity can represent a mixed blessing. On one hand, there are many work situations where managers typically want workers to conform to standard operating procedures. Katz and Kahn (1978) call this dependable role performance. On the other hand, employees must be sufficiently free to take advantage of what they believe to be unique or important opportunities on behalf of the organization. Katz and Kahn refer to this as innovative and spontaneous behavior. If pressures toward conformity are too strong, this spontaneity may be lost along with unique opportunities for the organization.

The importance of group cohesiveness for group effectiveness was discussed. Where it is desirable to develop highly cohesive groups, managers attempt to influence this process through tactics like showing employees how groups can help each other by working together. It is important to note, however, that group cohesiveness by itself does not guarantee increased group effectiveness. Instead, managers must take the lead in showing group members why they benefit from working toward organizational goals. One way to accomplish this is through the reward systems used by the organization.

MANAGEMENT BY GROUPS: THE CASE OF JAPANESE MANAGEMENT STYLE

A final factor to recognize when considering group dynamics is the role of culture. Clearly, variations in cultural patterns can play a significant role in how work groups perform. Indeed, culture can influence how management is defined in an organizational context. In Sweden, as we saw earlier, the role of management is seen as that of group facilitator, whereas in many Latin American companies managers have considerably more decision-making power.

A case in point is the role of management in Japan. Much has been written recently concerning so-called Japanese management style, a model of management based on group processes and consensual decision making. Because of the interest in this area, we will briefly examine this approach and consider its possible applicability to Western cultures.

EXHIBIT 11.6 · COMPARISON OF TRADITIONAL NORTH AMERICAN AND JAPANESE MANAGEMENT STYLES

	Traditional North American Management Style	Japanese Management Style
Employment:	Employment contracts last only as long as individual contributes.	Employment for life for most managers and senior male production workers.
Promotion:	Rapid promotion and feedback.	Slower rates of promotion.
Control System:	Explicit formal control systems.	Somewhat more implicit, less formal control systems.
Concern for Employees:	Little concern for the total person.	More concern for the total person.
Specialization:	Specialization of function with rotation only for people on a general management track.	More cross-functional rotation and emphasis on becoming a generalist.
Decision Making:	Individual, top-down decision making.	Relatively high level of participation and consensual decision making.
Responsibility Emphasis:	Emphasis on individual responsibility.	Emphasis on group responsibility.

Underlying Philosophy

A basic argument for Japanese management style rests on the unparalleled growth witnessed recently in the Japanese economy. Some feel that a primary reason for this success is the rather unique way in which Japanese companies are organized and run. How does this uniqueness compare with typical U.S. and Canadian firms? Ouchi (1981) draws a general distinction as shown in Exhibit 11.6. In essence, it is argued that in contrast to North American firms, Japanese firms are more paternalistic and holistic in their approach to employees, tend to employ people for life, have supervisors that look after personal as well as work-related needs of employees, use bottom-up consensual decision making, and encourage high levels of trust across both hierarchical level and functional specialization. It must be emphasized that the basic principles of Japanese management style can work and have worked in many U.S. and Canadian firms; that is, the style is *transferable* to Western culture. Consider the example of a Sony television factory in San Diego, described in Close-Up 11.5.

A Model of Japanese Management Style

Recently, a model was created to summarize Japanese management style in a manner that should be helpful to students of organization (Hatvany and

CLOSE-UP 11.5 SONY CORPORATION OF AMERICA

Can the Japanese management style work in America? Sony thought it could, and in 1972 the giant Japanese manufacturer opened a color television plant in San Diego. By 1981 production efficiency at the new facility rivaled the standards of Sony's Japanese plants, and the American workers had become so loyal that they voted against joining a union. How was this accomplished? Consider the following conditions at the San Diego plant:

In the San Diego facility employees and supervisors call each other by their first names and no one punches a time clock. Every month a management representative talks to the workers about the company's goals and listens to the workers' comments. Employee suggestions are taken seriously and often lead to immediate improvements. Because many of the plant's workers are Hispanic, one Japanese vice-president even learned to speak Spanish in order to improve communication.

This personal relationship with employees is reinforced by a company policy that favors promoting the plant's own workers rather than hiring from outside. Moreoever, when sales plummeted during a mid-seventies slump, Sony declined to take refuge in layoffs—not one person was furloughed. No wonder, then, that employees repeatedly voted against a union, even though the union pay scale would be higher.

By 1981 the plant accounted for a third of the Japanese manufacturer's overall output of color televisions, and Sony's managers were pleased and proud. From this success, it seems apparent that Japanese management techniques can be useful in America. In particular, close attention to workers' needs and ideas has paid dividends for Sony.

Source: Based on information in "Consensus in San Diego," *Time,* March 30, 1981, p. 58.

Pucik, 1981). Although any model must of necessity represent a simplification and generalization of the actual processes involved, this model captures the essence of the basic Japanese approach. The model consists of three parts: the focus, general strategies, and specific techniques (see Exhibit 11.7). Both the general strategy and the specific techniques reflect the primary focus of the model—an emphasis on developing human resources. The essence of management in major Japanese corporations is maximum development of employee talents and skills so that they may be used in attaining organizational goals.

General Strategies. As shown in the model, three primary general strategies can be identified. First, the organization is seen as an *internal labor market*. Employees are hired right after graduation and it is generally assumed that they will remain with the organization throughout their career. In Japan, this lifetime employment concept is possible because of two factors. First, the practice of subcontracting parts of their operations is widespread among major Japanese firms. As a result, in periods of economic downturn, these

EXHIBIT 11.7   A MODEL OF JAPANESE MANAGEMENT STYLE

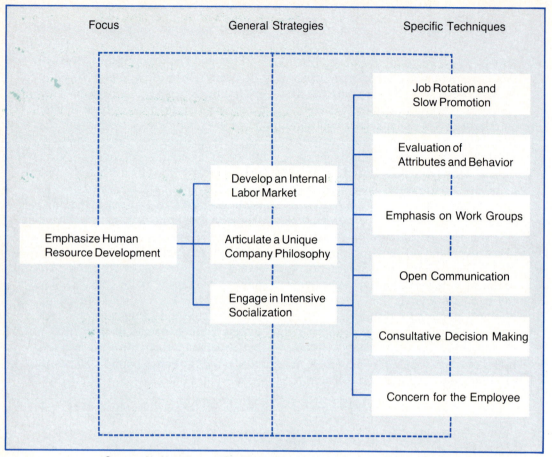

Source: N. Hatvany and V. Pucik, "An Integrated Management System: Lessons from the Japanese Experience," *Academy of Management Review 6* (1981): 470. Reprinted by permission.

subcontracted operations are absorbed back into the company so there is always work to be done by regular employees. Second, a "regular" employee is a male employee. Females are considered part of a temporary work force that is expendable in poor economic times. Hence, lifetime employment applies to regular male employees in major corporations—not male employees of smaller subcontractors, and not female employees.

A second general strategy is to *articulate a unique company philosophy*. Japanese companies go to great lengths to create a "family" atmosphere. Not only do employees work together, they often live together in company housing, vacation at company resorts, and socialize at company cultural centers. Moreover, their children may be born in a company hospital and educated in company schools. Employees can even expect to be buried in company cemeteries—clearly cradle-to-grave assistance! The ideal Japanese company reconciles two objectives: to make a profit and to perpetuate the company as a group. This philosophy is perhaps best summarized by the Japanese word *wa,* or harmony. The concept of *wa* is described as a "quality of relationships . . . teamwork comes to mind as a suitable approximation" (Rohlen, 1974, p. 74). In many ways, *wa* becomes a watchword for developing and enhancing both group consciousness and cooperation among employees.

The third general strategy can be seen in *intensive socialization* efforts. During the initial screening processes, young graduates are selected not only on technical merit, but also on the extent to which candidates are likely to be easily assimilated into the company. Moderate views and a harmonious personality are preferred. Once hired, new employees begin an initial training program of up to six months aimed at introducing them to the company. An employee is expected to exhibit the characteristics of a "company man," including strong loyalty and dedication to service. Functional specialization is of secondary importance. Beyond this, the employees are rotated laterally for several years to learn various aspects of the business and become familiar with co-workers. Through this process, employees become increasingly socialized in company culture and philosophy.

Specific Techniques. A variety of specific techniques can also be identified that are generally aimed at facilitating the accomplishment of the three general strategies (Hatvany & Pucik, 1981). For example, Japanese companies make extensive use of *job rotation,* and employ a *slow promotion* policy. Hence, most moves within the company are lateral rather than vertical. Extensive job rotation enhances the employee's experience and expertise across functional areas. Moreover, since employment is seen in terms of a lifetime commitment, less emphasis is placed on "getting to the top" and more concern is directed toward building the company. A major criticism of U.S. corporations is that they create a culture in which managers look after their own careers first and the company second. In Japan, this order of emphasis is reversed.

In addition, *evaluation techniques* differ in Japan. In particular, Japanese firms evaluate not only individual performance, but also *group* performance. Moreover, personality traits such as creativity, emotional maturity, and cooperation with others are also assessed. In the majority of companies, personality and behavior, not output, are the key to a successful personnel evaluation.

The *work group* has an important role in Japanese firms. Tasks are typically assigned to groups instead of individuals. This, along with group-based performance feedback and job rotation, leads to increased group cohesiveness. (Not surprisingly, these elements are also found at the core of work redesign programs such as those described earlier.) Work groups are given considerable autonomy and responsibility for task accomplishment and problem solving. In this way, a Japanese firm really consists of a series of *teams,* rather than a series of individuals.

The considerable emphasis on team spirit and the network of friendships that employees develop as they rotate throughout the organization encourage extensive *open communication* in Japanese firms. Work spaces are open, and few, if any, managers have private offices. Moreover, both foremen and senior plant managers are often seen on the shop floor examining problems, discussing work improvements, and instructing the less experienced employees. This open communication serves to better inform employees at all levels concerning various aspects of the operation. Each person knows where to go for help, and can also see how his or her own contribution fits into the larger organizational picture.

A widely publicized aspect of Japanese management is its emphasis on *consultative decision making.* Typically, a proposal is initiated by a middle manager who is concerned about some aspect of operations. The middle manager, with the blessing of top management, then discusses the idea with peers and supervisors. These discussions are usually informal and take a consultative form. Then, when everyone has had a chance to have input, a formal request for a decision is made and, because of the earlier consultations, is invariably accepted. As Rohlen (1974, p. 308) notes, "The manager will not decide until others who will be affected have had sufficient time to offer their views, feel they have been fairly heard, and are willing to support the decision even though they may not feel that it is the best one." As a result, although slow in coming, decisions once formally made can enjoy widespread support quickly. In contrast, a typical decision in a Western company will be made quickly at the top and then managers face the rather slow process of trying to secure subordinate support.

Finally, Japanese firms are often described as showing great *concern for employees.* Managers spend considerable time talking to employees about everyday matters. As a matter of fact, this quality of relationship with subordinates represents an important part of their performance evaluation. Concern for employees is shown not only through discussions with employees about their personal needs and problems, however. In addition, as noted above, the company is actively involved in the employees' lives by sponsoring cultural and athletic events, recreational activities, housing assistance, and so forth. Thus, a carefully balanced exchange relationship is established in which the employee feels the company is truly interested in his or her welfare and the company feels the employee is truly committed to the organization and its success. In this, the Japanese style of management has been described as a clear example of integrating personal and organizational goals.

Implications for Western Managers

Advocates of Japanese management style argue that the basic trends of such a model are applicable in Western organizations if Western managers are willing to create the proper climate to nurture the system (Ouchi, 1981; Pascale and Althos, 1981). Indeed, several examples of successful U.S. efforts are noted, including Intel, Dayton-Hudson Corporation, Rockwell International, Eli Lilly Company, and others.

However, the approach taken in Japan in its pure form is not without its critics. For instance, it was already noted that there is clear discrimination against women in Japan in such programs; women are considered temporary employees. Moreover, it was also noted above that such full-scale management styles are largely found in *major* Japanese firms. Smaller firms that live from one subcontract to another cannot afford the luxury of assuring lifetime employment. Indeed, one's status in the Japanese community is influenced by the size of the company for which one works. Being employed by Sony or Matsushita or Mitsubishi carries greater status than does working for a small subcontractor.

In addition, Schein notes that although the Japanese economy has been successful in recent years, there is no proof of a direct cause-and-effect relationship between management style in Japan and Japanese economic success. It may be that Japanese success is a reflection of some other historical, economic, and/or sociocultural factors. Schein cites the following examples: the role of postwar reconstruction; the close collaboration between industry and government; a strong sense of nationalism that produces high levels of motivation among all workers; trade restrictions by the Japanese government; the forced early retirement of most employees in their mid 50s; and a strong cultural tradition of duty, obedience, and discipline that favors a paternalistic form of organization.

Even so, such concerns do not deny the value of Japanese style management either in the East or the West. They simply caution against premature conclusions concerning the extent to which such a style will have an impact on organizational adaptation and effectiveness. As we have seen, there are clearly examples of successful U.S. and Canadian corporations using such techniques, whether they are called Japanese management style or something else. Hence the lesson for the Western manager appears to be to consider the Japanese approach in the context of the particular organization in question, and to adapt those aspects of the model that are appropriate. Such a conclusion cautions against acceptance or rejection, belief or disbelief. Rather, it suggests that managers must know their own corporation's goals, objectives, and culture, and utilize those techniques that have promise or merit.

SUMMARY

Based on the preceding section on individual behavior, we turned in this section to a consideration of group processes and behavior, identifying various types of groups, reasons for joining groups, and stages in group development. A framework for analyzing group processes in organizations was also reviewed.

Next, aspects of work group structure were examined. These included work group size, norms, roles, status, and group cohesiveness. To highlight these various aspects of work group structure, three studies were reviewed in some detail. The first, by Asch, examined the effects of group pressure for conformity on individual judgment. The second, by Trist and Bamforth, reviewed a classic study of the influences of group cohesiveness on a major organizational change. Finally, the third study reviewed the impact of cohesiveness on performance in a major automobile manufacturer.

Based on this discussion, several implications in group management were suggested. The primary focus of these recommendations was the need for managers to first understand the nature of group dynamics and behavior and then take a proactive approach to facilitating group effectiveness. In this way, group goals and organizational goals become compatible and both are achieved.

Finally, the influence of culture on the importance of groups and group processes in organizations was also explored. This influence was illustrated by the Japanese management style model, which served to emphasize that when group goals and organizational goals are compatible, both can be achieved.

KEY WORDS

conformity	role
group cohesiveness	role episode
interaction process analysis	role set
Japanese management style	status
norms	status incongruence
power	status systems
power dependencies	*wa*
return potential model	work groups

FOR DISCUSSION

1. What are the various types of groups often found in work situations?
2. Why do people join groups?
3. Describe the four stages of group development.
4. Critically analyze the model of groups in organizations described in Exhibit 11.1.
5. How does work group size influence individual and group behavior?
6. Discuss the role of work group norms in the work situation.
7. Describe Jackson's return potential model of group norms in organizations.
8. Consider how groups influence conformity and deviance in work situations.
9. What is the major conclusion of Asch's experiment on group pressure and individual judgment?
10. Describe a role episode.
11. Why is a knowledge of role relationships important for managers?
12. What purposes are served by status differentiations in work organizations? What problems emerge from these differentiations?
13. What determines group cohesiveness and what impact does it have on group behavior?
14. What are the major conclusions to be drawn from the British coal-mining study and the Saab-Scania examples given in Close-Ups 11.3 and 11.4?

15. Describe Japanese management style. What are its defining characteristics?
16. What limitations exist in North American cultures that may inhibit the effective implementation of Japanese management style?

NORTHWEST INDUSTRIES

Northwest Industries was a growing company that manufactured recreational vehicles. One of the factories was located in Salem, Oregon. The recreational vehicle market was strong in the western United States and there was good demand for Northwest's products. The market reached its peak in mid-June and tapered off during the winter months. The factory tried to maintain a fairly constant production flow by building up inventories during the low winter months. During the summer months, a number of college students were hired to help boost production and bring inventory back to the desired level.

Organization
The Salem plant had a three-leveled management structure (see Exhibit 1). Craig Hansen, age 52, was the general plant foreman. He had started working on the lines and had worked up to his position after seventeen years. Mr. Hansen knew "everything about trailers and could perform any separate job involved in the construction of a trailer within forty-five minutes." He was in charge of schedules for each run of trailers that was sent through. He also decided which line the trailers would go on and how long it would take to construct them.

Mr. Hansen was serious about the business and conferred with Northwest's home office several times each week.

Joe Mackay, age 35, was the assistant plant foreman. His job was to help the foremen solve any problems they couldn't handle and to see that all plant safety rules and regulations were complied with. He also was responsible for a raw materials inventory and ordering. The men viewed Joe as a walking bomb and, therefore, tried to stay out of his way. When he was called to help correct an error that had been made, Joe demanded to know who had made it and an explanation of "how the workman could be so . . . dumb."

Eight foremen constituted the third management layer. During the winter four of them worked in other areas of the plant, and weren't involved in construction. Each foreman was assisted by a lead man who helped manage the sixteen-man production crew. Foremen were salaried at $900 per month while lead men received 20 cents extra per hour, or $4.70 per hour.

Ted Nelson, age 28, was one of the regular foremen. He didn't have much, good or bad, to say about the college kids. On Ted's line, when a mistake was made, he would correct it himself and

---

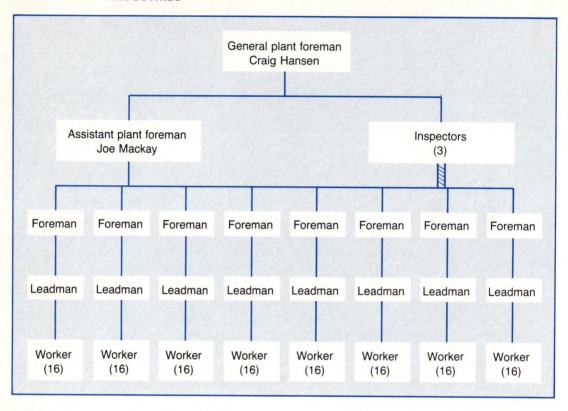

not say anything to the one who had made the mistake. If it happened again, Ted would point out the mistake to the worker and then correct it himself while the worker went back to his job. Ted also managed the time cards and handed out the paychecks.

Quality control in the plant was maintained by three inspectors who reported directly to Mr. Hansen. The inspector's position was considered prestigious, perhaps even above that of foreman, even though both received the same salary. Inspectors had to be especially knowledgeable and trustworthy and able to quickly find production mistakes.

Upon completion of each trailer, the foremen would call one of the inspectors who would examine the trailer and test all components. Any defects were noted on a "squawk sheet." These "squawks" then had to be fixed before the inspector would sign the release form. An average trailer generally had four or five minor squawks which a good "squawker" could repair within twenty to twenty-five minutes per trailer. The idea was to have a good squawker so people would not be pulled off the line and lose the time required to fix production errors.

Workers with some experience were hired on at $3.10 per hour, while unskilled help started at $2.40 per hour.

Provided the unskilled workers produced well, a raise would be given after two months on the job to $3.10 per hour. After four or five years, the workers usually earned $4.50 per hour.

The inspectors, year-round workers, and the foremen were a very close-knit group. They enjoyed many activities together such as parties, bowling, raft races, and occasionally light refreshments. Lunch and break times were looked forward to. All participated in a regular contribution to support the highly enjoyed numbers game which accompanied each pay period, as well as to fund such things as birthday or sympathy cards.

Most of the employees at Northwest had completed a high school education and had then started work with the company. These fellows worked hard and took pride in what they were making. Most men planned to stay with Northwest all their lives. About seventy-five men worked year-round with sixty-five seasonal employees helping out in the summer months.

Northwest's usual procedure was to run four of the eight production lines during the winter. During the summer, enough new people were hired to staff the entire eight lines. Most of the stations on a job required two people to complete each job and ample space existed between each station to permit a trailer to set in between each work area. This spacing procedure facilitated line moves and allowed for the time differences in performing each job.

The New Plan

This year, Mr. Hansen had decided to eliminate some of the problems experienced in the past. Six of the foremen had been complaining about the inefficiency of "those . . . college kids," who were reported to be stubborn, slow, know-it-alls. They admitted that the kids were hard to train and got bored easily but for the most part did a good job.

Mr. Hansen decided to run four lines as normal, leaving most of the older regular employees on those lines. The younger people that were already working for the company were distributed to two of the other lines, and as the college kids were hired, they were paired up with the younger but experienced workers for training. Mr. Hansen's strategy was that as the college kids learned, they would be able to expand to the other two lines and eventually all eight lines would be in full production.

The plan was readily adopted by the foremen. Four were assigned to the four lines with the regulars and the other four were assigned in pairs to the two new lines, with one designated as the foreman and the other as assistant foreman.

The new plan seemed to be working quite well. Halfway through July, the plant was running at full production. The lines with the newer workers enjoyed working together and a substantial rivalry had been created between them and the older workers. Mr. Hansen had seen to it that the younger lines were given routine, long production runs to work on. These runs generally consisted of thirty to forty units that were exactly the same, thus minimizing the training period and reducing errors. The other more experienced lines were given the shorter runs to work on.

At first the rivalry was in fun, but after a few weeks the older workers became resentful of the remarks that were being made and felt like those ". . . kids" should have to work on some of the other more difficult runs. The younger lines easily met production schedules, thus leaving some spare time for goofing around. It wasn't uncommon for someone from the younger lines to

go to another line, in guise of looking for some material, and then give the older workers a hard time. Some of the older workers resented this treatment and soon began to retaliate with sabotage. They would sneak over during breaks and hide tools, dent up metal, install something crooked, or in some small way do something which would slow the production in the lines with the younger workers.

To Mr. Hansen everything seemed to be going quite well and he was quite proud of himself and his plan. Towards the end of July, however, he began hearing reports of the rivalry and sabotage. As most of the longer production runs had been completed, Mr. Hansen decided that "those kids needed to quit playing around and get to work." He gave them some of the new runs which were basically the same as before except for a few changes in the interior walls and the wood roof.

Ted Nelson, the foreman of line C, one of the younger ones, heard about the new run coming onto his line so he decided to go ahead of the first trailer to help each station with the forthcoming changes. He carefully explained each change to the workers as the lead trailer came into their station and then went on

to the next. The kids seemed to be picking the changes up okay, so Ted didn't worry too much about the new run.

As the first trailer was pushed out ready for inspection, Ted called over the inspector. A half hour later, the inspector emerged with two pages of squawks —forty-nine of them. Not seeing Ted anywhere, the inspector called in Mr. Hansen and Joe to point out the uncommonly high number of squawks. It took about five minutes for things to completely explode. Ted walked onto the scene just in time to hear Mr. Hansen yell to Joe, "Get that line into gear in one week and get those . . . squawks fixed or fire the whole bunch!"

CASE DISCUSSION QUESTIONS

1. What is the basic problem in this case?
2. What factors led up to the problem?
3. How does your knowledge of group process help explain what is happening?
4. If you were Mr. Hansen, what would be your next step? What do you think would happen?

CHAPTER TWELVE

INTERGROUP BEHAVIOR AND CONFLICT

Life in organizations can be quite complex, due mostly to the endless string of awkward predicaments in which individuals and groups become embroiled. Consider the following examples:

- Should an organization promote women and minorities over more senior and equally qualified white males in order to overcome past discrimination? If so, couldn't white males then claim that *they* are being discriminated against by the organization? If not, wouldn't females and minorities protest that discrimination persists?

- Should a unionized employee follow the union's call to go out on strike, even if he or she disagrees with the union's case and even if it would risk the loss of home or car because of an inability to make the payments? What are the consequences if the employee does go on strike? If the employee does *not* go on strike?

- Should a sales representative follow company practices or suggestions to engage in unethical or "slightly" illegal behavior to make a big sale? What happens if he or she fails to do so? What happens if he or she does so, but is still not caught?

- Should aspiring managers work long hours to get ahead on the job, even if it jeopardizes the quality of their family relationships? In a true case, when a senior vice-president of a major corporation complained to the president that his long hours on the job were seriously interfering with the time he had for his wife, the president responded, "Then get rid of her!" What risks does one run politically in the organization? What risks does one run at home?

Problems such as these highlight two related issues of concern to contemporary managers. First, how do we manage the process by which several work groups or divisions interact within corporate boundaries? And second, how do we deal with the conflicts that inevitably arise from such group interactions? These two topics—intergroup relations and conflict —are the subject of this chapter.

IMPORTANCE OF TOPIC FOR MANAGERS

An organization is a collection of individuals and groups. If the organization is to succeed, a way must be found to harness the energies of these different groups for the overall good of the organization. After all, the well-being of employees rests on the success of the organization.

Some conflict in an organization is inevitable. Simply making a decision to do A instead of B often alienates the supporters of B, despite the soundness of the reasons behind the decision. But whatever the nature of the conflict and whatever its causes, it must be recognized and dealt with by managers. Hence, a knowledge of the causes of a conflict can help in identifying possible remedies.

The consequences of conflict can be costly to an organization, whether in labor-management disputes, conflicts between departments in the same organization, or conflicts between individuals. In an era of increasing business competition both from abroad and at home, reducing conflict is important. For these reasons, contemporary managers need a firm grasp of the dynamics of intergroup relations and conflict.

A MODEL OF INTERGROUP BEHAVIOR AND PERFORMANCE

To understand how groups interact with each other, it is important to identify the primary variables that characterize intergroup behavior. We can do this by

EXHIBIT 12.1   DETERMINANTS OF INTERGROUP PERFORMANCE

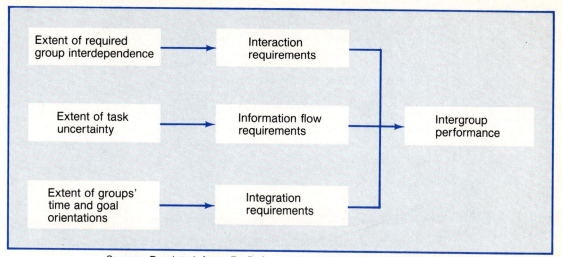

Source: Reprinted from R. Daft and R. Steers, *Organizations: A Micro/Macro Approach* (Glenview, Ill.: Scott, Foresman and Company, 1986), p. 498. Based on concepts in A. D. Szilagyi and M. J. Wallace, *Organizational Behavior and Performance,* 3rd ed. (Glenview, Ill.: Scott, Foresman and Company, 1983), p. 213.

using the model of intergroup performance suggested by Szilagyi and Wallace (1983), a version of which is shown in Exhibit 12.1. Intergroup performance is largely influenced by three variable requirements—for interaction, information flow, and integration. Each requirement, in turn, is influenced by the extent of required group interdependence, task uncertainty, and group time and goal orientation.

Interaction Requirements

Interaction requirements relate to the frequency and quality of interaction between groups that is required for successful task accomplishment. To successfully achieve corporate objectives, organizations must achieve enough intergroup interaction to coordinate resource allocation and utilization. The amount of required interaction is determined by the extent of *interdependence* between the groups. Group interdependence takes three primary forms:

- *Pooled interdependence* occurs when various groups are largely independent of each other, even though each contributes to and is supported by the larger organization. For example, while the physics and music departments may not interact frequently, both contribute to the larger goals of the university, and both use university resources.
- *Sequential interdependence* exists when the outputs of one unit or group become the inputs for another. For example, the shipping department is clearly dependent on manufacturing for the success of its own operation,

EXHIBIT 12.2   THREE TYPES OF GROUP INTERDEPENDENCE

Type of Interdependence	Degree of Dependence and Required Interaction	Description
Pooled	Low	Groups relatively independent of each other, although each contributes to overall goals of organization.
Sequential	Medium	One group's output becomes another group's input.
Reciprocal	High	Some of each group's outputs become inputs for the other.

Source: R. Daft and R. Steers, *Organizations: A Micro/Macro Approach* (Glenview, Ill.: Scott, Foresman and Company, 1986), p. 499.

whereas the manufacturing department is much less dependent on shipping.

- *Reciprocal interdependence* occurs when two or more groups depend on each other for inputs. For example, without product engineering, the marketing department would have nothing to sell. On the other hand, without consumer information from marketing, product engineering might not know what to manufacture. Both units are highly dependent on each other, thereby requiring a high degree of interaction.

In summary, the type of interdependence determines in large part the degree of interdependence (Exhibit 12.2), which in turn determines the extent of required interaction. High interdependence typically requires high intergroup interaction, while low interdependence typically requires relatively low intergroup interaction. An example of this can be seen in Close-Up 12.1.

Information Flow Requirements

The second requirement for successful intergroup performance is optimal *information flow*. To be successful, groups need the appropriate amount of information. Information flow is influenced to a large degree by the extent of *task uncertainty* (see Exhibit 12.3). When groups are working on highly uncertain tasks (e.g., a new product, an experiment, or an old product in a new environment), the need for communication increases. When task uncertainty is low, less information is typically needed.

Task uncertainty, as shown in Exhibit 12.3, is influenced by two factors. The first, *task clarity*, is the extent to which the requirements and responsibilities of the group are clearly understood by the group. The standard operating procedures often used in organizations are an example of a group requirement. They specify how operating procedures and routine decisions are to be made.

CLOSE-UP 12.1 REDUCING INTERGROUP CONFLICT

One of the most illuminating experiments on intergroup conflict processes and how conflict can be resolved was carried out in a classic study by Muzafer Sherif.

The study was carried out among boys attending a summer camp. In the experiment, Sherif created two cohesive groups and over time put the groups through a series of competitive exercises (win-lose situations) in which both group identity and intergroup conflict and hostility increased. Bitter resentment between groups surfaced and attitudes were adopted within each group to facilitate extreme criticism of members of the other group. The emergence of extreme hostility led Sherif to conclude early on in the experiment that when members of two groups are placed in a competitive situation where only one group can win, two situations occur: (1) the competitive activity soon engenders hostility between groups; and (2) the conflict between them facilitates solidarity within each group.

Based on these findings, Sherif set about to resolve the conflict. Several conflict resolution strategies were tried and failed. Among these were: (1) dispensing accurate and favorable information about the opposing groups; (2) appeals to moral values and brotherhood; and (3) the introduction of a common enemy to both groups.

Finally, Sherif placed the groups in a situation where both groups needed each other to solve a mutual problem. It was hypothesized that the conflict would be reduced by an appeal to a superordinate goal. Several mutual problems were presented to the groups (e.g., find a broken water pipe serving the camp, agree on one motion picture to be shown, work together to fix the camp truck so groceries could be secured).

In the experiment, it was found that the cumulative effect of having both groups pursue superordinate goals gradually reduced the conflict and hostility between them. The reinforced superordinate goals apparently led to the development of procedures for cooperating in specific activities. These activities, in turn, had transfer value to new situations, thus creating modes of intergroup cooperation. As the experiment drew to a close, members of previously opposing groups became overtly friendly.

Source: M. Sherif, *In Common Predicament: Social Psychology of Intergroup Conflict and Cooperation* (Boston: Houghton Mifflin, 1966).

The second factor is *task environment*—those factors inside and outside the organization that can affect the group's performance. Two aspects define the task environment: the number of groups that must be dealt with and the relative stability of the environment. Obviously, the more groups that must interact and the more dynamic the environment, the greater the task uncertainty. In a dynamic environment, groups tend to expand their information-gathering efforts to detect and cope with environmental changes. Hence, the greater the task uncertainty, the greater the need for comprehensive information flow systems.

EXHIBIT 12.3   RELATIONSHIP BETWEEN TASK UNCERTAINTY AND INFORMATION FLOW

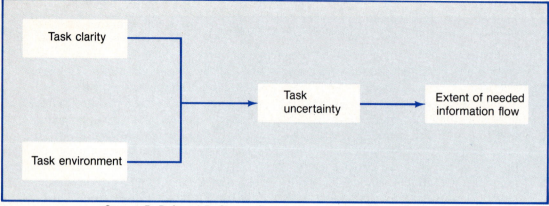

Source: R. Daft and R. Steers, *Organizations: A Micro/Macro Approach* (Glenview, Ill.: Scott, Foresman and Company, 1986), p. 501.

Integration Requirements

The final requirement for successful intergroup performance is *integration.* Integration requirements focus on the extent of collaboration, cooperation, or structural relationships between groups needed to ensure success. Chapters Two and Three, on organization design, demonstrated that different units within an organization have different goals and time orientations. A technical research department, for example, often sees its goals in scientific terms and has a long-term time perspective. A marketing department in the same company, on the other hand, focusing its goals on market considerations, would typically have a short-term time orientation. The production department, concerned with technical goals, would probably attempt to maintain a moderate time orientation in order to take advantage of the economies of scale associated with longer production runs.

A successful organization finds ways to integrate these various groups so they coordinate their efforts on behalf of corporate objectives. The trick is achieving some commonly acceptable coordinating mechanism, not achieving a state in which all units have the same goals and time orientations. The latter state would prove disastrous if the research unit looked for short-term results or the marketing department ignored short-term shifts in the marketplace. Through integration, various units can accommodate each other's needs while maintaining their individuality. In this way, the strengths of all groups are used in addressing organizational problems.

When we put these various requirements and their antecedents together, we can see why achieving intergroup coordination and performance is no easy task. Exhibit 12.4 shows the defining characteristics of four typical units of an organization: research, development, sales, and manufacturing. The interdependence, task uncertainty, and time and goal orientation of each unit are shown. In view of this exhibit, consider the complexities managers face in

EXHIBIT 12.4   INTERGROUP CHARACTERISTICS IN FOUR UNITS OF ONE COMPANY

Group	Interdependence Examples	Task Uncertainty	Time and Goal Orientation
Research	*Reciprocal* with development *Sequential* with market research *Pooled* with shipping	High	*Time:* Long term *Goal:* Science
Development	*Reciprocal* with market research *Sequential* with manufacturing *Pooled* with shipping	Moderate to High	*Time:* Long term *Goal:* Science and Techno-economic
Sales	*Reciprocal* with market research *Sequential* with manufacturing *Pooled* with personnel	Moderate	*Time:* Moderate term *Goal:* Market
Manufacturing	*Reciprocal* with accounting *Sequential* with shipping *Pooled* with research	Low	*Time:* Short term *Goal:* Techno-economic

Source: A. Szilagyi and M. Wallace, *Organizational Behavior and Performance,* 3rd ed. (Glenview, Ill.: Scott, Foresman and Company, 1983), p. 212. Reprinted by permission.

attempting to lead an organization efficiently and effectively. Indeed, business magazines are filled with examples of corporate failures that can be traced to management's failure to coordinate such units. These examples point to an endless array of potential sources of conflict that can reduce the capacity of a company to compete successfully in an ever-changing environment.

THE NATURE OF CONFLICT IN ORGANIZATIONS

By all standards, conflict is an important topic. Just how important can be seen in the results of one recent survey, which found that approximately twenty percent of top and middle managers' time was spent in dealing with some form of conflict (Thomas and Schmidt, 1976). Moreover, Graves (1978) found that managerial skill in handling conflict was a major predictor of managerial success and effectiveness.

A good example of the magnitude of the problems that conflict can cause in an organization is the case of General Concrete, Inc., of Coventry, Rhode Island (Eugene *Register Guard,* October 31, 1981). Operations at this concrete plant came to a halt for more than three weeks because the plant's one truck driver and sole member of the Teamsters Union began picketing after he was laid off by the company. The company intended to use other drivers from another of their plants. In response to the picketing, not a single employee of General Concrete crossed the picket line, thereby closing the plant and costing the company a considerable amount in lost production and profit.

In the sections that follow, several aspects of conflict in organizations are considered. First, conflict is defined and variations of conflict are considered by type and by level. Next, constructive and destructive functions of conflict are discussed, and the basic conflict process is examined. Factors that facilitate conflict are described, defense mechanisms are explored, and a general model of the conflict process is presented. Finally, both effective and ineffective strategies for conflict resolution are presented. We emphasize the role of conflict in work organizations and how such conflict can be effectively dealt with by managers.

Definition of Conflict

There are many ways to define conflict as it relates to work situations. Pondy (1967, p. 298) suggests four approaches, each dealing with one aspect of the conflict process:

> (1) *Antecedent conditions* (e.g., scarcity of resources, policy differences) of conflictful behavior; (2) *affective states* (e.g., stress, tension, hostility, anxiety); (3) *cognitive states* of individuals (i.e., their perception or awareness of conflictful situations); and (4) *conflictful behavior,* ranging from passive resistance to overt aggression.

Based on these approaches, Pondy and others have suggested that instead of arguing over which definition is more appropriate, it may be more functional to use the term conflict to refer to the entire process, including antecedent conditions, affective states, cognitive states, and actual conflictful behaviors. Use of this approach yields the following definition of *conflict.* "Conflict is the process which begins when one party perceives that the other has frustrated, or is about to frustrate, some concern of his" (Thomas, 1976, p. 891).

In other words, conflict involves situations in which the expectation or actual goal-directed behavior of one person or group is blocked—or about to be blocked—by another person or group. Hence, if a sales representative cannot secure enough funds to mount what he or she considers to be an effective sales campaign, conflict can ensue. Similarly, if A gets promoted and B doesn't, conflict can emerge. Finally, if a company finds it necessary to lay off valued employees because of difficult financial conditions, conflict can occur. Many such examples can be identified: in each, a situation emerges in which someone or some group cannot do what it wants to do (for whatever reason) and responds by experiencing an inner frustration.

Types of Conflict

The resulting frustration can lead to at least four distinct *types* of conflict. To begin, *goal conflict* can occur when one person or group desires a different outcome than others. This is simply a clash over whose goals are going to be pursued. Second, *cognitive conflict* can result when one person or group holds ideas or opinions that are inconsistent with others. This type of conflict is evident in political debates. *Affective conflict* emerges when one person's or group's feelings or emotions (attitudes) are incompatible with others. Such conflict is seen in situations where two individuals simply don't get along with each other. Finally, *behavioral conflict* exists when one person or group does something (i.e., behaves in a certain way) that is unacceptable to others. Dressing for work in a way that "offends" others and using profane language are examples of behavioral conflict.

Levels of Conflict

In addition to different types of conflict, there exist several different *levels* of conflict as well. Initially there is *intrapersonal* conflict, or conflict within one individual. We often hear about someone who has an approach-avoidance conflict; that is, he or she is both attracted to and repelled by the same object. Similarly, a person can be attracted to two equally appealing alternatives, such as two good job offers (approach-approach conflict) or repelled by two equally unpleasant alternatives, such as the threat of being fired if one fails to identify a co-worker guilty of breaking plant rules (avoidance-avoidance conflict).

Conflict can take an *interpersonal* form, where two individuals disagree on some matter, or it can take the form of *intragroup* or *intergroup* conflict. The possibility for conflict can thus be seen on all levels in an organization. A good example of interpersonal conflict can be seen in the case of the firing of the chief executive officer at Johns-Manville, described in Close-Up 12.2.

Constructive and Destructive Functions of Conflict

People often assume that all conflict is necessarily bad and should be eliminated. On the contrary, there are some circumstances in which a moderate amount of conflict can indeed be helpful. For instance, conflict can lead to the search for new ideas and new mechanisms as solutions to organizational problems. Conflict can stimulate innovation and change. It can also facilitate employee motivation in cases where employees feel a need to excel and, as a result, push themselves in order to meet performance objectives.

Conflict can at times help individuals and group members grow and develop self-identities. As noted by Coser (1956, p. 154):

> conflict, which aims at a resolution of tension between antagonists, is likely to have stabilizing and integrative functions for the relationship. By permitting immediate and direct expression of rival claims, such social systems are able to readjust their structures by eliminating their sources of dissatisfaction. The multiple conflicts which they experience may serve to eliminate the causes for dissociation and to reestablish unity. These systems avail themselves, through the toleration and institutionalization of conflict, of an important stabilizing mechanism.

CLOSE-UP 12.2 CONFLICT AT THE TOP

The politics of getting fired is indeed an interesting subject. Contrary to what one would expect, the reward for a chief executive officer who takes a dying company and pushes it into profitability can sometimes be termination from his job. Consider the case of W. Richard Goodwin, ex-president of Johns-Manville Corporation.

Goodwin was hired by the board of directors in 1969 to turn the building materials company around. He began immediately to reorganize the company, emphasizing long-range planning and return on investment. He got rid of much of the "deadwood" and brought in young, aggressive managers. As a result, sales rose ninety-one percent over the next five years, while profits rose 115 percent.

As he flew to a board of directors meeting in 1976, he intended to proudly report that the first half of that year had set a company record for earnings. Instead, as he was about to enter the board meeting, he was summarily fired.

Why? As Herbert E. Meyer observes, "The spectacular rise and fall of Dick Goodwin is a story of one man's style and personality—and how some of the very qualities that brought him so much success finally brought him down" (p.

148). In essence, Goodwin thought the company's impressive performance record gave him much more power and authority than the rather staid and conservative directors were actually willing to yield. One senior company executive suggested that Goodwin "just didn't accept the fact that they [the board of directors] were the bosses" (p. 154).

Goodwin's "crimes," and the actions that created so much conflict, involved two proposals that directly confronted the interests of board members. First, he proposed that a new upcoming stock offering be handled by several investment houses, instead of just one. This alienated one of the board members who also happened to be vice chairman of the investment house that heretofore had exclusive rights to J-M stock offerings. In addition, Goodwin proposed that the board be expanded from twelve to fifteen members, and eventually to twenty. We can only guess how the original twelve felt about diluting their power. What we do know is that, in spite of an enviable track record, the board decided it was time for new leadership and that Goodwin was "not the right man to steer J-M through the next phase of its history" (p. 154).

Source: Adapted from H. E. Meyer, "Shootout at the Johns-Manville Corral," *Fortune,* October 1976, pp. 146–151, 154. Reprinted by permission.

Even so, conflict can at the same time have negative consequences for both individuals and organizations when people divert energies away from performance and goal attainment while continuing their efforts to resolve the conflict. Continued conflict can take a heavy toll in terms of psychological well-being. As we shall see in the next chapter, conflict represents an important factor in influencing stress and the psychophysical consequences of stress. Finally, continued conflict can also affect the social climate of the group and inhibit group cohesiveness.

Thus, conflict can be either functional or dysfunctional in work situations, depending upon the nature of the conflict, its intensity, and its duration. The issue for management, therefore, is not how to eliminate conflict, but rather how to manage and resolve it when it occurs.

INFLUENCES ON CONFLICT IN ORGANIZATIONS

This section addresses two aspects of the conflict process. First, several factors that have been found to contribute to conflict will be identified. Following this, a model of conflict processes in organizations will be reviewed.

Factors Contributing to Conflict in Organizations

A number of factors have been identified that are known to facilitate organizational conflict under certain circumstances. In summarizing the literature, Miles (1980) points to several specific examples. The first conflict-contributing factor we will discuss here is *task interdependencies*. In essence, the greater the extent of task interdependence between individuals or groups (that is, the more they have to work together to accomplish a goal), the greater is the likelihood of conflict. This occurs in part because high task interdependency heightens the intensity of relationships. Hence, a small disagreement can very quickly get blown up into a major issue.

Status inconsistencies—differences in status levels between individuals or groups—can also facilitate opportunities for conflict. For example, managers in many organizations have the prerogative to take personal time off during workdays to run errands and so forth, while nonmanagerial personnel do not. Consider the effects this can have on the nonmanagers' view of organizational policies and fairness.

Conflict can also emerge from *jurisdictional ambiguities,* situations where it is unclear exactly where responsibility for something lies. For example, many organizations use an employee selection procedure in which applicants are evaluated both by the personnel department and by the department in which the applicant would actually work. Since both departments are involved in the hiring process, what happens when one department wants to hire an individual, but the other department does not?

The topic of communication is discussed thoroughly in Chapter 13. Suffice it to say that the various *communication obstacles* carry with them significant potential for conflict. When one misunderstands a message or when information is withheld, the individual often responds with frustration and anger. Another factor contributing to conflict that was discussed earlier in the text is the *dependence on common resource pools.* Whenever several departments must compete for scarce resources, conflict is almost inevitable. When resources are limited, a zero-sum game exists in which someone wins and, almost invariably, someone loses.

Differences in performance criteria and reward systems provide more potential for organizational conflict. In a single organization, different groups are evaluated and rewarded using varying criteria. For example, production personnel are often rewarded for their efficiency, and this efficiency is facilitated by the long-term production of a few products. Sales departments, on the other hand, are rewarded for their short-term response to market changes—often at the expense of long-term production efficiency. In such situations, conflict arises as each unit attempts to meet its own performance criteria.

Finally, as discussed in Chapter 4, *personal skills, abilities,* and *traits* can influence in no small way the quality and nature of interpersonal relations. Individual dominance, aggressiveness, authoritarianism, and tolerance for ambiguity all seem to influence how an individual deals with potential conflict. Indeed, such characteristics may determine whether or not conflict is created at all.

A Model of the Conflict Process

Having examined specific factors that are known to facilitate conflict, how does conflict come about in organizations? A model recently proposed by Kenneth Thomas attempts to answer this question by diagramming the basic conflict process. The model, shown in Exhibit 12.5, consists of four stages: (1) frustration; (2) conceptualization; (3) behavior; and (4) outcome.

Conflict situations originate when an individual or group feels *frustration* in the pursuit of important goals. This frustration may be caused by a wide variety of factors, including performance goals, promotion, pay raises, power, scarce economic resources, rules, and values. As Thomas (1976) notes, conflict can be traced to the frustration of anything a group or individual cares about.

In Stage 2, the *conceptualization* stage of the model, parties to the conflict attempt to understand the nature of the problem, what they themselves want as a resolution, what they think their opponents want as a resolution, and various strategies they feel each side may employ in resolving the conflict. This stage is really the problem-solving and strategy phase. For instance, when management and union negotiate a labor contract, both sides attempt to decide what is most important and what can be bargained away in exchange for these priority needs.

A major part of the conceptualization stage consists of strategy decisions concerning how each party will attempt to resolve the conflict. Thomas (1977) identified five modes for conflict resolution (after Lawrence and Lorsch, 1967) as shown in Exhibit 12.6: competing, collaborating, compromising, avoiding, and accommodating. Also shown in the exhibit are situations that seem appropriate for each strategy.

The choice of an appropriate conflict resolution mode depends to a great extent on the situation and the goals of the party. This is shown graphically in

EXHIBIT 12.5 A PROCESS MODEL OF CONFLICT EPISODES

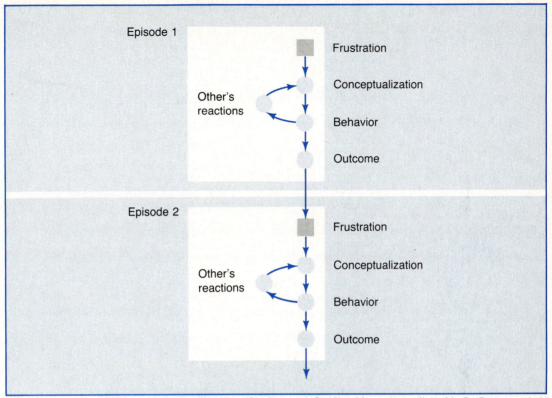

Source: Kenneth Thomas, "Conflict and Conflict Management," in M. D. Dunnette (ed.), *Handbook of Industrial and Organizational Behavior* (New York: John Wiley & Sons, Inc., 1976), p. 895. Copyright © 1976 by John Wiley & Sons, Inc. Reprinted by permission of John Wiley & Sons, Inc.

Exhibit 12.7. Depending upon the relative importance of one's own concerns, as opposed to the importance of the other party's concerns, the appropriate mode that a group or individual selects can vary significantly. Hence, if a union negotiator feels confident he or she can win on an issue that is of primary concern to union members (e.g., wages), a direct competition mode may be chosen. On the other hand, for issues on which the union either is indifferent or actually supports management's concerns (e.g., plant safety), we would expect an accommodating mode.

What is interesting in this process is the assumptions people make about their modes compared to their opponents'. In a study of executives, Thomas and Pondy (1967) discovered that the executives typically described themselves as using collaboration or compromise to resolve conflict, while these same executives typically described their opponents as using a competitive mode almost exclusively. In other words, the executives underestimated their opponents' concern for satisfying both sides. Executives saw their opponents

EXHIBIT 12.6   FIVE MODES OF RESOLVING CONFLICT

Conflict-handling Modes	Appropriate Situations
Competing	1. When quick, decisive action is vital—e.g., emergencies. 2. On important issues where unpopular actions need implementing —e.g., cost cutting, enforcing unpopular rules, discipline. 3. On issues vital to company welfare when you know you're right. 4. Against people who take advantage of non competitive behavior.
Collaborating	1. To find an integrative solution when both sets of concerns are too important to be compromised. 2. When your objective is to learn. 3. To merge insights from people with different perspectives. 4. To gain commitment by incorporating concerns into a consensus. 5. To work through feelings which have interfered with a relationship.
Compromising	1. When goals are important, but not worth the effort or potential disruption of more assertive modes. 2. When opponents with equal power are committed to mutually exclusive goals. 3. To achieve temporary settlements to complex issues. 4. To arrive at expedient solutions under time pressure. 5. As a backup when collaboration or competition is unsuccessful.
Avoiding	1. When an issue is trivial, or more important issues are pressing. 2. When you perceive no chance of satisfying your concerns. 3. When potential disruption outweighs the benefits of resolution. 4. To let people cool down and regain perspective. 5. When gathering information supersedes immediate decision. 6. When others can resolve the conflict more effectively. 7. When issues seem tangential or symptomatic of other issues.
Accommodating	1. When you find you are wrong—to allow a better position to be heard, to learn, and to show your reasonableness. 2. When issues are more important to others than yourself—to satisfy others and maintain cooperation. 3. To build social credits for later issues. 4. To minimize loss when you are outmatched and losing. 5. When harmony and stability are especially important. 6. To allow subordinates to develop by learning from mistakes.

Source: K. W. Thomas, "Toward Multidimensional Values in Teaching: The Example of Conflict Behaviors," *Academy of Management Review 2* (1977): Table 1, p. 487. Reprinted by permission.

as uncompromising. Simultaneously, the executives had perhaps flattering self-portraits of their own willingness to satisfy both sides in a dispute.

The third stage in Thomas' model is actual *behavior.* As a result of the conceptualization process, parties to a conflict attempt to implement their resolution mode by competing or accommodating in the hope of resolving problems.

EXHIBIT 12.7   A TWO-DIMENSIONAL MODEL OF CONFLICT BEHAVIOR

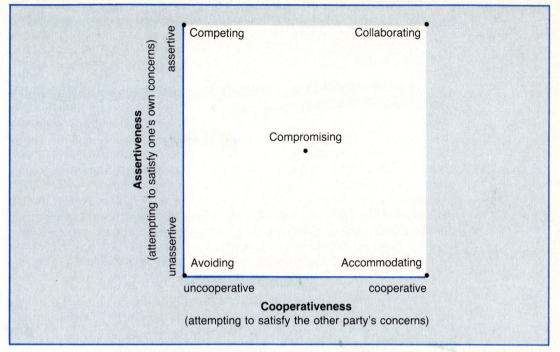

Source: Adapted from Kenneth Thomas, "Conflict and Conflict Management," in M. D. Dunnette (ed.), *Handbook of Industrial and Organizational Behavior* (New York: John Wiley & Sons, Inc., 1976), p. 900. Copyright © 1976 by John Wiley & Sons, Inc. Reprinted by permission of John Wiley & Sons, Inc.

Finally, as a result of behavior, both sides determine the extent to which a satisfactory resolution or *outcome* of the conflict can be achieved. Where one party to the conflict does not feel satisfied, or feels only partially satisfied, the seeds of discontent are sown for a later conflict as shown in Exhibit 12.5. One unresolved conflict episode can easily set the stage for a second episode. The importance of managerial action aimed at achieving quick and satisfactory resolution is vital. Failure to do so leaves the possibility (more accurately, the probability) that new conflicts will soon emerge.

STRATEGIES FOR RESOLVING CONFLICT IN ORGANIZATIONS

We have discovered that conflict is pervasive throughout organizations and that some conflict can be good for organizations. People often grow and learn from conflict, as long as the conflict is not dysfunctional. The challenge for managers is to select a resolution strategy appropriate to the situation and individuals involved. A review of past management practice in this regard reveals that managers often make poor strategy choices. That is, as often as not, managers select repressive or ineffective conflict resolution strategies.

Ineffective Conflict Resolution Strategies

At least five conflict resolution techniques commonly found in organizations fairly consistently prove to be *ineffective* (after Miles, 1980). In fact, in many cases, they serve to increase the problem. Perhaps the most common managerial response when conflict emerges is *nonaction*—to do nothing and ignore the problem. It may be felt that if the problem is ignored it will go away. Unfortunately, such is not often the case. In fact, ignoring the problem may serve only to increase the frustration and anger of the parties involved.

In some cases, managers will acknowledge that a problem exists, but then take little serious action. Instead, they continually report that a problem is "under study" or that "more information is needed." Telling a person who is experiencing a serious conflict that "these things take time" hardly relieves anyone's anxiety or solves any problems. This ineffective strategy for resolving conflict is aptly named *administrative orbiting*.

A third ineffective approach to resolving conflict is to set up a recognized procedure for redressing grievances, but at the same time ensuring that the procedure is long, complicated, costly, and perhaps even risky. The *due process nonaction* strategy is to wear down the dissatisfied employee while at the same time claiming that resolution procedures are open and available. This technique has been used repeatedly in conflicts involving race and sex discrimination.

Oftentimes, managers will attempt to reduce conflict through *secrecy.* Some feel that, by taking secretive actions, controversial issues or decisions can be carried out with a minimum of resistance. One argument for pay secrecy (that is, keeping employee salaries secret) is that such a policy makes it more difficult for employees to feel inequitably treated. Essentially, this is a "what they don't know won't hurt them" strategy. A major problem of this approach is that it leads to distrust of management. When managerial credibility is needed for other issues, it may be found lacking.

The final ineffective resolution technique to be discussed here is *character assassination.* The person with a conflict, perhaps a woman claiming sex discrimination, is labeled a "troublemaker." Attempts are made to discredit her and distance her from the others in the group. The implicit strategy here is that if the person can be isolated and stigmatized, he or she will either be silenced by negative group pressures or else will leave. In either case, the problem is "solved."

Strategies for Preventing Conflict

On the more positive side, there are many things managers can do to reduce conflict. These fall into two categories: actions directed at conflict *prevention* and actions directed at conflict *reduction.* We shall start by examining conflict prevention techniques, since preventing conflict is often easier than reducing it once it begins (Blake, Shepard, and Mouton, 1964). These include:

1. *Emphasizing organization-wide goals and effectiveness.* Focusing on organization-wide goals and objectives and the commitment to facilitating effective operations should prevent goal conflict. If larger goals are emphasized, employees are more likely to see the big picture and work together to achieve corporate goals.
2. *Providing stable, well-structured tasks.* When work activities are clearly defined, understood, and accepted by employees, conflict should be less likely to occur. Conflict is most likely to occur when task uncertainty is high; specifying or structuring jobs minimizes ambiguity.
3. *Facilitating intergroup communication.* Misperception of the abilities, goals, and motivations of others often leads to conflict, so efforts to increase the dialogue between groups and to share information should help avoid conflict. As groups come to know more about each other, suspicions often diminish, and greater intergroup teamwork becomes possible.
4. *Avoiding win-lose situations.* If win-lose situations are avoided, less potential exists for conflict. When resources are scarce, management can seek some form of resource sharing to achieve organizational effectiveness. Moreover, rewards can be given for contribution to overall corporate objectives, thus fostering a climate in which groups seek solutions acceptable to all.

These points bear a close resemblance to descriptions of the so-called Japanese management style (see Chapter Eleven). Considerable effort is invested by Japanese firms in preventing conflict. In this way, more energy is available for constructive efforts toward task accomplishment and competition in the marketplace (see Close-Up 12.3).

Strategies for Reducing Conflict

Where conflict already exists, something must be done, and managers may pursue one of at least two general approaches: change *attitudes* or change *behavior* (Neilsen, 1972). If they change behavior, open conflict is often reduced, but often groups still dislike each other; the conflict may simply become less visible as the groups are separated from each other. Changing attitudes, on the other hand, often leads to fundamental changes in the ways that groups get along. However, it also takes considerably longer to effect than behavior change because it requires a fundamental change in social perceptions, as described in Chapter Four.

Nine conflict resolution strategies are shown in Exhibit 12.8. The techniques near the top of the scale focus on changing behavior; those near the bottom focus on changing attitudes.

CLOSE-UP 12.3 PREVENTING CONFLICT BEFORE IT STARTS

Perhaps one of the best ways to prevent conflict is to ensure that all parties to a potential conflict keep in touch with each other. Open and continual communication allows problems to be dealt with before they become crises and before either side becomes committed to a particular resolution.

This emphasis on communication can be seen in fundamental changes occurring in collective bargaining efforts across North America. Some have described this occurrence as a quiet revolution in the way workers and managers reach contract agreements.

Consider the case of American Can Company. Until recently, operating schedules at American Can were discussed only at contract time. Now they are discussed and dealt with throughout the year. Corporate executives feel that changes happen so fast that year-round bargaining is necessary. As a result, potential conflicts and problems are dealt with when they arise, allowing both sides a better chance to find a remedy before resentment sets in and opposing positions harden. At American Can, this year-round approach to bargaining and labor relations seems to have prevented conflict in this area.

1. *Physical separation.* The quickest and easiest solution to conflict is physical separation. Separation is useful when conflicting groups are not working on a joint task or do not need a high degree of interaction. Though this approach does not encourage members to change their attitudes, it does provide time to seek a better accommodation.
2. *Use of rules and regulations.* Conflict can also be reduced through the increasing specification of rules, regulations, and procedures. This approach, also known as the bureaucratic method, imposes solutions on groups from above. Again, however, basic attitudes are not modified.
3. *Limiting intergroup interaction.* Another approach to reducing conflict is to limit intergroup interaction to issues involving common goals. Where groups agree on a goal, cooperation becomes easier. An example of this can be seen in recent efforts by firms in the United States and Canada to "meet the Japanese challenge."
4. *Use of integrators.* Integrators are individuals who are assigned a boundary-spanning role between two groups or departments. To be trusted, integrators must be perceived by both groups as legitimate and knowledgeable. The integrator often takes the "shuttle diplomacy" approach, moving from one group to another, identifying areas of agreement and attempting to find areas of future cooperation.
5. *Confrontation and negotiation.* In this approach, competing parties are brought together face-to-face to discuss their basic areas of disagreement. The hope is that, through open discussion and negotiation, means can be found to work out problems. Contract negotiations between union and management represent one such example. If a "win-win" solution can be

EXHIBIT 12.8   STRATEGIES FOR REDUCING INTERGROUP CONFLICT

Target of Change
Behavior

Conflict Reduction Strategy

1. Physical separation
2. Bureaucratic method
3. Limited interaction
4. Integrators
5. Confrontation and negotiation
6. Third-party consultants
7. Rotate members
8. Interdependent tasks and superordinate goals
9. Intergroup training

Attitudes

Source: Reprinted from R. Daft and R. Steers, *Organizations: A Micro/Macro Approach* (Glenview, Ill.: Scott, Foresman and Company, 1986). Adapted from concepts in E. H. Neilsen, "Understanding and Managing Conflict," in J. Lorsch and P. Lawrence (eds.), *Managing Group and Intergroup Relations* (Homewood, Ill.: Richard D. Irwin, 1972), pp. 329–43.

identified through these negotiations, the chances of an acceptable resolution of the conflict increase.

6. *Third-party consultation.* In some cases, it is helpful to bring in outside consultants who understand human behavior and can facilitate a resolution. An outside consultant not only serves as a go-between but can speak more directly to the issues because he or she is not a member of either group.

7. *Rotation of members.* By rotating from one group to another, individuals come to understand the frame of reference, values, and attitudes of other members; communication is thus increased. When those rotated are accepted by the receiving groups, change in attitude as well as behavior becomes possible. This is clearly a long-term technique, as it takes time to develop good interpersonal relations and understanding among group members.

8. *Identification of interdependent tasks and superordinate goals.* A further strategy for management is to establish goals that require groups to work together to achieve overall success—for example, when company survival is threatened. The threat of a shutdown often causes long-standing opponents to come together to achieve the common objective of keeping the company going.

9. *Use of intergroup training.* The final technique on the continuum is intergroup training. Outside training experts are retained on a long-term basis to help groups develop relatively permanent mechanisms for working together. Structured workshops and training programs can help forge more favorable intergroup attitudes and, as a result, more constructive intergroup behavior.

SUMMARY

This chapter's examination of intergroup relations and conflict began with a model of intergroup performance that recognized requirements for interaction, information flow, and integration. Conflict was shown to be either constructive or destructive; the reasons for intergroup conflict include the nature of task interdependencies, differences in performance criteria and reward systems, status inconsistencies, jurisdictional ambiguities, scarce resources, and poor communication.

The consequences of intergroup conflict as they relate to changes within and between groups were also examined. Potential changes within a group as a result of intergroup conflict include increased group cohesiveness, increased focus on task, and the rise of autocratic leadership. In addition, relations between groups also experience changes, such as more negative intergroup attitudes, distorted perceptions, decreased communication, and increased surveillance.

A four-part model of intergroup conflict and conflict resolution was presented. Conflict originates (Stage 1) when an individual or group experiences frustration in the pursuit of important goals. In Stage 2, the individual or group attempts to understand the nature of the problem and its causes. In Stage 3, efforts are made to change behavioral patterns in such a way that the desired outcome, or Stage 4, is achieved.

Finally, a series of possible strategies for resolving conflicts is divided into prevention and resolution strategies. Conflict prevention strategies include: (1) emphasizing organization-wide goals; (2) providing stable, well-structured tasks; (3) facilitating intergroup communication; and (4) avoiding win-lose situations. Conflict resolution strategies include: (1) physical separation of parties to the conflict; (2) increased use of rules and regulations; (3) limitation of intergroup interaction; (4) use of third-party integrators; (5) confrontation and negotiation; (6) third-party consultation; (7) rotation of members; (8) identification of interdependent tasks and superordinate goals; and (9) the use of intergroup training. It is almost always easier to prevent conflicts before they occur than to resolve them after they appear.

KEY WORDS

administrative orbiting	integration
affective conflict	interaction requirements
behavioral conflict	pooled interdependence
cognitive conflict	reciprocal interdependence
conflict	sequential interdependence
due process nonaction	task clarity
goal conflict	task environment
information flow system	task uncertainty

FOR DISCUSSION

1. Evaluate the utility of the intergroup performance model from the standpoint of managers. How might managers use this model to better understand possible problems between groups?
2. What would you do as a manager to facilitate better intergroup cooperation on tasks within an organization? Explain.
3. Identify the types of conflict commonly found in organizations and provide examples of each.
4. How can conflict be good for an organization?
5. Identify some reasons for the prevalence of intergroup conflict in organizations.
6. How does intergroup conflict affect behavior within a work group? Behavior between two or more work groups?
7. Review the intergroup conflict model. What lessons for management follow from this model?
8. Of the various strategies for resolving and preventing conflict that are presented in this chapter, which ones do you feel will generally be most effective? Least effective? Why?

EXERCISE

CONFLICT IN PROMOTION POLICIES

12.1

Purpose

To examine conflict in organizations and to attempt to develop an acceptable conflict resolution mechanism.

Instructions

Two groups of about five persons each should be selected from the class. Group 1 is assigned to represent the company and is responsible for ensuring the continued success of the business, although it cannot ignore the legitimate needs of all its employees. Group 2 is assigned to represent women and minorities within the company, although it cannot ignore the economic goals of the company.

Both the groups and the class will read the following case example. After doing so, Group 1 and Group 2 will each present an analysis of the case from the assigned perspective. Each group should propose a solution to the conflict, again keeping in mind its own assigned orientation.

Once the two proposed solutions have been presented, Group 1 and Group 2 will negotiate with each other to attempt to reach an acceptable compromise solution that best meets the conflicting goals of the parties involved.

The Case

A large multinational corporation does extensive business in the Middle East. Company policy requires that middle management spend time in one of the overseas offices. The rationale for this is that to move into top management, em-

ployees need experience in dealing with foreign clients, since this aspect of corporate operations contributes over forty-five percent of sales and fifty percent of profits. The path to top management is through the foreign office. The company's clients come from a society where women and blacks are not treated as equals, especially in business transac-tions. Consequently, the company has not transferred any of their women or black managers to positions of authority in their foreign operations, for fear of losing business. The company has at-tempted to utilize women and blacks in domestic operations; however, none have advanced into middle manage-ment.

CASE

UNIVERSAL INSURANCE COMPANY

12.1

At the Universal Insurance Company, in November, 1970, managers in the field agency department (with ninety to one hundred employees) decided to create the position of coordinator (job grade 6) in the field agency department. The co-ordinator's function would be to ensure that the work load among secretaries was more evenly divided than it had been. Up to that time, some secretaries had been consistently overworked while others frequently had much less work than they could do.

Obviously the qualifications for such a position would include intelligence, reliability, knowledge of the work, and insight into motivational and personali-ty differences among agency personnel, as well as ability to establish and main-tain good working relationships with secretaries and supervisors. Promotion from within was company policy, and job posting was a regular procedure.

To understand the importance of ef-fective coordination among secretaries, and the difficulties to be expected in achieving it, the reader needs a mini-mum of information about functions of the field agency department as well as responsibilities of agency supervisors and their secretaries.

The overall function of the field agen-cy department (in the home office) was to provide continuous contact with dis-trict managers in the field. Each of the ten to twelve agency supervisors served a marketing group in a specific geo-graphical area. Major objectives of all agency supervisors were to help district managers increase the number of policy-holders and to prevent policy lapses. For both purposes it was necessary to keep company representatives in the field fully informed as to all current develop-ments in the insurance business and any changes in home office procedures.

Meeting these liaison responsibilities required prompt and reliable response

Case 12.1 adapted from P. Pigors and C. A. Myers, *Personnel Administration: A Point of View and a Method,* 7th ed. (New York: McGraw-Hill, 1973). Used by permission.

to all correspondence and telephone inquiries. To help supervisors in this part of their job, each was assigned a personal secretary. However, the amount of activity, and therefore of correspondence, differed considerably among the various geographical areas covered by the agency supervisors. And this fact accounted for the unequal work load that had to be carried by the personal secretaries.

These secretaries had no understudies (though their work was supplemented by clerical employees in *information and service centers* who, supervised by unit heads, could be drawn upon as needed). As is customary, the personal secretaries enjoyed a special status. In this division, the vacation of each was timed to coincide with that of her boss (though normally the secretary's vacation was shorter). And she left for lunch at the same time as he did. (During her absence from the office, telephone calls were answered by any qualified clerical employee who happened to be in the office at the time.)

In 1971, two secretaries in the division were outstanding: Marilyn Wiener and Hope Tetzeli.

Marilyn started working for Universal in 1967, as a part-time clerk, during her last two years in high school. Immediately after her graduation (at eighteen, in June, 1969), she began full-time employment as a secretary (job grade 4) in Agency C of the field agency division. Her work was consistently outstanding, and she had received both of the annual merit increases that were open to employees at her level. In addition to her technical proficiency and reliability (she had never been tardy and rarely absent), she was well-liked because of her pleasant way with people. And, despite her quiet manner, her supervisor and associates were aware that she was ambitious. Some of her friends, but not her supervisor, also knew that by June, 1971, Marilyn had reached the conclusion that secretaries in the field agency department had little chance for promotion.[1] She was, therefore, tentatively planning to leave Universal during the next few months and to continue her education. In this way she hoped to qualify herself for a better position, if not at Universal, then in some other company.

Hope Tetzeli was another outstanding secretary in the field agency division at that time. She was secretary to Phil James (supervisor of Agency D). She first came to Universal in June, 1970, immediately after graduating from high school (at eighteen years of age). She prided herself on having been an honor student throughout her high-school career, having graduated in the top ten percent in her class of 550 students.

Her employment interviewer described her as "neat and well-dressed, petite, vivacious, with a markedly Latin temperament, deeply committed to equal rights for women, and with a keen sense of social justice." In her first performance appraisal, her supervisor (Phil James) rated the quality and quantity of her work as outstanding and commended her willingness to assume extra responsibilities when necessary. Like Marilyn, Hope had never been tardy and very rarely absent.

However, Hope's office conduct had occasionally been such as to elicit from John Lord (division manager) the comment "Hope is a self-elected moralist. She has an opinion on everything that happens, inside the department and out, and no hesitation about expressing her opinion however unfavorable it may be." In fact, Mr. Lord had gradually become convinced that Hope's outspokenness tended to create unrest in the office. That opinion had been formed on the basis of Hope's behavior in the following incidents.

Hope's "keen sense of social justice," as well as her outspokenness, first came to John Lord's attention in January, 1971, as a result of a misunderstanding that had occurred six months earlier. In July, 1970, Lord was orienting a group of relatively new women—including Hope. He told them that after six months they would receive an automatic salary increase. However, at the end of the six months several of the women, including Hope, did not receive the increase. Thereupon, Hope appeared in John Lord's office (with three other women whom she had apparently egged on to join her in making a protest). Serving as spokeswoman for the group, she demanded to know why they had not been given the promised increase. The division manager expressed regret for the misunderstanding, explaining that he must have forgotten to mention that the automatic increase applied only to low-level entry jobs (grades 1 through 3). He added that after this first automatic increase, pay raises were considered annually for all employees. The other women appeared to be satisfied with this explanation. But not long afterwards news reached Mr. Lord (through the grapevine) that Hope was harping on the "unjust treatment" that some of them had received in regard to the promised salary increase. When developing this theme in conversation with her friends, she reportedly cited the incident as proof that Mr. Lord "doesn't know what he's talking about when it comes to company policies."

When John Lord heard about these comments from Hope, he requested Phil James (her supervisor) to counsel her, explaining that her remarks were inappropriate in view of his apology and explanation—which should have ended the matter. James was reluctant to criticize the office conduct of an upstanding woman with whose technical performance he was more than satisfied. It seemed to him that her social shortcomings had nothing to do with her job performance. Therefore, his "counseling" of Hope consisted merely in saying: "You can't be a spokeswoman for all the women. Just keep on doing the excellent job you have been doing, and you're sure to get ahead."

A week later, another incident occurred which was reported differently by Hope and the other woman immediately involved. After an encounter in the ladies room, one of the women returned to the office in tears, complaining that Hope had humiliated her by talking in public about a "very personal matter." When asked about this incident, Hope replied that she had merely tried to console the woman (who was pregnant though unmarried), "and other women gathered around while I was talking."

When Mr. Lord heard about this encounter he sent for Hope and reproved her for "disturbing other employees and creating unrest in the office." According to Hope, he told her that in the future she should mind her own business and ended by saying, "If you keep on like this, I shan't be able to recommend you for promotion."

Shortly after this reprimand, Hope had her first progress review with the field agency department personnel assistant, Miss Page.[2] During this interview, Hope was full of complaints —ranging from the caliber of the company's medical clinic to the "injustice" she had suffered with regard to the "promised" salary increase. Miss Page suggested that Hope discuss her dissatisfactions with the division manager. But Hope refused. She said there would be

no point in doing so because Mr. Lord was obviously prejudiced against her. To substantiate this statement, Hope asserted that ever since the difficulty about the pay raise, Mr. Lord had "consistently picked on" her. She went on to say that Mr. Lord's prejudice extended to some of the other women also; that he had a few favorites; and that, owing to his "ignorance of company policy, he was a very ineffective manager." Miss Page then suggested that Hope should speak with the department manager, Mr. O'Hara. Hope dismissed that suggestion also, saying that "everyone" knew Mr. O'Hara took no interest in personnel matters.[3] She insisted instead on having a confidential interview with Mr. Ryan (department director). Miss Page, knowing that Mr. Ryan was a firm believer in the "open-door policy," acceded to Hope's request. The interview took place shortly thereafter.

During Hope's talk with the director, she apparently expressed the same critical views and strongly negative opinions about Mr. Lord as in the interview with Miss Page, though she stated that the supervisors were "fine."

Shortly after this interview, Mr. Lord's record as a manager was discreetly investigated. The results completely exonerated him (including charges of favoritism and inadequate information as to company policies).

During the early spring of 1971, Hope became convinced that she would never get ahead in the field agency department. She therefore kept track of posted job opportunities in other departments. In May she found one that appealed to her because it would entail a promotion. She therefore told Mr. James that she would like to apply for it. James, extremely anxious to keep his competent secretary, tried to dissuade her. Hope then went to Mr. Lord, who

acceded to her request. (Such a request and permission were standard operating procedure [S.O.P.] at Universal, a prepared form being signed by the management representative receiving the request.)

During the interview in the other department, Hope was told (according to her own later statement): "Don't get your hopes up, because this job requires a mature person." When the transfer failed to materialize, Hope jumped to the conclusion that Mr. Lord had stood in her way, because of his prejudice against her. Moreover, she was deeply offended by the implication that she was regarded as an immature person. On several later occasions, when criticizing behavior by other employees, she ended in a dramatic tone, "do you call *that* mature?" To cite one example: She told her friends that in the elevator one day she overheard an elderly man say to an associate, "There sure are lots of good-looking broads in this company." She added that although she regarded such a remark as evidence of extreme immaturity, she had made no official complaint because the man had a large family and could ill afford to lose his job.

On June 16, Hope had an encounter with Marilyn which brought about immediate and serious consequences. That afternoon (a Thursday), just before the end of the working day, Marilyn had been told that she was to be promoted to the position of coordinator as of the following Monday. She expressed delight at the prospect. The word spread like wildfire. Immediately after work, Hope waylaid Marilyn in the hallway. According to another woman who witnessed the encounter, Hope accused Marilyn of being unscrupulous in accepting the promotion since, by her own admission, she intended to leave Universal and "go back to school." Hope

added that such behavior on Marilyn's part was not only exceedingly immature, under the circumstances, but also selfish, and "unfair to us three women who want to make a career at Universal." According to another report that reached Miss Page, Hope's remarks were even more bitter. She accused Marilyn of "taking the bread out of other people's mouths," told her she was "greedy and ruthless," and also that "it is typical of your race to think only of yourselves."

After being the victim of this tirade, Marilyn burst into tears and rushed home.

News of the incident reached Mr. Lord the next morning, by telephone. Marilyn's mother called him to say that Marilyn would not be returning to Universal. She blamed Hope for this development. Mrs. Wiener was so angry that she almost hung up at this point. But when Mr. Lord urged her to tell him what had happened, she said that Hope had done "a complete job of character assassination" on Marilyn, who was "emotionally destroyed" and might require medical attention. She ended by saying that if this proved to be necessary, she would "hold the company morally and financially responsible."

Note

1. Usually the only way a secretary got ahead—except by a promotional transfer—was when her immediate supervisor was promoted. However, in the field agency department, even the director was only in his early forties.
2. At Universal, a departmental personnel assistant was responsible for scheduling and conducting progress reviews and for reporting her findings to the manager. But she was not expected to initiate any other action with personnel or to make suggestions to representatives of line management.
3. This opinion of Hope's was probably based on the fact that the department manager's responsibilities related entirely to the company representatives in the field, though this information had never been relayed to nonsupervisory employees.

CASE DISCUSSION QUESTIONS

1. Identify the types and levels of conflict in this case.
2. This chapter examined a number of factors that contribute to conflict situations in organizations. Which of these factors are particularly evident at Universal Insurance?
3. How would you describe Hope's handling of the conflict? What conflict resolution strategy did she use?
4. What method of conflict resolution was used by management? Was it effective?
5. If you were a manager, what would you have done differently?

CHAPTER THIRTEEN

COMMUNICATION IN ORGANIZATIONS

We now know that group processes combine with group structure to determine the nature and quality of group performance and behavior. With this understanding, we turn our attention to four specific group processes. Communication is the first of the four we will consider; decision making, power, and leadership are the other group processes to be explored in subsequent chapters.

Much has been written about the role of communication in organizational behavior. The following quotations reflect the emphasis given to the subject (Lillico, 1972, p. 1; Rogers and Rogers, 1976, p. 1):

> *In any exhaustive theory of organization, communication would occupy a central place, because the structure, extensiveness, and scope of the organization are almost entirely determined by communication techniques.*
> *Chester I. Barnard*

> *All human interaction takes place in a cross fire of information.*
> *Torsten Hägerstrand*

> *Communication is a good deal more talked about than understood.*
> *Lee Thayer*

Without communication there can be no sustained, organized social life. The health and performance of any social system, whether it be an organization, community, metropolitan area, family, or other such unit, depends upon the ease and certainty of communication. There must be transmission and reception of ideas, plans, instructions, values, feelings, and purposes.

Stanley E. Seashore

Clearly, if efforts are to be coordinated for achieving common goals and objectives, an understanding of communication processes is essential.

IMPORTANCE OF TOPIC FOR MANAGERS

Managers recognize that communication is one of the vital processes that make organizations run. The quality of the decisions that managers make rests squarely on the accuracy and amount of information they receive from other employees and from the external environment. The more timely and precise the information, the greater the likelihood that appropriate decisions will result.

There are several distinct types of communication used in organizational settings. The manager who is familiar with the various types has a greater array of techniques to apply on the job. In addition, a variety of strategies exist for improving accuracy and receptivity of communication in the work place. Managers can learn to clarify their own messages and to accurately receive messages from others.

Finally, it is useful to understand how communication breakdowns occur. When managers are aware of barriers to effective communication, they can take action to reduce or eliminate them.

INTERPERSONAL COMMUNICATION

In this chapter, we shall distinguish between communication primarily between two individuals—*interpersonal communication*—and communication between several individuals or groups—*organizational communication.*

We begin by turning our attention to interpersonal communication. Mintzberg (1973) found that managers tend to spend between fifty and eighty percent of their time in communication with others. Moreover, such managers were found not only to prefer face-to-face communication, but to devote a good deal of their time to such activity. Four aspects of interpersonal communication to be discussed here are: the purposes of such communication; a basic model of interpersonal communication; types of interpersonal communication; and major influences on interpersonal communication.

Purposes for Interpersonal Communication

Scott and Mitchell (1976) have suggested that interpersonal communication in organizations serves four basic purposes:

- To influence others
- To express feelings and emotions
- To provide, receive, or exchange information
- To reinforce the formal structure of the organization, such as using formal channels of communication

In other words, interpersonal communication allows employees at all levels of an organization to attempt to interact with others, to secure desired ends, to request or extend support, and to make use of the formal design of the organization. These purposes serve not only the individuals involved, but the larger aim of improving the quality of working life and organizational effectiveness as well.

A Basic Model of Interpersonal Communication

Any attempt to diagram communication between two individuals must necessarily be an oversimplification of what really happens. Even so, it is possible to represent the process, as shown in Exhibit 13.1. A simple communication episode consists of a communicator who encodes and sends a message to a receiver who decodes it and responds in some way, either verbally or behaviorally (Shannon and Weaver, 1948).

Encoding and Decoding. Two important aspects of this model are encoding and decoding. *Encoding* is simply the process by which individuals initiating the communication translate ideas into a systematic set of symbols (language). Encoding is influenced by the sender's previous experiences with the topic and people involved, his or her emotional state at the time, and the importance attached to the message. *Decoding,* on the other hand, is the process by which the recipient of the message interprets it. Decoding is influenced by factors like the receiver's previous experiences and frame of reference at the time of receiving the message.

EXHIBIT 13.1   A BASIC MODEL OF COMMUNICATION

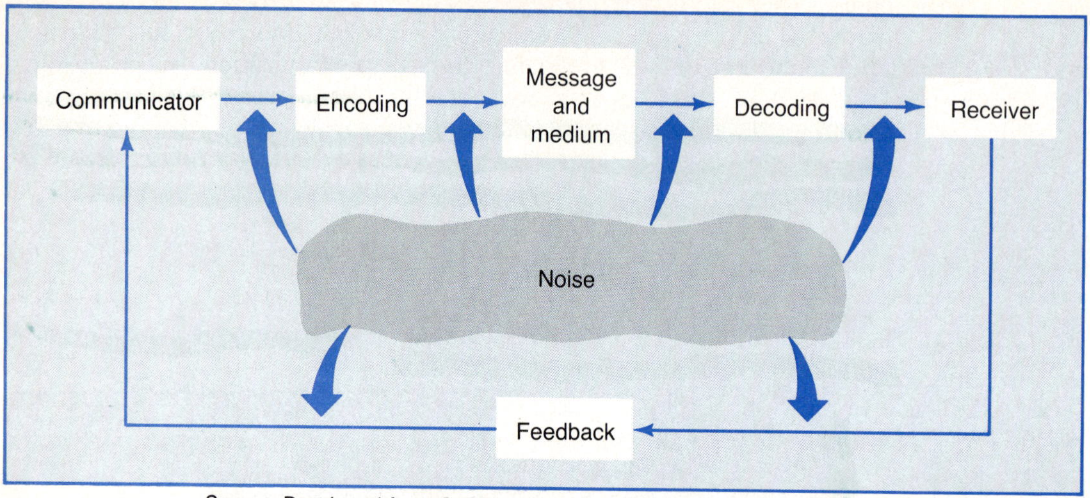

Source: Developed from C. Shannon and W. Weaver, *The Mathematical Theory of Communication* (Urbana: University of Illinois Press, 1948).

Feedback. As a result of the intended transmission of a message from the communicator to the receiver, several types of feedback are likely to result. *Feedback* can be seen as the final step in completing the communication episode and can take many forms, including a verbal response, a nod of the head, a question seeking further information, or no response at all. It has been suggested that there are three basic types of feedback (Kreitner, 1977). That is, feedback can be *informational* when the receiver simply provides nonevaluative information to the communicator. For instance, how many sales were made last month, or how many people are working on this problem? Feedback can be *corrective* when the receiver responds by challenging or correcting the original message. For instance, the receiver may point out that it is not his or her responsibility to monitor sales. Finally, feedback may be *reinforcing* when the receiver acknowledges clear receipt of the intended message. In this sense, a professor's grade on a term paper or examination is reinforcing feedback (positive or negative) to the student's original communication (the paper or exam).

Noise. Finally, there are a variety of ways in which the intended message can get distorted. Factors that distort message clarity are referred to as *noise*. Noise can occur at any point along the process shown in Exhibit 13.1. For example, a manager may be under considerable time pressure and issue a succinct message that lacks the needed clarity for employees to carry out a task correctly. The manager may tell his or her foreman, "I want this job done today, regardless of how much it costs," when in fact the manager does care how much it costs. Noise can also occur in the decoding process. As shown in Exhibit 13.2, there are many ways in which message transmission can be distorted.

EXHIBIT 13.2   EXAMPLES OF NOISE AND DISTORTION IN THE COMMUNICATION PROCESS

What the Manager Said	What the Manager Meant	What the Subordinate Heard
I'll look into hiring another person for your department as soon as I complete my budget review.	We'll start interviewing for that job in about three weeks.	I'm tied up with more important things. Let's forget about hiring for the indefinite future.
Your performance was below par last quarter. I really expected more out of you.	You're going to have to try harder, but I know you can do it.	If you screw up one more time, you're out.
I'd like that report as soon as you can get to it.	I need that report within the week.	Drop that rush order you're working on and fill out that report today.
I talked to the boss, but at the present time, due to budget problems, we'll be unable to fully match your competitive salary offer.	We can give you 95 percent of that offer and I know we'll be able to do even more for you next year.	If I were you, I'd take that competitive offer. We're certainly not going to pay that kind of salary to a person with your credentials.
We have a job opening in Los Angeles that we think would be just your cup of tea. We'd like you to go out there and look it over.	If you'd like that job, it's yours. If not, of course, you can stay here in Denver. You be the judge.	You don't have to go out to L.A. if you don't want to. However, if you don't, you can kiss good-bye to your career with this firm.
Your people seem to be having some problems getting their work out on time. I want you to look into this situation and straighten it out.	Talk to your people and find out what the problem is. Then get with them and jointly solve it.	I don't care how many heads you bust, just get me that output. I've got enough problems around here without you screwing things up too.

Source: *Organizational Behavior* by Richard M. Hodgetts and Steven Altman. Copyright © 1979 by W. B. Saunders Company. Reprinted by permission of Holt, Rinehart & Winston, Inc.

Types of Interpersonal Communication

In the communication episode, three types of communication can be used by either the communicator in the transmission phase or the receiver in the feedback phase. These three types are rather self-explanatory.

Oral Communication. This consists of all messages or exchanges of information that are spoken and by far represents the most prevalent type of communication.

Written Communication. This includes letters, reports, manuals, scribbled notes, and so forth. While most managers prefer oral communication for its efficiency and immediacy, some managers prefer written communications for important messages (e.g., contracts) where precision of language and documentation of message content is important.

Nonverbal Communication. A growing area of interest in managerial communication focuses on the transmission of messages without use of the spoken or written word. Two forms of nonverbal communication can be identified. *Physical or symbolic language,* such as traffic lights, sirens, and status symbols (e.g., office size), relates a message concerning something or someone important. *Body language,* such as facial expressions, posture, or eye movements, consciously or unconsciously relays messages to others. For example, some research has shown that people show tension by clenching their fists or crossing their arms. Boredom is conveyed by yawning or looking markedly disinterested.

In a classic book entitled *The Silent Language,* anthropologist Edward T. Hall (1959) points out that while most of us attain considerable proficiency in the use of the spoken word, we learn very little about the equally important area of nonverbal language—what Hall calls the "language of behavior." This silent language represents a significant influence on us and our success in organizations, yet we seem to be almost unaware of its existence.

The silent language, or nonverbal communication, in organizations can be seen in a multitude of ways. Consider the following examples:

- *Time.* One way to determine how important someone is considered to be in a particular situation is to see how long he or she has to wait to meet someone else. If you are kept waiting a long time, you are probably not considered very important.
- *Space.* When we enter someone's work space, we receive signals concerning who and how important they are. Private offices, large desks, wood paneling, scenic views, a private secretary—all indicate relative importance.
- *Dress.* Simply looking at someone helps us "classify" the individual. Do the clothes indicate a manager or a worker? A military officer or enlisted person?
- *Physical appearance.* Such factors as hair length, posture, and attractiveness send us signals (rightly or wrongly) about the person's personality, status, and even political philosophy.
- *Titles.* Our reactions to others can be influenced by the titles they possess. Examples include "Attorney at Law," "Senator," and "janitor."
- *Interpersonal interaction.* The way people behave toward us also sends signals concerning their status and intent. For example, in Japan it is customary to bow when meeting someone, and the depth of the bow is determined by the relative status of both parties. Similarly, most of us have seen "glad-hander" politicians and salespersons who raise questions in our minds about their sincerity or honesty.

In short, as Hall has suggested, there is a very pervasive silent language of behavior that significantly affects how we see others, how they see us, and how we interact with each other. As Marshall McLuhan said, "The medium is the message." That is, in many instances, how a message is conveyed may be far more important than what is said.

Major Influences on Interpersonal Communication

Regardless of the type of communication involved, the nature, direction, and quality of interpersonal communication processes can be influenced by several factors (R. Hall, 1977; Porter and Roberts, 1976). To begin, communication is clearly a social process. Obviously, it takes at least two participants to complete a communication episode. A variety of *social influences* can affect the accuracy of the intended message. For example, status barriers between employees on different levels of the organizational hierarchy influence modes of address (e.g., "Sir" vs. "Joe"). Prevailing norms and roles may dictate who initiates which kinds of messages, who speaks to whom, and how one responds. The social processes at work in a group or organization determine what is said, to whom it is said, and how it is said.

In addition, the communication process is heavily influenced by employees' *perceptual processes*. Thus, the extent to which employees accurately receive job instructions from supervisors may be influenced by their opinions of the supervisors, the extent to which the instructions are controversial or conflicting, or their interest in the job. If an employee has stereotyped the boss as an incompetent manager, chances are that little the boss says will be regarded seriously. On the other hand, if the boss is seen as influential in the company, everything he or she says may be interpreted as important, even when it is not.

Finally, the communication process is influenced by the *organization structure*. For instance, it has often been argued that a major reason to decentralize an organization is that such structures are more participative and lead to improved communications between parties. When messages must travel through several levels in the hierarchy, opportunities for message distortion are greatly increased, leading to problems that possibly would not occur if face-to-face communication was possible.

Other factors could be mentioned that influence communication processes in organizations. However, social, perceptual, and structural influences should be recognized as major constraints on communication processes. They play a role, regardless of the type of communication involved.

ORGANIZATIONAL COMMUNICATION

We come now to an examination of communication processes in the larger organizational context. In other words, what happens when individuals are put into groups? What happens when we impose structure on the patterns of interpersonal relationships? To consider these questions, we examine three related topics, the first being the impact of organization structure on communication patterns and resulting behavior and performance. Next, the direction of communication (upward, downward, and lateral) is considered. Lastly, we look at various roles played by individuals in ensuring the effectiveness of organizational communication.

Communication and Organization Structure

Chapters Two and Three discussed organization structure. It was noted, for example, that some organizations are "tall" while others are "flat" and that some organizations centralize decision-making authority while others decentralize it. What, then, are the effects of these variations in structure on communication patterns and behavior in organizations?

To answer this question, we will employ the concept of *communication networks*. A communication network is simply a diagram showing all communication patterns that are possible within a group of individuals. Clearly, patterns of communication—who is able or allowed to speak with whom —are quite varied in organizational situations, and this diversity in large part is determined by the structure of the organization itself.

In the literature on communication networks, four different types of networks are usually identified. These are the chain, the wheel or star, the circle, and the all channel, as shown in Exhibit 13.3. Each type depicts the possible interaction patterns of five people in a communication episode. The *chain* represents a communication pattern most frequently found in "tall" organization structures, where most communication flows up or down a formally defined chain of command. The chain shown in the exhibit can be thought of as five levels in the organization hierarchy, perhaps from the president of a company down through a first-line supervisor.

A *wheel* or *star* network shows the communication patterns most typically found in a work group where shop floor employees report to one supervisor, or in a "flat" organization structure where decision making is more decentralized. The *circle* network shows the interaction pattern among five members of a task force or committee. Although the task force may have a formal leader or chairperson, interaction patterns are clearly more diffuse among the members; that is, far more lateral or horizontal communication is possible. The circle also represents interaction patterns typically found in the autonomous work groups that characterize many work redesign efforts. Finally, an *all channel* network represents those situations (for instance, a grapevine) that exist outside the formal organization structure. In such situations, there is typically no leader (formal or informal) and communication can be initiated by anyone in the network to anyone else in the network.

Based on numerous studies (Bavelas and Barrett, 1951; Shaw, 1976; Rogers and Rogers, 1976), we have learned a good deal about the manner and effectiveness with which these different networks handle information. As would be expected, a chain-type network would exhibit considerable *centrali-*

EXHIBIT 13.3 CHARACTERISTICS OF FOUR DIFFERENT COMMUNICATION NETWORKS

	Chain	Wheel or Star	Circle	All Channel
Example	Chain of command	Formal work group	Committee or task force; autonomous work group	Grapevine; informal communication
Centralization of power and authority	High	Moderately high	Low	Very low
Speed of communication	Moderate	Simple tasks: Fast Complex tasks: Slow	Members together: Fast Members isolated: Slow	Fast
Accuracy of communication	Written: High Verbal: Low	Simple tasks: High Complex tasks: Low	Members together: High Members isolated: Low	Moderate
Level of group satisfaction	Low	Low	High	High
Speed of decisions	Fast	Moderate	Slow	
Group commitment to decisions	Low	Moderate	High	

Source: Adapted from A. Bavelas and D. Barrett, "An Experimental Approach to Organization Communication," *Personnel*, 1951; M. E. Shaw, *Group Dynamics: The Psychology of Small Group Behavior* (New York: McGraw-Hill, 1976); and E. M. Rogers and R. A. Rogers, *Communication in Organizations* (New York: The Free Press, 1976).

zation of power and authority, followed next by a wheel-type network. Power is more diffuse in circle networks and very diffuse or nonexistent in all channel networks.

The *speed of communication,* time spent in transmitting messages, is fastest in wheel networks (if the tasks are simple) and circles (if the task force is meeting together in one place). However, communication would be much slower in wheels where the tasks are complex, since the leader may become overloaded with information and feedback, and in circles where members are physically isolated. Communication in chains usually travels at moderate speeds, and in all channel networks such as grapevines it can travel very quickly.

The medium of the message determines the *accuracy of communication* in chains. Messages from top-level managers are highly accurate when communicated to lower-level employees in writing. On the other hand, with oral messages there is considerable opportunity for distortion as the message moves down the chain of command. The accuracy of the message in wheel networks would be typically high on simple tasks, yet low on complex tasks. Again, this can be explained by the large amount of often conflicting information and feedback involved in complex tasks with which the formal leader must deal. In circle networks, accuracy should be high if members are meeting or working together, but low if members are physically isolated from each other. Finally, all channel communication generally exhibits a moderate degree of accuracy, but wide variations can be expected, depending upon the impact the message has on the members of the network. That is, grapevines can be highly accurate in relaying inside information about who the next company president will be, but can be very inaccurate in circulating reports of impending staff layoffs.

The network members' feelings about the nature of the communication episodes is reflected in the *level of group satisfaction.* In general, chain and wheel networks do not lead to positive attitudes by employees, largely because of a lack of participation in the decision under consideration. Their role is more often than not that of a message recipient—not an active participant in a dialogue. In contrast, members of a circle network, like many committees or autonomous work groups, tend to report more positive attitudes about their role in communication episodes. Members of all channel networks likewise report positive attitudes; it seems people enjoy being part of a grapevine.

Another issue related to communication networks is *speed of decision making.* Insofar as speed is concerned, it has generally been found that chain networks lead to rapid decisions so long as relevant information is supplied to the decision maker. A major reason for this speed is found in the structure of the organization itself; that is, the manager has the formal authority to make the decision. The manager does not have to consult with group members unless he or she cares to do so. Wheel networks generally reach decisions with moderate speed. Again, this is explained by the power and authority of the formal leader; group members do not necessarily have to be consulted. The more decentralized nature of circle networks necessarily involves greater time to reach a decision as various members add their input into the problem. As for all channel networks, they are not part of the formal organization, and therefore do not make formal decisions.

Finally, what is the degree of *group commitment to decisions?* Members at the bottom of a chain network would not be likely to be highly committed to the decision made since they had little input in the decision-making process. Likewise, members of a wheel network, while probably at least consulted on the problem, were also typically allowed little real input into the actual decision. As such, group commitment would probably at best be moderate. In a circle network, however, greater opportunity is generally available for group discussion and debate. As a result, while the group may take longer to reach a decision, group commitment to the solution would generally be expected to be higher than for the other two networks.

In summary, communication networks play a significant role in several aspects of organizational behavior, including decision making, attitudes, information flow, and commitment. However, it must be remembered that trends are being discussed here. Exceptions or variations can easily be identified. Even so, an understanding of communication networks is useful for students of organizational behavior to help in comprehending the communication process in work organizations. Based on this information, we turn our attention now to a related aspect of organizational communication; namely, the direction of communication messages and their impact on behavior.

Direction of Organizational Communication

In the study of organizational communication, we typically identify three general directions in which a message can flow: upward, downward, and horizontally. *Horizontal,* or lateral, communication is more frequent than vertical communication in organizational settings since people feel more open and free communicating with peers than with superiors or subordinates (Downs, 1967). Because peers are most likely to share a common frame of reference, message distortion is less likely. In addition, horizontal communication is more likely to be informal and rapid since no formal levels in the organizational hierarchy are involved.

The one exception to this involves horizontal communication between individuals in *different* departments or divisions. In many ways, organization structures serve to discourage such horizontal communication by identifying proper chains of command through which messages are supposed to flow. Naturally, if followed, this would decrease the speed and accuracy of the message. Hence, most organizations acknowledge the right of individuals to cross departmental boundaries to secure or provide information that is germane to their own particular job. This process of circumventing formal organization structure was first recognized by Henri Fayol (1949), who noted, "There are many operations where success depends on rapid execution; we must find some means of reconciling respect for the hierarchic channel with the need for quick action." Thus, interdepartmental communication that goes outside the formal chain of command, but is necessary to task accomplishment, is often referred to as *Fayol's bridge.*

Whereas horizontal communication is typically used for coordinating activities of individuals or groups, *downward* communication (from superior to subordinate) is typically used to provide instructions and directions. *Upward* communication is typically used to provide feedback on operational performance. As such, vertical communication often carries messages that are potentially more threatening (Rogers and Rogers, 1976). Moreover, it has been found that vertical communication is far more likely to flow downward

EXHIBIT 13.4 RANKINGS OF THE EFFECTIVENESS OF VARIOUS UPWARD AND DOWNWARD COMMUNICATION TECHNIQUES

Rank	Upward Communication Techniques	Rank	Downward Communication Techniques
1	Informal discussion	1	Small group meeting
2	Meeting with supervisors	2	Direct organizational publications
3	Attitude surveys	3	Supervisory meetings
4	Grievance procedures	4	Mass meetings
5	Counseling	5	Letters to employees' homes
6	Exit interviews	6	Bulletin boards
7	Union representatives	7	Pay envelope inserts
8	Formal meetings	8	Public address system
9	Suggestion boxes	9	Posters
10	Employee newsletter	10	Annual reports, manuals, media advertising

Source: A. Szilagyi, *Management and Performance* (Glenview, Ill.: Scott, Foresman and Company, 1981), p. 384. Reprinted by permission.

than upward. For instance, Walker and Guest (1952) discovered in a study of assembly-line workers that seventy percent of the workers initiated communication with a supervisor less than once a month. Simon et al. (1950) suggested that this occurs because of the greater power and status that superiors have in dealing with subordinates.

When upward communication does occur, it is likely to be influenced to a considerable degree by what the subordinate thinks his or her superior wants to hear. A study by Read (1962), for example, found that when junior managers had strong aspirations of upward mobility and promotion, they tended to filter their upward communication such that positive messages were highlighted or exaggerated and negative messages were downplayed or omitted altogether. This study also revealed that the accuracy of upward communication was enhanced to the extent that the subordinates trusted their superiors and to the extent that they perceived that their superiors had little influence over their own career advancement. When trust was lacking or where an employee felt his or her superior had considerable influence over promotion decisions, however, upward messages became highly distorted.

Based on a review of relevant literature, Szilagyi (1981) attempted to rank various methods of upward and downward communication in terms of their effectiveness. These rankings are shown in Exhibit 13.4. As can be seen, effective downward techniques (like small group meetings or direct organizational publications) differ from effective upward communication methods (such as informal discussions or supervisory meetings). In view of the necessity of both forms of communication for organizational coordination and effectiveness, it seems important for managers to understand these various techniques, as well as when and where they are most likely to be successful.

EXHIBIT 13.5   INDIVIDUAL COMMUNICATION ROLES IN ORGANIZATIONS

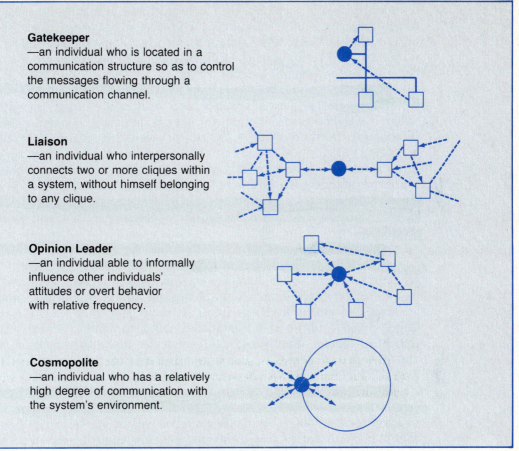

Gatekeeper
—an individual who is located in a communication structure so as to control the messages flowing through a communication channel.

Liaison
—an individual who interpersonally connects two or more cliques within a system, without himself belonging to any clique.

Opinion Leader
—an individual able to informally influence other individuals' attitudes or overt behavior with relative frequency.

Cosmopolite
—an individual who has a relatively high degree of communication with the system's environment.

Source: Reprinted with permission of The Free Press, a Division of Macmillan, Inc., from *Communication in Organizations* by Everett M. Rogers and Rekha Agarwala Rogers, p. 133. Copyright © 1978 by The Free Press.

Individual Communication Roles in Organizations

The third aspect of organizational communication to be addressed in this section focuses on the roles played by various individuals in facilitating communication effectiveness. Obviously, all individuals do not play the same role, nor are they equally important, in communication within the organization. In fact, Rogers and Rogers (1976) have identified four individual roles of people in such communication. These are the gatekeeper, the liaison, the opinion leader, and the cosmopolite (see Exhibit 13.5).

A *gatekeeper* is an employee who is located in such a position in the flow of information as to control certain messages into or away from a given channel. For example, secretaries have long been known to serve an important gatekeeper function by making screening decisions concerning which mail, telephone calls, and people are allowed to reach their bosses. Another example of gatekeepers are those individuals who have strong contacts outside the organization and serve as a primary source of information from the outside world. In using their contacts, such individuals decide what information is conveyed and to whom it is sent.

A *liaison* interpersonally connects two or more groups or departments within a system. The liaison is usually not a member of either group; rather he or she is a go-between who builds the bridges necessary to exchange needed information. In commenting on the role of liaisons in organizations, Rogers and Rogers (1976, p. 138) note, "The liaison role has important practical implications for organizational communication, as liaisons are undoubtedly crucial for the effective operation of an organization's interpersonal network. Liaisons occupy strategic positions within the organizations; they can be either expediters of information flow or bottlenecks in communication channels."

Opinion leaders have the ability to informally influence the attitudes or behaviors of others in a desired way and with relative frequency. They generally have considerable access to external sources of information and tend to hold respected positions within the organization such that their opinions are heard and valued. In comparison to their peers, opinion leaders are often characterized by: (1) a wide range of exposure to external and technically competent sources of information; (2) greater accessibility to their followers; and (3) higher conformity to the norms of the group they lead (Rogers and Rogers, 1976; Katz, 1957; Homans, 1961).

A *cosmopolite* (or cosmopolitan) is a person who has a high degree of interaction and communication with the organization's external environment. In a sense, cosmopolites represent a special type of gatekeeper in that they control communication flow by which new ideas enter the organization. In general, such individuals are characterized "by their wide travel, readership of nonlocal publications; national and international group affiliations, and membership in professional occupations with a high rate of migration" (Rogers and Rogers, 1976, p. 140).

It has been suggested that cosmopolites are concentrated at the very top and very bottom of an organization. At the top, executives travel widely and typically have memberships in a wide variety of external organizations. At the bottom, many employees come into daily contact with the "outside world" through their work with customers, suppliers, and so forth. In both cases, cosmopolites represent an important resource to the organization in helping it to learn more about and cope with the external environment.

In summing up their examination of the four individual communication roles in organizations, Rogers and Rogers (1976) conclude by suggesting the central role played by each of the four types in improving the effectiveness of communication networks. The gatekeeper helps prevent information overload by filtering and screening messages. The liaison integrates and interconnects the various groups or cliques in the network, while the opinion leader facilitates informal decision making in the network. Finally, the cosmopolite generally relates the organization to its external environment by providing an openness of ideas and an exchange of information. In all, then, each of the four functions plays an important role in facilitating organizational effectiveness by helping members of the organization collect, analyze, and act upon relevant information.

BARRIERS TO EFFECTIVE COMMUNICATION

If, as Chester Barnard said, communication forms the basis of organizations, then it is logical to consider several common problems associated with communication processes in organizations. Indeed, a very lengthy list of such problems, or barriers, could be generated with ease. In one such effort, Jackson (1959, p. 165) concluded that:

> What we call communication problems are often only symptoms of other difficulties which exist among persons and groups in an organization. To summarize . . . , I should like to point to four problems which people in organizations must solve in order to overcome barriers to communication:
>
> 1. *The problem of trust or lack of trust.* Communication flows among friendship channels. When trust exists, content is more freely communicated, and the recipient is more accurate in perceiving the sender's opinion.
> 2. *The problem of creating interdependence among persons: common goals and agreement about means for achieving them.* When persons have different goals and value systems, then it is especially important to create mutual understanding about needs and motives.
> 3. *The problem of distributing rewards fairly,* so that people's needs are being met and so that they are motivated to contribute to the overall objectives of the organization. Nothing can be so restrictive of the free flow of ideas and information, for example, as the feeling that you may not obtain credit for your contribution.
> 4. *The exceedingly important problem of understanding and coming to common agreement about the social structure of the organization.* I can think of nothing which would facilitate more the free and accurate flow of communication in an organization than consensus about questions of work, authority, prestige, and status relationships.[1]

For the sake of brevity, it is possible to summarize much of the available information on impediments to effective communication into a list of five barriers (Guetzkow, 1965; R. Hall, 1977): distortion, omission, overload, timeliness, and acceptance.

[1] Reprinted by permission of the International Communication Association, Austin, Texas.

Distortion

Communication *distortion* occurs when an intended message becomes altered as it passes through the information channel from sender to receiver. There are several reasons why distortion can occur, including: (1) differing frames of reference of the sender and receiver; (2) imprecision of language; (3) interpretation errors in the receipt of the message; (4) necessity to condense information for purposes of transmission; and (5) social distance or status barriers between sender and receiver.

A tragic example from history, known as the "black hole of Calcutta," serves to demonstrate what can happen when an intended message is distorted because of interpretation errors and status barriers between sender and receiver. In 1756, the Nawab of Calcutta led a successful uprising against the British East India Company in Calcutta. The British outpost surrendered and the Nawab ordered his lieutenants to place the 146 captives in prison for the night. He then went to bed. The only facility available for the prisoners was a small cell measuring 20 feet by 20 feet. It was referred to locally as the "black hole" and was used to hold occasional thieves. Interpreting the Nawab's orders strictly, all 146 captives were forced into the tiny cell. Without ample air and under claustrophobic conditions, panic broke out among the captives. Appeals to guards, who dared not wake the Nawab, went unanswered. By morning, 123 of the captives were dead. As a result, the black hole of Calcutta became a rallying cry in England symbolizing Indian hostility toward foreigners. Shortly thereafter, the British sent forces against the Nawab and won, and went on to colonize the remainder of India. As Watney (1974, p. 96) concluded of the incident, the tragedy began with a "not very bright subordinate who . . . obeyed [orders] in too literal a fashion. Later, no one . . . dared to take the responsibility of releasing the prisoners on their own incentive."

Examples of message distortion—both intentional and unintentional —are found throughout contemporary organizations (see Close-Up 13.1). They represent a primary cause of misunderstandings at the interpersonal, organizational, and international levels.

Omission

Omission occurs when only one part of an intended message is conveyed to the receiver. For example, a machine operator in a factory may tell his supervisor that his machine has broken down, but fail to point out that he failed to properly maintain the machine and caused the breakdown. Omission results either when the sender intentionally filters the intended message (perhaps because of fear of retribution) or when the sender is unable to grasp the entire message and therefore transmits incomplete information.

A rather interesting example of omission in message transmission can be seen in an episode from Richard M. Nixon's presidency, as described by Dan Rather and Gary Gates in *The Palace Guard* (1974, p. 109).

CLOSE-UP 13.1 THE ART OF COMMUNICATING WITH STOCKHOLDERS

An example of both distortion and omission in communication can often be found in the annual reports to stockholders issued by various corporations. It is common, as we would expect, for corporations to emphasize the positive in reviewing the year's activities. We even expect company reports to contain editorial comments, such as the phone company's arguments against regulations or steelmakers' complaints about imports.

However, recently we can also find in annual reports a series of statements to stockholders that seem to be highly distorted. A recent annual report from Apple Computers, for example, carried pictures of such celebrities as Lee Iacocca, Diane Feinstein, and David Rockefeller, although none are regular users of Apple products. And Mattel, Inc., buried in its accounting explanations the fact that it had to sell off its electronics business because of heavy losses. United Technologies noted that it elected a new president but neglected to say what happened to the old one.

Other examples could be cited. Apparently, some companies are more concerned with the image they convey than with presenting an even-handed analysis of the year's progress.

Source: Based on information in S. Prokesch, "The Creative Writing in This Year's Annual Reports," *Business Week,* April 15, 1985, p. 48.

The president was working alone, very late at night in a hotel room while on a trip. He opened the door, beckoned to a waiting aide and ordered, "Get me coffee." The aide immediately responded to the request. Most of the activities of the hotel including the kitchen were not operating at such a late hour. Hotel personnel had to be called in and a fresh pot of coffee brewed. All this took time and the president kept asking about coffee while waiting. Finally, a tray was made up with a carafe of coffee, cream, sugar and some sweet rolls and was rushed to the president's suite. It was only at this point that the aide learned that the president did not want coffee to drink, but rather wanted to talk to an assistant whose name was Coffee.

Overload

Oftentimes, a receiver is buried in an abundance of information and rational decision making and management suffers. This condition is called communication *overload.* Managers often face this problem when their subordinates fail to adequately screen information presented to the manager. As a result, managers are forced to spend so much time sorting through the information that they may fail to identify the major issues in time to take appropriate steps.

An example of this problem is provided by Allison (1971) in his analysis of the events leading up to the Cuban missile crisis of 1962. Allison found that the Central Intelligence Agency had sufficient information to assess accurately the deployment of missiles in Cuba and to take quiet diplomatic steps to solve the problem long before events reached crisis proportion. Unfortunately, however, the CIA possessed so much information that it was months behind in its intelligence processing. By the time the information was properly analyzed, opportunities for quiet, diplomatic conflict resolution had long passed.

Timeliness

A major factor in the effectiveness of communication is *timing*. Since messages are intended to stimulate action, it is important that their transmissions be timed so that they receive the necessary attention. Providing detailed instructions to employees on a task one month prior to the time the task is to be done, for example, may lead to problems of performance failure because of the lengthy time interval between task instruction and task performance. Conversely, we often see situations in which important memos are distributed to employees requesting actions but giving unrealistically short deadlines. If information is to be properly acted upon, it must arrive in a timely fashion. Close-Up 13.2 reviews a rather serious example of what can happen when messages are not transmitted at the proper time. One functional area at Chevrolet failed to communicate with another area and the results proved disastrous.

Acceptance

Even if all four of the above barriers could be overcome, it is necessary that there be *acceptance* of the message by the receiver if it is to be acted upon. If employees refuse to accept a message, perhaps because they feel it is inappropriate or comes from a noncredible source (e.g., a supervisor asks the secretary of another supervisor to type a letter), there is little reason to believe the message will be acted upon.

Recognition by managers of the existence of these barriers represents a first and useful step toward overcoming such problems. Once recognized, concrete actions can be initiated to improve speaking and writing capabilities, as well as listening capabilities. Managers and employees will learn not only *how* to communicate, but also *when* to communicate and with *whom* to communicate. In this way, considerable progress can be made in overcoming these barriers to effective communication.

STRATEGIES FOR IMPROVING COMMUNICATION EFFECTIVENESS

None of the above barriers to communication effectiveness is insurmountable. The problem for managers is how to improve the accuracy, flow, and

As one would expect, problems of communication are often magnified in larger organizations where more and more people must interact and coordinate their efforts for project completion. An example of the deleterious effects of poor communications in these large organizations can be seen in an event that occurred in 1968 at Chevrolet.

During this time, the sales staff decided to heavily promote a four-cylinder version of the Chevrolet Nova. A massive sales campaign was initiated, including media advertising, dealer promotions, local commercials, and so forth. Unfortunately, at the same time, the manufacturing group had decided to de-emphasize four-cylinder engine production because recent sales had fallen off. The four-cylinder equipment was removed from the plants and put to other uses. In fact, no one in management had bothered to check with manufacturing to see if the four-cylinder Novas being promoted were being built. They weren't.

The sales campaign was a success, but the results proved disastrous. Manufacturing was inundated with engine orders six times their capacity to build. As a result, everyone lost. Manufacturing couldn't meet dealer orders, dealers couldn't deliver cars they had sold, and customers couldn't get the cars they wanted. The company lost both customer goodwill and revenues.

Source: Based on information in J. Patrick Wright, *On A Clear Day You Can See General Motors* (New York: Avon, 1979), pp. 125–26.

acceptance of relevant communication so that uncertainty and distortion are reduced and acceptance is enhanced. The various remedies that exist to achieve this goal can be grouped for convenience according to the direction of the intended instructions: downward, upward, or horizontal (see Exhibit 13.6).

Improving Downward Communication

There are a variety of ways in which managers can facilitate improved communication with their subordinates. As shown in Exhibit 13.6, most of these techniques involve clarifying the nature of the job or task. The more employees understand about the nature of the job, including what they are to do and why, the less search behavior is required and the more goal-directed effort is available, assuming the employees accept the task and are motivated to perform.

In addition to clarifying job instructions and the rationale behind the instructions, managers can provide more feedback to keep employees on target. Managers can also use multiple communication channels (written and verbal messages simultaneously) and repeat messages to reinforce the impact of the intended message. By doing so, the chances are increased that the message will be received and understood. Finally, it is desirable at times to

EXHIBIT 13.6   STRATEGIES FOR IMPROVING COMMUNICATION EFFECTIVENESS

Downward Communications
1. Job instructions can be presented clearly to employees so they understand more precisely what is expected.
2. Efforts can be made to explain the rationale behind the required tasks to employees so they understand why they are being asked to do something.
3. Management can provide greater feedback concerning the nature and quality of performance, thereby keeping employees "on target."
4. Multiple communication channels can be used to increase the chances that the message is properly received.
5. Important messages can be repeated to ensure penetration.
6. In some cases, it is desirable to bypass formal communication channels and go directly to the intended receiver with the message.

Upward Communications
1. Upward messages can be screened so only the more relevant aspects are received by top management.
2. Managers can attempt to change the organizational climate so subordinates feel more free to transmit negative as well as positive messages without fear of retribution.
3. Managers can sensitize themselves so they are better able to detect bias and distorted messages from their subordinates.
4. Sometimes it is possible to utilize "distortion-proof" messages (Downs, 1967), such as providing subordinates with report forms requiring quantified or standardized data.
5. Social distance and status barriers between employees on various levels can be reduced so messages will be more spontaneous.

Horizontal Communications
1. Efforts can be made to develop interpersonal skills between group members and departments so greater openness and trust exist.
2. Reward systems can be utilized that reward interdepartmental cooperation and minimize "zero-sum game" situations.
3. Interdepartmental meetings can be used to share information concerning what other departments are involved in.
4. In some cases, the actual design of the organization itself can be changed to provide greater opportunities for interdepartmental contacts (e.g., shifting from a traditional to a matrix organization design).

Source: Reprinted from R. M. Steers, *Organizational Effectiveness: A Behavioral View* (Glenview, Ill.: Scott, Foresman and Company, 1977), p. 151.

bypass formal communication channels and to go directly to the intended receiver with the message, avoiding considerable noise and distortion in transmission.

Improving Upward Communication

Clearly one of the most important problems in upward communication is information overload. One popular way to reduce overload is *screening* —transmitting only the important aspects of a message through the hierarchy and omitting the peripheral aspects. Screening has several formats. One consists of a *management by exception* procedure, in which routine decisions and actions are handled through policy guidelines. Only exceptions, deviations, and emergencies are reported upward. A second approach is the *principle of sufficiency* (Dubin, 1959), where organizations intentionally regulate both the quantity and quality of upward information (e.g., where managers at each level in the hierarchy write summary reports for their superiors or where managers intentionally schedule meetings for less time than is thought to be needed so they can "get right to the point"). Finally, a third screening technique is *queuing,* where messages are handled sequentially by managers, usually in order of importance.

Another way to improve upward communication involves attempting to improve the organizational climate so subordinates have less fear about reporting negative or positive outcomes to their superiors. A major problem in upward communication is that bad news often gets filtered out as it moves up the hierarchy and quick remedial action is inhibited. If employees had less fear of negative consequences for admitting mistakes, superiors would be more likely to receive rapid and accurate information on trouble spots for which they could then seek remedy.

Other strategies can be employed as well, including the use of distortion-proof messages (Downs, 1967), where employees' messages are structured (perhaps using a standard form); the reduction of social and status barriers; and an increased awareness by managers of potential sources of bias in reporting. An alternative strategy is to recognize different individual communication roles in organizations, as discussed earlier in this chapter. As a result, managers should receive more accurate and timely information from employees who feel secure about reporting information upward.

Improving Horizontal Communication

If managers are to be successful in coordinating and integrating the efforts of individuals and groups in all areas of an organization, it is crucial that a concerted effort be made to develop accurate, rapid lines of horizontal communication. Work groups and departments must pool their efforts to achieve organizational effectiveness. But how can managers facilitate horizontal communication between groups?

As shown in Exhibit 13.6, several mechanisms exist. One is to foster high levels of interpersonal trust and openness between work groups. To the extent that these efforts are successful, more spontaneous efforts can emerge and less energy will be devoted to promoting group or departmental territoriality. Reward systems can be implemented to reward cooperation between departments instead of competition. One example would be to include in a manager's performance appraisal a question about the extent to which the manager helped *other* departments reach their goals. By such techniques, the propensity to conceal information that could be helpful to other groups and departments might be reduced.

CLOSE-UP 13.3 LEARNING TO LISTEN AT UNISYS

Beginning in 1979, the Sperry Corporation (now Unisys) experimented with an active listening program for its 90,000 employees. During this period, the main theme of its product advertising campaign was "We understand how important it is to listen." The project began when the company commissioned two research studies to discover what people thought about the corporation. A major trend in the results suggested that many people felt the company was different from other companies because their people listened—to customers and to each other.

As a result, a formal active listening program was initiated that consisted of a seven-hour seminar using audio and video cassettes and role playing. It covered some introductory concepts of listening as a learnable communication skill, as well as skill enhancement situations. The seminar was tailored to the special needs of each division. Hence, Sperry Univac used computer-related communication situations, while Sperry Vickers used manufacturing situations. The program stressed that listening goes beyond the mechanical art of hearing. It includes understanding, evaluating, interpreting, and ultimately, responding to what one has heard.

More than 10,000 employees went through the program, but phonograph records on listening went out to all employees. For those who were unable to attend the seminar, audio cassettes were developed that could be checked out and taken home by employees.

As Kenneth Thompson, Group Executive Vice-President noted, "Everywhere I go in the corporation . . . the listening thing is there. People are conscious of it." Added Thompson, "We're not trained to listen. We are trained to be good writers and readers, but I've never had a course in listening in my life. Maybe our mouth was given more powerful muscles than our ears." At Unisys, at least, efforts were made to change that.

Source: Adapted from J. L. Di Gaetani, "The Sperry Corporation and Listening: An Interview," *Business Horizons 25* (March–April 1982): 34–39.

Another technique involves having interdepartmental meetings (instead of, or in addition to, departmental meetings) where all members of two or more departments or groups come together and share information, problems, and possible solutions. In this way, members of one department can gain a better understanding of the problems of others and learn how to be of assistance. Using a matrix organization design is another way to accomplish the same end. There are many ways managers can facilitate improved communications at work so less effort is wasted and more energies are devoted toward goal attainment. However, managers must make it happen; they must take an active part in developing a climate best suited for open and accurate interchange between employees at various levels.

Success in these efforts also depends upon the ability of all people involved to actively listen to what is being said. The role of listening in communication effectiveness cannot be underestimated. In fact, at the Unisys Corporation, a major program was undertaken to train people to be better listeners. This program is described in Close-Up 13.3.

SUMMARY

This chapter examined various aspects of communication in organizations. To begin, it was pointed out that communication in organizational settings can be studied from at least two vantage points: the interpersonal and the organizational. It was noted that the determinants and the consequences of interpersonal communication and organizational communication can be quite different. A basic model of interpersonal communication was presented that included the elements of encoding, decoding, feedback, and noise. Moreover, different types of interpersonal communication—both verbal and nonverbal —were examined.

Under the topic of organizational communication, the relationship between communication processes and organizational structure was examined using the concept of a communication network. It was pointed out that there are at least four widely recognized communication networks, each with different implications for power and authority, speed and accuracy of communication, and group satisfaction.

An important point made in this chapter is that different individuals often serve various communication roles in organizations. Individuals may serve as gatekeepers, as liaisons, as opinion leaders, as cosmopolites, or as some combination of these roles. The point here is that, when studying communication, it is important to recognize that communication processes involve different people in different functions and that all of these functions are necessary in order to fulfill the organization's key objectives.

Several barriers to effective communication were examined as well, including distortion, omission, overload, timeliness, and acceptance. Strategies for improving upward, downward, and horizontal communication were also discussed.

KEY WORDS

body language
communication network
cosmopolite
decoding
distortion
encoding
Fayol's bridge
feedback
gatekeeper

interpersonal
    communication
liaison
management by exception
noise
omission
opinion leader
organizational communication
overload

principle of sufficiency   screening
queuing   symbolic language

FOR DISCUSSION

1. What is the importance of communication in organizations?

2. Distinguish between interpersonal and organizational communication.

3. Identify several commonplace sources of noise in a communication episode.

4. Compare and contrast the three primary forms of interpersonal communication.

5. Why is it important to understand variations in communication networks? What experience have you had personally with such networks?

6. Describe various individual communication roles in organizations. Which role is more important in facilitating managerial effectiveness?

7. Identify several barriers to effective communication. How can these barriers be overcome by managers?

EXERCISE

13.1

COMMUNICATION EXERCISE

Purpose

To consider the differences between one-way and two-way communication and how they relate to barriers to effective interpersonal communication.

Instructions

Select one member of the class to serve as the "leader," based on his or her recognized communication skills. All other students should have paper and pen ready and prepare to follow the leader's instructions.

In Stage One, the leader will stand with his or her back to the class and describe a picture (to be called Figure 1) that has been given to the leader. The leader will not answer any questions and will not use any gestures in giving instructions. Without consulting with one another, students will then be asked to draw the figure.

In Stage Two, the same leader faces the class and describes Figure 2. In this case, students can ask as many questions as they wish concerning the figure (although the leader still may not use any gestures). Again without consultation, students will be asked to draw the figure.

Next, the leader will draw both figures on the blackboard. The number of correct student drawings for both Figure 1 and Figure 2 should then be counted. Following this, the class should discuss the meaning of the results in terms of how both the leader and the class felt and performed under conditions of one-way and two-way communication.

Source: Based upon an exercise proposed in H. Leavitt and R. Mueller, "Some Effects of Feedback on Communication," *Human Relations 4* (1951): 401–10.

COMMUNICATION IN THE EXECUTIVE SUITE

The tasks of managers constitute a "social event," as William Henry put it, "not an individual event." One psychologist explained it this way: "The individual manager does not have a clearly bounded job with neatly defined authorities and responsibilities. Rather, he is placed in the middle of a system of relationships, out of which he must fashion an organization which will accomplish his objectives." Research on executive time use supports these propositions. In one study, four executives in England were found to spend eighty percent of their time talking. A Harvard Business School study estimated that fifty to sixty percent of a department head's time was spent talking to men other than his immediate subordinates. Robert Dubin found that in several samples as little as twenty-eight percent down to 6.3 percent of an executive's time was actually spent making decisions as opposed to other kinds of more social activities.[1]

That what managers did was communicate with people was certainly true at Indsco. A sample of twenty managers told me how they spent their time, and I generated this composite list: Paper work and mail; sales calls and negotiating contracts; reviewing telegrams at the office and at home; receiving and making phone calls (including unsuccessful repeat calls); talking to subordinates; interviewing recruits; reviewing with secretaries; teaching trainees; contracts,

monthly summaries, weekly summaries, forecasts, sales plans, and quarterly reviews; reviewing subordinates' expense accounts, career reviews (preparation and feedback); performance appraisals; meetings with others in the function, including technological, professional and associated functions; entertainment such as golf and skiing, travel; training programs; handling specific crises; entertaining out-of-town dignitaries; active recruiting on campus; discussions with others about competitors' activities; organizing meetings; reviewing business plans continuously; watching video tape cassettes sent from headquarters; travel, and time waiting for planes or appointments; solving problems of interface with people in other functions; and special task force meetings.

They estimated that from thirty percent to fifty-five percent of their time was spent actually in meetings with other people. This did not include time with secretaries, on the telephone, or in routine communication around the office. Time not spent talking could still involve communication. Many of them found, in fact, that the demands made by superiors for communication—even if those superiors were at a considerable distance, such as in the home office —could be quite irritating and represented distraction from a task they considered more important. Telegrams were one source of annoyance; they would even be sent to the manager's home.

One manager estimated that after being away from his office for two days, he could expect to find a stack of mail four inches deep when he returned, and "half of it not worth reading." Another commented, "The mail is important and we've got to pay attention to it, but there is too much of it. It is time-consuming and nonproductive to go through it. It gets worse and worse day by day because of the matrix. It is self-generating. If I write a note on a piece of mail and send it back, then my boss says, "You're not communicating." And, "We tend to over-communicate. I get more than one copy of the same thing. Neither one seems to know that he's sending the same thing." Still another manager estimated that he spent twenty percent of his time on the phone trying to make calls or actually talking.

Then there were the numerous special events that were deliberately social: Business luncheons. Dinners for trainees. Entertaining superiors who decided to drop in. "You have to be there when these cats, the heavies, the dignitaries, fly through and say, 'I want to spend a day with your people at Blump-te-de-blump.' And they come through and sit down in your office, from the corporate vice-president on down." Some people called them "snow birds"; others called them "the Monday evening supper club." Total time spent entertaining depended on the season, the customers, and demand on the managers. But one man estimated that he spent nine days during the first quarter of the year on entertainment, not including business lunches.

One typical day, a Monday in March in the Midwest, began at 7:30 when the manager arrived at the office. From 7:30 to 9:00 he finished reading his mail, wrote letters, and called headquarters.

From 9:00 to 10:30 he met informally with sales people and customer service people to discuss current problems and offer help. From 10:30 to 11:30 he interviewed a job candidate. From 11:30 to 12:00 he returned phone messages, and from 12:00 to 1:00 he had lunch with a sales person in order to conduct an informal performance appraisal before the formal meeting. From 1:00 to 2:00 he read more mail, and from 2:00 to 2:30 he answered phone messages, again from the headquarters office. At 2:30 he received a wire on the state of the business, which he was expected to communicate to the field and solicit a response to. He began on this and continued until 3:30. From 3:30 to 4:30 he worked on his quarterly review and at 4:30 left for home. Tuesday and Wednesday were spent out of town visiting another office. Thursday and Friday he returned to his own office, and Friday evening he attended a senior executive dinner from 7:00 to 11:00 P.M.

There were several striking features of the communication dominating managerial tasks, because of the sheer size, complexity, and geographic spread of the organization: Communication had to be rapid, since each episode was squeezed in among many more. It had to be accurate, since it was part of a network of interdependencies and contingencies. And it had to travel long distances, sometimes by impersonal means and through channels where people were not directly known to one another. Common language and common understanding were thus very important. People had neither the time nor the backlog of joint experience to make appropriate calibrations for differences in meaning systems or messages that seemed incomprehensible.

The structure of communication in-

volved in managerial jobs generated a desire for smooth social relationships and a preference for selection of those people with whom communication would be easiest. Indsco managers identified social and interpersonal skills as important characteristics of the "effective manager." After a group generated their list of twenty-four such attributes in a meeting, someone pointed out that missing from the list was "knowing the business you're in." But then another manager replied that he knew of many effective executives who knew nothing about their product or field. "Winning acceptance" and being able to communicate seemed much more important. And the group agreed that no one without peer acceptance could get ahead.

One way to ensure acceptance and ease of communication was to limit managerial jobs to those who were socially homogeneous. Social certainty, at least, could compensate for some of the other sources of uncertainty in the tasks of management. It was easier to talk to those of one's kind who had shared experiences—more certain, more accurate, more predictable. Less time could be spent concentrating on subtle meanings, and more time (such an overloaded resource for managers) on the task. The corporation's official language system and cryptic jargon (A/C scribbled at the bottom of a note signified "agreement and comprehension" of its message) could be supplemented by the certainty that socially similar communicators would have more basis for understanding one another. Hence, another force pushed for the confinement of managerial work to a closed circle of homogeneous peers, people who had been through the same things together and could readily understand one another.

There was a decided wish to avoid those people with whom communication was felt to be uncomfortable, those who took time to figure out or seemed unpredictable in their conduct. Deviants and nonconformists were certainly suspect for this reason. Even people who looked different raised questions, because the difference in appearance might signify a different realm and range of meanings in communication. It was all right to be somewhat controversial, as long as a person fit within the same value system and was consistent. ("All of our top executives have been 'radicals,'" a young manager who had worked for a time with officers remarked. "They sometimes did things differently and pushed the rest of us a little further, but they were always consistent. You knew where you stood.")

Women were decidedly placed in the category of the incomprehensible and unpredictable. There were many reports that managers felt uncomfortable having to communicate with women. "It took more time," they said. "You never knew where you stood." "They changed their minds all the time; I never knew what they'd do from one minute to the next." "With women's lib around, I never know what to call them, how to treat them." "They're hard to understand." "It takes a lot of toe testing to be able to communicate." "I'm always making assumptions that turn out to be wrong." Some managers were willing to admit that this was "ninety percent my problem, mostly in my head." But this was another example of the preference for dealing with people who were similar. The structure of the managerial role made it more comfortable to try to exclude those people seen as "different." A homogeneous network reinforced the inability of its members to incorporate heterogeneous elements.

Note

1. Although the names of the characters involved have been changed, this case is based on a study of an actual organization.

CASE DISCUSSION QUESTIONS

1. Identify examples of managers at Indsco engaging in oral communication, written communication, formal communication, and informal communication.

2. Which of Rogers and Rogers' organizational roles do managers serve at Indsco? Cite examples.

3. Certain factors contribute to making communication easier and more comfortable at Indsco. What are some of these factors?

4. If you were a manager, how might you improve communication processes at Indsco? Explain.

CHAPTER FOURTEEN

DECISION MAKING IN ORGANIZATIONS

Decision making, like communication, is a group process of significant concern to managers. Consider just a few of the many different decisions that must be made in organizations: how many employees to hire, and which applicants to choose; whether or not to roll out a new product; where to sell it; how to advertise it, etc. Obviously, it is vital for managers to understand the decision-making process in every sense. This knowledge must extend to recognizing decision-making pitfalls and learning how to avoid them, as well as practicing techniques for improving the quality of the decision itself.

IMPORTANCE OF TOPIC FOR MANAGERS

Making decisions has been clearly identified as one of management's primary responsibilities. Decisions may involve allocating scarce resources, hiring employees, investing capital, or introducing new products. If resources were abundant, few decisions would be necessary; however, such is typically not the case. Clearly, managers need to be aware of the basic processes by which decisions are made in organizations.

Several frameworks are available to help understand how decisions are made. Each framework is based on different assumptions about the nature of people at work. So, an informed manager should understand the models and the different assumptions underlying each.

Another management concern is the extent to which subordinates should be included in decisions affecting their jobs. When are group decisions superior (or inferior) to individual ones? How much participation can be accommodated in work organizations where managers still assume responsibility for group actions? The phenomena of groupthink and escalating commitment have emerged as important considerations in decision making. How do these phenomena affect decision quality?

Finally, what are some strategies that can be used by managers to improve decisions in organizations? A knowledge of these strategies can help managers make the most efficient use of their limited time and resources in their efforts to facilitate goal attainment.

THE NATURE OF DECISION MAKING

It has often been said that a common characteristic of effective leaders and effective work groups is their ability to make decisions that are appropriate, timely, and acceptable. If organizational effectiveness is defined as the ability to secure and utilize resources in the pursuit of organizational goals, the decision-making processes concerned with how these resources will be acquired and used emerge as a central topic in organizational analysis.

Because of the importance of this topic, we will consider several aspects. First, decision making will be defined. Next, three major models of decision-making processes will be compared, along with the assumptions underlying each model. Following this, individual and group decision making will be examined, including the concepts of participation in decision making and groupthink. In closing, several strategies for improving the quality and acceptability of decisions will be presented. Throughout, emphasis will focus

EXHIBIT 14.1   STAGES IN THE DECISION-MAKING PROCESS

on major lessons for management that will ease the responsibility of decision making.

For our purposes here, we define *decision making* as a process of selecting among available alternatives (Shull, Delbecq, and Cummings, 1970; MacCrimmon and Taylor, 1976). We look at how individuals and groups identify problem areas, consider potential solutions to problems, and select the most suitable solution (or solutions) in light of the particular situation.

If we take a close look at the decision-making process, it is possible to identify three relatively distinct stages (Simon, 1960). The first stage, as shown in Exhibit 14.1, is represented by *intelligence activities.* Individuals and groups attempt to recognize and understand the nature of the problem, as well as search for the possible causes and potential solutions. In the second phase of the process, *design activities,* alternative courses of action are formulated and assessed in light of known constraints. The third phase is represented by *choice activities,* where the actual choice among possible alternative decisions is made. It is believed that the quality of the resulting decision is largely influenced by the thoroughness of the intelligence and design phases combined with the rationality and goals of the decision makers themselves.

MODELS OF THE DECISION-MAKING PROCESS

It is no easy task to outline or diagram the general decision-making process. We actually know very little about how individuals and groups make decisions (Ungson and Braunstein, 1982). Even so, three different models of the decision-making process have been suggested. Each differs on the suppositions the model makes about the person or persons making the decision. These three models are (1) the econologic model; (2) the bounded rationality model; and (3) the implicit favorite model. Each model is useful for understanding the nature of decision processes in organizations.

Econologic Model

The *econologic model* represents the earliest attempt to model decision processes (Miller and Starr, 1967; Von Neumann and Morgenstern, 1953).

Briefly, this model rests on two assumptions: (1) it assumes people are economically rational; and (2) it assumes that people attempt to maximize outcomes in an orderly and sequential process. *Economic rationality,* a basic concept in many models of decision making, exists when people attempt to objectively maximize measured advantage, such as money or units of goods produced. That is, it is assumed that people will select the decision or course of action that has the greatest advantage or payoff from among the many alternatives. It is also assumed that they go about this search in a planned, orderly, and logical fashion. This model has also been referred to as the *economic man* model by Simon (1957).

A basic econologic decision model is shown in Exhibit 14.2. As can be seen, the model suggests the following orderly steps in the decision process based on the above two assumptions about the nature of people:

1. Discover the symptoms of the problem or difficulty.
2. Determine the goal to be achieved or define the problem to be solved.
3. Develop a criterion against which alternative solutions can be evaluated.
4. Identify all alternative courses of action.
5. Consider the consequences of each alternative, as well as the likelihood of occurrence of each.
6. Choose the best alternative by comparing the consequences of each alternative (step 5) with the decision criterion (step 3).
7. Act to implement the decision.

The simplicity of the econologic model is disarming. In fact, the model rests on two rather questionable foundations (Simon, 1957). First, the model portrays individuals or groups as having the capability to gather all necessary information for a decision. It assumes having complete information, which is rarely achieved. As a result, rationality itself is rarely achieved. As Simon (1957, p. 81) notes:

(1) Rationality requires a complete knowledge and anticipation of the consequences that will follow on each choice. In fact, knowledge of consequences is always fragmentary. (2) Since these consequences lie in the future, imagination must supply the lack of experienced feeling in attaching value to them. But values can be only imperfectly anticipated. (3) Rationality requires a choice among all possible alternative behaviors. In actual behavior, only a very few of all these possible alternatives ever come to mind.

In addition, the econologic model is based on the assumption that people can process the tremendous amount of information generated for one decision. It assumes that people can: (1) mentally store the information in some stable form; (2) manipulate the information in a series of complex calculations designed to provide expected values; and (3) rank all the consequences in a consistent fashion for purposes of identifying the preferred alternative. Unfortunately, a large body of research has shown that the human mind is simply incapable of executing such transactions at the level and magnitude

EXHIBIT 14.2   AN ECONOLOGIC MODEL OF DECISION MAKING

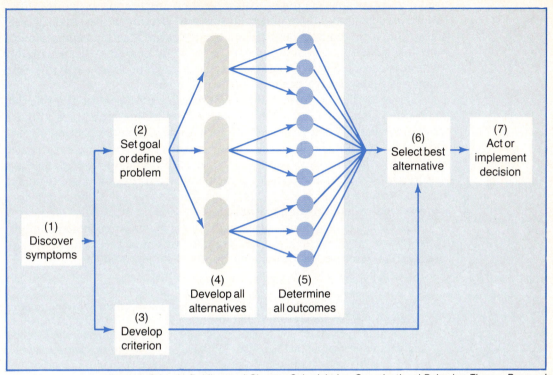

Source: Orlando Behling and Chester Schreisheim, *Organizational Behavior: Theory, Research, and Application* (Newton, Mass.: Allyn and Bacon, 1976), p. 19. Copyright © 1976 by Allyn and Bacon, Inc. Reprinted with permission.

that would be required for complex decisions. While the econologic model represents a useful representation of how decisions *should* be made (a *prescriptive* model), it seems to fall somewhat short concerning how decisions are actually made.

Bounded Rationality Model

An alternative model, one not bound by the above assumptions, has been presented by Simon (1957; March and Simon, 1958; Cyert and March, 1963). This is the *bounded rationality model,* also known as the *administrative man* model.

As the name implies, this model does not assume individual rationality in the decision process. Instead, it is assumed that people, while they may seek the best solution, usually settle for much less because the decisions they confront typically demand greater information processing capabilities than they possess. They seek a kind of bounded (or limited) rationality in decisions.

The concept of bounded rationality attempts to describe decision processes in terms of three mechanisms. With *sequential attention to alternative solutions,* people examine possible solutions to a problem one at a time. Instead of identifying all possible solutions and selecting the best (as suggested in the econologic model), the various alternatives are identified and evaluated individually. If the first solution fails to work it is discarded and another solution is considered. When an acceptable (though not necessarily the best) solution is found, search behavior is discontinued.

The second mechanism is the *use of heuristics.* A heuristic is a rule that guides the search for alternatives into areas that have a high probability for yielding satisfactory solutions. For instance, some companies continually hire MBAs from certain schools because in the past such graduates have performed well for the company. According to the bounded rationality model, decision makers use heuristics to reduce large problems to manageable propositions so decisions can be made rapidly. They look for obvious solutions or previous solutions that worked in similar situations.

Satisficing is the third mechanism. Whereas the econologic model focused on the decision maker as an optimizer, this model sees him or her as a satisficer. As described by March and Simon (1958, p. 140–41):

> An alternative is *optimal* if: (1) there exists a set of criteria that permits all alternatives to be compared, and (2) the alternative in question is preferred, by these criteria, to all other alternatives. An alternative is *satisfactory* if: (1) there exists a set of criteria that describes minimally satisfactory alternatives, and (2) the alternative in question meets or exceeds all these criteria. . . . Finding that optimal alternative is a radically different problem from finding a satisfactory alternative. . . . To optimize requires processes several orders of magnitude more complex than those required to satisfice.

Based on these three assumptions about decision makers, it is possible to outline the decision process as seen from the standpoint of the bounded rationality model. As shown in Exhibit 14.3, the model consists of eight steps:

1. Set the goal to be pursued or define the problem to be solved.
2. Establish an appropriate level of aspiration or criterion level (that is, when do you know that a solution is sufficiently positive to be acceptable, even if it is not perfect?).
3. Employ heuristics to narrow problem space to a *single* promising alternative.
4. If no feasible alternative is identified (a), lower the aspiration level, and (b) begin the search for a new alternative solution (repeat steps 2 and 3).
5. After identifying a feasible alternative (a), evaluate it to determine its acceptability (b).
6. If the individual alternative is unacceptable, initiate search for a new alternative solution (repeat steps 3–5).
7. If the identified alternative is acceptable (a), implement the solution (b).

EXHIBIT 14.3   A BOUNDED RATIONALITY MODEL OF DECISION MAKING

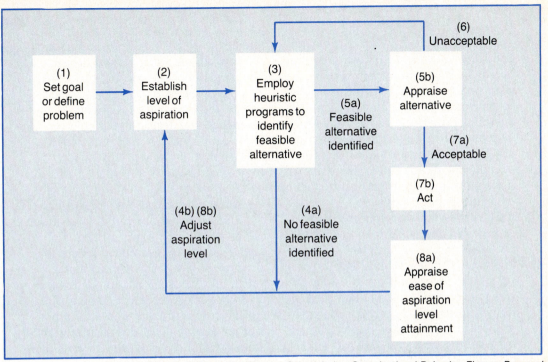

Source: Orlando Behling and Chester Schreisheim, *Organizational Behavior: Theory, Research, and Application* (Newton, Mass.: Allyn and Bacon, 1976), p. 29. Copyright © 1976 by Allyn and Bacon, Inc. Reprinted with permission.

8. Following implementation, evaluate the ease with which the goal was (or was not) attained (a), and raise or lower the level of aspiration accordingly on future decisions of this type (b).

Certainly, this decision process is quite different from the econologic model. In it we do not seek the best solution; instead, we look for a solution that is acceptable. The search behavior is sequential, evaluating one or two solutions at once. Finally, in contrast to the prescriptive econologic model, it is claimed that the bounded rationality model is *descriptive;* that is, it describes how decision makers actually arrive at the identification of solutions to organizational problems.

Implicit Favorite Model

A third model deals primarily with nonprogrammed decisions. *Nonprogrammed* decisions are decisions that are novel or unstructured, like seeking one's first job. *Programmed* decisions, in contrast, are more routine or

CLOSE-UP 14.1 GRESHAM'S LAW OF PLANNING AND MANAGEMENT DECISIONS

H. A. Simon distinguishes between *programmed* (routine, repetitive) decisions and *nonprogrammed* (unique, one-shot) decisions. While programmed decisions are typically handled through structured or bureaucratic techniques (standard operating procedures), nonprogrammed decisions must be made by managers using available information and their own judgment. As is often the case with managers, however, decisions are made under the pressures of time.

An important principle of organization design that relates to managerial decision making is Gresham's Law of Planning. This law states that there is a general tendency for programmed activities to overshadow nonprogrammed activities. Hence, if a manager has a series of decisions to make, those that are more routine and repetitive will tend to be made before those that are unique and require considerable thought. This

happens presumably because managers attempt to clear their desks so they can get down to the really serious decisions. Unfortunately, the desks very often never get cleared.

The implications of Gresham's law for managerial decision making is clear. Provisions must be made for ensuring that nonprogrammed decisions are completed in a timely fashion. This can be done, according to Simon, by creating specific organizational responsibilities and organizational units to assume the responsibility. Staff units in major organizations are examples. Where this is not possible, time management programs may be useful in training managers to better allocate their limited time. However it is accomplished, it is important for managers to see that important nonprogrammed decisions receive the attention they deserve.

Source: H. A. Simon, *The New Science of Management Decisions,* rev. ed. (Englewood Cliffs, N.J.: Prentice-Hall, 1977).

repetitious in nature, such as the procedures for admitting new MBAs to graduate school. (See Close-Up 14.1)

The *implicit favorite model,* developed by Soelberg (1967), rests strongly on the theory of cognitive dissonance described in Chapter Ten. It emerged when Soelberg observed the job choice processes of graduating business students and noted that, in many cases, the students identified implicit favorites very early in the recruiting and choice process. However, they continued their search for additional alternatives and quickly selected the best alternative candidate, known as the confirmation candidate. Next, the students attempted to develop decision rules that demonstrated unequivocally that the implicit favorite was superior to the alternative confirmation candidate. This was done through perceptual distortion of information about the two alternatives and through weighting systems designed to highlight the positive features of the implicit favorite. Finally, after a decision rule was derived that clearly favored the implicit favorite, the decision was announced. Ironically, Soelberg noted that the implicit favorite was typically superior to

EXHIBIT 14.4   AN IMPLICIT FAVORITE MODEL OF DECISION MAKING

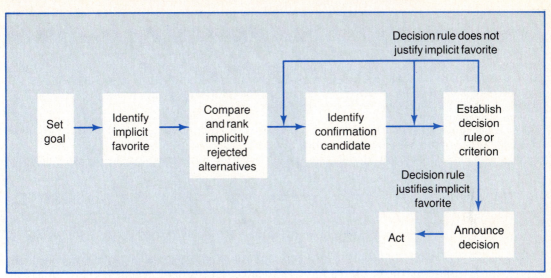

Source: Orlando Behling and Chester Schreisheim, *Organizational Behavior: Theory, Research, and Application* (Newton, Mass.: Allyn and Bacon, 1976), p. 32. Copyright © 1976 by Allyn and Bacon, Inc. Reprinted with permission.

the confirmation candidate on only one or two dimensions. Even so, the decision makers generally characterized their decision rules as being multidimensional in nature.

The process is shown in Exhibit 14.4. As noted, the entire process is designed to justify to the individual, through the guise of scientific rigor, a nonprogrammed decision that has already been made in an intuitive fashion. By doing so, the individual becomes convinced that he or she is acting in a rational fashion and making a logical, reasoned decision on an important topic.

INDIVIDUAL AND GROUP DECISION MAKING

The three models of the decision-making process can be used for examining both how individuals make decisions and how groups and organizations make decisions. The basic processes remain the same. For instance, using the econologic model, we observe that both individuals and groups often identify money as an objective to be sought. Both individuals and groups in some cases attempt to identify all possible outcomes before selecting one. Similarly, both individuals and groups are often observed engaging in satisficing behavior or using heuristics in the decision process. Finally, both individuals and groups

EXHIBIT 14.5   ASSETS AND LIABILITIES OF GROUP DECISION MAKING

Assets	Liabilities
▪ Groups can accumulate more knowledge and facts. ▪ Groups have a broader perspective and consider more alternative solutions. ▪ Individuals who participate in decisions are more satisfied with the decision and are more likely to support it. ▪ Group decision processes serve an important communication function, as well as a useful political function.	▪ Groups often work more slowly than individuals. ▪ Group decisions involve considerable compromise that may lead to less than optimal decisions. ▪ Groups are often dominated by one individual or a small clique, thereby negating many of the virtues of group processes. ▪ Overreliance on group decision making can inhibit management's ability to act quickly and decisively when necessary.

develop implicit favorites and attempt to justify those favorites by procedures that appear to others to be rationalization. In fact, recent research indicates that people often stick with a prior decision even when they know it to be wrong (Staw and Ross, 1978).

Advantages and Disadvantages of Group Decision Making

However, while the general models of the decision process are similar, there are differences in the *outcomes* of individual and group decision making. There are situations where group decision making can be an asset and other times when it can be a liability (Maier, 1967). Several of these are described in Exhibit 14.5.

In summarizing what we know about the impact of groups on the decision-making process—particularly in *non*programmed decisions—Harrison (1975) concluded the following:

▪ In *establishing objectives,* groups are typically superior to individuals in that they possess greater cumulative knowledge to bring to bear on problems.

▪ In *identifying alternatives,* individual efforts are important to ensure that different and perhaps unique solutions are identified from various functional areas that later can be considered by the group.

▪ In *evaluating alternatives,* group judgment is often superior to individual judgment because it brings into play a wider range of viewpoints.

▪ In *choosing an alternative,* involving group members often leads to greater acceptance of the final outcome.

▪ In *implementing the choice,* individual responsibility is generally superior to group responsibility. Regardless of whether decisions are made individually or collectively, individuals perform better in carrying out the decision than groups do.

Hence, it is not possible to conclude that one form of decision making (individual or group) is superior. Rather, both specific situations and the individuals involved must be considered before choosing a decision technique. The major variables affecting the choice are considered in the next section as we examine the details of participation in decision making.

Participation in Decision Making

A central issue facing managers in carrying out their responsibilities is the extent to which they should allow their subordinates in the work group to participate in decisions affecting their jobs. Participation represents one method of decentralizing authority and influence throughout an organization. It is believed that this action will in many cases lead to improved decision quality, increased commitment of members to decision outcomes, and increased satisfaction resulting from involvement. These results are often associated with effective organizations.

The subject of participation in decision making is closely related to the nature of supervisory style. While a close scrutiny of this relationship is reserved until later, it is possible to summarize much of what is known about what happens when managers allow greater group input into decisions. (See Locke and Schweiger, 1979, for an in-depth review of the subject.)

Based on a series of studies on managerial decision-making behavior, Vroom and Yetton (1973) found evidence to support the conclusion that managers tend to be *more* participative when the quality of the decision is important and when subordinate acceptance of the decision is critical for its effective implementation. Also, managers tend to be more participative when they trust their subordinates to focus on organizational rather than personal goals and when conflict among subordinates is minimal.

On the other hand, managers tend to be *less* participative when they have all the necessary information to make a high-quality decision. This is also the case when the immediate problem is well structured or where there is a common solution that has been applied in similar situations in the past. In addition, managers tend to participate less when time is limited and immediate action is required.

Along with understanding the circumstances in which managers are more or less likely to allow group input in the decision process, it is also useful to know the effects of participation on subsequent behavior and attitudes. Available research indicates that members of supportive, participative groups experience greater satisfaction and cooperation on task activities and have less turnover, absenteeism, and job-related stress (Filley, House, and Kerr, 1975; Steers and Porter, 1974; Vroom, 1964). Job performance is sometimes higher in participative groups, although the results are certainly not consistent (Dubin, 1965).

One question about the effects of participation remains to be asked: that is, why does participation seem to work in many instances? A partial answer to this question has been offered by Ebert and Mitchell (1975). First, they suggest that participation clarifies organizational contingencies so employees understand more fully what is expected of them. Second, it increases the likelihood that employees will work for rewards and outcomes they value. Third, it heightens the effects of social influence on behavior. Finally, it enlarges the amount of control employees have over their own behavior. In many cases, participation in decision making can represent a useful vehicle for facilitating both organizational goal attainment and personal need satisfaction.

GROUPTHINK

Increased attention has been focused on a phenomenon known as *groupthink*. This phenomenon, first discussed by Janis (1971), refers to a mode of thinking in a group in which the seeking of concurrence among members becomes so dominant that it overrides any realistic appraisal of alternative courses of action. The concept emerged from Janis' studies of high-level policy decisions by government leaders. These included decisions by the U.S. government about Vietnam, the Bay of Pigs, and the Korean War. By analyzing the decision process leading up to each action, Janis found numerous indications pointing to the development of group norms that improved morale at the expense of critical thinking.

Symptoms of Groupthink

In studies of both government and business leaders, Janis identified eight primary symptoms of groupthink. The first is the *illusion of invulnerability*. Group members often reassure themselves about obvious dangers and become overly optimistic and willing to take extraordinary risks. Members fail to respond to clear warning signals. For instance, in the disastrous Bay of Pigs invasion, the United States operated on the false assumption that they could keep the fact that the United States invaded Cuba secret. Even after news of the plan leaked out, government leaders remained convinced of their ability to keep it a secret.

Victims of groupthink also tend to collectively engage in *rationalizations* aimed at discounting warning signs and other types of negative feedback that could lead to a reconsideration of the course of action if taken seriously. When General Motors introduced its down-sized X-cars (e.g., Citation) in 1979, a leading competitor commented that it was "no big thing" since his company already had such cars. In fact, these cars captured a major share of the auto market.

Group members often believe in the inherent morality of the group. Because of this *illusion of morality,* they ignore the ethical or moral consequences of their decisions. Leading tobacco companies continue to run advertisements about free choice in decision making about smoking, completely ignoring all the medical evidence on the hazards involved.

Stereotyping the enemy is another symptom of groupthink. In-group members often stereotype leaders of opposition groups in so harsh a fashion as to rule out any need to negotiate with them on differences of opinion. Often they also place tremendous *pressure to conform* on members who temporarily express doubts about the group's shared illusions or who raise questions about the validity of the arguments supporting the decisions of the group.

Moreover, group members often use *self-censorship* to avoid deviating from what appears to be a group consensus. They often minimize to themselves the seriousness of their doubts. Partly because of self-censorship by group members, another symptom of groupthink, the *illusion of unanimity,* is often created. Members assume everyone holds the same opinion. It is assumed that individuals who remain silent are in agreement with the spoken opinions of others.

Finally, victims of groupthink often appoint themselves as *mindguards* to protect the leader and other members of the group from adverse information that may cause conflict in the group over the correctness of a course of action. This can be done by telling the dissident that he or she is being disruptive or nonsupportive, or by simply insulating the dissident from other group members. For many years, FBI agents in the Washington headquarters who expressed views contrary to the party line found themselves transferred to less desirable locations.

Consequences of Groupthink

Groupthink can have several deleterious consequences on the quality of decision making. First, groups often limit their search for possible solutions to one or two alternatives and avoid a comprehensive analysis of all possible alternatives. Second, groups frequently fail to reexamine their chosen course of action after new information or events suggest a change in course. Third, group members spend little time considering whether there are any nonobvious advantages to alternative courses of action that indicate alternatives may be preferable to the chosen course of action. Fourth, groups often make little or no attempt to seek out the advice of experts either inside or outside their own organization. Fifth, members show positive interest in facts that support their preferred decision alternative and either ignore or show negative interest in facts that fail to support it. Finally, groups often ignore any consideration of possible roadblocks to their chosen decision and, as a result, fail to develop contingency plans for potential setbacks.

Overcoming Groupthink

In view of the potentially serious consequences that can result from the emergence of a groupthink mentality in organizations, questions are logically raised about what can be done to minimize its effects. Janis (1971) suggests several strategies. To begin, group leaders can reduce groupthink by encouraging each group member to be a critical evaluator of proposals. Also, by refraining from stating their own positions and instead promoting open inquiry, leaders can ensure that the group considers a range of alternatives.

Other strategies for preventing groupthink involve getting more suggestions for viable solutions. This can be accomplished by assigning the same problem to two independent groups. Or, at intervals before the group reaches a decision, members can take a respite and seek advice from other parts of the organization. Another technique is to invite experts from outside the group to challenge members' views at group meetings.

Groupthink may also be prevented with strategies that directly involve the group members themselves. For example, for each group meeting, a member can be appointed to serve as a devil's advocate to challenge the majority position. Another means to stop groupthink is to split the group into two sections for independent discussions. They can then compare results. An additional tactic is, after reaching a preliminary consensus on a course of action, to schedule a second-chance meeting. This allows group members an opportunity to express doubts and rethink the issue.

In other words, if groups are aware of the problems of groupthink, several specific and relatively simple steps can be taken to minimize the likelihood of falling victim to this problem. As is usually the case, recognizing the problem represents half the battle in the effort to make more effective decisions in organizational settings.

ESCALATING COMMITMENT TO A DECISION

Whereas groupthink helps to explain how policy-making groups put blinders on and stifle dissenting opinions when making major decisions, the concept of *escalating commitment* to decisions explores why decision makers adhere to a course of action after they know it is incorrect (that is, why managers "throw good money after bad"). To understand the problem of escalating commitment, consider the following true examples (Staw, 1981, pp. 577–78).

> At an early stage in the U.S. involvement in the Vietnam War, George Ball, then Undersecretary of State, wrote the following in a memo to President Johnson: "The decision you face now is crucial. Once large numbers of U.S. troops are committed to direct combat, they will begin to take heavy casualties in a war they are ill equipped to fight in a noncooperative if not downright hostile countryside. Once we suffer large casualties, we will have started a well-nigh irreversible process. Our involvement will be so great that we cannot—without national humiliation—stop short of achieving our complete objectives. Of the two possibilities, I think humiliation would be more likely than the achievement of our objectives—even after we have paid terrible costs. . . .

A company overestimates its capability to build an airplane brake that will meet certain technical specifications at a given cost. Because it wins the government contract, the company is forced to invest greater and greater effort into meeting the contract terms. As a result of increasing pressure to meet specifications and deadlines, records and tests of the brake are misrepresented to government officials. Corporate careers and company credibility are increasingly staked to the airbrake contract, although many in the firm know the brake will not work effectively. At the conclusion of the construction period, the government test pilot flies the plane; it skids off the runway and narrowly misses injuring the pilot. . . .

An individual purchased a stock at $50 a share, but the price has gone down to $20. Still convinced about the merit of the stock, he buys more shares at this lower price. Soon the price declines further and the individual is again faced with the decision to buy more, hold what he already has, or sell out entirely.

How do we account for such commitment by individuals and groups to obvious mistakes? At least three explanations are possible. First, we can point to individual limitations in information processing and suggest that people are limited in both their desire and ability to handle all of the information necessary for such complex decisions. As a result, errors in judgment are possible. A second approach is to explain decisional errors by suggesting that a breakdown in rationality occurred due to interpersonal elements such as group dynamics. For example, power considerations may outweigh the more rational aspects of organizational decision making. While both of these explanations may contribute to a better understanding of decisional error, Staw (1981) suggests that they do not go far enough. "A salient feature of the preceding case examples is that a *series* of decisions is associated with a course of action rather than an isolated choice" (p. 578).

In order to help explain such behavior, Staw turned to the social psychological literature on *forced compliance* (Wicklund and Brehm, 1976). In studies of forced compliance, individuals are typically induced to perform an unpleasant or dissatisfying act (e.g., eating worms) when no compensating external rewards are present. In general, after compliance, individuals will bias their own attitudes in a positive direction so as to justify their previous behavior. This biasing of attitudes is most likely to occur when the individuals feel personally responsible for the negative consequences, and when the consequences are difficult to undo.

Based on these findings, Staw and his colleagues (Staw, 1976; Staw and Fox, 1977; Staw and Ross, 1978) carried out a series of experiments focusing on how willing people would be to continue to commit valued resources to a course of action after it is clear that the original decision had been in error. It was found in these experiments that decision makers actually allocated more money to company divisions that were showing poor results than to those that were showing good results. Also, decision makers allocated more money to a division when they themselves (instead of another party) had been responsible for the original decision to back the division. In short, decision makers were

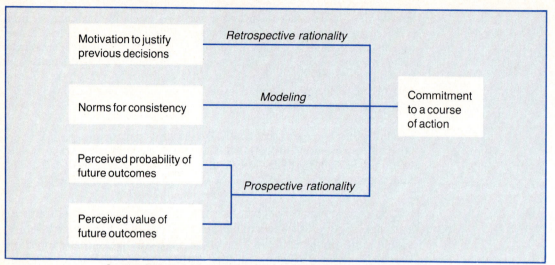

Source: Developed from B. M. Staw, "The Escalation of Commitment to a Course of Action," *Academy of Management Review 6* (1981): 582. Used by permission.

most likely to spend money on projects that had *negative* consequences for which *they* were responsible.

To find out why, Staw (1981) suggested a model of escalating commitment, as shown in Exhibit 14.6. In this abbreviated model, we can see that four basic determinants of commitment to a course of action can be identified. First, people are likely to remain committed to a course of action (even when it is clearly incorrect) due to a desire or need to justify previous decisions. When people feel a responsibility for negative consequences, and at the same time feel a need to demonstrate their own competence, they will often stick to a decision in hopes of "turning the situation around" or "pulling a victory out of defeat." This is referred to as *retrospective rationality*: that is, the individual seeks to appear competent in *previous* as opposed to future actions. This process can be seen in the example from the Vietnam War cited above.

In addition, commitment to a previous decision is influenced by a norm for consistency. That is, in most contemporary societies, managers who are consistent in their actions are often considered better leaders than those who switch around from one course of action to another. For instance, in a Gallup poll of President Carter's popularity, respondents who were dissatisfied with his performance consistently described him as "inconsistent" (Gallup, 1978). Hence, we often see a "we'll *make* it work" syndrome, caused by an unwillingness on the part of a manager (or government leader) to change course in the midst of turmoil or threat. Often, these norms for consistency result from managers who model their behavior after people they see as successful, either within the organization or in society.

Finally, two additional factors—the perceived probability of future outcomes and the perceived value of future outcomes—jointly influence what is called *prospective rationality*. Prospective rationality is simply one's belief that future courses of action are rational and correct. When people feel they can "turn the situation around" or that "prosperity is just around the corner," and when the goal is highly prized, we would expect strong commitment to a continued course of action, influenced in part by the feeling that it is the proper thing to do at that point in time.

In summarizing the model, Staw (1981, p. 584) argues:

> Thus, commitment decisions to a course of action may be determined as much by a desire to rectify past outcomes as to attain future ones. In addition, because the decisions are associated with each other, norms for consistency in action may override SEU [subjective expected utility] or economic considerations.

Staw (1981, p. 585) suggests when this "escalation hypothesis" is expected to be most common:

> Prime candidates for escalation therefore include resource allocation or investment decisions that are identified by an entering and exit value, life choices that are linked together with the label of a career, and policy decisions for which administrators are held accountable by others in the organization or by the general public.

In summary, when considering effective decision-making processes in organizations, special attention must be given to the two related threats of groupthink and escalating commitments. Each process has the potential to constrain or subvert even the most carefully considered decisions. As such, managers need to be alert to the existence of both and to initiate positive actions to reduce their impact in organizations.

STRATEGIES FOR IMPROVING DECISION MAKING

Up to now, we have considered decision processes in a general way. We have noted attempts to model the process, differences between individual and group decisions, participation in decision making, and the concept of groupthink. Throughout, various limitations to the process were noted. Several of these limitations are shown in Close-Up 14.2. Based on this discussion, we are now in a position to consider ways of improving the decision-making process beyond those discussed above.

Much of the discussion so far has focused on what is called the *interacting* (or discussion) group. That is, the pertinent people in a decision meet together and discuss the problem and possible solutions. This is certainly the most common form of group decision making. Two alternative methods of

CLOSE-UP 14.2 ROADBLOCKS TO EFFECTIVE DECISION MAKING

In the early stages of any decision process, there is the likelihood that a variety of perceptual biases may interfere with problem analysis or the identification of possible solutions. Elbing has identified several roadblocks that can impede managerial effectiveness in arriving at the most suitable decision.

- The tendency to evaluate before one investigates. Early evaluation precludes inquiry into a fuller understanding of the situation.
- The tendency to equate new and old experiences. This often causes managers to look for what is similar rather than what is unique in a new problem.
- The tendency to use available solutions, rather than consider new or innovative ones.
- The tendency to deal with problems at face value, rather than ask questions that might illuminate reasons behind the more obvious aspects of the problem.
- The tendency to direct decisions toward a single goal. Most problems involve multiple goals that must be handled simultaneously.
- The tendency to confuse symptoms and problems.
- The tendency to overlook unsolvable problems and instead concentrate on simpler concerns.
- The tendency to respond automatically or to act before thinking.

Problems like these often cause managers to act in haste before the facts are known and often before the actual underlying problem is recognized or understood. A knowledge of these roadblocks will assist managers in their attempts to analyze problem situations and make reasoned decisions.

Source: A Elbing, *Behavioral Decisions in Organizations,* 2nd ed. (Glenview, Ill.: Scott, Foresman and Company, 1978).

group decision making have been suggested that attempt to structure the decision environment in a way that reduces or overcomes many of the problems inherent in the interacting technique. These are the nominal group technique and the delphi technique.

Nominal Group Technique

This technique, typically referred to as NGT, consists of four phases in the group decision-making process (Delbecq, Van de Ven, and Gustafson, 1975). First, individual members meet as a group (as in the interacting technique), but begin by sitting silently and independently generating their ideas on a problem in writing. This silent period is followed by a round-robin procedure in which each group member presents an idea to the group. No discussion of the idea is allowed at this time. The ideas are summarized and recorded (perhaps on a blackboard). After all individuals have had an opportunity to present their ideas, each idea is discussed for the purpose of clarification and evaluation. Finally, the group members conclude the meeting by silently and independently recording their rank-ordering of the various ideas or solutions to the problem. The final decision is determined by the pooled outcome of the members' votes on the issue.

The NGT allows the group to meet formally, but does not allow members to engage in much discussion or interpersonal communication; hence, the term *nominal* group technique. A chief advantage of this procedure, then, is to ensure that everyone independently considers the problem without influence from other group members. As we found, the influence represents one of the chief obstacles to open-minded discussion and decision making.

Delphi Technique

In contrast to NGT, the delphi technique never allows decision participants to meet face-to-face. Instead, a problem is identified and members are asked through a series of carefully designed questionnaires to provide potential solutions. These questionnaires are completed independently. Results of the first questionnaire are then circulated to other group members (who are still physically separated). After viewing the feedback, members are again asked their opinions (to see if the opinions of others on the first questionnaire caused them to change their own minds). This process may continue through several iterations until group members' opinions begin to show a consensus on a prospective solution to the problem (Dalkey, 1969).

The NGT and delphi methods are compared in Exhibit 14.7. Many structural differences can be noted, as well as differences in process. Whether one technique is superior, however, remains an open question. From a managerial perspective, perhaps the best advice is to consider the nature of the problem and the people involved before selecting one method over the other.

These two techniques of decision making represent proof that poor decisions do not have to be tolerated in organizations. Clearly, there are a variety of problems in decision-making processes. Individuals and groups have various biases and personal goals that may lead to suboptimal decisions. Groups often censor themselves, as noted earlier in the discussion on groupthink. Even so, techniques such as NGT and delphi aim to minimize many of these problems by insulating individual participants from the undue influences of others. This allows individuals greater freedom of expression, and the group receives far less filtered or slanted information with which to make its decision. Thus, while not perfect, these techniques can assist managers in need of mechanisms to improve both the quality and the timeliness of decisions made in work organizations.

SUMMARY

This chapter discussed decision making as it relates to organizational behavior. It began by noting three stages of most decision processes: intelligence activities, design activities, and choice activities.

EXHIBIT 14.7 **COMPARISON OF QUALITATIVE DIFFERENCES BETWEEN THREE DECISION PROCESSES BASED UPON EVALUATIONS OF LEADERS AND GROUP PARTICIPANTS**

Dimension	Interacting Groups	Nominal Groups	Delphi Technique
Overall methodology	Unstructured face-to-face group meeting High flexibility High variability in behavior of groups	Structured face-to-face group meeting Low flexibility Low variability in behavior of groups	Structured series of questionnaires and feedback reports Low-variability respondent behavior
Role orientation of groups	Socioemotional Group maintenance focus	Balanced focus on social maintenance and task role	Task-instrumental focus
Relative quantity of ideas	Low; focused "rut" effect	Higher; independent writing and hitchhiking round-robin	High; isolated writing ideas
Search behavior	Reactive search Short problem focus Task-avoidance tendency New social knowledge	Proactive search Extended problem focus High task centeredness New social and task knowledge	Proactive search Controlled problem focus High task centeredness New task knowledge
Normative behavior	Conformity pressures inherent in face-to-face discussion	Tolerance for non-conformity through independent search and choice activity	Freedom not to conform through isolated anonymity
Equality of participation	Member dominance in search, evaluation, and choice phases	Member equality in search and choice phases	Respondent equality in pooling of independent judgments
Method of problem solving	Person-centered Smoothing over and withdrawal	Problem-centered Confrontation and problem solving	Problem-centered Majority rule of pooled independent judgments
Closure decision process	High lack of closure Low felt accomplishment	Low lack of closure High felt accomplishment	Low lack of closure Medium felt accomplishment
Resources utilized	Low administrative time and cost High participant time and cost	Medium administrative time, cost, preparation High participant time and cost	High administrative time, cost, preparation
Time to obtain group ideas	1½ hours	1½ hours	Five calendar months

Source: A. H. Van de Ven and A. L. Delbecq, "The Effectiveness of Nominal, Delphi, and Interacting Group Decision-Making Processes," *Academy of Management Journal 17* (1974): 618. Reprinted by permission.

Next, three distinct models of the decision-making process were presented. The econologic, bounded rationality, and implicit favorite models each rest on different assumptions about the nature of people. In addition, each predicts a different outcome. New concepts introduced here include heuristics, satisficing, and programmed/nonprogrammed decisions.

Following this was a comparison of the relative merits of individual and group decision making. Disadvantages and advantages of each were noted. Participation in decision making was also discussed.

The concepts of groupthink and escalating commitment were introduced as major potential flaws in many group decision efforts. Symptoms and outcomes of groupthink were considered, along with techniques for its prevention. Escalating commitment was discussed in a similar fashion.

At the close of the chapter, two relatively new techniques for improving group decisions were examined—nominal group technique and delphi technique—and compared to the more commonplace interacting method.

KEY WORDS

administrative man
bounded rationality model
decision making
delphi technique
econologic model
economic man
economic rationality
escalating commitment
forced compliance
Gresham's law of planning

groupthink
implicit favorite model
mindguards
nominal group technique
nonprogrammed
   decisions
programmed decisions
prospective rationality
retrospective rationality
satisficing

FOR DISCUSSION

1. What are the three stages in decision making?
2. What is the basic premise of the econologic model of decision making? How does it differ from the bounded rationality model?
3. What are the primary advantages of the bounded rationality model of decision making?
4. What is satisficing?
5. How does the implicit favorite model of decision making work?
6. Describe Gresham's law of planning and management decision making.
7. Discuss the advantages and disadvantages of group decision making compared to individual decision making.
8. When is it more appropriate for a manager to be more participative in decision making?
9. Describe the phenomenon of groupthink. What are its symptoms? What are its outcomes?

10. How can we overcome groupthink?
11. Can you identify examples in your own life of escalating commitment to past decisions?
12. How can managers work to overcome the effects of escalating commitment to past decisions?
13. Compare and contrast the nominal group technique and the delphi technique of decision making.
14. What are some of the more prominent roadblocks to effective managerial decision making?

LAYOFF EXERCISE

Purpose

To examine how to weigh a set of facts and make a difficult personnel decision about laying off valued employees during a time of financial hardship. To examine your own values and criteria used in the decision-making process.

The Problem

Walker Space (WSI) is a medium-sized firm, located in Connecticut. The firm essentially has been a subcontractor on many large space contracts which have been acquired by firms such as North American Rockwell and others.

With the cutback in many of the National Aeronautics and Space Administration programs, Walker has an excess of employees. Stuart Tartaro, the head of one of the sections, has been told by his superior that he must reduce his section of engineers from nine to six. He is looking at the following summaries of their vitae and pondering how he will make this decision.

1. *Roger Allison,* age 26, married, two children. Allison has been with WSI for a year and a half. He is a very good engineer, with a degree from Rensselaer Polytech. He's held two prior jobs and lost both of them because of cutbacks in the space program. He moved to Connecticut from California to take this job. Allison is well liked by his co-workers.

2. *LeRoy Jones,* age 24, single. Jones is black and the company looked hard to get Jones because of affirmative action pressure. He is not very popular with his co-workers. Since he has been employed less than a year, not too much is known about his work. On his one evaluation (which was average) Jones accused his supervisor of bias against blacks. He is a graduate of Detroit Institute of Technology.

3. *William Foster,* age 53, married, three children. Foster is a graduate of "the school of hard knocks." After getting out of World War II, he started to go to school. But his family expenses were too much, so he dropped out. Foster has worked at the company for 20 years. His ratings were excellent for 15 years. For the last five years they have been average.

Foster feels his supervisor grades him down because he doesn't "have sheepskins covering my office walls."

4. *Donald Boyer,* age 32, married, no children. Boyer is well liked by his co-workers. He has been at WSI five years, and he has a B.S. and M.S. in engineering from Purdue University. Boyer's ratings have been mixed. Some supervisors rated him high, some average. Boyer's wife is an M.D.

5. *Mel Shuster,* age 29, single. Shuster is a real worker, but a loner. He has a B.S. in engineering from the University of California. He is working on his M.S. at night, always trying to improve his technical skills. His performance ratings have been above average for the three years he has been employed at WSI.

6. *Sherman Soltis,* age 37, divorced, two children. He has a B.S. in engineering from Ohio State University. Soltis is very active in community affairs: Scouts, Little League, United Appeal. He is a friend of the vice-president through church work. His ratings have been average, although some recent ones indicate that he is out-of-date. He is well liked and has been employed at WSI for 14 years.

7. *Warren Fortuna,* age 44, married, five children. He has a B.S. in engineering from Georgia Tech. Fortuna headed this section at one time. He worked so hard that he had a heart attack. Under doctor's orders, he resigned from the supervisory position. Since then he has done good work, though because of his health, he is a bit slower than the others. Now and then, he must spend extra time on a project because he did get out-of-date during the eight years he headed the section. His performance evaluations for the last two years have been above average. He has been employed at WSI for 14 years.

8. *Robert Treharne,* age 47, single. He began an engineering degree at M.I.T. but had to drop out for financial reasons. He tries hard to stay current by regular reading of engineering journals and taking all the short courses the company and nearby colleges offer. His performance evaluations have varied, but they tend to be average to slightly above average. He is a loner and Tartaro thinks this has negatively affected his performance evaluations. He has been employed at WSI 16 years.

9. *Sandra Rosen,* age 22, single. She has a B.S. in engineering technology from Rochester Institute of Technology. Rosen has been employed less than a year. She is enthusiastic, a very good worker, and is well liked by her co-workers. She is well regarded by Tartaro.

Tartaro doesn't quite know what to do. He sees the good points of each of his section members. Most have been good employees. They all can pretty much do each other's work. No one has special training.

He is fearful that the section will hear about this and morale will drop. Work would fall off. He doesn't even want to talk to his wife about it, in case she'd let something slip. Tartaro has come to you, Edmund Graves, personnel manager at WSI, for some guidelines on this decision—legal, moral, and best personnel practice.

Assignment

You are Edmund Graves. Write a report with your recommendations for termination and a careful analysis of the criteria for the decision. You should also carefully explain to Tartaro how you would go about the terminations and recommend a reasonable termination pay. You should also advise him about the pension implications of this deci-sion. Generally 15 years' service entitles you at least to partial pension.

Source: William F. Glueck and George E. Stevens, *Cases and Exercises in Personnel,* 3rd ed. (Dallas, Texas: Business Publications, 1983).

LYNDON JOHNSON'S DECISION

When Lyndon Johnson was Senate Majority leader during the Eisenhower years, he was adamantly opposed to any American involvement in Indo-China. It was widely believed that it was his opposition which, in 1954 after the French defeat in Vietnam, made Eisenhower rule out any American military intervention against the strong pressure for it on the part of his Secretary of State, John Foster Dulles, his Vice-President, Richard Nixon, and his Chairman of the Joint Chiefs of Staff, Admiral Radford. Johnson continued his opposition to any American involvement in Indo-China when he became President Kennedy's Vice-President. He was outspoken about his desire to withdraw the American advisors whom Eisenhower had sent to bolster the South Vietnamese regime; and he strongly opposed the plunge into Vietnamese politics on the part of the Kennedy Administration when, in the fall of 1963 —shortly before President Kennedy's assassination—it countenanced the coup against President Diem and thereby made the American government the guarantor of the successor regime, and the actual power in South Vietnam. Johnson continued this position after becoming President and resisted all through 1964 pressures for increased American involvement, especially from the Foreign and Defense Secretaries he had inherited from Mr. Kennedy. He strongly emphasized during his election campaign of 1964 his resistance to any attempt to expand the war in Vietnam or to make it an American war. Indeed, his opposition to our involvement in Vietnam was so great and so well known that it was widely feared in the Pentagon and the State Department—and even more in Saigon—that Johnson was encouraging the North Vietnamese to attack by, in effect, promising them that the U.S. would not resist.

Then, in the spring of 1965, Hanoi adopted a new and aggressive policy. Previously, Hanoi had confined itself to supporting insurgents in South Vietnam —with arms, advisors, and money. It had, in other words, matched the American policy of support for the South Vietnamese government and also the American decision not to become involved militarily on a large scale. Beginning in the spring of 1965—only a few weeks after Johnson was sworn in for his second term—North Vietnam began to send North Vietnamese Regulars, heavi-

ly armed with Russian armor and artillery, into South Vietnam, where they took over military operations from the South Vietnamese Viet Cong guerrillas. In late spring these North Vietnamese troops—by now the equivalent of about fifteen American divisions—launched a massive attack clearly aimed at cutting South Vietnam in two. North Vietnam's objective suddenly seemed to be a "military solution," that is, the defeat and destruction of the South Vietnamese military. In the face of this situation, Johnson changed his basic position. He decided that force had to be met with force. He sent a major American military force to Vietnam to take over the main burden of fighting the North Vietnamese. He argued—enough documents have been published to make this clear—that the South Vietnamese would not rise to join the North Vietnamese, as indeed they did not. In this situation a defeat of Hanoi's military thrust would rapidly induce Hanoi to re-establish the uneasy truce that had prevailed before, if not to replace it, as had happened in Korea ten years earlier, with a long-term armistice. Militarily the U.S. was at first fully successful. The North Vietnamese were beaten back with very heavy losses in manpower and almost complete loss of their equipment. By fall of 1965, the North Vietnamese were in full retreat, pulling their badly mauled divisions back into North Vietnam. There was every reason to believe that Johnson's basic premise, that such a defeat would lead to a valid armistice, would be proven right. We know that active negotiations via Moscow were going on and that around Christmas, 1965, an armistice was thought "to be in the bag" in Moscow, apparently as well as in Washington.

What happened then we do not know. One theory is that Brezhnev, until then only one of the three top men in the Soviet hierarchy, made his bid for supreme power in late 1965 and needed the support of the military (and it seems, especially of the Navy) which he only got by turning "hawk." To support this theory there is the fact that Russia began suddenly to step up military supplies to Hanoi—after telling Hanoi and the world in 1965 that supplies would be limited to replacement of lost equipment; that at the same time the Soviet Union, after long hesitation, decided on a crash program to build a three-ocean navy; and that it took over supplying India with arms on a massive scale. Another theory argues that the balance of power in Hanoi, between "doves" and "hawks," shifted decisively toward the "hawks," as Ho Chi Minh suffered a heart attack or stroke and could no longer control events (though he did not die until 1969). Another theory—the least likely one, by the way—maintains that growing American resistance to the Vietnamese war encouraged the Communists; but there was still very little resistance to the Vietnamese war in this country in early 1966, though it was beginning to grow and to be more vocal.

In any event, by January or February 1966, it had become clear that events were not following Lyndon Johnson's expectations. Hanoi had broken off truce negotiations. Instead it was pouring back supplies and men into South Vietnam. The Russians who, only a few months earlier, had acted as intermediaries between Washington and Hanoi were stepping up their support for Hanoi and refusing to use their influence to persuade Hanoi to moderate its demands for total surrender. And so President Johnson had to face the fact that his policy, despite its resounding military success, had been a political failure.

When he sat down with his advisors —mostly the crew he had inherited two years earlier from President Kennedy —no one felt very good about the situation. But prevailing sentiment—and Johnson agreed reluctantly—was that there was really no choice but to hang on. It was now clear that the North Vietnamese could not win a military victory against American forces. It was equally clear that the South Vietnamese, while perhaps not enthusiastic about their regime, did not support the North Vietnamese government. So, the consensus ran, "sooner or later" Hanoi or their "real master," Moscow, would have to see the futility of the drive for a "military solution," and until then all the U.S. could do was to hang on.

No one liked this conclusion. But everyone—Rusk, McNamara, McGeorge Bundy, the Joint Chiefs of Staff —went along, reluctantly. The only dissenter in the group, according to all reports, was George Ball, Undersecretary of State. He was primarily con-cerned with economic affairs, and until then, very far away from the Vietnam problem. Ball is reported to have said: "I don't know, Mr. President, what the right answer is. But I do know that continuing last year's policy is the wrong thing to do. It cannot work and must end in disaster. For it violates basic principles of decision-making."

CASE DISCUSSION QUESTIONS

1. Describe the decision model used by Johnson and his cabinet in this case.
2. How does the groupthink phenomenon help explain the decision process?
3. Examine Johnson's decisions as an example of escalating commitment to a course of action.
4. What could President Johnson have done to ensure a better decision process? Why wasn't such a process followed?

POWER AND POLITICS IN ORGANIZATIONS

People often feel uncomfortable discussing or even acknowledging the existence of power relationships in organizations. Yet power is very much a part of group functioning. Within work groups, power relationships determine group structure and reinforce role relationships and norms. Moreover, communication patterns and the actual messages themselves are often influenced by power distributions. Decision making, too, is constrained and guided by who has power over whom. In short, power and the political process are facts of organizational life, and managers must be equipped to deal with them.

IMPORTANCE OF TOPIC FOR MANAGERS

Organizations are composed of coalitions and alliances of different parties that continually compete with one another for available resources. As such, a major influence on how decisions are made is the distribution of power among the decision makers. Unequal distribution of power in organizations can have critical effects on many aspects of work life, including employee motivation, job satisfaction, absenteeism and turnover, and stress. Hence, an awareness of the nature and pervasiveness of power and politics is essential for a better understanding of these other behavioral processes.

The concept of power is closely related to the concepts of authority and leadership. It is important to understand when one method of influence ceases and another begins. For example, when does a manager stop using legitimate authority in a work situation and start using unauthorized power?

Moreover, on an individual level, various people attempt to exercise influence in organizations by using power tactics. An awareness of such tactics helps managers to recognize them and to take appropriate actions. Keep in mind that attempts by others to exercise power do not have to be successful. A number of mechanisms are available to countermand or neutralize influence attempts. Knowledge of these strategies gives a manager greater latitude in his or her response to power plays by others.

In short, power and political processes in organizations represent a topic of central importance to students of organizational behavior. Along with other group processes such as communication and decision making, power and politics can considerably influence both the behavior and the attitudes of employees at various levels of the organization. In addition, they can further influence the extent to which various units within the organization secure the necessary resources for task accomplishment and ultimate organizational success.

POWER IN INTERPERSONAL RELATIONS

In this chapter, we shall examine various aspects of power in organizations, beginning with the topic of power in interpersonal relations. Here, power is defined and distinguished from the related concepts of authority and leadership, and several bases of power and aspects of power dependency are discussed. While these aspects of power also relate to group situations, they are most germane to interpersonal relations.

EXHIBIT 15.1 THREE MAJOR TYPES OF INFLUENCE

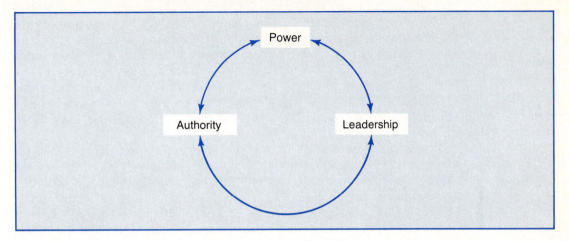

Definition of Power

Numerous definitions of power abound in the literature on organizations. One of the earliest was suggested by Max Weber (cited in Henderson and Parsons, 1947, p. 152), the noted German sociologist, who defined power as "the probability that one actor within a social relationship will be in a position to carry out his own will despite resistance." Similarly, Emerson (1962, p. 32) noted, "the power of actor A over actor B is the amount of resistance on the part of B which can be potentially overcome by A." Following these and other definitions, we shall define *power* for our purposes as an interpersonal (or intergroup) relationship in which one individual (or group) has the ability to cause another individual (or group) to take an action that would not be taken otherwise.

In other words, power involves one person changing the behavior of another. It is important to note that in most organizational situations, we are talking about *implied* force to comply, not necessarily actual force. That is, person A has power over person B if person B believes that person A can in fact force person B to comply.

Power, Authority, and Leadership

Clearly, the concept of power is closely related to the concepts of authority and leadership (see Exhibit 15.1). In fact, power has been referred to by some as "informal authority" (Barnard, 1938), while authority has been called "legitimate power" (Grimes, 1978). However, these three concepts are not the same, and important differences among the three should be noted.

As stated previously, power represents the capacity of one person or group to secure compliance from another person or group. Nothing is said here about the right to secure compliance—only the ability. In contrast, *authority* represents the right to seek compliance by others. In other words, the exercise of authority is backed by legitimacy. If a manager instructs a secretary to type certain letters, he or she presumably has the authority to make such a request. However, if the same manager asked his or her secretary to run personal errands, this would be outside the bounds of the legitimate exercise of authority. While the secretary may still act on this request, the secretary's compliance would be based on power or influence considerations, not authority.

Hence, the exercise of authority is based on group acceptance of the right of someone to exercise legitimate control. As Grimes (1978, p. 726) notes, "What legitimizes authority is the promotion or pursuit of collective goals that are associated with group consensus. The polar opposite, power, is the pursuit of individual or particularistic goals associated with group compliance."

Finally, as we shall see in Chapter Sixteen, *leadership* is the ability of one individual to exercise influence over and above required or mechanical compliance, with directives of others. It is this voluntary aspect of leadership that sets it apart from power and authority. Hence, we often differentiate between headship and leadership. A department head may have the right to require certain actions, while a leader has the ability to inspire certain actions. Although both functions may be served by the same individual, such is clearly not always the case.

Bases of Power

If power is one's ability to secure compliance by others, how is such power exercised? On what is it based? At least two efforts have been made to identify the bases of power. The first model was proposed by Etzioni (1964), identifying three types of power. In fact, it is argued that organizations can be classified according to which of the three types of power is most prevalent. *Coercive* power involves forcing someone to comply with one's wishes. A prison organization is an example of a coercive organization. *Utilitarian* power is power based on performance-reward contingencies; that is, a person will comply with his or her supervisor in order to receive a pay raise or promotion. Business organizations are thought to be essentially utilitarian organizations. Finally, *normative* power rests on the beliefs of the members in the right of the organization to govern their behavior. An example here would be a religious organization.

Although useful for comparative analysis of divergent organizations, this model may have limited applicability since most business and public organizations rest largely on utilitarian power. Instead, a second model developed by French and Raven (1968) of the *bases of power* may be more helpful. French and Raven identified five primary ways in which power can be exerted in social situations.

Reward power exists when person A has power over person B because A controls rewards that B wants. These rewards can cover a wide array of possibilities, including pay raises, promotions, desirable job assignments, more responsibility, new equipment, and so forth. Research by Shetty (1978) has indicated that reward power often leads to increased job performance as employees see a strong performance-reward contingency. However, in many organizations, supervisors and managers really do not control very many rewards. For example, salary and promotion among most blue-collar workers is based on a labor contract, not a performance appraisal.

Coercive power is based primarily on fear. Here, person A has power over person B because A can administer some form of punishment to B. Thus, this kind of power is also referred to as punishment power. As Kipnis (1976) points out, coercive power does not have to rest on the threat of violence. "Individuals exercise coercive power through a reliance upon physical strength, verbal facility, or the ability to grant or withhold emotional support from others. These bases provide the individual with the means to physically harm, bully, humiliate, or deny love to others" (p. 77). Examples of coercive power in organizations include the ability (actual or implied) to fire or demote someone, transfer someone to an undesirable job or location, or strip them of valued perquisites. Indeed, it has been suggested that a good deal of organizational behavior (such as prompt attendance, looking busy, avoiding whistleblowing) can be attributed to coercive, not reward, power. As Kipnis (1976, p. 77) explains, "Of all the bases of power available to man, the power to hurt others is possibly the most often used, most often condemned and most difficult to control."

Legitimate power exists when person B submits to person A because B feels that A has a right to exert power in a certain domain. Legitimate power is really another name for authority, as explained earlier. A supervisor has a right, for instance, to assign work. Legitimate power differs from reward and coercive power in that it depends on the official position a person holds, and not on his or her relationship with others.

Legitimate power derives from three sources: first, prevailing cultural values can assign power to some group. In Japan, for instance, older employees derive power simply because of their age. Second, legitimate power can be attained as a result of the accepted social structure. For example, many Western European countries, as well as Japan, have royal families that serve as a cornerstone to their societies. Third, legitimate power may be designated, as in the case of a board of directors choosing a new company president, or a person being promoted into a managerial position. Whatever the reason, people exercise legitimate power because subordinates assume they have a right to exercise it. A principal reason given for the downfall of the Shah of Iran is that the people came to first question and then denounce his right to legitimate power.

In some cases, person B looks up to or admires person A and, as a result, B follows A largely because of A's personal qualities, characteristics, or reputation. In this case, A can use *referent* power to influence B. Referent power has also been called charismatic power because allegiance is based on interpersonal attraction of one individual for another. Examples of referent power can be seen in advertising, where companies use celebrities to recommend their products; it is hoped that the star appeal of the person will rub off on the products. In work environments, junior managers often emulate senior managers and develop subservient roles based more on admiration and respect than authority.

Finally, *expert power* is demonstrated when person A gains power because A has knowledge or expertise relevant to B. For instance, professors presumably have power in the classroom because of their mastery of a particular subject matter. Other examples of expert power can be seen in staff specialists in organizations (e.g., accountants, labor relations managers, management consultants, and corporate attorneys). In each case, the individual has credibility in a particular—and narrow—area as a result of experience and expertise, and this credibility gives the individual power in that domain.

We have seen, then, that at least five bases of power can be identified. In each case, the power of the individual rests on a particular attribute of the powerholder, the follower, or their relationship. In some cases (e.g., reward power), power rests in the superior; in others (e.g., referent power), power is given to the superior by the subordinate. In all cases, the exercise of power involves delicate and sometimes threatening interpersonal consequences for the various parties involved. Moreover, the nature of the subordinate's response to the attempted use of power is often contingent upon a series of factors collectively known as power dependencies, the next topic to be discussed.

Power Dependencies

In any situation involving power, at least two persons (or groups) can be identified: the person attempting to influence others and the target or targets of that influence. Until recently, attention focused almost exclusively on how people tried to influence others. Only recently has equal attention been given to how people respond to influence attempts. In particular, we now recognize that the extent to which influence attempts are successful is determined in large part by the *power dependencies* of those on the receiving end of the influence attempts. In other words, all people are not subject to (or dependent upon) the same bases of power. What causes some people to be more submissive or vulnerable to power attempts? At least three factors have been identified (Mitchell, 1978).

Subordinate's Values. To begin, person B's values can influence his or her susceptibility to influence attempts. For example, if the outcomes that A can influence are important to B, then B is more likely to be open to influence attempts than if the outcomes are unimportant. Hence, if an employee places a high value on money and believes the supervisor actually controls pay raises, we would expect the employee to be highly susceptible to the supervisor's influence. Indeed, when we hear comments about how young people don't really want to work hard anymore, perhaps a part of this response is a feeling

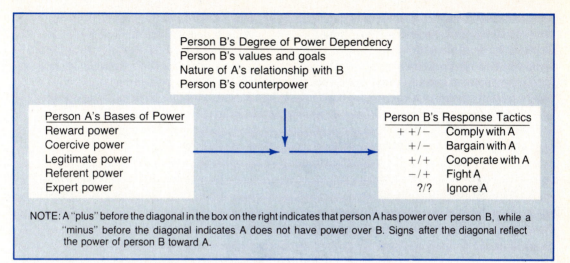

Person B's Degree of Power Dependency
Person B's values and goals
Nature of A's relationship with B
Person B's counterpower

Person A's Bases of Power
Reward power
Coercive power
Legitimate power
Referent power
Expert power

Person B's Response Tactics
+ +/−	Comply with A
+/−	Bargain with A
+/+	Cooperate with A
−/+	Fight A
?/?	Ignore A

NOTE: A "plus" before the diagonal in the box on the right indicates that person A has power over person B, while a "minus" before the diagonal indicates A does not have power over B. Signs after the diagonal reflect the power of person B toward A.

that some young people don't place a high value on those traditional things (for example, money) that are used to influence their behavior. In other words, such complaints may really be saying that young people are more difficult to influence than they used to be.

The Nature of Relationships. In addition, the nature of the relationship between A and B can be a factor in power dependence. Are A and B peers, or a superior and a subordinate? Is the job permanent or temporary? A person on a temporary job, for example, may feel less need to acquiesce since he or she won't be holding the position for long. Moreover, if A and B are peers or good friends, the influence process would likely be more delicate than if they are superior and subordinate.

Counterpower. Finally, a third factor to consider in power dependencies is counterpower. The concept of counterpower focuses on the extent to which B has other sources of power to buffer the effects of A's power. For example, if B is unionized, the union's power may serve to negate A's influence attempts. The use of counterpower can be clearly seen in a variety of situations where various coalitions attempt to bargain with each other and check the power of their opponents.

Exhibit 15.2 is a rudimentary model that combines the concepts of bases of power with the notion of power dependencies. As can be seen, person A's bases of power interact with person B's extent of power dependency to determine B's response to A's influence attempt. If A has significant power

CLOSE-UP 15.1 POWERLESSNESS AMONG WOMEN IN MANAGEMENT

The traditional problems of women in management are illustrative of how formal and informal practices often combine to cause powerlessness. Historically, women in management have found their opportunities in the more routine, low-profile staff functions, where they serve in support capacities to (male) line managers, but have little real power.

One of the reasons for this powerlessness arises from the behavior of male managers toward their female counterparts. For instance, male managers can make a woman powerless by patronizingly overprotecting her. That is, when a woman (or man for that matter) is put into a "safe" job, not exposed to high risk, not given visible assignments, or not given enough to do to prove capability, then there is little opportunity to demonstrate responsibility and earn the respect—and power—for making substantive contributions to the organization.

In addition, women can be rendered powerless when other managers show obvious signs of a lack of managerial support. For example, allowing someone supposedly in authority to be easily bypassed means that no one else has to take that person seriously.

Since power is closely related to the nature of interpersonal relationships, women can lose power simply by not being included in the "social life" of an organization. By consistently not inviting a woman manager to management parties or social occasions, opportunities to develop close social ties with other managers are lost.

Finally, even when women are able to acquire some power, they are often unable to translate such personal credibility into an organizational power base. Power bases are typically developed when the powerholder can pass on or share power with subordinates via a sponsorship or mentor system. Historically, women have been seen by both men and women as the recipients of such sponsorship, not as the sponsors. As such, little opportunity is provided to develop a power network in which the woman is the central figure.

Through mechanisms such as these, it becomes relatively easy to impede the ability of anyone—man or woman—to acquire or use power in an organizational setting. Whether this situation will change dramatically in the near future will depend on women's continued drive to acquire a greater power base and men's willingness to provide a more supportive environment where power accrues according to ability, not gender.

Source: Based on information in R. M. Kanter, "Power Failure in Management Circuits," *Harvard Business Review,* July–August, 1979, pp. 65–75.

and B is highly dependent, we would expect person B to comply with A's wishes.

If A has more modest power over B but B is still largely power dependent, B may try to bargain with A. Despite the fact that B would be bargaining from a point of weakness, this strategy may serve to protect B's interests better than outright compliance. For instance, if your boss asked you to work overtime, you might attempt to strike a deal whereby you would get compensatory time off at a later date. If successful, although you would not have decreased your working hours, at least they would not have been increased.

Where power distribution is more evenly divided, B may attempt to develop a cooperative working relationship with A in which both parties gain from the exchange. An example of this position is labor contract negotiations where labor-management relations are characterized by a balance of power and a good working relationship.

If B has more power than A, B will more than likely reject A's influence attempt. B may even become the aggressor and attempt to influence A. Finally, when B is not certain of the power relationships, he or she may simply try to ignore A's efforts. In doing so, B will discover either that A does indeed have more power, or that A cannot muster the power to be successful. A good illustration of this last strategy can be seen in some companies' response to early governmental efforts to secure equal opportunities for minorities and women. These companies simply ignored governmental efforts until new regulations forced compliance.

An examination of power distribution in organizations today would be incomplete if it did not include the special problems women face in acquiring power. Powerlessness of women in management can result from a variety of causes. Close-Up 15.1 discusses the situation.

Symbols of Managerial Power

How do we know when a manager has power in an organizational setting? Kanter (1979) has identified several of the more common symbols of managerial power. For example, managers have power to the extent that they can intercede favorably on behalf of someone in trouble with the organization. Moreover, managers have power when they can get a desirable placement for a talented subordinate or get approval for expenditures beyond their budget. Other manifestations of power include the ability to secure above-average salary increases for subordinates and the ability to get items on the agenda at policy meetings.

Furthermore, we can see the extent of managerial power when someone can gain quick access to top decision makers or can get early information about decisions and policy shifts. Finally, power is evident when top decision makers seek out the opinions of a particular manager on important questions. Through such actions, the organization sends clear signals concerning who has power and who does not. In this way, the organization reinforces or at least condones the power structure in existence.

Interpersonal Power in Use

The final question concerning interpersonal power relationships deals with the extent to which powerholders actually use the power they have. Research indicates that those who hold power typically make use of it. A study by

Kipnis (1972) found that when managers had power they: (1) sent more messages to subordinates; (2) rated their subordinates less highly on performance appraisals; (3) indicated less willingness to meet socially with subordinates; and (4) were more likely to attribute subordinate performance to managerial expertise than to subordinate ability.

From the subordinate's standpoint, the findings are also clear. People do not like power to be used on them and often resist the attempts. However, when the exercise of power is based on legitimate, expert, or referent power, resistance is less likely than when based on coercion. Moreover, while the use of reward power may lead to greater performance, it often does so at the expense of job satisfaction. People usually prefer to do something for someone else because they enjoy doing so or because they respect the person, rather than because they will be rewarded for it. Contemporary managers—who typically hold considerable power themselves—must be sensitive to how their influence attempts are received. In this regard, the issue is not so much getting the job done but *how* one goes about trying to get the job done. Some strategies obviously have fewer undesirable side effects than others.

POLITICS IN ORGANIZATIONS

Closely related to the concept of power is the equally important topic of politics. In any discussion of the exercise of power—particularly in intergroup situations—a knowledge of basic political processes is essential. Based on this discussion, we shall then be in a good position to consider political strategies for acquiring and maintaining power in intergroup relations.

Definition of Politics

Perhaps the earliest definition of politics was offered by Lasswell (1936), who described it as who gets what, when, and how. Even from this simple definition, one can see that politics involves the resolution of differing preferences in conflicts over the allocation of scarce and valued resources. Politics represents one mechanism to solve allocation problems when other mechanisms, such as the introduction of new information or the use of a simple majority rule, fail to apply. For our purposes here, we will adopt Pfeffer's (1981, p. 7) definition of *politics* as involving "those activities taken within organizations to acquire, develop, and use power and other resources to obtain one's preferred outcomes in a situation in which there is uncertainty or dissensus about choices."

In comparing the concept of politics with the related concept of power, Pfeffer (1981, p. 7) notes:

> If power is a force, a store of potential influence through which events can be affected, politics involves those activities or behaviors through which power is

developed and used in organizational settings. Power is a property of the system at rest; politics is the study of power in action. An individual, subunit or department may have power within an organizational context at some period of time; politics involves the exercise of power to get something accomplished, as well as those activities which are undertaken to expand the power already possessed or the scope over which it can be exercised.

In other words, from Pfeffer's definition it is clear that political behavior is activity that is initiated for the purpose of overcoming opposition or resistance. In the absence of opposition, there is no need for political activity. Moreover, it should be remembered that political activity need not necessarily be suboptimal for organization-wide effectiveness. In fact, many managers often believe that their political actions on behalf of their own department are actually in the best interests of the organization as a whole. Finally, we should note that politics, like power, is not inherently bad. In many instances, the survival of the organization depends on the success of a department or coalition of departments challenging a traditional but outdated policy or objective. That is why an understanding of organizational politics, as well as power, is so essential for managers.

Political Realities in Organizations

Contemporary organizations are highly political entities. Indeed, much of the goal-related effort produced by an organization is directly attributable to political processes. In the realm of interpersonal and intergroup behavior, as Miles (1980, p. 182) observes, "conditions that threaten the status of the power or encourage the efforts of those wishing to increase their power base will stimulate the intensity of organizational politics and increase the proportion of decision-making behavior that can be classified as political as opposed to rational."

In fact, Miles (1980) identifies five major reasons why organizational behavior is often more political than rational. These are as follows:

1. *Scarcity of resources.* Politics surfaces when resources are scarce and allocation decisions must be made. If resources were ample, there would be no need to use politics to claim one's "share."
2. *Nonprogrammed decisions.* A distinction was made in the previous chapter between programmed and nonprogrammed decisions. When decisions are not programmed, conditions surrounding the decision problem and the decision process are usually more ambiguous, leaving room for political maneuvering. Programmed decisions, on the other hand, are typically specified in such detail that little room for maneuvering exists. Hence, we are likely to see more political behavior on major questions, such as long-range strategic planning decisions.
3. *Ambiguous goals.* Similarly, when the goals of a department or organization are ambiguous, more room is available for politics.
4. *Technology and environment.* In general, political behavior is increased

when the nature of the internal technology is nonroutine and when the external environment is dynamic and complex (see Chapter Three).

5. *Organizational change.* Periods of organizational change also present opportunities for political rather than rational behavior. Efforts to restructure a particular department, open a new division, introduce a new product line, and so forth, are invitations to all to join the political process, as different factions and coalitions fight over territory (see Chapter Two).

Since most organizations today have scarce resources, ambiguous goals, increasingly complex technologies, and more sophisticated and unstable external environments, it seems reasonable to conclude that a large proportion of contemporary organizations are highly political in nature. As a result, contemporary managers must be sensitive to political processes as they relate to the acquisition and maintenance of power in organizations.

This brings up the question of why we have policies and standard operating procedures (SOPs) in organizations. Actually, such policies are frequently aimed at reducing the extent to which politics influences a particular decision. This effort to encourage more "rational" decisions in organizations was a primary reason behind Max Weber's development of the bureaucratic model (see Chapter Two). That is, increases in the specification of policy statements often are inversely related to political efforts, as shown in Exhibit 15.3. This is true primarily because such actions reduce the uncertainties surrounding a decision and hence the opportunity for political efforts.

POLITICAL STRATEGIES IN INTERGROUP RELATIONS

Up to this point, we have examined the related concepts of power and politics and studied a simple model of the exercise of power in interpersonal relations. Shifting our focus from the individual or interpersonal to the intergroup level of analysis, the picture becomes somewhat more complicated. In developing a portrait of how political strategies are used to attain and maintain power in intergroup relations, we will highlight two major aspects of the topic. The first is the relationship between power and the control of critical resources. The second is the relationship between power and the control of strategic contingencies. Both cases will illustrate how subunit control leads to the acquisition of power in organizational settings.

Power and Control of Critical Resources

Earlier in the text, Pfeffer and Salancik's (1978) *resource dependence model* of organization-environment relations was presented. This model also serves our

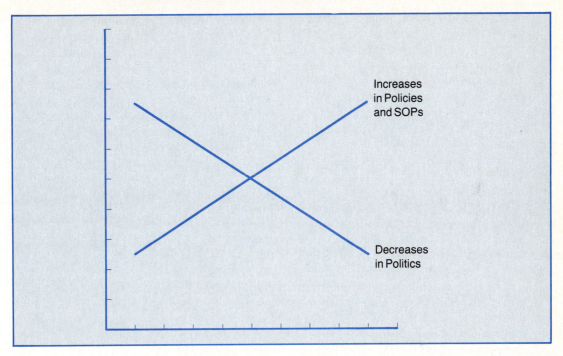

purpose here as we consider how power is attained by the various subunits of an organization. Refer back to Chapter Three for a review of the discussion.

When one subunit of an organization controls a scarce resource that is needed by another subunit, that subunit acquires power. As such, it is in a better position to bargain for the critical resources it needs from the organization. Hence, while all subunits may contribute something to the organization as a whole, power allocation within the organization will be influenced by the relative importance of the resources contributed by each unit. To quote Salancik and Pfeffer (1974, p. 470):

> Subunit power accrues to those departments that are most instrumental in bringing or in providing resources which are highly valued by the total organization. In turn, this power enables these subunits to obtain more of those scarce and critical resources allocated within the organization. Stated succinctly, power derived from acquiring resources is used to obtain more resources, which in turn can be employed to produce more power—"the rich get richer."

To document their case, Salancik and Pfeffer (1974) carried out a major study of university budget decisions. As shown in Close-Up 15.2, politics and power played a major role in such decisions.

In a study of power tactics used by various subunits, Salancik and Pfeffer examined the relationship between control of resources and subsequent power and favorability of decision outcome among various academic departments of a major state university. The aim of the study was to test the hypothesis that departments that controlled critical resources attained more power in the university and were able to secure more favorable decision outcomes.

In the study, power was measured both by having the various department heads rate the amount of power each department had to influence decisions and by examining the extent of departmental representation on important university-wide committees. The key resources needed by the university were number of students; national prestige of departments; amount of outside grant support; public visibility of department activities; administrative and service contributions of departments to the university; and the extent of professional and business contacts outside the university.

The investigation found that the best predictors of the extent of departmental power were: (1) the department's ability to provide outside funds to the university in the form of contracts and grants; (2) the size of the department's graduate student body; and (3) the national prestige of the department. In all, the amount of outside funding generated by a department proved to be the best single predictor of departmental power.

In addition, the study examined how three common resource allocation decisions were made. The three resources were the amount of funds to support graduate student fellowships, faculty research grants, and summer faculty fellowships. It was found that the more scarce the resource, the more political (as opposed to rational) was the decision-making process. Moreover, the amount of departmental power was found to be related to the allocation decisions on these three resources.

In summary, Salancik and Pfeffer concluded that departments or subunits who had more power found it easier to secure a greater share of the scarce resources available and that these resources served to reinforce their power. Hence, a continual cycle was established whereby power led to increased resources, which led to continuation of power, and so forth.

Source: G. Salancik and J. Pfeffer, "The Bases and Use of Power in Organizational Decision Making," *Administrative Science Quarterly* 19 (1974): 453–73.

Power and Control of Strategic Contingencies

In addition to the control of critical resources, subunits can also attain power by controlling what are termed *strategic contingencies.* A contingency is defined by Miles (1980, p. 170) as "a requirement of the activities of one subunit that is affected by the activities of other subunits." For example, the business office of most universities represents a strategic contingency for the various colleges within the university because it has veto or approval power over financial expenditures of the schools. Its approval of a request to spend money is far from certain. Thus, a contingency represents a source of uncertainty in the decision-making process. A contingency becomes strategic when it has the potential to alter the balance of interunit or interdepartmental power in such a way that interdependencies between the various units are changed (Hickson et al., 1971).

Perhaps the best way to illustrate this is to consider the example of power distribution in various organizations attempting to deal with a major source of uncertainty—the external environment. In a classic study by Lawrence and Lorsch (1967; see Chapter Three), influence patterns were examined for companies in three divergent industries: container manufacturing, food processing, and plastics. It was found that for *successful* firms, power distribution conformed to the firm's strategic contingencies. For example, in the container manufacturing companies where the critical contingencies were customer delivery and product quality, the major share of power in decision making resided in the sales and production staffs. In contrast, in the food processing firms where the strategic contingencies focused on expertise in marketing and food sciences, major power rested in the sales and research units. In other words, those who held power in the successful organizations were in areas that were of central concern to the firm and its survival at a particular point in time. The functional areas that were most important for organizational success were under the control of the decision makers. For less successful firms, this congruence was not found.

The changing nature of strategic contingencies can be seen in the evolution of power distribution in major public utilities. Many years ago, when electric companies were developing and growing, most of the senior officers of the companies were engineers. Technical development was the central issue. More recently, however, as utilities face greater litigation, government regulation, and controversy over nuclear power, lawyers are predominating in the leadership of most companies. This example serves to emphasize that "subunits could inherit and lose power, not necessarily by their own actions, but by the shifting contingencies in the environment confronting the organization" (Miles, 1980, p. 169).

A related illustration of the influence of strategic contingencies on organizational behavior can be seen in a classic study of bureaucracy by Crozier, as shown in Close-Up 15.3.

Following from earlier work by Hickson and his associates (Hickson et al., 1971), it is possible to develop a simplified model of the use of strategic contingencies by various subunits and groups in acquiring and maintaining power. The model is shown in Exhibit 15.4. Basically, it is argued that subunit power is influenced by three factors: (1) the ability to cope with uncertainty; (2) the degree of substitutability of coping activities; and (3) the centrality of the coping activities.

Ability to Cope with Uncertainty. According to advocates of the strategic contingencies model of power, the primary source of subunit power is the unit's ability to cope with uncertainty on behalf of the other subunits of the

CLOSE-UP 15.3 POWER RELATIONSHIPS ON THE SHOP FLOOR

In a classic study of a large government-owned manufacturing facility, Michael Crozier, a French sociologist, examined the patterns of influence existing between groups of production workers and maintenance workers on the shop floor.

The two groups had dramatically different backgrounds. Production workers were recruited from among people legally entitled to government employment under French law. This included war widows, orphans, disabled veterans, and ex-military personnel. Production workers enjoyed considerable job security through civil service tenure, were protected against unfair disciplinary action, and could not be replaced or transferred arbitrarily. These people, while secure, were less skilled than the maintenance workers, and tended to be more heterogeneous. Maintenance workers, on the other hand, were highly skilled technicians recruited through difficult competitive examinations. They tended to have similar backgrounds and shared similar values.

A further difference between the two groups was the reward systems in use. Production workers used a piece-rate incentive plan such that their wages increased with their production. In contrast, maintenance workers were salaried and governed by strict seniority.

As would be expected from the above details, Crozier found that the Achilles' heel in terms of power was the control the maintenance workers had over machine stoppages and "repairs." In this otherwise highly predictable, highly routine factory, machine stoppages were the only major events that could not be predicted or programmed. As such, production workers (on a piece-rate system) were clearly dependent upon the salaried maintenance workers who, in turn, were *not* dependent upon the production workers. As such, maintenance workers alone could control the primary strategic contingency of the factory.

To protect their position, maintenance workers "built a fence" around their jobs. They adhered to a guild apprenticeship system to restrict entry of others; they disregarded blueprints and maintenance directions; they used ambiguous machine settings; and overall they kept their skills at a rule-of-thumb level. Not even supervisors had enough expertise or knowledge to check their work. As a result, they succeeded in protecting their base of power in the factory and could successfully bargain with the production workers for what they wanted.

Source: M. Crozier, *The Bureaucratic Phenomenon* (Chicago: University of Chicago Press, 1964).

organization (Miles, 1980). In other words, if our group can help your group reduce the uncertainties associated with *your* job, then our group has power over your group. As Hickson et al. (1971, pp. 219–20) put it:

Uncertainty itself does not give power; coping gives power. If organizations allocate to their various subunits task areas that vary in uncertainty, then those subunits that cope most effectively with the most uncertainty should have most

EXHIBIT 15.4   A STRATEGIC CONTINGENCIES MODEL OF SUBUNIT POWER

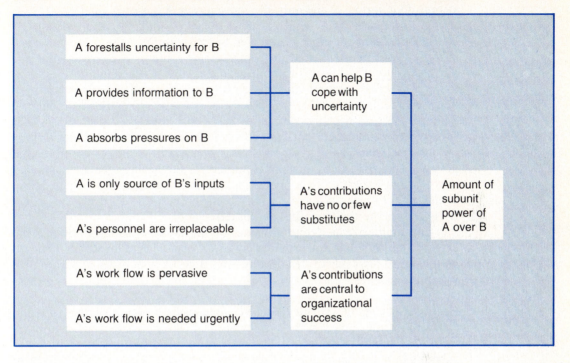

power within the organization, since coping by a subunit reduces the impact of uncertainty on other activities in the organization, a shock absorber function.

As shown in Exhibit 15.4, three primary types of coping activities relating to uncertainty reduction can be identified. The letters "A" and "B" are used in this exhibit to denote the two subunits involved in the power relationship. To begin, some uncertainty can be reduced through steps by one subunit to *prevent or forestall uncertainty*. Crozier's study (Close-Up 15.3) showed how maintenance units could use preventive maintenance to reduce uncertainty about machine performance if they desired. Second, a subunit's ability to cope with uncertainty is influenced by its capacity to *provide or collect information*. Such information can forewarn of probable disruptions or problems so corrective action can be taken promptly. Many business firms use various forecasting techniques to predict sales, economic conditions, and so forth. The third mechanism for coping with uncertainty is the unit's ability to *absorb pressures* that actually impact on the organization. For instance, if one manufacturing facility runs low on raw materials and a second facility can supply it with needed materials, this second facility effectively reduces some of the uncertainty of the first facility—and in the process gains influence over it.

In short, one subunit (designated "A" in Exhibit 15.4) gains power over another subunit (designated "B") if A can help B cope with the contingencies and uncertainties facing it. The more dependent that B is upon A to ensure the smooth functioning of the unit, the more power A has over B.

Nonsubstitutability of Coping Activities. Substitutability is the capacity for one subunit to seek needed resources from alternate sources. Two factors influence the extent to which substitutability is available to a subunit. First, the *availability of alternatives* must be considered. If a subunit can get the job done using different products or processes, it is less susceptible to influence. Perhaps one reason many companies may resist buying word processors for their offices is that other options are available, such as standard typewriters. Second, the *replaceability of personnel* is important. A major reason for the power of staff specialists (personnel managers, purchasing agents, etc.) is that they possess expertise in a specialized area of value to the organization. Consider, for example, a reason for closed-shop union contracts: they effectively reduce the replaceability of workers.

To summarize, a second influence on the extent of subunit power is the extent to which subunit A provides goods or services to B for which there are no (or only a few) substitutes. In this way, B needs A in order to accomplish subunit objectives.

Centrality of Coping Activities. Finally, one must consider the extent to which a subunit is interlinked in the system of organizational activities, or in other words, the subunit's *centrality*. The more interlinked subunit A is with other subunits in the organization, the more "central" it is. This centrality, in turn, is influenced by two factors. First, *work flow pervasiveness* is the degree to which the actual work of one subunit is connected with other subunits. If subunit B cannot complete its own tasks without the help of the work activities of subunit A, then A has power over B. An example of this is an assembly line where units toward the end of the line are highly dependent upon units at the beginning of the line for inputs. The second factor, *work flow immediacy*, relates to the speed and severity with which the work of one subunit affects the final outputs of the organization. For instance, companies that prefer to keep low inventories of raw materials (perhaps for tax purposes) are in effect giving their outside suppliers greater power than those companies that keep large reserves of raw materials.

When examined as a whole, then, the strategic contingency model of intergroup power suggests that subunit power is influenced: when one subunit can help another unit reduce or cope with its uncertainty; when the subunit is difficult to replace or irreplaceable; and when the subunit is central to continued operations. The more these three conditions prevail, the more power will become vested in the subunit. Even so, it should be recognized that the power of one subunit or group can shift over time. As noted by Hickson et al. (1971, p. 227), "As the goals, outputs, technologies, and markets of organizations change, so, for each subunit, the values of the independent variables [such as coping with uncertainty, nonsubstitutability, and centrality] change, and the patterns of power change." In other words, the strategic contingency model suggested here is a dynamic one that is clearly subject to change over time as various subunits and groups negotiate, bargain, confront, and compromise with each other in an effort to secure a more favorable position in the organizational power structure.

SPECIFIC POWER TACTICS IN ORGANIZATIONS

The two models of intergroup power discussed previously—the resource dependence model and the strategic contingencies model—imply various tactics that can be employed to gain power. Based on this discussion, we are now in a position, by way of summary, to review several specific power tactics that can be found in organizational settings. Since a very large number of such tactics can be identified, we have selected several of the more common ones to examine (Mechanic, 1962; DuBrin, 1974; Pettigrew, 1975; Pfeffer, 1981).

Most decisions rest on the availability of relevant information, so persons *controlling access to information* play a major role in decisions made. A good example of this is the common corporate practice of pay secrecy. Only the personnel department and senior managers typically have salary information—and power—for personnel decisions. Another related power tactic is the practice of *controlling access to persons.* A well-known reason contributing to President Nixon's downfall was his isolation from others. His two senior advisors had complete control over who saw the President.

Very few organizational questions have one correct answer; instead, an appropriate decision is made that best fits the criteria to be achieved. As such, significant power can be exercised by those who can practice *selective use of objective criteria* that will lead to a decision favorable to themselves. According to Herbert Simon, if an individual is permitted to select decision criteria, he or she needn't care who actually makes the decision. Attempts to control objective decision criteria can be seen in faculty debates in a university or college over who gets hired or promoted. One group tends to emphasize teaching and will attempt to set criteria for employment dealing with teacher competence, subject area, interpersonal relations, and so on. Another group may emphasize research, and will try to set criteria related to number of publications, reputation in the field, etc.

One of the simplest ways to influence a decision is to ensure that it never comes up for consideration in the first place. There are a variety of strategies used for *controlling the agenda.* Efforts may be made to order the topics at a meeting in such a way that the undesired topic is last on the list. Failing this, opponents may raise a number of objections or points of information concerning the topic that cannot be easily answered, thereby tabling the topic until another day.

Still another means to gain an advantage is by *using outside experts.* The unit wishing to exercise power may take the initiative and bring in experts from the field or experts known to be in sympathy with their cause. Hence, if a dispute arises between spending more money on research or more on actual production, we would expect differing answers from outside research consultants and outside production consultants. Most consultants have experienced situations in which their clients feed them information and biases they hope the consultant will repeat in a meeting.

In some situations, the organization's own policies and procedures provide ammunition for power plays, or *bureaucratic gamesmanship*. For instance, a group may drag its feet on making changes in the work place by creating red-tape work slowdowns, or "working to rule." In this way, they let it be known that the work flow will continue to slow down until they get their way.

The final power tactic to be discussed here is that of *coalitions and alliances*. One unit can effectively increase its power by forming an alliance with other groups that share similar interests. This technique is often used when multiple labor unions in the same corporation join forces to gain contract concessions for their workers. It can also be seen in the tendency of corporations within one industry to form trade associations to lobby for their position. While the various members of a coalition need not agree on everything—and, indeed, they may be competitors—sufficient agreement on the problem under consideration is necessary as a basis for action.

Although other power tactics could be discussed, these examples serve to illustrate the diversity of techniques available to those interested in acquiring and exercising power in organizational situations. In reviewing the major research carried out on the topic of power, Pfeffer (1981, p. 370) states:

> If there is one concluding message, it is that it is probably effective and it is certainly normal that these managers do behave as politicians. It is even better that some of them are quite effective at it. In situations in which technologies are uncertain, preferences are conflicting, perceptions are selective and biased, and information processing capacities are constrained, the model of an effective politician may be an appropriate one for both the individual and for the organization in the long run.

SUMMARY

In this chapter we examined the role of power and politics in work organizations. While the topic of power and politics may be a controversial one, it must nevertheless be recognized as a prominent force in organizational dynamics that can be managed to enhance organizational effectiveness.

Power was defined as an interpersonal or intergroup relationship in which one individual or group has the ability to cause another individual or group to take an action that would not be taken otherwise. In other words, someone's behavior is being changed under conditions of threat. It is important to note here that we are not necessarily talking about the use of actual force, but rather the use of implied force. Power was also distinguished from the related concepts of authority and leadership.

Next, the five bases of power and their relationships in organizations were examined. The interactions between these five bases of power and power dependencies were also discussed. For example, it was pointed out that recipients of influence attempts often have at their disposal various mechanisms by which to counter or neutralize such influence attempts. In this way we recognize a balance of influence efforts between the two parties, emphasizing that power and influence attempts may not always be successful.

In addition to the topic of power, several aspects of politics in organizations were discussed in this chapter. In particular, there are several reasons the political realities of organizations must be clearly recognized. Behavior is often more political than rational because of: the scarcity of resources, nonprogrammed decisions, ambiguous goals, technology and environment, and the constant change in organizations.

Politics was defined as those activities taken within organizations to acquire, develop, and use power and other resources to obtain one's preferred outcomes in a situation in which there is uncertainty or dissension about possible choices. Two models of power and politics in organizations were discussed; the resource dependence model and the strategic contingency model. Based on these two models, several specific power tactics were discussed as they relate to influence efforts in organizations.

KEY WORDS

authority	legitimate power
bases of power	politics
bureaucratic	power
gamesmanship	power dependencies
coercive power	referent power
counterpower	resource dependence
expert power	reward power
leadership	strategic contingencies

FOR DISCUSSION

1. Compare and contrast power, authority, and leadership.
2. Identify five bases of power and provide an example of each. Which base (or bases) of power do you feel would be most commonly found in organizations?
3. Discuss the concept of power dependencies. What is the relationship between power dependencies and bases of power?
4. What is counterpower? Provide an example of counterpower from your own experience.
5. Why is it important to understand political behavior in organizations?
6. Define politics. How does politics differ from power?

7. Compare and contrast the resource-dependence model of power and politics with the strategic-contingency model.
8. Identify several specific power tactics in organizations and provide an example of each.

EXERCISE

15.1

POWER RELATIONSHIPS IN UNIVERSITIES

Purpose
To examine bases of power and power dependencies in university settings and to consider how power and politics can facilitate personal and organizational goal attainment.

Part One
Consider your classroom as a political environment. The major power groups are: (1) the professor; and (2) the class. For each group, provide your own estimate of the percentage of power held by that group (e.g., 50%–50%? 40%–60%?). Next, identify any bases of power that the group has at its disposal to influence the direction and outcome of the class. Also, identify any power dependencies for each group that may influence direction and outcome. In your responses, attention should obviously focus on who has power, and why, but may also focus on how you might change the balance (or imbalance) of power.

Part Two
Consider the university as a whole as a political environment. Here the major power groups are: (1) the faculty; (2) the student body; (3) the administration; and (4) clerical and blue-collar workers. For each group, identify the primary sources of power that can be used by that group to pursue its own objectives. For each source of power, how might other groups attempt to nullify such power?

Note: Both parts of this exercise can be done either in groups of five or six students, or as a class.

CASE

15.1

THE UNITED FUND

A recent investigation of financial allocation to local social service agencies that were members of various United Funds provides evidence on the use of power in budgeting. The United Fund was established to achieve economies of scale in fund raising, as well as to cope with employer complaints about multiple agencies requesting permission to solicit payroll-deduction contributions at the work place. The United Fund has as its goal the inclusion of as much of the local fund-raising effort as possible. In return for receiving a share of the United Fund's annual income, the local agency, such as the Boy Scouts, a home for unwed mothers, a disease prevention center, mental health or other social

service agency, foregoes any other solicitation in the community, at the work place particularly, although other fund-raising activities such as sales, lotteries, and so forth are permitted. This arrangement has made the United Fund, although private, an important source of funds for many public-sector social service organizations in many American communities.

A sample of sixty-six United Fund budget allocations to member agencies for the years 1962, 1967, and 1972 were examined by Pfeffer and Leong.[1] These authors argued that the power of a member agency in the Fund was negatively related to the agency's dependence on the Fund, measured as the proportion of the agency's budget obtained from the Fund. The power of a member agency in the Fund was also expected to be positively related to the Fund's dependence on the agency, measured as the proportion of the total United Fund budget that went to each member agency. The agency needed the Fund allocations for its operating budget, and the higher the proportion of this budget that was obtained from the United Fund, the greater the dependence and therefore, the less the power. At the same time, however, the Fund needed agency participation to legitimize its own activities, and also the United Fund came to define its goal as including as much of the local agency fund raising as possible. The net power of a particular social service agency vis-à-vis its United Fund, therefore, was the net result of its dependence on the United Fund and the United Fund's dependence on the social service agency. As Pfeffer and Leong (p. 779) state:

> The individual agency's power within the United Fund is a function of its importance to the United Fund and its ability to articulate a credible threat of withdrawal. The ability to threaten withdrawal is de-

termined by the agency's ability to raise funds on its own outside the Fund . . . the greater the amount of outside funds raised, the higher the allocation from the United Fund. . . . Our argument suggests that this causal relationship will be stronger (a) the smaller the proportion of the agency's budget received from the United Fund (the less dependent the agency is on the Fund), and (b) the larger the proportion of the United Fund's budget that goes to a given agency (the larger, and hence, the more important, the agency is to the Fund).

The hypothesis was supported following an examination of financial allocations across cities to eleven agencies in 1962, fifteen agencies in 1967, and eighteen agencies in 1972. In virtually no case was there a significant association between any demographic variable and the allocations to social service agencies. The allocations to agencies serving primarily black constituencies were unrelated to the proportion of blacks in the area; allocations to agencies providing financial assistance were unrelated to median income or to the proportion of the population falling below the poverty line; and allocations to agencies serving youth (the so-called character-building agencies) were unrelated to the age distribution of the population in the areas served. Seventeen demographic variables, ranging from population size, income distribution, age distribution, and occupational distribution, to the crime and divorce rate were examined. The inability of these variables to account for financial allocations to the various social service agencies provides some evidence that politics intervened in the resource allocation process.

Typically, the most powerful groups in the United Fund have been the Boy and Girl Scouts and YMCA and

YWCA. All are fairly large, but most importantly, all service the employees and their families who constitute the core of the United Fund's contributors. Agencies serving the poor and those otherwise in distress typically provide fewer direct services to the United Fund contributors. Thus, the United Fund has found itself in a paradoxical position: it collects most of its contributions basically from the working middle class, and then provides a great share of its budget to support agencies and programs such as community centers, scouts, and the Y's that service the middle class. While there is some redistribution of benefits away from the contributors, it is not as much as might be suggested by relative need, because these agencies have the power to threaten withdrawal from the Fund.

Two examples serve to illustrate this power and how it can be employed. In Champaign-Urbana, the two cities in which the University of Illinois is located, the pattern of United Fund contributions and budgeting is similar to that found elsewhere. Most of the funds come from employees of the university and other major employers in the area, and the bulk of the budget goes to the scouts, the Y's, and the various community centers. The board of the United Fund one year decided to rationalize its decision-making process. Instead of just having agencies make budget proposals (which were typically based on last year's budget plus an increment), the board required the agencies to identify the type of services provided and the specific client population groups (identified by sex, race, and income level) which were served by the various programs. Then, the board determined to provide more funding to the various agencies which provided more important services to client groups which

would not otherwise be served without the Fund's assistance. This was done with little debate or discussion. After all, if they worked out the indicators of program criticality and client group need, how could anyone object to basing budget decisions on a criterion that would better serve the social welfare of the community?

When the criteria and then the new funding decisions based on these criteria were announced, the scouts and the Y's were outraged. They were the big losers in the process, since recreational services for the middle class fared poorly by the criteria when compared to health services, job training, and other forms of social welfare for much poorer parts of the population. The aggrieved agencies soon discovered their common plight and formed a coalition. This coalition formation process was facilitated by the overlapping memberships on some of the boards, and the fact that these four agencies were the ones most dominated by university faculty or their families. After much discussion among the agencies, they determined a course of action. They went to the local United Fund board as a group and argued that unless they got their previous share of the allocation, they would withdraw and form a separate fund-raising organization among themselves. After much discussion and debate and negotiating, the United Fund determined that the agencies were serious, at which point they got back their previous allocations.

Even so, the United Fund still had a problem. It had kept important member agencies but it had also just had every agency go through this new budget request process, and announced to the world its new criteria for budget allocations. There were board members and others in the community who agreed with the new directions. It would be

embarrassing, to say the least, to announce that it had disregarded the very procedures and rules it had just formulated, particularly when it would have done so as the result of a pure power play. What the Fund did, of course, was to use the new rules, forms, information and procedures, but somehow the allocations came out looking much as they had in the past. It turns out that there was enough latitude even in these new procedures to permit the Fund to do just about what it wanted, which was to allocate resources in a way which was in large measure based on the political clout of the requesting agencies. Thus, the objective criteria were selectively used, and the coalition of member agencies got what they wanted from the United Fund. The use of power had proved successful.

The second example comes from the San Francisco Bay area. Here, the charities which primarily served the black population were distressed by the United Fund's allocations. They thought that it was wrong to recycle such a large proportion of the budget to those agencies that served the relatively more affluent parts of the population. After several years of negotiation for a larger share, a set of charities which served the black community withdrew as a group from the United Fund and formed their own organization for raising and allocating money. Although initially United Fund collections were hurt by all the attendant negative publicity, after a few years contribution levels pretty much recovered and now there are probably more people in the area who do not even know that such a splinter group broke off or that it still exists. Organizations

fail to take account of power only at some peril; if they do respond to power, most of the time they seem to survive in fairly good condition.

Note
1. J. Pfeffer and A. Leong, "Resource Allocation in United Funds: Examination of Power and Dependence," *Social Forces,* 55, 1977, pp. 775–90.

CASE DISCUSSION QUESTIONS

1. Identify the power tactics used by (a) the Scouts and Y's in Urbana-Champaign, and (b) the charities serving the black community in the San Francisco Bay area.
2. Pfeffer and Leong proposed a positive relationship between a member agency's power and the United Fund's dependence on that agency. How do the activities of the Urbana-Champaign Scouts and Y's support this hypothesis?
3. Pfeffer and Leong also proposed a negative relationship between a member agency's power and that agency's dependence on the Fund. How do the activities of the San Francisco black community charities support this hypothesis?
4. What might be done realistically to reduce the exercise of power and politics in the allocation decisions of such agencies?

Source: Based on J. Pfeffer, *Power in Organizations* (Marshfield, Mass.: Pitman, 1981), pp. 239–43.

CHAPTER SIXTEEN

LEADERSHIP AND GROUP EFFECTIVENESS

For many people, the concept of leadership is synonymous with management. Managers, functioning as leaders, coordinate employee effort and guide the direction in which an organization moves. Without the element of leadership, how could management be successful?

This chapter presents a thorough examination of leadership, including definitions, functions, patterns, attributes, and behaviors. Three contemporary models of leadership will be discussed as well. In closing, some constraints on leadership will be examined together with means for improving leadership effectiveness.

IMPORTANCE OF TOPIC FOR MANAGERS

Because leaders can have a substantial impact on group performance, it is essential for managers to understand the various facets of the leadership process. How does the process work, and what prevents it from working?

When faced with constraints on leadership—situations where leadership may not work—managers need to be acquainted with viable substitutes. They should also be familiar with mechanisms for improving leadership effectiveness. Several contemporary models of leadership exist, and each suggests methods for sharpening leadership skills.

The need for understanding and appreciating the importance of the leadership process becomes clearer with knowledge of the work functions that leadership performs in organizations. This chapter introduces the topic by focusing on the nature of leadership.

THE NATURE OF LEADERSHIP

In general, at least three approaches to a definition of leadership can be identified. Leadership has been viewed as an attribute of position (e.g., president of a corporation), a characteristic of a person ("she's a natural-born leader"), and a category of behavior. From the standpoint of understanding the nature of people at work, perhaps the most useful approach is to consider leadership as a category of behavior, as something one person does to influence others.

Following this approach we will employ Katz and Kahn's (1978, p. 528) definition of *leadership* as "the influential increment over and above mechanical compliance with routine directives of the organization." Leadership occurs when one person can influence others to do something of their own volition instead of doing something because it is required or because they fear the consequences of noncompliance. It is this voluntary aspect of the response to leadership that sets it apart from other influence processes such as power or authority.

Functions of Leadership

One may well ask why leadership is necessary in contemporary work organizations. Most organizations are highly structured, have relatively clear lines of authority, stated objectives, and momentum to carry them forward. Why, then, do employees need leadership?

Four reasons, or functions of leadership, have been advanced by Katz and Kahn (1978). To begin, there is the incompleteness of organization design to take into account. Because it is not possible to design the perfect organization and account for every member's activities at all times, something must ensure that human behavior is coordinated and directed toward task accomplishment. This something is leadership. In addition, one must consider changing environmental conditions. Leadership helps maintain the stability of an organization in a turbulent environment by allowing for rapid adjustment and adaptation to changing environmental conditions. Third, there are internal dynamics of organizations, as well. Leadership can assist in the internal coordination of diverse organizational units, particularly during periods of growth and change. It can act as a buffer between conflicting parties. Finally, the nature of human membership in organizations must be recognized. Organizations consist of individuals who pursue various needs and make difficult demands. Leadership can play a major role in maintaining a stable work force by facilitating personal need satisfaction and personal goal attainment.

Leadership plays a crucial role in organizational dynamics. It fills many of the voids left by conventional organization design, allows for greater organizational flexibility and responsiveness to environmental changes, provides a way to coordinate the efforts of diverse groups within the organization, and facilitates organizational membership and personal need satisfaction. In short, it is the quality of managerial leadership that differentiates effective from ineffective organizations.

Leadership Patterns

In addition to a knowledge of the reasons leadership is necessary in work organizations, it is useful to understand basic differences in leadership patterns. How does the leadership role of top administrators and executives differ from the role of middle-level or lower-level managers and supervisors? This question has been answered by Katz and Kahn (1978), who suggest three different leadership patterns for three levels in the managerial hierarchy (see Exhibit 16.1).

The three basic types of leadership patterns are:

- *Origination,* or the introduction of structural change or policy formulation.
- *Interpolation,* or piecing out the incompleteness of existing formal structure and attempting to supplement or develop structure.
- *Administration,* or the use of the structure that is formally provided to keep the organization in motion and in effective operation.

The exercise of each of these three patterns of leadership calls for different cognitive styles, as well as different affective (or attitudinal) characteristics. Top-level executives concerned with origination need a system-wide

EXHIBIT 16.1 LEADERSHIP PATTERNS, THEIR LOCUS IN THE ORGANIZATION, AND THEIR SKILL REQUIREMENTS

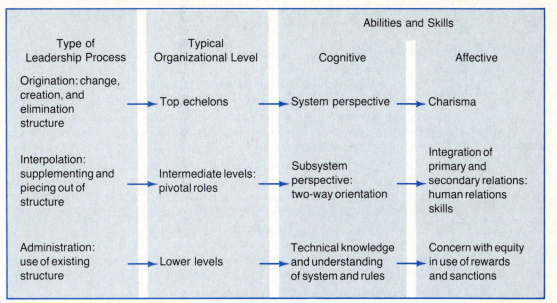

Type of Leadership Process	Typical Organizational Level	Abilities and Skills	
		Cognitive	Affective
Origination: change, creation, and elimination structure	→ Top echelons	→ System perspective	→ Charisma
Interpolation: supplementing and piecing out of structure	→ Intermediate levels: pivotal roles	→ Subsystem perspective: two-way orientation	→ Integration of primary and secondary relations: human relations skills
Administration: use of existing structure	→ Lower levels	→ Technical knowledge and understanding of system and rules	→ Concern with equity in use of rewards and sanctions

Source: D. Katz and R. Kahn, *The Social Psychology of Organizations,* 2nd ed. (New York: John Wiley & Sons, Inc., 1978), p. 539. Copyright © 1978 by John Wiley & Sons, Inc. Reprinted by permission of John Wiley & Sons, Inc.

perspective when making policy decisions. They are primarily concerned with goal formulation, strategic decision making, and buffering the effects of the external environment. Their concern must be almost exclusively "macro." The type of leadership they exhibit, as seen by the rank-and-file employee, is charismatic; they symbolize the organization and what it stands for.

Middle-level managers, on the other hand, are largely concerned with subsystem decisions. They are responsible for a department or a division and the people and activities contained therein. Their focus is shorter term than executives', although typically not directed at routine activities on the shop floor. Although human relations skills are clearly necessary, many interpersonal relations are impersonal and distant.

Finally, the lower-echelon managers or supervisors are primarily responsible for day-to-day operations in a single work group. Their technical knowledge of operations is important, as is their understanding of rules and policies made higher up in the hierarchy. These managers deal continually with the rewards and punishments that accrue to individual employees, and are responsible for ensuring that work is accomplished in a timely fashion.

Although this distinction among three levels of managers is somewhat arbitrary (and exceptions no doubt exist), the framework is useful in emphasizing the fact that all leaders do not do the same thing. Some leaders are almost the embodiment of the organization while others are simply people trying to work through people to get their group's performance goals accomplished. This distinction should be kept in mind as we examine the various contemporary models of leadership effectiveness.

Leader-Follower Transactions

It has been suggested that a solid understanding of the basic nature of leadership processes can be achieved by examining the *transactions* between leaders and followers (Hollander, 1978). Following this approach, effective leaders are those individuals who "give" something and who "get" something in return. In other words, leadership is viewed as a social exchange process.

This social exchange, or transactional, approach involves three basic variables: the leader, the followers, and the situation (see Exhibit 16.2). Leaders bring to a situation their personalities, motivations, competencies, and legitimacy, while followers bring their personalities, motivations, competencies, and expectations. Each situation has its own unique characteristics, including the availability of resources and nature of the tasks, social structure and rules, physical setting, and history. Where these three areas overlap, there exists what Hollander calls the *locus of leadership,* or that realm where leader and followers are bound together in a relationship within a situation. Leader and followers all contribute something to the relationship and each receives something in return. Neither is self-sufficient.

In view of this model, it becomes clear that in a systematic study of leadership processes in organizations we must examine all three variables: leaders, followers, and situations. Much of the current work on the topic attempts to do this. In examining this material, we will first review some of the basics; specifically, research that has been done on leader attributes and leader behavior. Following this, we will focus on several contemporary theories of leadership that attempt to account for the variables involved in the locus of leadership.

LEADER ATTRIBUTES AND BEHAVIOR

The earliest work on leadership, dating from ancient Greek times, assumed that great leaders were born to their greatness. This view, later termed *the great man* theory of leadership, took a historical approach and concluded that in most instances leaders were destined for positions of influence as a result of birth. This position was popular throughout the nineteenth century. In 1869, for example, Sir Francis Galton wrote a widely read book entitled *Hereditary Genius* in which he argued that leadership qualities were based on heredity. As we entered the twentieth century, belief in inherited leader traits diminished, although belief in the importance of the traits themselves remained popular.

EXHIBIT 16.2   THREE ELEMENTS INVOLVED IN LEADERSHIP

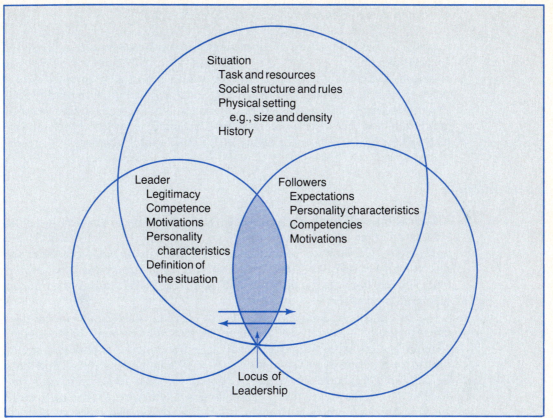

Source: Reprinted with permission of The Free Press, a Division of Macmillan, Inc., from *Leadership Dynamics* by Edwin P. Hollander, p. 8. Copyright © 1978 by The Free Press.

Leader Attributes

Much of the research in the first half of the twentieth century focused on attempts to identify the traits great leaders throughout history had in common. Ignoring the situation and followers, this research assumed that a person who exhibited these traits would be successful in leading any group. This research on leader attributes was brought together in a classic work by Ralph Stogdill in 1948.

Stogdill reviewed 124 empirical studies of leader attributes covering twenty-seven recurring characteristics. Among these studies, he discovered some consistencies. Successful leaders generally exhibited the following characteristics: (1) *height*—leaders tended to be taller than the average height of the followers; (2) *intelligence*—leaders tended to be rated higher on IQ tests, verbal fluency, overall knowledge, originality, and insight; and (3) *initiative*

—leaders tended to show high levels of energy, ambition, and persistence. Interestingly, no clear relationship was found between leader success and characteristics like emotional stability or extraversion.

In addition to the above attributes, Stogdill's review pointed to a conclusion that led the way to subsequent, more comprehensive research. He found that in many instances, the profile of a successful leader varied with the situation! Different groups and different group activities required different types of leaders. As a result of this finding, emphasis shifted in the early 1950s toward looking into how leaders interacted with groups under various conditions and how these interactions succeeded or failed. Much of this research focused on leader behavior as the basic unit of analysis.

Leader Behavior

Based on this early work, studies were begun in the 1950s to discover just what leaders did that caused others to follow. Two major research projects are noteworthy. The first was conducted at the University of Michigan under the direction of Rensis Likert and his associates, and the second was done at Ohio State University under the direction of Ralph Stogdill, Edwin Fleishman, John Hemphill, and others.

The results of both projects led to similar conclusions. Essentially, effective leader behavior was found to be multidimensional, implying that effective leaders exhibit different behavior in different situations. This multi-dimensional nature of leadership is clearly shown in the case of the Ohio State Leadership Studies, which began by identifying nine leader behaviors (see Exhibit 16.3). However, when these nine behaviors were examined more closely (through a procedure known as factor analysis), two relatively distinct behaviors emerged. These were:

- *Consideration,* including leader behaviors like helping subordinates, ie., doing favors for them, looking out for their welfare, and explaining things.
- *Initiating Structure,* including behaviors like getting subordinates to follow rules and procedures, maintaining performance standards, and making the leader and subordinate roles explicit.

Consideration has also been called by other terms, including socio-emotional activities and employee-centeredness, while initiating structure has been labeled instrumental activity, production centeredness, and task orientation.

In summarizing research on consideration (socio-emotional orientation) and initiating structure (task-orientation), House and Baetz (1979, p. 359) concluded:

1. Task-oriented leadership is necessary for effective performance in all working groups.
2. Acceptance of task-oriented leadership requires that the task-oriented leader

EXHIBIT 16.3   NINE DIMENSIONS OF LEADER BEHAVIOR

Initiation—originates, facilitates, or resists new ideas and new practices.

Membership—mixes with the group, stresses informal interaction between self and members, or interchanges personal services with members.

Representation—defends the group against attack, advances the interests of the group, and acts in behalf of the group.

Integration—subordinates individual behavior, encourages pleasant group atmosphere, reduces conflicts between members, or promotes individual adjustment to the group.

Organization—defines or structures own work, the work of other members, or the relationships among members in the performance of their work.

Domination—restricts the behavior of individuals or the group in action, decision making, or expression of opinion.

Communication—provides information to members, seeks information from them, facilitates exchange of information, or shows awareness of affairs pertaining to the group.

Recognition—engages in behavior which expresses approval or disapproval of group members' behavior.

Production—sets levels of effort or achievement or prods members for greater effort or achievement.

Source: Carroll L. Shartle, *Executive Performance and Leadership,* © 1956, renewed 1984, p. 116. Reprinted by permission of Prentice-Hall, Inc., Englewood Cliffs, New Jersey.

allows others to respond by giving feedback, making objections, and questioning the task-oriented leader.

3. Socio-emotionally oriented leadership is required in addition to task-oriented leadership when groups are not engaged in satisfying or ego-involving tasks.

4. Groups requiring both kinds of leadership behavior will be more effective when these leader behaviors are performed by one person rather than divided among two or more persons.

5. When the leadership roles are differentiated, groups will be most effective if those assuming the roles are mutually supportive and least effective when they are in conflict with each other.

6. When formally appointed leaders fail to perform the leader behaviors for group success, an informal leader will emerge and will perform the necessary leader behaviors, provided success is desired by the group members.

In other words, research on leader behaviors has demonstrated rather conclusively that *both* consideration and initiating structure are necessary (albeit at different times) for group effectiveness. If the manager cannot provide leadership in both these areas, the group will often find someone else who can, and will develop a surrogate leader to accommodate group needs.

The major drawback to these findings was the limited attention given to situations. While leader-follower interactions were rather carefully considered, little effort was made to examine how situational differences might influence leader effectiveness. This important variable was considered, however, in subsequent leadership research commencing in the 1960s and culminating with the publication of several contemporary theories of leadership. In contrast to earlier work on leader attributes or behaviors, these theories attempt to explain leadership dynamics within the context of the larger work situation.

Several such theories can be identified; however, major attention has focused on three. These are: (1) Fiedler's Contingency Theory; (2) Vroom and Yetton's Normative Theory; and (3) House's Path-Goal Theory. We now turn our attention to an examination of each of these models.

CONTINGENCY THEORY OF LEADERSHIP

Certainly one of the most popular contemporary theories is the *contingency theory,* advanced by Fred Fiedler (1967). Fiedler's model argues that group performance or effectiveness is dependent upon the interaction of leadership style and the favorableness of the situation. We shall examine each of these two factors separately and then put them together to consider how the theory works.

Situational Factors

Fiedler's model suggests that the situation in which the leader operates can be characterized by three factors:

- *Leader-member relations.* This refers to the degree of confidence, trust, and respect followers have for the leader. Is the leader accepted? Do leader and members get along well or poorly?
- *Task structure.* How clear are the task-goals and role assignments? Does everyone know precisely what to do (e.g., an assembly-line worker), or is the job more ambiguous (e.g., a research scientist)? The more task structure, the easier it is for the leader to tell group members what to do.
- *Position power.* Finally, who holds the power, the leader or the group? The more rewards and punishments leaders can use, the more influence they will have.

By differentiating these three dimensions, it is possible to develop a list of eight leadership situations (called octants). These eight situations are shown in Exhibit 16.4. In other words, leader-member relations can be either good (octants 1–4) or bad (octants 5–8); task structure can be high (octants 1, 2, 5, and 6) or low (octants 3, 4, 7, and 8); and leader position power can be strong (octants 1, 3, 5, and 7) or weak (octants 2, 4, 6, and 8). These octants contain all possible permutations or combinations of the three major situational variables.

EXHIBIT 16.4   FIEDLER'S CLASSIFICATION OF SITUATION FAVORABLENESS

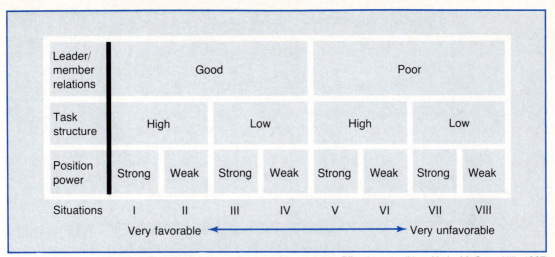

Source: Fred E. Fiedler, *A Theory of Leadership Effectiveness* (New York: McGraw-Hill, 1967). Reprinted by permission.

Once the situation is defined according to these three major situational variables, questions are raised about which octant or situation represents the most desirable from the leader's situation. Fiedler proposes that *situation favorableness* is highest (from the leader's viewpoint) in octant 1 and lowest in octant 8. A leader is in a far superior position when leader-member relations are good, when task structure is high, and when position power is strong (as in octant 1) than when the reverse is true (as in octant 8).

Leadership Orientation

The second key variable in this model is the leader. Fiedler suggests that two basic leader-orientations are useful, following earlier leadership research. These are relationship-oriented (a more lenient, people-oriented style) and task-oriented (where task accomplishment is a prominent concern).

These orientations are measured by the *least preferred co-worker* (LPC) scale. On this scale, the individual is asked to think of the person with whom he or she has worked who was least preferred as a co-worker, and to describe this person on several bipolar scales (efficient–inefficient, tense–relaxed, frustrating–helpful). (See Exercise 16.2.) A favorable description of the least preferred co-worker (high LPC) suggests a relationship-oriented leader, while an unfavorable description (low LPC) suggests a task-oriented leader.

Finally, combining leader LPC scores with situation favorableness, Fiedler examined the statistical correlations between LPC scores and group performance for each situational octant. As shown in Exhibit 16.5, negative correlations emerged at both ends of the situational continuum, while positive

EXHIBIT 16.5   RESULTS FROM CONTINGENCY THEORY RESEARCH

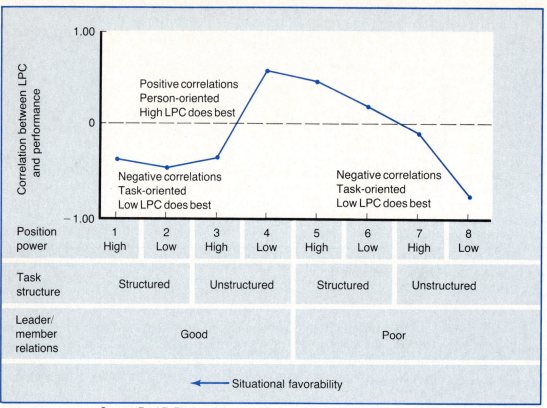

Source: Fred E. Fiedler, *Leadership* (Morristown, N.J.: General Learning Press, 1971). Reprinted by permission of the author.

correlations were found toward the middle of the continuum. It was concluded that high LPC (relationship-oriented) leaders were more effective in facilitating group performance when the situation was moderately favorable or moderately unfavorable (that is, toward the middle of the continuum). Here, the leader is moderately liked, has some power, and supervises jobs that are somewhat vague. A leader with high interpersonal skills can exert the necessary leadership in such situations to help clarify task ambiguity through discussions and participation.

On the other hand, when the situation is *either* highly unfavorable *or* highly favorable (that is, at either end of the continuum), Fiedler argues that a low LPC (task-oriented) leader is more effective in securing group performance (if not satisfaction). The logic of this argument is simple. If the situation is highly favorable (everyone gets along, the task is clear, and the leader has power), all that is needed is for someone to take charge and show direction (that is, a low LPC person). Similarly, if the situation is highly unfavorable (exhibiting the opposite characteristics), the leader is placed in a battle of wills with the group members. In this situation, Fiedler contends that a strong leader (low LPC) is necessary to counterbalance the power of the group and show direction in an ambiguous task environment. Since leader-member relations are already poor, being task-oriented in this situation does not run the risk of making the leader unpopular.

Research on the Contingency Model

During the past twenty-five years, Fiedler and his colleagues have carried out a series of studies on a variety of military and civilian samples. In general, consistent support has emerged for his hypothesis concerning the relationship between LPC and group performance for the various degrees of situation favorableness (see Exhibit 16.5). The results suggest that the model has some utility in helping managers understand leadership processes in organizations.

Even so, the model has also been criticized on several grounds (House and Baetz, 1979). In particular, critics have questioned the use of the LPC scale to measure leader orientation. It is argued that better and more reliable measures of leader orientation are needed. In addition, critics have suggested that Fiedler's classification system of situations is overly simplistic and that additional factors should be included in a more comprehensive description of situation favorableness or unfavorableness. While these criticisms may be justified, however, they do not diminish the utility of the basic model as a tool to help understand some of the variables that combine to influence leadership effectiveness in work organizations.

NORMATIVE THEORY OF LEADERSHIP

It is difficult to determine whether this next model is really a model of leadership or a model of decision making. In essence, the model focuses on the extent to which subordinates should be allowed to participate in decisions affecting their jobs. In addition, however, the model also considers how managers should behave in decision-making situations. Suffice it to say that the Vroom and Yetton (1973) model is a theory of how leaders should approach group-related decisions.

In contrast to Fiedler, Vroom and Yetton present a *normative theory of leadership.* It attempts to prescribe correct leader behavior by way of participation. The model rests on several assumptions, assuming (like Fiedler) that there is no single leadership style that is appropriate for all situations. Instead, leaders must develop a repertoire of responses ranging from autocratic to consultative and employ the style that is most appropriate to the decision situation. Unlike Fiedler, however, this model assumes that leaders must adapt their style to the situation. Fiedler, in contrast, argues that situations should be altered to match what he considers a fairly unalterable leader style.

Decision Effectiveness: Quality, Acceptance, and Timeliness

While Fiedler uses group performance as the evaluation criterion to determine whether or not a leader is effective, Vroom and Yetton use decision effectiveness. Decision effectiveness is characterized by three factors. *Decision quality* refers to the extent to which decisions under consideration are important for facilitating group performance. For instance, a decision on where to place a water cooler in a plant requires low decision quality since it has little impact on group performance, while a decision on performance goals or on work assignments requires high decision quality. *Decision acceptance* refers to how important it is for group members to accept decisions in order for them to be successfully implemented. Some decisions do not require group acceptance to be successfully executed (what color to paint the walls in an office), while others must be accepted by group members in order to be successful (setting sales performance objectives). *Time required to reach decision* is the third factor. Decisions must be made in a timely fashion. Some decisions can be made slowly (choice of color when repainting an office), while others may require immediate action (whether or not to invest in a particular stock).

This model suggests that a decision is effective to the extent that it satisfactorily accommodates these three factors. These criteria are in stark contrast to Fiedler—so much so that it has been suggested by some that the two models really examine different areas of leader behavior. While Vroom and Yetton consider how leaders make decisions, Fiedler examines how they achieve a satisfactory performance level in light of power considerations and co-worker relations.

Leader Decision-Making Styles

Based on the above definition of what constitutes an effective decision, the normative model next turns its attention to how leaders might behave relative to group members in order to arrive at these decisions. The model suggests that leaders have five decision-making styles open to them and that these five styles can be placed on a continuum from highly autocratic to highly participative. The five styles are shown in Exhibit 16.6. As shown, *A* represents a more autocratic style of leadership, *C* represents a more consultative style, and *G* represents a highly consultative or group decision.

Again, remember that one manager should be able to exhibit all five different styles, depending upon particular situations. The manager may be called upon to make an *A I* decision at one time, followed by a *G II* decision a short time later. Needless to say, this presumes the manager has the intuition to recognize the appropriate style for a given problem and the flexibility to implement that style.

EXHIBIT 16.6   FIVE DECISION STYLES

Decision Style	Definition
A I	Manager makes the decision alone.
A II	Manager asks for information from subordinates but makes the decision alone. Subordinates may or may not be informed about what the problem is.
C I	Manager shares the problems with subordinates and asks for information and evaluations. Meetings take place as dyads, not as a group, and the manager then goes off alone and makes the decision.
C II	Manager and subordinates meet as a group to discuss the problem, but the manager makes the decision.
G II	Manager and subordinates meet as a group to discuss the problem, and the group makes the decision.

Note: A = autocratic; *C* = consultative; *G* = group

Source: Reprinted from *Leadership and Decision-Making* by Victor H. Vroom and Philip W. Yetton by permission of the University of Pittsburgh Press. © 1973 by University of Pittsburgh Press.

Decision Rules of the Normative Model

In order to select the appropriate decision strategy, Vroom and Yetton have suggested seven decision rules aimed at simplifying the process. By following these rules, it is argued that managers can easily discover the quickest and most acceptable way to arrive at a quality decision. The first three rules focus on assuring decision quality, while the remaining four deal with decision acceptance.

- *The Leader Information Rule.* If the quality of the decision is important and if the leader does not have sufficient information or expertise to solve the problem alone, *A I* style is eliminated from the feasible set, since using it risks a low-quality decision.
- *The Goal Congruence Rule.* If the quality of the decision is important but the leader is not sure subordinates share the goals of the organization (that is, cannot be trusted to base their problem-solving efforts on these goals), then *G II* style is eliminated from the feasible set. In this case, the leader cannot afford to allow the group to make the decision alone.
- *The Unstructured Problem Rule.* If the quality of the decision is important but the leader lacks sufficient information and expertise *and* the problem is unstructured (that is, it is not clear exactly what information is needed or where it is located), then *A I, A II,* and *C I* are eliminated from the feasible set. In such cases, the ambiguity of the problem requires interaction between leader and subordinates to clarify the problem and possible solution.

- *The Acceptance Rule.* If acceptance of the decision by subordinates is crucial to effective implementation, and if it is not certain that an autocratic decision made by the leader would receive acceptance, then *A I* and *A II* are eliminated from the feasible set.
- *The Conflict Rule.* If acceptance of the decision is crucial, an autocratic decision is not certain to be accepted, *and* subordinates are likely to be in conflict or disagreement over the appropriate solution, then *A I, A II,* and *C I* are eliminated from the feasible set. Conflict is probably best resolved here by allowing greater participation and interchange among group members.
- *The Fairness Rule.* If the quality of the decision is *un*important but acceptance is critical and not certain to result from an autocratic decision, then *A I, A II, C I,* and *C II* are eliminated from the feasible set. Since group acceptance is the only relevant consideration, a *G II* style is likely to generate acceptance more effectively than less participative styles.
- *The Acceptance Priority Rule.* If acceptance is critical and not certain to result from an autocratic decision, and if subordinates are motivated to pursue organizational goals, then methods that provide equal partnership in the decision-making process will lead to greater acceptance without risking decision quality. Because of this, *A I, A II, C I,* and *C II* are eliminated from the feasible set.

Although these rules may seem imposing, careful reflection leads one to conclude that they are potentially of considerable heuristic value to managers. The rules serve to narrow the options open to managers and point to the most appropriate strategy, the right participation for a decision.

Vroom and Yetton (1973) have attempted to simplify the selection of an appropriate decision strategy for leaders. They suggest a decision tree that allows leaders to select a strategy by answering a series of questions relating to the decision rules. As shown in Exhibit 16.7, a manager begins at the left side of the flow chart with question A: does the problem possess a quality requirement? If the answer is yes, the manager then proceeds to question B. If the answer is no, the manager proceeds to question D, since questions B and C are irrelevant if quality is not a requirement. By working across the flow chart, the manager finally arrives at the strategies most appropriate for the particular situation. If a manager has a choice of acceptable strategies, it is recommended that the most autocratic within the feasible set be used, since this will save time, without reducing decision quality or acceptance. An example of this process is shown in Close-Up 16.1.

Research on the Normative Model

Because the normative model has only been recently introduced, verification research is still light. Vroom and Yetton (1973) carried out a study involving 181 actual decision situations, using the model to predict which decisions

EXHIBIT 16.7   **DECISION TREE FOR DETERMINING APPROPRIATE DECISION STRATEGY**

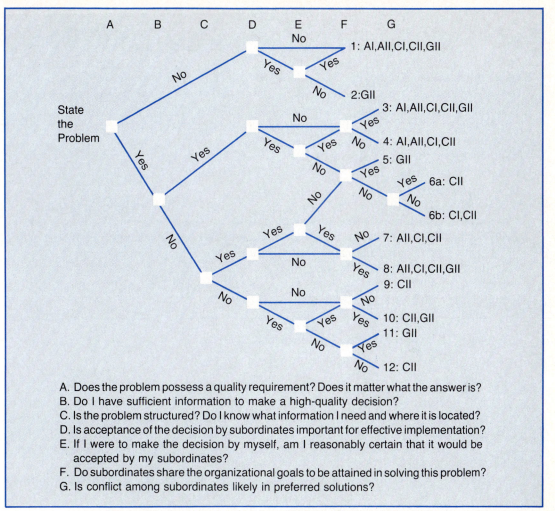

A. Does the problem possess a quality requirement? Does it matter what the answer is?
B. Do I have sufficient information to make a high-quality decision?
C. Is the problem structured? Do I know what information I need and where it is located?
D. Is acceptance of the decision by subordinates important for effective implementation?
E. If I were to make the decision by myself, am I reasonably certain that it would be accepted by my subordinates?
F. Do subordinates share the organizational goals to be attained in solving this problem?
G. Is conflict among subordinates likely in preferred solutions?

Source: Reprinted from *Leadership and Decision-Making* by Victor H. Vroom and Philip W. Yetton by permission of the University of Pittsburgh Press. © 1973 by University of Pittsburgh Press.

would be effective (that is, those in which the leader actually chose an acceptable style according to the model). Results were in support of the model. In the situations where leader behavior agreed with the feasible set of acceptable styles, sixty-eight percent were judged to have been successful. On the other hand, in those cases where leader behavior violated the feasible set of acceptable styles, only twenty-two percent were judged successful.

In other research, an attempt was made to consider how managers actually make decisions, instead of how they should make them according to the model. Several interesting results emerged. It was found that managers as a group tend to be more participative than is required by the model (Vroom and

CLOSE-UP 16.1 EXAMPLE OF VROOM AND YETTON MODEL

The following example demonstrates how the Vroom and Yetton model works. Consider yourself the supervisor of a group of twelve engineers. Their formal training and work experience are very similar, permitting you to use them interchangeably on projects. Today you were informed that an overseas affiliate had requested that four of your engineers be sent abroad for a period of from six to eight months to assist the affiliate. Your supervisor concurred with this request, even though such overseas assignments are not generally regarded as desirable by company engineers. Your job is to select the four persons who will go. All of your people are capable of handling the assignment and there is no reason why any particular engineer should be retained over others.

How would you make this decision? Would you make it yourself, consult with the group, or let the group itself make the decision? Using Vroom and Yetton's framework (Exhibit 16.7), we would proceed as follows:

Question A (Quality requirement?): No

Question D (Subordinate acceptance critical?): Yes

Question E (Is acceptance likely without participation?): No

Feasible set of decision procedures: *G II* (only)

Source: Based on Victor H. Vroom and Philip W. Yetton, *Leadership and Decision-Making* (Pittsburgh: University of Pittsburgh Press, 1973).

Jago, 1974). It has also been found that females tend to be more participative managers than males (Steers, 1977b). Finally, business school students were found to be more participative than actual managers (Jago and Vroom, 1978), and high-level managers were more participative than were low-level managers (Jago, 1977).

In summary, the normative model of leadership and decision making appears to represent a significant breakthrough both in terms of understanding how managers make decisions and in terms of training future managers to reach high-quality decisions in a timely fashion. Now we turn to a third theory of leadership that will further expand our knowledge of leadership processes in work organizations.

PATH-GOAL THEORY OF LEADERSHIP

In the third leadership model to be discussed, we approach the topic from quite a different perspective than the first two. Fiedler's (1967) contingency theory focuses on how leaders can best facilitate performance by manipulating power, leader-member relations, and task clarity or structuring, attempting to engineer the job to fit the manager. Vroom and Yetton's (1973) normative model focuses on how much participation leaders should allow subordinates in decisions relating to their jobs. In contrast, the *path-goal theory* emphasizes how leaders can facilitate task performance by showing subordinates how performance can be instrumental in achieving desired rewards. The path-goal model builds heavily on the expectancy/valence theory of work motivation.

The path-goal model of leadership can be traced to the work of Martin Evans (1970), and was developed more fully by Robert House (1971; House and Dessler, 1974; House and Baetz, 1979). Essentially, the model focuses on how managers influence subordinate perceptions of work, personal goals, and various paths to goal attainment. The basic emphasis is on the extent to which managerial behavior is motivating or satisfying for subordinates. It is argued that managerial behavior is motivating or satisfying to the extent that it increases goal attainment by subordinates and clarifies the paths to these goals.

Path-Goal Leader Behaviors

In the original model, Evans (1970, 1974) noted that leadership served two important functions. The first he called *path clarification*. This dealt with the extent to which the leader helps subordinates understand the kind of behavior necessary to accomplish goals and obtain valued rewards. The second function of the leader was to increase the *number of rewards* available to subordinates by being supportive and paying attention to their welfare, status, and comfort.

In expanding on Evans' original formulation, House (1971) argued that a comprehensive theory of leadership must recognize at least four distinctive types of leader behavior. They are:

- *Directive leadership.* Provides specific guidance, standards, and schedules of work, as well as rules and regulations; lets subordinates know what is expected of them.
- *Supportive leadership.* Shows concern for the status, well-being, and personal needs of subordinates; focuses on developing satisfactory interpersonal relations among group members.
- *Achievement-oriented leadership.* Sets challenging goals, emphasizes improvement in performance, and establishes high expectations of subordinates' ability to meet improved standards of excellence.
- *Participative leadership.* Consults with subordinates, solicits suggestions and advice in decision making.

In contrast to Fiedler, House (1971) asserts that these four styles can be practiced by the same manager at varying times and in varying situations. Fiedler, we remember, argues that managers can have considerable difficulty changing styles. House's model is similar to that of Vroom and Yetton, however, in that the latter also argue for changing leader behaviors.

Basic Propositions of Path-Goal Theory

The path-goal theory of leadership rests on two primary propositions:

- Leader behavior will be acceptable and satisfying when subordinates perceive it as an immediate source of satisfaction or as instrumental in future satisfaction.
- Leader behavior will be motivating to the extent that it makes subordinate satisfaction contingent upon effective performance *and* to the extent that it complements the subordinate's work environment by providing necessary guidance, clarity of direction, and rewards for effective performance.

Leaders have at their disposal a variety of mechanisms to facilitate increased subordinate motivation. Among these mechanisms are: (1) recognize and arouse subordinates' needs for outcomes over which leaders have some control; (2) increase personal payoffs to subordinates for effective performance or goal attainment; (3) clarify the path to those payoffs, through either coaching or additional direction; (4) help subordinates clarify expectancies; (5) reduce obstacles or frustrations that inhibit goal attainment; and (6) increase opportunities for personal satisfaction for effective performance. Leaders and managers have several available strategies for facilitating goal attainment by integrating employees' personal goals with organizational goals. When these two sets of goals are congruent, conflict is reduced and employees can pursue what they desire most by simultaneously pursuing managerial directives.

Contingency Factors

Like the two previous theories, the path-goal theory represents a situational model. It holds that effective leadership is a function of the interaction between leader behaviors and situational or contingency variables. In particular, House (see also House and Mitchell, 1974) identifies two basic contingency factors. These are shown in Exhibit 16.8 along with the other two factors, subordinate characteristics and environmental factors, involved in the theory.

Subordinate Characteristics. The personal characteristics of subordinates determine how they will react to leader behavior. Several personality characteristics have been found to be related to the way in which subordinates respond to influence attempts. The first of these is an individual's *authoritarianism.* High authoritarian subordinates tend to be less receptive to a participative style of leadership and more responsive to directive leadership (House and Baetz, 1979).

In addition, it has been discovered that an individual's *locus of control*

EXHIBIT 16.8   SUMMARY OF PATH-GOAL RELATIONSHIPS

Leader Behavior and	Contingency Factors	Cause	Subordinate Attitudes and Behavior
Directive	Subordinate characteristics: Authoritarianism	Personal perceptions	Job Satisfaction: Job → Rewards
Supportive	Locus of control Ability		Acceptance of leader: Leader → Rewards
Achievement-oriented	Environmental factors: The task	Motivational stimuli	Motivational behavior: Effort → Performance
Participative	Formal authority system	Constraints	Performance → Rewards
	Primary work group	Rewards	

Source: R. J. House and T. R. Mitchell, "Path-Goal Theory of Leadership," *Journal of Financial and Quantitative Analysis 5* (1974): 81–94. Reprinted by permission.

also affects responses. Individuals who have an internal locus of control (they believe rewards are contingent upon their own efforts) are generally more satisfied with a participative leadership style, while individuals who have an external locus of control (they believe rewards are beyond their own control) are generally more satisfied with a directive style (Runyon, 1973; Mitchell, Smyser, and Weed, 1974).

Finally, individuals' own *abilities* can influence how they respond to different leadership styles. Where individuals feel they have high levels of task-related abilities, we do not expect them to be receptive to a close or directive leadership style (House and Baetz, 1979). Instead, these individuals may prefer a more challenging achievement-oriented style.

Environmental Factors. In addition to subordinate characteristics, the path-goal model suggests that at least three environmental factors moderate the impact of leader style on outcomes (see Exhibit 16.8). These factors are: (1) the nature of the *task* performed by subordinates; (2) the *formal authority system* of the organization; and (3) the *primary work group*.

These factors can influence an individual's response to leader behavior in a variety of ways. They may *motivate* individuals, such as when a person performs an intrinsically satisfying job. Or, they may *constrain* variability on the job, such as on an assembly line where behavior is prescribed by technology. Finally, they may clarify and provide *rewards* for satisfactory performance. For instance, group members may give praise to individuals who did most to help the group achieve its performance objectives. As House and Dessler (1974, p. 40) point out, "when goals, and paths to desired goals, are apparent because of the routine nature of the task, clear group norms, or objective controls of the formal authority system, attempts by the leader to clarify paths and goals would be redundant and would be seen by subordinates as an imposition of unnecessarily close control."

Subordinate Attitudes and Behavior

Finally, what is the outcome of this interaction between leader behavior and contingency factors? According to the model, three possible outcomes exist. First, individual perceptions, which are influenced by subordinate characteristics, can lead an employee to determine that the job itself can indeed lead to the receipt of rewards; hence, *job satisfaction* may be increased. Personal perceptions can also lead employees to conclude that the leader does, in fact, control many of the desired rewards; hence, *leader acceptance* may be increased. Finally, the motivational stimuli, constraints, and potential rewards can serve to heighten *motivational behavior*. They can increase an employee's expectations that effort will lead to rewards. The model leads to very specific outcomes that are useful if not imperative in the pursuit of organizational effectiveness.

Research on the Path-Goal Model

To date, little substantive work has been done to test the basic tenets of the path-goal theory of leadership. The research that is available is often clouded by methodological problems brought on by the complicated nature of the theory itself.

Even so, the studies that are available lend some credence to the model (Downey, Sheridan, and Slocum, 1976; Dessler and Valenzi, 1977). These studies have suggested that the model is probably more complex than first thought and that additional variables, like conflict and structure, should be incorporated into future versions of the model.

COMPARING THE THREE LEADERSHIP MODELS

We have now examined three quite different ways of approaching the study of leadership dynamics in groups and organizations. How are these models similar and different and what can be learned from a comparative analysis of them?

The distinctiveness of orientations of the three models can be seen in Exhibit 16.9. Fiedler's model is based on leader style (high versus low LPC) and how this style interacts with group power and the nature of the task. Vroom and Yetton focus on decision-making processes and the role of leaders in facilitating participation in decisions. Finally, House clearly rests his model on the motivational bases of organizational behavior.

All three models use somewhat different outcome criteria for evaluating the extent to which influence attempts are successful. Fiedler emphasizes

EXHIBIT 16.9 A COMPARISON OF ELEMENTS IN THREE SITUATIONAL THEORIES OF LEADERSHIP

Model	Leader Behavior	Contingency Factors	Outcome Criteria
Fiedler's LPC	Task-oriented (Low LPC) Relationship-oriented (High LPC)	Leader-member relations Task structure Leader position power	Group effectiveness
Vroom and Yetton's Decision Making	Autocratic, Consultative Group style	Importance of decision quality Degree needed information is available to leader and followers Problem structure Followers' probable acceptance and motivation regarding decision Disagreement among followers about preferred solutions	Quality of decision Acceptance of decision by flowers Time required to reach decision
House's Path-Goal	Directive Supportive Achievement-oriented Participative style	Subordinate characteristics and personal perceptions Environmental factors: task, authority system, primary work group	Follower satisfaction Acceptance of leader Effort to gain rewards

Source: Reprinted with permission of The Free Press, a Division of Macmillan, Inc., from *Leadership Dynamics* by Edwin P. Hollander. Copyright © 1978 by The Free Press.

group performance, Vroom and Yetton focus on decision quality, acceptance, and timeliness, and House focuses on follower satisfaction, leader acceptance, and motivational force aimed at achieving desired rewards.

Finally, each model differs with respect to the contingency factors that are thought to be at work in determining successful influence attempts. These differences are summarized in Exhibit 16.9. What this exhibit shows is not that one theory is superior to the others, but rather that each model focuses on a different aspect of the leadership process. Managers can learn much from each theory.

This accumulation of knowledge about leadership processes should help managers to better understand leadership in broad terms and to employ the model that best suits the particular situation or problem. That is, if a decision must be made dealing with some aspect of group behavior, Vroom and Yetton's normative model may be most suitable. On the other hand, if the problem is one of facilitating performance, the other two models may be of more use. In any case, a thorough knowledge of the models can improve a manager's ability to understand the options open and to make an informed choice about the way in which a problem or situation is approached.

PROBLEMS AND PROSPECTS OF LEADERSHIP AT WORK

Up to this point, we have assumed that leaders were relatively free to act on their environment and that they behaved according to theory with few constraints. Obviously, this is not always the case. There are many factors that inhibit leader behavior. We now turn our attention to these problems in the leadership process, as well as what managers can do to minimize them.

Constraints on Leadership

An important part of knowing how leadership processes work is recognizing occasions when they may not work, or when they have a diminished impact on employee behavior. If we view leadership as a central process in facilitating group performance and effectiveness, then constraints on the process must be clearly recognized. At least six constraints on leadership effectiveness have been suggested (Steers, 1977c):

- Extent to which managerial decisions and behavior are preprogrammed due to precedent, structure, technological specificity, or the absence of familiarity with available alternative solutions.
- Traits and skills (particularly leadership skills) of the manager. Research has indicated, for instance, that effective leaders tend to exhibit specific personal attributes. Good leaders demonstrate expertise in their own area of endeavor (such as the foreman who can perform any departmental job). A lack of skills may preclude effective leader behavior to some extent.
- Inability of leaders to vary their behavior to suit the particular situation. Rigid patterns of behavior may be inappropriate for many situations requiring certain styles of leadership.
- Extent to which a leader controls rewards desired by subordinates, such as pay raises and promotions.
- Characteristics of the situation, such as how much power a leader has, the importance of a given decision or action, and the quality of interpersonal relations between leader and subordinate.
- Openness of the organization to variations in leader behavior (e.g., a participative leadership style may be discouraged or prohibited in a military organization).

These constraints to a large extent set the stage on which influence attempts transpire. The greater the skills and abilities of the leader or manager, the more easily constraints can be handled. To the extent these constraints are recognized and accounted for, the leader can use available latitude to best advantage in securing the support of subordinates for task accomplishment.

Substitutes for Leadership

Partially because of the modest support that contemporary leadership theories have received and because of the recognition of constraints on leader behavior, recent attention to influence processes has taken note of what has been called *substitutes for leadership.* As argued by Kerr and Jermier (1978, p. 375):

> While disagreeing with one another in important respects, these theories and models (of leadership) share an implicit assumption that while the style of leadership likely to be effective may vary according to the situation, *some* leadership style will be effective *regardless* of the situation. It has been found, however, that certain individual, task, and organizational variables act as "substitutes for leadership," negating the hierarchical superior's ability to exert either positive or negative influence over subordinate attitudes and effectiveness.

In other words, there are factors in the environment that act as a structure of support for subordinates, and leader behavior is at times irrelevant to subordinate performance or satisfaction. A list of possible substitutes is outlined in Exhibit 16.10. This exhibit differentiates between relationship-oriented and task-oriented leader behavior, since this distinction is common in the literature on leadership. For each leader behavior, Kerr and Jermier (1978) identify which substitutes (of the subordinate, the task, or the organization) serve to neutralize which behavior.

The point here is that there are many ways managers—and subordinates—can get something done. Only one of these is through the exercise of leadership. Other ways include making use of the personal characteristics of individuals (ability or experience), structuring tasks, or relying on the structure of the organization itself. The existence of these substitutes adds a note of realism to our study of influence processes and cautions against the naive belief that leader behavior alone will have a great impact on subordinate performance.

Improving Leadership Effectiveness

Although leader behavior may not be a panacea for all performance ills of organizations, there are many instances in which leaders can make a real difference. It is important to understand how managers can develop leadership talent so that such talents can be put to use in facilitating organizational effectiveness. Many techniques could be suggested here. However, for the sake of brevity, we shall mention only five general strategies for improving leadership effectiveness (Steers, 1977c). These are (1) managerial selection and placement; (2) leadership training; (3) rewarding leader behavior; (4) reward-

EXHIBIT 16.10 SUBSTITUTES FOR LEADERSHIP

Characteristics	Substitutes for Leadership Will Tend To Neutralize	
	Relationship-oriented, Supportive, People-centered Leadership: Consideration, Support, and Interaction Facilitation	Task-oriented, Instrumental, Job-centered Leadership: Initiating Structure, Goal Emphasis, and Work Facilitation
Of the Subordinate		
1. Ability, experience, training, knowledge		X
2. Need for independence	X	X
3. "Professional" orientation	X	X
4. Indifference toward organizational rewards	X	X
Of the Task		
5. Unambiguous and routine		X
6. Methodologically invariant		X
7. Provides its own feedback concerning accomplishment		X
8. Intrinsically satisfying	X	
Of the Organization		
9. Formatization (explicit plans, goals, and areas of responsibility)		X
10. Inflexibility (rigid, unbending rules and procedures)		X
11. Highly-specified and active advisory and staff functions		X
12. Closely-knit, cohesive work groups	X	X
13. Organizational rewards not within the leader's control	X	X
14. Spatial distance between superior and subordinates	X	X

Source: S. Kerr and J. Jermier, "Substitutes for Leadership: Their Meaning and Measurement," *Organizational Behavior and Human Performance* 22 (1978): 378. Reprinted by permission.

ing subordinate behavior; and (5) organizational engineering. As we shall see, many of these suggestions have their roots in the leadership theories discussed above.

Managerial Selection and Placement. Improved leadership effectiveness can be facilitated by increasing the likelihood that those in command possess the necessary skills to influence their subordinates on task-related activities. Following Fiedler's model, for example, we might wish to select a task-oriented (low LPC) person to supervise a work group characterized by high task structuring, centralized power, and distant leader-member relations. On the other hand, a relationship-oriented (high LPC) leader may be more appropriate when the task structuring is less concrete, power is diffused, and leader-member relations are cordial but not overly warm. The notion of matching people to leadership roles contradicts the current practice in many organizations of promoting employees to supervisory positions based on seniority or even based on good job performance. Although good job performance may be a desirable trait for supervisors to possess, it does not by itself ensure good supervisory skills.

Leadership Training. Attempts can also be made to develop individuals already in leadership positions to their fullest potential as managers through a variety of training techniques (Bass and Vaughn, 1966; Goldstein, 1975, 1980). Training can take many forms, including general management skills programs, human relations training, problem-solving and decision-making programs, and a variety of specialized programs.

Rewarding Leader Behavior. A third method of improving leadership effectiveness involves designing reward systems so desired leader behavior is amply rewarded. If pay and promotions are based on a manager's ability to elicit successful subordinate efforts on goal-directed activities, then managers will see effective leader behavior as instrumental in obtaining desired rewards. A performance-reward contingency should serve to make managers more aware of the role of leadership in task accomplishment, making them more likely to attempt to improve their capacity for leadership activity.

Rewarding Subordinate Behavior. In addition, it is also possible to structure reward systems to stimulate rather than inhibit desired subordinate behavior. By giving managers greater discretion in rewarding subordinates, the probability that subordinates will follow managerial directives is increased since this behavior would be instrumental to their own personal goal attainment. House's path-goal theory is essentially based on this relationship: to the extent that subordinates see following a manager's directives as instrumental to the accomplishment of their own goals, they will be more likely to follow them.

Organizational Engineering. Finally, in some instances, it is more suitable to adopt a structural (as opposed to a behavioral) approach to improving leader effectiveness. Here, one attempts to modify either the manager's job or the way jobs are clustered (reporting procedures, lines of authority, decentralization) and allow the structure itself to facilitate task accomplishment. In other words, as Fiedler (1965, p. 115) describes it, organizations may wish to "engineer the job to fit the manager." This approach is particularly useful when a specific individual (e.g., an R&D scientist) is necessary to the organization, yet does not possess the requisite interpersonal skills for leadership. In these cases, the job can be engineered around the individual so many necessary leadership roles are fulfilled by other means.

SUMMARY

Clearly, one of the most popular and important topics in organizational behavior is leadership. This concept is also one of the least understood and most controversial. Despite several decades of serious attention, there is little agreement over what is meant by leadership or how it is brought about.

In this chapter, we considered this controversy, beginning with a discussion on the nature of leadership. The functions of leadership were examined, along with variations in leadership patterns. In addition, leader attributes and behaviors were discussed using the concept of leader-member transactions.

Next, three divergent theories of leadership were presented, along with their empirical support and their managerial implications. Finally, on a more general level, consideration was given to constraints on leader behavior and to possible substitutes for leadership. This was followed by an examination of various techniques managers can use to improve leader effectiveness on the job.

KEY WORDS

consideration
contingency theory
initiating structure
leadership
least preferred co-worker
locus of leadership
normative theory

organizational
  engineering
path clarification
path-goal theory
situation favorableness
substitutes for leadership

FOR DISCUSSION

1. What is meant by the term *leadership?* the term *manager?*
2. What functions do leaders serve?
3. Describe the leader-follower transactional process. What role does the locus of leadership play in this process?
4. What are some rather generalizable leader traits?
5. What major conclusion can be drawn from the research on consideration and initiating structure?
6. What is the basic thesis of Fiedler's contingency theory of leadership? How does it differ from the other two theories of leadership discussed in this chapter?
7. What is the least preferred co-worker?
8. Why is Vroom and Yetton's model called the normative theory of leadership? What is really new about this model?

9. Discuss the decision rules of the normative model.
10. What different implications for management follow from the three models of leadership? What similar implications for management follow?
11. Describe several constraints on leader behavior.
12. What is meant by substitutes for leadership?
13. How can managers improve their leadership effectiveness?

LEADERSHIP AND PARTICIPATION IN DECISION MAKING

16.1

Purpose

This exercise allows you to examine in some detail how Vroom and Yetton's normative theory of leadership works. Actual practice is provided using the basic framework of the model.

Instructions

Below are three short cases in which a manager must make a decision. Based on these three cases, you should make two sets of decisions. First, on your own, read each case and state whether you would make the decision by yourself; consult with your subordinates and then make the decision; or let the group of subordinates make the decision. Remember, you are the supervisor and your job is to state how you would arrive at the decision. You are not asked to actually make the decision.

Second, review Vroom and Yetton's normative theory of leadership, as presented in this chapter, and read through the cases again. This time, however, you are asked to use the decision tree in Exhibit 16.7 to assist you in identifying a decision style. Following this, compare the results of your first decisions with those of your second. What do you think accounts for the difference?

Case I

You are a manufacturing manager in a large electronics plant. The company's management has recently installed new machines and put in a new simplified work system, but to the surprise of everyone, yourself included, the expected increase in productivity was not realized. In fact, production has begun to drop, quality has fallen off, and the number of employee separations has risen.

You do not believe that there is anything wrong with the machines. You have had reports from other companies that are using them and they confirm this opinion. You have also had representatives from the firm that built the machines go over them and they report that they are operating at peak efficiency.

You suspect that some parts of the new work system may be responsible for the change, but this view is not widely shared among your immediate subordinates who are four first-line supervisors, each in charge of a section, and your supply manager. The drop in production has been variously attributed to poor training of the operators, lack of an adequate system of financial incentives, and poor morale. Clearly, this is an issue

about which there is considerable depth of feeling within individuals and potential disagreement among your subordinates.

This morning you received a phone call from your division manager. He has just received your production figures for the last six months and was calling to express his concern. He indicated that the problem was yours to solve in any way that you think best, but that he would like to know within a week what steps you plan to take.

You share your division manager's concern with the falling productivity and know that your workers are also concerned. The problem is to decide what steps to take to rectify the situation.

Case II

You are general foreman in charge of a large gang laying an oil pipeline and have to estimate your expected rate of progress in order to schedule material deliveries to the next field site.

You know the nature of the terrain you will be working across and have the historical data needed to compute the mean and variance in the rate of speed over that type of terrain. Given these two variables, it is a simple matter to calculate the earliest and latest times at which materials and support facilities will be needed at the next site. It is important that your estimate be reasonably accurate. Underestimates result in idle foremen and workers, and an overestimate results in tying up materials for a period of time before they are to be used.

Progress has been good, and your five foremen and other members of the gang stand to receive substantial bonuses if the project is completed ahead of schedule.

Case III

You are on the division manager's staff and work on a wide variety of problems of both an administrative and technical nature. You have been given the assignment of developing a standard method to be used in each of the five plants in the division for manually reading equipment registers, recording the readings, and transmitting the scorings to a centralized information system.

Until now there has been a high error rate in the reading and/or reporting of data. Some locations have considerably higher error rates than others, and the methods used to record and transmit the data vary among plants. It is probable, therefore, that part of the error variance is a function of specific local conditions rather than anything else, and this will complicate the establishment of any system common to all plants. You have the information on error rates but no information on the local practices that generate these errors or on the local conditions that necessitate the different practices.

Everyone would benefit from an improvement in the quality of the data; the data is used in a number of important decisions. Your contacts with the plants are through the quality-control supervisors who are responsible for collecting the data. They are a conscientious group committed to doing their jobs well, but they are highly sensitive to interference on the part of higher management in their own operations. Any solution that does not receive the active support of the various plant supervisors is unlikely to reduce the error rate significantly.

Source: Cases reprinted from *Leadership and Decision-Making* by Victor H. Vroom and Philip W. Yetton by permission of the University of Pittsburgh Press. © 1973 by University of Pittsburgh Press.

LEAST PREFERRED CO-WORKER (LPC) SCALE

Purpose

This instrument was designed by Fred Fiedler to measure your LPC score as described in the contingency theory of leadership.

Instructions

Think of the person with whom you work least well. He or she may be someone you work with now, or may be someone you knew in the past. He or she does not have to be the person you like least well, but should be the person with whom you now have or have had the most difficulty in getting a job done. Describe this person as he or she appears to you by circling the number between each pair of adjectives that you believe best describes that person. Do this for each pair of adjectives. Then transfer the numbers to the spaces provided at the right. Add up the numbers in this column and write the value in the box marked "LPC Score." Your instructor will then explain the meaning of your score.

	LPC Scale (Circle One Number for Each Line)		Transfer the Numbers to These Spaces
Pleasant	: 8 : 7 : 6 : 5 : 4 : 3 : 2 : 1 :	Unpleasant	_____
Friendly	: 8 : 7 : 6 : 5 : 4 : 3 : 2 : 1 :	Unfriendly	_____
Rejecting	: 1 : 2 : 3 : 4 : 5 : 6 : 7 : 8 :	Accepting	_____
Helpful	: 8 : 7 : 6 : 5 : 4 : 3 : 2 : 1 :	Frustrating	_____
Unenthusiastic	: 1 : 2 : 3 : 4 : 5 : 6 : 7 : 8 :	Enthusiastic	_____
Tense	: 1 : 2 : 3 : 4 : 5 : 6 : 7 : 8 :	Relaxed	_____
Distant	: 1 : 2 : 3 : 4 : 5 : 6 : 7 : 8 :	Close	_____
Cold	: 1 : 2 : 3 : 4 : 5 : 6 : 7 : 8 :	Warm	_____
Cooperative	: 8 : 7 : 6 : 5 : 4 : 3 : 2 : 1 :	Uncooperative	_____
Supportive	: 8 : 7 : 6 : 5 : 4 : 3 : 2 : 1 :	Hostile	_____
Boring	: 1 : 2 : 3 : 4 : 5 : 6 : 7 : 8 :	Interesting	_____
Quarrelsome	: 1 : 2 : 3 : 4 : 5 : 6 : 7 : 8 :	Harmonious	_____
Self-Assured	: 8 : 7 : 6 : 5 : 4 : 3 : 2 : 1 :	Hesitant	_____
Efficient	: 8 : 7 : 6 : 5 : 4 : 3 : 2 : 1 :	Inefficient	_____
Gloomy	: 1 : 2 : 3 : 4 : 5 : 6 : 7 : 8 :	Cheerful	_____
Open	: 8 : 7 : 6 : 5 : 4 : 3 : 2 : 1 :	Guarded	_____
		Total LPC Score =	_____

Source: Fred E. Fiedler, *A Theory of Leadership Effectiveness* (New York: McGraw-Hill, 1967). Reprinted by permission.

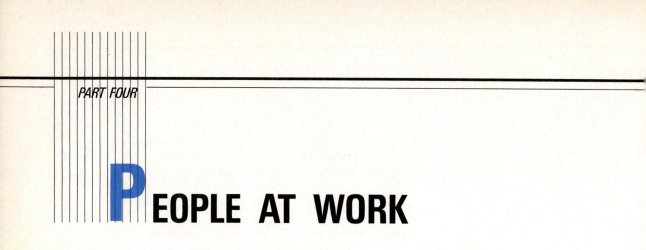

PART FOUR

PEOPLE AT WORK

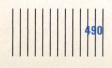

WORK AND STRESS

Almost every day, the news carries a tale of blue-collar blues or white-collar woes. Soaring costs, depressed sales figures, inflation, wage and hiring freezes, product recalls, bankruptcy, and layoffs all contribute to the stressful environment in organizations of the eighties. Workers of all ages, occupations, and backgrounds are often discontented and suffer from various maladies of the work place.

From a corporate standpoint, these woes translate into considerable losses in both human and financial terms. Consider the following cases (King, 1985):

- An employee at Raytheon Company with 22 years seniority suffered a nervous breakdown when told she would be transferred to another department. The Massachusetts Supreme Judicial Court ruled that she was entitled to worker's compensation benefits since her breakdown was a "personal injury arising out of and in the course of . . . employment."
- In Louisville, a white sanitation supervisor blamed his depressions on the stress of being forced to work with blacks. The Kentucky Workers' Compensation Board awarded him maximum benefits and ordered the city to return him to an all-white job setting.
- In Oregon, a deputy sheriff blamed his depression on the belief that his supervisor was persecuting him. The Oregon Supreme Court upheld his claim for worker's compensation benefits.

In California alone, the number of mental stress injuries reported to the Workers' Compensation Board has more than tripled in the last five years. Throughout the United States, it is estimated that companies spend $18 billion yearly on these claims alone. Clearly, work-related stress is a problem for companies as well as individuals.

IMPORTANCE OF TOPIC FOR MANAGERS

An understanding of work adjustment and job-related stress is important to managers. Prolonged stress has been shown to have deleterious physical and psychological side effects on individuals. Thus, employee health, as well as employee contribution to the organization, is jeopardized. Studies show that these effects are particularly pronounced in managerial personnel.

Stress is a major cause of employee turnover and absenteeism, inhibiting the effectiveness of an organization. And stress experienced by one employee can jeopardize the safety of others. This is clearly seen in the air traffic controllers' and machine operators' jobs.

In recent years we have gained sufficient knowledge concerning stress and work adjustment to see that much of the stress experienced at work is needless. Reducing stress can improve an employee's contribution to an organization. In addition, lowering stress levels can increase satisfaction with the job itself.

PROBLEMS OF WORK ADJUSTMENT

Failure to adjust to work represents a major problem in industry today. It has been estimated that between eighty and ninety percent of industrial accidents are caused by personal factors (Yolles, 1967). Turnover, absenteeism, drug abuse, alcoholism, and sabotage remain relatively permanent fixtures of most contemporary work organizations. To the extent that individuals are unable to adjust to work, we would expect them to persist in counterproductive behavior.

In a study of why people have problems adjusting to work, Neff (1968) identified five major reasons. Following type theory of personality, he suggests that each of the five types represents a "clinical picture of different varieties of work psychopathology" (p. 208):

Type I: People who lack motivation to work. These individuals have a negative conception of the work role and choose to avoid it.

Type II: People whose predominating response to the demand to be productive is fear or anxiety.

Type III: People who are characterized predominantly by open hostility and aggression.

Type IV: People who are characterized by marked dependency. These people often exhibit the characteristic of helplessness, constantly seeking advice from others, and are unable to initiate any action on their own.

Type V: People who display a marked degree of social naiveté. These individuals lack perception when it comes to the needs and feelings of others and may not realize that their behavior elicits reactions from and has an effect on others. Typically, these individuals are socially inept and unaware of appropriate behavior in ordinary social situations.

Several important points follow from Neff's analysis. First, note that failure to adjust to a normal job or work schedule does not automatically imply that an individual is lazy or stupid. Several deeply ingrained psychological problems keep people from making normal adjustment in many cases.

Second, note that only one of the five types (Type I) represents a motivational problem. Managers must look beyond motivation for answers to the psychopathology of work. Third, one type (Type V) represents a form of personality disorder, or at least social immaturity.

The remaining three types—anxiety, aggression, and dependency —relate not only to personality, but more importantly to how the nature of the job affects that personality. In fact, anxiety, aggression, and dependency are major factors inherent in stressful jobs in organizations. Hence, it seems that at least three of the five reasons for failure to adjust to work relate to the extent to which the job is experienced as stressful and causes the individual to want to withdraw.

It has been wisely observed, "If, under stress, a man goes all to pieces, he will probably be told to pull himself together. It would be more effective to help him identify the pieces and to understand why they have come apart" (Ruddock, 1972, p. 94). This is the role of the contemporary manager in dealing with stress. Managers cannot simply ignore the existence of stress on the job. Instead, they have a responsibility to understand stress and its causes.

We will explore the somewhat ambiguous topic of work-related stress in several stages, first examining major organizational and personal influences on stress, then considering several outcomes of stress, and finally exploring methods for coping with stress on the job. Throughout, emphasis will be placed on how stress and its consequences affect people at work and what role managers can play in attempting to minimize the effects of stress on both the individual and the organization. (See Cooper and Payne [1978] for an in-depth discussion of research relating to stress at work.)

THE NATURE OF WORK-RELATED STRESS

Stress refers to the reaction of individuals to characteristics of the environment that pose a threat. It points to a poor fit between individuals and an environment in which either excessive demands are being made or individuals are ill-equipped to handle a given situation (French, 1976). Under stress, individuals are unable to respond to environmental stimuli without undue psychological and/or physiological damage such as chronic fatigue, tension, or high blood pressure. This damage resulting from experienced stress is usually referred to as *strain*.

Before examining the concept of work-related stress in detail, several important points need to be made. First, stress is pervasive in the work environment (McGrath, 1976). Most of us experience stress at some time. For instance, a job may require too much or too little from us. In fact, almost any aspect of the work environment is capable of producing stress. Stress can result from excessive noise, light, or heat; too much or too little responsibility; too much or too little work to accomplish; or too much or too little supervision.

Second, it is important to note that all people do not react in the same way to stressful situations, even in the same occupation. One individual (a high need achiever) may thrive on a certain amount of job-related tension; this tension may serve to activate the achievement motive. A second individual may respond to this tension by worrying about his or her inability to cope with the situation. Managers must recognize the central role of individual differences in the determination of experienced stress.

Third, all stress is not necessarily bad. Although highly stressful situations invariably have dysfunctional consequences, moderate levels of stress often serve useful purposes. A moderate amount of job-related tension not only keeps us alert to environmental stimuli (possible dangers and opportunities), but in addition often provides a useful motivational function. Some experts argue that the best and most satisfying work that employees do is work performed under moderate stress. Some stress may be necessary for psychological growth, creative activities, and the acquisition of new skills. Learning to drive a car or play a piano or run a particular machine typically creates tension that is instrumental in skill development. It is only when the level of stress increases or when it is prolonged that physical or psychological problems emerge.

General Adaptation Syndrome

The general response to stressful events is believed to follow a fairly consistent pattern known as the *General Adaptation Syndrome* (Selye, 1956). This syndrome consists of three stages. The first stage, *alarm,* occurs at the first sign of stress. Here the body prepares to fight stress by releasing hormones from the endocrine glands. During this initial stage, heartbeat and respiration increase, blood-sugar level rises, muscles tense up, pupils dilate, and digestion slows. Following this initial shock, the body moves into the second stage, *resistance.* The body attempts to repair any damage and return to a condition of homeostasis. If successful, physical signs of stress will disappear. If the stress continues long enough, however, the body's capacity for adaptation becomes exhausted. In this third stage, *exhaustion,* defenses wear away and the individual experiences a variety of stress-related illnesses, including headaches, ulcers, and high blood pressure. This third stage is the most severe, and presents the greatest threat both to individuals and to organizations.

Types of Stress: Frustration and Anxiety

There are several different ways to categorize stress. However, from a managerial perspective, it is useful to focus on only two forms: frustration and anxiety. *Frustration* refers to an obstruction or impediment to goal-oriented behavior. Frustration occurs when an individual wishes to pursue a certain course of action but is prevented from doing so. This obstruction may be externally or internally caused. Examples of frustration include a salesperson who continually fails to make a sale, a machine operator who cannot keep pace with the machine, or even an inability to get back correct change from a coffee machine. The prevalence of frustration in work organizations should be obvious from this and other examples.

Whereas frustration is an obstruction in instrumental activities or behavior, *anxiety* is a feeling of inability to deal with anticipated harm. Anxiety occurs when people do not have appropriate responses or plans for coping with anticipated problems. It is characterized by a sense of dread, a foreboding, and a persistent apprehension of the future for reasons that are sometimes unknown to the individual.

What causes anxiety in work or organizations? Hamner and Organ (1978, p. 202) suggest several factors:

Differences in power in organizations which leave people with a feeling of vulnerability to administrative decisions adversely affecting them; frequent changes in organizations, which make existing behavior plans obsolete; competition, which creates the inevitability that some persons lose "face," esteem, and status; and job ambiguity (especially when it is coupled with pressure). To these may be added some related factors, such as lack of job feedback, volatility in the organization's economic environment, job insecurity, and big visibility of one's performance (successes as well as failures). Obviously, personal, nonorganizational factors come into play as well, such as physical illness, problems at home,

EXHIBIT 17.1   MAJOR INFLUENCES ON WORK-RELATED STRESS

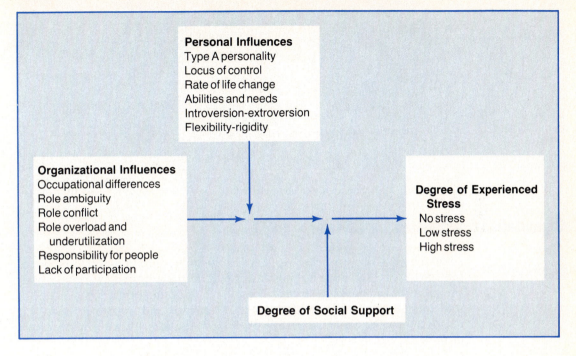

Personal Influences
Type A personality
Locus of control
Rate of life change
Abilities and needs
Introversion-extroversion
Flexibility-rigidity

Organizational Influences
Occupational differences
Role ambiguity
Role conflict
Role overload and
    underutilization
Responsibility for people
Lack of participation

**Degree of Experienced
    Stress**
No stress
Low stress
High stress

Degree of Social Support

unrealistically high personal goals, and estrangement from one's colleagues or one's peer group.

We will consider in more detail various factors that have been found to influence both frustration and anxiety by presenting a general model of stress, including its major causes and its outcomes. Following this, we will explore several mechanisms by which employees and their managers cope with or reduce experienced stress in organizations.

MAJOR INFLUENCES ON WORK-RELATED STRESS

The model of stress presented here draws heavily on the work of several social psychologists with the Institute for Social Research at the University of Michigan, including John French, Robert Caplan, Robert Kahn, and Daniel Katz. In essence, the proposed model identifies two major sources of stress: organizational sources and individual sources. In addition, the moderating effects of social support are considered. These influences are shown in Exhibit 17.1.

EXHIBIT 17.2   HIGH- AND LOW-STRESS JOBS

High-Stress Jobs	Low-Stress Jobs
Manager	Farm laborer
Secretary	Maid
Foreman	Craft worker
Waitress/waiter	Stock handler
Office manager	Heavy equipment operator
Inspector	College professor
Clinical lab technician	Personnel worker

Source: Study conducted by the National Institute for Occupational Safety and Health, Department of Health, Education and Welfare, cited in *U.S. News & World Report,* March 13, 1978, pp. 80–81.

Organizational Influences on Stress

Although many factors in the work environment have been found to influence the extent to which people experience stress on the job, six factors have been shown to be particularly strong. These are: (1) occupational differences; (2) role ambiguity; (3) role conflict; (4) role overload and underutilization; (5) responsibility for people; and (6) lack of participation. We will consider each of these factors in turn.

Occupational Differences. Tension and job stress are prevalent in our contemporary society and can be found in a wide variety of jobs. Consider, for example, the following quotes from interviews with working people (Terkel, 1972).[1] The first is from a bus driver (p. 275):

> You have your tension. Sometimes you come close to having an accident, that upsets you. You just escape maybe by a hair or so. Sometimes maybe you get a disgruntled passenger on there, and starts a big argument. Traffic. You have someone who cuts you off or stops in front of the bus. There's a lot of tension behind that. . . . Most of the time you have to drive for the other drivers, to avoid hitting them. So you take the tension home with you. Most of the drivers, they'll suffer from hemorrhoids, kidney trouble, and such as that. I had a case of ulcers behind it.

Or, consider the plight of a bank teller (p. 348):

> Some days, when you're aggravated about something, you carry it after you leave the job. Certain people are bad days. (Laughs). The type of person who will walk in and says, "My car's double-parked outside. Would you hurry up, lady? . . . You want to say, "Hey, why did you double-park your car? So now you're going

[1]From *Working: People Talk About What They Do All Day and How They Feel About What They Do,* by Studs Terkel. Copyright © 1972, 1974 by Studs Terkel. Reprinted by permission of Pantheon Books, a Division of Random House, Inc., and by permission of Gower Publishing Company Ltd.

EXHIBIT 17.3 CAUSES OF STRESS NAMED BY SECRETARIES

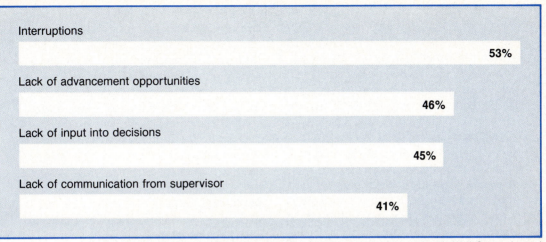

Interruptions

53%

Lack of advancement opportunities

46%

Lack of input into decisions

45%

Lack of communication from supervisor

41%

to blame me if you get a ticket, 'cause you were dumb enough to leave it there?" But you can't. That's the one hassle. You can't say anything back. The customer's always right.

Stress is experienced in many jobs: secretary, assembly-line worker, foreman, waitress, or executive. In fact, it is difficult to find jobs that are without some degree of stress. We seldom talk about jobs without stress; instead, we talk about the degree or magnitude of the stress.

The work roles (or occupations) that people fill have a substantial influence on the degree to which they experience stress (Cooper and Payne, 1978; French and Caplan, 1972). These occupational differences do *not* follow the traditional blue-collar/white-collar dichotomy, however. In general, available evidence suggests that high-stress occupations are those in which incumbents have little control over their jobs, work under relentless time pressures or threatening physical conditions, or have major responsibilities for either human or financial resources.

A recent survey of 130 occupations by the National Institute for Occupational Safety and Health (NIOSH) attempted to identify those occupations that were most (and least) susceptible to occupational stress *(U.S. News & World Report,* March 13, 1978). By examining death rates and admission records to hospitals and mental health facilities, NIOSH was able to rank the various occupations by fairly objective measures of stress. The results are presented in Exhibit 17.2. As shown, high-stress occupations (managers, secretaries, foremen) are typified by the stress-producing characteristics noted above, while low-stress occupations are not. It can be concluded that a major source of general stress emerges from the occupation at which one is working. A second survey, among secretaries, examined the specific causes of such stress. These results are shown in Exhibit 17.3.

CLOSE-UP 17.1 JOB STRESS IN THE CONTROL TOWER

Certainly one of the most stressful jobs in contemporary society is that of the air traffic controller, the person who monitors and guides airplanes in for take-off and landing. Nowhere is this stress more acute than in Chicago's O'Hare airport, the busiest airport in the world and called the "ulcer factory" by the controllers who work there. O'Hare airport handles 1900 flights per day and has one take-off or landing every twenty seconds during peak hours. Because of this pressure, controllers are only allowed to work ninety minutes at a stretch during peak hours, landing a plane every two minutes while simultaneously monitoring a half dozen more.

The Problem. This pressure, combined with the ever-present fear of causing a crash or collision (known with studied casualness as creating an "aluminum shower") places controllers under tremendous stress on the job. Of the ninety-four controllers at O'Hare, only two have been there more than ten years; most controllers don't reach five years. Two-thirds of those remaining either have ulcers or ulcer symptoms. Most exhibit signs of prolonged stress: high blood pressure, arthritis, colitis, skin disorders, headaches, allergies, and upset stomachs. Other controllers struggle with more severe problems, like alcoholism, depression, persistent nightmares, and acute anxiety. In one year alone, seven men had to be carried from the O'Hare control tower on stretchers, victims of acute hypertension. And since 1970, more than forty controllers have been permanently removed from their jobs for medical reasons.

Lack of Remedies. Although the nature and extent of the problem is fully acknowledged, the prevailing work environment and Federal Aviation Administration (FAA) policies seem to conspire to thwart a workable solution. First, controllers contend that their supervisors and FAA policies place them in a no-win situation since FAA regulations require proper spacing of all aircraft, yet the volume of traffic makes this spacing unrealistic. Supervisors encourage controllers to overlook these regulations and prevent delays, but if an error is made or a near-miss occurs, the controller is disciplined for not following regulations. Second, the controllers charge the FAA with understaffing, computer malfunctions, inadequate training programs, unrealistic transfer policies, and nerve-wracking conditions that jeopardize their health and public safety. However, a lawsuit filed by the controllers against the FAA to remedy these conditions was dismissed in court on the grounds that the controllers had not pursued other avenues of redress. Third, controllers who experience high stress are subject to a catch-22 transfer policy. Since O'Hare is understaffed, the FAA is hesitant to transfer healthy controllers to smaller, less stressful airports. Yet when a controller becomes unable to cope with the pressure at O'Hare, the FAA prefers to terminate the controller rather than transfer him to a smaller airport, where he could use his skills in a less stressful environment. Finally, while the FAA maintains a staff of qualified flight surgeons, controllers seldom visit them for fear that their stress-related disorders will be reported to the

FAA. Hence, the controller's only way out is through some form of physical ailment.

Postscript. In August 1981, the U.S. air traffic controllers went on an illegal strike, insisting something had to be done to address the problem of job fatigue (and demanding more money). Within days, President Reagan's re-sponse was to terminate about 12,000 striking controllers. New controllers were hired and trained at considerable expense, yet many of the same problems emerged. In 1987, after repeated unsuc-cessful attempts to secure some remedy to their stressful job conditions, the new air traffic controllers voted to form a new union.

Sources: D. Martindale, "Sweaty Palms in the Control Tower," *Psychology Today,* February 1977, pp. 71–73; and "The Constant Quest for Safety," *Time,* April 11, 1977.

Although not included in the NIOSH study, one of the most stressful occupations is that of air-traffic controller. Controllers consistently confront tasks that not only tax their mental and physical capabilities, but also have serious personal risks to the passengers whose safety depends on their judgment and skill. The plight of these air-traffic controllers is discussed in Close-Up 17.1.

Role Ambiguity. The first organizational influence on stress to be discussed here is *role ambiguity.* When individuals have inadequate information con-cerning their roles, they experience role ambiguity. Uncertainty over job definition takes many forms, including not knowing expectations for perfor-mance, not knowing how to meet those expectations, and not knowing the consequences of job behavior (Kahn et al., 1964). Role ambiguity is particu-larly strong among managerial (as opposed to nonmanagerial) jobs, where role definitions and task specification lack clarity. Role ambiguity can also occur among nonmanagerial employees (e.g., secretaries) where supervisors fail to take sufficient time to clarify role expectations for subordinates, thus leaving them unsure of how to best contribute to departmental—and organizational —goals. (Note that a major benefit ascribed to management-by-objectives programs is that they substantially reduce role ambiguity by specifying task goals.)

How prevalent is role ambiguity at work? In two independent surveys of employees, it was found that thirty-five percent of one sample (a national random sample of male employees) and sixty percent of the other sample (primarily scientists and engineers) reported some form of role ambiguity (Kahn et al., 1964; French and Caplan, 1972). Hence, ambiguity of job role is not an isolated event.

Role ambiguity has been found to lead to several negative stress-related outcomes. French and Caplan (1972) summarized their study findings as follows:

> In summary, role ambiguity, which appears to be widespread, (1) produces psychological strain and dissatisfaction; (2) leads to underutilization of human resources; and (3) leads to feelings of futility on how to cope with the organizational environment (p. 36).

In other words, role ambiguity has far-reaching consequences beyond experienced stress—consequences that include employee turnover and absenteeism, poor coordination and utilization of human resources, and increased operating costs due to inefficiency.

It should be noted, however, that not everyone responds in the same way to role ambiguity. Studies have shown that some people have a higher *tolerance for ambiguity* and are less affected (in terms of stress, reduced performance, or propensity to leave) than those with a low tolerance for ambiguity (Kahn et al., 1964).

Role Conflict. Another organizational influence on stress, *role conflict* may be defined as "the simultaneous occurrence of two (or more) sets of pressures such that compliance with one would make more difficult compliance with the other" (Kahn et al., 1964, p. 19). In other words, role conflict occurs when an employee is placed in a situation where contradictory demands are placed upon him or her. For instance, a factory worker may find himself in a situation where the supervisor is demanding greater output, yet the work group is demanding a restriction of output. Similarly, a secretary who reports to several supervisors may face a conflict over whose work to do first.

One of the best known studies of role conflict and stress was carried out by Robert Kahn and his colleagues at the University of Michigan. Kahn studied fifty-three managers and their subordinates (a total of 381 people), examining the nature of each person's role and how it affected subsequent behavior. As a result of the investigation, the following conclusions emerged:

> Contradictory role expectations give rise to opposing role pressures (role conflict), which generally have the following effects on the emotional experience of the focal person: intensified internal conflicts, increased tension associated with various aspects of the job, reduced satisfaction with the job and its various components, and decreased confidence in superiors and in the organization as a whole. The strain experienced by those in conflict situations leads to various coping responses—social and psychological withdrawal (reduction in communication and attributed influence) among them.
>
> Finally, the presence of conflict in one's role tends to undermine his reactions with his role senders, to produce weaker bonds of trust, respect, and attraction. It is quite clear that role conflicts are costly for the person in emotional and interpersonal terms. They may be costly to the organization, which depends on effective co-ordination and collaboration within and among its parts (1964, pp. 70–71).

Other studies have found similar results about the serious side effects of role conflict both for individuals and organizations (House and Rizzo, 1972; Miles and Perreault, 1976). It should be recognized, however, that personality differences may serve to moderate the impact of role conflict on stress. In particular, it has been found that introverts and people who are more flexible respond more negatively to role conflict than do others (French and Caplan, 1972). Even so, role conflict should not be overlooked by managers as a primary source of stress and strain needing serious attention.

Role Overload and Underutilization. In addition to role ambiguity and conflict, a third aspect of role processes has also been found to represent an important influence on experienced stress, namely, the extent to which employees feel either overloaded or underutilized in their job responsibilities. *Role overload* is a condition in which individuals feel they are being asked to do more than time or ability permits. Individuals often experience role overload as a conflict between quantity and quality of performance. *Quantitative* overload consists of having more work than can be done in a given time period. It can be visualized as a continuum ranging from too little to do to too much to do. *Qualitative* role overload, on the other hand, consists of being taxed beyond one's skills, abilities, and knowledge. It can be seen as a continuum ranging from too easy work to too difficult work. It is important to note that *either* extreme represents a bad fit between the abilities of the employee and the demands of the work environment (French and Caplan, 1972). A good fit occurs at that point on both scales of workload where the abilities of the individual are relatively consistent with the demands of the job.

There is evidence that both quantitative and qualitative role overload are prevalent in our society. A review of findings suggests that between forty-four to seventy-three percent of white-collar workers experience a form of role overload (French and Caplan, 1972). What induces this overload? As a result of a series of studies, French and Caplan (1972) concluded that a major factor influencing overload is the high achievement needs of many managers. Need for achievement correlated .42 with the number of hours worked per week and .25 with questionnaire measures of role overload. Much overload is apparently self-induced.

Similarly, the concept of *role underutilization* should also be acknowledged as a source of experienced stress. Role underutilization occurs when employees are allowed to use only a few of their skills and abilities, even though they are required to make heavy use of these. The most prevalent form of role underutilization is monotony, where the worker performs the same routine task (or set of tasks) over and over. Other examples of underutilization include total dependence on machines for determining work pace and sustained positional or postural constraint. Several studies have found that underutilization often leads to low self-esteem, low life satisfaction, and increased frequency of nervous complaints and symptoms (Gardell, 1976). Underutilization has also been found to lead to increased absenteeism and lower participation (even in union activities).

EXHIBIT 17.4   RELATIONSHIP AMONG ROLE OVERLOAD, UNDERUTILIZATION, AND STRESS

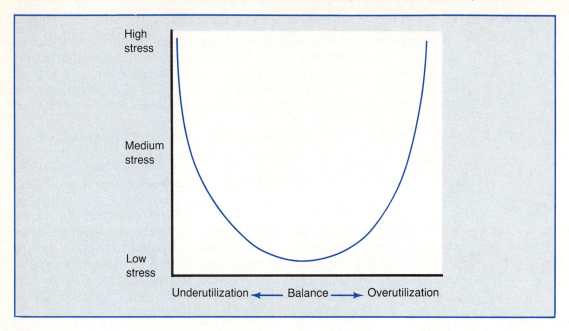

Both role overload and role underutilization have been shown to influence psychological and physiological reactions to the job. This U-function relationship between the extent of role utilization and stress is shown in Exhibit 17.4. As shown, the least stress is experienced at that point where an employee's abilities and skills are in balance with the requirements of the job. Recall that many of the current efforts to redesign jobs and improve the quality of work are aimed at minimizing overload or underutilization in the work place and achieving a more suitable balance between abilities and skills used on the job.

Responsibility for People. Some evidence suggests that managers and supervisors—people who are responsible for other people—experience considerable stress as a result of responsibility. Studies in the United States and abroad indicate that these individuals consistently have more ulcers and experience more hypertension than the people they supervise (Cooper and Payne, 1978; Katz and Kahn, 1978). Responsibility for people was found to represent a greater influence on stress than responsibility for nonpersonal factors like budgets, projects, equipment, and other property. As noted by French and Caplan (1972, p. 48):

> If there is any truth to the adage that "man's greatest enemy is himself," it can be found in these data—it is the responsibility which organizational members have for other organizational members, rather than the responsibility for impersonal

aspects of the organization, which constitutes the more significant organizational stress.

Lack of Participation. The final organizational influence on stress we will consider here is the extent to which employees are allowed to participate in decisions affecting their work. To the extent that employees' opinions, knowledge, and wishes are excluded from organizational decision processes, the resulting lack of participation can lead not only to increased stress and strain, but also to reduced productivity (Coch and French, 1948; French, Israel, and As, 1960).

The importance of employee participation in decision making (or PDM) in reducing stress is reflected in the French and Caplan (1972) study. After a major effort to uncover the antecedents of job-related stress, these investigators concluded (p. 51):

> Since participation is also significantly correlated with low role ambiguity, good relations with others, and low overload, it is conceivable that its effects are widespread, and that all the relationships between these other stresses and psychological strain can be accounted for in terms of how much the person participates. This, in fact, appears to be the case. When we control or hold constant, through statistical analysis techniques, the amount of participation a person reports, then the correlations between all the above stresses and job satisfaction and job related threat drop quite noticeably. This suggests that low participation generates these related stresses, and that increasing participation is an efficient way of reducing many other stresses which also lead to psychological strain.

So convinced were French and Caplan of the centrality of participation in decision making in reducing dysfunctional behavior and increasing organizational effectiveness that they have suggested a series of hypothetical consequences of PDM. These consequences, shown in Exhibit 17.5, are based on their review of a series of studies. As illustrated in the exhibit, PDM is hypothesized to lead to a wide variety of desirable consequences that not only improve the quality of work for individuals but also improve the level of effectiveness of the organization. Many of these outcomes (increased performance, commitment, and innovation, and decreased turnover and absenteeism) have been repeatedly identified in the literature as indicators of organizational effectiveness. While the extent to which PDM actually determines or influences these outcomes may be questioned, it appears that increased employee participation in decisions affecting their jobs seems to be an important factor in reducing various dysfunctional psychological and behavioral reactions to the work place.

Personal Influences on Stress

The second major category of stress-causing factors at work are the personal characteristics of individuals. It was noted at the beginning of this chapter that

EXHIBIT 17.5   CHARACTERISTICS OF PERSONS WHO PARTICIPATE IN DECISIONS THAT AFFECT THEIR WORK

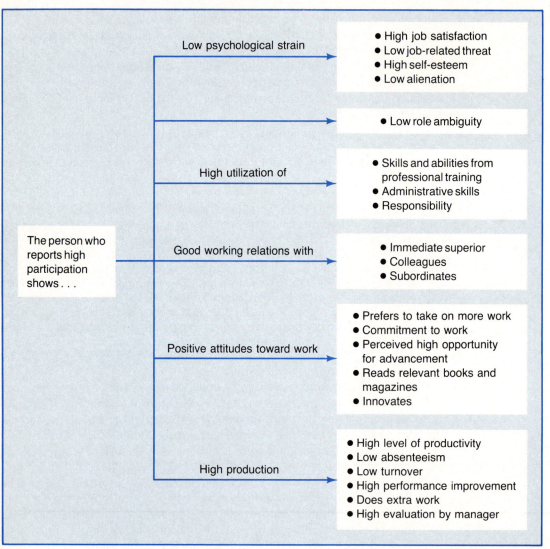

individual differences play a major role in determining the extent to which people experience stress. All people do not react the same way to potentially stressful events. Here we will consider five personal influences on stress: (1) Type A personality; (2) locus of control; (3) rate of life change; (4) abilities and needs; and (5) other personality traits, particularly introversion-extroversion and flexibility-rigidity.

Type A Personality. Research over the past decade has focused on what is perhaps the single most dangerous personal influence on experienced stress and subsequent physical harm. This characteristic was first introduced by Friedman and Rosenman (1974) and is called *Type A personality* (as opposed to Type B personality). Type A and Type B personalities are felt to be relatively stable personal characteristics exhibited by individuals.

Type A personality is frequently observed in managers. Indeed, one study found that sixty percent of managers were clearly identified as Type A, while only twelve percent were clearly identified as Type B (Howard, Cunningham, and Rechnitzer, 1976). It has been suggested that Type A personality is most helpful in rising through the ranks of an organization. It is characterized by impatience, restlessness, aggressiveness, competitiveness, polyphasic activities (having many "irons in the fire" at one time), and being under considerable time pressure. Work activities are particularly important to Type A individuals, and they tend to freely invest long hours on the job to meet pressing (and recurring) deadlines. Type B people, on the other hand, experience no pressing deadlines or conflicts and are relatively free of any sense of time urgency or hostility.

The importance of Type A personality in producing stress is exemplified by the relationship between this behavior and heart disease. Rosenman and Friedman (1971) studied 3500 men over an eight and one-half year period and found Type A individuals to be twice as prone to heart disease, five times as prone to a second heart attack, and twice as prone to fatal heart attacks when compared to Type B individuals. Similarly, Jenkins (1971) studied over 3000 men and found that, of 133 coronary heart disease sufferers, ninety-four were clearly identified as Type A in early test scores. The rapid rise of women in managerial positions suggests that they too may be subject to this same problem. Hence, Type A behavior very clearly leads to one of the most severe outcomes of experienced stress.

One irony of Type A is that, although this behavior is helpful in securing rapid promotion to the top of an organization, it may be detrimental once the individual has arrived. That is, while Type A employees make successful managers (and salespeople), the most successful *top* executives tend to be Type B. They exhibit patience and a broad concern for the ramifications of decisions. As Dr. Elmer Green, a Menninger Foundation psychologist who works with executives, notes, "This fellow—the driving A—can't relax enough to do a really first-rate job, at the office or at home. He gets to a level that dogged work can achieve, but not often to the pinnacle of his business or profession, which requires sober, quiet, balanced reasoning" *(Business Week,* October 17, 1977, p. 137). The key is to know how to shift from Type A behavior to Type B.

How does a manager accomplish this? The obvious answer is to slow down and relax. However, many Type A managers refuse to acknowledge either the problem or the need for change since they feel it may be viewed as a sign of weakness. In these cases, several small steps can be taken, including scheduling specified times every day to exercise, delegating more significant work to subordinates, and eliminating optional activities from the daily calendar. Some companies have begun experimenting with retreats, where managers are removed from the work environment and engage in group psychotherapy over the problems associated with Type A personality. Initial results from these programs appear promising *(Business Week,* October 17, 1977). Even so, more needs to be done if we are to reduce job-related stress and its serious health implications.

Locus of Control. The concept of *locus of control* was discussed in some detail in Chapter Four. This concept has implications with respect to how persons respond to a potentially stressful environment. In essence, locus of control can influence experienced stress by affecting perceived ability to cope with and possibly alter a stressful environment. That is, internals (individuals who feel that surrounding events are largely under their own control) are more likely to be upset by threats to the control of surrounding events than are externals (those who believe they are largely controlled by surrounding events). Recent evidence indicates that internals react to situations over which they have little or no control, such as goal frustration, with aggressiveness—presumably in an attempt to reassert control over ongoing events (Carver and Glass, 1978). On the other hand, externals tend to be more resolved to external control, are much less involved in or upset by a turbulent work environment, and do not react as emotionally to organizational stress factors.

However, when internals face a potentially stressful situation over which they *do* have control (such as the amount of time and effort spent studying for an examination), these individuals are likely to take charge of modifying the environment and reducing or eliminating stresses. The extent to which the environment can be changed has a significant impact on the reactions of internals and externals in potentially stressful situations.

Rate of Life Change. A third personal influence on experienced stress is the degree to which individuals' lives are stable or turbulent. A long-term research project by Ruch and Holmes (1971) has attempted to document the extent to which *rate of life change* generates stress in individuals and leads to the onset of disease or illness. As a result of their research, Ruch and Holmes identified a variety of life events and assigned points to each event to reflect its impact on stress and illness (see Exhibit 17.6).

The death of a spouse was seen as the most stressful change and was assigned 100 points. Other events were scaled proportionately in terms of their impact on stress and illness. It was found that the accumulation of more than 200 points in a single year led to a better than fifty percent chance that a person would encounter a serious illness the following year. Apparently, the influence of life changes on stress and illness is brought about by the endocrine system. This system provides the energy needed to cope with new or unusual situations. When the rate of change surpasses a given level, the system

EXHIBIT 17.6   SCALING THE LIFE-CHANGE UNITS FOR VARIOUS EXPERIENCES

Life Event	Scale Value
Death of spouse	100
Divorce	73
Marital separation	65
Jail term	63
Death of a close family member	63
Major personal injury or illness	53
Marriage	50
Fired from work	47
Marital reconciliation	45
Retirement	45
Major change in health of family member	44
Pregnancy	40
Sex difficulties	39
Gain of a new family member	39
Business readjustment	39
Change in financial state	38
Death of a close friend	37
Change to a different line of work	36
Change in number of arguments with spouse	35
Mortgage or loan for major purchase (home, etc.)	31
Foreclosure of mortgage or loan	30
Change in responsibilities at work	29
Son or daughter leaving home	29
Trouble with in-laws	29
Outstanding personal achievement	28
Wife begins or stops work	26
Begin or end school	26
Change in living conditions	25
Revision of personal habits	24
Trouble with boss	23
Change in work hours or conditions	20
Change in residence	20
Change in schools	20
Change in recreation	19
Change in church activities	19
Change in social activities	18
Mortgage or loan for lesser purchase (car, etc.)	17
Change in sleeping habits	16
Change in number of family get-togethers	15
Change in eating habits	15
Vacation	13
Christmas	12
Minor violations of the law	11

Source: Reprinted with permission from L. O. Ruch and T. H. Holmes, "Scaling of Life Change: Comparison of Direct and Indirect Methods," *Journal of Psychosomatic Research 15* (1971): 224. Copyright 1971, Pergamon Journals, Ltd.

experiences overload and malfunctions. The result is a lowered defense against viruses and disease.

It is important to realize, however, that potentially dysfunctional life changes may be positive changes (changing a job, shift in job responsibilities) as well as negative changes (being fired, trouble with boss).

Abilities and Needs. Another influence on the extent to which stress is experienced is the closeness of fit between employee abilities and needs and the demands of the work environment (French and Caplan, 1972). To the extent that an individual's job-related abilities are commensurate with job demands *and* to the extent that an individual's needs are satisfied by the job, we predict less stress will be experienced. A clerk-typist's job would cause much less stress for someone with excellent typing skills than for a beginning typist. A person with a high need for affiliation would tend to experience much less anxiety or frustration when working in a group as opposed to working alone (Schachter, 1959). This view of the "goodness of fit" between the individual and the work environment as the central determinant of experienced stress forms the basis for one of the major theories of job-related stress (French and Caplan, 1972).

Other Personality Traits. Finally, several additional personality traits have been found to influence the way people respond to potentially stressful situations. In particular, it has been found that role conflict produces much greater job-related tension in introverts than in extroverts. Introverts are generally less sociable and more independent than extroverts, and they have more difficulty coping with conflict because it occurs in social situations and threatens their independence. Similarly, flexible people also experience greater stress as a result of role conflict than rigid people. Since flexible people more often blame themselves when things go wrong, and rigid people blame others (Kahn et al., 1964), it is reasonable to assume that flexible people turn the blame for conflict inward, resulting in greater job-related tension. Rigid persons typically blame someone else for the conflict, thus removing themselves from the center of controversy.

Buffering Effects of Social Support

We have seen in the previous discussion how a variety of organizational and personal factors influence the extent to which individuals experience stress on the job. While many factors, or stressors, have been identified, their effect on psychological and behavioral outcomes is not always as strong as we might expect. This lack of a direct stressor-outcome relationship suggests the existence of a moderator variable that buffers the effects of potential stressors on individuals. Recent research has identified *social support* as a major buffer in this relationship (Katz and Kahn, 1978). The effect of social support on stress is shown in Exhibit 17.1. Social support is simply the extent to which organization members feel their peers can be trusted, are interested in each

CLOSE-UP 17.2 STRESS AND SOCIAL BEHAVIOR

Stanley Schachter and his colleagues carried out a series of studies to better understand the effects of stress (particularly anxiety) on affiliative behavior.

The study was carried out among a sample of female college students. Subjects were divided into an experimental group and a control group. None of the subjects knew each other.

The experimental group was brought into a room filled with scientific-looking equipment, replete with electric wires and switches. A sinister-looking "doctor" then entered the room and explained to the subjects that they were about to take part in a series of experiments examining the effects of electric shock on humans. While the shocks would be painful, the doctor explained, they would not cause permanent injury.

This procedure was used to create a strong sense of fear in the experimental group. (No such treatment was administered to the control group.) Subjects were then informed that there would be a short delay in the experiment and given the option of waiting either by themselves or in a group.

In the experimental group (fear condition), the subjects overwhelmingly preferred to wait in a group. Not only did the subjects prefer to wait in a group, they further preferred to wait with the others in the same condition (fear), rather than with others who were not in the same condition. But in the control group (no fear condition) where participants were still uninformed about the nature of the experiment, subjects tended to prefer to wait alone. In other words, the creation of threatening conditions increased the affiliative need substantially.

The Schachter study points out how powerful anxiety and fear can be in their influence on the social behavior of individuals. For instance, we often observe that union solidarity is strongest prior to and during a strike. Solidarity results in part from fear of the unknown. (Will the company settle? How long will the strike last? Can we afford to hold out?) Having others around who are in the same condition can provide ego support and the reassurance needed to continue everyday activities.

Source: S. Schachter, *The Psychology of Affiliation* (Palo Alto, Calif.: Stanford University Press, 1959).

other's welfare, respect one another, and have a genuine positive regard for one another. When social support is present, individuals feel that they are not alone as they face the more prevalent stressors. This "misery loves company" factor is well established, dating from a classic study by Stanley Schachter (see Close-Up 17.2). The feeling that those around you really care about what happens to you and are willing to help blunts the severity of potential stressors and leads to less painful side effects.

Much of the rigorous work on the buffering effects of social support in stress comes from the field of medicine, but has relevance for organizational behavior. In a series of medical studies, it was consistently found that high peer support reduced negative outcomes of potentially stressful events (surgery, job loss, hospitalization) and increased positive outcomes. These results clearly point to the importance for group relations and processes in individual well-being. These results also indicate that managers should be aware of the importance of building cohesive, supportive work groups, particularly on jobs (such as on an assembly line) that are most subject to stress. We will continue discussing what managers can do to reduce employee stress later in this chapter. First, however, by way of summary, several of the more important outcomes of stress in organizational settings will be examined.

CONSEQUENCES OF WORK-RELATED STRESS

In exploring major influences on stress, it was pointed out that the intensity with which a person experiences stress is a function of organizational factors and personal factors, moderated by the degree of social support in the work environment. We come now to an examination of major *consequences* of work-related stress. Here we will attempt to answer the "so what?" question. Why should managers be interested in stress and resulting strain?

As a guide for examining the topic, we recognize three intensity levels of stress—no stress, low stress, and high stress—and will study the outcomes of each level. These outcomes are shown schematically in Exhibit 17.7. Three major categories of outcomes will be considered: stress and health; stress and performance; and stress and counterproductive behavior.

Stress and Health

High degrees of stress are typically accompanied by severe anxiety and/or frustration, high blood pressure, and high cholesterol levels. These psychological and physiological changes contribute to the impairment of health in several different ways. Most importantly, high stress contributes to heart disease (Cooper and Payne, 1978). The relationship between high job stress and heart disease is well established. In view of the fact that well over a half-million people die of heart disease every year, the impact of stress is important (Glass, 1976).

High job stress also contributes to a variety of other ailments, including peptic ulcers (Susser, 1967), arthritis (Cobb, 1971), and several forms of mental illness. In a study by Cobb and Kasl (1970), for example, it was found that individuals with high educational achievement but low job status exhibited abnormally high levels of anger, irritation, anxiety, tiredness, depression, and low self-esteem. In another study, Slote (1977) examined the effects of plant closing in Detroit on stress and stress outcomes. While factory closings are fairly common, the effects of these closings on individuals have seldom been examined. Slote found that the plant closing led to "an alarming

EXHIBIT 17.7   MAJOR CONSEQUENCES OF VARIOUS LEVELS OF WORK-RELATED STRESS

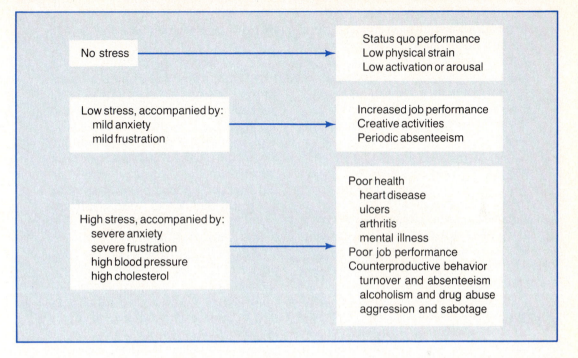

rise in anxiety and illness," with at least one-half the employees suffering from ulcers, arthritis, serious hypertension, alcoholism, depression requiring medical help, and even hair loss. Clearly, this life change event took its toll on the mental and physical well-being of the work force. Another example of the effect of stress on health is seen in the recent studies of workers on night shifts, as described in Close-Up 17.3.

Finally, in a classic study of mental health of industrial workers, Kornhauser (1965) studied a sample of automobile assembly-line workers. Of the employees studied, he found that forty percent had symptoms of mental health problems. His main findings may be summarized as follows:

- Job satisfaction varied consistently with employee skill levels. Blue-collar workers holding high-level jobs exhibited better mental health than those holding low-level jobs.
- Job dissatisfaction, stress, and absenteeism were all related directly to the characteristics of the job. Dull, repetitive, unchallenging jobs were associated with the poorest mental health.
- Feelings of helplessness, withdrawal, alienation, and pessimism were widespread throughout the plant. As an example, Kornhauser noted that fifty percent of the assembly-line workers felt they had little influence

CLOSE-UP 17.3 JOB STRESS ON THE NIGHT SHIFT

A fact unknown to most managers and organizational analysts is that fully one-sixth of the U.S. work force, or ten million people, work on night shifts. Moreover, the proportion of night workers continues to grow. Yet little is known about the special problems of such employees.

For some, working the night shift represents almost a primordial attraction. There is usually more freedom from close supervision, power struggles, and office intrigues; reduced work loads and a more casual working atmosphere; less traffic to and from work; and solitude. In short, night work offers workers more "elbow room."

At the same time, however, such shifts can create serious problems, sometimes called *industrial jet lag*. Although we don't know precisely how night work affects the body and mind, it appears to be linked to several physical and emotional problems. Primary among these problems is poor sleep, brought on in part by a drastic change in the body's natural twenty-four-hour rhythm, and in part by the greater noise levels and interruptions during the day when night workers attempt to sleep. The result of this sleep deprivation is increased fatigue, gastrointestinal complaints, and inefficiency. Moreover, increased divorce rates and excessive drinking are commonly associated with night work.

In view of these problems, why do night shifts continue? From the organization's standpoint, night shifts are important to ensure higher utilization of machinery. Moreover, in industries such as steel, chemicals, and pulp and paper, the processes and machinery are designed to run continuously and cannot simply be turned off until morning. From the employees' standpoint, the motivation is simple—they make more money working at night.

What is being done about the stress problems created by shift work? In France, companies are encouraged to rotate employees on and off night shifts. And in Japan, many factories have simply placed cots on the shop floor so workers can catnap on them instead of on the assembly line. Finally, in the U.S., night shift is considered by unions and management to be one of many issues (along with vacations, overtime, and rest breaks) for collective bargaining. Primarily, the U.S. solution is an economic one. No doubt other strategies for reducing night work stress will evolve, but in the meantime, research interest continues to grow as we learn more about the possible health hazards of the night shift.

Source: Based on information in "The Lonely World of Night Work," *Fortune,* December 15, 1980, pp. 108–14.

over the future course of their lives; this compares to only seventeen percent for nonfactory workers.
- Employees with the lowest mental health also tended to be more passive in their nonwork activities: typically, they did not vote or take part in community activities.

EXHIBIT 17.8   RELATIONSHIP BETWEEN STRESS AND JOB PERFORMANCE

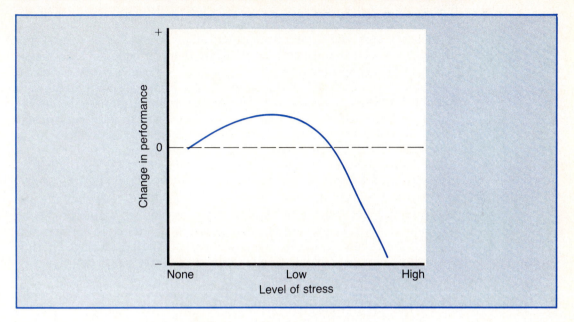

In conclusion, Kornhauser (1965) noted:

> Poor mental health occurs whenever conditions of work and life lead to continuing frustration by failing to offer means for perceived progress toward attainment of strongly desired goals which have become indispensable elements of the individual's self-esteem and dissatisfaction with life, often accompanied by anxieties, social alienation and withdrawal, a narrowing of goals and curtailing of aspirations—in short . . . poor mental health.

Managers need to be concerned about the problems of physical and mental health because of their severe consequences both for the individual and for the organization. Health is often related to performance, and to the extent that health suffers, so too does performance. Given the importance of performance for organizational effectiveness, we will now examine how it is affected by stress.

Stress and Job Performance

A major concern of management is the effects of stress on job performance. The relationship is not as simple as might be supposed. The stress-performance relationship resembles an inverted J-curve, as shown in Exhibit 17.8. At very low or *no stress* levels, individuals maintain their current level of performance. Under these conditions, individuals are not activated (Scott, 1966), do not experience any stress-related physical strain, and probably see no reason to change their performance level. Note that this performance level may be high or low. In any event, an absence of stress probably would not cause any change (Gowler and Legge, 1975).

On the other hand, under conditions of *low stress,* studies indicate that people are activated sufficiently to motivate them to increase performance. For instance, salespeople and many managers perform best when they are experiencing mild anxiety or frustration. Stress in modest amounts acts as a stimulus for the individual, as when a manager has a tough problem to solve. The toughness of the problem often pushes managers to their performance limits. Similarly, mild stress can also be responsible for creative activities in individuals as they try to solve difficult (stressful) problems.

Finally, under conditions of *high stress,* individual performance drops markedly, as shown in Exhibit 17.8. Here, the severity of the stress consumes attention and energies, and individuals focus considerable effort on attempting to reduce the stress (often employing a variety of counterproductive behaviors as noted below). Little energy is left to devote to job performance, with obvious results. (For a detailed discussion of the effects of high stress on job performance, see Chapter 2 in Cooper and Payne [1978].)

Stress and Counterproductive Behavior

Finally, it is useful from a managerial standpoint to consider several forms of counterproductive behavior that are known to result from prolonged stress. These counterproductive behaviors include turnover and absenteeism, alcoholism and drug abuse, and aggression and sabotage.

Turnover and Absenteeism. Although they are temporary, turnover and absenteeism represent convenient forms of withdrawal from a highly stressful job. Results of several studies have indicated a fairly consistent, if modest, relationship between stress and subsequent turnover and absenteeism (Porter and Steers, 1973; Steers and Rhodes, 1978; Mobley et al., 1979). In fact, one survey found that while there has been a twenty-two percent rise over the last fifteen years in the amount of absenteeism attributable to purely physical diseases, during the same period absenteeism associated with psychological ills increased 152 percent for men and 302 percent for women (Kearns, 1973). These forms of withdrawal may indeed represent two of the less undesirable consequences of stress, particularly when compared to alternative choices such as alcoholism, drug abuse, or aggression. While high turnover and absenteeism may inhibit productivity, at least they do little physical harm to the individual or co-workers. It must be remembered, however, that many other factors contribute to this type of withdrawal.

Alcoholism and Drug Abuse. It has long been known that stress is linked to alcoholism and drug abuse among employees at all levels in the organizational hierarchy. These two forms of withdrawal offer a temporary respite from severe anxiety and severe frustration. A recent study by the Department of

Health, Education, and Welfare (1973, p. 85) reported, "Our interviews with blue-collar workers in heavy industry revealed a number who found it necessary to drink large quantities of alcohol during lunch to enable them to withstand the pressure or overwhelming boredom of their tasks." A similar study by the New York Narcotics Addiction Control Commission (1971) revealed a surprising amount of drug abuse by young employees on blue-collar jobs, especially among assembly-line employees and long-haul truck drivers. A third study of a UAW local involving 3,400 workers found fifteen percent of the work force addicted to heroin (Executive Office of the President, 1972).

In other words, both alcohol and drugs are used by a significant proportion of employees to escape from the rigors of a routine or stressful job. Although many companies have begun in-house programs aimed at rehabilitating chronic cases, these forms of withdrawal seem to continue to be on the increase, presenting another serious problem for modern managers. One answer to this dilemma involves reducing stress on the job that is creating the need for withdrawal from organizational activities.

Aggression and Sabotage. Severe frustration can also lead to overt hostility in the form of aggression toward other people and toward inanimate objects. Aggression occurs when individuals feel frustrated and can find no acceptable, legitimate remedies for the frustration. For instance, a busy secretary may be asked to type a stack of letters, only to be told later that the boss changed his mind and no longer needs the letters typed. The frustrated secretary may react by covert verbal abuse or an intentional slowdown on subsequent work. A more extreme example of aggression can be seen in the periodic reports in newspapers about a worker who "goes berserk" (usually after a reprimand or punishment) and attacks fellow employees.

One common form of aggressive behavior on the job is sabotage. As a recent H.E.W. (1973, p. 83) study reported:

> The roots of sabotage, a frequent aspect of industrial violence, are illustrated by this comment of a steelworker: "Sometimes, out of pure meanness, when I make something, I put a little dent in it. I like to do something to make it really unique. Hit it with a hammer deliberately to see if it'll get by, just so I can say I did it." In a product world where everything is alike, sabotage may be a distortion of the guild craftsman's signature, a way of asserting individuality in a homogeneous world—the only way for a worker to say, "That's mine." It may also be a way of striking back against the hostile, inanimate objects that control the worker's time, muscles, and brain. Breaking a machine in order to get some rest may be a sane thing to do.

The extent to which frustration leads to aggressive behavior is influenced by several factors, often under the control of managers (Hamner and Organ, 1978). Aggression tends to be subdued when: (1) employees anticipate that it will be punished; (2) the peer group disapproves; and (3) it has not been reinforced in the past (that is, when aggressive behavior failed to lead to positive outcomes). It is incumbent upon managers to avoid reinforcing undesired behavior and, at the same time, to provide constructive outlets for frustration. In this regard, Levinson (1959) has suggested that organizations provide official channels for the discharge of aggressive tendencies. Many companies have experimented with ombudsmen, whose task it is to be impartial mediators of employee disputes. Results have proved positive. These procedures or outlets are particularly important for nonunion personnel who do not have contractual grievance procedures.

COPING WITH WORK-RELATED STRESS

We come now to the most important question from a managerial standpoint: What can be done to reduce job-related stress? Many suggestions for coping with stress are implicit in the previous discussions. However, it is possible to summarize several important actions employees and managers can take in order to provide a more desirable work environment and improve employee adjustment to work.

Individual Strategies

There are many things people can do to help eliminate the level of experienced stress or, at the very least, to help cope with continuing high stress. For example, individuals can increase their own *self-awareness* of how they behave on the job. They can learn to know their own limits and recognize signs of potential trouble. Employees should know when to withdraw from a situation (known to some as a "mental health day" instead of absenteeism) and when to seek help from others on the job in an attempt to relieve the situation.

In addition, individuals can develop *outside interests* to take their minds off work. This solution is particularly important for Type A people, whose physical health depends on toning down their drive for success. Employees can ensure that they get regular *physical exercise* to relieve pent-up stress. Many companies sponsor athletic activities and some have built athletic facilities on company premises to encourage employee activity.

Another means individuals can use to cope with stress is through a variety of *personal* or *unique solutions*. For instance, here is how one manager described his reaction to a stressful situation *(U.S. News & World Report,* March 13, 1978, p. 81): "If someone finally bugs me, I politely hang up the phone and then pound the hell out of my typewriter, saying all the things on paper I wanted to say to that person on the phone. It works every time. Then, I rip up the paper and throw it into the trash can."

Sometimes, however, an employee may be unable to improve his or her situation. Individuals may in some instances find it necessary (i.e., healthful) simply to *leave the organization* and find alternative employment. While this is clearly a difficult decision to make, there are times when turnover is the only answer.

Organizational Strategies

Since managers usually have more control over the working environment than subordinates, it seems only natural that they have more opportunity to contribute to a reduction of work-related stress. Among their activities, managers may include the following seven strategies.

First, they can pay more attention in the *selection and placement* process to the fit between job applicants, the job, and the work environment. As French and Caplan (1972) point out, current selection and placement procedures are devoted almost exclusively to preventing qualitative role overload by ensuring that people have the required education, ability, experience, and training for the job. Managers could extend these selection criteria to include a consideration of the extent to which job applicants have a tolerance for ambiguity and can handle role conflict. In other words, managers could be alert in the job interview and subsequent placement process to potential stress-related problems and the ability of the applicant to deal successfully with them.

Second, stress can be reduced in some cases through better job-related *skills-training* procedures, where employees are taught how to do their jobs more effectively with less stress and strain. For instance, an employee might be taught how to reduce overload by taking shortcuts or by being provided with new or expanded skills. These techniques would only be successful, however, if management did not follow this increased effectiveness by raising work quotas. Along with this could go a greater effort by managers to specify and clarify job duties to reduce ambiguity and conflict. Employees could also be trained in human-relations skills in order to improve their interpersonal abilities so that they might encounter less interpersonal and intergroup conflict.

Third, managers can change certain aspects of jobs or the ways people perform these jobs. Much has been written about the benefits of *job enrichment.* Enriching a job may lead to improved task significance, autonomy, responsibility, and feedback. For many people, these jobs will present a welcome challenge, thus improving the job-person fit and reducing experienced stress. It should be noted, however, that all people do not necessarily want an enriched job. Enriching the job of a person with a very low need for achievement or external locus of control may only increase anxiety and fear of failure. Care must be taken in job enrichment to match these efforts to employee needs and desires. In addition to job enrichment, a related technique aimed at reducing stress is *job rotation.* Job rotation is basically a way of spreading stress among employees and providing a respite—albeit temporary —from particularly stressful jobs.

Several companies and universities have begun experimenting with *counseling programs,* the fourth strategy suggested here. For instance, Stanford University's executive program includes a module on coping with stress, and the Menninger Foundation conducts a one-week antistress seminar in Topeka. A recent experiment by Sarason et al. (1978) among police officers examined the value of a stress-management program. In the program, which consisted of six two-hour sessions, officers were told about the nature and causes of stress, were shown useful relaxation exercises, and were put through several simulated stressful situations such as role playing the handling of an arrest. Throughout, emphasis was placed on reinforcing the officers' confidence that they could, in fact, successfully cope with on-the-job stress. The results of the program showed that those officers who went through the program performed better, exhibited greater self-control, and experienced less stress than officers in comparable positions who did not go through the program. Similar findings have emerged in a variety of business organizations. Once again, much work-related stress can be reduced simply by encouraging managers to be more supportive and to provide the necessary tools for people to cope with stress.

Fifth, managers can allow employees greater *participation* in decisions affecting their work. As noted above, participation increases job involvement and simultaneously reduces stress by relieving ambiguity and conflict. However, while the benefits of increased participation are many, it should be noted that being more participative is no easy task for some supervisors. One recent study, for example, found significant differences in the extent to which different supervisors would allow their subordinates to participate in decision making (Steers, 1977b). Females were found to allow more participation than males. Supervisors with high-achievement needs, high levels of confidence in the abilities of their subordinates, and low feelings of being threatened by others allowed more subordinate participation. The issue of participation does not appear to be whether subordinates desire it; instead, it appears to be whether superiors will allow it.

Sixth, managers can attempt to build *work group cohesiveness.* Team-building efforts are common in industry today. These efforts focus on developing groups so they are both more productive and mutually supportive. A critical ingredient in the extent to which stress is experienced is the amount of social support employees receive. Team building represents one way to achieve this support.

Finally, as discussed in Chapter Ten, managers can open *communication* channels so employees are more informed about what is happening in the organization. With greater knowledge, role ambiguity and conflict are reduced. Managers must be aware, however, that communication is a two-way street and should allow and be receptive to communication from subordinates. To the extent that subordinates feel their problems and complaints are being heard, they experience less stress and are less inclined to engage in counterproductive behavior.

Here, then, are seven specific techniques that have proven useful in work organizations in reducing the amount of experienced stress. None is particularly costly. However, all require an acknowledgement by management that stress is a significant problem on the job and a commitment by management to take positive actions to change the work environment. The alleviation of work-related stress is mostly in the hands of management, not employees, and solutions to the problem seem well within the reach of those who are concerned.

SUMMARY

This chapter examined the relationship between work and stress. First, the dimension of the problem was discussed, followed by an examination of the basic processes involved in stress, the general adaptation syndrome, and frustration and anxiety.

Next, major influences on stress were identified using a model of work-related stress. In addition, the consequences of experienced stress and strain were reviewed. It was noted that stress can influence health and job performance and can in many cases lead to counterproductive behavior.

Finally, a variety of individual and organizational strategies for coping with stress were suggested. Emphasis was placed on the need for managers to be sensitive to the emergence of stressful situations at work and to act quickly to attempt a remedy. These actions benefit both the employees and the organization.

KEY WORDS

anxiety	role underutilization
frustration	social support
general adaptation syndrome	strain
locus of control	stress
role ambiguity	tolerance for
role conflict	ambiguity
role overload	Type A personality

FOR DISCUSSION

1. Discuss the five types of problems related to employee work adjustment.
2. Define stress. How does it differ from strain?
3. How does the general adaptation syndrome work?
4. Contrast frustration with anxiety.
5. Identify the major categories of variables that have been found to influence stress. What role does social support play in the process?
6. In Close-Up 17.1, the plight of air-traffic controllers was discussed. What realistic suggestions would you make to relieve the tension and stress of this job?
7. Compare and contrast role conflict with role ambiguity.
8. How does a manager achieve a useful balance in a person-job fit so neither role overload nor role underutilization occurs?
9. How should a manager deal with a subordinate who is clearly a Type A personality? How should a manager who is a Type A personality handle his or her own stress?
10. Of what utility is the rate-of-life-change concept?

11. In organizations with which you are familiar, which of the many suggestions for coping with stress would be most applicable? Are the strategies you selected individual or organizational strategies?
12. What suggestions do you have for improving the work environment of night shift employees?

CASE

SCOTT TRUCKS, LTD.

17.1

"Mr. McGowan will see you now, Mr. Sullivan," said the secretary. "Go right in."

Sullivan looked tired and tense as he opened the door and entered McGowan's office. He had prepared himself for a confrontation and was ready to take a firm approach. McGowan listened as Sullivan spoke of the problems and complaints in his department. He spoke of the recent resignation of Tobin and the difficult time he had in attracting and keeping engineers. McGowan questioned Sullivan as to the quality of his supervision and direction, emphasizing the need to monitor the work and control the men.

"You have got to let them know who is boss and keep tabs on them at all times," said McGowan.

"But Mr. McGowan, that is precisely the point; my engineers resent surveillance tactics. They are well-educated, self-motivated people. They don't want to be treated like soldiers at an army camp."

The discussion was beginning to heat up. McGowan's fist hit the table. "Listen Sullivan, I brought you in here as a department manager reporting to me. I don't need your fancy textbook ideas about leading men. I have 10 years as a military officer, and I have run this plant from its inception. If you can't produce the kind of work I want and control your

men, then I will find someone who can. I don't have complaints and holdups from my other managers. We have systems and procedures to be followed, and so they shall or I will know the reason they aren't."

"But that is just the point," continued Sullivan, "my men do good work and contribute good ideas and, in the face of job pressures, perform quite well. They don't need constant supervision and direction and least of all the numerous and unnecessary interruptions in their work."

"What do you mean by that?" asked McGowan.

"Well both Tobin and Michaels have stated openly and candidly that they like their work but find your frequent visits to the department very disconcerting. My engineers need only a minimal amount of control, and our department has these controls already established. We have weekly group meetings to discuss projects and routine work. This provides the kind of feedback that is meaningful to them. They don't need frequent interruptions and abrasive comments about their work and the need to follow procedures."

"This is my plant and I will run it the way I see fit," screamed McGowan. "No department manager or engineer is going to tell me otherwise. Now I suggest, Mr. Sullivan, that you go back to

522   Work and Stress

EXHIBIT 1   **ORGANIZATIONAL CHART, SCOTT TRUCKS**

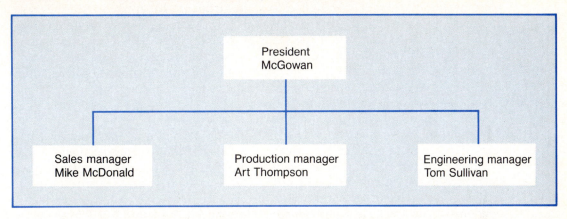

your department, have a meeting with your men, and spell out my expectations."

By this time Sullivan was intimidated and very frustrated. He left the office hastily and visibly upset. McGowan's domineering style had prevailed, and the meeting had been quite futile. No amount of pleading or confrontation would change McGowan's attitude.

Sullivan returned to his department and sat at his desk quite disillusioned with the predicament. His frustration was difficult to control and he was plagued with self-doubt. He was astonished at McGowan's intractable position and stubbornness.

He posted a notice for a meeting that would be held the next day with his department. He outlined an agenda and included in it mention of resignation. He left the plant early, worrying about the direction he should take.

Background

Scott Trucks is housed in an old aircraft hangar in the Debert Industrial Park, near Truro, Nova Scotia. The government of Nova Scotia sold the building for a modest sum as it no longer had use for the hangar after the armed forces

had abandoned it. The facility, together with the financial arrangements organized by Mr. McGowan, the president of Scott, made the enterprise feasible.

Inside the building, renovations have provided for an office area, a production operation, and an engineering department. The main offices are located at the front of the building, housing the sales team and the office clerks. The sales manager, Mike McDonald (see Exhibit 1), and two assistants make up the sales team at the Debert location of Scott Trucks. Three or four field representatives work in southern Ontario and the United States.

Mike is considered a good salesman and often assumes a role much broader than sales. Customer complaints, ordering, and replacement parts also fall into his domain. The production manager frequently makes reference to Mike's ability to talk on two phones at the same time!

Art Thompson has been production manager at Scott Trucks for eight years. The area he manages is behind the sales office and takes up most of the space in the building. The engineering department, comprising small offices, is located behind the production department

which is divided into two areas by a long, narrow corridor. The shop floor is divided into basic sections of assembly with a paint, a welding, and a cab section as well as other areas used to assemble the large Scott trucks.

Owing to the limited capacity of the plant, only two or three truck units are in production at any one time. Another constraint on capacity is the nature of the system used to produce the trucks. There are no pulleys, belts, or assembly lines used in the system; rather the production takes place in large bays where sections of the trucks are individually completed in preparation for the final assembly.

The truck units are used for a variety of functions, particularly where a heavy truck requirement is in demand. Fire trucks, highway maintenance trucks, and long-distance hauling trucks are some of the units produced by Scott. To some extent the trucks are custom-made, as each purchaser will request changes on the basic design. The engineers also adapt the trucks to meet the various standards and specifications of the Canadian government and the vigorous Canadian climate.

Tom Sullivan, who is a recent graduate of Nova Scotia Technical Institute with a degree in engineering, is the newest of the managers at Scott. He shows good promise as an engineer but, as with his predecessor, is having adjustment problems as a manager. Tom received an M.B.A. from Dalhousie University and majored in management science and organizational behavior. He completed project work in participative management styles under the direction of a specialist in this area. He tries to practice this approach in his new position and enjoys the ideas and flow of discussion at the department meetings. Tom works in a department with men much

his senior and is the youngest of the department managers at Scott Truck. He works hard and is well liked by his subordinates. Personal satisfaction, though infrequent, comes as a direct result of the open and participative management style he uses.

The Engineers

The composition of the group of engineers at Scott is unusual. One of the group is not an engineer by qualification but had many years of practical experience. He moved from Detroit to Truro, having worked with Ford Trucks for 15 years. Since his recruitment by McGowan he has worked with Scott for eight years. Retirement for this man is not far off, a fact he frequently makes known to the group. His work is good, and he seems to have many answers to difficult problems—a redeeming factor in the absence of an engineering degree. Don Jones, another member of the group, is a good engineer. His workday is solid. However, most evenings are spent at a local tavern. His wife was killed recently, and he does not seem to care any more. The remainder of the group are a combination of senior and junior men who have been with the company for a number of years. Two engineers had just left the group for better jobs and for a "less confining" atmosphere, as they put it. Tom Sullivan's effort to lead the group is proving to be a difficult task.

The Production Workers

Work for the men in the production plant is reasonably stable. A good-paying job in production in Truro is difficult to find, a situation of which the men are fully aware; many of them have experienced the monotony of unemployment and job hunting before this opening presented itself.

With the exception of a few French-Canadian welders, the workers are Maritimers whose experience and skills range from those of a skilled tradesman to those of a casual laborer. The local trades school in Truro has provided the organization with a number of good machinists, welders, and painters that the foreman hired and began to develop.

The morale on the plant floor has been very good, particularly since the company has improved its sales position. The once-frequent layoffs that were due to work shortage have ceased in the presence of higher demand for the trucks. The new field sales group contributes significantly to the situation with their efforts in southern Ontario and the northern United States. The pay scale is above average for the area and there is a good rapport between the production manager and the workers.

Administrative Control

Administrative control in the plant has been accomplished by two methods: one in terms of the quality of the product and the other in terms of its cost. Attention has been paid to the quality control function through a quality control supervisor whose task it is to examine the end product in a thorough manner using rigorous criteria. The other method of control is that implemented by the accounting office. Through the adoption of a standard cost program, material labor and overhead variances are accumulated and presented on data report sheets.

The production manager, Art Thompson, is responsible for collecting cost data and for sending it to the office on a weekly basis. Art is not an easygoing person; he frequently gets upset when problems occur on the shop floor. He is closely watched by Mr. McGowan, the president. Consequently, to Art the monthly meetings of the managers are a real ordeal, since McGowan, as owner, tries to watch the costs very carefully and to make sure the plant is running as efficiently as possible.

McGowan uses three approaches to managing the operation at Scott Trucks. The first is a monthly meeting with the three managers. The second technique is a series of interdepartmental memos that interpret the results of cost figures presented to him throughout the month. The third method is by frequent plant visits and observations.

None of these controls is favorably received by the managers, as they feel they are being watched too carefully. Interdepartmental memos may read as follows:

May 12, 19—
To: Mr. Art Thompson, production manager
From: Mr. McGowan, president, Scott Trucks
Re: Materials quantity variance

I noticed a considerable amount of material quantity variance in your production reports for last week. The standard cost system has been implemented for six weeks now, and it no longer suffices to say that you are still "working the bugs out of the system." It is time you paid closer attention to the amount of materials going into the production process and to avoiding any spoilage.

Another example of an interdepartmental memo reads as follows:

May 20, 19—
To: Mr. Art Thompson, production manager
From: Mr. McGowan, president, Scott Trucks
Re: Inaccurate recording of time, and use of time cards

I noticed last week on your labor cost submissions that a number of employees have been neglecting to

punch time cards. Please see that this system is properly followed.

Art Thompson's reaction to these memos has been one of apprehension and concern. It is the practice of the foreman and himself to try to resolve the problems as quickly as possible, and together they have been able to rectify these difficulties quite rapidly as the men are eager to cooperate.

The plant visits to the production area made by Mr. McGowan are frequent and effective. He has been known to come out in shirt-sleeves and literally assume the workman's job for a period of time. This is particularly true of a new worker or a young worker, where he will dig in and instruct the individual on how he should be doing his job. On such occasions he will give specific instructions as to how he wants things done and how things should be done.

It makes McGowan feel right at home when he is involved with the workers. He spent 15 years as a navy commander, and he often used to remark that there was only one way to deal with his subordinates. The reaction of the workers to this approach is mixed. Some of the production people dislike this "peering over the shoulders"; others do not seem to mind and appreciate McGowan's concern for a "job well done." The workers grumble at McGowan's approach but feel most of his criticisms to be constructive.

McGowan's management approach in the monthly meetings is not considerably different from that with the production workers. McGowan assumes a very authoritarian style in dealing with his managers.

The monthly meetings are an integrative effort among engineering, sales, and production, with the purpose of ironing out difficulties both on a personality

basis and on a work basis. The workload in the engineering department has been growing for the last six months at a considerable rate. This reflects the increase in production and the need for people in the area of engineering and design to provide a high quality of technical expertise.

The number of engineers currently working at Scott is eight. Relations between the engineering department and other departments have been less than satisfactory, and a good deal of conflict has occurred over a number of issues. For example the reports from quality control at Scott have been poor from time to time, and increasingly the problem has been traced to unclear engineering specifications. Upset about these conditions, McGowan has expressed strong disapproval in his memos to the department.

Lately the engineers have been bombarded with McGowan's memos, the results of more frequent complaints about the engineering department from the quality control manager and the production manager. Along with other factors, they have provided the ammunition McGowan needed to confront the engineering department. The engineers, however, have resisted, refusing to accept these memos in the same way that the production people have. As a result of these memos, complaints and misunderstandings have arisen. The engineers have responded by suggesting that the production people cannot interpret the blueprints and that they never bother to question them when a change is not understood or clear.

Disturbed by this situation, McGowan has made it a point to visit the engineering section at regular intervals, and his tactics have been much the same as with the production people. Unfortunately the engineering manager, Tom

Sullivan, was feeling the pressure and could not seem to keep his department running smoothly. Being new to the job, he did not know how to handle McGowan. The two engineers had quit recently and left the company, not explaining their discontent but only referring to better jobs elsewhere.

Tom Sullivan had reacted poorly to this situation and had been in a somber mood for about two months. His work and his adjustment had not been successful. The veterans in the department, though understanding his frustration, could not help Sullivan, who felt he was better off trying to accommodate McGowan than resisting him. To make matters worse the two engineers who had recently quit had left a large backlog of work incomplete, and efforts to recruit new engineers had been a strain on Sullivan. The marketplace quickly absorbed all the engineers graduating from Nova Scotia Tech, and Debert, Nova Scotia, had few attractions available to enable it to compete with larger centers.

Tom did get a big break, however, in his recruiting drive when he discovered through a contact in Montreal two engineers who were wishing to return to the Maritimes. Both men were young and had experience and good training in engineering. In their interview they discussed their experiences and their ability to work independently. Moreover both were looking for a quieter environment. Sullivan liked their credentials and hired the two men.

McGowan had been on vacation at the time and had not met the new engineers until a month after they had been on the job. His first encounter, however, was a cordial meeting with the two engineers and, although the climate in the department was always unpredictable and changing, activities and relations were smooth for a month or two much

to the relief of Sullivan. McGowan maintained his surveillance of the plant, including the engineers. Tim Michaels and Bill Tobin, the new engineers, felt uncomfortable with McGowan around but just proceeded with their work and ignored the long stares and the continued presence of the "boss."

One Friday afternoon McGowan walked into the engineering section with a smug look on his face. It was near the end of the month, just prior to the monthly meeting. Sullivan looked up immediately as McGowan moved towards Tobin's drafting table. McGowan was irate. He began talking to Tobin in a loud voice. Shaking his fist, he threw down a report on a change proposed by Tobin for the interior of the cabs made at Scott.

"What gives you the right to implement such a change without first going to Sullivan, then to me?" screamed McGowan. "You have only been with this company for two and a half months and already you feel you can ignore the 'system.'"

"Well, Mr. McGowan, I thought it was a good idea, and I have seen it work before," responded Tobin, flustered by McGowan's attack.

In the meantime Sullivan came out of his office to see what the problem was about. McGowan turned to him and asked him why he couldn't control his men, adding that the changes were totally unauthorized and unnecessary. Sullivan glanced at the blueprint and was taken by surprise when he examined it more carefully. In the meantime McGowan raved on about Tobin's actions.

"Oh, um, ah, yes, Mr. McGowan, you're right; this should have been cleared between, uh, you and me before production got it; but, ah, I will see that it doesn't happen again."

McGowan stormed out, leaving

Tobin and Sullivan standing by the desk. Tobin was upset by "this display of rudeness," as he put it.

"Tom," he went on, "this was a damn good idea and you know it."

Sullivan shook his head. "Yes, you're right. I don't know how to deal with McGowan; he wears me down sometimes. But also Bill, you have to channel your changes through the system."

Tobin turned back to his table and resumed his afternoon work.

For the next six weeks the plant operated smoothly as production picked up and more people were hired. Work in the engineering department increased correspondingly as people wanted new and better parts on their trucks. New engine and cab designs were arriving and put an increased burden on the engineering department. In fact it fell well behind in its efforts to change and adapt the truck specifications to meet the Canadian environment. The lengthy review process required to implement change also put an added burden on the operation at Scott.

These difficulties were compounded further by the fact that engineers were hard to find, and at Scott they were also hard to keep. Moreover summer was approaching, which meant decreased manpower owing to the holidays.

McGowan's frequent visits added to the difficult situation in the engineering department. Sullivan had taken to group meetings once a week with the engineers in an attempt to solve engineering problems and personal conflicts. At each meeting Tobin and Michaels discussed their work with the group and showed signs of real progress and development. They were adjusting well and contributing above expectations. At these meetings, however, they both spoke openly and frankly about McGowan's frequent visits and his abrasive style. A month had passed since they first suggested to Sullivan that he talk to McGowan about the problems he presented to the engineers by his visits to the department. At first the rest of the group agreed passively to the idea that Sullivan confront McGowan on this issue, but by the fourth week the group was being very firm with Sullivan on this issue, insisting he talk with McGowan.

Tom Sullivan knew the time had come and that he would have to face McGowan. That very morning he had received a call from a local company about Mr. Tobin and the quality of his work. Presumably Tobin had been looking for work elsewhere. This was the last straw. Sullivan picked up the phone and asked the secretary for an appointment with Mr. McGowan.

He wondered as he hung up the phone how he would deal with the problems he faced in his department and with Mr. McGowan.

CASE DISCUSSION QUESTIONS

1. Describe the basic nature of the stress in this case.
2. What do you feel has caused this stress? In your analysis, make use of the materials outlined in the chapter.
3. As a manager, what would you do to resolve the conflict and reduce the stress levels?

Source: Reprinted by permission of Lakehead University, Thunder Bay, Ontario.

WORK DESIGN

People are often overheard saying things like "I hate my job" or "My job is one of the worst in the world." Obviously, some jobs are less rewarding than others. For example, Walters (cited in Dickson, 1975, p. 57) identifies what he claims are the "Ten Worst Jobs." These, in no specific order, are:

- assembly-line worker
- highway toll collector
- car-watcher in a tunnel
- pool typist
- bank guard
- copy-machine operator
- bogus typesetter (those who set type that is not to be used)
- computer-tape librarian (a fancy title for a person whose job is rolling up spools of tape all day)
- housewife (not to be confused with mother)
- automatic-elevator operator

Although we could disagree with specific choices here, these jobs do lack the status, challenge, and rewards that are found in other jobs such as airplane pilot, line manager, engineer, architect, systems analyst, or chemist. Jobs differ, and our concern in this chapter is the nature of these differences and what managers can do to improve the integrity and quality of certain jobs.

The problems of employee discontent have been well documented throughout the previous chapters. In Chapter One we saw the various negative ways in which people describe their jobs. In Chapters Six and Seven, we discussed models of employee motivation and how many organizational environments fail to provide a motivating work environment. We now come to an examination of one of the major ways in which many of these problems can be reduced—namely, attempts to redesign the job and work environment.

IMPORTANCE OF TOPIC FOR MANAGERS

Managers should be familiar with work design in organizations for several reasons. Work design experiments have become increasingly popular in recent years. Why? What is behind the technique, and how does it relate to a particular organization? Answers to these questions help a manager to determine whether a similar program is appropriate for his or her situation.

Work design represents an important tool in a manager's repertoire of skills for improving organizational effectiveness. Many studies have shown that recent experiments in work design have resulted in increased job performance and/or attitudes.

As with any attempt to change the work place, however, problems sometimes arise that stifle managerial efforts. Before adopting a particular work design technique, managers should know possible drawbacks of the technique, as well as methods for overcoming the obstacles.

EARLY APPROACHES TO WORK DESIGN

Serious efforts to efficiently structure jobs that people perform date from the early 1800s and the rise of the industrial revolution. As factories grew in size and developed in sophistication, greater efforts were made to break down workers' jobs so they could be performed more quickly and with less training cost and time. It was reasoned that, since workers were mostly economically motivated, efforts at job fractionization would benefit both companies and workers. Companies would benefit because of increased efficiency and output. Workers would benefit, it was thought, because the piece-rate compensation

EXHIBIT 18.1   EVOLUTION OF WORK DESIGN

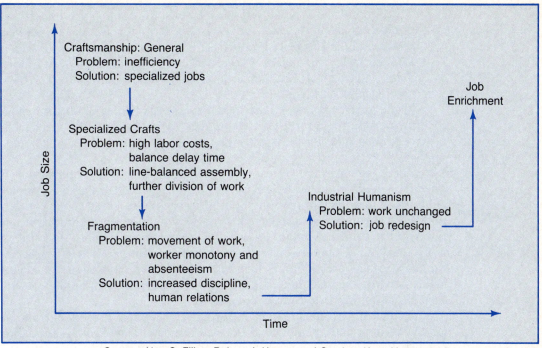

Source: Alan C. Filley, Robert J. House, and Stephen Kerr, *Managerial Process and Organizational Behavior* (Glenview, Ill.: Scott, Foresman and Company, 1976), p. 339. Reprinted by permission.

system tied monetary rewards directly to output: the greater the production, the higher the wages.

Scientific Management

Attempts to simplify job design reached their zenith from a technological standpoint in the assembly-line production techniques that became popular in the early 1900s (see Exhibit 18.1). A study of assembly-line technology in automobile manufacturing (Walker and Guest, 1952) identified six predominant characteristics of job fractionization:

- *Machine pacing.* The production rate is determined by the speed of the conveyor belt and not by the workers.
- *Repetitiveness.* Tasks are performed over and over during a single work shift. On auto assembly lines, for example, typical *work cycles* (that is, the time allowed for an entire piece of work) range from between thirty seconds to one and one-half minutes. This means the worker performs the same task up to 500 times per day.

- *Low skill requirements.* Because of the simplified task requirements, jobs can be easily learned and workers are easily replaced.
- *Task specialization.* Each job consists of only a few operations. Final product assembly is often done elsewhere in the factory so workers seldom see the complete product.
- *Limited social interaction.* Because of the speed of the assembly line, noise, and physical separation, it is difficult to develop meaningful social relationships on the job.
- *Tools and techniques specified.* Staff specialists (usually industrial engineers) select the tools and techniques to be used by the workers to maximize efficiency of operations.

These principles are typical of the techniques suggested by advocates of *scientific management* (such as Frederick Taylor). Although these techniques led to early successes on the shop floor, drawbacks also began to appear that nullified many of the advances made. First, job fractionization or fragmentation ignored human needs for growth and development. Taylor (1911, p. 59) noted that "one of the very first requirements for a man who is fit to handle pig iron as a regular occupation is that he more nearly resembles in his mental makeup the ox than any other type." This view of employees hardly encouraged efforts to improve working conditions.

Second, it became apparent in the early 1920s that job fractionization led to boredom and unauthorized breaks (Vernon, 1924). People simply did not like the jobs, and they reacted by not cooperating with the wishes of management. Sabotage and unionization efforts also became prevalent during this period.

Industrial Humanism

Partly as a result of these problems, concern for improving job attitudes at work began in the 1930s. Behavioral scientists turned to seriously examining the plight of the worker and, under the rubric of *industrial humanism* (also known as the Human Relations movement), efforts were made to make employees happier on their jobs. Human relations training came into vogue, as did company newspapers, employee awards, and company social events. However, the basic nature of the job itself remained unchanged and the problems persisted. It was not until the late 1950s that the concept of job enrichment emerged as a potential solution to problems of worker aberration and poor performance.

Herzberg's Contribution to Job Enrichment

One of the most significant early contributors to job design was Frederick Herzberg (Herzberg, Mausner, and Snyderman, 1959). Based on a study of accountants and engineers, Herzberg discovered that employees tended to describe satisfying experiences in terms of factors that were intrinsic to the job itself. These factors were called *motivators* and included variables like achievement, recognition, responsibility, advancement, and personal growth. On the other hand, these same employees described dissatisfying experiences (called *hygiene* factors) in terms of non–job-related factors. Hygiene factors included salary, company policies, supervisory style, and co-worker relations; all of these were factors that surrounded but did not include the job activities themselves.

Based on these findings, Herzberg argued against the efforts toward industrial humanism that prevailed at the time. These efforts treated hygiene factors, while the roots of employee motivation lay in the job itself. The implication of this conclusion for managers is clear: employee motivation can be enhanced through changes in the nature of the job (job enrichment). Efforts to change or enrich the job could include the following:

- *Control over resources.* Employees should have maximum control over the mechanisms of task performance.
- *Accountability.* Employees should be held accountable for their performance.
- *Feedback.* Supervisors have a responsibility to provide direct, clear, and frequent feedback.
- *Work pace.* Within limits, employees should be able to set their own work pace.
- *Achievement opportunities.* Jobs should allow employees to experience a feeling of accomplishment.
- *Personal growth and development.* Employees should be able to learn new and different procedures on the job and should be able to experience some degree of personal growth.

A quick comparison of this list with the earlier list pertaining to attributes of scientific management will show a marked difference in management philosophies over the nature of tasks in the work place. The philosophy underlying job enrichment takes a more optimistic view of the nature of workers and their needs, drives, and aspirations. It assumes that employees want to tackle problems at work and want to show their creative abilities. In this sense, it assumes that money, while important, is clearly not the only important motivator of good performance.

Herzberg's model has not escaped critique. It has been sharply criticized on several points (Steers and Porter, 1987): (1) it ignores individual differences, it assumes *all* employees want an enriched job; (2) the existence of two independent factors (motivators and hygiene factors) has not been substantiated; (3) the theory itself is open to different interpretations and Herzberg failed to present an unambiguous statement of the model; and (4) the model remains moot concerning *how* factors like achievement and recognition influence motivation. It does not describe the psychological processes underlying job design and motivation. Despite its limitations, however, Herzberg deserves considerable credit for ushering in the concept of job enrichment as a central topic in the study of people at work. In fact, much of the current work on job design can be traced directly to the early formulations proposed by Herzberg.

A CONTEMPORARY APPROACH TO WORK DESIGN

Today there exist several contemporary and often overlapping approaches to changing the design of work. These include job enlargement, job enrichment, sociotechnical systems, and others (see Steers and Mowday [1977] for a discussion of different approaches). Recently, Richard Hackman (1976), a leading figure in job redesign theory, has suggested that instead of comparing the nuances or finer points of these models, we may make better progress by simply combining the various models into the study of work redesign. According to Hackman, *work redesign* refers to any activities that involve the alteration of specific jobs (or interdependent systems of jobs) with the intent of increasing both the quality of employees' work experience and their productivity.

Why Redesign Work?

Redesigning jobs does not offer a panacea for organizational problems. Nor is it always appropriate in all situations. Rather, work redesign represents a systematic technique that has been found to be useful for improving life at work in a number of situations.

Why has work redesign proved successful as a change strategy? Hackman (1976) suggests four basic reasons. The first is that *work redesign alters the basic relationship between people and their jobs.* It is based on the premise that the work itself can be a powerful influence on motivation, performance, and satisfaction. By changing the job, intrinsic motivation can be increased.

The fact that *work redesign directly changes behavior* is a second reason for its success. Instead of attempting to change attitudes and hope that attitude changes get translated into changed behavior, work redesign focuses directly on what employees do—their behavior. By changing the job, employees must change what they do. As a result of experiencing more rewarding work, it is thought that employees develop more favorable attitudes which then reinforce behavior. Hence, the behavior tends to remain changed.

Also, *work redesign opens numerous opportunities for initiating other changes.* Advocates of systems theory note the importance of recognizing that changes in one area often cause changes in other areas. So it is with work redesign. The very act of implementing such techniques points to other areas within the organization where changes could be made (like the need for supervisory training or skills training or a career-development program). The ability to initiate one change in a work situation often makes it easier to initiate others.

A fourth reason for its success is that *work redesign can ultimately result in organizations that rehumanize rather than dehumanize people at work.* In contrast to the effects of assembly-line technology, work redesign can help individuals experience feelings of personal growth and development as a result of engaging in challenging work activities. People are rewarded for creative activities and for accepting responsibility for task accomplishment. As a result, they may find it easier to satisfy their higher-order needs at work.

In short, work redesign offers the promise that organizations can develop work environments that challenge employees and make better use of their human resources. If properly carried out, work redesign can help managers facilitate organizational effectiveness while at the same time improving the quality of working life.

The Job Characteristics Model

Several recent attempts have been made to develop a model of how work redesign influences employees and their behavior (Hackman and Oldham, 1976; Staw, 1976). To date, the model that has received the widest attention is that proposed by Hackman and Oldham (1976), known as the *Job Characteristics Model.* This model summarizes and integrates much of the earlier work in the area (Turner and Lawrence, 1965; Trist, 1970; Hackman and Lawler, 1971).

The job characteristics model, shown in Exhibit 18.2, consists of four parts. As shown, five core job dimensions influence three critical psychological states which in turn influence several desired personal and work outcomes. The links between job dimensions and psychological states and between psychological states and outcomes are moderated by employee growth-need strengths. We will briefly review this process.

Critical Psychological States. According to the model, an employee's motivation and satisfaction are influenced by three psychological states:

- *Experienced meaningfulness of the work.* Employees must feel that the work is important, worthwhile, and valuable.
- *Experienced responsibility for work outcomes.* Employees must feel personally responsible and accountable for the results of the work they perform.
- *Knowledge of results.* Employees must receive regular feedback concerning the quality of their performance.

As Hackman (1976, p. 129) explains, "The model postulates that internal rewards are obtained by an individual when he *learns* (knowledge of results) that he *personally* (experienced responsibility) has performed well on a task that he *cares about* (experienced meaningfulness)." The more these three psychological states are present on a job, the more satisfied individuals will feel when they perform well. These internal rewards act as incentives for

EXHIBIT 18.2   THE JOB CHARACTERISTICS MODEL OF WORK MOTIVATION

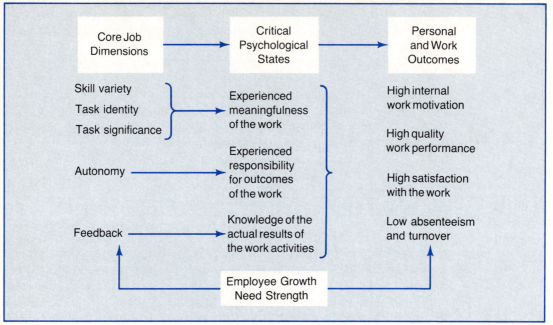

Source: J. R. Hackman and G. R. Oldham, "Motivation Through the Design of Work: Test of a Theory," *Organizational Behavior and Human Performance 16* (1976): 250–79. Reprinted by permission.

individuals to continue their efforts to perform in order to obtain additional intrinsic rewards. When individuals fail to perform well, positive reinforcement is not experienced and they may be motivated to try harder on subsequent tasks in order to regain the intrinsic rewards.

Core Job Dimensions. What activates these psychological states? According to Exhibit 18.2, five core job dimensions combine to determine motivational level. *Skill variety* is the degree to which a job requires a variety of different activities that involve the use of a number of different skills and talents. *Task identity* is the degree to which the job requires completion of a whole and identifiable piece of work; that is, doing a job from beginning to end with a visible outcome. *Task significance* is the degree to which a job has a substantial impact on the lives or work of other people, in the immediate organization or in the external environment. *Autonomy* is the degree to which a job provides substantial freedom, independence, and discretion to an individual in scheduling work and in determining the procedures to be used in carrying it out. The fifth core job dimension is *feedback*—the degree to which carrying out work activities required by the job results in individuals obtaining direct and clear information about the effectiveness of their performance.

The first three job dimensions above are believed to influence the experienced meaningfulness of work, as shown in the exhibit. Autonomy influences experienced responsibility for work outcomes, while feedback influences knowledge of results. Any work redesign effort should, according to the model, attempt to develop jobs that are high in these core dimensions.

The job dimensions are often measured using a questionnaire developed by Hackman and Oldham (1976). Based on this questionnaire, it is possible to calculate a *motivating potential score* (MPS) that simply reflects the extent to which employees see their jobs as motivating. According to the model, a high motivating potential score is only possible if a job is high on at least one of the three dimensions that influence experienced meaningfulness, *and* high on autonomy *and* high on feedback. The existence of these three dimensions creates the necessary work environment for all three critical psychological states. Mathematically, then, the MPS can be calculated as follows:

$$\begin{array}{c} \text{Motivating} \\ \text{Potential} \\ \text{Score} \end{array} = \frac{\left[\begin{array}{c} \text{Skill} \\ \text{variety} \end{array} + \begin{array}{c} \text{Task} \\ \text{identity} \end{array} + \begin{array}{c} \text{Task} \\ \text{significance} \end{array} \right]}{3} \times \text{Autonomy} \times \text{Feedback}$$

This formula shows that a near-zero score on any of the three factors will reduce the MPS score to near-zero. Again, it is important to note that all three factors are imperative in redesigning work.

Employee Growth Need Strength. Hackman and Oldham use *growth need strength* to refer to a collection of higher-order needs (achievement, affiliation, autonomy) that they believe moderate the way in which employees react to the work environment. This influence emerges at two points in the model (see Exhibit 18.2). First, employees with high growth need strengths (GNS) are more likely to experience the desired psychological states when their objective job has been enriched than those with low GNS. This occurs because, based on their needs, they are more sensitive to (have a greater demand for) these job characteristics.

Second, high GNS individuals tend to respond more favorably to the psychological states when they occur than do low GNS individuals, since these states are more likely to facilitate the satisfaction of these higher-order needs. For instance, a person who has a high need for achievement can satisfy that need by successfully performing challenging tasks (high MPS). On the other hand, a person with a low *n Ach* may experience frustration or anxiety by being placed on such a job. The role of individual differences must be emphasized when designing work for people. It must be recognized that enriched jobs may have greater impact on some people (high GNS individuals) than on others.

Personal and Work Outcomes. Finally, the model indicates that several personal and work-related outcomes result from the combination of psychological states and GNS. Specifically, when people experience the psychological states described above, one would expect them to exhibit high levels of internal work motivation, high quality of performance, high job satisfaction, and low turnover and absenteeism. While the psychological states are clearly not the only variables to affect these outcomes, they are believed to be an important influence.

Research on the Job Characteristics Model. As with any conceptual model of human behavior, it is difficult to adequately test it. While much research on the model has emerged recently, most of it takes the form of correlational designs instead of experimental designs. Although caution is advised in evaluating the results, it is possible to summarize the research to date on the validity of the model.

On the positive side, several studies have found that people who work on jobs high in the core job dimensions are more motivated and satisfied than people who work on jobs low in these dimensions. Similar (though weaker) findings exist for absenteeism. Second, the MPS-outcome relationship has been found to be stronger for employees with a high GNS than for those with a low GNS. Third, some inferential evidence is claimed that core job dimensions work *through* psychological states to influence outcomes (Hackman and Oldham, 1976; Steers and Mowday, 1977).

On the negative side, however, several limitations should be noted. First, the forecasting powers of the model are far less significant in predicting performance than job satisfaction. In fact, the model is rather poor at predicting performance, although this may be caused by our inability to accurately measure the study variables. In addition, considerable trouble has been experienced in attempting to demonstrate conclusively that core job dimensions work through psychological states to influence outcomes (Wall, Clegg, and Jackson, 1978). In view of the fact that we are dealing with psychological (and nonobservable) variables, this difficulty is understandable.

In summary, the Job Characteristics Model does appear to represent a useful conceptual framework for understanding how and why work redesign influences employee behavior and attitudes. While more work on the topic is needed, the utility of the model for management practice should not be overlooked.

Principles for Redesigning Work

Based on the Job Characteristics Model (and earlier work on the topic), Hackman (1976) has proposed five principles, or guidelines, for enriching jobs and redesigning work. These principles suggest ways in which managers can make substantive work changes, as well as how such changes will affect the core job dimensions (see Exhibit 18.2). Together, the principles illustrate very clearly how the model can be applied to work situations.

To the extent possible, workload should be divided into natural work units—pieces of work that logically fit together. For instance, a typist may be assigned all the typing responsibilities for a person or department instead of spreading the work around to various typists who never see completed projects. *Forming natural work units* allows employees to increase their ownership of the work and to see its significance. Similarly, jobs can be enlarged by combining several of their related aspects. By *combining tasks,* skill variety and task identity are both increased.

Jobs that are designed traditionally (assembly-line or fractionated jobs) provide little or no contact between the producer (employee) and the clients, whether these clients are inside or outside the organization. By *establishing client relationships,* several things occur. First, feedback increases because the ultimate user is now in a position to respond to the quality of the product or service. Second, skill variety may increase since the producer (employee) now needs to develop the interpersonal skills necessary to interact with clients. Third, autonomy may also increase as the producer now has the responsibility to decide how to manage the relationship with the clients.

Hackman's fourth principle, the principle of *vertical loading,* aims at closing the gap between the doing and controlling aspects of work. For example, employees are permitted to select their own work methods, inspect their own work, choose their hours of work, or participate in decisions affecting their job or the organization. By doing so, employee autonomy is increased.

A manager can make a fifth substantive work change, according to Hackman, by *opening feedback channels.* Most employees receive supervisor-provided feedback about their job performance. However, using work redesign, another source of feedback emerges: job-provided feedback. When jobs are designed so they provide built-in feedback mechanisms (having employees check their own work), employees are continually reminded of their performance quality and these reminders come from the job without the interpersonal problems inherent in supervisor-provided feedback.

While these principles may sound fine in theory, how do they work in actual practice? How do we take a dull job and apply the principles to improve the quality of work? Hackman and associates (Hackman, Oldham, Janson, and Purdy, 1975) provide one answer in the example shown in Close-Up 18.1.

The principles suggested here are meant to illustrate the types of interventions that can be used in organizations. Through techniques like these, it may be possible to build core job dimensions that sufficiently cue psychological states and lead to employee motivation and satisfaction. But as we shall see in the examples below, this is easier said than done.

EXAMPLES OF WORK REDESIGN EXPERIMENTS

The recent literature on organizational behavior and management is filled with examples of successful (and sometimes unsuccessful) work redesign efforts (Gyllenhammer, 1977; Cummings, Molloy, and Glen, 1977). We continually see vignettes of simple ways in which work can be made both more satisfying and more productive. Consider the following examples:

The Problem. Perhaps one of the clearest examples of the application of the Job Characteristics Model can be seen in one effort to redesign the job of keypunch operators at Traveler's Insurance Company. Using the core job dimensions described in the model, the job of keypunch operator prior to enrichment can be described as follows:

- *Skill variety.* None. Only a single skill was needed: the ability to accurately punch data on cards.
- *Task identity.* Little. Batches were assembled to provide an even work load, but not whole identifiable jobs.
- *Task significance.* Not apparent. While keypunching is a necessary step in providing service to company customers, the individual operators were isolated by an assignment clerk and a supervisor from any knowledge of what the operation meant to the receiving department, let alone to the ultimate consumer.
- *Autonomy.* Little. The operators had no freedom to arrange their daily tasks to meet schedules, to resolve problems with receiving departments, or even to correct information that was obviously wrong.
- *Feedback.* None. Once a batch was completed, the operators received no feedback on performance quality.

Work Redesign. The investigators, using the Job Characteristics Model, made the following simple changes:

- *Natural work units.* Instead of randomly assigning batches of work, each operator was assigned continuing responsibility for certain accounts (particular departments or recurring jobs). All work for an account was given to the same operator.
- *Task combination.* Some planning and controlling functions were integrated with the main task of keypunching.
- *Client relationships.* Each operator was given several channels of direct contact with clients. Operators, not assignment clerks, could now examine documents for legibility and autonomy. When a problem arises, the operator, not the supervisor, contacts the client.
- *Feedback.* In addition to client feedback, the operators also receive feedback from the job itself. For example, all incorrect cards are returned to the operator for correction. Weekly computer printouts are provided listing error rates and productivity. These are sent directly to the operator, not the supervisor.
- *Vertical loading.* Operators were given authority to correct obvious errors on their own. They could also set their own schedules and plan their daily work.

Results. As a result of the work redesign experiment, several desired outcomes emerged: (1) While the control group (where no changes were made) showed an increase in productivity of 8.1 percent during the trial period, the work redesign group showed an increase of 39.6 percent. (2) Prior to the study the experimental group had an error rate of 1.53 percent; following the intervention, the average error rate fell to 0.99 percent. (3) During the study period, absenteeism in the experimental group declined 24.1 percent, while it increased

29 percent in the control group. (4) While no attitude changes occurred in the control group, overall job satisfaction increased 16.5 percent in the experimental group after intervention. (5) Because of the improved operator proficiency, fewer controls were necessary, reducing supervisory needs. (6) Since the operators took over many of the mundane supervisory responsibilities, supervisors were now able to devote more time to developing feedback systems, setting up work modules, overseeing the enrichment effort, and planning. In short, supervisors were now able to manage instead of dealing with day-to-day problems.

Source: J. R. Hackman, G. Oldham, R. Janson, and K. Purdy, "A New Strategy for Job Enrichment," *California Management Review 17* (4) (1975): 57–71.

- At Southern Central Bell Telephone Company, employees who were responsible for compiling telephone directories were given the right to establish their own cut-off dates for the sale of Yellow Page advertisements. On their own, the employees consistently set later deadlines than management had previously allowed. As a result, in one year, this practice gave the company a total of three extra weeks of sales time and led to an increase of $100,000 in additional advertising sold.
- At Möet and Chandon, the famous French champagne producer, each portion of the production process is broken down into small profit centers that "buy" the produce in process from the group before it and "sell" it to the next. The "profit" (that is, the value added to the product) in excess of the norm—a standard negotiated between management and labor—is returned to the workers as a bonus.
- Taking a simple approach to increased employee participation, the 3M Company, in an effort to reduce manufacturing costs, simply asked employees to set up their own cost-cutting programs. Within one year, costs had been reduced by $10 million.
- In Denmark, Sadolin and Holmblad, manufacturers of printing ink, asked workers to design the new plant the company intended to build. The company supplied the architects and technical help and agreed within reason to abide by the outcomes. The finished product was "perhaps eighty percent like the factory which the bosses would have created on their own." In addition to subtle design changes, the workers installed a swimming pool that doubled as a water reservoir required for fire protection. As a result of the changes, the absenteeism rate dropped from ten percent to five percent per day, turnover dropped to zero for the first two years of operation, and productivity increased fifteen percent (with no changes in production technology or machinery).
- At the Communications Division of Motorola, Inc., a single person is

now responsible for the assembling, testing, and packaging of Pageboy II pocket radio-paging devices. Previously, these devices were made using assembly-line technology that consisted of 100 steps (and people). As a result, both the quantity and quality of production have increased, while turnover and absenteeism have decreased.

Examples like these are often cited as proof that work redesign represents a useful technique for simultaneously improving the quality of work and organizational effectiveness. However, these vignettes often fail to document the developmental work that preceded the changes and the possible problems or side-effects that resulted. To understand the whole picture, it is necessary to examine case histories of work redesign in some detail. We will do so here by reviewing three work redesign experiments that have been carried out among different types of employees performing different jobs. All too often, we are given one case history that may be industry specific and may be difficult to apply to other types of workers in a broad range of industries. The following examples demonstrate the widespread application of the technique. As you read each case, consider the principles of the Job Characteristics Model for guidance.

Xerox Corporation: Service Representatives

Several years ago, Xerox Corporation initiated a trial project in work redesign focusing on a sample of field technical representatives (Jacobs, 1975). Xerox employs 7000 representatives to service their copying machines at customer locations. The representatives provide maintenance at regular intervals and emergency maintenance for breakdowns. In the experiment, a sample of ninety representatives in one branch was selected for the experimental group, while several other branches served as control groups.

The Program. The primary emphasis in the program was to increase the authority and responsibility of the representatives. Prior to work redesign, representatives could not order parts or tools for maintenance; these were ordered by the field service managers. Under the new program, representatives were given full responsibility for ordering parts and tools to maintain their own inventory. When they needed technical assistance, they were allowed to call branch, region, or headquarters offices for advice (instead of going through the field service manager). Representatives were allowed to determine their own schedules for maintenance and installation as well as their own work hours, as long as the hours conformed to customer needs. They were authorized to work overtime and approve repairs without prior approval. Finally, some representatives helped interview and train new representatives. These changes were instituted a few at a time over a period of three months.

Results. As a result of the changes, several outcomes were noted:

- Employee attitudes (particularly with respect to responsibility, recognition, and challenge) increased significantly in the experimental group, while no changes were noted in the control groups.
- Absenteeism decreased by forty percent in the experimental group.
- Performance also improved somewhat during the project. Before the experiment, the branch under study ranked next to last among sixteen branches in the region. After the initial fourteen-month trial period, the experimental group had achieved a median ranking.

As a result of the early success, field service managers (the representatives' immediate superiors) began to show concern as to the abilities of the representatives to exercise good judgment in carrying out their new responsibilities. After discussions about the utility of the experiment, the managers developed a wait-and-see attitude. As time went on and they began to see that work redesign was successful in improving performance and attitudes, the commitment of the senior managers increased and their uneasiness and hostility subsided. Hence, the experiment made some contribution toward developing greater confidence and trust between levels within the organization. Based on these results, efforts continue at Xerox to expand the parameters of employees' jobs in various areas of the company.

General Foods—Topeka: Production Workers

Whereas the Xerox work redesign efforts focused on field representatives, a program using the same basic principles was attempted among production workers at the Gaines Pet Food Plant of General Foods in Topeka, Kansas. This case history is noteworthy both for its far-reaching change efforts and for the chronology of events that followed program implementation (Glaser, 1976).

The Program. In 1968, General Foods decided to construct a new plant to manufacture pet foods. As a result of several serious labor problems at an existing plant in Kankakee, Illinois, including sabotage, shutdowns, product waste, and low morale, management determined to build the new plant (in a separate geographic region) following basic principles of work redesign. Every effort was made to design both the factory and the work to provide challenging, meaningful jobs.

Although many new innovations were introduced, several important changes included:

- *Autonomous work groups.* Production processes were built around seven-to fourteen-member work teams. Teams were created for: (1) processing; (2) packaging and shipping; and (3) office duties. Each member was assigned to a team, but not to fixed job duties within the team. Each team had the responsibility for work assignments, screening and selecting new members, and other major decisions affecting group function.

- *Self-governance.* Teams were responsible for determining policies and procedures as they saw fit, instead of abiding by formal plant rules. As a result, fewer rules were issued and freedom of action increased.
- *Job enrichment.* Each job was designed to maximize variety, autonomy, significance, and feedback. The boring or repetitive aspects of work were eliminated where possible.
- *Job mobility and rewards for learning.* As a result of having enriched jobs, it was possible to have a single job classification for all workers. Pay raises were then based on ability to learn new skills or master new jobs. Workers were paid for what they were capable of doing instead of what they actually were allowed to do.
- *Freedom of access to information.* All information pertinent to the operation of the plant—production output, quality control data, economic forecasts—was made available to the work teams.
- *Elimination of status symbols.* Efforts were made in plant design to reduce needless status differentiation between managers and workers. The plant contained only one dining facility (no executive dining room), one parking lot (no reserve spaces), and one office decor.
- *Continuous monitoring of attitudes and output.* Plant productivity and worker morale were continually evaluated and changes were made only after their impact on these outcomes was considered.

During the implementation stage, several problems had to be recognized and overcome. The first problem was compensation rates. Pay rates were based on attained skill level and were determined by the team leader. Everyone began at the same rate but soon some workers received raises because they demonstrated new skills. As a result, other workers complained about both the equity of the decisions and the availability of opportunities to learn new skills and qualify for raises.

Second, from the start, the management at corporate headquarters was lukewarm about the project. This lack of enthusiasm possibly resulted from traditional resistance to innovation (Walton, 1975).

Finally, several rather minor problems arose among the team members themselves. Some individuals felt uneasy in group meetings or in participating in spontaneous mutual-help patterns of behavior. Some team leaders had difficulty overcoming an inclination to act like traditional authority figures. Excessive group pressure was often applied to workers who failed to meet the output norms set by the group. Even so, the initial program was allowed to continue to provide a fair test of the program.

Results. What happened as a result of these changes in work design? A summary of the findings to date was presented by Dulworth (1976), the original Topeka plant manager:

- Cost savings were between twenty percent and forty percent greater at Topeka than at other plants. The savings amounted to about $2 million per year.

- Quality control improved. Rejects were about eighty percent less than is normal for the industry.
- No sabotage or worker-caused shutdowns were experienced.
- Absenteeism ran about one and one-half percent and eighty percent of that was with the knowledge and approval of management.
- Turnover was about ten percent, compared to fifteen percent for the company as a whole. About one-half the turnover was company initiated.
- Compared to other plants, about three times as many employees have taken advantage of outside educational programs.
- Job attitudes and organizational commitment were higher than at similar plants.

With results like these, it is difficult not to become an advocate of work redesign efforts. Even so, caution is in order in interpreting these results. Mitchell Fein (1974), an industrial engineer, summarizes many of the problems as follows:

> General Foods—Topeka is a controlled experiment; a small plant with conditions set up to achieve desired results. The employees are not a cross section of the larger employee population; or even of Topeka. The plant and its operations are not typical of those in industry today. The results obtained are valid only for this one plant. What are other managers to do? Should they screen out nine of ten possible candidates and hire only from the select group that remains [like Topeka] . . . ?
>
> If the investigators had shown how they converted a plant bursting with labor problems into one where management and employees told glowingly of their accomplishments, the study would truly merit the praise it has received. Instead, they turned their backs on the company's parent plant in Kankakee, which has many of the problems of big city plants. Even worse, they tantalize management with the prospect that, in building a new plant with new equipment, carefully selected employees, and no union, productivity will be higher (pp. 71–72).

Clearly, while the prospects for a Topeka-like work redesign project should not be discounted, we should not be oblivious to the potential spurious effects often found in such experiments.

Aftermath. By 1976, the project had been operating for some time and serious problems began to emerge, not with the work design techniques, but with the political environment surrounding it. As described by *Business Week* (1977, p. 78):

> The problem has been not so much that the workers could not manage their own affairs as that some management and staff personnel saw their own positions threatened because the workers performed almost too well. One former employee says the system—built around a team concept—came squarely up against the company's bureaucracy. Lawyers, fearing reaction from the National Labor Relations Board, opposed the idea of allowing team members to vote on pay raises. Personnel managers objected because team members made hiring decisions. Engineers resented workers doing engineering work.

As one former employee noted:

Creating a system is different from maintaining it. There were pressures almost from the inception, and not because the system didn't work. The basic reason was power. We flew in the face of corporate policy. People like stable states. This system has to be changing or it will die.

As a result of this power struggle, many managers who instituted the program left the company. In response to concerns expressed by various professional groups, several changes were made. These included more job classifications, less participation, more supervision, and the addition of seven management positions to the plant, including controller, plant engineering manager, and manufacturing services manager. Despite these setbacks, General Foods describes the experiment as a success and has implemented similar—though scaled-down—programs at several other sites. As one of the ex-managers notes, "Every time you make a mistake, you wonder if White Plains (corporate headquarters) thinks that maybe if we had a traditional system there wouldn't have been a mistake. . . . Still, it's the best place I ever worked."

Federal Government: Clerical Workers

This work redesign experiment differs from the earlier ones in at least two respects: it focuses on clerical workers and it was carried out in a federal agency, not in a private corporation. In contrast to the General Foods experiment, this program was implemented in an ongoing organization exhibiting severe morale problems. Finally, it represents one of the more rigorous studies of workers on the job. It provides additional evidence of the wide range of applications of work redesign techniques.

The Program. This experiment focused on a large sample of clerical workers (mostly at the GS-3 level) in one federal bureaucracy (Locke, Sirota, and Wolfson, 1976). The jobs generally consisted of sorting incoming mail, searching for lost or misplaced files, and filing. The site was selected because of its widely known morale problems and history of labor-management conflict. Attitudes toward all aspects of the work environment as measured by standardized questionnaires were particularly negative prior to the intervention.

Three experimental work units were identified and were matched with three control units. In the experimental units, the following changes were made:

- Employees in the mail-posting department were divided into four six-person teams instead of working independently. Three teams worked on sorting and one worked on miscellaneous mail room jobs on a rotating basis. The teams could decide for themselves how to divide the

EXHIBIT 18.3   SUMMARY OF RESULTS OF JOB ENRICHMENT EXPERIMENT

Measure	Group	
	Experimental Units	Control Units
Productivity	+23%	+2%
Absenteeism	−5%	+7%
Turnover	−6%	+20%
Complaints and disciplinary actions	0	4
Attitudes	No change	No change

Source: E. A. Locke, D. Sirota, and A. D. Wolfson, "An Experimental Case Study of the Successes and Failures of Job Enrichment in a Government Agency," *Journal of Applied Psychology 61* (1976): 708. Copyright 1976 by the American Psychological Association. Reprinted by permission of the publisher and authors.

various operations rather than being assigned specific tasks. Daily productivity was recorded and posted.

▪ For those responsible for searching for misplaced files, the experimental units were allowed to decide for themselves what needed to be done. If materials could not be found, they decided on the next step rather than referring it to their supervisor. Clerks allotted time to various tasks based on what needed to be done rather than on what was assigned them. They kept their own records. A team captain was selected on a rotating basis to screen incoming work, complete unit time cards, dispatch outgoing work and telephone other units regarding file problems. Meetings were also held to discuss common problems.

▪ For those employees charged with filing, fixed production standards were eliminated. Employees could switch back and forth between tasks at will instead of being told what to do each hour. All clerks were trained to do the advanced tasks rather than being assigned to carry out only one small task. Employees kept track of their own production and these records were posted daily.

Results. Pre- and post-measures on attitudes and behaviors were taken. Results are shown in Exhibit 18.3. As shown, productivity in the experimental units increased substantially while absenteeism, turnover, and complaints decreased. Job attitudes remained unchanged in both groups, however.

While these results are impressive, the authors caution against interpreting them as highly supportive of job enrichment efforts (Locke et al., 1976). For instance, they attribute productivity increases to the following factors (p. 708):

(a) more efficient use of manpower as a result of enrichment, since after enrichment, employees could work where they were needed rather than where they were assigned;

(b) elimination of some unnecessary work procedures;

(c) more precise and/or frequent feedback regarding performance; and

(d) competition among employees.

Similarly, reduced absenteeism and turnover may have resulted in part from the enrichment efforts, but also in part from *initial* changes in attitudes resulting from program implementation. The implementation of the program served to heighten workers' expectations and, when all of these expectations were not met, attitudes returned to their previous (lower) levels. Locke et al. (1976, pp. 709–710) continue:

> Another group that complained about not having enough enrichment was reminded that they were being given substantially new responsibilities, which were formerly held by GS-4 employees in another unit, even as the experiment ended. Their reply was, "How come they are giving us their work? Don't they want it?" When pressed for why they viewed the new work in this way, they indicated that since they were not getting any practical rewards for their higher level work, their unit must be considered, in effect, a repository for unwanted tasks.
>
> It was clear from the interviews that these employees viewed their jobs *instrumentally,* that is, as a means to an end. Their comments . . . indicated that the concept of intrinsically satisfying work was not psychologically real to them. Their greatest concern was to get good ratings so that they could get promoted and get more pay. When these outcomes did not follow the enrichment program, the employees were angry and bitter.

Hence, while this study found that the work redesign program was a partial success (particularly in terms of improving productivity), the findings may have resulted as much from improved efficiency and job engineering as from job enrichment. This study clearly shows that major changes in the work situation often create new employee expectations which, if unmet, lead to additional problems for management.

As a postscript, it should be noted that upon receiving the report from the investigators summarizing the results of the study, the agency lost interest in the job enrichment idea. While two of the three experimental units were allowed to remain as they were, the enrichment idea failed to spread to other units in the agency.

ADDITIONAL TECHNIQUES OF WORK REDESIGN

From reading the above cases, one forms the impression that most work redesign efforts are built principally upon job enrichment. However, several other changes in the work place have also been tried with varying success. In many cases, these additional techniques are possible when job enrichment is not. Included among these other techniques of work redesign are: (1) job rotation; (2) four-day work week; (3) flexitime; (4) job sharing; and (5) quality control circles. Each will be briefly described.

Job Rotation

When an organization has a series of routine jobs that cannot be combined or enriched, it is possible to rotate workers from one job to the next over time. The aim of this *job rotation* is to minimize the routine and boredom to the extent possible through a change in activities. The employee learns different jobs and the company develops a more flexible work force. Even so, job rotation does not solve the basic problem of unenriched and unchallenging jobs and should be used only as a temporary or last-resort technique.

Four-Day Work Week

Beginning in the early 1970s, the *4/40* (four days/forty hours) *work week* emerged as a popular experiment in work redesign. It is estimated that close to two thousand companies employing over one million people now use the 4/40 plan (Dickson, 1975). The major push behind the 4/40 plan came from companies who hoped to gain greater productivity and efficiency and workers who wanted more leisure time. The 4/40 aims at accomplishing both without changing the job technology.

In a 1972 survey by the American Management Association, 143 companies using the 4/40 plan were asked to evaluate the plan. Results showed that the plan increased production in sixty-two percent of the companies, increased efficiency in sixty-six percent, and boosted profits for fifty-one percent. Similarly, a Bureau of Labor Statistics study showed that companies that had installed the plan generally met their objectives, whether they were to reduce costs, improve efficiency, reduce absenteeism, or improve job satisfaction (Dickson, 1975).

On the negative side, the AMA study revealed that 4/40 plans often presented problems for working mothers, as well as shipping and receiving problems, customer confusion about new hours, and occasionally cost increases. Clearly, an organization must consider the characteristics of the work force and whether the product or service performed lends itself to a four-day week before committing to the strategy.

Flexitime

One approach to change in the work place that has received increasing attention in recent years is *flexitime*. It is currently being used in over 5000 firms of varying sizes. Flexitime is a technique that allows employees more latitude and freedom in determining their own work schedules. It differs from plans like the four-day work week in that, while the employees have a certain degree of choice over starting and quitting time, they are all required to be present during certain daily core hours, so that necessary interpersonal and interdepartmental communication can take place.

Perhaps an example will clarify the technique. A New Jersey company, Sandoz-Wander, introduced a flexitime program that contained the following parameters (Dickson, 1975):

Earliest starting time:	7:30 AM
Latest starting time:	9:30 AM
Earliest leaving time:	4:00 PM
Latest leaving time:	6:00 PM
Lunch period:	12:00–2:00 PM
Maximum lunch period:	2 hours
Minimum lunch period:	1 hour
Core hours (when everyone must be present):	9:30–12:00 noon 2:00–4:00 PM
Average work week:	37.5 hours
Maximum work week:	40 hours
Minimum work week:	22.5 hours
Average workday:	7.5 hours
Maximum workday:	9.5 hours
Minimum workday:	4.5 hours

Within these guidelines, employees are free to select the working hours that best fit their own needs and desires. Following this plan, then, does not alter the basic nature of the job, but does provide employees with some discretion as to when to perform. Results of a series of experiments summarized in Golembiewski and Proehl (1978) reveal fairly consistent positive results. Both attitudes and behaviors (particularly in the form of reduced absenteeism and turnover) are generally improved.

Job Sharing

Finally, another strategy for relieving job fatigue while at the same time accommodating the needs of part-time workers is *job sharing*. Job sharing consists of two or more persons who jointly cover one job over a normal forty-hour week. For instance, two manuscript typists may share one job, with one working in the morning and one in the afternoon. The typing gets done and both employees have ample time for outside activities. While job sharing does not change the basic nature of the work, it does allow an organization to tap previously unavailable labor markets.

Quality Control Circles

A central aspect of Japanese management style, discussed in Chapter Eleven, is the involvement of production workers in decisions concerning improvements in productivity and product quality. This involvement manifests itself in the *quality control (Q.C.) circle.* A Q.C. circle consists of all employees who work closely together on one particular job. The circle leader may be a worker or a supervisor. In any case, the group meets periodically (e.g., one hour per week) to discuss production problems and look for useful solutions.

The idea behind quality control circles is simple. As L. J. Hudpeth, vice-president for corporate productivity at Westinghouse, says, "They [shop-floor workers] know more about operations than you do" *(Newsweek,* September 8, 1980, p. 59). That is, the employees themselves are best able to identify problems and suggest improvements, assuming, of course, that they have the necessary problem-solving skills, the necessary data, the time, and the financial support. Employees are given training ·in problem-solving tactics, including technical information and data analysis techniques. Moreover, they are given time off to conduct their enquiries.

Quality control circles were invented in the United States about thirty years ago, but were widely ignored until the past few years when U.S. firms realized how effective they have been in Japan. In Japan, one out of every eight workers belongs to a Q.C. circle. In the last few years, several hundred U.S. firms have joined the trend (Willis, 1980). (See Close-Up 18.2.)

Consider the following examples. A Q.C. circle at Northrup became concerned because the bits used to drill holes in titanium for F-5 fighter planes kept breaking. After investigating the problem, the group suggested that the drilling angle be changed and that bits from harder steel be used. As a result, the change—as small as it may seem—saved Northrup $70,000 in lost time. Similarly, Ford Motor Company recently adopted a variation on the Q.C. theme by giving workers forty-eight hours of special training at the two plants that they were gearing up to manufacture Ford Escorts and Mercury Lynxes. The training was intended to help workers spot start-up problems on the assembly line, saving Ford trouble later on. Early results suggest that the technique is successful, since the new cars have been far more trouble-free than comparable new introductions.

A third example of a Q.C. effort in action can be seen in the rather dramatic turnaround at the G.M. plant in Terrytown, New Jersey. In the early 1970s, the plant was plagued by violence and absenteeism. Car quality was extremely poor, and each year employees filed about 3000 grievances. As a result of the introduction of worker-management teams, car quality has improved substantially, and grievances fell to about forty per year. As suggested by Irving Bluestone, a retired U.A.W. vice-president, the new spirit of cooperation may have actually prevented the big facility from closing *(Newsweek,* September 8, 1980, p. 59).

Rewards to employers for participating in Q.C. circles vary. At Northrup, for example, the circle receives ten percent of any dollar savings resulting from the suggestion. In most situations, however, no monetary reward is used. Instead, it is believed that the increased employee involvement and resulting pride in accomplishment is sufficient. In any case, the technique continues to gain in popularity and continues to increase organizational efforts to facilitate effectiveness.

If one had to attempt to identify the primary reasons for the success of

CLOSE-UP 18.2 QUASAR ELECTRONICS: A CASE FOR QUALITY CONTROL

One of the earliest examples of the introduction of so-called Japanese management style into a U.S. firm is the case Quasar Electronics. In 1974, Matsushita, one of Japan's largest corporations, purchased the Motorola TV factory. Prior to the takeover, Motorola experienced 150 defects per 100 sets. After conversion to the new management style, Quasar (the new company name) reduced its defect rate to three or four defects per 100 sets using the same workers and the same quality control people. The only difference was the Japanese approach to quality management.

What exactly did Quasar do to cause such a dramatic improvement in product quality? A study by Juran (1978) suggests several factors that accounted for the change:

1. *Scrubdown of new products.* New products are carefully tested *before* they go into production to eliminate bugs. Previously, much of this "scrubdown" was often done *during* production in order to "save" production costs.
2. *Emphasis on quality characteristics.* A TV set has three principal quality characteristics: picture quality, cabinet appeal, and reliability. Many U.S. television companies focused on the first two of these characteristics, but ignored the third. In contrast, Japanese companies place higher emphasis on reliability. As a result, U.S. color TV sets failed in service at a rate five times higher than Japanese TV sets.
3. *Components.* Japanese companies carefully test all components before putting them into the set, while Americans typically do less testing. Japanese also give greater attention to quality (as well as price) in selecting vendors.
4. *Training.* Training is emphasized at all levels. Top managers attend classes on production quality and design engineers must work in operations prior to designing new products so they understand production problems. Most production workers are trained in quality control (Q.C.) circles as a regular part of their jobs. Such practices are typically not found in comparable U.S. firms.
5. *Employee relations.* Japanese companies emphasize teamwork and worker responsibility for quality control. Line managers and workers both have greater inputs into decision making about products and, as a result, feel greater responsibility, accountability, and pride than their U.S. counterparts.

Through the application of these simple techniques, Quasar Electronics found it could turn around a manufacturing plant in a short period of time and in the process improve both productivity and employee job satisfaction.

Source: J. M. Juran, "Japanese and Western Quality—A Contrast," *Quality Progress,* December 1978.

Q.C. circles, three reasons would probably stand out. First, in order to be successful, workers must be adequately trained in problem-solving techniques so they have the necessary skills to analyze the problem. Second, workers must be assured that suggested changes will not lead to their being penalized in any way (e.g., increased layoffs, increased job fractionization). And third, workers must feel that top management clearly and actively supports Q.C. efforts. Without this support, it is difficult to imagine Q.C. circles being taken seriously by employees.

WORK REDESIGN: PROBLEMS AND PROSPECTS

Problems with Work Redesign

Although work redesign holds much promise for improving both employee performance and the quality of working life, it is by no means a panacea. In fact, several rather serious problems have been identified by various researchers that suggest caution in work redesign attempts (Fein, 1974; Hackman, 1975; Walton, 1975).

Several recent studies have shown that some employees respond more positively to enriched jobs than others. For instance, for an employee with a high need for achievement, an enriched job may serve to cue the achievement motive, facilitating increased effort (Steers and Spencer, 1977). However, *failure to recognize individual differences*—putting employees with *low* need for achievement on an enriched job—may only heighten their anxiety, frustration, and dissatisfaction. And in many cases, the nature of the job does not lend itself to enrichment or redesign. Such *technical constraints* are present in continuous-process jobs, where the jobs are paced by machines. In these circumstances, job rotation or flexitime may perhaps offer a partial solution.

In many cases, *costs* of work redesign efforts are simply very high. These increased costs include additional expenditures for training, tools, construction, start-up, and sometimes wages. The problem is whether the consumers are willing to pay the additional costs associated with work redesign, passed along in the form of higher prices. Often, companies exhibit a *lack of proper diagnosis prior to introduction*. In their haste to be the first in innovation, companies fail to carefully consider the nature and costs of the problems they are facing, as well as what constitutes the best approach to solving them.

Many failures in job redesign have been traced to *failure to actually change the work*. No substantive changes were made in the job itself. Instead, lip service was paid by indifferent or hostile managers. Since the jobs were not changed, no changes were recorded in attitudes or behavior. Managers may occasionally feel threatened by the increased autonomy given to workers under work redesign (see General Foods example). They may fear loss of both power and status. This *managerial resistance* may be demonstrated in dragging feet and efforts sabotaged in numerous ways.

Similarly, *unions often resist* work redesign efforts, surprisingly for many of the same reasons as managers. Unions develop power bases as a result of their ability to represent workers to management. Work redesign often allows a more direct interchange between workers and management and bypasses the union. Unions frequently feel that these efforts are simply another attempt to increase productivity. One union official described work redesign as a "speed-up in sheep's clothing." Traditional unions tend to have traditional demands (wage, hours, job security), and as a result, are oftentimes less innovative than management when it comes to improving the quality of working life.

Overcoming Problems with Work Redesign

The seriousness of work redesign problems must not be overlooked. Even so, there are several steps that managers can take to help reduce the impact of these problems and enhance the chances for program success (Hackman, 1976). Begin by *diagnosing the work system prior to change.* Know what the problems are (union resistance, individual differences, etc.) before beginning to seriously consider changing the work place. As much as possible, get the union involved in the diagnosis.

Next, *keep the focus on the work itself.* Keep personal differences outside the discussion. Suspend, at least for the moment, the "it can't be done" syndrome. Assume it can be done and *prepare ahead of time for unexpected problems.* Develop contingency plans ahead of time and be ready for possible problems that could sidetrack redesign efforts.

Another suggestion is to *evaluate continuously.* Whether evaluation is done by outside consultants or by union-management teams, continuous feedback can assist in pinpointing potential trouble spots so remedial action can be taken. In addition, don't bury important issues or potential problems in the hope they will disappear. *Confront difficult problems early.* If management is not committed to change, consider ways of increasing (not bypassing) their commitment.

Finally, *design change processes that facilitate change objectives.* Utilize implementation procedures that are congruent with change objectives. For instance, if you want to develop work teams that exhibit high levels of participation and autonomy, use a participative change strategy. Get workers involved in designing job changes. By using techniques in the design and planning phases that you wish continued in the actual program, employees become introduced to the techniques gradually and have an opportunity to test management's sincerity and commitment to the proposed changes.

By following these guidelines, managers can provide a work environment conducive to experimentation in redesigning work. While these changes by themselves certainly do not guarantee that the quality of working life will be significantly improved, they will at least make a useful contribution in that direction.

SUMMARY

This chapter examined the concept of work design. Initially, consideration was given to early approaches to work design. Next, a contemporary model of work design was presented. Based on the model, other principles for redesigning jobs were discussed.

In moving from the theoretical to the practical, specific examples of work redesign experiments were reviewed. These examples came from both public and private organizations and covered several different types of employees.

Next, additional techniques of work redesign were discussed, including job rotation, the four-day work week, flexitime, job sharing, and quality control circles. In closing, several problems with work redesign were discussed, as were techniques for overcoming these problems. It was emphasized that although work redesign can be a valuable management test in many situations, it should not be seen as a panacea for all organizational ills.

KEY WORDS

autonomous work groups
core job dimensions
critical psychological states
flexitime
four-day work week
growth need strength
hygiene factors
industrial humanism
job characteristics model

job rotation
job sharing
motivating potential score
motivators
quality control circles
scientific management
vertical loading
work cycle
work redesign

FOR DISCUSSION

1. In view of the history of job redesign efforts, how far have we actually come in improving productivity and the quality of working life?
2. What are the main characteristics of scientific management?
3. Herzberg has been given credit for making substantial contributions to the field of work redesign. Describe the nature of these contributions.
4. Provide reasons why a manager would want (or would not want) to implement work redesign.
5. What implications for management follow from the Job Characteristics Model?
6. In Close-Up 18.1, a work redesign experiment among keypunch operators was described. What techniques other than work redesign might managers have attempted in order to increase productivity and satisfaction?
7. What general lessons for management emerge from reviewing the various work redesign experiments discussed in this chapter?
8. How useful do you think techniques like job rotation or the four-day work

week are for improving performance and satisfaction? What limitations exist for these techniques?

9. What are some reasons Q.C. circles may not work in manufacturing situations?

10. Identify several important problems with work redesign. How might these problems be overcome?

JOB DIAGNOSTIC SURVEY

Purpose

To gain firsthand experience in using an instrument designed to measure job characteristics in work settings and to consider how variations in work design can affect attitudes and behavior.

Instructions (Part One)

Please describe your present job (or a previous paid or unpaid job you have had) using the questionnaire below. For each question, circle the number (1 through 7) that best describes your own job. Be as objective as possible in describing this job on the various scales.

Name of the job to be described: _____

1. How much *variety* is there in your job? That is, to what extent does the job require you to do many different things at work, using a variety of your skills and talents?

1.....................2.....................3.....................4.....................5.....................6.....................7

Very little; the job requires me to do the same routine things over and over again.

Moderate variety.

Very much; the job requires me to do many different things, using a number of different skills and talents.

2. To what extent does your job involve doing a *"whole"* and *identifiable piece of work?* That is, is the job a complete piece of work that has an obvious beginning and end? Or is it only a small part of the overall piece of work, which is finished by other people or by automatic machines?

1.....................2.....................3.....................4.....................5.....................6.....................7

My job is only a tiny part of the overall piece of work; the results of my activities cannot be seen in the final product or service.

My job is a moderate-sized "chunk" of the overall piece of work; my own contribution can be seen in the final outcome.

My job involves doing the whole piece of work, from start to finish; the results of my activities are easily seen in the final product or service.

Source: Exercise 18.1 is based on the work of J. R. Hackman and G. R. Oldham, *Work Redesign,* pp. 277–79. © 1980, Addison-Wesley Publishing Company, Inc., Reading, Massachusetts. Reprinted with permission.

3. In general, *how significant or important* is your job? That is, are the results of your work likely to significantly affect the lives or well-being of other people?

1.....................2.....................3.....................4.....................5.....................6.....................7

Not very significant; the outcomes of my work are *not* likely to have important effect on other people.

Moderately significant.

Highly significant; the outcomes of my work can affect other people in very important ways.

4. How much *autonomy* is there in your job? That is, to what extent does your job permit you to decide on *your own* how to go about doing the work?

1.....................2.....................3.....................4.....................5.....................6.....................7

Very little; the job gives me almost no personal "say" about how and when the work is done.

Moderate autonomy; many things are standardized and not under my control, but I can make some decisions about the work.

Very much; the job gives me almost complete responsibility for deciding how and when the work is done.

5. To what extent does *doing the job* itself provide you with information about your work performance? That is, does the actual *work* itself provide clues about how well you are doing—aside from any "feedback" co-workers or supervisors may provide?

1.....................2.....................3.....................4.....................5.....................6.....................7

Very little; the job itself is set up so I could work forever without finding out how well I am doing.

Moderately; sometimes doing to job provides "feedback" to me; sometimes it does not.

Very much; the job is set up so that I get almost constant "feedback" as I work about how well I am doing.

Instructions (Part Two)

Based on your answers to the Job Diagnostic Survey, you can now calculate your Motivating Potential Score (see text). The MPS represents a summary score indicating how motivating the job you have described is. Insert your scores on the Job Diagnostic Survey (the numbers 1 through 7) into the following formula to calculate your MPS.

Finally, chart your own individual JDS score against national norms on the graph provided as Exhibit 1 (page 558). Based on this exercise, how does your own job (past or present) compare to the national norms? How does it compare to the jobs described by other students? What are the implications for improving your own job?

$$MPS = \frac{[\text{skill variety} + \text{task identity} + \text{task significance}]}{3} \times \text{autonomy} \times \text{feedback}.$$

Your MPS = _____ (National average = 128).

EXHIBIT 1

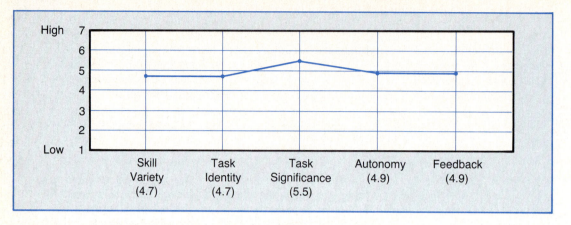

Skill Variety (4.7)	Task Identity (4.7)	Task Significance (5.5)	Autonomy (4.9)	Feedback (4.9)

CASE

THE NATIONAL INSURANCE COMPANY

18.1

Jerry Taylor has been involved with the administrative functions of the National Insurance Company for almost twenty years. About three months ago, Jerry was appointed group manager of the Policyholder Service and Accounting Departments at the home office. Before he actually assumed the job, Jerry was able to get away for a three-week management development program at the State University College of Business. One of the topics covered in the program was the concept of job enrichment, or job redesign. Jerry had read about job enrichment in several of his trade journals, but the program was his first opportunity to think about the concept in some detail. In addition, several of the program participants had had some experience (both positive and negative) with job redesign projects.

Jerry was intrigued with the idea. He knew how boring routine administrative tasks could become, and he knew from his previous supervisory work that turnover of clerical personnel was a real problem. In addition, his conversations with the administrative vice-president and Joe Bellows, the personnel manager, led him to believe that some trials and redesigning the work would be supported and favorably regarded.

Description of the Work
Group Policyholder Service Department. The principal activities undertaken in this department are the sorting and opening of incoming mail and then matching to accounting files; reviewing of group insurance bills from policyholders; and coding required changes to policies (e.g., new employees and termi-

Case 18.1 from Randall S. Schuler and Dan R. Dalton, *Case Problems in Management,* 3rd ed. (St. Paul: West, 1986), pp. 175–179. The case and the analysis are adapted (with permission) from Antone F. Alber, *An Exploratory Study of the Benefits and Costs of Job Enrichment,* Ph.D. dissertation, The Pennsylvania State University, 1977. Several figures are reproduced directly, and major portions of the text are quoted directly. The case was written in conjunction with Henry P. Sims, Jr., and Andrew D. Szilagyi, Jr.

EXHIBIT 2   POLICYHOLDER SERVICE DEPARTMENT WORK FLOW AND TASKS

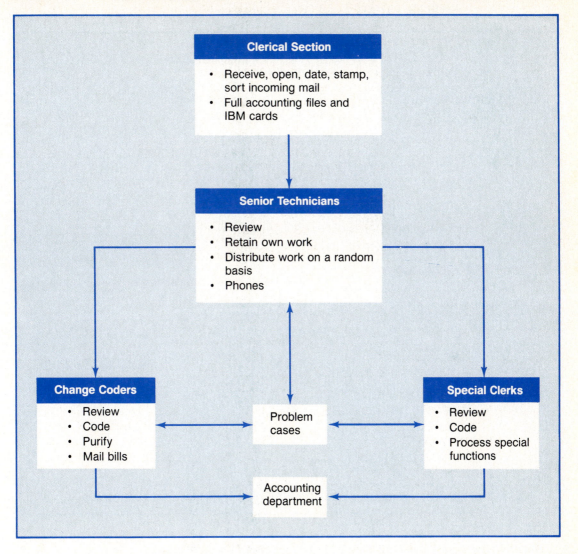

nations). These activities are carried out by approximately twenty-eight people; 53 percent of them are over age thirty-five, 82 percent female, 89 percent high school graduates, and 53 percent have less than two years' experience in their current job.

Organizationally, the department is headed by a manager. The employees are grouped into the four functional categories of clerical support, senior technician, change coder, and special clerk. The general work flow and a more specific list of the tasks carried out within each functional category are shown in Exhibit 2.

The Group Policyholder Service Department shares the same physical working area as the Accounting Department. The people within Policyholder

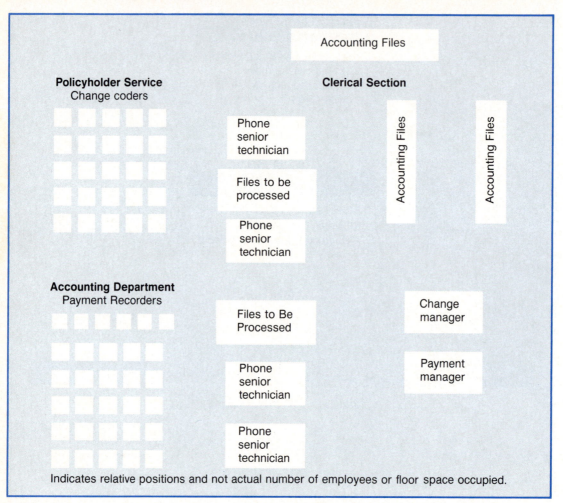

Policyholder Service
Change coders

Accounting Files

Clerical Section

Phone senior technician

Accounting Files

Accounting Files

Files to be processed

Phone senior technician

Accounting Department
Payment Recorders

Files to Be Processed

Change manager

Phone senior technician

Payment manager

Phone senior technician

Indicates relative positions and not actual number of employees or floor space occupied.

Service who work in the different functional categories are in very close proximity to one another, frequently just one desk away. The files for the department are located at one corner of the work area and the supervisors have offices along one side (see Exhibit 3).

In the last few months, Jerry has observed that the functional breakdown and the accompanying physical arrangement of people and files lead to a number of problems. Since work is assigned or selected on a random basis, there is no personal accountability for it. Files are at one corner of the work area where they can be retrieved by the clerical group and distributed to a senior technician who randomly distributes them to be processed. After a file is coded, it is placed in a holding area for processing by the Accounting Department. Here, assignment of work is also done on a

EXHIBIT 4   ACCOUNTING DEPARTMENT WORK FLOW AND TASKS

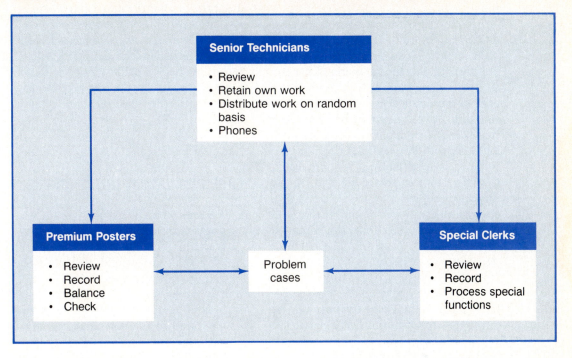

random basis. It is difficult to respond to phone calls or written requests for information promptly, because it is frequently difficult to find a file. In fact, several people are kept busy doing nothing but looking for files.

The typical employee performs a job which consists of two tasks on approximately an eleven-minute cycle. All work is cross-checked. The training for the job is minimal and there are a number of individuals performing the same set of tasks on files randomly issued. A clerk occasionally corresponds with a policyholder, but all correspondence goes out with the manager's signature on it. The manager thus receives all phone calls and correspondence from policyholders.

Because of the random distribution of work, individual performance is difficult to measure. There are spot checks on some completed work by someone other than the doer, but it is difficult or impossible to determine the specific individual who was responsible. Consequently, it is not possible to provide specific information to individuals at regular intervals about their work performance.

Accounting Department. The Accounting Department processes the files, bills, and checks received from the Group Policyholder Service. Premiums are posted on IBM cards and worksheets. Necessary adjustments are made to accounts and the checks, cards, and worksheets are balanced. Approximately twenty-eight people are employed at any one time performing these tasks. Seventy-seven percent of the work force are under thirty-five years of age. Everyone has at least a high school degree and 54 percent have less than two years' experience in the job they are performing.

The department has both a manager and a supervisor. The employees are divided into senior technicians, premium posters, and special clerks. The general work flow and tasks carried out in each of these functional areas are shown in Exhibit 4. As shown in Exhibit 3, the Accounting Department shares its work and files with Policyholder Service.

Work is selected on a random basis. Clerks go to a bookcase file and choose the cases they wish to do. Occasionally, correspondence with a policyholder is necessary, and is signed by the manager.

The Problem of Change

Jerry believes that if the work in his department can be *properly* redesigned, then departmental effectiveness can be improved. In addition, he believes that substantial improvements can be made in terms of individual employee work satisfaction.

In thinking about redesigning the work, Jerry has separated the problem into two parts. First, he is concerned about the *process* of change. How can he best accomplish a job redesign project? Second, Jerry has been concerned with the arrangement of the tasks themselves. Before he begins such a project, Jerry hopes to have at least some preliminary ideas about the feasibility of such a change.

CASE DISCUSSION QUESTIONS

1. If you were Jerry, how would you approach the process of redesigning the jobs?
2. Exactly how would you redesign the jobs if you were Jerry?
3. In doing so, how would you employ the enriching variables incorporated in the Job Characteristics Model?
4. In addition to work redesign, what else might Jerry do to improve employee attitudes and performance?

CAREERS AND ORGANIZATIONAL ATTACHMENT

In their classic book, *Organizations,* March and Simon (1958) distinguish between the "decision to produce" and the "decision to participate." The decision to produce is basically the issue of motivation to perform on the job; it has been dealt with extensively in this text. The second issue is the decision to participate. Here we are concerned with factors that influence people to join organizations, to develop attachments to those organizations, and to want to come to work and remain with the organization. Also at issue here is the concept of career, both from the individual's standpoint and from the organization's.

In this chapter, we consider several aspects of employee careers and organizational attachment. First, the issue of organizational entry is examined, and we ask how individuals choose organizations and how organizations choose individuals. Next, we examine the concept of careers in organizations. Socialization processes are reviewed as they relate to employee behavior and performance. Next, the topic of employee commitment to the organization is discussed. Finally, the related topics of employee absenteeism and turnover are reviewed. Hence, in this chapter, we highlight the employee attachment process, from entry to exit. Throughout, implications for management are considered.

IMPORTANCE OF TOPIC FOR MANAGERS

Several reasons account for the concept of employee participation in (or attachment to) organizations having received increased attention by managers in recent years. By better understanding the processes individuals go through in choosing and joining organizations, managers can be more prepared in the recruitment and selection process. For instance, providing employees with realistic job previews gives both sides a better opportunity to accurately assess the potential match between individual and organization. Research has consistently demonstrated that activities such as the realistic job preview can lead not only to improvements in job performance and satisfaction levels, but also to reduced turnover.

Employees experience differing needs and goals as they develop and mature in the work place. By understanding the concept of careers and career stages, managers can improve employee counseling efforts and can recognize these changing needs. Socialization and individualization represent primary vehicles by which individuals and organizations attempt to mold and shape each other to adapt and survive. This never-ending process has important implications for both employee behavior and attitudes and for managerial action.

The concept of organizational commitment has emerged in recent years as a primary concern of management. In the pursuit of organizational goals, committed employees play a major part. High organizational dedication has been fairly consistently shown to lead to increased employee effort and reduced turnover. Simply by being aware of the primary factors leading up to withdrawal—absenteeism or turnover—can help managers take steps to minimize it where possible.

ORGANIZATIONAL ENTRY

For several decades, industrial psychologists have studied employee recruitment and selection processes from the organization's standpoint. These processes constitute a major part of any contemporary text on industrial psychology or human resources management. It is only recently, however, that psychologists have focused attention on recruitment and selection from the *employee's* standpoint. This study of the manner in which a newcomer moves from outside to inside the organization—from the individual standpoint—is an area known as *organizational entry* (Wanous, 1977).

Organizations are continually involved in matching processes with individuals. Prospective employees bring their skills and abilities to an organization and attempt to match them with an organization's job requirements. In addition, prospective employees also bring a variety of human needs, in search of an organization climate in which these needs can be satisfied. In many respects, organizations focus their attention during the recruitment process on the first match (skills and abilities versus job requirements), while individuals focus on the second match (needs vs. climate). The end result of these two matching processes determines how satisfied both individuals and organizations are with the choice and how likely each is to want to continue the relationship.

The topic of organizational entry generally addresses four questions: (1) How do individuals choose organizations? (2) How accurate and complete is the information that prospective employees have about organizations? (3) What is the impact of organizational recruitment on matching individuals and organizations? (4) What are the consequences of matching or mismatching individuals and organizations? Answers to these questions help managers gain an understanding of the individual's point of view in the recruitment process and allow managers and potential employees to make more informed choices that benefit both.

Choosing an Organization

The most common approach to analyzing how people choose from among various organizations is based on expectancy theory. A simplified model of this choice process is shown in Exhibit 19.1, which is adapted from the work of Vroom (1966) and Lawler (1973). As this model shows, it is important to distinguish among three stages in the choice process: (1) the relative attractiveness of an organization; (2) the amount of effort directed toward joining the organization; and (3) the actual choice of an organization from among the job offers the individual receives. Hence, attractiveness, effort, and choice refer to the entry process from an individual's point of view (Wanous, 1977).

In Stage 1, the relative attractiveness of an organization is determined by a combination of expectations about the characteristics of each organization and valences attached to each of those characteristics. Vroom (1966) studied a group of MBA students as they chose their first job. Students' job expectations and job valences were measured for each organization being considered. As it turned out, the students' overall organizational attractiveness score (expectations × valences) accurately predicted seventy-six percent of actual subsequent job choices. These findings offer strong confirmation of the role of expectancies and valences in choice behavior.

During this information-gathering stage, individuals often ask a number of questions concerning the organization in an effort to gain additional insight into the decision. These questions commonly cover topics such as the following:

1. How large is the organization's industry and what are its prospects for growth?

EXHIBIT 19.1   THE ORGANIZATIONAL CHOICE PROCESS

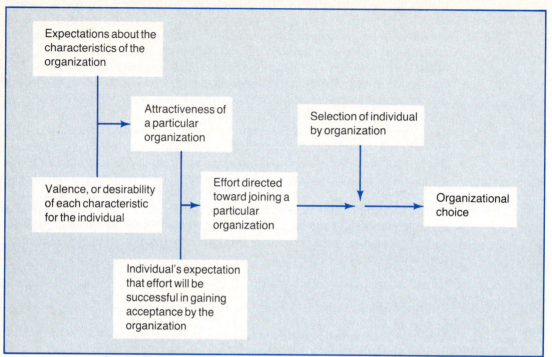

Source: Based on V. H. Vroom, "Organizational Choice: A Study of Pre- and Post-decision Processes," *Organizational Behavior and Human Performance 1* (1966): 212–25; and E. E. Lawler, *Motivation in Work Organizations* (Monterey, Calif.: Brooks/Cole, 1973).

2. What goods and services does it produce?
3. How large is the organization (people, assets, sales volume)?
4. Where does it have other plants or divisions?
5. What are the organization's compensation policies? Performance appraisal practices? Training and development practices?
6. What do people generally like or dislike about the organization?
7. What are the organization's plans for the future?
8. What jobs have top executives held during their careers with the organization?

In Stage 2, individuals must determine the amount of energy to devote toward joining an organization. Here applicants put their best foot forward. The decision to make this effort is influenced by both the attractiveness of the organization and the belief that the effort will in fact be successful in gaining acceptance (that is, a job offer).

As a result of this effort, organizations make *their* selections and offer positions to their favored candidates. Once offers are made, individuals select among alternative offers in Stage 3. Most individuals select the position that appears to offer the greatest attractiveness in either the short or long term.

The model of job choice suggested here is intentionally oversimplified to highlight many prominent aspects of the choice process. Obviously, other factors enter into actual job-choice decisions. Some people do not follow anything like a rational or quasi-rational process in their decision, but rather take positions almost by caprice. Even so, the model is helpful in identifying some of the factors that influence decisions.

Two additional aspects of the organizational choice process need to be mentioned. The first is the cognitive distortions that occur in the decision process. The act of choosing from among job alternatives often causes us to distort our perceptions of the characteristics (and desirability) of the various alternatives. Once we have chosen a particular job (but before we report for work), we often *increase* our perceptions of the chosen job (increase organizational attractiveness) and *decrease* our perceptions of the alternative positions (Lawler et al., 1975; Vroom, 1966). This is done to justify our choice and to reduce possible dissonance about the decision.

However, studies have also shown that once individuals actually join and work in an organization, they become less satisfied with their decision than they were before, or immediately after, making it (Vroom and Deci, 1971). This reality shock occurs as a result of incomplete or inaccurate information people have about the future job. Once they arrive at work they are confronted with aspects of the job that they either failed to recognize or thought were less important. As a result, satisfaction with their decision diminishes and propensity to leave increases. In fact, in many industries, a major share of all turnover (often seventy percent or higher) occurs during the first year of employment.

Realistic Job Previews

Obviously, many people are led to expect a work environment quite different from what confronts them upon arrival at work. The existence of reality shock raises questions about the accuracy of the information people use in choosing among alternative organizations. How incomplete is this information and what can be done to increase the accuracy of it?

Several studies indicate that company recruiters tend to give glowing descriptions of jobs to prospective employees rather than balanced descriptions (Dunnette, Arvey, and Banas, 1973; Ward, 1972). This is probably done in the hope of attracting desirable candidates in a competitive job market. As a result, however, the inflated expectations of many employees are not met, and the disappointed employees subsequently leave (Porter and Steers, 1973).

There are two important ways in which employee expectations can be met. The first is to increase the positive outcomes experienced by the employee (perhaps through pay increases, better supervision, job enrichment, new office furniture, or increased social activities). By doing so, the likelihood of meeting an employee's inflated expectations is enhanced. Unfortunately, this is often difficult to accomplish for a variety of reasons. The second

EXHIBIT 19.2 A COMPARISON OF TRADITIONAL AND REALISTIC JOB PREVIEWS

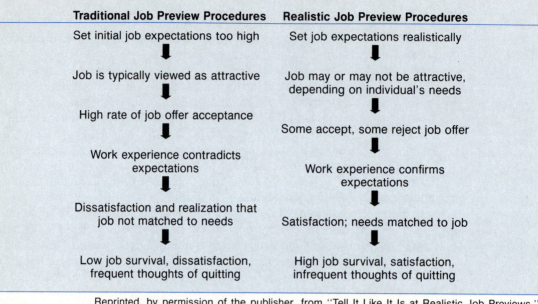

Traditional Job Preview Procedures	Realistic Job Preview Procedures
Set initial job expectations too high	Set job expectations realistically
⬇	⬇
Job is typically viewed as attractive	Job may or may not be attractive, depending on individual's needs
⬇	⬇
High rate of job offer acceptance	Some accept, some reject job offer
⬇	⬇
Work experience contradicts expectations	Work experience confirms expectations
⬇	⬇
Dissatisfaction and realization that job not matched to needs	Satisfaction; needs matched to job
⬇	⬇
Low job survival, dissatisfaction, frequent thoughts of quitting	High job survival, satisfaction, infrequent thoughts of quitting

approach is to reduce expectations so they more accurately reflect organizational reality. This is done through realistic job previews.

A *realistic job preview* (RJP) attempts to provide prospective employees with accurate job information. When they have been given such information, employees have more realistic (as opposed to inflated) initial expectations and can make more informed and appropriate choices. A realistic job preview emphasizes specific facts about the job and presents both the positive and negative aspects. Based on these facts, employees are more likely to identify a suitable match between their own needs and those of the organization. In contrast, the traditional approach typically attempts to sell the job and present it in its most favorable light (see Exhibit 19.2).

Several experiments have been done in industry in an attempt to compare the relative advantage of realistic job previews with the traditional approach. In the realistic job previews, job information was presented to candidates in either a film about the job, a booklet describing the job, a practice session, or interviews with actual job incumbents.

What effect did the previews have? Several benefits were noted (Wanous, 1977). First, contrary to expectations, RJPs did not impair the organization's ability to recruit and hire desired candidates. People were still willing to take the positions, despite less positive impressions. Second, several studies show that RJPs clearly lowered job expectations, and created more realistic perceptions of what the actual job would be like. Third, RJPs led to more positive job attitudes after the initial employment period, as well as fewer thoughts about leaving. Finally, RJPs consistently led to reduced turnover compared to traditional methods. Employees exposed to realistic job previews in a wide array of work organizations exhibited turnover rates between ten to twenty percent lower than other employees. While realistic job previews should not be seen as a panacea for all organizational ills, they do appear to represent another factor contributing to the overall effectiveness of the organization and its management.

CAREER PLANNING AND DEVELOPMENT

Employee career patterns vary considerably. Some employees join a particular organization at an early age and remain with that same organization through retirement. Others change jobs—and even vocations—almost at will. Despite these differences, it is possible to develop a portrait of the average pattern by studying career stages. We can do so by asking questions about the way employees become attached to or separated from their employers.

Definition of Career

Hall (1976, p. 4) defines a *career* as an "individually perceived sequence of attitudes and behaviors associated with work-related experiences and activities over the span of the person's life." Underlying this definition are four rather important assumptions:

- The notion of a career as such does not imply success or failure. A career is viewed as a lifelong series of events rather than an evaluation of how successful someone has been over his or her lifetime.
- Career success or failure is best judged by the person whose career is being considered, not by the normative opinions of others.
- A career consists of the events that happen to an individual over time. It is what an individual does and feels at work.
- A career is best viewed as a process of work-related experiences. These experiences may include a series of promotions within a single company, or they may involve different jobs in varied organizations.

Career Stages

When viewed in this manner, it is possible to identify a series of relatively discrete *career stages.* (Of course, these stages must be presented in a

EXHIBIT 19.3   STAGES IN CAREER DEVELOPMENT

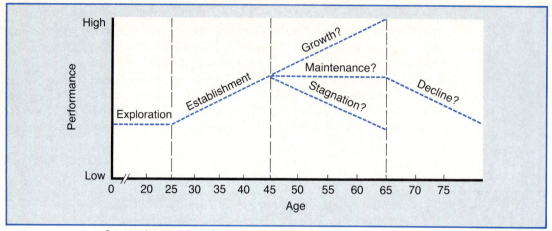

Source: Adapted from D. T. Hall, *Careers in Organizations* (Glenview, Ill.: Scott, Foresman and Company, 1976), p. 57. Used by permission.

generalized form, and variations on this pattern must be recognized). Following Super (1957) and others, we can identify at least four stages: (1) exploration; (2) establishment; (3) maintenance; and (4) decline. These are shown in Exhibit 19.3.

In general, the *exploration* stage consists of the time period when individuals are completing school and seeking initial employment. (This stage is closely related to the process of *organizational entry,* which is discussed in the next section.) Here, individuals try to match their needs, abilities, and skills with organizational requirements. This search usually continues throughout the early months on the job, during which individuals question whether the correct job choice was made.

In the *establishment* stage, individuals begin to better understand the work environment and organizational demands and strive to establish their worth in the organization. This is also a period when the organization is often carefully evaluating individuals to determine their long-term worth.

Next, in the *maintenance* stage, individuals have usually entrenched themselves in the organization. In this stage, they frequently experience fairly strong linkages to the organization and often find it difficult, if not impossible, to leave and go elsewhere. Also, during this stage individuals' performance levels can be expected to vary considerably. Some individuals continue to grow and develop, while others begin to stagnate and retreat. Certainly, in terms of wasted employee time and energy, this stage is where the greatest problem lies.

Finally, in the *decline* stage, individuals approach retirement. Often,

EXHIBIT 19.4 CONCERNS OF MANAGERS BY CAREER STAGE

Age Group	Career Stage	Career Concerns
15–22	Exploration	Finding the right career Getting the appropriate education
22–30	Early career: Trial	Getting the first job Adjusting to daily work routine and supervisors
30–38	Early career: Establishment	Choosing specialty and deciding on level of commitment Transfers and promotions Broadening perspective of occupation and organization
38–45	Middle career: Growth	Establishing professional or organizational identity Choosing between alternative career paths (e.g., technical vs. managerial)
45–55	Middle career: Maintenance	Being an independent contributor to the organization Taking on more areas of responsibility
55–62	Later career: Plateau	Training and developing subordinates Shaping the future direction of the organization Dealing with threats to position from younger, more aggressive employees
62–70	Later career: Decline	Planning for retirement Developing one's replacement Dealing with a reduced work load and less power

Source: Reprinted by permission from H. J. Arnold and D. G. Feldman, *Organizational Behavior* (New York: McGraw-Hill, 1986), p. 548. Based on the work of E. H. Schein, *Career Dynamics: Matching Individual and Organizational Needs* (Reading, Mass.: Addison-Wesley, 1978), pp. 40–46; G. W. Dalton, P. H. Thompson, and R. L. Price, "The Four Stages of Professional Careers: A New Look at Performance by Professionals," *Organizational Dynamics 6* (1977): 19–42; J. Van Maanen and E. H. Schein, "Career Development," in J. R. Hackman and J. L. Suttle (eds.), *Improving Life at Work* (Santa Monica, Calif.: Goodyear, 1977), pp. 54–57.

however, physical age does not reflect mental age, and individuals may be capable of contributing far more to the organization than the organization allows.

Throughout this process, individuals typically ask themselves a number of questions relating to their position on the career ladder. Arnold and Feldman (1986, p. 548) have attempted to summarize these concerns by career stage (see Exhibit 19.4).

Career Development

Many contemporary organizations take an active role in developing their employees. In fact, as we saw at the beginning of the book, a hallmark of the human resource management approach is an active effort by management to identify, develop, and utilize the full human potential of the company's human resources. In this effort, career development—by both the company and the individual—is actively pursued.

The corporation can do many things to facilitate career development (Arnold and Feldman, 1986). These include:

1. *Career counseling.* Either through workshops or one-on-one counseling, employees receive guidance concerning career opportunities throughout the organization and whatever unique skills they have to exploit these opportunities.
2. *Career pathing.* Some organizations are beginning to plan job changes well in advance for employees in such a way that up-and-coming people get well-planned, broad job experiences. Moved in a logical way, people can use their present skills and develop new skills that can be of use to them and the organization over time.
3. *Career information systems.* Organizations make an active effort to post all new job openings so prospective applicants can apply. In some cases, computers are used to organize job openings systematically so career counselors have ready access to career opportunities.
4. *Human resource planning.* Many companies have developed computerized skills inventories of their employees. When a job opening occurs, ready access to all employees who have certain skills is available (e.g., Who speaks French? Who has an MBA?). In some systems, managers are required to document the efforts they have made to train their subordinates in preparation for promotions.
5. *Training.* In a wide variety of cases, advanced training is used to facilitate career development. This training can be done in-house or through external sources; it can also be done informally through workshops and seminars or more formally through degree programs (e.g., in MBA programs).

However they are undertaken, career development activities represent an important investment by companies interested in developing their employees so that they can make their maximum contribution.

EMPLOYEE ADAPTATION: SOCIALIZATION AND INDIVIDUALIZATION

When individuals join an organization, they enter an unknown world filled with new experiences, challenges, and potential threats. This initial employment period is important for both the individual and the organization since so much turnover (voluntary and involuntary) occurs during this matching period. Many employees discover that they simply cannot handle—or do not wish to handle—their assigned jobs. For a variety of reasons they discover somewhat too late that a mistake has been made and choose to leave. Others learn to cope, to adapt, to even enjoy their new position, and decide to remain.

What causes differences in the reactions of employees? First, many employees are simply not equipped technically to handle the job. Perhaps they cannot type, make decisions, deal with people, or make sales. Under these circumstances, people either seek additional training or leave. In addition to technical factors, several psychological factors account for success or failure in adaptation and development. Two points are relevant here. First, there are the related processes of socialization and individualization. Second is the concept of organizational commitment. Each relates to employee ability to successfully adapt to an organization.

One way to view the employment relationship is as a process of exchange between employees and organizations. Levinson and associates (1962) refer to this as a *psychological contract* in which both parties create mutual expectations of each other that govern their relationship. Ironically, both sides are often unaware of the expectations of the other party and assume that their own view of the exchange is shared by the other party. Included in this psychological contract is a series of legitimate demands (level of output, types of work activities) placed on the individual by the organization. The individual accepts these demands as part of the contract in exchange for receiving valued outcomes (salary, job security) from the organization.

In this process, organizations typically attempt to exert—overtly or covertly—subtle pressures on employees to shape them into the kinds of employees desired. This process is called *socialization.* Simultaneously, individuals continue to attempt to shape the work environment so it meets their own needs. This process is called *individualization.* The interaction of these two processes, operating continuously, creates the work place in which everyone works and lives. Thus, it is important to understand how these processes work.

Socialization is vital to the efficient operation of any work organization. As noted by Schein (1968, p. 2), "the speed and effectiveness of socialization determine employee loyalty, commitment, productivity, and turnover. The basic stability and effectiveness of organizations therefore depends upon their ability to socialize new members." Without some degree of socialization, employees would diffuse their work efforts, often in conflicting directions, because of disagreements over the major purposes and values of the organization.

Stages in Socialization

The socialization process consists of three stages (see Exhibit 19.5). In the *prearrival stage,* individuals typically enter organizations with preconceptions

EXHIBIT 19.5   STAGES IN EMPLOYEE SOCIALIZATION

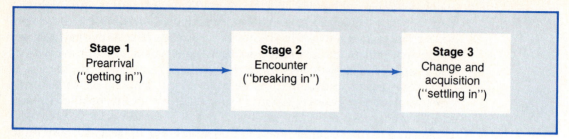

about the nature of the organization and job. These preconceptions are formed as a result of previous education, work experiences, and contacts with organization members. For instance, a dominant attitude taught in many business schools is the need for an efficient, dedicated work force. Hence, many individuals who are exposed to this idea are already well on the way to socialization before actual organizational entry.

Once inside the organization, the individual enters the *encounter stage.* He or she encounters other members who exhibit accepted attitudes and behavior. These day-to-day interactions, combined with positive reinforcements for behaving in a similar fashion (and punishment for contrary behavior), condition the individual over time to accept the status of peers and superiors.

Initial encounters, along with their conditioning and reinforcement attempts, ultimately lead to solidifying the new attitudes and behaviors individuals have learned. In the *change and acquisition stage,* people develop new self-images more consistent with other members". They develop new social relationships, often with members of the same organization. Finally, they develop new values and new modes of behavior. At this point, the individual has been transformed from an outsider into a member.

The success of socialization attempts is influenced by two factors (Schein, 1968). First, attempts are more successful if individuals are highly motivated upon entry. If individuals are eager to join a firm, for instance, they are more likely to put up with initial discomforts and to be more receptive to company-sanctioned norms and values. In addition, socialization attempts are usually more successful if the organization offers inducements to remain with the organization and comply with its dictates. Offering an employee perquisites not offered elsewhere (a private office, a company car) can often entice the individual to remain.

Techniques of Socialization

How do organizations socialize their employees? Several common methods can be identified (Caplow, 1964). Through *employee selection,* employers and interviewers seek the "right kind of person." This search often translates into a search for individuals who already share common values. Once inside the organization, employees participate in *training and development* activities. They are often exposed to a series of programs designed to instill in them certain beliefs and values that are desired by the organization. These programs may take the form of new employee orientation, management development workshops, and departmental meetings.

Apprenticeships are another means of socializing employees. Here a senior employee assumes responsibility for socializing a new employee. Under this "buddy system," the senior advisor is in an advantageous position to instill in the new employee both technical skills and work-place norms and values. Failure to comply with these efforts can lead to expulsion from the apprentice program, thereby adding significant reinforcing power to socialization attempts. A more dramatic socialization technique is the *debasement experience.* The employee undergoes something that causes him to detach himself from earlier attitudes and to substitute a more humble self-perception that allows for easier socialization attempts. Periodically, an old hand or a supervisor will set up a new employee in such a way that the employee fails on a task or is publicly embarrassed. As a result of the experience, the employee is more prone to look up to the supervisor for advice and knowledge.

The *anticipatory socialization* process consists of an individual accepting the beliefs and values of a group he aspires to become a member of, but to which he does not already belong. In essence, the person socializes himself in the hope that it may facilitate membership and acceptance by the group or organization. Anticipatory socialization can be seen among students in many professional schools (business, law, medicine) as they prepare for their careers and develop belief systems that are compatible with the profession.

Finally, socialization often occurs almost by *trial and error.* Organizations do not control the daily activities of all their employees. They must allow the employees to experience various aspects of the organization and, in the process, learn about the organization. While these nonprogrammed efforts may not be as systematic as other methods, they are nevertheless a necessary part of organizational life.

Individualization

The second half of the psychological contract consists of efforts by individuals to change the work place to meet their needs (Porter, Lawler, and Hackman, 1975). While the organization attempts to socialize individuals to accept its beliefs and values, individuals often respond in several ways aimed at nullifying or reducing these attempts and maintaining a certain degree of control over their own work life. Efforts directed at asserting individualization can be classified into three broad categories (Schein, 1968).

At one extreme, an individual may respond to socialization attempts with *rebellion*—open rejection and hostility. This rejection, however, may lead to the individual being dismissed (perhaps as a nonconformist). Alternatively, it could lead to actual change in the organization. More likely, it would result in an attempt by the organization to "co-opt" the rebel and blunt the attack.

Toward the middle of the individualization continuum is *creative individualism*. Individuals choose to accept the basic aspects of the organization's norms and values, but reject the peripheral ones and substitute their own. In essence, this is a compromise position where both parties attempt to make peace: the individual will accept certain aspects of organizational life, while the organization allows room for dissent and unconventional behavior.

At the other extreme is *conformity*. Many individuals adapt to organizational life by simply giving up their individuality and conforming to corporate norms. The "organization man" (or woman) is a prime example. However, as noted previously, the personal costs associated with such behavior can be high.

We have seen how individuals and organizations attempt to accommodate one another and create relatively stable situations in which both can survive and prosper. As individuals continue on the job, they come to think more about the nature of their relationship with the organization. Do they agree with the goals and values of the organization? Are they motivated to work hard to help the organization realize the goals? Do they wish to remain with the organization or go elsewhere? Answers to questions like these focus on the extent to which employees feel committed to the organization. Because of the relationship between socialization and organizational commitments —particularly during the initial employment period—we now turn to an examination of the nature of commitments in organizations.

EMPLOYEE COMMITMENT TO ORGANIZATIONS

Management concern over the strength and quality of the linkages between an organization and its employees has increased significantly in recent years. As William H. Whyte asks (*Fortune,* February 9, 1981, p. 54), "Whatever happened to corporate loyalty?" During the 1950s, corporations were considered by some to be the "citadel of belongingness" and the prevailing feeling of the time was "to be loyal to the company, and the company will be loyal to you." Clearly, in the 1980s the situation has changed. As noted by Whyte, turnover among managers out of college less than five years has increased four-fold since 1960. In fact, today the average corporation can expect to lose at least half of its college recruits within the first five years of their employment. The evidence of this disaffection can be seen in Exhibit 19.6, which charts employee attitudes toward companies and managers.

Because of this, increased concern has focused on how employee commitment to the organization can be enhanced (see Close-Up 19.1). Briefly defined, *organizational commitment* refers to the relative strength of an

EXHIBIT 19.6 DECLINE IN EMPLOYEE COMMITMENT TO ORGANIZATIONS

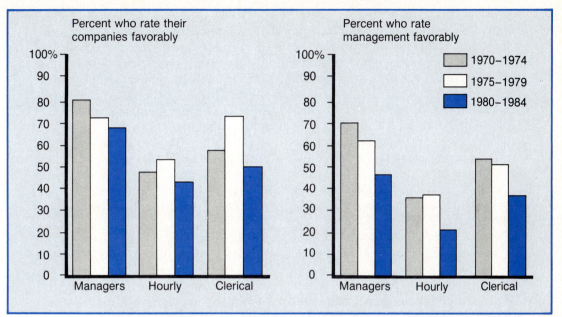

individual's identification with and involvement in an organization (Mowday, Porter, and Steers, 1982). It can be characterized by at least three factors: (1) a strong belief in and acceptance of the organization's goals and values; (2) a willingness to exert considerable effort on behalf of the organization; and (3) a strong desire to maintain membership in the organization.

When viewed in this way, commitment represents something beyond mere passive loyalty to an organization. Instead, it involves an active relationship with the organization in which individuals are willing to give something of themselves in order to help the organization succeed and prosper. As noted by March and Simon (1958), real commitment often evolves into an exchange relationship in which individuals attach themselves to the organization in return for certain rewards or outcomes.

As an attitude, commitment differs in several ways from the more widely studied attitude of job satisfaction. First, commitment involves a wider perspective, reflecting an individual's feelings toward an organization as a whole. Job satisfaction, on the other hand, focuses on a person's responses either to the job or to certain aspects of the job. Job satisfaction levels can change rapidly over time in response to immediate changes in the work environment, while commitment attitudes develop more slowly, but consistently, over time (Porter et al., 1974).

Numerous examples of companies with highly committed employees can be identified. Most such companies are typified by senior managements who are truly concerned about the welfare of their employees (as well as the productivity of the firm). Hence, philosophy of management is an important aspect of building commitment. Consider the following examples.

At IBM, turnover has always been low and has been cut in half since the 1960s. Executives at IBM are imbued with the corporate credo, "Dignity and respect for the individual. Pursuit of excellence. Dedication to service." W. E. Burdick, vice-president for personnel, notes, "We'd be foolish to expect MBAs to walk in through the door and be loyal. Loyalty is something you've got to win." As part of this "winning" process, every step up the executive ladder is marked by a return visit to IBM's management development center for discussions concerning corporate philosophy and responsibility.

"Promotion, remuneration, and recognition are the building blocks of loyalty," says Carl Luis, public affairs director for the 3M Company. The company has expanded so rapidly over the past two decades that its employees enjoy considerable opportunities for advancement. Moreover, 3M has a strong policy of promotion from within and has created a "dual ladder" system of promotion for its scientists who choose not to enter line management. In view of this, it is no surprise that 3M employees have a reputation for commitment *and contribution* to the company.

Finally, at Hewlett-Packard, turnover among engineers runs only about ten percent per year compared to an industry average of sixty percent. Why the difference? Chairman David Packard says, "We make sure our people share in the successes they create." For example, Hewlett-Packard has a well-established profit-sharing plan and uses decentralized operating control. Salaries are no more than its competitors. However, each of forty divisions has its own research budget so "nobody has to come, hat in hand, begging for R&D money." Notes Packard, "It's this freedom that our people are after."

Although such managerial philosophies clearly do not work magic, they have been shown in many instances to facilitate or add to a climate in which employees feel they have a greater stake in the organization and the organization has a greater stake in them. Under such circumstances, it is not surprising that turnover would be low and commitment high.

Source: Based on Roy Rowan, "Rekindling Corporate Loyalty," *Fortune,* February 9, 1981, pp. 54–58. Reprinted by permission.

Influences on Employee Commitment

Considerable work has been done to identify the primary antecedents of employee commitment. As shown in Exhibit 19.7, influences on commitment are indeed widespread (see Steers, 1977a, and Mowday, Porter, and Steers,

EXHIBIT 19.7 ANTECEDENTS AND CONSEQUENCES OF ORGANIZATIONAL COMMITMENT

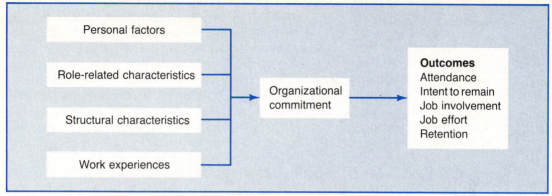

Sources: Adapted from R. M. Steers, "Antecedents and Outcomes of Organizational Commitment," *Administrative Science Quarterly* 22 (1977): 46–56; and R. T. Mowday, L. W. Porter, and R. M. Steers, *Employee-Organization Linkages: The Psychology of Commitment, Absenteeism, and Turnover* (New York: Academic Press, 1982).

1982, for summaries). To begin, several *personal factors* have been found to be related to commitment. In particular, older and more tenured employees consistently report higher commitment scores. Women tend to be more committed as a group than men, and more highly educated employees tend to be *less* committed.

In addition, several *role-related characteristics* influence commitment. In general, employees working on enriched jobs and employees reporting low levels of role conflict and ambiguity tend to be more committed. Several *structural characteristics* can influence commitment as well. Most notably, employers in decentralized organizations and in worker-owned cooperatives report higher commitment levels. Finally, a series of *work experiences* has been found to be related to commitment. For example, higher employee commitment can be expected when employees feel the organization is dependable and is truly interested in their welfare; when employees feel their jobs are particularly important to the organization; when employees are highly involved socially in organizational activities; and when in general employees feel their expectations have been met on the job. In other words, major influences on employee commitment can be found in the person, the job, *and* the situation or work environment. In view of this, the job of building commitment is certainly no easy task.

Consequences of Employee Commitment

If commitment represents part of the adaptation process, how do high levels of commitment influence employee behavior? Specifically, at least four consequences are apparent. To begin, employees truly committed to the goals and values of an organization are more likely to participate actively in organizational activities (March and Simon, 1958). High employee commitment is reflected in lower absenteeism.

In addition, highly committed employees generally have a stronger desire to remain with their employer and will continue to contribute toward the attainment of the organizational objectives with which they agree. Considerable empirical support exists for this position. Commitment has been consistently found to be inversely related to turnover (Mowday, Steers, and Porter 1979). In fact, although job satisfaction may represent a better predictor of employee turnover during the *initial* development period, commitment becomes a stronger predictor than satisfaction as time goes on and employees begin to identify more with the organization and its goals.

Third, as employees continue to identify themselves with the organization and to believe in its objectives, they may become more involved in their jobs, since their jobs represent the key mechanism by which they can contribute to the attainment of organizational goals. This relationship may not be overly strong, however. It is possible, for instance, that a nurse's aide could be highly committed to the public health goals of a hospital, but not become involved in the more distasteful aspects of caring for the sick. Here, an employee may continue to be committed to the organization—and faithfully perform the job—yet remain uninvolved in the actual task requirements of the job itself.

Fourth, we expect highly committed employees to be willing to expend a good deal of effort on behalf of the organization. This follows from the definition of commitment itself. While such effort may at times be translated into actual job performance (Mowday et al., 1974), this would not always be the case. Job performance is a function of several factors. While effort is certainly one of these factors, it is not in itself sufficient to determine actual performance level.

Building Employee Commitment

Given the importance of employee commitment to the attachment process, what can managers do to facilitate or increase commitment? Several strategies are available. First, when employees are placed in situations where they have opportunities to achieve goals that are personally meaningful to them, they may come to link personal outcomes with organizational outcomes instead of being in conflict with them (Argyris, 1957). Workers should be shown that management and other employees are truly concerned about their welfare. Many times managers are in fact concerned, yet fail to indicate it. Third, it is possible under some circumstances to modify jobs so employees have greater autonomy and responsibility and can identify with the actual tasks they perform. Finally, managers can attempt to foster better employee understanding of organizational goals and objectives. Why are the goals meaningful and how can employees contribute toward goal attainment? Actions like these can help create an atmosphere of mutual trust and support between employee and employer, where both contribute something to the attainment of the other's goals, and where an exchange is made with adequate consideration for employee needs and goals.

It is important to note, however, that high employee commitment to organizations can sometimes have adverse effects. For instance, as noted by Mowday, Porter, and Steers (1982), high employee commitment often serves to reduce one's mobility and career advancement by holding the employee in one organization. In many cases, a person can advance more rapidly by changing organizations. Moreover, commitment in the extreme may create tension or stress in one's family life as this aspect of human development becomes increasingly ignored. High commitment may also create a "group-think" phenomenon, where employees feel so strongly about the organization that they are reluctant to criticize it.

It should also be noted that high commitment may cause problems for the organization itself. First, if high commitment leads to very little turnover, the chances for employee advancement are reduced. Second, without this infusion of new people brought about by turnover, fewer opportunities for the introduction of new ideas may result. But perhaps the most tragic example of overcommitment by employees is seen in the 1980 case of Takuya Sakai, the fifty-three-year-old captain of the Japanese freighter *Fuji Maru* (Eugene *Register Guard,* August 28, 1980). As captain of a ship carrying 1500 cars from Japan to Los Angeles, Sakai felt personally responsible when the ship experienced ballast problems in high seas and took on 1500 tons of water. As a result, some 200 cars were damaged. Unable to escape a deep sense of guilt over the damage to the ship and its cargo, Sakai brought the ship safely into port in Los Angeles and promptly committed *hara-kiri.*

The point here is not that employee commitment in itself is detrimental. Quite the contrary is true. Even so, managers should exercise caution to see that the development of employee commitment is balanced with an equally strong concern for the development of other aspects of the employee's life.

EMPLOYEE ABSENTEEISM

Each year, approximately 400 million work days are lost in the U.S. as a result of employee absenteeism. This amounts to about 5.1 days lost per employee per year (Yolles, Carone, and Krinsky, 1975). In fact, many industries, particularly those characterized by highly stressful jobs, have proportionately higher absenteeism rates, often approaching fifteen to twenty percent per day. Over ten years ago, Mirvis and Lawler (1977) estimated that the cost of nonmanagerial absenteeism is about $66 per day per employee, including salary, fringe benefits, costs associated with temporary replacement, and estimated profit loss. Today, the figure is closer to $86. Combining this figure with the number of workdays lost yields an estimated annual cost of absenteeism in this country of $34.4 billion! Clearly, absenteeism represents a significant problem for managers and organizations that must be understood and dealt with if effectiveness of operations is to be achieved.

Many managers assume that absenteeism and turnover represent similar behaviors and are caused by the same factors. This is not the case, however. Absenteeism differs from turnover in several ways that require special managerial attention (Porter and Steers, 1973). First, the negative consequences associated with absenteeism for the employee are usually much less than those associated with turnover. Second, absenteeism is more likely to be a spontaneous and relatively easy decision, while the act of termination is more carefully considered over time. Finally, absenteeism often represents a substitute form of behavior for turnover, particularly when alternative forms of employment are unavailable. These differences justify the study of employee absenteeism as a separate category of behavior and not simply as a part of the turnover process.

In this section, we will consider a model of the major influences on employee absenteeism or attendance (after Steers and Rhodes, 1978). The model addresses two basic questions: What causes attendance motivation (a desire or willingness to come to work) and what causes actual attendance? It is important to clearly recognize that the answers to these two questions are quite different. Both sets of factors are depicted in Exhibit 19.8.

Causes of Attendance Motivation

First, let's examine the major causes of attendance motivation. Based on available data, *attendance motivation* appears to be influenced by two primary factors: (1) satisfaction with the job situation, and (2) various pressures to attend. If employees enjoy the work situation and the tasks associated with the job, they are more likely to *want* to come to work, since the work experience is a pleasurable one. In addition, even if the job is not a pleasurable one, there are many conditions (pressures) under which it would be in employees' best interest to attend. We will consider both of these factors separately.

Satisfaction with the Job Situation. With what we know about the nature of job attitudes, we can suggest that people are more satisfied when the job and the surrounding work environment meet their personal values and job expectations (Locke, 1976). The job situation may be characterized by many factors, including job scope, job level, and role stress. These factors are evaluated by employees in light of their own values on job expectations to determine the extent to which employees have positive or negative attitudes about the work situation. Job expectations, in turn, are influenced by several personal characteristics. For example, tenured employees or employees with more education often expect more from a job, making it harder for the job situation to satisfy their demands.

An example will help clarify this situation. An employee who has considerable seniority (a personal characteristic) comes to expect certain perquisites as a result of longevity on the job. These expectations may include higher-grade jobs, greater status, or being first in line for promotion. Under this circumstance, we expect the individual to be satisfied when these

EXHIBIT 19.8   MAJOR INFLUENCES ON EMPLOYEE ATTENDANCE

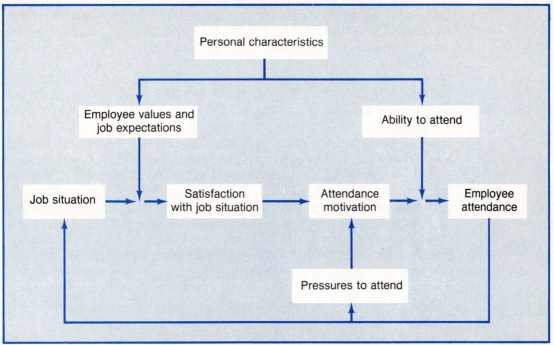

Source: R. M. Steers and S. R. Rhodes, "Major Influences on Employee Attendance: A Process Model," *Journal of Applied Psychology 63* (1978). Copyright 1978 by the American Psychological Association. Reprinted by permission of the publisher.

expectations are met by the job situation. When expectations are not met, satisfaction with the job situation diminishes.

Pressures to Attend. The second factor in attendance motivation consists of a series of what may be called pressures to attend. These pressures are conditions, characteristics, or incentives that make it desirable to attend —from an employee viewpoint—even if the job itself is not attractive or satisfying. As shown in Exhibit 19.8, these pressures may include: (1) economic and market conditions, including options in finding alternative employment; (2) incentive/reward systems, or the extent to which pay and other rewards are contingent upon good attendance; (3) work group norms about attendance behavior; (4) personal work ethic, or the belief that an individual has a moral obligation to attend; and (5) organizational commitment, or the extent to which an employee identifies with the organization and its goals and wants to help attain them.

These pressures, and one's relative satisfaction with the overall job situation, are the primary causes of attendance motivation. In this process, we expect different factors to be more important to different employees. For instance, a traveling sales representative who works alone would probably not be significantly influenced by work group norms, particularly when compared to an assembly-line worker. Similarly, financial incentives would probably not motivate someone who has more than sufficient income (or whose family has sufficient income) to come to work. Even so, we expect the sum total of these various pressures to combine with satisfaction levels to influence attendance motivation.

Causes of Employee Attendance

Now we come to the second question: how do we get from attendance motivation to actual attendance? As was pointed out above, an employee's *desire* to come to work is not the same as the *ability* to come to work. As shown in the model (Exhibit 19.8), actual attendance is a result of *both* factors: attendance motivation and ability to attend.

At least three limitations on people's ability to attend can be identified: (1) illness and accidents; (2) family responsibilities; and (3) transportation problems. Probably the most significant problem is illness and accidents. It has been estimated that nearly sixty percent of all absences are due to health-related causes. Over forty million work days are lost every year as a result of work-related accidents (Hedges, 1973). Illness and accidents clearly are major causes of absenteeism.

Family responsibilities also place limitations on ability to attend. For instance, statistics show that women are absent from work more often than men. However, in examining the reasons for this we discover that much of the difference in absence rates can be attributed both to differences in the kinds of jobs women typically hold and in the traditional roles and responsibilities assigned to them. It is generally the wife or mother who stays home and cares for sick children. As a result, as family size increases so does female absenteeism.

Transportation represents a third influence on one's ability to attend. Transportation problems involve travel distance, weather conditions, and the reliability of the mode of transportation.

In many ways, ability to attend serves as gatekeeper in the attendance process. Assuming the ability to come to work, attendance motivation fairly accurately predicts actual attendance. The higher the motivation the more regular the attendance. However, when an employee is sick or has car problems, attendance motivation alone will probably not suffice. Both factors must be present for us to expect high levels of attendance at work.

One final note: Exhibit 19.8 contains a feedback arrow indicating that the model is cyclical in nature. Superior attendance is often seen as an indicator of good performance and readiness for promotion. Poor attendance may adversely influence relationships with supervisors and co-workers and could even result in changes in these relationships. Widespread absenteeism may cause the company to alter its incentive or control programs. In short, absence or attendance behavior should not be seen solely as an end result.

They cause other aspects of the work situation to change which, in turn, may also affect future attendance.

Managing Attendance Behavior

The purpose of any model like the one proposed here is to explain human behavior. What can managers learn from the model to aid them in reducing avoidable absenteeism from the work place? The model described here leads to several recommendations.

First, before any action is taken, a *systematic* analysis of the problem can be made. The model suggested here provides a framework for diagnosis and points to several areas in which major problems may be found. By working through the model, major problem areas may become apparent. As a result, efforts aimed at eliminating the problem can be more focused.

Second, if diagnosis reveals that a major problem exists with the *satisfaction* component of the model, efforts can be made in this area. Several strategies can be suggested:

- Implement job enrichment
- Reduce job stress
- Build group cohesiveness and co-worker relations
- Improve leadership training
- Clarify job expectations
- Provide employee career counseling

Third, if the problem seems to be in the area of *pressures or incentives to attend,* other remedies may be attempted (see Close-Up 19.2):

- Clarify rewards for good attendance
- Review sick leave policies
- Encourage an attendance-oriented work group norm
- Foster a personal work ethic
- Facilitate organizational commitment

Finally, if *ability to attend* is the problem, several remedies are:

- Encourage sound physical health (perhaps through company-sponsored exercise programs and physical examinations)
- Institute employee counseling programs to foster sound mental health
- Be sensitive to problems of alcoholism and drug abuse and provide relevant programs where necessary
- Consider company-sponsored or supported day-care facilities
- Consider shuttle buses for employees living in outlying areas

This list of possible remedies to problems of employee absenteeism illustrates some of the kinds of actions management can take. Through actions

We have all heard of sick pay, but at least one firm is experimenting quite successfully with well pay. The firm, Parsons Pine Products of Ashland, Oregon, views well pay as the opposite of sick pay. It is an extra eight hour's wages that the company gives employees who are neither absent nor late for a full month.

Well pay was begun as a response to chronic tardiness and absenteeism in the manufacturing plant. After its introduction, tardiness was reduced to "almost zero" and absenteeism dropped more than Parsons wanted, since employees started coming to work even when they were sick. This practice increased the possibility of illness-related accidents on the job. As a result, Parsons introduced retro pay.

Retro pay offers a bonus to employees based on any reductions in the premiums from the state industrial accident insurance fund. Before the retro plan, the company had an accident rate eighty-six percent above the statewide base and paid into the fund accordingly. Under the retro pay plan, any savings that resulted from reduced accidents would be distributed to the employees. As a result, the accident bill in one year dropped from $28,500 to $2,500. After deducting for administrative expenses, the state returned over $89,000 of the $100,000 premium, or some $900 per employee.

By using simple techniques such as well pay and retro pay, employees saw a fairly direct benefit in coming to work and avoiding accidents. As a result, attendance (and performance) increased, accidents decreased, and employees benefited.

Source: Based on information in "How to Earn Well Pay," *Business Week,* June 12, 1978, pp. 143–46.

like these, serious efforts can be made to reduce the occurrence of absenteeism, thereby creating conditions more conducive to organizational effectiveness.

EMPLOYEE TURNOVER

One of the most widely studied topics in the area of organizational behavior is employee turnover. In fact, well over 1000 articles on the subject have been published in the last few decades (Mobley, 1982; Price, 1977; Steers and Mowday, 1981). As a result of these studies, several useful models of the turnover process have been proposed. We shall examine one model here, developed by William H. Mobley, and then consider what managers can learn from the model to help reduce turnover on the job.

The model presented here is basically a cognitive model in that it assumes employees typically make conscious decisions to leave their jobs. It is

EXHIBIT 19.9   THE EMPLOYEE TURNOVER PROCESS

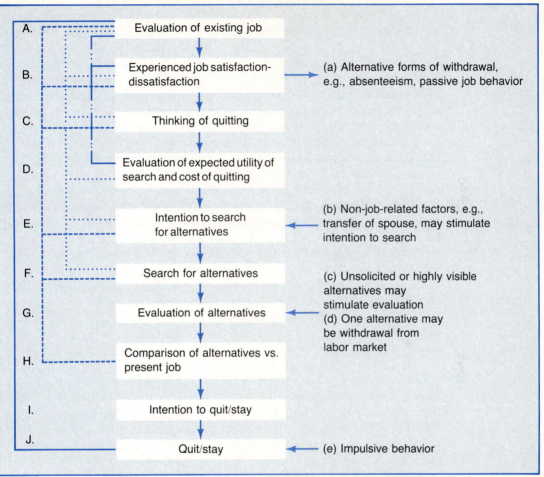

Source: W. H. Mobley, "Intermediate Linkages in the Relationship Between Job Satisfaction and Employee Turnover," *Journal of Applied Psychology 62* (1977): 238. Copyright 1977 by the American Psychological Association. Reprinted by permission of the publisher and author.

a process model in that it describes the processes leading up to actual termination. A schematic diagram of this model is shown in Exhibit 19.9 (Mobley, 1977, 1982).

The starting point in this model is an employee's evaluation of his or her existing job (shown in block A). As employees think about the positive and negative aspects of their jobs, they experience various levels of job satisfaction or dissatisfaction (block B). When dissatisfaction is experienced, at least two outcomes often result. First the employees may begin thinking about quitting (block C) and making alternate plans for employment. At the same time, however, employees may also begin engaging in several alternative forms of withdrawal (absenteeism, reduced job effort) as shown by arrow a in Exhibit 19.9.

Thoughts of quitting, in turn, often cause employees to consider the utility and costs associated with searching for (and possibly accepting) a new job (block D). The expected utility of search would include factors like the chances of finding another job, the desirability of alternative jobs, and the costs of search (travel costs, time away from the job). The evaluation of the costs of quitting might also include a consideration of loss of seniority and loss of vested benefits in retirement programs. In short, employees consider whether it is worth the trouble to look for a job elsewhere.

If employees determine that the costs of leaving are fairly high and/or that the expected utility of searching for a new job is low, they may decide to remain. In fact, employees may then reevaluate the existing job and begin to see it in a more positive light. On the other hand, if the costs of searching are reasonable and the expected utility of a search is high, we predict that the employee will develop a behavioral intention to search for alternatives (block E). This intention would also be influenced by a series of nonwork factors (arrow b), like a spouse's employment situation and geographic preferences. One may decide not to leave a dissatisfying job because one wishes to stay in the same geographic area or because one's spouse has a job nearby. Similarly, these nonwork factors may stimulate search behavior—even if an employee is satisfied with the job—if one's spouse is about to be transferred. These intentions to search, however activated, generally lead to actual search behavior (block F).

If an individual is successful in identifying alternative job opportunities or if a unique opportunity is presented to the individual by others (arrow c), these opportunities must be evaluated (block G). In this process, the alternatives are compared to the present job (block H) to determine the relative merits of both staying and leaving. The end result of this decision process is an intent to either stay or leave (block I), followed by the actual behavior of staying or leaving (block J).

Finally, arrow e suggests that some individuals may bypass this somewhat rational decision process and act impulsively. They may quit simply because of an argument with a co-worker or supervisor. Whatever the reason, it is important to recognize that the process is not entirely a rational one, as the model may suggest. Exceptions to the process may occur at any stage in the model. Still, the model is helpful in highlighting some of the major influences leading up to the decision to stay or leave.

Managing Turnover Behavior

Several avenues are open to managers who are interested in reducing employee turnover (Mowday, Porter, and Steers, 1982). Although other management implications than those that follow can be identified, the point is that, based on the model depicted in Exhibit 19.9, there *are* things managers can do to reduce employee turnover and develop a more stable work force for the pursuit of organizational effectiveness.

A manager can begin by clarifying job expectations for new and prospective employees. Realistic job previews have been shown to lead to reduced turnover since resulting expectations are more easily met by the actual job situation. Also, he or she should make sure that expected rewards or outcomes are closely tied to desired behaviors. In this way, it is more likely that employee expectations will be met following suitable performance.

When examining turnover rates, differentiate between turnover among high performers and low performers. These two groups may leave for quite different reasons. While reducing turnover among high performers may be desirable, there are many reasons why a *high* turnover rate among poor performers may be desirable.

In addition, recognize the importance of job attitudes (both job satisfaction and organizational commitment) since these attitudes can have important repercussions in terms of influencing both subsequent job performance and intent to leave. As much as possible, recognize individual characteristics in the selection and placement process and match people to jobs. (An alternative approach—matching jobs to people—was discussed in Chapter Eighteen). In matching, it is more likely that individuals will have the requisite skills to succeed on the job and may develop more positive attitudes toward staying with the organization.

Organizations can endeavor to increase commitment by convincing employees that management is truly concerned about their welfare. One way to accomplish this is through career counseling programs (D. T. Hall, 1976) where employees are shown the various options available to them should they remain. Recognize nonwork factors as a potent influence on intent to leave, as well. Many employees leave not by choice, but because of nonwork-related reasons, as discussed earlier. In some situations, organizations may be able to help. Successful examples include subsidizing day-care centers, policies that allow the company to hire spouses, or policies that attempt to take family considerations into account in promotions and transfers.

Finally, as discussed earlier in the text, it may be desirable in some cases to monitor employee attitudes toward the job and organization at regular intervals (perhaps annually) as an early warning system for potential turnover. If attitudes drop substantially, management is alerted to the problem and can take remedial action aimed at solving the problem and reducing the probability of increased terminations.

We have now come full circle in this chapter. We began by considering the attachment cycle, the process by which individuals join organizations, become socialized, and grow and develop with experience. We also considered absenteeism and turnover, the latter being the final stage in the attachment cycle. People tend to consider the earlier stages in this cycle as positive and the latter stages as negative. However, this view is overly simplistic.

There are many situations in which some turnover is desirable. For instance, turnover among poor performers allows an organization to replace them with more skilled and motivated employees. Turnover can be beneficial to many of the employees who choose to leave when it facilitates their seeking other positions that may be more suitable to their own personal goals and needs. In this regard, it should be noted that some employees have to be pushed out of the nest before they will attempt something more rewarding. Turnover can serve this function. Turnover can also reduce entrenched conflict: long-standing situations where two individuals or groups oppose each other's actions to the point of being dysfunctional for the organization as a whole (Staw, 1980). Finally, turnover opens up avenues of promotion for those who aspire to make a career with the organization, yet find upward mobility slow.

On the other hand, it should also be recognized that adverse results accompany turnover that offset many of these benefits. Disadvantages include increased recruitment and selection costs, increased training and development costs, disruption of ongoing group processes, and possible demoralization of remaining members. Managers should not automatically set out to reduce turnover. Only after assessing potential costs and benefits should a decision be made regarding actions aimed at reducing turnover and stabilizing the work force.

SUMMARY

This chapter shifted attention from motivating employee performance to motivating employee participation—that is, to the major influences on the psychological linkages that develop between individuals and organizations and the ways that these linkages themselves affect withdrawal behavior.

First we considered the topic of organizational entry and realistic job previews. Following this, the concept of careers and career development was introduced. The benefits of having management take an active role in career development was stressed.

Socialization processes were also reviewed as they relate to the manner by which organizations attempt to enculturate employees as they fit with the organization. At the same time, however, it was noted that employees often attempt to individualize the organization.

A model of employee absenteeism was presented as a way to better understand the major influences on the decision—and ability—to come to work. Finally, employee turnover was considered. A model of turnover was introduced, and implications for management were again suggested. Throughout, the point was made that reducing employee turnover and absenteeism requires the active efforts of management.

KEY WORDS

absenteeism	career
anticipatory socialization	career development
attendance motivation	career information system

career pathing	psychological contract
career stages	realistic job preview
debasement experience	retro pay
human resource planning	socialization
individualization	turnover
organizational commitment	well pay
organizational entry	

FOR DISCUSSION

1. What major factors influence a person's choice of an organization? In general, how accurate is the information most people have in making this choice?
2. How do realistic job previews differ from traditional ones? What are some advantages and disadvantages of realistic job previews?
3. What is a psychological contract? How does it work?
4. Describe the typical career stages through which many employees go. How might exceptions to this typical pattern occur?
5. How do socialization processes work in organizations?
6. What are some techniques used to socialize employees?
7. Describe the process of individualization. How do employees attempt to individualize their jobs?
8. Define organizational commitment. How does an organization build organizational commitment?
9. Discuss several outcomes of organizational commitments.
10. What are the major causes of employee absenteeism?
11. Distinguish between attendance and attendance motivation.
12. What role do pressures to attend play in actual attendance? What role does ability to attend play?
13. Identify several major strategies that can be used by managers to reduce absenteeism.
14. How do the major causes of turnover differ from those of absenteeism? How are they similar?
15. What can managers do to reduce turnover?

EXERCISE

MANAGING ORGANIZATIONAL CAREERS: SOME PROBLEMS

19.1

Purpose

To practice your skills in making organizational decisions and planning programs to facilitate employees' career development.

Introduction

Many of the conditions necessary for better career development seem disarmingly straightforward—e.g., provide more initial job challenge, more realistic

job previews, more opportunities for women and minorities. However, when put into practice, some of the unintentioned consequences and system effects (such as uncooperative supervisors or co-workers) come into play, indicating that organization development as well as career development is occurring. In the following problems you will be given a chance to try to find organizational solutions to some thorny career issues.

Procedure

Step 1. Formation (5 minutes). Divide the class into groups of four to six people. Assign each group one of the problems at the end of the exercise.

Step 2. Preparation (20 minutes). Each group will develop a solution to its problem and prepare a five-minute presentation to the rest of the class. In this presentation, the group will identify the problem and develop a persuasive case for the group's solution, while the rest of the class acts as a "board of directors."

Step 3. Presentations (5 minutes per group). Each group will have five minutes to present their solutions.

Step 4. Discussion (varying time). Compare the various solutions in an open discussion. What are the costs and benefits of each? What resistance would each encounter? How could this resistance be reduced?

Career Problem: The "Dead-End" Employee

Jim Duncan is a fifty-two-year-old department manager in your large manufacturing organization. He has been in this job for eight years. His performance has been very good, but lately has dropped off. He has had more sick days this year than ever before in his career.

Jim is not seen by top management or by personnel experts as having the ability to progress to a higher management position. He seems ideally placed in his present job.

You are Jim's boss, the plant manager. What action would you take to improve his performance and morale?

Career Problem: The "Deadwood" Employee

Ralph Hamner is seen by most employees as "deadwood." He was hired when the organization was much smaller, when you only had a few engineers, who had to be generalists. Now you have an engineering department of fifty people, most with advanced degrees and specialized backgrounds to deal with the increased complexity of your products —calculators and photographic equipment.

Ralph is now a senior engineer and just does not have the new knowledge necessary for most of your products. It has been hard to find projects on which he can use his present knowledge. At the same time, he is blocking the advancement of several promising junior engineers. Ralph is a well-liked guy, but he seems a bit defensive about his technical competence.

You are the personnel manager. What action would you recommend regarding Ralph Hamner?

Career Problem: Loss of Talented Young Employees

Your organization has traditionally been very attractive to college graduates as a place to work. The turnover among new employees has been about average for your industry. However, a recent study has just revealed a critical piece of information: the turnover is now occurring among your highest-performing new employees. The people you'd like to lose are staying, and those you want to keep are leaving.

Exit interviews indicate that young people are frustrated by low challenge and low advancement opportunities. You have a lot of people in their fifties in middle management who are blocking promotions now and who are threatened by sharp young employees. But you won't have any good middle managers in ten years (when the present managers retire) if all your best young people leave now. Business has been rather slow lately, and no new positions through growth seem likely for several years.

What should be done to retain more of your promising young employees?

Source: D. T. Hall, *Careers in Organizations* (Glenview, Ill.: Scott, Foresman and Company, 1976), pp. 220–21. Reprinted by permission.

EXERCISE

19.2

CONTROLLING EMPLOYEE TURNOVER

Purpose

To examine the primary causes of employee turnover among a clerical sample and to design an intervention strategy to attempt to reduce such turnover.

Instructions

Read the following true case. Based on the case, groups of five or six persons should develop a strategy for reducing employee turnover among the bank tellers. In doing so, keep several issues in mind. First, the program cannot use money in the form of pay raises, bonuses, etc. Second, the program must have the active support of branch managers in order to be successful. Finally, the program should be realistic.

Each group should take about forty minutes to develop its program. Following this, the class should meet as a whole to compare programs.

The Bank Case

The bank in question is a large west-coast bank. Among its bank tellers, annual turnover consistently averages around fifty percent. To make matters worse, about eighty percent of this turnover occurs during the first six months of employment. These turnover rates are comparable to industry averages. Moreover, salaries paid to bank tellers are a little above industry averages. In fact, management is so convinced that money is not the principal cause of turnover that they have forbidden you to alter compensation policies in any way.

To solve the turnover problem, the bank has agreed that you can have fifty separate bank branches to experiment with. Twenty-five of these branches will serve as a control group and twenty-five as your experimental group. The two groups have been matched as much as possible, and at the end of your intervention, the bank plans to compare your results with the experimental branches against the "uncontaminated" control groups. Branches range in size from two to fifteen tellers.

A preliminary study among the tellers suggests that many tellers are concerned about such issues as professional growth and development, relationships with their supervisor (the branch manager), and communication to and from management. All tellers are female, typically with a high-school education or some college (but no degree). Ages are evenly dispersed from eighteen to fifty-five.

The top management of the bank (your client) has noted that for any intervention to be a success it must have the active support of the branch managers.

LOYALTY AT INDSCO

Managers have a great deal of discretion over how they use their time and when they leave their desk and sometimes even where they work; but the organizational situation surrounding business management has made it among the most absorptive and time-consuming careers. In the midst of organizations supposedly designed around the specific and limited contractual relationships of a bureaucracy, managers may face, instead, the demand for personal attachment and a generalized, diffuse, unlimited commitment.[1]

The importance of loyalty in corporate careers was made clear in several different places on my sales force survey. Nearly half of those responding (forty-two percent) indicated that they had considered leaving Indsco within the last six months; only five percent said that they had never considered leaving. But in response to an open-ended question about why they had stayed, seventeen percent of the potential leavers wrote that they had stayed out of *loyalty* to the company, even in the absence of concrete rewards such as a better job at Indsco. Another set of items asked people to rate themselves in terms of their strength on twenty-seven personal characteristics, on a five-point scale, running from "very strong" to

"weak, need improvement." "Loyal" netted the highest mean rating (1.9), beating out "ambitious" (in second place with a mean rating of 2.1), and only closely followed by "helpful" and "friendly" (tied at 2.2). ("Knows business trends" received the lowest mean rating, at 3.1.) Loyalty was thus an important part of the self-perception of Indsco's upper-level workers, and it showed in their acceptance of demands for unbounded commitment.

Indsco managers tended to put in many more hours than workers, and they spent more of their so-called leisure time in work-related activities. One manager even dreamed about the company. At 4:30, when the working day ended, people stuffed the elevators in the rush to get out. Some of the men stayed behind for an occasional dinner or training program or important meeting. Into the briefcase went those inevitable papers or a trade publication or even a book on work-related issues that certainly could not be read in the office. "No one would believe that an executive was working if he were found at his desk reading a book," one commented. (On the other hand, another manager said that *visibly* working very long hours could also be slightly suspect. People would begin to wonder about the com-

petence of someone who seemed to have to work much longer than others at the same job.)

Managers routinely felt that too many people were making too many demands on their time: "There's *no way* this is a forty-hour week." "When I walk through the office five people will say, 'Slow down.'" "It's a juggling act. There are twenty balls up in the air at any one time." "There's no such thing as relaxing or thinking time." "Part of *my* time I have to spend placating my wife for all the rest of the time I'm not spending with her." "Going up the line, it doesn't get better." Sixty-hour work weeks were typical. Sales managers agreed that even though some functions do not spend as much time traveling as do people in sales, they spend more time in team meetings. Furthermore, the tendency of Indsco to do more and more work through committees and task forces put an additional pressure on managers. They were on committees to work on transportation, packaging, training, corporate relocation, minority relations, or to solve particular organizational problems. The immediate response to any problem in the corporation was to form a committee, and managers were likely to get an announcement in the mail that they were appointed to one. In the sales force survey, eighty-three percent of 205 respondents reported that they now did what they considered "extra work," beyond the bounds of a reasonable working day.

Some managers and professionals work so hard because the organization piles on tasks; others do it to get ahead; still others because they love the work. When asked why they did extra work, the sales force respondents indicated it was because of the work load (forty-six percent), commitment to the company (twenty-four percent), or interest in the work itself (twenty-one percent). (It is striking that interest in job content was mentioned with least frequency.) In any case, many companies resemble Indsco in actively encouraging work-absorption. A first-line manager told this story, which sent sympathetic chords through a group at Indsco to whom I showed it: "I used to work for another firm, and they really pushed for production, which was okay with me. I can work as hard as the next guy. My line produced as much as any of the others and more than most. You won't believe this, but upper management expected you to come in on Sundays too —not to work, but just to be seen on the premises—supposed to show how much you loved the damn place. . . . Well, I have a family. What are you supposed to do, live at the plant? Lots of the foremen came down to the lounge on Sunday and drank coffee for a couple of hours. I did a few times, and then said to hell with it—it's not worth it. . . . I started to get passed over on promotions, and I finally asked why. My boss said they weren't sure about my attitude and for me to think about it. Attitude! How does that grab you? So I quit and came here."

The organization's demands for a diffuse commitment from managers is another way to find concrete measures of trust, loyalty, and performance in the face of uncertainties. It is the answer to a series of questions about control over the performance of people given responsibility for the organization's fate. *Question:* How do managers show they are trustworthy? *Answer:* By showing they care about the company more than anything else. *Question:* How does the organization know managers are doing their jobs and that they are making the best possible decisions? *Answer:* Because they are spending every moment at it and thus working to the limits of human possibility. *Question:* When has a manager finished the job? *Answer:* Never. Or at least, hardly ever. There is always something more that could be done.

There is an expectation, furthermore, that people in management form their careers largely around one organization. This expectation not only built loyalty but it also ensured that managerial personnel have a common core of organizational experience that would establish trustworthiness and translate into smooth and accurate communication. Thus, managers became members of Industrial Supply Corporation rather than of a community or even a nation. Those on management ladders at Indsco planned their career, sought jobs within the company, as though all of life could be encapsulated within the corporation. They resigned themselves to the necessity of geographic relocations, and even built this expectation into the rhythm of their family. Houses were selected for their resale value, and they were often identical versions of the same suburban split-level all over the country. When the company announced a decision to move headquarters to X-ville, some managers answered my question about how they spent their time by a joking reference to having to move: "I spend my time looking for property in X-ville." One manager had considered himself very lucky. In twenty years with the company, he had been able to remain at or near headquarters and to establish solid roots in a suburban community. He "loved the city," he said, and both he and his wife dreaded moving, yet if the corporation moved, he would go with it. He never even considered looking for another job so that he could stay in his community.

A number of analysts have commented on the multiple functions served by frequent personnel transfers on the managerial level, beyond the official reason of "broadening a manager's experience, providing wide exposure": to break up cliques, to reduce directly personal competition by shuffling people through locations. But it is also clear that transfers serve to reduce the efficacy of commitments other than to the corporation. Just as long-lived utopian communities built commitment in part by establishing strong boundaries between themselves and the outside world, making it difficult for people to maintain any ties outside the community, so do corporations like Indsco create organizational loyalty by ensuring that for its most highly paid members the corporation represents the only enduring set of social bonds other than the immediate family. And the family, too—at least the wife—can be drawn in. The demands of executive work have often had two effects: time demands reduce the participation of men in their families, and demands on wives have sometimes absorbed them into the realm of corporate loyalty and corporate control.

The concern with organizational commitment showed in a number of other ways. People who seemed to have competing loyalties were considered slightly suspect. It was a bad sign when someone in the sales force turned into a "customers' man"—identifying with the customers and looking out for their interests—even if this resulted in higher sales. Similar reasoning might be behind the traditionally lower status of people in staff positions in corporations. Certainly staff are immune from the direct responsibilities for production that characterize line managers, and therefore their contribution to the organization's functioning is even more uncertain. But also, their professional affiliations make their loyalties flow outward but not necessarily upward, so to

questions of the worth of the staff function are added concerns about the loyalty of staff people themselves. Indeed, at Indsco one highly promising manager with a shot at a vice presidency fell from grace after he took a temporary personnel staff assignment and began to devote himself to the professional aspects of the work, joining outside associations, attending meetings, and seeming to become more the professional and less the company man.

If pressures for total dedication sometimes serve to *include* wives in peripheral and auxiliary roles, they also serve to *exclude* many other women from employment as managers. Women have been assumed not to have the dedication of men to their work, or they have been seen to have conflicting loyalties, competing pulls from their other relationships. Successful women executives, as Margaret Hennig showed in her interviews with a hundred of them, have often put off marriage until rather late so that they could devote their time during the important ladder-climbing years to a single-minded pursuit of their careers.

Concerns expressed by men in management about the suitability of women for managerial roles reflect these themes. Questions about turnover, absenteeism, and ambition are frequently raised in meetings at Indsco, when affirmative action officers try to enlist the support of other managers. Sets of statistics and information countering prevalent myths have been prepared to hand out in response to such likely questions. The issue behind them often has to do with marriage.

The question of marriage is experienced by some women in professional, managerial, or sales ladders at Indsco as full of contradictory injunctions. Sometimes they got the message that being single was an advantage, five women reported, sometimes that it was just the opposite. Two single women, one of them forty, in quite different functions, were told by their managers that they could not be given important jobs because they were likely to get married and leave. One male manager said to a female subordinate that he would wait about five years before promoting a competent woman to see if she "falls into marriage." On the other hand, they were also told in other circumstances that married women cannot be given important jobs because of their family responsibilities: their children, if they are working mothers; their unborn children and the danger they will leave with pregnancy, if currently childless. One woman asked her manager for a promotion, to which he replied, "You're probably going to get pregnant." So she pointed out to him that he told her that eight years ago, and she hadn't. A divorced woman similarly discussed promotion with her manager and was asked "How long do you want the job? Do you think you'll get married again?" One working mother who had heard that "married women are absent more," had to prove that she had taken only one day off in eleven years at Indsco.

A male manager in the distribution function who supervised many women confirmed the women's reports. He said that he never even considered asking a married woman to do anything that involved travel, even if this was in the interests of her career development, and therefore he could not see how he could recommend a woman for promotion into management.

Note

1. Although the names have been disguised, this case is based on a real organization.

CASE DISCUSSION QUESTIONS

1. Identify some employee behaviors that indicate commitment to Indsco. How do these behaviors fit the definition of commitment given in this chapter?

2. What sorts of situations are considered conflicting loyalties by Indsco, and how does the organization respond to people who exhibit these tendencies?

3. What sort of negative consequences might Indsco face as a result of its intolerance of outside commitments?

4. As a manager at Indsco, what might you do differently insofar as employee commitment to the organization is concerned?

ORGANIZATIONAL CHANGE AND DEVELOPMENT

The ability to adapt successfully to a changing environment is one of the most important characteristics of effective managers. Such adaptation is not easy in view of the often conflicting demands of employees and the complex environment facing an organization. In addition, organizational change must not be random or initiated merely for the sake of change; management must balance the need for adaptation and innovation with the equally important need for stability and continuity. As Kast and Rosenzweig (1974) suggest:

> Management is charged with the responsibility for maintaining a dynamic equilibrium by diagnosing situations and designing adjustments that are most appropriate for coping with current conditions. A dynamic equilibrium for an organization would include the following dimensions:
>
> 1. Enough stability to facilitate achievement of current goals,
> 2. Enough continuity to ensure orderly change in either ends or means,
> 3. Enough adaptability to react appropriately to external opportunities and demands as well as changing internal conditions,
> 4. Enough innovativeness to allow the organization to be proactive (initiate changes) when conditions warrant (pp. 574–75).

The administrators' ability to create these four conditions simultaneously largely determines whether an organization survives and how well it grows in a turbulent environment.

In this chapter we will examine several related topics. First, we will consider several forces for change in organizations. Next, we will discuss resistance to change, and then we will describe the planned change process in organizations. We will consider strategies for planned change, ending with a discussion of organizational development as a technique for planned change.

IMPORTANCE OF TOPIC FOR MANAGERS

Effective managers recognize change as a fact of organizational life. Organizations exist in turbulent environments, and planned organizational change will keep the organization current and capable of adapting successfully. To capably plan change, managers must fully understand the array of change techniques available to them.

Successful managers must both recognize the need for change and understand the various techniques for facilitating it in order to keep their organizations competitive in a dynamic environment.

THE CHALLENGE OF ORGANIZATIONAL CHANGE

The need for organizational change becomes apparent when managers sense that an organization's activities, goals, or values are deficient in some way. When there is a noticeable gap between what an organization is trying to do and what it actually is accomplishing, management must take positive steps to reduce this disparity. For instance, several years ago many scientists and mathematicians—and a great number of college students—considered a slide rule essential for their required computations. Almost overnight, however, the introduction of inexpensive, electronic pocket calculators made the slide rule a thing of the past (see Chapter Two)—one company watched its slide rule sales drop 75 percent in just two years. The technology of calculating instruments changed radically, necessitating change in organizations that produced such instruments. Only companies that were aware of trends and began planning early for change were able to maintain their positions in the

EXHIBIT 20.1   EXTERNAL AND INTERNAL FORCES FOR ORGANIZATIONAL CHANGE

External Forces for Change

Economic and market changes
Technological changes
Legal/political changes
Resource availability
  changes

The Organization

Internal Forces for Change

Employee goal changes
Job technology changes
Organizational structure
  changes
Organizational climate
  changes
Organizational goal changes

market. Other companies either disappeared or moved on to other fields, leaving behind a lucrative market.

The forces necessitating organizational change can be found both inside and outside organizations. If managers are to take a comprehensive view of innovation and adaptation, they must be aware of both types of forces and be able to account for both in their actions.

External Forces for Change

There are a wide variety of external forces for organizational change that require managerial action (see Exhibit 20.1). These include (1) changes in economic or market conditions, such as a sudden decline in demand for a company's products; (2) changes in product or manufacturing technology, such as the discovery of a less expensive manufacturing process by a competitor; (3) changes in the legal or political situation, such as a new consumer protection law that affects current products or practices; and (4) changes in resource availability, such as an increase in cost or sudden unavailability of a major input such as oil.

These forces create performance problems that can severely threaten organizational stability—and even survival—if not remedied. For instance, the oil shortage of the mid-1970s resulted in corporate distribution policies that led to the demise of many independently owned service stations that lacked the resources necessary to survive and compete with company-owned stations. Simply put, the independent stations did not have the capacity to respond adequately to external forces for change; as a result, they were forced out of business.

Internal Forces for Change

In addition, several factors within an organization can be important forces for organizational change. These factors include (1) changes in the composition or personal goals of employees, such as the hiring of newer or younger employees with a work ethic different from that of employees with more seniority; (2) changes in job technology, such as the replacement of workers on craft-type jobs by automated equipment; (3) changes in organizational structure, such as new divisions necessitated by company growth; (4) changes in organizational climate, such as the creation of a climate of distrust, hostility, and insecurity as a result of mass layoffs; and (5) changes in organizational goals (goals may change because management realizes its initial expectations were too high, too low, or misdirected for some reason).

These forces for change create unstable conditions within organizations and jeopardize goal-directed efforts. When stability and continuity are threatened, organizations must adapt their structure or behavior to ensure long-term growth and survival. Before we consider such change processes, however, we should discuss several reasons why change in organizational settings is often difficult to accomplish.

RESISTANCE TO CHANGE

An important lesson learned by most managers who introduce changes is that resistance to such efforts can be found throughout an organization. The reasons for resistance can be either personal or organizational. Some of the more prominent personal and organizational reasons for resistance are listed in Exhibit 20.2.

Individual Reasons

As shown in Exhibit 20.2, employees may resist new techniques or methods because they feel secure under existing conditions and fear that changes will destroy interpersonal relationships that have developed through the years. Some employees may not fully understand the reasons behind a change or how it will affect their own situations. Group norms may operate to resist any change in work procedures for fear that it will lead to higher output without commensurate rewards or compensation.

Employees who do not identify with proposed changes often create passive resistance and drag their feet in implementation. This reaction often has been cited as a reason for the failure of affirmative action programs that attempt to increase minority hiring. Current nonminority employees often are simply indifferent to the goals of affirmative action. It is important to realize that most personal reasons for resisting change are not the result of any overt intention to interfere with goal attainment. Instead, such resistance often results from a fear of the consequences of change and a preference for the known over the unknown.

EXHIBIT 20.2   PERSONAL AND ORGANIZATIONAL REASONS FOR RESISTANCE TO CHANGE

Personal Sources	Organizational Sources
1. Misunderstanding of purpose, mechanics, or consequences of change	1. Reward system may reinforce status quo
2. Failure to see need for change	2. Interdepartmental rivalry or conflict, leading to an unwillingness to cooperate
3. Fear of unknown	3. Sunk costs in past decisions and actions
4. Fear of loss of status, security, power, etc. resulting from change	4. Fear that change will upset current balance of power between groups and departments
5. Lack of identification or involvement with change	5. Prevailing organizational climate
6. Habit	6. Poor choice of method of introducing change
7. Vested interests in status quo	7. Past history of unsuccessful change attempts and their consequences
8. Group norms and role prescriptions	8. Structural rigidity
9. Threat to existing social relationships	
10. Conflicting personal and organizational objectives	

Source: Reprinted from R. M. Steers, *Organizational Effectiveness: A Behavioral View* (Glenview, Ill.: Scott, Foresman, and Company, 1977), p. 167.

Organizational Reasons

The nature and character of the organization itself also can influence the extent to which change is accepted. For instance, the prevailing reward structure may favor existing behavior, such as when an organization pays salespeople solely on the basis of total sales and ignores effort and time spent in developing new customers. When various departments see one another as rivals, they may subvert cooperative efforts aimed at change for fear of encroachment on their territory. Managers may consider themselves bound by past decisions and actions because of large investments made previously in a particular product or technology, sometimes preferring to live with past decisions than to admit that a mistake was made or that conditions have changed. In addition, if previous organizational attempts at change were ill-conceived and unsuccessful, employees will lack confidence in the success of any new change efforts.

There are many other reasons for resistance to change, but the important point is that management must be aware of the various sources of this resistance and be able to minimize them. Managers must accurately assess the nature of and need for change, and then lay the groundwork for the change by addressing the possible sources of resistance. The manner in which change is implemented is at least as important for success as the actual change itself. With this in mind, we now turn to a consideration of the change process in

EXHIBIT 20.3   BASIC CHANGE PROCESSES IN ORGANIZATIONS

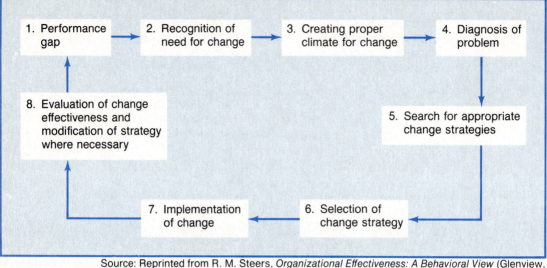

Source: Reprinted from R. M. Steers, *Organizational Effectiveness: A Behavioral View* (Glenview, Ill.: Scott, Foresman and Company, 1977), p. 169.

organizations, with particular emphasis on the way planned change is introduced.

PLANNED CHANGE IN ORGANIZATIONS

The ideal organizational change process is a series of fairly distinct, sequential steps leading from the recognition of the problem to the introduction and execution of the change strategy. Although actual change may be far more complex, a flow diagram can highlight some of the more important steps in the process. The steps in a simplified change process are represented in Exhibit 20.3.

Performance gaps initially emerge because of changes in the environment, structure, technology, or membership of an organization. These gaps may take the form of a loss of sales revenue, reduced productivity, or increased absenteeism and turnover. Once managers recognize such gaps, they can try to create a climate that is conducive to change. If sufficient time and effort are invested at the outset in eliminating the causes for resistance, a more open approach to the change process can be taken. Next, the manager diagnoses the extent of the problem. Based on this analysis, he or she makes recommendations for appropriate adjustments to remedy the situation and eliminate or reduce the performance gaps. After the implications, costs, and benefits of the alternatives are considered, a decision on a particular change strategy is made and implemented. Once implementation is complete, management can assess how well strategy reduced the performance gap. The manager then can take steps to reinforce and maintain the new program as long as it serves the needs of the organization, its members, and its stakeholders.

Consider the following true example. For twenty years, a major U.S. research laboratory specializing in valves and gauges spent most of its time and effort designing hardware for aerospace projects. Most of its income came from government contracts. As government funds became scarce, however, the laboratory was faced with a performance gap. Because it could see no further contracts coming from the government, management recognized the need for change and began laying the groundwork for a shift from aerospace engineering. After diagnosing the situation, management concluded that with minimal organizational disturbance the laboratory's technical expertise could be applied to hardware problems in the automotive industry. Thus, management shifted the laboratory's goals to providing precision valves and gauges for automobiles instead of space vehicles. Assessment of the change revealed that the process had been carried out with minimal loss of personnel and that the laboratory had sufficient revenues to continue operations in an area in which it had ample expertise. The organization responded to environmental changes by adapting its goals to maintain stability and continuity, thereby enhancing its chances for survival, growth, and development.

STRATEGIES FOR PLANNED CHANGE

The success or failure of change efforts rests not only on accurate identification of the problem and successful reduction of resistance to change but also on the appropriateness of the selected strategy for implementing the change. Understanding the problem is not enough, nor is having employees who are willing to change. Managers must make the right selection among a wide variety of strategies of change. The three general strategies of change differ in the direction of efforts to change, targeting structure, technology, or people. As noted by Leavitt (1964), these three key ingredients interact with more general organizational activities to create conditions that enable organizations to be more effective (see Exhibit 20.4). We shall consider each of these three approaches briefly.

Structural Approaches to Change

Changes in an organization's *structure* can take several forms. Glueck (1979, p. 427) summarized some of the more common techniques:

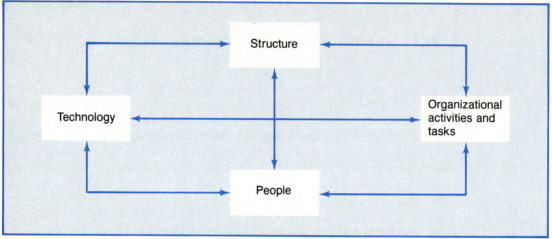

Source: H. J. Leavitt, "Applied Organization Change in Industry: Structural, Technical, and Human Approaches," in W. W. Cooper, H. J. Leavitt, and M. W. Shelly (eds.), *New Perspectives in Organization Research* (New York: John Wiley & Sons, Inc., 1964), p. 56. Copyright © 1964 by John Wiley & Sons, Inc. Reprinted by permission of John Wiley & Sons, Inc.

- Effecting changes in job design that permit more specialization or enrichment
- Clarifying the job descriptions
- Altering the basis of departmentation (changing from a functional organization to a department system based on products, for example)
- Increasing or decreasing the span of control and therefore the height of the hierarchy
- Modifying the organization manual and its description of policies and procedures
- Clarifying coordination mechanisms, such as policies and procedures
- Changing the power structure (moving from a centralized to a decentralized authority, for example)

Structural changes are fairly common in organizations. A major purpose of structural change is to create conditions that facilitate and reward goal-directed efforts. For example, a matrix organization (discussed in Chapter Three) may be introduced in a situation in which divergent areas of expertise must be integrated and coordinated for a particular product or project, such as a space satellite. The underlying assumption of this approach is that behavior, performance, and effectiveness are largely determined by the way an organization or work group is structured. An example of this theory in action can be seen in Chase Manhattan Bank's efforts to change its prevailing reward system and corporate culture (see Close-Up 20.1).

CLOSE-UP 20.1 CHANGING CORPORATE CULTURE AT CHASE MANHATTAN

You can't see it or feel it, but one of the most important aspects of an organization is its culture. A culture is a pattern of beliefs and expectations shared by the members of an organization that establishes the norms and rules governing acceptable employee behavior. The culture of an organization can have a profound effect on behavior within it. Many people believe that serious efforts to change an organization can only succeed if managers are successful in changing its culture first.

Consider the example of Chase Manhattan Bank. David Rockefeller, the youngest of John D. Rockefeller's six grandchildren, became president of Chase Manhattan in 1961, having risen to the top the easy way. Once there, he ran the nation's third-largest bank like a club. Bank officers tended to "worry more about how many oils from the Chase art collection they had on their walls than about profits," said one Wall Street analyst.

By 1977 profits had plummeted. Return on assets fell to $.33 per $100, and bad debts totaled $1.9 billion. Numerous poor business decisions had been made, and many of the bank's most experienced executives had resigned.

It was David Rockefeller himself who decided at last to change the culture from one that rewarded people for appearance to one that would reward them for performance. He set himself a goal of making the three years until his mandatory retirement "the most productive of my career."

The first thing Rockefeller and a group of his top executives did was draw up a three-page statement of the bank's goals. "We will only do those things we can do extremely well and with the highest level of integrity," the statement said. Those things included closing 50 unprofitable branches in New York, turning away risky loans, replacing about 600 executives with new young talent, and updating the bank's customer services. In addition, the bank made efforts to increase communication both up and down in the hierarchy—a marked change from the previous top-down approach.

The results speak for themselves. Three years later assets had risen from $45 billion to $65 billion, while bad debts had declined from $269 million to $93 million; net income had risen from $116 million to $303 million. Chase Manhattan had created a new culture. David Rockefeller proudly took his share of the credit when he told a financial correspondent for *Time* magazine, "I helped to create a climate that has finally produced a really professional management team, which was essential to our success."

Sources: "The Change at David's Bank," *Time,* September 1, 1980, p. 49; "Corporate Culture," *Business Week,* October 27, 1980, pp. 148–60.

Technological Approaches to Change

A second general approach to change involves alterations in the prevailing *technology.* Research has shown consistently that when the nature of job technology—how we do our jobs—changes, the work environment also changes, although not necessarily for the better (see Chapter Eighteen). Examples of technological approaches to change include:

- Altering the techniques used for doing work, such as using human factors engineering to change worker-machine relations
- Changing the equipment used in work—for example, by introducing robots on an assembly line
- Modifying production methods, such as shifting from an assembly-line method to an autonomous work-group method
- Changing engineering processes, such as by introducing microprocessors or chips into a product to replace more cumbersome or less reliable mechanical equipment

The principal assumption underlying technological change is that improved technology or work methods can lead to more efficient operations and either increased productivity or improved working conditions, perhaps through the elimination of more tedious tasks. A good example can be seen in discussions surrounding the introduction of word processors in offices. It is argued that word processors allow typists to become more efficient and productive, thereby saving the company money and presumably offsetting the cost of the equipment. Unfortunately, in many situations no one bothers to ask the typists for *their* opinions on such changes. The consequence is often diminished results, negative attitudes, or, at the very least, misunderstandings. It is important to consult and involve the employees concerned when attempting to introduce technological change.

People Approaches to Change

The third approach to change focuses on attempts to change *individuals*. Strategies aimed at changing people tend to emphasize improving employee skills, attitudes, or motivation. These approaches assume that behavior in organizations—and ultimately organizational effectiveness—are largely determined by the characteristics and actions of the members of the organization. If these people can be changed in some way, it is believed that they will work harder to achieve the organization's goals.

Individual change strategies take many forms, including a wide variety of personnel training programs, such as skills training, communication effectiveness, and decision-making training; attitude motivation training; and socialization efforts to develop a "company man" or "company woman" (see Chapter Nineteen).

Most such strategies rely on a basic model of individual change that was first advanced by Kurt Lewin (1943) and later developed by Ed Schein (1968). The model consists of four basic steps, as shown in Exhibit 20.5.

- *Desire for change.* Before change can occur, the individual must feel a

EXHIBIT 20.5   THE INDIVIDUAL CHANGE PROCESS

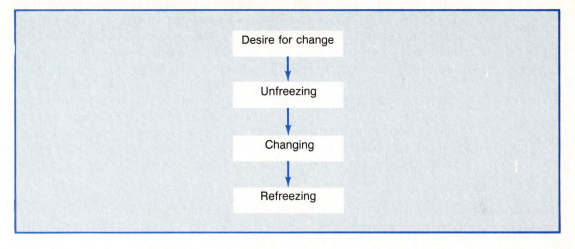

need for it. This need can result from a perceived deficiency, actual dissatisfaction, or a desire for improvement.

- *Unfreezing.* As Schein (1968, p. 62) notes, unfreezing involves "an alteration of the forces acting on the individual, such that his stable equilibrium is disturbed sufficiently to motivate him and to make him ready for change; this can be accomplished either by increasing the pressure to change or by reducing some of the threats or resistance to change."

- *Changing.* According to Schein (1968, p. 62), changing involves "the presentation of a direction of change and the actual process of learning new attitudes. This process occurs basically by one of two mechanisms: (a) *identification*—the person learns new attitudes by identifying with and emulating some other person who holds those attitudes; or (b) *internalization*—the person learns new attitudes by being placed in a situation where new attitudes are demanded of him as a way of solving problems which confront him and which he cannot avoid."

- *Refreezing.* In refreezing, the changed attitudes are integrated into the individual's personality in such a way that they become part of his or her way of thinking.

Although this model is simple, it highlights the basic processes involved in attempts to change people. Managers who are aware of this process stand a far greater chance of succeeding with planned change attempts than those who ignore the people involved.

Overall, then, the appropriate change technique depends on the nature and character of the problem, the goals of the change, the orientations of the people implementing the change, and the resources available. For instance, if poor communication is seen as a barrier to effective performance, management may decide to make structural changes, such as using a matrix design to change reporting procedures and lines of authority, fostering more interaction and exchanges of views and thereby improving communications. On the other hand, management may also simply institute communications training programs to improve both interpersonal and communications skills. Both of these approaches address barriers to effective communication, though their techniques and underlying assumptions are quite different. The important point is that a primary responsibility of managers is to recognize the need for change in organizations, diagnose the nature and extent of the problems that create this need, and implement the most effective change strategy they can devise. Without such leadership, an organization's ability to respond to both internal and external threats to stability and continuity is greatly diminished, reducing the organization's ability to operate effectively in the long run.

ORGANIZATION DEVELOPMENT

We have reviewed three general approaches to planned organizational change: changes to structure, technology, and people. These approaches are usually aimed at fairly specific goals within the organization, such as improving employees' achievement motivation through training or improving job efficiency through job redesign. An integrated approach to change, however, focuses not on one aspect or problem within the organization but on long-term, global change and development throughout the organization. *Organization development,* as we shall see, is an ongoing and system-wide developmental approach. It seeks to improve both productivity and efficiency on the one hand and the quality of working life on the other.

The topic of organizational development is broad and includes many different and often conflicting approaches (see, for example, the discussion in Beer, 1980, p. 198). Even so, the following definition for organization development is broad enough to encompass most of the different activities (French and Bell 1973):

> [Organization development is] a long-range effort to improve an organization's problem-solving and renewal processes, particularly through a more effective and collaborative management or organization culture—with special emphasis on the culture of formal work teams—with the assistance of a change agent, or catalyst, and the use of the theory and technology of applied behavioral science, including action research.

Several dimensions emerge from this definition. First, organization development is a problem-solving process used to alleviate threats to organizational survival or well-being or to capitalize on a unique opportunity. Second, its goal is to help the organization *renew* itself and become more vital. Third, it stresses *collaborative management;* that is, change efforts involve the active participation of all affected parties. Fourth, major organization development efforts are attempts to change an organization's *culture* and *work climate.* Finally, a central aspect of many organization development efforts is *action research.* Action research is the process by which behavioral research findings are collected and then fed back to participants, who discuss the results and use them as a foundation for planned change. Thus, organization development is a mechanism for change that is highly participatory, broad in scope, and evolutionary in design. As such, it truly represents an integrative approach to planned organizational change.

Basic Assumptions of Organization Development

Any approach to change rests on certain assumptions and values espoused by its advocates. Some of the more general assumptions of organization development about what life in organizations should be like, how change should occur, and how individual employees, group relationships, and organizational relationships should work are discussed in the following sections.

Assumptions about individuals. Organization development advocates often assume that employees want and need personal growth and that they need fulfillment on the job. They also assume that people generally can contribute more to the organization than they are typically encouraged or allowed to. In other words, organization development assumes that most people are "premotivated" to perform at high levels. Its purpose, then, is to develop a work environment that encourages this motivation and allows employees to realize their full potential within organizations.

Assumptions about groups. Organization development practitioners also hold several assumptions concerning the nature of group relations. In many organizations, for example, there is less interpersonal trust and mutual support among group members than is desirable for maximum effectiveness. Organization development holds that leadership responsibilities, instead of being concentrated in one person, can be more widely shared among group members. This emphasizes facilitating group activities and group cooperation; open communication is stressed as a means to secure the active participation of everyone and to root out potential problems or conflicts. Advocates also believe that developing an *ésprit de corps* among group members will support positive feelings about one another and genuine interest in the welfare of group members.

Assumptions about organizations. The third set of assumptions underlying many organization development activities is that change in one part of an organization, such as the marketing department, will necessarily influence and be influenced by other parts, such as engineering or production. As we have said, organization development is a system-wide change effort. In addition, the members of an organization not only are involved in their own groups but also must interact with other groups—hence the emphasis on intergroup relations. Efforts to reduce conflict emphasize *non–zero-sum games;* that is, efforts are made to avoid situations in which someone wins and someone loses. Instead, a search is made for a solution to the conflict that will satisfy all parties. Finally, if organization development is to succeed, it must have the full and active support of top management. This last point cannot be emphasized enough.

While these assumptions vary somewhat, the major thrust of organization development activities can succeed only in environments characterized largely by these values. Organization development is as much a philosophy of change as a technology of change. It assumes that people are open to change and that organizations and their managers are willing to change. Without this willingness, organization development attempts are doomed to failure.

The Organization Development Process

The basic change process used in organization development follows the steps shown in Exhibit 20.3. As a change technology, however, it emphasizes several features not typically found in more focused or narrow efforts. Organization development as a process typically consists of several rather distinct steps (Glueck, 1979):

1. *Initial diagnosis.* At this stage, fundamental questions are asked: What is the basic problem? Can the problem be solved using organization development techniques?
2. *Data collection.* Data are collected through interviews and question-naires to verify the initial diagnosis and suggest possible solutions.
3. *Feedback and confrontation.* The findings from the survey are fed back to the participants, discussed, and examined as they relate to the group. Priorities for change are identified.
4. *Planning and problem solving.* Problem-solving groups are established to tackle major problem areas and goals.
5. *Team building.* Conscious efforts are made to develop work groups into cohesive teams rather than isolated individuals who happen to work together.
6. *Intergroup development.* Efforts are made to build and solidify good working relationships among the various teams.
7. *Follow-up and evaluation.* Results are compared against initial goals, and steps are identified to ensure that resulting change sticks. New change goals are established when necessary to overcome previous problems.

The final outcome of this process should be a more cohesive organization with highly integrated work teams, good intergroup relations, less conflict, and greater focus and consensus on organizational goals. Though of course the results are not always positive, organization development has in many situations contributed to substantial improvements in organizational function. It is because of this, perhaps, that most of the top Fortune 500 companies have adopted some form of organization development activities.

Approaches to Organization Development

Several approaches are available to people interested in organization development. These include survey feedback, process consultation, team building, and grid organization development.

Survey Feedback. Survey feedback is a relatively straightforward technique in which employees are surveyed with a questionnaire or interview and the results are given back to them in an aggregate or summarized form. Next, the employees discuss the meaning of the results. Topics commonly surveyed include the general level of job satisfaction, perceptions of leadership styles, openness of communication, and conflict. As a result of these discussions, training and development activities are initiated to solve the problems the survey has identified.

Process Consultation. In process consultation, an external agent observes a group at work, assessing such aspects as leadership styles, communication, conflict and cooperation, and decision-making processes. The change agent's observations, when shared with group members, serve as the basis for a discussion concerning ways to improve the situation. The change agent may discover, for example, that decisions are highly centralized—made by the general sales manager, perhaps—but that people far down in the hierarchy who are seldom consulted, such as sales representatives, have important information bearing on these decisions. As a result, useful information is ignored. Such a conclusion and possible remedies would then be considered.

Team Building. In team building, the manager attempts to analyze the effectiveness of a work group and help it discover how to work more effectively as an integrated and cohesive team. Methods for team building include discussions with group members about possible barriers to cohesiveness, and behavioral techniques, such as sensitivity training, that increase awareness of how other people respond to an individual's behavior in a group setting.

Grid Organization Development. An approach that has received considerable attention in recent years is Grid® organizational development. This approach was developed by Blake and Mouton (1985) and represents one of the more comprehensive and systematic approaches to change. The technique is based on Blake and Mouton's managerial grid, which suggests that two key outcome variables are important to organizations: a concern for people and a concern for production. The Grid, shown in Exhibit 20.6, identifies the possible combinations of these two concerns.

In Exhibit 20.6, concern for people is plotted on the vertical axis of the Grid and concern for production is plotted on the horizontal axis. Five major intersections between these two concerns are shown, beginning with what is labeled a "1, 1" management style, in which managers show little concern for either people or production. In "1, 9" and "9, 1" management styles, managers emphasize one concern at the expense of the other. Managers with a

EXHIBIT 20.6   THE MANAGERIAL GRID

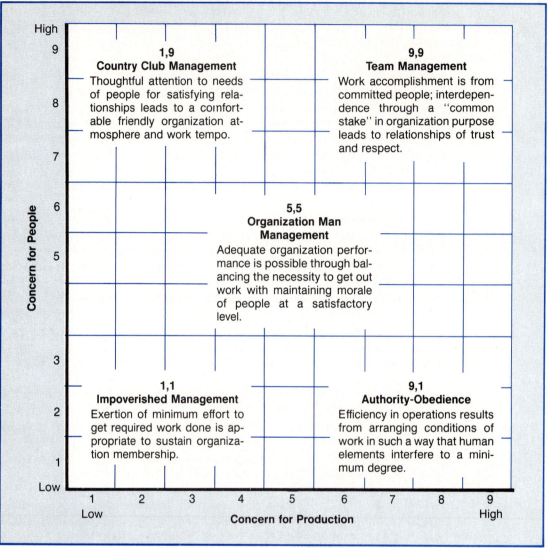

Source: Robert R. Blake and Jane Srygley Mouton, *The Managerial Grid III: The Key to Leadership Excellence* (Houston: Gulf Publishing Company, Copyright © 1985), p. 12. Reproduced by permission.

"5, 5" style attempt to compromise and show "sufficient" attention to both. The ideal form—a "9, 9" management style—emerges when managers are successful in developing highly committed, cohesive, and satisfied work teams that are dedicated to maximum production and organizational effectiveness.

Change agents help managers locate themselves on the Grid. Ideally, this self-evaluation will serve as a starting point for development of a "9, 9" manager. The program through which such managers are developed consists of six steps:

- *Phase 1: Training.* After top management has concluded that Grid organizational development may help solve the organization's problem, key managers attend a week-long seminar to learn the basic concepts of the program. They assess their own managerial styles and work to improve their communication, group problem-solving abilities, and team-development skills. Following this seminar, each key manager returns to the organization and attempts to put the program into effect.
- *Phase 2: Team development.* Managers and their subordinates work together to improve their interrelationship and to develop cohesive teams capable of operating on a "9, 9" level.
- *Phase 3: Intergroup development.* Efforts are made to reduce conflict and increase cooperation in intergroup relations. The goal is for the entire organization to work together and for individual members to help one another work toward organizational goals.
- *Phase 4: Organizational goal setting.* Once intergroup cooperation is achieved, the organization as a whole can consider what changes are needed in long-term corporate goals. Active participation at all levels is encouraged in the attempt to define what the organization will or should look like in the future.
- *Phase 5: Goal attainment.* Effort is directed toward making the ideal organization a real one. Concern focuses on removing obstacles to organizational objectives.
- *Phase 6: Stabilization.* The entire program is evaluated to determine where success has been achieved and where more effort is needed. When necessary, new improvement goals are set to remedy past failures. Finally, the positive outcomes that have been achieved throughout the process are stabilized and secured.

A Guide to Successful Interventions

The history of organization development interventions is difficult to interpret. Most of the research carried out to evaluate the effectiveness of such interventions has been done by organization development consultants, who have an obvious interest in positive results. Even so, organization development remains a popular form of change. Many managers feel that though imperfect, organization development represents one of the better approaches to planned change in organizations.

Efforts can be made to enhance the likelihood of success in organization development interventions. French and Bell (1973) have listed eleven factors:

1. Recognize that the organization has problems. Without this recognition, no change effort can succeed.
2. Use an *external* change agent. Internal change agents usually lack

necessary experience or expertise and typically have greater political problems in orchestrating serious change.

3. Elicit strong support from top managers for the organization development intervention efforts. Such support is necessary if the efforts are to succeed.

4. Make use of action research. Decisions should be guided by facts, not opinions.

5. Achieve a small success in some part of the organization to motivate employees to participate actively in the program. A small success indicates that the program can work.

6. Make sure that employees understand what organization development is and is not, and that they are aware of why it is being used. In this way, apprehension and resistance to the unknown are reduced.

7. Ensure that change agents do not condescend to managers or employees.

8. Ensure that managers from the personnel department are actively involved. Internal expertise concerning an organization's human resources can be incorporated into the change efforts.

9. Begin to develop internal expertise in organization development. In this way the internal facilitators can assume responsibility from the external change agents in time and assure the continuity of the program.

10. Monitor the results continuously and be sensitive to deviations from the program or to weakening support for the program.

11. Ensure that valid and reliable measures are taken before and after the intervention to provide an accurate indicator of actual change. Without such data, it becomes virtually impossible to determine whether the efforts were successful.

SUMMARY

In organizational settings, the need for change becomes apparent when there is a noticeable gap between what an organization is trying to do and what it actually is accomplishing. The reasons for these performance gaps can be found both within and outside the organization. External forces for change include changes in economic or market conditions, product or manufacturing technology, the legal or political situation, and resource availability. Unless these gaps are remedied, they can lead to threats to organizational stability and survival. Internal forces for change include changes in the composition or personal goals of employees, job technology, organizational structure, and organizational goals. When stability and continuity are threatened, organizations must adapt their structure or behavior to ensure long-term growth and survival. Resistance to change can come from employees or from the nature and character of the organization itself.

The change process ideally is a series of distinct, sequential steps leading from recognition of the problem to the introduction and assessment of the change strategy. Three general strategies for change are structural, which includes alterations in job design, job descriptions, and the power structure; technological, which includes alterations in the techniques or equipment used; and personal, in which people are changed in some way by improving their skills, attitudes, or motivation. The strategy used depends on the nature of the problem, the goals of the change, the orientation of the people implementing the change, and the available resources.

Organization development is a long-range problem-solving process aimed at helping the organization renew itself. It stresses collaborative management in an attempt to change an organization's culture and work climate. Action research is a central aspect of many organization development efforts. Organization development consists of seven steps: initial diagnosis, data collection, feedback and confrontation, planning and problem solving, team building, intergroup development, and follow-up and evaluation. Several of the more common techniques available to change agents are survey feedback, process consultation, team building, and Grid organization development, which stresses a concern for people and production. The likelihood of success in organization development interventions can be enhanced by the actions of both management and the change agent.

KEY WORDS

freezing   structural change
Grid organization development   survey feedback
individual change   team building
organization development   technological change
process consultation   unfreezing

FOR DISCUSSION

1. What are several external and internal forces for change in organizations? How would such factors be expected to change across organizations?
2. What are some of the more important sources of resistance to change in organizations?
3. What are performance gaps? How do they emerge?
4. Outline a basic change process. What is the role of management at each stage of the process?
5. Distinguish a structural approach to change from a technological approach. Where would each approach be most effective?
6. What is meant by a "people approach" to change? How is it unique?
7. Define *unfreezing*.
8. What is organization development? How does it differ from the approaches described earlier?
9. Outline the organization development approach to change.

10. Define and provide examples of: (a) survey feedback; (b) process consultation; and (c) team building.
11. Describe how Grid organization development works. Do you support this approach to organizational change?

MATSUSHITA ELECTRIC COMPANY

The Matsushita Electric Company ranks among the fifty largest corporations in the world. Its products are sold under various brand names, including National, Panasonic, Quasar, and Technics. The phenomenal growth that has enabled Matsushita to rank so highly is itself impressive. But when we consider its deliberate development as a tightly knit culture, its integration with Japanese society, and its achievement of an enduring effectiveness that seems likely to persist beyond the departure of its founder-builder, we can see that it is not merely its relatively short term financial success that is impressive.

What accounts for this organizational success? A major factor in Matsushita's success involves its structure. The firm has always been at the forefront of organizational innovation. In the period 1933–1936, paralleling U.S. efforts to develop the divisionalized organization, Konosuke Matsushita was evolving a similar concept in Japan. Matsushita (with only 1,600 employees at the time) conceived of divisional organization as a means of keeping things small and entrepreneurial. During this period, Matsushita manufactured radios and other small consumer appliances. What at-

tracted him to the divisional approach were not only the advantages of increased organizational clarity and control but also the *behavioral* advantages of the arrangement. Each division could be set afloat, each ship to its own hull. Division managers would thus be motivated to keep a sharp eye on the marketplace as surely as a ship's captain watches the weather.

In Matsushita's view, there were four factors that motivated his organizational innovations of the 1930s. First, he wished to establish distinct product categories and independent managers whose performance could be measured clearly. Second, as a result of their self-sufficiency, managers would be driven to establish a strong consumer orientation (a factor Matsushita viewed as a key to success). Third, through this arrangement, he sought to gain the advantages of smaller companies—particularly flexibility. Finally, Matsushita reasoned, the divisions would evolve specialized expertise and their managers would become seasoned much more rapidly. Thus, the divisional system would serve to train a cadre of general managers who would be needed as the company grew.

Case 20.1 based on R. T. Pascale and A. G. Athos, *The Art of Japanese Management* (New York: Simon & Schuster, 1981), pp. 28–35. Copyright © 1981 by Richard Tanner Pascale and Anthony G. Athos. Reprinted by permission of Simon & Schuster, Inc.

Matsushita recognized that there were also inherent disadvantages of this system. As the divisions became independent, they would tend to move away from central control, and there would be difficulties in promoting interdivisional cooperation. Also, highly specialized divisions might not have the perspective or strength to cope with major threats to a whole product group. Matsushita thus counterbalanced his strong thrust toward decentralization by centralizing four key functions, which remain centralized to the present day. First, he created a group of controllers reporting to headquarters and a comprehensive centralized accounting system. Second, he instituted a company "bank" into which divisional profits flowed and from which divisions had to solicit funds for capital improvements. Third, viewing people as the critical resource of his company, he centralized the personnel function. (To this day, no employee with more than a junior high school education is hired without central personnel prescreening. All managerial promotions are carefully reviewed by headquarters as well.) Fourth, and finally, Matsushita centralized training. All Matsushita employees undergo a basic training program that includes a heavy emphasis on Matsushita values.

As Matsushita's organizational structure evolved, he alternatively added and subtracted company-wide functions such as R&D centers and centralized production engineering. In 1953, he organized his divisions into product groups, with division managers reporting vertically to the president of Matsushita and horizontally to their group vice-presidents, who served as specialists with detailed knowledge of a whole family of products. This concept of having employees report to two bosses was anathema to managers of his day. Mat-

sushita reckoned, however, that we all grow up under two bosses—a mother and a father—and that it is the nature of life to have to endure complexities that arise from such arrangements. Here was the makings of a matrix organization, perhaps ten years ahead of its widespread appearance in the United States.

Matsushita was among the first to recognize that the conflict between centralization and decentralization is unresolvable and that great organizations must have both. Thus, despite the extraordinary efficiency of his divisionalized system, Matsushita continually tinkered with it as a way of ensuring his organization's vitality. Yasau Okamoto, an authority on Matsushita, writes: "When we look at the overall characteristics of Matsushita's structure, we see decentralization and centralization revolving in a kind of spiral. That is to say, it's not that decentralization replaces centralization and then reverses itself again, but rather that the two forms of organization swing back and forth in an ever more complex marriage." According to Okamoto, between 1945 and 1952, responding to postwar confusion and recession, Matsushita dismantled his divisional organization and strongly centralized under his own authority. At one point in this period, he ran the Advertising Department personally in addition to being the CEO.

Why? In the recessionary postwar economy, Matsushita believed that the firm needed to stimulate consumer confidence in the future as well as demand for new products through advertising. By the early fifties, these problems had passed. In the period from 1953 to 1955, with competition increasing, Matsushita perceived a need to respond flexibly on many fronts at once. This gave rise to a period of decentralization, institution of independent product

groups, and addition of separate marketing, administrative, and R&D functions. From 1955 to 1960 there was another swing toward centralization—a period of high growth and penetration of international markets. Then came the early sixties and another period of recession and stagnation. This time, Matsushita decentralized to give more initiative to the field; for the first time, each product group was given full responsibility for its marketing and sales activities. This thrust continued through 1973, with the gradual elimination of headquarters staff. Then, with the onset of the oil crisis and the stagnation of the mid- and late seventies, the trend moved back again toward more centralized control.

Thus, Matsushita contrived to shift organizational structure to meet the environmental challenge. As this account suggests, Matsushita's conception of organizations was always fluid. He never took his organizational charts too literally, and he built in safety valves to make them human. For example, his controllers and other headquarters staff were always referred to as "coordinators." To further harness line/staff tensions, he insisted on the location of staff controllers within the factories they served—not at the head office.

As the organization evolved, so, it seems, did the founder prepare the firm for his succession. In 1959, at the age of sixty-five, Matsushita established a three-person Executive Council, which met daily and handled major decisions. One of its members was in charge of short-term strategy and domestic operations; another was charged with finance, accounting, and international operations; Matsushita retained primary responsibility for long-term strategy and the authority of final decision maker. Over the next ten years, Matsushita

played a more or less active role—sometimes remaining relatively uninvolved for periods of as long as a year, then reappearing when crisis occurred. By 1971 he resigned as president and assumed the title of chairman. He commented: "A danger arises when firms outgrow the generation that founded them. There is a tendency to depend too much on the founder, and I have felt of late that our management had not operated smoothly. I have a fear that our organization is looking too much to one man. Therefore, I have decided to resign so that my successors can be cultivated."

In the position of chairman, Matsushita adopted a grandfatherly role. But in 1977, in the face of environmental difficulties, he emerged again to reshuffle senior management, having been convinced that the man he had earlier appointed as president (his adopted son) was not capable of handling the job. Promoting his son to chairman, the founder adopted the title of honorary chairman. Now, at age eighty-six, he is once again relatively inactive. Four years have passed since his last significant intervention. Perhaps the organization is ready?

CASE DISCUSSION QUESTIONS

1. Describe Konosuke Matsushita's basic philosophy of organizational change.
2. Describe the major organizational changes that Matsushita Electric went through during its growth as a firm. Did these changes make the company more or less effective and efficient?
3. What role did the founder's personality play in the selection of suitable approaches to change and development?

4. One could argue that the changes occurring at Matsushita Electric ignored the need for long-term stability in the firm and that the frequent changes may have hurt the organization's overall performance. What do you think?

PART FIVE

PREDICTIONS FOR THE FUTURE

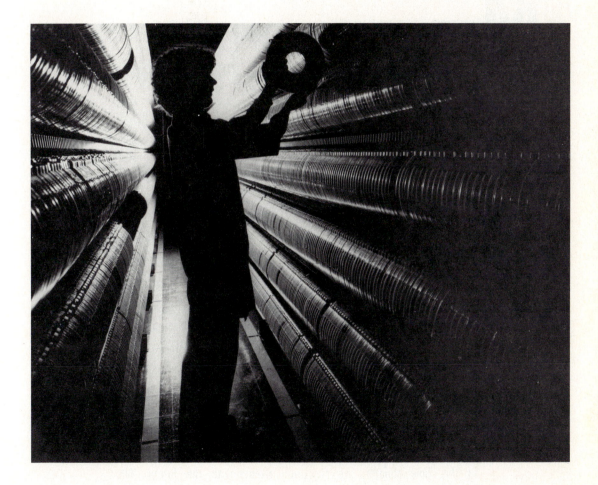

MANAGING PEOPLE AT WORK: THE FUTURE

We come now to the end of this introductory study of organizational behavior. Throughout the text, we have examined various aspects of the association of people and organizations. We began by considering the nature of organizations, both in terms of their design and the strategic contingencies with which they must deal as they interact with their environment. Next, we focused on individual behavior on the job, including perception, motivation, and learning. Following this, attention shifted to work group dynamics and the roles of communication, decision making, power, and leadership. Finally, we put these various factors together and examined people at work, exploring the topics of work design, reward systems, job attitudes, employee attachment, conflict, and stress.

For each aspect of organizational behavior discussed, we focused on what students could learn that would aid them in effectively managing organizations. Hence, each topic was considered only to the extent that it was relevant to management. This approach was chosen to bridge the gap between the behavioral sciences and the needs of managers.

In this final chapter, we turn our attention to the future. What developments are on the horizon that have the potential to change the way organizations are structured and managed? Will employee expectations be substantially different in the future? How will changes in the economy affect the work place? Questions such as these are dealt with here as we speculate about the future of the work place.

FUTURE ISSUES IN ORGANIZATIONAL BEHAVIOR

This text focused on the role of organizational behavior in the management of contemporary organizations, emphasizing what could be learned to facilitate both increased productivity and improved quality of work. However, contemporary organizations are, in a very real sense, products of their environment, and this environment is dynamic. More than ever, managers of work organizations must be alert to future changes as they relate to organizational adaptation and effectiveness both within and outside of the organization.

What major changes can we expect that will have an impact on organizational behavior? Although it is difficult to predict the future, several trends can be identified (Porter and Angle, 1980; Mowday et al., 1982): (1) socionormative changes; (2) demographic changes; (3) economic changes; and (4) technological changes. The way in which managers address these changes and challenges will determine how successful organizations will be at surviving, growing, and developing in the next decades.[1]

Societal changes influence employee behavior and attitudes, not directly, but rather through their influence on the work environment. As shown in Exhibit 21.1, changes in our society, such as changing work norms or changing technology, alter the work environment, affecting both employees' productivity and their job satisfaction.

Socionormative Changes

The socionormative aspect of the external environment focuses on the constraints that society as a whole places on correct or acceptable behavior. Socionormative changes could include the work ethic, aspiration levels, attitudes toward authority, sex-role stereotypes, and trust in organizations and institutions. These changes can influence the work environment in at least three ways: (1) through the socialization process that all employees encounter; (2) through the normative beliefs other employees bring to the work place that can influence the focal individual; and (3) through the individual's general knowledge of what is happening in society, based on the media, communications, travel, and so forth. Thus, external forces influence the nature of the work environment which, in turn, influences how people behave and feel on the job.

The socionormative changes currently facing contemporary work organizations have been described as the "great . . . cultural revolution in the work

[1]The following section draws heavily on the work of Porter and Angle (1980) and Mowday, Porter, and Steers (1982).

EXHIBIT 21.1 THE INFLUENCE OF SOCIETAL CHANGES ON EMPLOYEE ATTITUDES AND BEHAVIOR

Source: Adapted from R. T. Mowday, L. W. Porter, and R. M. Steers, *Employee-Organization Linkages: The Psychology of Commitment, Absenteeism, and Turnover* (New York: Academic Press, 1982).

force" (Kerr, 1979). It is suggested that, in the next few years, more people will want jobs and more people will want *good* jobs. There will be an increasing emphasis on personal self-fulfillment and individual rights. Yankelovich (1979, pp. 10–11), who has similarly identified a "new breed" of employees, states, "[They will] feel that success is not enough to satisfy their yearnings for self-fulfillment. They are reaching out for something more and for something different. . . . in effect, they demand full enjoyment as well as full employment."

Katzell (1979, p. 48) has summarized current cultural changes that will apparently have a strong influence on the work environment. Among these are the following:

- Revised definitions of success, with less emphasis on material achievement and more on personal fulfillment
- More flexible and equal division of work roles between the sexes
- Growing psychology on entitlement to the good life
- Shifting emphasis from bigness and growth to smallness and conservation
- Growing beliefs that work organizations are obliged . . . to contribute to the quality of life and society
- Rising concern with the welfare of consumers
- Greater awareness of issues pertaining to health, both physical and mental
- Greater social acceptance of ethnic minorities
- Growing conviction that there is more to life than working

From these predicted societal changes, Katzell (1979, p. 49) continues with suggestions of how such changes will influence employee job attitudes at work:

- [More concern with] the long-range implications of . . . jobs, in contrast to here-and-now considerations
- [Greater relative importance of] autonomy, responsibility, achievement, and related psychic rewards in relation to material or comfort considerations
- [Desire for] more of a voice in what goes on [in one's own organization]
- [More concern with] conditions furthering . . . "quality of working life," even at the expense of productivity and profits
- [Less motivation] to work long and hard just out of habit of conscience; increasingly greater expectations of explanations and payoffs in both material and psychological terms

In essence, then, it must be recognized that changes of a socionormative nature are indeed occurring and can have a profound effect on the work place of the future.

Demographic Changes

In addition, changes are also occurring in the nature and composition of the labor force. Of particular interest are sizable changes in the educational level of the work force, the age level, the percentage of women and minorities entering managerial levels, and the percentage of dual-career or multiple-wage-earner households.

We face a future in which the number of employees with college degrees will continue to increase. Moreover, the number of employees between twenty-five and forty-five years of age will rise dramatically. Women and minorities will continue to press for greater quality in both personnel selection and promotion as prevailing court decisions consistently back up these demands. And finally, the percentage of families with only one (typically male) wage earner will decline from its current twenty-five percent of all households to a lower figure.

The result will be increased heterogeneity and diversity in the work force. Treating employees as though they were a single type or group will become increasingly difficult. As Yankelovich (1979, pp. 21–22) has suggested, "The work of managing diverse incentive packages poses an administrative and bureaucratic nightmare. Understandably, therefore, most managers choose to ignore the problem. Under the old value system they could do so with impunity; under the new value system they cannot. In the 1980s they will be obliged to face this new reality."

Economic Changes

Economic changes can influence work life in at least two ways. Short-term changes in the economy can have rather marked effects on employee income level, experienced stress, absenteeism, and turnover. That is, during short-term economic downturns, job security emerges as a more central issue among employees as they attempt to protect their basic standard of living. Moreover, brief economic downturns can easily create uncertainty, anxiety, and stress for employees. Finally, during such times, an employee's attachment to the organization may also be affected. For instance, if few alternative jobs are available, absenteeism may increase as an escape mechanism since turnover is less likely.

In the long term, major shifts in the economy can affect general levels of affluence and the amount of leisure time available. For instance, it has been suggested by some that the recent economic problems plaguing both North America and Western Europe call for a *reduction* of our standard of living. Although not pleasant to contemplate, it is likely that economic conditions will continue for some years to be less than ideal. This, in turn, creates increased difficulties for both managers and employers as they attempt to build a better work place. With less money available—and with many jobs eliminated or threatened—it is difficult to initiate the kind of changes deemed necessary in order to provide an improved work experience.

Technological Changes

The fourth major area in which change can be expected in the future is technological innovation. Technological change is evident in several areas. To begin, there has been a sharp increase in the amount of automated equipment used both in the office and in the plant. The introduction of advanced computers, electronic mail, robots, etc. must of necessity change how we do our jobs—as well as how many people are needed to do those jobs.

Increased technological sophistication brings with it an increased need for technical experts or professionals to handle the software and hardware. This has obvious implications for both the personnel selection and placement process and the employee training and development function. In essence, it will become easier for employees to become technically obsolete, and efforts must be taken to countermand this threat.

Finally, because of the huge investments in capital equipment, increased pressure is emerging to use such equipment around the clock. Hence, shift work is on the increase. The implications of this for both individual well-being and for family life are only beginning to be explored.

SUMMARY

In summary, we can expect significant changes in the years to come. Most of these changes will come whether we like them or not. The job for managers, then, is to attempt to be ready for such changes to the greatest extent possible, and to continue efforts to develop both employees and organizations so they can successfully adapt to changes. In this way, it is likely that potential problems can be transformed into opportunities. If this effort is to be successful, however, it is clear that organizations will need to be managed by those who are creative, assertive, and informed. Managers will need to be proactive rather than reactive and guide their actions by a deep understanding of human behavior in organizations.

Managers with an appreciation of the problems of individuals and groups at work and an understanding of possible solutions can use their knowledge to facilitate organizational effectiveness. Familiarity with human behavior and problems inherent in working should place managers in a position to take intelligent actions aimed at improving both productivity and the quality of work. This is the basic charge of management, and it is hoped that the material presented here will help managers to carry out this charge. This hope rests on the assumption that the informed manager is better able to make reasonable decisions relating to the design of work activities. In this regard, we are reminded of J. M. Clark's quotation, "Knowledge is the only instrument of production that is not subject to diminishing returns." It is hoped that this book has contributed to your knowledge and helped to lay a solid foundation for understanding behavior in organizations.

SCIENTIFIC METHOD IN ORGANIZATIONAL RESEARCH

It is common for students of management to make pleas against following "theoretical" or "abstract" approaches to a subject and to argue instead in favor of "relevant" and "applied" approaches. The feeling is that there usually exist two distinct ways to study a topic, and from a managerial standpoint, a focus on application is the preferred way. Serious reflection about this problem may suggest a somewhat different approach, however. Consider the following situation:

As a personnel manager for a medium-sized firm, you have been asked to discover why employee turnover in your firm is so high. Your boss has told you that it is your responsibility to arrive at a well-documented assessment of this problem, as well as to offer suggestions aimed at reducing turnover. What will you do? Several possible strategies come to mind. You may decide to:

- Talk with those who have quit the organization
- Talk with those who remain
- Talk to the employees' supervisors
- Consult with personnel managers in other companies
- Measure job satisfaction
- Examine company policies and practices
- Examine the jobs where most turnover occurs

None of these actions will likely be very successful in helping you arrive at sound conclusions, however. Talking with those who have left usually yields a variety of biased responses by those who either want to "get back at" the company or who fear criticism will negatively affect their chances for future recommendations. Talking with those still employed has similar problems:

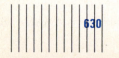

why should they be candid and jeopardize their jobs? Talking with supervisors will not help if they themselves are the problem. Asking other personnel managers, while comforting, ignores major differences between organizations. Measuring job satisfaction, examining company policies, or examining the jobs themselves may help if one is fortunate enough to hit upon the right problem, but the probability of doing so is minimal. In short, many of the most obvious ways a manager can choose to solve a problem may yield biased results at best, and possibly no results at all.

A more viable approach would be to view it as a research problem and to use widely accepted methods of scientific inquiry to arrive at a solution that minimizes potentially biased results. Most of what we know about organizational behavior results from people's efforts to apply such methods in solving organizational problems (e.g., How do we motivate employees? How do we develop effective leaders? How do we reduce stress at work?). Since an awareness of the nature of scientific inquiry is useful both for understanding how we learned what we know about organizations and in facilitating managers' efforts to solve behavioral problems at work, we shall examine this process.

THEORY-BUILDING IN ORGANIZATIONS

Theory Defined

Briefly stated, a *theory* is a set of statements that serve to amplify the manner in which certain concepts or variables are interrelated. These statements result both from our present level of knowledge on the topic and from our assumptions about the variables themselves, allowing us to deduce logical propositions, or hypotheses, that can be tested in the field or laboratory. In short, a theory is simply a technique or model that permits us to better understand how different variables fit together. Their use in research and in management is invaluable (see Dubin, 1976).

Uses of a Theory

Why do we have theories in the study of organizational behavior? Hamner and Organ (1978) suggest at least three reasons. First, theories help us *organize* knowledge about a given subject into a pattern of relationships that lends meaning to a series of observed events. They provide a structure for understanding. For instance, rather than struggling with a lengthy list of factors found to relate to employee turnover, a theory of turnover might suggest how such factors fit together and are related.

Second, theories help us to *summarize* diverse findings so that we can focus on major relationships and not get bogged down in details. A theory "permits us to handle large amounts of empirical data with relatively few propositions" (Shaw and Costanzo, 1970, p. 9).

Finally, theories are useful in that they *point the way* to future research efforts. They raise new questions and suggest answers. In this sense, they serve a useful heuristic value in helping to differentiate between important and trivial questions for future research. Theories are useful both for the study and management of organizations. As Kurt Lewin often said, "There is nothing so practical as a good theory."

What Is a Good Theory?

Abraham Kaplan (1964) discusses in detail the criteria for evaluating the utility or soundness of a theory. At least five such criteria can be mentioned:

- *Internal consistency.* Are the propositions inherent in the theory free from contradiction? Are they logical?
- *External consistency.* Are the propositions of a theory consistent with observations from real life?
- *Scientific parsimony.* Does the theory contain only those concepts that are necessary to account for findings or to explain relationships? Simplicity of presentation is preferred unless added complexity furthers understanding or clarifies additional research findings.
- *Generalizability.* In order for a theory to have much utility, it must apply to a wide range of situations or organizations. A theory of employee motivation that applies only to one company hardly helps us understand motivational processes or apply such knowledge elsewhere.
- *Verification.* A good theory presents propositions that can be tested. Without an ability to operationalize the variables and subject the theory to field or laboratory testing, we are unable to determine its accuracy or utility.

To the extent that a theory satisfies these requirements, its usefulness both to researchers and managers is enhanced. However, a theory is only a starting point. Based on theory, researchers and problem solvers can proceed to design studies aimed at verifying and refining the theories themselves. These studies must proceed according to commonly accepted principles of scientific method.

SCIENTIFIC METHOD IN ORGANIZATIONAL BEHAVIOR RESEARCH

Many years ago, Cohen and Nagel (1943) suggested that there were four basic "ways of knowing." Managers and researchers use all four of these techniques: tenacity, intuition, authority, and science. When managers form a belief (e.g.,

EXHIBIT A.1   A MODEL DEPICTING THE SCIENTIFIC METHOD

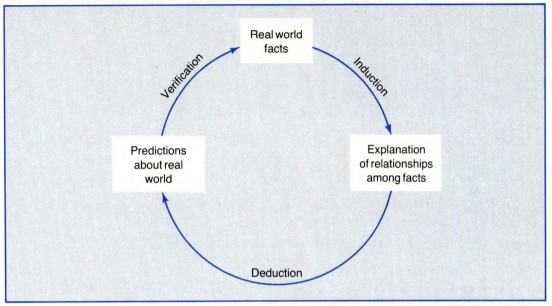

Source: E. F. Stone, *Research Methods in Organizational Behavior* (Glenview, Ill.: Scott, Foresman and Company, 1978), p. 8. Reprinted by permission.

a happy worker is a productive worker) and continue to hold that belief out of habit and often in spite of contradictory information, they are using *tenacity*. They use *intuition* when they feel the answer is self-evident or when they have a hunch about how to solve a problem. They use *authority* when they seek an answer to a problem from an expert or consultant who supposedly has experience in the area. Finally, they use *science*—perhaps all too seldom —when they are convinced that the three previous methods allow for too much subjectivity in interpretation.

In contrast to tenacity, intuition, and authority, the scientific method of inquiry "aims at knowledge that is *objective* in the sense of being intrasubjectively certifiable, independent of individual opinion or preference, on the basis of data obtainable by suitable experiments or observations" (Hempel, 1965, p. 141). In other words, the scientific approach to problem solving sets some fairly rigorous standards in an attempt to substitute objectivity for subjectivity.

The scientific method in organizational behavior consists of four stages: (1) observation of the phenomena (facts) in the real world; (2) formulation of explanations for such phenomena using the inductive process; (3) generation of predictions or hypotheses about the phenomena using the deductive process; and (4) verification of the predictions or hypotheses using systematic, controlled observation (Stone, 1978). This process is shown in Exhibit A.1.

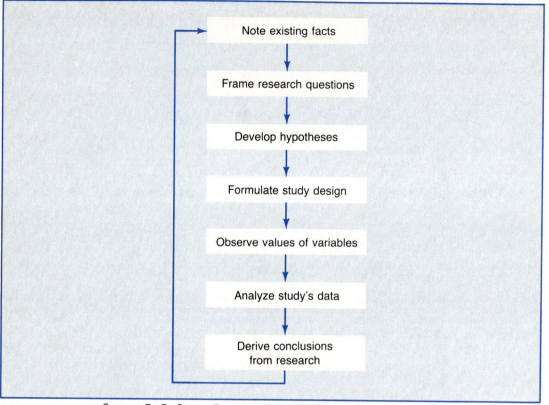

Source: E. F. Stone, *Research Methods in Organizational Behavior* (Glenview, Ill.: Scott, Foresman and Company, 1978), p. 17. Reprinted by permission.

When this rather abstract description of the steps of scientific inquiry is shown within the framework of an actual research study, the process becomes much clearer. A basic research paradigm is shown in Exhibit A.2. In essence, a scientific approach to research requires that the investigator or manager first recognize clearly what research questions are being posed. To paraphrase Lewis Carroll, if you don't know where you're going, any road will take you there. Many managers identify what they think is a problem (e.g., turnover) only to later discover that their "problem" turnover rate is much lower than comparable industries. Or, some managers look for the solution to poor employee morale and performance and ignore what may be the *real* problem (e.g., poor leadership).

Based on the research questions, specific hypotheses are identified. These hypotheses represent our best guesses about what we expect to find. We set forth hypotheses to determine if we can predict the right answer so we can select a study design that allows for a suitable testing. Based on the study design (to be discussed shortly), we observe the variables under study, analyze the data we collect, and draw relevant conclusions and management implications. By following this process, the risks of being guided by our own opinions or prejudices are minimized and we arrive at useful answers to our original research questions.

BASIC RESEARCH DESIGNS

While a detailed discussion of the various research designs is beyond the scope of this appendix (see Stone, 1978; Mowday and Steers, 1979; Dunnette, 1976), we can review several common research designs that have been used to collect data in the study of people at work. Specifically, we will examine five different research designs that are frequently used to study behavior at work: (1) naturalistic observation; (2) survey research; (3) field study; (4) field experiment; and (5) laboratory experiment. In general, the level of rigor of the design increases as we move from naturalistic observation toward laboratory study. Unfortunately, so do the costs in many cases.

Criteria for Evaluating Research Designs

Before examining the five designs, it will be helpful to consider how a researcher selects from among the various designs. Clearly, no one strategy or design is superior in all cases. Each has its place, depending upon the research goals and the constraints placed on the research.

However, when choosing among the potential designs, researchers generally must consider several things. For example, does the design require that you *specify* a priori *hypotheses?* If you specify such hypotheses and are able to confirm them, then you can predict behavior in organizations. As a manager, being able to predict behavior in advance allows you to intervene and make necessary changes to remedy problem situations. The ability to accurately predict behavior is clearly superior to simply being able to explain behavior after the fact.

Other factors to examine are the *method of measurement* and the *degree of control* to be used. Does the method of measurement use qualitative or quantitative measures? While qualitative measures may be useful for generating future hypotheses, it is generally felt that quantitative measures add more rigor to results. Also, if you are interested in demonstrating causal relationships, it is necessary to have a high degree of control over the study variables. You must be able to manipulate the primary study variable to determine the results of this manipulation, while at the same time keeping other potentially contaminating variables constant so they do not interfere in the results.

In addition, a researcher must know to what extent he or she can generalize the results from the study to apply to other organizations or situations. Results that are situation-specific are of little use to managers. *External validity* is of key importance. And, of course, in practical terms how much is it going to cost to carry out the study and discover a solution? *Cost* can be measured in many ways, including time and money.

The analysis of the previous five criteria provides insight concerning the *overall level of rigor* of the research design. The more rigorous the design, the more confidence one has in the results. This is because more rigorous designs typically employ more accurate measures or interventions and attempt to control for contaminating influences on study results. With this in mind, we can now consider various research designs.

Naturalistic Observation

Naturalistic observations represent the most primitive (least rigorous) method of research in organizations. Simply put, *naturalistic observations* represent conclusions drawn from observing events around us. At least two forms of such research can be identified: authoritative opinions and case studies.

In essence, *authoritative opinions* are the opinions of experts in the field. When Henri Fayol wrote his early works on management, for example, he was offering his advice as a former industrial manager. Based on his experience in real work situations, Fayol and others suggest that what they have learned can be applied to a variety of work organizations with relative ease. Other examples of authoritative opinions can be found in Barnard's *The Functions of the Executive,* Sloan's *My Years with General Motors,* and Townsend's *Up the Organization.* Throughout their works, these writers attempt to draw lessons from their own practical experience that can help other managers assess their problems.

The second use of naturalistic observation can be seen in the *case study.* Case studies attempt to take one situation in one organization and to analyze it in detail with regard to the interpersonal dynamics between the various members. For instance, we may have a case of one middle manager who appears to have burned out on the job; his performance seems to have reached a plateau. The case would then review the cast of characters in the situation and how each one related to this manager's problem. Moreover, the case would review any actions that were taken to remedy the problem. Throughout, emphasis would be placed on what managers could learn from this one real-life problem that can possibly relate to other situations.

Survey Research

Many times, managers wish to know something about the extent to which employees are satisfied with their jobs, are loyal to the organization, or experience stress on the job. In such cases, the managers (or the researchers) are interested mainly in considering how high or low the responses are. Questionnaires designed to measure such variables are an example of *survey research.* Here we are not attempting to relate the results to subsequent events. We simply wish to assess the general feelings and attitudes of employees.

These surveys are particularly popular with managers today as a method of assessing relative job attitudes (see Chapter Sixteen). Hence, we may make an annual attitude survey and track changes in attitudes over time. If attitudes begin to decline, management is alerted to the problem and can take steps to remedy the situation.

Field Study

In a *field study,* the researcher is interested in the relationship between a *predictor* variable (e.g., job satisfaction) and a subsequent *criterion* variable (e.g., employee turnover or performance). Measures of each variable are taken (satisfaction, perhaps through a questionnaire, and turnover, from company records) and are compared to determine the extent of correlation. No attempt is made to intervene in the system or to manipulate any of the variables, as is the case with experimental approaches.

To continue the simple example we began with, a manager may have an hypothesis that says that satisfaction is a primary indicator of employee turnover. After measuring both, it is found that there is a moderate relationship between the two variables. Hence, the manager may conclude that the two are probably related. Even so, due to the moderate nature of the relationship, it is clear that other factors also influence turnover; otherwise, there would be a much stronger relationship. The manager concludes that, while efforts to improve job satisfaction may help solve the problem, other influences on turnover must also be looked at as well, such as salary level and supervisory style.

Field Experiment

A *field experiment* is much like a field study with one important exception. Instead of simply measuring job satisfaction, the manager or researcher makes efforts to actually change satisfaction levels. In an experiment, we attempt to manipulate the predictor variable. This is most often done by dividing the sample into two groups: an experimental group and a control group. In the experimental group, we intervene and introduce a major change. Perhaps we alter the compensation program or give supervisors some human relations training. The control group receives no such treatment. After a period of time, we compare turnover rates in the two groups. If we have identified the correct treatment (that is, a true influence on turnover), turnover rates would be reduced in the experimental group but not in the control group.

In other words, in a field experiment, as opposed to a field study, we intentionally change one aspect of the work environment in the experimental group and compare the impact of the change with the untreated control group. Thus, we can be relatively assured that the solution we have identified is in fact a true predictor variable and is of use to management.

Laboratory Experiment

Up to this point, we have considered a variety of research designs that all make use of the actual work environment, the *field*. In this last design, *laboratory experiments,* we employ the same level of rigor as that of the field experiment and actually manipulate the predictor variable, but we do so in an artificial environment instead of a real one.

We might, for instance, wish to study the effects of various compensation programs (hourly rate versus piece-rate) on performance. To do this, we might employ two groups of business students and have both groups work on a simulated work exercise. In doing so, we are *simulating* a real work situation. Each group would then be paid differently. After the experiment, an assessment would be made of the impact of the two compensation plans on productivity.

Comparing Research Designs

Now that we have reviewed various research designs, the obvious question that remains is which designs are best? This is not an easy question. All designs have been used by managers and researchers in studying problems of people at work. Perhaps this question can best be answered by considering the relative strengths and weaknesses of each, based on our earlier discussion of the criteria for evaluating research designs (see Exhibit A.3). We should then have a better idea of which design or designs would be appropriate for a particular problem or situation.

Specification of hypotheses in advance. It was noted earlier that the ability to specify *a priori* hypotheses adds rigor to the study. In general, hypotheses are not set forth for naturalistic observations or survey research. These two techniques are used commonly for exploratory analyses and for identifying pertinent research questions for future, more rigorous study. On the other hand, the remaining three designs (field study, field experiment, and laboratory experiment) do allow explicitly for *a priori* hypotheses. Hence, they are superior in this sense.

Qualitative vs. quantitative measures. Naturalistic observations typically involve qualitative data, while field studies and both forms of experiments typically involve quantitative data. Survey research most often provides for both. Hence, if it is important to provide hard data to one's superior concerning a problem (e.g., what is the magnitude of the relationship between satisfaction and turnover?), quantitative designs would clearly be preferred. On the other hand, if one's superior is more concerned about identifying major reasons for turnover and little prior knowledge about the problem exists, qualitative data may be preferred and survey research may be a better research strategy. The selection of an appropriate design hinges in part on the intended uses for the information.

Control. As noted earlier, control represents the extent to which potentially contaminating influences can be minimized in a study. Clearly, experi-

EXHIBIT A.3   A COMPARISON OF VARIOUS RESEARCH DESIGNS

Research Design	*A priori* Hypotheses	Qualitative vs. Quantitative Measures	Control	External Validity	Cost	Overall Level of Rigor
Naturalistic observation	No	Qualitative	Low	Low	Low	Low
Survey research	No	Qualitative and quantitative	Low	High	Low	Medium
Field study	Yes	Quantitative	Medium	High	Medium	Medium
Field experiment	Yes	Quantitative	High	High	High	High
Laboratory experiment	Yes	Quantitative	High	Low	High	High

Note: This table represents general trends; exceptions can clearly be identified.

mental procedures allow for better control than do nonexperimental ones. The researcher or manager can systematically structure the desired work environment and minimize irrelevant or contaminating influences. As a result, conclusions concerning causal relations between variables can be made with some degree of certainty. Where it is not possible to secure such high control, however—perhaps because the organization does not wish to make a major structural change simply for purposes of the experiment—a field study represents a compromise design. It allows for some degree of control but does not require changing the organization.

External validity. The question of external validity is crucial to any study. If the results of a study in one setting cannot be applied with confidence to other settings, the utility of the results for managers is limited. In this regard, survey research, field studies, and field experiments have higher levels of external validity than naturalistic observations or laboratory experiments. Naturalistic observations are typically based on nonrandom samples, and such samples often exhibit unique characteristics that may not allow for transfers of learning from one organization to another. A clear example can be seen in the case of a small company in which the president implemented a unique compensation plan that proved successful. Whether such a plan would work in a major, multinational corporation would be highly doubtful because of the radically different nature of the organizations. Similarly, there is some question about how realistic a work environment is actually created in a laboratory situation. If managers are to learn from the lessons of other organizations, they should first learn the extent to which the findings from one kind of organization are applicable elsewhere.

Cost. As one would expect, the quality of information and its price covary. The more rigorous the design (and thus the more accurate the information), the higher the cost. Costs can be incurred in a variety of ways and include such things as actual out-of-pocket expenses, time invested, and residue costs. The organization is left with the aftermath of an experiment, which could mean raised employee expectations and anxieties, as well as the possibility of disillusionment if the experiment fails. It should be noted that, in survey research, a large amount of general information can be gathered rather quickly and cheaply.

Overall level of rigor. In summary, then, the real answer to the question concerning which strategy is best lies in the degrees of freedom a manager has in selecting the design. If an experiment is clearly out of the question (perhaps because one's superior doesn't want anything altered), a field study may be the best possible strategy given the constraints. In fact, field studies are often considered a good compromise strategy in that they have a medium amount of rigor but are also fairly quick and inexpensive. On the other hand, if one simply wishes to take an attitude survey, survey research is clearly in order. If one is not allowed to do anything, authoritative opinions from others may be the only information available. However, if constraints are not severe, experimental methods are clearly superior in that they allow for greater certainty concerning major influences on the criterion variable and on the problem itself.

REFERENCES

Abegglen, J. C. "Personality Factors in Social Mobility: A Study of Occupationally Mobile Businessmen." *Genetic Psychology Monographs* (August, 1958): 101–59.

Adams, J. S. "Injustice in Social Exchange." In L. Berkowitz (ed.), *Advances in Experimental Social Psychology.* Vol. 2. New York: Academic Press, 1965.

Adler, A. "Individual Psychology." Translated by S. Langer, in C. Murchison (ed.), *Psychologies of 1930.* Worcester, Mass.: Clark University Press, 1930: 398–99.

Adorno, T. W., Frenkel-Brunswik, E., Levinson, D. J., and Sanford, R. N. *The Authoritarian Personality.* New York: Harper & Row, 1950.

Alderfer, C. P. *Existence, Relatedness, and Growth.* New York: The Free Press, 1972.

Alderfer, C. P. "A New Theory of Human Needs." *Organizational Behavior and Human Performance 4* (1969): 142–75.

Allison, G. T. *Essence of Decision.* Boston: Little, Brown, 1971.

Allport, G. W. "Attitudes." In C. Murchison (ed.), *Handbook of Social Psychology.* Worcester, Mass.: Clark University Press, 1935: 798–844.

Allport, G. W. *Pattern and Growth in Personality.* New York: Holt, Rinehart & Winston, 1961.

Allport, G. W., and Odbert, H. S. "Trait Names: A Psycho-lexical Study." *Psychological Monographs 47* (1936): 211.

American Institutes For Research. *Project Talent: Progress in Education, A Sample Survey.* Washington, D.C., 1971.

Andrews, J. D. W. "The Achievement Motive and Advancement in Two Types of Organizations." *Journal of Personality and Social Psychology 6* (1967): 163–68.

Argyle, M. *The Social Psychology of Work.* Harmondsworth, Middlesex: Penguin, 1972.

Argyris, C. *Personality and Organization.* New York: Harper & Row, 1957.

Argyris, C. "Personality and Organization Theory Revisited." *Administrative Science Quarterly 18* (1973): 141–67.

Arnold, H. J., and Feldman, D. C. *Organizational Behavior.* New York: McGraw-Hill, 1986.

Asch, S. "Forming Impressions of Personality." *Journal of Abnormal and Social Psychology 41* (1946): 258–90.

Asch, S. "Studies of Independence and Conformity: A Minority of One Against a Unanimous Majority." *Psychological Monographs 20* (1955): 416.

Atkinson, J. W. *An Introduction to Motivation.* Princeton, N.J.: Van Nostrand, 1964.

Atkinson, J. W., and Raphelson, A. C. "Individual Differences in Motivation and Behavior in Particular Situations." *Journal of Personality* (1956): 349–63.

Bales, R. F. *Interaction Process Analysis: A Method for the Study of Small Groups.* Cambridge, Mass.: Addison-Wesley, 1950.

Bales, R. F., and Borgatta, E. F. "Size of Group as a Factor in the Interaction Profile." In A. P. Hare, E. F. Borgatta, and R. F. Bales (eds.), *Small Groups.* New York: Knopf, 1956.

Barnard, C. *The Functions of the Executive.* Cambridge, Mass.: Harvard University Press, 1938.

Barnowe, J. T., Mangione, T. W., and Quinn, R. P. The Relative Importance of Job Facets as Indicated by an Empirically Derived Model of Job Satisfaction. Unpublished paper. Survey Research Center, University of Michigan, 1972.

Bartol, K. M., and Butterfield, D. A. "Sex Effects in Evaluating Leaders." *Journal of Applied Psychology* 61 (1976): 446–54.

Bass, B. M. *Leadership, Psychology and Organizational Behavior.* New York: Harper & Row, 1960.

Bass, B. M. and Vaughn, J. A. *Training in Industry: The Management of Learning.* Belmont, Ca.: Wadsworth, 1966.

Bavelas, A., and Barrett, D. "An Experimental Approach to Organization Communication." *Personnel* 27 (1951): 366–71.

Beer, M. *Organization Change and Development.* Glenview, Ill.: Scott, Foresman and Company, 1980.

Behling, O., and Schriesheim, C. *Organizational Behavior: Theory, Research, and Application.* Boston: Allyn and Bacon, 1976.

Bem, D. J. "Self-perception Theory." In L. Berkowitz (ed.), *Advances in Experimental Social Psychology.* New York: Academic Press, (1972): 1–62.

Bernardin, J. J., and Walter, C. S. "The Effects of Rater Training and Diary Keeping on Psychometric Error in Ratings." *Journal of Applied Psychology* 61 (1977): 64–69.

Bertalanffy, L. Von. "The History and Status of General Systems Theory." *Academy of Management Journal* 15 (1972): 407–26.

Birch, D., and Veroff, J. *Motivation: A Study of Action.* Monterey, Ca.: Brooks/Cole, 1966.

Blake, R., and Mouton, J. S. *The Managerial Grid III: The Key to Leadership Excellence.* Houston: Gulf Publishing Company, 1985.

Blake, R., Shepard, H. A., and Mouton, J. S. *Managing Intergroup Conflict in Industry.* Houston: Gulf Publishing Company, 1985.

Blum, P. M. *The Dynamics of Bureaucracy.* Chicago: University of Chicago Press, 1955.

Bossom, J., and Maslow, A. H. "Security of Judges as a Factor in Impressions of Warmth in Others." *Journal of Abnormal and Social Psychology* 55 (1957): 147–48.

Bray, D., and Moss, J. "Personnel Selection." *Annual Review of Psychology.* Palo Alto, Ca.: Annual Reviews (1972): 545–76.

Brief, A. P., and Aldag, R. J. "Employee Reactions to Job Characteristics: A Constructive Replication." *Journal of Applied Psychology* 60 (1975): 182–86.

Brody, N. *Personality: Research and Theory.* New York: Academic Press, 1972.

Bruner, J. S., and Postman, L. "On the Perception of Incongruity: A Paradigm." *Journal of Personality* 18 (1949): 206–23.

Bruner, J. S., and Tagiuri, R. "The Perception of People." In G. Lindzey (ed.), *Handbook of Social Psychology.* Vol. 2. Reading, Mass.: Addison-Wesley, (1954): 601–33.

Burke, R. J. "Occupational and Life Strains, Satisfaction, and Mental Health." *Journal of Business Administration* 1 (1969): 35–41.

Burns, T., and Stalker, G. M. *The Management of Innovation.* London: Tavistock, 1961.

Business Week. "Productivity Gains from a Pat on the Back." January 23, 1978, 56–62.

Business Week. "Stonewalling Plant Democracy." March 28, 1977, 78–79.

Campbell, J. P., Dunnette, M. D., Lawler, E. E., and Weick, K. E. *Managerial Behavior, Performance, and Effectiveness.* New York: McGraw-Hill, 1970.

Campbell, J. P., and Pritchard, R. D. "Motivation Theory in Industrial and Organizational Psychology." In M. D. Dunnette (ed.), *Handbook of Industrial and Organizational Psychology.* Chicago: Rand McNally, 1976, 63–130.

Caplow, T. *Principles of Organization.* New York: Harcourt, Brace, and World, 1964.

Cartwright, D., and Zander, A. *Group Dynamics: Research and Theory.* 3rd ed. New York: Harper & Row, 1968.

Carver, C. S., and Glass, D. C. "Coronary-prone Behavior Pattern and Interpersonal Aggression." *Journal of Personality and Social Psychology 36* (1978): 361–66.

Cattell, R. B. *The Scientific Analysis of Personality.* Chicago: Aldine, 1965.

Chadwick-Jones, J. K. *Automation and Behavior.* New York: Wiley, 1969.

Chandler, A. *Strategy and Structure.* Cambridge, Mass.: MIT Press, 1962.

Chapple, E. D., and Sayles, L. R. *The Measure of Management.* New York: Macmillan, 1961.

Cherrington, D. J. "Satisfaction in Competitive Conditions." *Organization Behavior and Human Performance 10* (1973): 47–71.

Cleland, D. I., and King, W. R. *Systems Analysis and Project Management.* New York: McGraw-Hill, 1968.

Cobb, S. *The Frequency of the Rheumatic Diseases.* Cambridge, Mass.: Harvard University Press, 1971.

Cobb, S., and Kasl, S. "Blood Pressure Changes in Men Undergoing Job Loss: A Preliminary Report." *Psychosomatic Medicine,* January/February, 1970.

Coch, L., and French, J. R. P. "Overcoming Resistance to Change." *Human Relations 1* (1948): 512–33.

Cohen, M., and Nagel, E. *An Introduction to Logic and Scientific Method.* New York: Harcourt, Brace and Co., 1943.

Cohen, S. L., and Bunker, K. A. "Subtle Effects of Sex Role Stereotypes on Recruiters' Hiring Decisions." *Journal of Applied Psychology 60* (1975): 566–72.

Cooper, C., and Payne, R. *Stress at Work.* London: Wiley, 1978.

Coser, L. *The Functions of Social Conflict.* New York: The Free Press, 1956.

Costello, T. W., and Zalkind, S. S. *Psychology in Administration: A Research Orienta-* *tion.* Englewood Cliffs, N.J.: Prentice-Hall, 1963.

Crutchfield, R. S. "Conformity and Character." *American Psychologist 10* (1955): 191–98.

Cummings, L. L., and Berger, C. J. "Organization Structure: How Does It Influence Attitudes and Performance?" *Organizational Dynamics 5* (2) (1976): 34–49.

Cummings, T. G., Malloy, E. S., and Glen, R. "A Methodological Critique of Fifty-eight Selected Work Experiments." *Human Relations 30* (1977): 675–708.

Cyert, R., and March, J. G. *A Behavioral Theory of the Firm.* Englewood Cliffs, N.J.: Prentice-Hall, 1963.

Dalkey, N. *The Delphi Method: An Experimental Study of Group Opinion.* Santa Monica, Ca.: The Rand Corporation, 1969.

Davis, S. M., and Lawrence, P. R. *Matrix.* Reading, Mass.: Addison-Wesley, 1977.

Dean, J. *Blind Ambition.* New York: Simon & Schuster, 1976.

Dearborn, D. C., and Simon, H. A. "Selective Perception: A Note on Departmental Identification of Executives." *Sociometry 21* (1958): 142.

DeCharms, R. C. "Affiliation Motivation and Productivity in Small Groups." *Journal of Abnormal and Social Psychology 55* (1957): 222–76.

Deci, E. L. "The Effects of Contingent and Noncontingent Rewards and Controls on Intrinsic Motivation." *Organizational Behavior and Human Performance 8* (1972): 217–29.

Delbecq, A., Van de Ven, A., and Gustafson, D. *Group Techniques for Program Planning.* Glenview, Ill.: Scott, Foresman and Company, 1975.

Department of Health, Education, and Welfare. *Work in America.* Cambridge, Mass.: MIT Press, 1973.

Dessler, G., and Valenzi, E. R. "Initiation of Structure and Subordinate Satisfaction: A Path Analysis Test of Path-goal Theory." *Academy of Management Journal 20* (1977): 251–59.

Dickson, P. *The Future of the Workplace.* New York: Wybright and Talley, 1975.

Downey, H. K., Sheridan, J. E., and Slocum, J. W. "The Path-goal Theory of Leadership: A Longitudinal Analysis." *Organizational Behavior and Human Performance 16* (1976): 156–76.

Downs, A. *Inside Bureaucracy.* Boston: Little, Brown, 1967.

Dubin, R. "Stability of Human Organizations." In M. Haire (ed.), *Modern Organization Theory.* New York: Wiley, 1959.

Dubin, R. "Supervision and Productivity: Empirical Findings and Theoretical Considerations." In R. Dubin, G. Homans, F. Mann, and D. Miller (eds.), *Leadership and Productivity.* San Francisco: Chandler, 1965.

Dubin, R. *Theory Building.* New York: The Free Press, 1976.

Dubin, R. *World of Work.* Englewood Cliffs, N.J.: Prentice-Hall, 1958.

DuBrin, A. *Fundamentals of Organizational Behavior.* Elmsford, New York: Pergamon, 1974.

Dulworth, E. R. "The Changing World of Work." Cited in E. M. Glaser, *Productivity Gains Through Worklife Improvements.* New York: Harcourt, Brace, Jovanovich, 1976: 61–62.

Duncan, R. B. "The Characteristics of Organizational Environments and Perceived Environmental Uncertainty." *Administrative Science Quarterly 17* (1972): 313–27.

Dunnette, M. D. *Handbook of Industrial and Organizational Psychology.* Chicago: Rand McNally, 1976.

Dunnette, M. D. *Performance Equals Ability and What?* Working paper. University of Minnesota, Minneapolis, 1972.

Dunnette, M. D., Arvey, R. D., and Banas, P. A. "Why Do They Leave?" *Personnel* (1973): 25–39.

Dunnette, M. D., and Kirchner, W. K. *Psychology Applied to Industry.* New York: Appleton-Century-Crofts, 1965.

Ebert, R. J., and Mitchell, T. R. *Organizational Decision Processes: Concepts and Analysis.* New York: Crance, Russak, and Co., 1975.

Emerson, R. "Power-Dependence Relations." *American Sociological Review 27* (1962): 31–41.

Emery, F., and Trist, E. L. "The Causal Texture of Organizational Environments." *Human Relations 18* (1965): 21–32.

Esposito, J. P., and Richards, H. C. "Dogmatism and the Congruence Between Self-reported Job Preference and Performance Among School Supervisors." *Journal of Applied Psychology 59* (1974): 389–91.

Etzioni, A. *A Comparative Analysis of Complex Organizations.* (Rev. ed.) New York: The Free Press, 1975.

Etzioni, A. *Modern Organizations.* Englewood Cliffs, N.J.: Prentice-Hall, 1964.

Evans, M. "Effects of Supervisory Behavior: Extensions of Path-goal Theory of Motivation." *Journal of Applied Psychology 59* (1974): 172–78.

Evans, M. "The Effects of Supervisory Behavior on The Path-goal Relationship." *Organizational Behavior and Human Performance 5* (1970): 277–98.

Exline, R. V. "Interrelations Among Two Dimensions of Sociometric Status, Group Congeniality and Accuracy of Social Perception." *Sociometry 23* (1960): 85–101.

Fayol, H. *General and Industrial Management.* London: Pitman, 1949.

Fein, M. "Job Enrichment: A Reevaluation." *Sloan Management Review,* Winter 1974: 69–88.

Feshback, S., and Singer, R. "The Effects of Personal and Shared Threat upon Social Prejudice." *Journal of Abnormal and Social Psychology* (1957): 411–16.

Festinger, L. "Informal Social Communication." *Psychological Review 57* (1950): 271–82.

Festinger, L. *A Theory of Cognitive Dissonance.* Palo Alto, Ca.: Stanford University Press, 1957.

Fiedler, F. "Engineer the Job to Fit the Manager." *Harvard Business Review 43* (1965): 115–22.

Fiedler, F. *A Theory of Leadership Effectiveness.* New York: McGraw-Hill, 1967.

Fiedler, F., and Chemers, M. *Leadership and Effective Management.* Glenview, Ill.: Scott, Foresman and Company, 1974.

Filley, A., House, R. J., and Kerr, S. *Managerial Process and Organizational Behavior.* Glenview, Ill.: Scott, Foresman and Company, 1975.

Fishbein, M., and Ajzen, I. *Belief, Attitude, Intention and Behavior: An Introduction to Theory and Research.* Reading, Mass.: Addison-Wesley, 1975.

Fitch, S. K. *Insights into Human Behavior.* Boston: Holbrook Press, 1970.

Fleishman, E. A., and Harris, E. F. "Patterns of Leadership Behavior Related to Employee Grievances and Turnover." *Personnel Psychology 15* (1962): 43–56.

Frauenfelder, K. J. "A Cognitive Determinant of Favorability of Impression." *Journal of Social Psychology 94* (1974): 71–81.

French, E. "Some Characteristics of Achievement Motivation." *Journal of Experimental Psychology 50* (1955): 232–36.

French, E. "Effects of the Interaction of Motivation and Feedback on Task Performance." In J. W. Atkinson (ed.), *Motives in Fantasy, Action, and Society.* Princeton, N.J.: Van Nostrand, 1958: 400–08.

French, J. R. P. *Job Demands and Worker Health.* Paper presented at the 84th Annual Convention of the American Psychological Association. September 1976.

French, J. R. P., and Caplan, R. D. "Organizational Stress and Individual Strain." In A. J. Morrow (ed.), *The Failure of Success.* New York: AMACOM, 1972.

French, J. R. P., Israel, J., and As, D. "An Experiment on Participation in a Norwegian Factory." *Human Relations 13* (1960): 3–19.

French, J. R. P., and Raven, B. "The Bases of Social Power." In D. Cartwright and A. Zander (eds.), *Group Dynamics.* New York: Harper & Row, 1968.

French, W., and Bell, C. *Organization Development.* Englewood Cliffs, N.J.: Prentice-Hall, 1973.

Freud, S. *Das unbehagen in der kultur.* Vienna, 1929 (Eng. trans. Joan Riviere, *Civilization and its discontents,* Hogarth Press, 1930).

Freud, S. Lecture XXXIII. *2 New Introductory Lectures on Psychoanalysis.* New York: Norton, 1933, 153–86.

Friedman, M., and Rosenman, R. *Type A Behavior and Your Heart.* New York: Knopf, 1974.

Galbraith, J., and Cummings, L. L. "An Empirical Investigation of the Motivational Determinants of Task Performance: Interactive Effects Between Valence-instrumentality and Motivation-ability." *Organizational Behavior and Human Performance 2* (1967): 237–58.

Gallup, G. *The Gallup Opinion Index.* Princeton, N.J.: American Institute of Public Opinion, March 1978.

Gardell, G. *Arbetsinnehall och livskvalitet.* Stockholm: Prisma, 1976.

Georgopoulos, B. S., Mahoney, G. M., and Jones, N. "A Path-goal Approach to Productivity." *Journal of Applied Psychology 41* (1957): 345–53.

Gerwin, D., and Tuggle, F. "Modeling Organizational Decisions Using the Human Problem-Solving Paradigm." *Academy of Management Review 3* (1978): 762–73.

Ghiselli, E. E. *Explorations in Managerial Talent.* Pacific Palisades, Ca: Goodyear, 1966.

Ghiselli, E. E. *The Validity of Occupational Aptitude Tests.* New York: Wiley, 1966.

Gibson, J., Ivancevich, J., and Donnelly, J. *Organizations: Structure, Process, and Behavior.* Dallas: Business Publications, Inc., 1979.

Glaser, E. M. *Productivity Gains Through Worklife Improvements.* New York: Harcourt, Brace, Jovanovich, 1976.

Glass, D. C., "Stress, Competition, and Heart Attacks." *Psychology Today 10* (7) (1976): 55–57, 134.

Glueck, W. F. *Personnel: A Diagnostic Approach.* Dallas: Business Publications, Inc., 1979.

Goldstein, I. L. *Training: Program Development and Evaluation.* Monterey, Ca.: Brooks/Cole Publishing Co., 1975.

Goldstein, I. L. "Training in Work Organizations." In M. Rosenzweig and L. Porter (eds.). *Annual Review of Psychology.* Palo Alto, Ca.: Annual Reviews, 1980.

Golembiewski, R. T., and Proehl, C. W. "A Survey of the Empirical Literature on Flexible Workhours: Character and Consequences of a Major Innovation." *Academy of Management Review 3* (1978): 837–55.

Gomez-Mejia, Luis; McCann, Joseph E.; and Page, Ronald C. "The Structure of Managerial Behaviors and Rewards." *Industrial Relations 24* (1985): 147–154.

Goodman, P. S. "Social Comparison Processes in Organizations." In B. M. Staw and G. R. Salancik (eds.), *New Directions in Organizational Behavior.* Chicago: St. Clair, 1977: 97–131.

Goodman, P., and Pennings, J. *New Perspectives on Organizational Effectiveness.* San Francisco: Jossey-Bass, 1977.

Gowler, D., and Legge, K. (eds.). *Managerial Stress.* London: Wiley, 1975.

Graen, G. "Instrumentality Theory of Work Motivation: Some Experimental Results and Suggested Modification." *Journal of Applied Psychology 53* (1969): (2, Part 2).

Graves, J. P. "Successful Management and Organizational Mugging." In J. Paap (ed.), *New Directions in Human Resource Management.* Englewood Cliffs, N.J.: Prentice-Hall, 1978.

Greene, C. N. "The Satisfaction-Performance Controversy." *Business Horizons 15* (5) (1972): 31–41.

Greer, F. L. *Small Groups Effectiveness.* Institute Report No. 6, Institute for Research in Human Relations, Philadelphia, 1955.

Grimes, A. J. "Authority, Power, Influence, and Social Control: A Theoretical Synthesis." *Academy of Management Review 3* (Oct., 1978): 725.

Gross, B. M. "What Are Your Organization's Objectives? A General Systems Approach to Planning." *Human Relations 18* (1965): 195–215.

Grove, B. A., and Kerr, W. A. "Specific Evidence on Origin of Halo Effect in Measurement of Employee Morale."

Journal of Social Psychology 34 (1951): 165–70.

Guetzkow, H. "Communications in Organizations." In J. G. March (ed.), *Handbook of Organizations.* Chicago: Rand McNally, 1965: 534–73.

Gyllenhammer, P. G. "How Volvo Adapts Work to People." *Harvard Business Review.* (July-August 1977): 102–13.

Hackman, J. R. "Group Influence on Individuals." In M. D. Dunnette (ed.), *Handbook of Industrial and Organizational Psychology.* Chicago: Rand McNally, 1976.

Hackman, J. R. "Is Job Enrichment Just a Fad?" *Harvard Business Review* (September-October 1975): 129–39.

Hackman, J. R. "Work Design." In J. R. Hackman and J. L. Suttle, *Improving Life at Work.* Santa Monica, Ca.: Goodyear, 1976: 96–162.

Hackman, J. R., and Lawler, E. E. "Employee Reactions to Job Characteristics." *Journal of Applied Psychology 55* (1971): 259–86.

Hackman, J. R., and Morris, C. G. "Group Tasks, Group Interaction Process, and Group Performance Effectiveness: A Review and Proposed Integration." In Berkowitz (ed.), *Advances in Experimental Social Psychology.* Vol. 8. New York: Academic Press, 1975: 45–99.

Hackman, J. R., and Oldham, G. R. "Motivation Through the Design of Work: Test of a Theory." *Organizational Behavior and Human Performance 16* (1976): 250–79.

Hackman, J. R., Oldham, G., Janson, R., and Purdy, K. "A New Strategy for Job Enrichment." *California Management Review 17* (1975): 57–71.

Haire, M. "Role-perception in Labor-management Relations: An Experimental Approach." *Industrial and Labor Relations Review 8* (1955): 204–16.

Haire, M., and Grunes, W. F. "Perceptual Defenses: Processes Protecting an Organized Perception of Another Personality." *Human Relations 3* (1950): 403–12.

Hall, D. T. *Careers in Organizations.* Glenview, Ill.: Scott, Foresman and Company, 1976.

Hall, R. H. *Organizations: Structure and Process.* Englewood Cliffs, N.J.: Prentice-Hall, 1977.

Hamner, W. C. "How to Ruin Motivation with Pay." *Compensation Review, 7 (3)* (1975): 17–27.

Hamner, W. C. "Reinforcement Theory." In H. L. Tosi and W. C. Hamner (eds.), *Organizational Behavior and Management: A Contingency Approach.* Chicago: St. Clair, 1977: 93–112.

Hamner, W. C., and Hamner, E. P. "Behavior Modification on the Bottom Line." *Organizational Dynamics 4* (4) (1976): 3–21.

Hamner, W. C., and Organ, D. *Organizational Behavior: An Applied Psychological Approach.* Dallas: Business Publications, Inc., 1978.

Hare, A. P. *Handbook of Small Group Research.* New York: The Free Press, 1976.

Harrison, E. F. *The Managerial Decision-making Process.* Boston: Houghton Mifflin, 1975.

Hatvany, N., and Pucik, V. "An Integrated Management System: Lessons from the Japanese Experience." *Academy of Management Review 6* (1981): 469–80.

Hedges, J. N. "Absence from Work: A Look at Some National Data." *Monthly Labor Review 96* (1973): 24–31.

Heider, F. *The Psychology of Interpersonal Relations.* New York: Wiley, 1958.

Hempel, C. G. *Aspects of Scientific Explanation.* New York: The Free Press, 1965.

Henderson, A. M., and Parsons, T. *Max Weber: The Theory of Social and Economic Organization.* New York: The Free Press, 1947.

Herman, J. B., Dunham, R. B., and Hulin, C. L. "Organizational Structure, Demographic Characteristics, and Employee Responses." *Organizational Behavior and Human Performance 13* (1975): 206–32.

Herzberg, F., Mausner, B., and Snyderman, B. *The Motivation to Work.* New York: Wiley, 1959.

Hickson, D. J., Hinings, C., Lee, C., Schneck, R., and Pennings, J. "A Strategic Contingencies Theory of Intraorganizational Power." *Administrative Science Quarterly 16* (1971): 216–27.

Hickson, D. J., Pugh, D. S., and Pheysey, D. C. "Operations Technology and Organizational Structure: An Empirical Reappraisal." *Administrative Science Quarterly 14* (1969): 378–97.

Hilgard, E., and Atkinson, R. C. *Introduction to Psychology.* New York: Harcourt, Brace, and World, 1967.

Hodgetts, R., and Altman, S. *Organizational Behavior.* Philadelphia: Saunders, 1979.

Hollander, E. P. *Leadership Dynamics.* New York: The Free Press, 1978.

Hollman, T. D. "Employment Interviewer's Errors in Processing Positive and Negative Information." *Journal of Applied Psychology 56* (1972): 130–34.

Homans, G. *The Human Group.* New York: Harcourt, Brace, and World, 1950.

Homans, G. *Social Behavior: Its Elementary Forms.* New York: Harcourt, Brace, and World, 1961.

Hoppock, R. *Job Satisfaction.* New York: Harper & Row, 1935.

House, R. J. "A Path-goal Theory of Leader Effectiveness." *Administrative Science Quarterly 16* (1971): 321–38.

House, R. J., and Baetz, M. L. "Leadership: Some Generalizations and New Research Directions." In B. M. Staw (ed.), *Research in Organizational Behavior.* Greenwich, Conn.: JAI Press, 1979.

House, R. J., and Dessler, G. "The Path-goal Theory of Leadership: Some *Post hoc* and *A priori* Tests." In J. G. Hunt and L. L. Larson (eds.), *Contingency Approaches to Leadership.* Carbondale, Ill.: Southern Illinois University Press, 1974.

House, R. J., and Mitchell, T. R. "Path-goal Theory of Leadership." *Journal of Contemporary Business 5* (1974): 81–94.

House, R. J., and Rizzo, J. R. "Role Conflict and Ambiguity as Critical Variables in a Model of Organizational Behavior." *Organizational Behavior and Human Performance 7* (1972): 467–505.

Hovland, C., Janis, I., and Kelley, H. *Com-*

munication and Persuasion. New Haven: Yale University Press, 1953.

Howard, J. H., Cunningham, D. A., and Rechnitzer, P. A. "Health Patterns Associated with Type A Behavior: A Managerial Population." *Journal of Human Stress 2* (1) (1976): 24–31.

Ivancevich, J. M., and McMahon, J. T. "A Study of Task-goal Attributes, Higherorder Need Strength, and Performance." *Academy of Management Journal 20* (1977): 552–63.

Ivancevich, J. M., Szilagyi, A. D., and Wallace, M. J. *Organizational Behavior and Performance.* Glenview, Ill.: Scott, Foresman and Company, 1977.

Jackson, J. M. "The Organization and its Communication Problems." *Journal of Communication 9* (1959): 158–67.

Jackson, J. M. "Structural Characteristics of Norms." In I. D. Steiner and M. Fishbein (eds.), *Current Studies in Social Psychology.* New York: Holt, Rinehart & Winston, 1965.

Jacobs, C. D. "Job Enrichment of Field Technical Representatives—Xerox Corporation." In L. E. Davis and A. B. Cherns (eds.), *The Quality of Working Life.* Vol. II. New York: The Free Press, 1975, 285–99.

Jago, A. *Hierarchical Level Determinants of Participative Leader Behavior.* Ph.D. dissertation. Yale University, 1977.

Jago, A., and Vroom, V. H. "Predicting Leader Behavior from a Measure of Behavioral Intent." *Academy of Management Journal 21* (1978): 715–21.

Janis, I. L. "Groupthink." *Psychology Today,* November 1971.

Janis, I. L. *Victims of Groupthink: A Psychological Study of Foreign-policy Decisions and Fiascos.* Boston: Houghton Mifflin, 1972.

Jenkins, C. D. "Psychologic and Social Precursors of Coronary Disease." *New England Journal of Medicine 284* (1971): 244–55 and 307–17.

Jones, S. "Self and Interpersonal Evaluations." *Psychological Bulletin 80* (1973): 185–99.

Kahn, R. L. "The Meaning of Work: Inter-

pretations and Proposals for Measurement." In A. A. Campbell and P. E. Converse (eds.), *The Human Meaning of Social Change.* New York: Basic Books, 1972.

Kahn, R. L., Wolfe, D. M., Quinn, R. P., Snoek, J. D., and Rosenthal, R. A. *Organizational Stress: Studies in Role Conflict and Ambiguity.* New York: Wiley, 1964.

Kanfer, F. H. "Vicarious Human Reinforcement: A Glimpse into the Black Box." In L. Kresner and L. P. Ullman (eds.), *Research in Behavior Modification.* New York: Holt, Rinehart & Winston, 1965, 244–67.

Kanfer, F. H., and Karoly, P. "Self-control: A Behavioristic Excursion into the Lion's Den." *Behavior Therapy 3* (1972): 398–416.

Kanter, R. "Power Failure in Management Circuits." *Harvard Business Review* (July-August 1979).

Kaplan, A. *The Conduct of Inquiry.* San Francisco: Chandler, 1964.

Kasl, S. V., Sampson, E. E., and French, J. R. P. "The Development of a Projective Measure of the Needs for Independence: A Theoretical Statement and Some Preliminary Evidence." *Journal of Personality 32* (1964): 556–86.

Kast, F., and Rosenzweig, J. *Organization and Management.* New York: McGraw-Hill, 1974.

Katz, D. "Determinants of Attitude Arousal and Attitude Change." *Public Opinion Quarterly 24* (1960).

Katz, D., and Kahn, R. *The Social Psychology of Organizations,* 2nd ed. New York: Wiley, 1978.

Katz, E. "The Two-step Flow of Communication: An Up-to-date Report on an Hypothesis." *Public Opinion Quarterly 21* (1957): 61–78.

Katzell, R. A. "Changing Attitudes Toward Work." In C. Kerr and J. Rostow (eds.), *Work in America: The Next Decade.* New York: Van Nostrand, 1979.

Katzell, R. A. "Personal Values, Job Satisfaction, and Job Behavior." In H. Borow (ed.), *Man in a World of Work.* Boston: Houghton Mifflin, 1964, 341–63.

Kearns, J. D. *Stress in Industry.* London: Priory Press, 1973.

Kelley, H. H. "Attribution Theory in Social Psychology." In D. Levine (ed.), *Nebraska Symposium on Motivation.* Lincoln, Neb.: University of Nebraska, 1967.

Kemp, C. G. *Perspectives on Group Processes.* Boston: Houghton Mifflin, 1970.

Kerr, C. "Industrialism with a Human Face." In C. Kerr and J. Rostow (eds.), *Work in America: The Next Decade.* New York: Van Nostrand, 1979.

Kerr, S., and Jermier, J. "Substitutes for Leadership: Their Meaning and Measurement." *Organizational Behavior and Human Performance 22* (1978): 375–403.

Kimble, G. A., and Garmezy, N. *Principles of General Psychology.* New York: Ronald Press, 1963.

King, R. W. "Stress Claims Are Making Business Jumpy." *Business Week* (October 14, 1985): 152–54.

Kipnis, D. "Does Power Corrupt?" *Journal of Personality and Social Psychology 24* (1972): 33–41.

Kipnis, D. *The Powerholders.* Chicago: University of Chicago Press, 1976.

Klimoski, R. J., and Strictland, W. J. "Assessment Centers: Valid or Merely Prescient." *Personnel Psychology 30* (1977): 353–61.

Kluckhohn, C., and Murray, H. A. *Personality in Nature, Society, and Culture.* 2nd ed., revised and enlarged. New York: Alfred A. Knopf, 1953.

Kogan, N., and Wallach, M. A. "Group Risk Taking as a Function of Members' Anxiety and Defensiveness." *Journal of Personality 35* (1967): 50–63.

Korman, A. K. *Organizational Behavior.* Englewood Cliffs, N.J.: Prentice-Hall, 1977.

Kornhauser, A. *Mental Health of the Industrial Worker.* New York: Wiley, 1965.

Kreitner, R. "People are Systems, Too: Filling the Feedback Vacuum." *Business Horizons 20* (November 1977): 54–58.

Kretch, D., Crutchfield, R. S., and Ballachey, E. L. *Individual in Society.* New York: McGraw-Hill, 1962.

Lang, J., Dittrich, J., and White, S. "Managerial Problem-Solving Models: A Review and a Proposal." *Academy of Management Review 3* (1978): 854–66.

Lasswell, H. D. *Politics: Who Gets What, When, How.* New York: McGraw-Hill, 1936.

Latham, G. P., and Yukl, G. "A Review of Research on the Application of Goal-setting in Organizations." *Academy of Management Journal 18* (1975): 824–45.

Lawler, E. E. *Motivation in Work Organizations.* Monterey, Ca.: Brooks/Cole, 1973.

Lawler, E. E. "New Approaches to Pay Administration." *Personnel 53* (5) (1976): 11–23.

Lawler, E. E. *Pay and Organizational Effectiveness.* New York: McGraw-Hill, 1971.

Lawler, E. E. *The Design of Effective Reward Systems.* Technical Report. University of Southern California, April 1983.

Lawler, E. E. *Whatever Happened to Incentive Pay?* Technical Report. University of Southern California, May 1983.

Lawler, E. E., Kuleck, W. J., Jr., Rhode, J. G., and Sorensen, J. E. "Job Choice and Post Decision Dissonance." *Organizational Behavior and Human Performance 13* (1975): 133–45.

Lawler, E. E., Mohrman, A. M., and Resnick, S. M. *Performance Appraisal Revisited.* Technical Report. University of Southern California, March 1983.

Lawler, E. E., and Suttle, J. L. "Expectancy Theory and Job Behavior." *Organizational Behavior and Human Performance 9* (1973): 482–503.

Lawrence, L. C., and Smith, P. C. "Group Decision and Employers' Participation." *Journal of Applied Psychology 39* (1955): 334–37.

Lawrence, P. R., and Lorsch, J. W. *Organization and Environment.* Boston: Harvard University, Division of Research, Graduate School of Business Administration, 1967.

Leavitt, H. J. "Applied Organization Change in Industry: Structural, Technical, and Human Approaches," in W. W. Cooper, H. J. Leavitt, and M. W. Shelley (eds.), *New Perspectives in Organization Research.* New York: Wiley, 1964.

Leventhal, G. S. "Fairness in Social Relationships." In J. Thibaut, J. Spence, and R. Carson (eds.), *Contemporary Topics in Social Psychology.* Morristown, N.J.: General Learning Press, 1976.

Levinson, H. "The Psychologist in Industry." *Harvard Business Review 37* (1959): 93–99.

Levinson, H., Price, C. R., Munden, H. J., and Salley, C. M. *Men, Management, and Mental Health.* Cambridge. Harvard University Press, 1962.

Lewin, K. *The Conceptual Representation and the Measurement of Psychological Forces.* Durham, N.C.: Duke University Press, 1938.

Lewin, K. *A Dynamic Theory of Personality.* New York: McGraw-Hill, 1935.

Lewin, K. "Forces Behind Food Habits and Methods of Change." *Bulletin of the National Research Council 108* (1947): 35–65.

Lieberman, S. "The Effects of Changes in Roles on the Attitudes of Role Occupants." *Human Relations 9* (1956): 385–402.

Likert, R. *New Patterns in Management.* New York: McGraw-Hill, 1961.

Lillico, M. *Managerial Communication.* London: Pergamon, 1972.

Lippman, L. *Attitudes Toward the Handicapped: A Comparison Between Europe and the United States.* Springfield, Ill.: Charles C. Thomas, 1972.

Litwin, G. H., and Stringer, R. A., Jr. *Motivation and Organizational Climate.* Boston: Harvard University, Graduate School of Business Administration, Division of Research, 1968.

Locher, A. H., and Teel, K. S. "Performance Appraisal: A Survey of Current Practices." *Personnel Journal,* May 1977.

Locke, E. A. "The Motivational Effects of Knowledge of Results: Knowledge or Goal-setting?" *Journal of Applied Psychology 51* (1967): 324–29.

Locke, E. A. "The Myths of Behavior Mod in Organizations." *Academy of Management Review 2* (1977): 543–53.

Locke, E. A. "The Nature and Causes of Job Satisfaction." In M. D. Dunnette (ed.), *Handbook of Industrial and Organization-*

al Psychology. Chicago: Rand McNally, 1976.

Locke, E. A. "Toward a Theory of Task Performance and Incentives." *Organizational Behavior and Human Performance 3* (1968): 157–89.

Locke, E. A. "What is Job Satisfaction?" *Organizational Behavior or Human Performance 4* (1969): 309–36.

Locke, E. A., and Schweiger, D. M. "Participation in Decision Making: One More Look." In B. M. Staw (ed.), *Research in Organizational Behavior.* Greenwich, Conn.: JAI Press, 1979, 265–340.

Locke, E. A., Sirota, D., and Wolfson, A. D. "An Experimental Case Study of the Successes and Failures of Job Enrichment in a Government Agency." *Journal of Applied Psychology 61* (1976): 701–11.

Lofquist, L., and Dawis, R. *Adjustment to Work: A Psychological View of Man's Problems in a Work-oriented Society.* New York: Appleton-Century-Crofts, 1969.

Luthans, R. *Organizational Behavior.* New York: McGraw-Hill, 1977.

Lynch, B. P. "An Empirical Assessment of Perrow's Technology Construct." *Administrative Science Quarterly 19* (1974): 338–56.

McClelland, D. C. *The Achieving Society.* Princeton, N.J.: Van Nostrand, 1961.

McClelland, D. C. *Assessing Human Motivation.* New York: General Learning Press, 1971.

McClelland, D. C. "Power is the Great Motivation." *Harvard Business Review 54* (2) (1976): 100–10.

McClelland, D. C. *Power: The Inner Experience.* New York: Irvington, 1975.

McClelland, D. C. "Toward a Theory of Motive Acquisition." *American Psychologist* (1965): 321–33.

McClelland, D. C., Atkinson, J. W., Clark, R. A., and Lowell, E. L. *The Achievement Motive.* New York: Appleton-Century-Crofts, 1953.

Maccoby, M. *The Gamesman.* New York: Simon & Schuster, 1976.

McCormick, E. J., and Tiffin, J. *Industrial Psychology.* 6th ed. Englewood Cliffs, N.J.: Prentice-Hall, 1976.

MacCrimmon, K., and Taylor, R. "Decision Making and Problem Solving." In M. D. Dunnette (ed.), *Handbook of Industrial and Organizational Psychology.* Chicago: Rand McNally, 1976, 1397–1453.

McDavid, J., and Harari, M. *Social Psychology: Individuals, Groups, Societies.* New York: Harper & Row, 1968.

McDougall, W. *An Introduction to Social Psychology.* London: Methuen, 1908.

McGrath, J. E. *Social Psychology: A Brief Introduction.* New York: Holt, Rinehart & Winston, 1964.

McGrath, J. E. "Stress and Behavior in Organizations." In M. D. Dunnette (ed.), *Handbook of Industrial and Organizational Psychology.* Chicago: Rand McNally, 1976.

McGregor, D. *The Human Side of Enterprise.* New York: McGraw-Hill, 1960.

McGuire, W. J. "Personality and Attitude Change: An Information-processing Theory." In A. G. Greenwald, T. C. Brock, and T. M. Ostrom (eds.), *Psychological Foundations of Attitudes.* New York: Academic Press, 1968, 171–196.

Macy, B. A., and Mirvis, P. H. "Measuring the Quality of Work and Organizational Effectiveness in Behavioral-economic Terms." *Administrative Science Quarterly 21* (1976): 212–26.

Maier, N. R. F. "Assets and Liabilities in Group Problem Solving: The Need for an Integrative Function." *Psychological Review 47* (1967): 239–49.

Maier, N. R. F. *Psychology in Industrial Organizations.* Boston: Houghton Mifflin, 1973.

March, J. G., and Simon, H. A. *Organizations.* New York: Wiley, 1958.

Marlatt, G. A. "A Comparison of Vicarious and Direct Reinforcement Control of Verbal Behavior in an Interview Setting." *Journal of Personality and Social Psychology 16* (1970): 695–703.

Maslow, A. H. *Motivation and Personality.* New York: Harper & Row, 1954.

Maslow, A. H. *Toward a Psychology of Being.* 2nd ed. New York: Van Nostrand, 1968.

Mason, D. J. "Judgments of Leadership Based upon Physiognomic Cues." *Journal of Abnormal and Social Psychology 54* (1957): 273–74.

Mathis, R. L., and Jackson, J. H. *Personnel: Contemporary Perspectives and Applications.* 2nd ed. St. Paul: West Publishing Co., 1979.

Mechanic, D. "Sources of Power of Lower Participants in Complex Organizations." *Administrative Science Quarterly 7* (1962): 349–64.

Mesdag, L. M. "Are You Underpaid?" *Fortune* (March 19, 1984): 20–25.

Meyer, H., Kay, E., and French, J. R. "Split Roles in Performance Appraisal." *Harvard Business Review 43* (1965): 123–29.

Miles, R. E., Porter, L. W., and Craft, J. A. "Leadership Attitudes Among Public Health Officials." *American Journal of Public Health 56* (1966): 1990–2005.

Miles, R. H. *Macro Organizational Behavior.* Glenview, Ill.: Scott, Foresman and Company, 1980.

Miles, R. H., and Perreault, W. D. "Organizational Role Conflict: Its Antecedents and Consequences." *Organization Behavior and Human Performance 17* (1976): 19–44.

Milgram, S. "Behavioral Study of Obedience." *Journal of Abnormal and Social Psychology 67* (1963): 371–78.

Milgram, S. *Obedience to Authority.* New York: Harper & Row, 1973.

Miller, D., and Starr, M. *The Structure of Human Decisions.* Englewood Cliffs, N.J.: Prentice-Hall, 1967.

Miner, J. B. *The Management Process: Theory, Research, and Practice.* New York: Macmillan, 1973.

Miner, J. B., and Dachler, H. P. "Personnel Attitudes and Motivation." *Annual Review of Psychology,* Palo Alto, Ca.: Annual Reviews, 1973, 379–402.

Mintzberg, H. *The Nature of Managerial Work.* New York: Harper & Row, 1973.

Mirvis, P. H., and Lawler, E. E. "Measuring the Financial Impact of Employee Attitudes." *Journal of Applied Psychology 62* (1977): 1–8.

Mitchell, T. R. "Cognitive Complexity and Leadership Style." *Journal of Personality and Social Psychology 16* (1970): 166–74.

Mitchell, T. R. "Expectancy Models of Job Satisfaction, Occupational Preference and Effort: A Theoretical, Methodological and Empirical Appraisal." *Psychological Bulletin 81* (1974): 1096–112.

Mitchell, T. R. *People in Organizations.* New York: McGraw-Hill, 1978.

Mitchell, T. R., Smyser, C. M., and Weed, S. E. "Locus of Control: Supervision and Work Satisfaction." *Academy of Management Journal 18* (1974): 263–360.

Mobley, W. H. *Employee Turnover: Causes, Consequences, and Control.* Reading, Mass.: Addison-Wesley, 1982.

Mobley, W. H. "Intermediate Linkages in the Relationship Between Job Satisfaction and Employee Turnover." *Journal of Applied Psychology 62* (1977): 237–40.

Mobley, W. H., Griffeth, R. W., Hand, H. H., and Meglino, B. M. "Review and Conceptual Analysis of the Employee Turnover Process." *Psychological Bulletin 86* (1979): 493–522.

Morgan, C. T., and King, R. A. *Introduction to Psychology.* 3rd ed. New York: McGraw-Hill, 1966.

Morris, J. H. *Organizational Antecedents and Employee Responses to Role Ambiguity and Role Conflict.* Unpublished doctoral dissertation. Graduate School of Management, University of Oregon, 1976.

Mowday, R. T. "Equity Theory Predictions of Behavior in Organizations." In R. M. Steers and L. W. Porter (eds.), *Motivation and Work Behavior.* 2nd ed. New York: McGraw-Hill, 1979.

Mowday, R. T., Porter, L. W., and Dubin, R. "Unit Performance, Situational Factors, and Employee Attitudes in Spatially Separated Work Units." *Organizational Behavior and Human Performance 12* (1974): 231–48.

Mowday, R. T., Porter, L. W., and Steers, R. M. *Employee-Organization Linkages: The Psychology of Commitment, Absenteeism, and Turnover.* New York: Academic Press, 1982.

Mowday, R. T., and Steers, R. M. *Research in Organizations: Issues and Controversies.* Santa Monica, Ca.: Goodyear, 1979.

Mowday, R. T., Steers, R. M., and Porter, L. W. "The Measurement of Organizational Commitment." *Journal of Vocational Behavior 14* (1979): 224–47.

Muchinsky, P. M. "Employee Absenteeism: A Review of the Literature." *Journal of Vocational Behavior 10* (1977): 316–40.

Murray, H. A. *Explorations in Personality.* New York: Oxford University Press, 1938.

Mussen, P. H. *The Psychological Development of the Child.* Englewood Cliffs, N.J.: Prentice-Hall, 1963.

Nadler, D. A., Hackman, J., and Lawler, E. *Managing Organizational Behavior.* New York: Little, Brown, 1979.

Nadler, D. A., and Tushman, M. L. "A Model for Diagnosing Organizational Behavior." *Organizational Dynamics 9* (2) (1980): 35–51.

Neff, W. S. *Work and Human Behavior.* New York: Atherton, 1968.

Newman, J. E. "Understanding the Organizational Structure–Job Attitude Relationship Through Perceptions of the Work Environment." *Organizational Behavior and Human Performance 14* (1975): 371–97.

New York Narcotics Addiction Control Commission. *Differential Drug Use Within the New York State Labor Force.* July, 1971.

Norman, R. D. "The Interrelationships Among Acceptance-rejection, Self-other, Insight into self, and Realistic perception of others." *Journal of Social Psychology 37* (1953): 205–35.

Norton, S. "The Empirical and Content Validity of Assessment Centers vs. Traditional Methods of Predicting Managerial Success." *Academy of Management Review 2* (1977): 442–53.

Omwake, K. T. "The Relation Between Acceptance of Self and Awareness of Others Shown by Three Personality Inventories." *Journal of Consulting Psychology 18* (1954): 443–46.

Opsahl, R. L., and Dunnette, M. D. "The Role of Financial Compensation in Industrial Motivation." *Psychological Bulletin 66* (1966): 94–96.

O'Reilly, C. A., and Roberts, K. H. "Individual Differences in Personality, Position in the Organization, and Job Satisfaction." *Organizational Behavior and Human Performance 14* (1975): 144–50.

Organizational Dynamics. "At Emery Air Freight: Positive Reinforcement Boosts Performance." Vol. 1, No. 3 (Winter 1973): 41–50.

Ouchi, W. *Theory Z.* Reading, Mass.: Addison-Wesley, 1981.

Palmore, E. "Predicting Longevity: A Follow-up Controlling for Age." *The Gerontologist 9* (1969): 247–50.

Parsons, T. *Essays in Sociological Theory: Pure and Applied.* New York: The Free Press of Glencoe, 1949.

Pascale, R. and Althos, A. *The Art of Japanese Management.* New York: Simon & Schuster, 1981.

Payne, R. B., and Hauty, G. T. "Effect of Psychological Feedback upon Work Decrement." *Journal of Experimental Psychology 50* (1955): 343–51.

Perrow, L. A. "A Framework for the Comparative Analysis of Organization." *American Sociological Review 32,* (1967): 194–208.

Pettigrew, A. M. "Towards a Political Theory of Organizational Intervention." *Human Relations 28* (1975): 191–208.

Pfeffer, J. *Power in Organizations.* Marshfield, Mass.: Pitman, 1981.

Pfeffer, J., and Salancik, G. *The External Control of Organizations.* New York: Harper & Row, 1978.

Pondy, L. R. "Organizational Conflict: Concepts and Models." *Administrative Science Quarterly 12* (1967): 296–320.

Porter, L. W. "A Study of Perceived Need Satisfaction in Bottom and Middle Management Jobs." *Journal of Applied Psychology 45* (1961): 1–10.

Porter, L. W., and Angle, H. Manager-Organization Linkages. In K. Duncan, M. Gruneberg, and D. Wallis (eds.), *Changes in Working Life.* Chichester, Eng.: Wiley, 1980.

Porter, L. W., and Lawler, E. E. *Managerial Attitudes and Performance.* Homewood, Ill.: Irwin, 1968.

Porter, L. W., and Lawler, E. E. "Properties of Organization Structure in Relation to Job Attitudes and Job Behavior." *Psychological Bulletin 64* (1965): 23–51.

Porter, L. W., Lawler, E. E., and Hackman, J. R. *Behavior in Organizations.* New York: McGraw-Hill, 1975.

Porter, L. W., and Roberts, K. H. "Communication in Organizations." In M. D. Dunnette (ed.), *Handbook of Industrial and Organizational Psychology.* Chicago: Rand McNally, 1976.

Porter, L. W., and Steers, R. M. "Organizational, Work, and Personal Factors in Employee Turnover and Absenteeism." *Psychological Bulletin 80* (1973): 151–76.

Porter, L. W., Steers, R. M., Mowday, R. T., and Boulian, P. V. "Organizational Commitment, Job Satisfaction, and Turnover Among Psychiatric Technicians." *Journal of Applied Psychology 59* (1974): 603–09.

Price, J. *The Study of Turnover.* Ames: Iowa State University Press, 1977.

Pritchard, R. D. "Equity Theory: A Review and Critique." *Organizational Behavior and Human Performance 4* (1969): 176–211.

Rachlin, H. *Modern Behaviorism.* San Francisco: W. H. Freeman, 1970.

Rather, D., and Gates, G. *The Palace Guard.* New York: Harper & Row, 1974.

Read, W. "Upward Communication in Industrial Hierarchies." *Human Relations 15* (1962): 3–16.

Reitan, H. T., and Shaw, M. E. "Group Membership, Sex Composition of the Group, and Conformity Behavior." *Journal of Social Psychology 64* (1964): 45–51.

Roethlisberger, F., and Dickson, W. J. *Management and the Worker.* Cambridge, Mass.: Harvard University Press, 1939.

Rogers, E. M., and Rogers, R. A. *Communication in Organizations.* New York: The Free Press, 1976.

Rohlen, T. *For Harmony and Strength.* Berkeley: Univ. of California Press, 1974.

Rokeach, M. *The Nature of Human Values.* New York: The Free Press, 1973.

Rokeach, M. *The Open and Closed Mind.* New York: Basic Books, 1960.

Rosen, B., and Jerdee, T. H. "The Influence of Age Stereotypes on Managerial Decisions." *Journal of Applied Psychology 61* (1976): 428–32.

Rosen, B., and Jerdee, T. H. "Influence of Sex-role Stereotypes on Personnel Decisions." *Journal of Applied Psychology 59* (1974): 9–14.

Rosen, C., Klein, K., and Young, K. "When Employees Share the Profit." *Psychology Today.* (January 1986): 30–36.

Rosenbaum, M. E. "Social Perception and the Motivational Structure of Interpersonal Relations." *Journal of Abnormal and Social Psychology 59* (1959): 130–33.

Rosenman, R., and Friedman, M. "The Central Nervous System and Coronary Heart Disease." *Hospital Practice 6* (1971): 87–97.

Rotter, J. B. "Generalized Expectancies for Internal vs. External Control of Reinforcement." *Psychological Monographs 80* (1966): 1–28.

Ruch, F. L. *Psychology and Life.* 10th ed. Glenview, Ill.: Scott, Foresman and Company, 1983.

Ruch, L. O., and Holmes, T. H. "Scaling of Life Change: Comparison of Direct and Indirect Methods." *Journal of Psychosomatic Research 15* (1971): 221–27.

Ruddock, R. (d.) *Six Approaches to the Person.* London: Routledge and Kegan Paul, 1972.

Runyon, K. E. "Some Interactions Between Personality Variables and Management Style." *Journal of Applied Psychology 57* (1973): 288–94.

Salancik, G. "Commitment and the Control of Organizational Behavior and Belief." In B. M. Staw and G. R. Salancik (eds.), *New Directions in Organizational Behavior.* Chicago: St. Clair Press, 1977, 1–21.

Salancik, G. R., and Pfeffer, J. "The Bases and Use of Power in Organizational Decision Making." *Administrative Science Quarterly 19* (1974): 453–73.

Sanford, F. H., and Wrightsman, L. S., Jr. *Psychology.* 3rd ed. Monterey, Ca.: Brooks/Cole, 1970.

Sarason, I. G., Johnson, J. H., Berberich, J. P., and Siegel, J. M. *Helping Police Officers Cope with Stress: A Cognitive-behavioral Approach.* Technical report. Department of Psychology, University of Washington, February, 1978.

Sarbin, T. R., Taft, R., and Bailey, D. E. *Clinical Inference and Cognitive Theory.* New York: Holt, Rinehart & Winston, 1960.

Schachter, S. "Deviation, Rejection, and Communication." *Journal of Abnormal and Social Psychology 46* (1951): 190–207.

Schachter, S. *The Psychology of Affiliation.* Stanford, Ca.: Stanford University Press, 1959.

Scheibe, K. E. *Beliefs and Values.* New York: Holt, Rinehart & Winston, 1970.

Schein, E. H. "Organizational Socialization and the Profession of Management." *Industrial Management Review 9* (1968): 1–16.

Schein, V. E. "Relationships Between Sex Role Stereotypes and Requisite Management Characteristics Among Female Managers." *Journal of Applied Psychology 60* (1975): 340–44.

Schroder, H. M., Driver, M. H., and Streufert, S. *Human Information Processing.* New York: Holt, Rinehart & Winston, 1967.

Schwab, D. P., and Cummings, L. L. "Theories of Performance and Satisfaction: A Review." *Industrial Relations 7* (1970): 408–30.

Scott, W. E. "Activation Theory and Task Design." *Organizational Behavior and Human Performance 1* (1966): 3–30.

Scott, W. G. *Organization Theory.* Homewood, Ill.: Irwin, 1967.

Scott, W. G., and Mitchell, T. R. *Organization Theory: A Structural and Behavioral Analysis.* Homewood, Ill.: Irwin, 1976.

Sears, R. R. "Experimental Studies of Perception: Attribution of Traits." *Journal of Social Psychology 7* (1936): 151–63.

Seashore, S. E., and Barnowe, J. T. *Demographic and Job Factors Associated with the "Blue collar Blues."* Working paper. University of Michigan, 1972.

Secord, P. F. "The Role of Facial Features in Interpersonal Perception." In R. Tagiuri and L. Petrullo (eds.), *Person Perception and Interpersonal Behavior.* Stanford, Ca.: Stanford University Press (1958): 300–315.

Secord, P. F., and Backman, C. W. *Social Psychology.* New York: McGraw-Hill, 1964.

Selye, H. *The Stress of Life.* New York: McGraw-Hill, 1956.

Shannon, C., and Weaver, W. *The Mathematical Theory of Communication.* Urbana: University of Illinois Press, 1948.

Shartle, C. L. *Executive Performance and Leadership.* Englewood Cliffs, N.J.: Prentice-Hall, 1956.

Shaw, M. E. *Group Dynamics: The Psychology of Small Group Behavior.* New York: McGraw-Hill, 1976.

Shaw, M. E., and Costanzo, P. R. *Theories of Social Psychology.* New York: McGraw-Hill, 1970.

Shetty, Y. "Managerial Power and Organizational Effectiveness: A Contingency Analysis." *Journal of Management Studies 15* (1978): 178–81.

Shull, F. A., Delbecq, A. L., and Cummings, L. L. *Organizational Decision Making.* New York: McGraw-Hill, 1970.

Simon, H. A. *Administrative Behavior.* 2nd ed. New York: The Free Press, 1957.

Simon, H. A. *The New Science of Management Decision.* New York: Harper & Row, 1960.

Simon, H. A., et al. *Public Administration.* New York: Knopf, 1950.

Skinner, B. F. *Beyond Freedom and Dignity.* New York: Knopf, 1971.

Skinner, B. F. *Contingencies of Reinforcement: A Theoretical Analysis.* Englewood Cliffs, N.J.: Prentice-Hall, 1969.

Skinner, B. F. "Operant Behavior." *American Psychologist 18* (1963): 503–15.

Skinner, B. F. *Science and Human Behavior.* New York: Macmillan, 1953.

Slote, A. *Termination: The Closing at Baker Plant.* Ann Arbor: Institute for Social Research, University of Michigan, 1977.

Smith, P. C., Kendall, L. M., and Hulin, C. L. *The Measurement of Satisfaction in Work and Retirement.* Chicago: Rand McNally, 1969.

Soelberg, P. O. "Unprogrammed Decision Making." *Industrial Management Review 8* (1967): 19–29.

Spencer, D. G. *The Influence of Intrasubjective Normative Expectations on Turnover Intent.* Unpublished doctoral dissertation. Graduate School of Management, University of Oregon, 1979.

Stagner, R. *Psychology of Industrial Conflict.* New York: McGraw-Hill, 1956.

Staw, B. M. "The Consequences of Turnover." *Journal of Occupational Behavior,* 1980.

Staw, B. M. "The Escalation of Commitment to a Course of Action." *Academy of Management Review 6* (1981): 577–87.

Staw, B. M. *Intrinsic and Extrinsic Motivation.* Morristown, N.J.: General Learning Press, 1976.

Staw, B. M. "Knee-deep in the Big Muddy: A Study of Escalating Commitment to a Chosen Course of Action." *Organizational Behavior and Human Performance 16* (1976): 27–45.

Staw, B. M., and Fox, F. V. "Escalation: The Determinants of Commitment to a Chosen Course of Action." *Human Relations 30* (1977): 431–50.

Staw, B. M., and Ross, J. "Commitment to a Policy Decision: A Multitheoretical Perspective." *Administrative Science Quarterly 23* (1978): 40–64.

Steers, R. M. "Problems in the Measurement of Organizational Effectiveness." *Administrative Science Quarterly 20* (1975): 546–58.

Steers, R. M. "Task-goal Attributes, *n* Achievement, and Supervisory Performance." *Organizational Behavior and Human Performance 13* (1975): 392–403.

Steers, R. M. "Factors Affecting Job Attitudes in a Goal-setting Environment." *Academy of Management Journal 19* (1976): 6–16.

Steers, R. M. "When is an Organization Effective? A Process Approach to Understanding Effectiveness." *Organizational Dynamics* 5 (2) (1976): 50–63.

Steers R. M. "Antecedents and Outcomes of Organizational Commitment." *Administrative Science Quarterly* 22 (1977): 46–56. (a)

Steers, R. M. "Individual Differences in Participative Decision Making." *Human Relations* 30 (1977): 837–47. (b)

Steers, R. M. *Organizational Effectiveness: A Behavioral View*. Glenview, Ill.: Scott, Foresman and Company, 1977. (c)

Steers, R. M., and Braunstein, D. N. "A Behaviorally Based Measure of Manifest Needs in Work Settings." *Journal of Vocational Behavior* 9 (1976): 251–66.

Steers, R. M., and Mowday, R. T. "Employee Turnover and Post-decision Accommodation Processes." In L. L. Cummings and B. M. Staw (eds.), *Research in Organizational Behavior*. Greenwich, Conn.: JAI Press, 1981.

Steers, R. M., and Mowday, R. T. "The Motivational Properties of Tasks." *Academy of Management Review* 2 (1977): 645–58.

Steers, R. M., and Porter, L. W. *Motivation and Work Behavior*. 4th ed. New York: McGraw-Hill, 1987.

Steers, R. M., and Porter, L. W. "The Role of Task-goal Attributes in Employee Performance." *Psychological Bulletin* 81 (1974): 434–51.

Steers, R. M., and Rhodes, S. R. "Major Influences on Employee Attendance: A Process Model." *Journal of Applied Psychology* 63 (1978): 391–407.

Steers, R. M., and Spencer, D. G. "The Role of Achievement Motivation in Job Design." *Journal of Applied Psychology* 4 (1977): 472–79.

Stogdill, R. *Handbook of Leadership*. New York: The Free Press, 1974.

Stogdill, R. "Personal Factors Associated with Leadership: A Survey of the Literature." *Journal of Psychology* 25 (1948): 35–71.

Stone, E. F. *Research Methods in Organizational Behavior*. Glenview, Ill.: Scott, Foresman and Company, 1978.

Strickland, L. H. "Surveillance and Trust." *Journal of Personality* 26 (1958): 200–215.

Super, D. *The Psychology of Careers*. New York: Harper & Row, 1957.

Susser, M. "Causes of Peptic Ulcer: A Selective Epidemiologic Review." *Journal of Chronic Diseases* 20 (1967).

Szilagyi, A. D. *Management and Performance*. Glenview, Ill.: Scott, Foresman and Company, 1981.

Szilagyi, A. D., and Wallace, M. J. *Organizational Behavior and Performance*. 3rd ed. Glenview, Ill.: Scott, Foresman and Company, 1983.

Taylor, F. W. *The Principles of Scientific Management*. New York: Harper & Row, 1911.

Taylor, R. N., and Dunnette, M. D. "Influence of Dogmatism, Risk-taking Propensity, and Intelligence on Decision-making Strategies for a Sample of Industrial Managers." *Journal of Applied Psychology* 59 (1974): 420–23.

Taylor, R. N., and Thompson, M. "Work Value Systems of Young Workers." *Academy of Management Journal* 19 (1976): 522–36.

Terkel, S. *Working*. New York: Avon, 1972.

Thibaut, J. W., and Kelley, H. H. *The Social Psychology of Groups*. New York: Wiley, 1959.

Thibaut, J. W., and Riecker, H. W. "Authoritarianism, Status, and the Communication of Aggression." *Human Relations* 8 (1955): 95–120.

Thomas, K. W. "Conflict and Conflict Management." In M. D. Dunnette (ed.), *Handbook of Industrial and Organizational Psychology*. Chicago: Rand McNally, 1976.

Thomas, K. W. "Toward Multi-dimensional Values in Teaching: The Example of Conflict Behaviors." *Academy of Management Review* 2 (1977): 484–90.

Thomas, K. W., and Pondy, L. R. "Toward an Intent Model of Conflict Management Among Principal Parties." *Human Relations* 30 (1977): 1089–102.

Thomas, K. W., and Schmidt, W. H. "A

Survey of Managerial Interests with Respect to Conflict." *Academy of Management Journal* (1976): 315–18.

Thompson, J. D. *Organizations in Action.* New York: McGraw-Hill, 1967.

Thorndike, E. L. *Animal Intelligence.* New York: Macmillan, 1911.

Tolman, E. C. "Principles of Purposive Behavior." In S. Koch (ed.), *Psychology: A Study of a Science.* Vol. 2. New York: McGraw-Hill, 1959.

Tosi, H., and Carroll, S. *Management-by-Objectives.* New York: Macmillan, 1973.

Tosi, H., Rizzo, J. R., and Carroll, S. "Setting Goals in Management by Objectives." *California Management Review* *12*(4) (1970): 70–78.

Triandis, H. C. *Attitude and Attitude Change.* New York: Wiley, 1971.

Trist, E. *A Socio-technical Critique of Scientific Management.* Paper presented at the Edinburgh Conference on the Impact of Science and Technology. University of Edinburgh, May 1970.

Trist, E., and Bamforth, K. "Some Social and Psychological Consequences of the Longwall Method of Goal-getting." *Human Relations 4* (1951): 1–38.

Trotter, W. *Instincts of the Herd in Peace and War.* New York: Macmillan, 1916.

Tubbs, M. E. "Goal-setting: A Meta-analytic Examination of the Empirical Evidence." *Journal of Applied Psychology 71* (1986): 474–83.

Tuckman, B. W. "Developmental Sequence in Small Groups." *Psychological Bulletin 64* (1965): 384–99.

Turner, A. N., and Lawrence, P. R. *Industrial Jobs and the Worker.* Cambridge, Mass.: Harvard University Press, 1965.

Ungson, G., and Braunstein, D. *Decision making.* Boston: Kent, 1982.

U.S. Department of Labor. *Job Satisfaction: Is There a Trend?* Manpower Research Monograph No. 30, 1974.

Valecha, G. K. "Construct-Validation of Internal-External Locus of Reinforcement Related to Work-Related Variables." *Proceedings,* 80th Annual Convention of the American Psychological Association (1972): 455–56.

Van de Ven, A., and Joyce, W. F. *Perspectives on Organization Design and Behavior.* New York: Wiley, 1981.

Van Maanen, J. *Organizational Careers: Some New Perspectives.* New York: Wiley, 1977.

Vernon, H. M. *On the Extent and Effects of Variety in Repetitive Work.* Industrial Fatigue Research Board, Report No. 26. London: Her Majesty's Stationery Office, 1924.

Von Neumann, J., and Morgenstern, O. *Theory of Games and Economic Behavior.* Princeton: Princeton University Press, 1953.

Vroom, V. H. "Organizational Choice: A Study of Pre- and Post-decision Processes." *Organizational Behavior and Human Performance 1* (1966): 212–25.

Vroom, V. H. *Some Personality Determinants of the Effects of Participation.* Englewood Cliffs, N.J.: Prentice-Hall, 1960.

Vroom, V. H. "Some Personality Determinants of the Effects of Participation." *Journal of Abnormal and Social Psychology 59* (1959): 322–27.

Vroom, V. H. *Work and Motivation.* New York: Wiley, 1964.

Vroom, V. H., and Deci, E. L. "The Stability of Post-decisional Dissonance: A Follow-up Study of the Job Attitudes of Business School Graduates." *Organizational Behavior and Human Performance 6* (1971): 36–49.

Vroom, V. H., and Jago, A. "Decision Making as a Social Process: Normative and Descriptive Models of Leader Behavior." *Decision Sciences 5* (1974): 743–69.

Vroom, V. H., and Yetton, P. W. *Leadership and Decision-Making.* Pittsburgh: University of Pittsburgh Press, 1973.

Wahba, M. A., and Bridwell, L. G. "Maslow Reconsidered: A Review of Research on the Need Hierarchy Theory." *Organizational Behavior and Human Performance 15* (1976): 212–40.

Walker, C. R., and Guest, R. H. *The Man on*

the *Assembly Line.* Cambridge, Mass: Harvard University Press, 1952.

Wall, T. D., Clegg, C. W., and Jackson, P. R. "An Evaluation of the Job Characteristics Model." *Journal of Occupational Psychology 51* (1978): 183–96.

Walton, R. E. "The Diffusion of New Work Structures: Explaining Why Success Didn't Take." *Organizational Dynamics,* Winter 1975, 3–22.

Wanous, J. P. "Effects of a Realistic Job Preview on Job Acceptance, Job Attitudes, and Job Survival." *Journal of Applied Psychology 58* (1973): 327–32.

Wanous, J. P. "Organizational Entry: Newcomers Moving from Outside to Inside." *Psychological Bulletin 84* (1977): 601–18.

Ward, L. B., and Athos, A. G. *Student Expectations of Corporate Life.* Boston: Harvard University, Graduate School of Business Administration, Division of Research, 1972.

Watney, J. *Clive in India.* London: Saxon House, 1974.

Watson, J. B. *Behavior: An Introduction to Comparative Psychology.* New York: Holt, Rinehart & Winston, 1914.

Webber, R. A. "Perceptions of Interactions Between Superiors and Subordinates." *Human Relations 23* (3) (1970): 235–48.

Weber, M. *The Theory of Social and Economic Organization.* New York: Free Press, 1947.

Weick, K. E. "The Concept of Equity in the Perception of Pay." *Administrative Science Quarterly 11* (1966): 414–39.

Weiner, B. *Achievement Motivation and Attribution Theory.* Morristown, N.J.: General Learning Press, 1974.

White, R. W. "Motivation Reconsidered: The Concept of Competence." *Psychological Review, 66* (5) (1959): 297–333.

White, S. E., Mitchell, T. R., and Bell, C. H. "Goal-setting, Evaluation Apprehension, and Social Cues as Determinants of Job Performance and Job Satisfaction in a Simulated Organization." *Journal of Applied Psychology 62* (1977): 665–73.

Wilensky, H. "Work as a Social Problem." In H. S. Becker (ed.), *Social Problems: A Modern Approach.* New York: Wiley, 1966.

Willis, J. "Quality Circles Breed Enthusiasm." *Minneapolis Star,* April 2, 1980.

Woodward, J. *Industrial Organization: Theory and Practice.* Oxford: Oxford University Press, 1965.

Woodward, J. *Management and Technology.* London: Her Majesty's Stationery Office, 1958.

Worthy, J. C. "Organizational Structure and Employee Morale." *American Sociological Review 15* (1950): 169–79.

Wright, Patrick. *On a Clear Day You Can See General Motors.* New York: Avon Books, 1979.

Wyatt, S., Langdon, J. N., and Stock, F. G. "Fatigue and Boredom in Repetitive Work." Industrial Health Research Board, Report No. 37, Great Britain, 1937.

Yankelovich, D. "We Need New Motivational Tools." *Industry Week,* August 6, 1979.

Yolles, S. A. "Mental Health at Work." In A. McLean (ed.), *To Work Is Human: Mental Health and the Business Community.* New York: Macmillan, 1967.

Yolles, S. F., Carone, P. A., and Krinsky, L. W. *Absenteeism in Industry.* Springfield, Ill.: Charles C. Thomas, 1975.

Zaleznik, A. "Power and Politics in Organizational Life." *Harvard Business Review* (May–June 1970): 47–60.

Zalkind, S. S., and Costello, T. W. "Perception: Some Recent Research and Implications for Administration." *Administrative Science Quarterly 9* (1962): 218–35.

Zander, A., and Newcomb, T. "Group Levels of Aspiration in United Fund Campaigns." *Journal of Personality and Social Psychology* (1967): 157–62.

Zimbardo, P. G., and Ruch, F. L. *Psychology and Life.* Glenview, Ill.: Scott, Foresman and Company, 1975.

Zwerman, W. L. *New Perspectives of Organizational Theory.* Westport, Conn.: Greenwood Press, 1970.

NAME INDEX

Ludwig, Daniel, 79
Luis, Carl, 578
Luthans, R., 219

McCann, Joseph E., 19
McClelland, David, 164, 165,
    167–69, 171, 173–75
Maccoby, M., 172
McCormick, E. J., 123, 221
MacCrimmon, K., 411
McDavid, J., 324
McDougall, W., 157
McGrath, J. E., 330, 495
McGregor, D., 114, 159
McGuire, W. J., 291
McMahon, J. T., 196
Mahoney, G. M., 198
Maier, N. R. F., 124, 418
Mangione, T. W., 303
March, J. G., 186, 413–14, 563,
    577, 580
Marlatt, G. A., 235
Maslow, A. H., 103, 158–64,
    166–67
Mason, D. J., 100
Mathis, R. L., 268
Mausner, B., 532
Mechanic, D., 453
Mesdag, L. M., 265
Meyer, H., 228, 364
Miles, R. E., 153
Miles, R. H., 67, 304, 365, 370,
    445, 448–50, 503
Miller, D., 411
Miner, J. B., 114–15, 164
Mintzberg, H., 382
Mirvis, P. H., 581
Mitchell, T. R., 103, 106, 132, 196,
    286, 303, 326, 329, 337, 383,
    419, 440, 478, 479
Mobley, W. H., 305, 516, 586–87
Mohr, 67, 68
Mohrman, A. M., 252
Molloy, E. S., 539
Morgan, C. T., 97
Morgenstern, O., 411
Morris, C. G., 324
Morris, J. H., 304
Moss, J., 259
Mouton, J. S., 371, 613
Mowday, R. T., 185, 187, 190, 262,
    534, 538, 577, 578, 580, 581,
    586, 588, 625, 635
Muchinsky, P. M., 306
Murray, H. A., 124–25, 158,
    164–75

Nadler, D. A., 16, 17
Nagel, E., 632
Neff, W. S., 494
Neilsen, 371
Newcomb, T., 194

Newman, J. E., 305
Nixon, Richard M., 432, 453
Norman, R. D., 103
Norton, S., 259

Odbert, H. S., 137
O'Reilly, C. A., 304
Oldham, G. R., 304, 535, 537–39
Omwake, K. T., 103
Opsahl, R. L., 264
Organ, D., 231, 496, 613
Ouchi, W., 344, 348

Packard, David, 578
Page, Ronald, C., 19
Parsons, T., 31, 335, 437
Pascale, R., 348
Pavlov, I., 216
Payne, R. B., 194, 495, 499, 504,
    512
Pennings, J., 33, 68
Perreault, W. D., 304, 503
Perrow, L. A., 68
Pettigrew, A. M., 453
Pfeffer, J., 78–81, 444–48, 457
Pondy, L. R., 362, 367
Porter, L. W., 26, 153, 161, 185,
    192, 193, 198, 201–2, 262,
    295, 302–4, 306–7, 328–30,
    387, 419, 516, 533, 567, 575,
    577, 578, 580–82, 588, 625
Porter, R. M., 262
Postman, L., 98
Price, J., 586
Pritchard, R. D., 190, 201–3
Poehl, C. W., 550
Pucik, V., 345, 347
Pugh, D. S., 64
Purdy, K., 539

Quinn, R. P., 303

Rachlin, H., 222
Radford, Admiral, 432
Raft, R., 286
Raphelson, A. C., 170
Rather, Dan, 396–97
Raven, B., 438
Read, W., 392
Rechnitzer, P. A., 507
Reitan, H. T., 332
Resnick, S. M., 252
Rhode, J. G., 292
Rhodes, S. R., 306, 329, 516, 582
Richards, J. P., 131
Riecker, H. W., 101
Rizzo, J. R., 197, 503
Roberts, K. H., 304, 387
Rockefeller, David, 607
Roethlisberger, F., 155, 325
Rogers, E. M., 388, 391, 393, 394
Rogers, R. A., 388, 391, 393, 394

Rohlen, T., 347, 348
Rokeach, M., 131, 287
Rosen, B., 110–12
Rosen, C., 268
Rosenbaum, M. E., 102
Rosenman, R., 507
Rosenzweig, J., 599
Ross, J., 418, 423
Rotter, J. B., 105
Ruch, F. L., 220
Ruch, L. O., 98, 508
Ruddock, R., 494
Runyon, K. E., 479
Rusk, Dean, 434

Sakai, Takuya, 581
Salancik, G. R., 78–81, 446–48
Sampson, E. E., 170
Sanford, F. H., 169
Sarason, I. G., 519
Sarbin, T. R., 286
Sayles, L. R., 60
Schachter, S., 130, 333, 510, 511
Scheibe, K. E., 285
Schein, E. H., 573–75, 608–9
Schein, V. M., 110–112
Schlesinger, Arthur, 333
Schmidt, W. H., 361
Schroder, H. M., 132
Schwab, D. P., 306–7
Schweiger, D. M., 419
Scott, W. G., 103, 303, 335, 383,
    515
Sears, R. R., 116
Secord, P. F., 97, 98, 101, 116
Shannon, C., 383
Shaw, M. E., 127, 129, 130, 324,
    332, 338, 388, 632
Shepard, H. A., 371
Sheridan, J. E., 480
Sherif, Muzafer, 359
Shull, F. A., 411
Simon, H. A., 44, 83, 102, 114,
    115, 186, 411–14, 416, 453,
    563, 577, 580
Singer, R., 115
Sirota, D., 546
Skinner, B. F., 218, 222, 227, 235
Sloan, Alfred P., Jr., 38, 636
Slocum, J. W., 480
Slote, A., 512
Smith, Adam, 41
Smith, Frederick W., 168
Smith, P. C., 194, 295, 296, 303
Smyser, C. M., 106, 479
Snyderman, B., 532
Soelberg, P. O., 416
Sorenson, J. E., 292
Spenser, D. G., 167, 331, 553
Stagner, R., 111
Stalker, G. M., 68, 72–74
Starr, M., 411

Staw, B. M., 290, 296, 418, 422–25, 535, 590
Steers, R. M., 33, 38, 167, 170, 171, 182, 185, 192, 193, 196, 262, 295, 302, 304, 306, 307, 329, 419, 476, 482, 483, 516, 520, 533, 534, 538, 553, 567, 577, 578, 580–82, 586, 588, 635
Stogdill, R., 130, 303, 465–66
Stone, E. F., 304, 633, 635
Streufert, S., 132
Strickland, L. H., 102
Strictland, W. J., 259
Stringer, R. A., 171
Super, D., 570
Susser, M., 512
Suttle, J. L., 203
Szilagyi, A. D., 217, 357, 392

Tagiuri, R., 114
Taylor, F. W., 41, 154, 532
Taylor, R. N., 11, 131, 411
Teel, K. S., 248–49, 252
Terkel, Studs, 5, 498
Thibaut, J. W., 101, 339
Thomas, K. W., 361, 362, 366, 367
Thompson, J. D., 61, 68, 71
Thompson, M., 11
Thorndike, E. L., 158, 218
Tiffin, J., 123, 221
Tolman, E. C., 158, 220
Tosi, H., 197, 257
Triandis, H. C., 110, 283, 291

Trist, E. L., 71, 340, 341
Trotter, W., 170
Tubbs, M. E., 193
Tuckman, B. W., 326
Turner, A. N., 535
Tushman, M. L., 16

Ungson, G., 411

Valecha, G. K., 107
Valenzi, E. R., 480
Van de Ven, A., 426
Vaughn, J. A., 221, 485
Vernon, H. M., 532
Veroff, J., 170
Von Neumann, J., 411
Vroom, V. H., 128–29, 156, 171, 198, 234, 292, 293, 296, 298, 303, 305–7, 419, 468, 471–77, 480–81, 565, 567

Wahba, M. A., 162–63
Walker, C. R., 392, 531
Wall, T. D., 538
Wallace, M. J., 217, 357
Wallach, M. A., 131
Walter, C. S., 252
Walton, R. E., 544, 553
Wanous, J. P., 564, 565, 568
Ward, L. B., 567
Watney, J., 396
Watson, J. B., 218
Weaver, W., 383
Webber, R. A., 108

Weber, Max, 34, 437, 446
Weed, S. E., 106, 479
Weick, K. E., 82, 185
Weiner, B., 105, 106
Welsh, John, 168
White, Jerry, 168
White, Robert, 161
White, S. E., 196
Whyte, William H., 576
Wicklund, 423
Wilensky, H., 301
Willis, J., 551
Wolfson, A. D., 546
Woodward, J., 60
Worthy, J. C., 37
Wright, Patrick, 250
Wrightsman, L. S., Jr., 169
Wyatt, S., 307

Yagiuri, R., 113
Yankelovich, D., 10, 626, 627
Yetton, P. W., 156, 419, 468, 471–77, 480–81
Yolles, S. A., 493
Yolles, S. F., 581
Young, K. C., 268
Yukl, G., 195, 196

Zaleznik, A., 174
Zalkind, S. S., 102, 113, 224, 287, 289
Zander, A., 194, 324, 338, 340
Zimbardo, P. G., 220
Zwerman, W. L., 68

SUBJECT INDEX